A POLICY OF
DISCONTENT

THE MAKING OF
A NATIONAL ENERGY STRATEGY

VITO STAGLIANO

Copyright© 2001 by
PennWell Corporation
1421 South Sheridan
Tulsa, Oklahoma 74112
800-752-9764
sales@pennwell.com
www.pennwell-store.com
www.pennwell.com

Cover and book design by Amy Spehar

Library of Congress Cataloging-in-Publication Data

Stagliano, Vito A.
A policy of discontent : the making of a national energy
strategy / by Vito A. Stagliano.
p. cm.
Includes bibliographical references and index.
ISBN 0-87814-817-5
1. Energy policy--United States. 2. Power resources--
Government policy--United States. I. Title.

HD9502.U52 S72 2001
333.79'0973--dc21
2001033939

Printed in the United States of America

1 2 3 4 5 05 04 03 02 01

For John Bernotavicz

In Memoriam

TABLE OF CONTENTS

Foreword

by Paul T. Ruxin

Administrations come and go, politicians' stars rise and fall, but the work of government goes forward, carried out by professional staffs surprisingly (to those cynical about bureaucracy at least) dedicated, competent, and hard working. To the extent government policy is informed by an institutional memory, it is essentially the memory of the Staff. To the degree there is continuity and consistency in the rulemakings and statutes that emerge from legislative committees and agency hearing rooms, it reflects, to a large degree, the presence and efforts of career employees. Insofar as the "regulatory expertise" to which reviewing courts so often defer actually exists, it resides in the Staff.

These professionals are, often, all that stand between the country's unsuspecting citizens and their elected representatives or appointed regulators, mindful only of Everett Dirkson's maxim that the politician's first duty is to get re-elected. Playing for the next election, the next vote, the temptation to make policy with a view to the popular sentiment of the moment is great indeed. The complexity of the subject, the technical knowledge required to legislate or regulate wisely, the history of an issue, and the long-term consequences of the law or rule or policy at stake often present problems of a sophistication exceeding that of those temporarily in charge, who may well have come to the task by political appointment or by accident, rather than by virtue of experience, training, or formal qualification.

No area of our collective governmental experience demonstrates this reality as well as energy. Highlighted today by the wave of restructuring that rippled across the country beginning in the 1990's, the economic complexity of the energy supply, demand, and resource relationship has overwhelmed politicians and regulators in a variety of ways. The results to date—worst in California—are not encouraging. Electricity should not cost ten times more in the wholesale markets of the West than in those of the Midwest and the East. Natural gas, in plentiful supply to meet the needs of decades of future use, should not be subject to volatile prices and extreme spikes. Oil—simply because much of it must come from abroad—should not be a weapon of foreign policy blackmail in the hands of its suppliers and domestic hysteria in the minds of American consumers. Conservation and "green" energy and nuclear power should be exploited, not for political purposes, but to meet realistic economic and environmental objectives. To the extent these issues are addressed and resolved sensibly, we as a people will be indebted to those who, without much public recognition or even awareness, educate and discipline and restrain those decision-makers who appear in the news media to take credit for happy results and lay blame for unhappy ones.

Today's gasoline-pump prices and rolling blackouts are only the nightly news' focal point, a kind of media-minimalist take, on the complex and interwoven issues the "energy problem" represents in sum. Consumer expectations and reactions may highlight the news, but the real issues involve the often seemingly irreconcilable interests of the producers (and producing regions) and the consumers. Not merely our own Eastern vs. Western problem, but domestic vs. foreign considerations, from the market manipulations of OPEC and the politics of the Arab world, to the investment alternatives and tax incentives available to American capital, figure in the energy equation. The need to meet the demand created by fuel-guzzling, exhaust-emitting SUVs owned by a public that also wants (or claims to want) pristine natural preserves, reminds the thoughtful that the economics of energy conservation, properly assessed, require a balancing of the costs and the benefits of increased production to meet increased, and sometimes frivolous, demand. How we measure the full cost of the incremental barrel of oil or kilowatt-hour will also reflect how we, as a people, truly value nature, convenience, and comfort.

Vito Stagliano's book addresses not only these questions, but also the political implications of resolving them. Why, for example, did the hands-off approach of administrations as different as those of Presidents Reagan and Clinton seem to succeed, while the well-intentioned activism of the Carter and Bush I regimes saw "crisis" only as part of a two-word phrase beginning with "energy?" Bad timing? Regulatory lag? The story told here helps makes sense out of what, on the surface, seems counter-intuitive.

It is also a story both interesting and useful on a variety of levels. Very specifically, it is a history of the National Energy Strategy, finally developed under Secretary of Energy James Watkins in the late 1980's and legislatively transformed into the Energy Policy Act of 1992, but actually the ultimate response to the Arab oil embargo of 1973. As Stagliano demonstrates, however, the need for such a strategy, and the "crisis" declared in 1973, had even earlier and deeper roots, and our failure to develop a coherent policy before 1973 explains much of what came after including, in part, the Gulf War and its aftermath. This story is a compelling one, compellingly told.

Those interested in energy matters will find it both informative and instructive, a cautionary tale of the dangers of inaction, reaction, and over-reaction, specifically illustrated by detailed pictures of those people, moments, and events that led to our present day uncertainty. The still-raging debates include those over the impossible dream of petroleum independence, the need for drilling in the Alaska Natural Wildlife Refuge, as well as under Lake Erie and offshore Florida and California, the renewed development of nuclear power resources and, fittingly enough, the future of windmills. The energy novice and specialist alike will both learn from and be entertained by this unfolding saga of the shaping and mis-shaping of our present energy posture.

But this is not a book for the energy specialist alone. In fact it would be a remarkably good text for political science courses. It is, by analogy, the story of how government policy and regulatory decisions are often made. It is the story of the interplay of foreign and domestic policies, of external events with profound internal implications. It is the story of political appointments, political ambitions, grandstanding, special interests, and entitlements: the "sausage-making" aspects of legislation Bismark warned against exposing to the public view. It is also, however, the story of the hard work, intelligence, and dedication that professional staff and enlightened political leaders can bring to bear on difficult subjects, and how those virtues can affect—and effect—national policy.

Most of all, this is the story of the necessity of compromise in public life and political action. Without it, little would happen, and most of that unfortunate. Such compromise is the result of the need to recognize a wide variety of legitimate civic objectives, and the need to reconcile and respect multiple interests and positions. Such a process is necessarily shaped by the personalities—the human qualities—of the participants. Here, too Stagliano serves us, and history, well. Thus, his book is not only an excellent history of energy policy, and an illuminating case study of the political process, it is a personal record of real people, of how they conducted their professional lives, and used their skills and talents, and were limited as well as freed, by their natures.

One of the small ironies of our time is that for every hundred people who remember that "those who do not learn from history are doomed to repeat it," only one can tell us who George Santayana was. So it is too often with the work of dedicated public servants, the fruit of whose efforts we all share, but whose names we do not know. With this book, however, many who will benefit from an expanded understanding of how government works, who will be better informed about what our national energy policy should and can be, will know, with gratitude, Vito Stagliano.

Paul T. Ruxin

Chairman, Jones, Day, Reavis & Pogue
Energy Industry Practice Group

Chicago, Illinois
May 2001

PROLOGUE

Although short-lived, and unsuccessful in its aim to influence U.S.–Middle Eastern policy, the Arab oil embargo of 1973 profoundly affected American thinking about the fuels and technology that power the world's economy. The embargo rekindled concerns about security first experienced in the 19th century, when navies made the transition from coal- to oil-fired ships. No less seductive for being elusive, the quest for energy security launched the United States, as well as Western Europe and industrialized Asia, into costly policy experimentation to mitigate the foreign policy and economic consequences of over reliance on oil from the Persian Gulf.

Access to secure supplies of petroleum has preoccupied governments, in war and peace, for a century or more, but U.S. reactions to the 1973 oil embargo surpassed reasonable concern about the availability of an essential fuel, amounting to a crisis of national confidence. Between 1973 and 1980, U.S. public policy was held virtually hostage to what came to be known as the energy crisis. The crisis, in retrospect more psychological than real, was to ultimately contribute to the destruction of Jimmy Carter's presidency.

Can hydrocarbons and electrons shape the fate of nations? It seemed so in the 1970s, perhaps because a failure of policy—oil policy—took on the dimensions of human inability to manage human affairs. The roots of national dissatisfaction with energy policy ran deep, in any case. Congress excoriated Roosevelt's New Dealers for intruding in the electric utility field with the vast Federal hydropower projects of the 1930s. Truman was berated for allowing American oil companies to manage the consequences of Iran's nationalization of its oil fields. Eisenhower was damned for his imposition of controls on oil imports. Only Kennedy, Johnson, and Clinton, among post–WW II presidents, escaped public wrath on the issue, but only because they relegated energy policy to a sidebar of the nation's business.

U.S. energy policy evokes passions not normally associated with technical subjects. It has caused conflict among energy producing and energy-consuming States and regions. It has instigated shameful displays of prejudice, as in the case of Americans cursing all things Arab while standing in line for scarce gasoline. It has pitted the myriad social and economic interests represented in the energy economy one against the other. Coal producers have inveighed against natural gas producers, environmentalists have decried the wanton use of fossil fuels, protectors of rivers have battled against hydropower developers, and operators of nuclear power plants have been vilified for having adapted an instrument of war to the generation of electricity.

The energy debate was no less polarized during the two years in which Energy Secretary James Watkins undertook the development of what came to be known as the National Energy Strategy (NES) and the further two years it took to translate the NES into the Energy Policy Act (EPAct) of 1992. The NES effort was launched, albeit reluctantly, by the Administration of George H.W. Bush in order to reverse the perception of benign neglect engendered by a decade of Reagan energy policy. There were neither crises nor specific issues demanding attention when the NES effort was begun, merely a sense that the time was ripe for a thorough review of the subject.

Watkins was directed by his President to find a balance among competing, perhaps irreconcilable, goals of energy at reasonable cost, economic efficiency, energy abundance, environmental protection and energy security. The NES was to be comprehensive in scope, addressing supply and demand requirements with equal care. It was to search for common ground between the liberal view of energy as a social good and the conservative faith in free markets. The NES was also to be the means of determining, by other than Congressional allocation of fiscal pork, how

Federal research and development priorities for energy technology might be established.

The making of policy is inherently a human task. It cannot be mechanized nor given to faith. It is crafted by men and women with knowledge and prejudice, pride and ideology, and varying skill in the exercise of power. And so it was with the NES; hammered into shape by dissension as great within the senior ranks of the Bush Administration as among members of Congress and the special interest community. As in all human undertakings, the development of the NES produced villains as well as heroes, personal aggrandizement and uncelebrated achievement.

Begun in political calm, the NES was completed in the charged atmosphere of the Iraqi war. That it was completed at all is testament to the tenacity required of modern-day Cabinet officials to succeed in any policy development effort of national significance. That it inspired the enactment of substantive legislation—EPAct—by a Congress dominated by Bush's opposition party is evidence that bi-partisanship is not after all a political illusion.

Like all public policy, the NES resulted from compromise; the prudence of its proposals perhaps its greatest virtue. It did not, like Nixon's "Project Independence," measure national sovereignty by the quantity of imported energy. It did not, as in the case of Carter's "National Energy Plan," seek civic virtue in the regulation of consumer behavior. The NES, rather, met the expectations of the political center: encouragement of conservation, shared private and public financing of research on technology, a prod in the direction of greater competition in the electric power sector, and government sponsorship of alternative transportation fuels.

Future analysts and policy-makers—including those charged with it in the second Bush presidency—might come to value the National Energy Strategy, above all, for its central tenet. This was the proposition that, contrary to the conclusions presented in the vast majority of previous energy policy plans, the security of a great nation is not, indeed should not be threatened by barrels of oil, carbon molecules, or electrons.

This is the story of how the NES was constructed and the Energy Policy Act enacted. It is also the story of how policy is crafted and shaped by the people and institutions of the Executive and Legislative branch of the Federal Government—those who arrive in the city after every election, and those who labor anonymously in the professional ranks of the Federal civil service. The story is important because, the technical brittleness of the subject notwithstanding, energy policy affects our social and economic life in critical ways and contributes directly to our personal comfort and well-being. Indeed, modern life would be unthinkable without seamless access to affordable energy.

CHAPTER ONE

A BRIEF HISTORY OF U.S. ENERGY POLICY AND ITS MAKERS

From Roosevelt to Reagan

ROOSEVELT & TRUMAN: THE RISE OF THE ENERGY BUREAUCRACY

Natural resources planning became a function of the federal government during Franklin D. Roosevelt's first term in office. Energy was only a part of the natural resources equation, but no less important an instrument of federal authority that New Dealers would harness to support their aim of social and economic change. Responsibility for natural resources management resided then as now in the Department of the Interior, but authority for natural resources policy was assigned to the National Resources Board, created in 1934. The board was one of many extra-statutory bodies Roosevelt created to do what he believed established bureaucracies would not: infuse federal power with vigorous idealism and apply it to resolve pressing national problems.

Repeatedly reorganized over the subsequent decade and by 1939 renamed the National Resources Planning Board, its new Rooseveltian bureaucrats over time spread their reach over vast areas of public policy. The board occupied what historian Arthur Schlesinger has described as the convergence of public interests represented by "land, water, forests; erosion control, flood control, navigation, irrigation, reclamation; dams, power, poverty, politics."[1] This broad domain offered extraordinary opportunity for government activism, precisely as envisaged and pursued by the idealists of the New Deal.

The New Deal was given practical expression in great public works projects aimed at stimulating social and economic development, particularly in regions prone to poverty and lacking the essential infrastructure necessary to business development and job creation. The New Deal created the Tennessee Valley Authority (TVA), the Bonneville Power Administration (BPA), California's Central Valley Project, and other rural development structures to harness the energy of America's great river systems (the Columbia, the Missouri and the Colorado). These projects provided cheap electricity to millions, water for irrigation and recreation, and, most of all a stimulus to further local entrepreneurial initiative. They also established a federal responsibility for a range of socioeconomic obligations to discrete constituencies and regions of the nations, which, in time became—and remain—federal budgetary entitlements. New Deal energy projects were a source of great controversy, contributing then as energy policy has done since, to profound political divisions. Congress set the tone of the national discourse on energy policy as soon as TVA was established in 1933. It focused its displeasure on David Lilienthal, a committed New Dealer, who shaped and directed TVA in its first decade. As David McCullough notes in his biography of Truman, Republican members of Congress considered TVA to be a "hotbed of Communism"[2] and labeled Lilienthal "a typical power hungry bureaucrat."[3]

The creation of TVA was merely the start of New Deal activism in the energy sector. The construction of hydropower dams engendered the requirement to regulate the marketing of electricity generated at federal installations, and more broadly, the need to oversee the rapidly expanding interstate electric grid. And so, in 1935, Roosevelt proposed, and Congress enacted the Federal Power Act (FPA). FPA, which also created the Federal Power Commission (FPC), brought the full authority of the federal government into a sector of the economy previously regulated by states and forever changed how electricity would be generated, transmitted, and distributed in the United States. FPC's powers were further expanded in 1938 with enactment of the Natural Gas Act. This statute established federal authority over the interstate transportation and sale of natural gas, concurrently creating the dichotomy of federal and state regulation of the natural gas market, which would defy rationalization for more than forty years.

The federal role in the petroleum market was, by contrast, nearly passive and might have remained so for some time, had fuel requirements for the war effort not surfaced as a federal preoccupation. The *de facto* oil policymakers of the 1930s were American oil companies and the states of the Southwest. The Interstate Oil Compact Commission essentially controlled U.S. oil production. The federal government's chief responsibility of the period was to superficially oversee the commission's decisions. Acting under authority of the Connolly Hot Oil Act of 1935, the Interior Department provided data on national oil demand requirements, which the commission then used to set production quotas. The Interior Department's Petroleum Conservation Division was charged with enforcement of the quotas.[4]

During World War II, Roosevelt faced the possibility of an oil supply shortage. The advice he was given to address this eventuality has echoed in the nation's energy policy debate in every subsequent decade. Interior Secretary Harold Ickes warned Roosevelt, "We have no national policy with respect to petroleum."[5] The policy Ickes had in mind was the creation of a Federal Petroleum Reserve Corporation to purchase oil outside the United States for use by American allies, and, subsequently, to acquire and manage domestic oil reserves for use in domestic emergencies.

Other advisers to Roosevelt also concluded for reasons other than Ickes' that future U.S. oil supplies were better secured overseas. In 1942, Sumner Pike, a member of Roosevelt's Petroleum Administration for War, suggested that "instead of stimulating (oil) discoveries in this country by incentive prices, we should, as a long-range policy, be not only willing but happy to...purchase substantial (foreign) quantities of our domestic needs as long as they can be had cheaply."[6] The reasoning behind the advice was fundamentally economic, but nonetheless influenced by the theory that neither private American producers nor foreign suppliers could be entrusted with the provision of a commodity that had become the only means of assuring mobility to modern armies.

Ickes eventually prevailed and was authorized by Roosevelt to buy and sell foreign oil as necessary to ensure supplies to U.S. allies during the entire course of the war. Moreover, the Interior Department was authorized to control domestic prices of oil products, ration supplies, and allocate production to defense and civilian use. The war effort was viewed as ample justification for government's pervasive presence in the oil market. Ickes thus cemented the policy view that energy generally, and oil in particular, were strategic assets, access to which was a matter of national security. This view, and its logical sequitur that government has a duty to be engaged in energy matters has remained a consistent, largely unchallenged tenet of U.S. energy policy deliberation.

POST WAR POLICY

The end of war should have seen a reduction of the federal role in the energy sector and a return to civilian management of the economy. However, newly empowered President Harry Truman was confronted with a number of highly charged energy issues immediately upon taking office.

First, he had to consider whether nuclear power, the most destructive force known to man, should be adopted for use by the private sector. Second, he faced a controversy created by the first-ever antitrust investigation of U.S. oil companies. Third, he was being pressed by his interior secretary to authorize a precedent-setting federal involvement in the production of synthetic fuels. Truman, like many of his successors, neither sought nor welcomed these issues to his policy agenda. They were, rather, thrust upon him by bureaucracies unwilling to relinquish powers granted extraordinarily during a war and by agencies seeking domain over technological change.

The debate on the peaceful use of the atom began soon after nuclear fission became a reality, and intensified with the creation in 1946 of the Atomic Energy Commission (AEC). Truman policymakers were concerned about the implications for the defense and intelligence establishment of releasing secret data on weapons technology into publicly available means of controlling a nuclear reaction to produce electricity. Public utilities and other private interests, by contrast, saw nuclear power as a potentially lucrative new industry. According to McCullough, Truman was determined that civilians rather than military leaders assume control of the nation's nuclear affairs.[7]

An advisory group chartered by the AEC determined in 1948 that "the need for Government monopoly in certain important areas, coupled with secrecy, seems to erect an impenetrable barrier to a wish for knowledge (about nuclear power)."[8] The impenetrable barrier was exactly what the defense establishment had in mind. "I am alarmed," Truman was told by his air force aide, General Robert Landry, "about the amount and kind of information concerning atomic energy activities...that appears in public articles."[9] The advent of the Korean War permitted Truman to put in abeyance the issue of civilian use of nuclear power, but the analysis and debate carried out in his administration set the stage for Eisenhower's Atoms for Peace program, which effectively launched America's civilian nuclear industry.

On the oil policy front, however, decisions could not be postponed. In a series of events that were to be replayed to the same script in the 1970s, Iranian workers at the Abadan oil refinery—then the largest in the Middle East—shut down production in a dispute over wages with the Anglo-Iranian Oil Company. The U.S. Interior Department confronted the Iranian crisis by creating a Foreign Petroleum Supply Committee, made up exclusively of oil industry representatives, charged with investigating problems of supply shortfalls and recommending corrective action.[10] The committee interpreted its charter very broadly.

Although U.S. interests were not threatened—the British-owned Abadan refinery supplied Europe and not the Western Hemisphere—the committee, having obtained a grant of antitrust immunity from Congress, proceeded to assume virtual control of the international oil market.[11] The committee devised a "voluntary agreement" for worldwide allocation of oil stocks, which was used, in effect, to allocate supplies among the committee's own members. In time, the agreement was transformed into an instrument of foreign and commercial policy managed by privately owned oil companies. It became the means to reward and punish Middle Eastern governments that did not cooperate with the committee's mandate to "determine the supplies of petroleum in free friendly states in order to anticipate supply shortages which it would be necessary to meet."[12]

The committee managed the supply shortfall created by the Iranian crisis by increasing product prices to U.S. and European consumers. This policy, reasonable on the merits of balancing the market by inducing reductions in demand, also served to enhance the profits of committee members, who believed that their antitrust immunity would protect them from adverse public reactions. The belief proved naive. Attacked by Congress and the media, viewed with extreme suspicion by the public, the voluntary agreement and the committee itself came finally to symbolize federal surrender of public policy to a private industry that would use a political crisis for the purpose of self-enrichment.[13]

The Foreign Petroleum Supply Committee came under investigation by the Federal Trade Commission (FTC) in 1950. Two years later, the FTC issued a report, titled *The International Petroleum Cartel*, which was initially suppressed for its provocative conclusions, but soon released to the clamor of Congress. The report accused the oil industry of collusion to create a worldwide oligopoly with the power to control the supply and price of oil. The FTC recommended that criminal charges be pursued by the Justice Department against the entire membership of the Foreign Petroleum Supply Committee.[14]

The decision to proceed or not with prosecution of committee members landed on Truman's desk in January 1953. Truman was faced on the one hand with the culpability of his own Interior Department, which had permitted the committee to operate without effective government oversight, and on the other by his duty to act on the findings of FTC. In the end, he ordered criminal proceedings dropped but directed the Justice Department to pursue civil damages.[15]

Refinement of policy analysis

On the analytical front, the Truman administration fostered the use of energy sector analysis as an increasingly sophisticated element of federal policy planning. The credit goes to Harold J. Barnett, an economist on the staff of Truman's Interior Secretary Julius Krug. Barnett, perhaps the modern age's first energy policy analyst, compiled a report titled, *Energy Uses and Supplies, 1939, 1947, 1965*. The report, completed in 1948, made use of then-novel energy supply and demand projections. Barnett argued that "most fuels were finite in quantity, could not be increased in production or substituted for each other without substantial lead time, were developed only with very large investments, and were produced frequently in non-competitive industries."[16] But perhaps the most telling element of *Energy Uses and Supplies* was Barnett's conclusion that the United States would in the future require a "substantial increase in crude (oil) imports on combined grounds of (domestic production) cost and American company ownership of important foreign reserves."[17]

Unlike the institution he served, Barnett would later, as a private analyst unconstrained by bureaucratic deference, deepen his understanding of the energy sector to the point of refuting the theory of finite resources that underlay his original report. But Barnett's post-government service thinking would not dissuade the Interior Department from seeking alternatives to what it regarded as a virtually assured national over-dependence on unreliable oil imports. The alternative was coal. The department determined that liquid fuels produced from America's vast resources of coal and shale held the promise of energy independence; a future solely dependent on home- grown technology and free of worries about the Persian Gulf's perennially volatile politics.

Synthetic fuels

The first federal synthetic fuels (synfuel) research program began with a modest investment of $225,000 by Interior's Bureau of Mines.[18] The program was given a congressional charter and public visibility with passage of the Synthetic Liquid Fuels Act of 1944. The legislation drew immediate fire. It was considered by the oil industry to be a challenge to its preeminence in the liquid fuels market and an unwarranted expansion of the government's already pervasive role in the energy sector of the economy. The oil industry attacked the program as an Interior Department effort to "...frighten and propagandize Congress,"[19] and initially succeeded in stalling its implementation. But congressional support for the program remained steady, as did federal financial support, albeit at modest levels through the 1940s.

In 1951, Interior Secretary Krug, again confronted by the uncertainties of a new war, as well as the need to secure fuel supplies for civilian and military use, obtained from the Treasury Department $455 million in federal loan guarantees that could be extended to those willing to build synthetic fuel plants.[20] The impetus to invest federal funds in a crash program of questionable economic value came from the crisis atmosphere of the Korean War. Still, the Krug initiative did not last long. In less than a year, the executive branch and Congress became convinced that the program was of dubious value and, by late 1951, Interior's own staff questioned "the objectives, technology, economics, government support" of the synfuel effort.[21]

The Krug synfuel program expired in 1952. In its brief operational life, the effort demonstrated that it was possible to liquefy coal and produce oil from shale, but at costs substantially higher than those of conventionally produced petroleum. The poor economics of synfuels did not, as might have been expected, discourage their pursuit. The two initial failures, rather, whetted the appetite of Interior Department researchers for a domestic answer to what they saw as the perennial threat posed by imports of cheap oil. The flame of synfuels' promise was kept alive in research laboratories operated by the Bureau of Mines in Morgantown, West Virginia, and Pittsburgh, Pennsylvania. In those two centers, men with deep roots in Appalachia's culture of coal production—and despair—held tenaciously to the expectation that sooner or later federal policymakers would see the tantalizing prospects of producing limitless fuels from coal.

Every administration since Truman's has glimpsed in synthetic fuels the promise of U.S. energy independence. Federal energy plans promulgated from 1950 to 2000 have contained a financial commitment—sometimes modest but frequently substantial—to reach the elusive goal of enticing cost-competitive gaseous or liquid energy from America's vast coal reserves. Synfuels served as the opiates of energy policy most especially in the wake of the 1973 energy crisis, touted as the answer to America's energy problems by Republican and Democratic administrations alike.

As detailed in later chapters, coal researchers and energy policymakers have repeatedly assured presidents and members of Congress that the cost of synfuels could be reduced sufficiently to make them competitive with crude oil. In 1950, the difference in cost between synfuels and crude oil was projected to be bridged in five years. Later, it was to be bridged—again in five years—for Nixon's Project Independence, and by the same time period for Carter's National Energy Plan. For George H. W. Bush's National Energy Strategy, the cost difference was projected to be closed by the turn of the century, provided that the real price of crude oil would, on a sustainable basis, be no lower than $29 per barrel.[22]

EISENHOWER:
MANDATORY OIL IMPORTS CONTROL

From his predecessor, General Eisenhower inherited a recession, pending antitrust litigation against U.S. oil companies, political trouble in Iran, the demilitarization of nuclear power, and an energy policy report from a federal commission chaired by William Paley. The Paley Commission had been chartered by Truman to assess long-range prospects for minerals and resources independently of assessments typically carried out by competing, self-interested bureaucracies. Paley, chairman of Columbia Broadcasting System, had had no previous involvement in energy policy matters. He proceeded to examine energy issues on a system-wide basis shunning the fuel-by-fuel approach that had until then characterized both the analytical agenda and the functional alignment of the federal energy establishment.[23] Meticulous analysis, complex modeling and brilliant graphic presentations characterized Paley's final report. But the report, true to its analytical character and Paley's personal modesty, was agnostic on specific policy recommendations. These, in Paley's view, were political decisions beyond the scope of his mandate.

Among the matters of concern to the incoming Eisenhower administration was the impact on domestic production of increasing imports of cheap foreign oil. By the early 1950s, crude oil imports accounted for about ten percent of domestic consumption. This was considered troubling because it represented a doubling of U.S. oil import dependence in less than a decade. Trends were similarly worrisome for the entire Western Alliance, which, like the United States, had increased its reliance on external sources of oil from politically volatile geographic regions.

The relatively modest level of U.S. oil imports was viewed by the Eisenhower administration in the context of the need by Europe and Japan to meet the bulk of their civilian and military oil requirements through commercial arrangements with Persian Gulf producers. These arrangements had not been considered problematic in the past because Middle Eastern oil was owned, produced, transported, refined and retailed by the Seven Sisters—Standard Oil of New Jersey, Texaco, Gulf, Standard

Oil of California, Mobil, British Petroleum, and Royal Dutch/Shell. But political events in Iran were changing the geopolitics of world oil as well as U.S. energy policy preoccupations.

As Henry Linden recounts in his 1987 essay "World Oil"[24], "In June 1951, the Mossadegh regime began in earnest the process of nationalizing the Anglo-Iranian Oil Company. This precipitated a lock-out of British oil technicians by Iranian troops...and Iranian crude production of 700,000 barrels per day—more than 6 percent of the world's total at the time—was virtually shut down." Iranian attempts to operate its production and refining industry with the assistance of technicians from other countries were thwarted by the Seven Sisters. The oil companies' intent was to deny the technological means of production to nations that were considered politically too primitive to be allowed control of their own resources. Oil production in Iran did not resume until the Eisenhower administration worked out a production arrangement between the Iranian government and a consortium of Western producers. Interestingly, the consortium included many U.S. oil companies that were parties to the antitrust suit begun under Truman and still pending at the Eisenhower Justice Department.

The arrangement with Iran proved temporarily workable, but in 1955 the continuing prospect of unstable political conditions in the Middle East led the Eisenhower administration to experiment with a voluntary program to reduce oil imports. The program sought to curb imports rather than reduce demand and was therefore generally ignored by the international oil companies, which saw their business as meeting their customers' needs. As a consequence, oil imports continued to grow, in line with the robust demand induced by steady growth in the U.S. vehicle fleet. This led, on March 10, 1959, to the issuance by Eisenhower of a presidential proclamation establishing mandatory quotas on oil imports.[25] He acted under authority of the Trade Agreement Extension Act of 1955, which provided to the president the authority to establish quotas whenever imports were deemed to adversely affect national security.

The mandatory controls on oil imports distorted U.S. oil policy for the entire period in which they were in effect. It is noteworthy that the impact of controls was very well understood by the analytical community and by

Eisenhower's own advisers. In December 1958, Clarence Randall, chairman of the Council on Foreign Economic Policy, warned the administration that mandatory controls "cannot be justified on grounds of security or those of economic policy."[26] Randall argued that controls would have the effect of raising domestic consumer prices while concurrently accelerating the depletion of domestic resources. He concluded that controls would be counterproductive to U.S. international leadership on reduction of trade barriers and would undermine the U.S. position on the General Agreement on Tariffs and Trade.

Douglas Bohi and David Montgomery noted in a 1982 study of mandatory controls that the Eisenhower program was "significant in the history of oil import controls because it was implemented specifically for national security reasons.[27]" If national security had been the intent of the curb on oil imports, the consequences proved the contrary, as Eisenhower's State Department learned immediately after the controls were imposed.

Venezuela, whose exports of residual fuel oil to the United States were affected by the mandatory controls, lost no time in reminding the Eisenhower administration that two could play the market intervention game. The card played by Venezuela was to call a meeting of the world's then major oil producers for the purpose of creating what came to be known as the Organization of Petroleum Exporting Countries (OPEC).

It can be argued that the U.S. mandatory oil import control program not only created the conditions needed to coalesce the interests of OPEC members, but served also to accelerate the nationalization of oil production in Latin America, Africa, and the Persian Gulf. Eisenhower's State Department foresaw clearly the control policy's outcome. A staff paper of July 1959 stated that "given the nationalistic climate which today prevails in Venezuela, it is doubtful that the line can be held at any point short of total government control, if not expropriation." More importantly, the paper went on to say: "if Venezuela demonstrates that it is capable of taking these measures, it is wishful thinking to assume that the line (against nationalization) could be held in the Near and Far East."[28]

If the international costs of protectionism are measured in the imprecise currency of diplomatic consequence, domestic costs can, by contrast, be measured as specific economic impacts on consumers and the economy. The cost consequences of the mandatory import program were calculated in 1970 by a cabinet task force chartered by President Nixon, which reached the conclusion—never challenged—that in the single year of 1969, American consumers paid $5 billion more for petroleum products than would have been the case without the program.[29]

As to the policy costs? The Eisenhower quota program contributed to the policy confusion surrounding the oil embargo of 1973. As Bohi and Russell note in *Limiting Oil Imports*, the program was "perceived to have effects that were due instead to changes in underlying market forces and to price controls."[30] The Nixon administration was later to react to the confusion by lifting Eisenhower's controls on imports but retaining those on price, thereby aggravating the energy crisis of 1973.

The mandatory quota program exposed the nation to economic and diplomatic costs, as well as to policy risks whose full dimensions did not become fully evident until a decade later. The program also established a pattern of modern-day government intervention in the petroleum market that was not to change fundamentally until 1981. Oil policy—usually the result of difficult and querulous political compromises—acquires institutional inertia that can be redirected only by determined congressional action. On energy policy, Congress is prone to deliberate with exceptional slowness, and to typically reverse course only after the policy's economic costs have become unbearable. In the case of oil policy, Congress pondered the issue of controls for two decades before agreeing to a cautious decontrol schedule proposed by President Carter and finally completed by President Reagan.

Eisenhower on other fronts

Eisenhower launched the Atoms for Peace program in 1953, committing the United States to civilian application of nuclear technology at home and abroad. The initiative was deemed more a matter of cold war policy than an issue of energy policy. The program was intended to provide an example to the world of how the United States could treat openly and without undue secrecy, technology like nuclear fission that, by contrast, the Soviet Union held under absolute state control. Congress codified the Atoms for Peace program in the Atomic Energy Act of 1954, which authorized the newly created AEC to develop prototype nuclear reactors for electricity generation and provide to utilities, under license, the fissionable fuel needed to operate them.

Natural gas policy also received attention during the Eisenhower administration, but from the Supreme Court. In 1954, the Court handed down its ruling in *Phillips Petroleum v Wisconsin,* supporting Wisconsin's position that the Natural Gas Act of 1938 indeed required the federal government to regulate the wellhead price of natural gas sold in interstate commerce. The *Phillips* decision, a literal interpretation of a bad law, led to the creation of a dual natural gas market, unregulated as to price when the fuel was sold within the state of production, but regulated in the case of interstate sales.

The court's decision shaped natural gas production and consumption for nearly four decades and contributed to the view that the natural gas sector was more closely related to the structure of electric and water utilities than to a commodity market. Consumers felt the full brunt of the *Phillips* decision in the mid-1970s when acute shortages of gas were experienced in the federally regulated interstate market while the fuel was in surplus in intrastate markets. It would take thirty-five years from the *Phillips* decision for Congress to be persuaded of the irrationality of natural gas price regulation.

Controls of the source, production, and price of oil and gas had a pernicious effect on federal energy policy for two decades after Eisenhower's administration. In that period, energy policy became premised on the duality of federal and state regulatory processes and on the prerogatives of each to divorce consumers' interests from the replacement costs of fuels. Consequently, the economics and market fundamentals of natural resources were generally disregarded as matters of policy. This regulatory frame of reference would prove fatally inappropriate when the time arrived to confront the crisis that Arab oil producers orchestrated in 1973.

KENNEDY & JOHNSON: NUCLEAR VS. FOSSIL

OPEC was established in 1960, to the general indifference of the incoming Kennedy administration. At the time, responsibility for energy policy was dispersed among numerous specialized agencies that, in the absence of visible White House coordination and control, exercised the prerogatives of bureaucratic fiefdoms. The AEC promoted nuclear power. The Interior Department concerned itself with domestic production of oil, gas, and coal. The Bureau of Reclamation built hydropower dams, as did the Army Corps of Engineers. The FPC regulated the interstate sale of electric power, natural gas, and oil. The State Department held domain over the international aspects of energy policy, which consisted mainly of keeping a close, if futile, watch on U.S. oil companies' operations in the Middle East. The president's Office of Science and Technology oversaw federal research and development (R&D) policy.

Then, as now, specialized federal agencies saw their first duty as protecting—if not expanding—the boundaries of their statutory mission. Cabinet secretaries had no incentive to coordinate common, inter-agency policy unless specifically directed to do so by White House staff and leadership. Agencies' self-contained structures reflected the programmatic territory delineated by congressional oversight committees whose interest lay in safeguarding budgetary turf. Policy integration paid no dividends for the executive or the legislative branches of government. There was, in short, no practical institutional incentive to subordinate agency missions to broader public policy interests and no organizational vehicle to assess the full dimension of events such as the creation of OPEC.

OPEC came into being ostensibly to oppose the power of multinational oil companies—the famed Seven Sisters—to set the price of oil, with or without the consent of the nations whose oil they sold. The explanation would seem simplistic in retrospect. The ability of the five OPEC founders—Venezuela, Saudi Arabia, Iran, Iraq, Kuwait—to mobilize nations and governments as diverse as the thirteen which ultimately joined the organization most probably stemmed from multiple and complex causes. The evidence suggests that the federal energy establishment was unprepared to assess the cause and effects of OPEC's creation. As Crauford Goodwin would later note, the United States had failed to develop "a sizable and capable body of disinterested and broad-gauged specialists competent to deal with complex issues of energy policy."[31]

Seaborg's reign

Those who held positions of power in the energy establishment of the Kennedy administration were advocates of particular fuels and technologies. Chief among them was the leader of the AEC, who viewed himself as the champion of nuclear technology, rather than its regulator.

Kennedy's AEC Chairman, Glenn Seaborg, sought adherence to his vision of a nuclear future—a future of *electricity too cheap to meter*—by raising doubts about the size and extraction cost of U.S. fossil fuel reserves. To the extent that his view was not supported by evidence of availability of economically competitive fuels and technology, Seaborg, a Nobel Laureate, raised doubts about his opponents' data and assumptions. AEC staff was given the task of promoting the need for nuclear energy by discrediting Interior Department estimates of coal, oil, and natural gas reserves. AEC claimed that fossil fuel estimates were exaggerated and unreliable and that the size of the energy resource base was insufficient to meet future U.S. energy demand.[32]

In early 1963, to arbitrate the irreconcilable differences between AEC and the Interior Department, Kennedy established the Interdepartmental Energy Study Group under the chairmanship of Donald Horning, director of the White House Office of Science and Technology. Co-chaired by Walter Heller, a member of the Council of Economic Advisers (CEA), the group was directed to undertake "a comprehensive study of the development and utilization of our total energy resources, to aid in determining the most effective allocation of our R&D resources."[33] Ali Bulent Cambel of Northwestern University was retained to conduct the study. Cambel completed his work in late 1963 and submitted to the White House a massive technical report recommending major federal support for energy technology development—especially nuclear—while concurrently concluding that conventional energy supplies were ample.[34]

In a pattern that was to be reflected in subsequent administrations and in future attempts to achieve government-wide consensus on energy policy, the agencies represented on the Study Group responded to Cambel by questioning all of his conclusions and demanding equal time at policy analysis and recommendation. The agencies took issue with data, assumptions, analysis, the methodology, and results of virtually every section of the Cambel report. For nearly two years that Cambel worked on the project, they delivered a steady stream of comments, critiques, questions and objections, until they succeeded in burying the report.[35] Kennedy's assassination finally sealed Cambel's effort.

There was in fact no obvious reason to embark upon energy policy initiatives during the early 1960s. Composite fuel oil prices had been in decline since 1953, domestic oil reserve estimates were up, as was production, and natural gas proven reserves were increasing even in the face of counterproductive regulation. The Paley report had forecast stable or slightly rising prices up to its planning horizon of 1975 and the Study Group had not substantially departed from the Paley forecast. The sanguine view of resource availability was further reinforced by a 1960 study directed by Sam Schurr at Resources for the Future, who declared that "[t]he United States is *not* (emphasis added) compelled to adopt particular policies because of impending resource exhaustion in any of the mineral fuels, or the threat of steeply rising costs."[36]

The crowded Johnson agenda

Lyndon Johnson, an impatient man with broad political shoulders, wanted to hit the policy ground running when finally free of the Kennedy shadow. During his 1964 election campaign, he chartered a series of task forces to provide policy advice for his forthcoming administration. One such task force, led by Joseph Fisher, the president of Resources for the Future, was commissioned to prepare a report, *Resources Policy for a Great Society*.

The Fisher report was delivered to the president immediately after his landslide victory over Barry Goldwater. It contained prudent advice on most issues. On R&D policy, Fisher recommended a balanced portfolio of federal investments in energy technology and a departure from emphasis on construction of nuclear reactors. It was, however, the report's analysis of the oil market that displayed uncommon foresight. Fisher and his group called for the creation of a presidential energy commission to address some critical questions about the future direction of national oil policy. The issues raised by Fisher's group almost precisely anticipated conditions the nation was to confront a decade later, including the political evolution of OPEC and the probability of an oil supply disruption. Among the many policy questions raised by Fisher were the following:[37]

- What percentage of total oil consumption could be imported by the United States without endangering its national security?
- What advance provisions should be made to cope with interruptions in oil supply?
- To what extent would the nation be placed at risk "by the emergence of an organization of oil exporting countries for concerting [*sic*] policy and action?"[38]

Like Paley's, Fisher's work advanced the art of energy analysis but not of policy formulation and decision-making. Task force advice was, in any case, soon lost in the frantic pace of Johnson's social agenda and his eventual absorption in the Vietnam war. The absence of White House attention to the broader aspects of energy policy, however, had the unintended effect of leaving the field open for the AEC to press ahead with rapid development of the civilian nuclear power industry.

Light water reactors of American design, adapted from the Navy's nuclear propulsion program, captured the world market by the mid-1960s. Even so, the AEC was not satisfied with the success of this first generation technology, believing that the future of nuclear power lay in the technology of breeder reactors. The AEC made the case for breeders—by definition capable of producing new fuel from used uranium—by arguing, as it previously had in regard to fossil fuels, that uranium resources were limited and exhaustible and subject to curtailment by unfriendly states.[39] With this highly dubious thesis, the AEC persuaded Congress to finance construction of a prototype breeder reactor at Clinch River in Tennessee. The program survived ten years of annual congressional appropriations (and cost overruns) until abolished by President Jimmy Carter, a nuclear engineer.

As with synfuels, the history of federal involvement in the nuclear sector is one of exaggerated expectations as to the benefits that the nation would obtain from taxpayer support of research, development, demonstration, and deployment of nuclear generating plants. Usually a favorite of Republican administrations, federal nuclear programs have typically been trimmed but never quite eliminated by Democratic presidents. Carter's determination to bury the Clinch River project ran into his successor's equally strong determination to revive it.

Johnson apparently cared little about nuclear technology or about energy policy. As if by Delphic design, however, he was forced to contend with the 1967 Arab-Israeli war, which would sow the seeds of explosive Arab rage over American and Western European policy in the Middle East. The policy of unconditional Western support for Israel served to mold Arab oil producers into a cohesive political force that, in 1973, brought to the United States and the world at large, the first experience of a crisis in energy.

NIXON & FORD:
THE FIRST ENERGY CRISIS

Fate chose Richard Nixon to manage the United States' first energy crisis. Unlike his recent predecessors, who had been spared any serious concerns about the energy sector, Nixon was beset by energy issues throughout his administration. Although there are few references to energy matters in Nixon's memoirs, or in most of his later writings, the public record indicates a recurrent and intense preoccupation of his administration with the intractability and political and social dimensions of energy matters.

Nixon sent his first energy policy message to Congress on June 4, 1971. He sent his last message on July 2, 1974.[40] During the intervening three years he unsuccessfully harangued and cajoled Congress for action on the energy front. Frustrated by congressional inaction, he undertook initiatives designed to test the limits of executive authority over the energy sector. He experimented with a variety of policy instruments and structures within the White House and the executive branch in an effort—never quite successful— to bring cohesion to energy policymaking.

By the end of his term in office, Nixon had substantially restructured the federal apparatus charged with energy regulatory and R&D functions, and had nearly persuaded Congress to enact the first comprehensive energy legislation of modern times. But he had also established powerful precedents of indiscriminate federal intervention in the energy sector and a willingness to trade environmental protection for assured energy supplies. As in other aspects of his presidency, his words were frequently more enlightened than his actions. On the foreign policy front, his administration watered the seeds of the Iranian revolution, thereby setting the stage for what would become the United States' second energy crisis in 1979.

"For most of our history, " Nixon told Congress in his 1971 *Program to Insure an Adequate Supply of Clean Energy in the Future,* "a plentiful supply of energy is something the American people have taken very much for granted." But in light of electricity brownouts experienced in the Northeast during the winter of 1970, continued worries about potential shortfalls of fuel oil and concomitant increases in fuel prices in the winter of 1970–71 and growing pressure from the environmental community to address ecological degradation caused by fossil fuel consumption, Nixon came to the conclusion that "we cannot take our energy supply for granted any longer."[41]

To address the nation's energy problems, Nixon proposed a sweeping R&D and regulatory reform program aimed at enhancing supplies and curbing demand. He requested funds for the Environmental Protection Agency (EPA) to pursue demonstration of sulfur oxide control technology, a precursor to the Reagan administration's Clean Coal Technology Program. He directed the AEC to develop and commercialize a nuclear breeder reactor that he called "our best hope today for meeting the nation's growing demand for economical clean energy." He supported federal funding for coal gasification, coal liquefaction, and magnetohydrodynamic technology (forcing gasified coal through a magnetic field at high temperature to generate electricity). He called for development of advanced nuclear reactors and directed the National Aeronautics and Space Administration (NASA) to assess solar energy.[42]

Believing that the United States would face imminent shortages of natural gas, Nixon advocated broader access to federal lands, tax incentives to accelerate the search for new sources of gas, and, incredibly, "*nuclear stimulation experiments which seek to produce natural gas from tight geologic formations.* (emphasis added)" He further proposed negotiations with Canada to enhance U.S. imports of natural and liquefied gas.[43] On energy conservation and efficiency, Nixon unexpectedly framed the policy debate in unusually enlightened terms with views well ahead of the then prevailing wisdom. "We must," Nixon stated in 1971, "get back on the road of increased efficiency," in part by "*pricing energy on the basis of its full cost to society.* (emphasis added)"[44]

Fully aware of the fragmentation of energy policy and program responsibility among myriad federal agencies, Nixon proposed to consolidate energy functions into a new department of energy and natural resources, exclusive of AEC, which was to remain an independent agency. In the interim, he assumed direct control of energy policy and directed it from the Oval Office for most of his term in office.

Congress pondered Nixon's first energy message but took no action. On April 18, 1973, Nixon forwarded a second energy message to Congress, in which he warned that in the years ahead "we must face up to the possibility of occasional energy shortages and some increase in energy prices." He added, "We should not be misled into pessimistic predictions of an energy disaster. But neither should we be lulled into a false sense of security." Concerning oil imports, Nixon advised Congress that he would, by presidential proclamation, remove all existing tariffs on imported crude oil and products and would "suspend direct control over the quantity of crude oil and refined products which can be imported."[45]

Thus were Eisenhower's mandatory oil import quotas abolished, their impact on the national economy finally recognized as contrary to the national interest. Nixon's elimination of the program might have amounted to enlightened, perhaps even decisive, policy in the context of the energy crisis ahead. However, Nixon then proceeded to impose price and allocation controls on petroleum, as part of his effort to mitigate inflationary pressures. These would prove even more economically damaging than Eisenhower's import quotas and would last nearly as long.[46]

On the organizational front, in 1973 Nixon established, by executive order, a number of departmental and White House positions to better coordinate federal energy policy. He undertook these measures because, in his words, "the 92nd Congress did not act"[47] on his 1971 proposal to create a new department of energy and natural resources. His executive order created a counselor to the president for natural resources, an assistant secretary of Interior for Energy and Minerals, and the first Federal Office of Energy Conservation. The order also directed the Department of Commerce to work with EPA on a program of voluntary energy efficiency labels for major home appliances, established a new division of Energy and Science in the Office of Management and Budget (OMB) and brought the Oil Policy Committee, which coordinated oil import policy, under the Treasury Department. "The need for action is urgent," Nixon wrote in the conclusion of his second energy message to Congress, "I hope Congress will act with dispatch."[48]

Congress has historically proven unable to act with dispatch on energy matters. And so, in June 1973, Nixon once again took direct action. He appointed John Love, governor of Colorado, to direct a new White House Energy Policy Office. He once again requested that Congress create a cabinet level department for energy and natural resources, but added a proposal to establish a separate Energy Research and Development Administration (ERDA) without specifying differences in the mission of the two agencies. He proposed a $10 billion, five-year program of energy technology R&D and launched a national conservation drive to "reduce anticipated personal consumption of energy by 5 percent over the next twelve months." With unexpected foresight, Nixon warned: "Unless we act swiftly and effectively, we could face a genuine energy crisis in the foreseeable future."[49]

On September 8, 1973, with the Middle East essentially at war, and the war's repercussions manifest in the international oil market, Nixon emerged from a cabinet meeting that had been devoted entirely to a discussion of energy matters to reassure the nation that things were not as bleak as they seemed. "We have heard a lot about a crisis," he stated, but "I do not use that term because we do not face a crisis in the sense of the word. I would simply say that in the short term we face a problem."[50] Nixon was dissembling; the nation was in fact confronting the first energy crisis in its history.

On September 10, Nixon sent yet another message to Congress, pleading for action on at least some of the legislative initiatives he had earlier proposed. He requested that Congress act to authorize construction of the Alaska oil pipeline, underwrite the construction of new deepwater ports capable of accommodating supertankers, allow deregulation of prices of natural gas from new wells, and enact standards for reclamation of land after surface mining. "It is absolutely essential," wrote Nixon, "that the Congress not wait for the stimulation of energy shortages to provide the legislation necessary to meet our needs."[51]

The first (energy) oil crisis

Congress remained unmoved by Nixon's pleas. The second Arab-Israeli war broke out in October 1973. On October 20, in response to the U.S. policy of resupplying Israel with weapons, the Organization of Arab Petroleum Exporting Countries (OAPEC) announced an embargo of oil shipments to the United States, Canada and the Netherlands. OAPEC also reduced its overall production levels and counted on further headaches to the West being provided by the closure of the Suez Canal. Oil supplies to the international market were reduced by an average of 1.6 million barrels per day (MMB/D). World oil prices quadrupled, rising from about $3 per barrel before the embargo to over $11 at its conclusion.[52]

Nixon addressed the nation on the energy emergency on November 7, 1973. "We are heading," he said, "toward the most acute shortages of energy since World War II." He went on to describe emergency measures he had taken to assure basic needs, appealed to the American spirit to weather this latest national crisis and announced a bold new energy initiative. "Let us unite in committing the resources of this Nation to a major new endeavor, an endeavor that in this bicentennial era we can appropriately call 'Project

Independence.' Let us set as our national goal, in the spirit of Apollo, with the determination of the Manhattan Project, that by the end of this decade we will have developed the potential to *meet our own energy needs without depending on any foreign energy sources.* (emphasis added)"[53]

The 1973 Arab oil embargo, spectacularly successful from OAPEC's perspective—all the more so because of Western inexperience in the management of supply interruptions—inspired jingoistic rhetoric in the political class, fear and loathing of all things Arab among American consumers, and apocalyptic scenarios from the analytical community. The political call to arms, the respected analysts' dire predictions of resource scarcity, and the public willingness to accept simple explanations for complex causes inflamed the energy policy debate for over a decade.

"Since the first price explosion of 1973," wrote Henry Kissinger in his introduction to Charles Ebinger's *The Critical Link*, "we have learned that the energy crisis is not a mere problem of transitional adjustment; it is a grave challenge to the political and economic structure of the free world." In the same book, Ebinger notes that the price shock of 1973–74 "generated fear in international financial circles that ever escalating oil prices...could lead to a collapse of the international financial system."[54]

The energy crisis precipitated by the 1973 Arab oil embargo had numerous underlying causes, many traceable to federal and state control of fossil fuel production. The regulation of natural gas and coal production, each for different reasons, had forced consumers to turn to oil in order to meet growth in demand. Oil use had expanded beyond the transportation sector, to serve the electricity generation and industrial sectors. Yet domestic oil production had also been constrained and the rise in demand fostered by the switch from other fuels had been met by imports.

The embargo found the United States particularly vulnerable to interruption in the supply of its most important fuel, especially because forty years of policy experimentation had failed to provide a market environment in which oil could be efficiently produced and traded. Douglas Bohi traces the roots of difficulty with U.S. oil policy to a collusive agreement worked out in 1933 by U.S. oil-producing states. Acting under the leadership of the Texas Railroad Commission, the states of Texas, Louisiana, and Oklahoma agreed to limit total U.S. oil production "to an amount that would just cover demand at a pre-determined price."[55] As previously noted, the states' agreement was codified by Congress in the Connolly Hot Oil Act, prohibiting interstate sale of crude oil produced in violation of state allowances. This system was briefly threatened by the rise of oil imports in the 1950s, but Eisenhower's imposition of import quotas—limiting oil imports to twelve percent of total domestic consumption—gave it new life.

Throughout the 1960s, states strictly controlled oil production through rationing, regulations and price caps. Interstate commerce of oil was regulated by the federal government, as were imports. Persian Gulf producers controlled their production as well. The only unregulated segment of the oil market was consumption, which for the previous two decades had been growing at substantially higher rates than had either U.S. or OPEC production.

As the 1973 crisis deepened, Nixon sought and received from Congress emergency authority to restrict private and public consumption of energy and to ration and allocate energy supplies. He also assured the nation, in a radio address on January 19, 1974, that he would do everything in his power to "hold down the price of foreign oil." He added: "Scare stories that the American people will soon be paying a dollar for a gallon of gas are just as ridiculous as the stories that will say that we will be paying a dollar for a loaf of bread." He promised, in direct contradiction of the position he had taken three years earlier in his first energy message to Congress, "Americans cannot afford to pay such prices, and I can assure you that we will not have to pay them."[56]

It seems unusual in retrospect that virtually none of Nixon's energy policy pronouncements contained reference to market functions. The option of freeing oil prices to rise in order for the market to adjust to lower supplies does not appear to have been given serious consideration. Yet the fundamental economic theory that markets would reach supply and demand equilibrium if left relatively unencumbered was well established. Also surprising, given the administration's conventionally rigid response to the embargo, is the fact that Nixon had impressive economic expertise at his disposal. During the 1973–74 period, the president's senior advisers on energy included Charles Shultz, an eminent economist; Charles DiBona, who had joined the White House from the Center for Naval Analysis; Ezra Solomon and Edward Mitchell, both economists at CEA, and William Simon, an investment banker.

In truth, all of the actors in the drama were caught in a script written for governments and not for markets. In 1973, the buying and selling of oil was carried out mainly through diplomatic arrangements among government officials. The oil market resembled a geopolitical chess board on which, internationally, U.S. and European agents alternately jockeyed and colluded for political and economic influence in the Persian Gulf, and where domestically the accommodation of federal and state governmental interests took precedence over the efficient delivery of fuel to consumers.

In sum, there was no oil market available for self-adjustment in 1973. Production and consumption of oil, domestically and internationally, was in the political domain from wellhead to burner tip. Furthermore, the economies of the United States, Europe and Japan were far more oil intensive than would be the case in subsequent years, and the embargo's effects were consequently felt across a broad range of economic and social activity: electricity generation, industrial production, heating, and cooking. The impact of the embargo was amplified, as well, by its timing. The American people were living in an age of trauma. In the ten years before the oil crisis, they had experienced assassinations, riots and war. In 1973 they were living in the grip of stagflation.

By March 1974, the embargo was over, but Congress had only just begun to legislate. It passed the Energy Emergency Act, requested by Nixon several months earlier. Nixon vetoed the legislation because he believed that it set domestic crude oil prices at such a level as to discourage domestic production and increase reliance on imports.[57] On May 7, however, Nixon signed into law the Federal Energy Administration Act of 1974, which established the Federal Energy Administration (FEA) as a successor to the ad hoc White House Federal Energy Office. FEA was given authority for fuel allocation and petroleum pricing regulations, energy data collection and analysis, planning for Project Independence, and energy conservation. In signing the FEA act, Nixon noted that not less than sixteen additional energy policy proposals were awaiting action by the ever-reluctant Congress.[58]

Nixon transmitted his last energy message to Congress on July 2, 1974, in which he indicated that the United States should develop what he called the capacity for self-sufficiency in energy. With that last vain hope, Nixon

left office in disgrace, and it became then the responsibility of Gerald
to cope with the after effects of the embargo and give practical expression
what came to be known as Project Independence.

Ford's blueprint

With Ford's ascension to the presidency, Project Independence became the responsibility of Eric Zausner, assistant FEA administrator for policy planning. Zausner, working with a 500-member staff borrowed from other agencies, produced the massive 800-page *Project Independence Blueprint* in November 1974. The *Blueprint* was innovative in the pioneering use of general equilibrium models (PIES—Project Independence Evaluation System) to measure the impact of policy options on the energy sector and the economy. But it reflected in most of its component elements the prevailing wisdom of the time that the energy crisis would be resolved by making it a function of the federal government.

The *Blueprint* was no sooner released than it became mired in a bureaucratic struggle for control of energy policymaking between FEA Administrator John Sawhill and Treasury Secretary William Simon, also known as the energy czar. The central policy issue was the degree of oil market supply and price decontrol that could be allowed in order to achieve future energy policy objectives without aggravating short-term inflation. FEA itself was divided over the issue. Treasury favored rapid and full decontrol. The CEA, fearing inflationary pressures, favored progressive decontrol. OMB could not quite stake out an independent position because its personnel were staffing the recently created FEA. The issue was placed before President Ford, who took an unexpectedly strong pro-deregulation position.[59]

Meanwhile, in October 1974, Congress finally enacted the Energy Reorganization Act earlier proposed by Nixon. This legislation created ERDA, the Energy Resources Council, and the Nuclear Regulatory Commission (NRC). These organizations joined FEA in the crowded field of energy policymaking, even as the 1973 embargo began to fade into memory. Ford himself began to rethink the aggressive concept of achieving U.S. energy independence and adopted instead the more modest goal of seeking "reasonable self-sufficiency."[60]

To achieve this reasonable self-sufficiency, Ford nonetheless believed in mobilizing the full powers of the federal government. In a television and radio address broadcast on January 13, 1975, he underscored the interlocking aspects of energy, economic and security policy. "We must," he said, "wage a simultaneous three-front campaign against recession, inflation and energy dependence."[61] He carried the message—and a plan—to Congress two days later in his first State of the Union Address, by declaring his intent to establish three national energy policy goals:[62]

- A 1 million barrel per day (MMB/D) reduction of oil imports by the end of 1975 and a 2 MMB/D reduction by 1977;
- By 1985, the end of vulnerability to economic disruption by foreign oil suppliers;
- Development of domestic energy resources and technology sufficient to meet a "*significant share of the energy needs of the Free World*" (emphasis added) by the year 2000.

To accomplish these goals, Ford requested that Congress in effect legislate the most sweeping federal intervention in the energy sector in U.S. history. The proposals included a massive program to increase energy supplies, with emphasis on production on federal lands and on the U.S. Outer Continental Shelf (OCS). In direct challenge to prevailing congressional expectations, Ford recommended the imposition of a $1 per barrel tariff on imported oil effective February 1, 1975. The fee, which he planned to impose under then existing Economic Stabilization Act authority, would rise to $3 per barrel by April 1975. Ford further called for deregulation of new natural gas production coupled with an excise tax, a windfall profits tax and full decontrol of domestic crude oil prices.[63]

To reduce energy consumption by 3 to 5 MMB/D by 1985, Ford requested that Congress enact efficiency standards for all new buildings, provide a $150 tax credit per household for home insulation, establish a federal program to help low-income homeowners purchase insulation supplies, and direct that a forty percent improvement in automobile fuel efficiency be achieved by 1980. Ford proposed that automotive pollution standards be deferred for five years in order to concentrate attention on achieving higher fuel economy.[64]

On the security front, Ford proposed the creation of a one billion-barrel strategic oil storage program for civilian use and a 300 million-barrel reserve for defense purposes. This, he stated, "would make the United States invulnerable to foreign disruptions."[65]

Ford's technology R&D agenda was equally ambitious. He set the goal of achieving one million barrels of synthetic fuels and shale oil production by 1985, build 200 nuclear power plants, 250 new coal mines, 150 coal-fired plants, 30 oil refineries, and 20 synthetic fuel plants over ten years. He furthermore called for drilling "many thousands" of new oil wells, insulating eighteen million homes, and manufacturing "millions of new automobiles, trucks and buses that use much less fuel."[66] This represented a federal energy agenda of monumental proportions and cost. Nothing similar had ever been proposed by a U.S. president.

Congress was stunned by the sweep of Ford's program and unable to digest its dimensions. Instead, in March 1975, ignoring Ford's request that comprehensive energy legislation was needed within ninety days of his State of the Union Address, Congress delivered to the president a single legislative act: to postpone the imposition of Ford's proposed tariff on oil imports. The act was consistent with Congress' historical aversion to oil taxes—an aversion that has remained constant to date. Ford vetoed the bill.[67]

In May 1975, Congress passed the Surface Mining and Reclamation Act, a statute rife with unworkable, overlapping federal and state regulation of the mining industry. Its effect would have been to substantially curb coal production, eliminate nearly forty thousand jobs in the industry, and enable states to ban surface mining on federal lands. Ford vetoed the bill, taking the opportunity to remind Congress that "we are today more vulnerable to the disruption of oil supplies than we were during the Mid-East oil embargo [of 1973]."[68]

Congress continued, in Ford's words, to "drift, dawdle and debate forever with [sic] America's future," until October, when it enacted the Energy Policy and Conservation Act (EPCA). Ford was not entirely happy with the bill, but decided after several weeks of deliberation to sign it into law on December 22, 1975. Signing of the bill came in the wake of intense debate about its oil price control provisions. In essence, Congress wanted to roll back oil prices to near pre-embargo levels plus inflation. Ford wanted aggressive decontrol of prices, but un-elected and facing a tough forthcoming campaign, he was not in a position to fight the Democratic Congress.[69] Ford's misgivings notwithstanding, EPCA gave the president authority to progressively dismantle the price and allocation control regime, subject to disapproval by either house of Congress.

EPCA contained authorization for a strategic petroleum reserve, fuel efficiency standards for automobiles, federal assistance to state conservation programs, U.S. participation in the newly created International Energy Agency, and a broad energy R&D program. It was probably the best that could be achieved under the circumstances. Memories of the oil embargo were fading and fuel shortages had disappeared. Opinion polls indicated that most Americans believed the energy crisis had not been, after all, OPEC's doing, but the work of the major oil companies.[70]

Congress had an easier time of it with EPCA's stepchild. In the summer of 1976, with the presidential election campaign in high gear, Congress easily mustered the consensus to enact the Energy Conservation and Production Act. ECPA (to be thenceforth permanently confused with EPCA) authorized up to $2 billion in federal loan guarantees for investments in conservation by business, industry, nonprofit organizations and state and local governments. ECPA deregulated stripper oil well production and production of oil by the use of enhanced technology. ECPA also required the president to prepare a plan for reorganization of federal energy and natural resources functions, which set the stage for creation of the Department of Energy (DOE) under President Carter. ECPA also established an Office of Energy Information and Analysis, forecasting the future Energy Information Administration (EIA). Thus, in the forty-first year from the start of the twentieth century's energy legislation, and the third year of the energy crisis era, Congress adjourned.

CARTER:
THE MORAL EQUIVALENT OF WAR

Jimmy Carter assumed the presidency of the United States on an overcast day in January 1977. He inherited the knowledge of what had been debated, accepted and rejected by Congress as energy policy in the previous four years. He was equipped with the authority of the EPCA of 1975 and of ECPA of 1976. He was probably better prepared than most of his twentieth century predecessors to understand issues of technology. He also believed, as he noted in *Keeping Faith*, his first book of memoirs, that energy markets were fundamentally uncompetitive and had to be managed by the federal government in order to ensure the common good.

When Carter took office, the energy crisis mentality of 1973 was abating among the general population, but not within the analytical community. Studies of the energy sector and of energy policy abounded. In 1975, ERDA had commissioned the National Academies of Science to assess future U.S. energy requirements. The assessment, known as the CONAES study, for the Committee on Nuclear and Alternative Energy Systems, involved 250 analysts and took more than four years to complete. CONAES produced an impressive energy database and state-of-the-art models. It also contributed to the energy debate by providing the common sense advice that energy policy comprises social and political as well as technological choices, the former being far less well understood than the latter.[71]

The CONAES reasoned effort stood in sharp contrast to the 1974 Ford Foundation's "A Time to Choose, America's Energy Future." The Ford Foundation study, led by S. David Freeman, saw a world manipulated by domestic and international energy companies whose influence on government policy was pernicious. Writing later in *Energy, The New Era*,[72] Freeman would reveal the depth of antagonism he had carried to the Ford study:

> America's energy policy amounted to a blind act of faith that the oil companies and the utilities would indefinitely continue to deliver the goods...Even after the fuel shortages

became a reality in the winter of 1972/1973, the Federal government played down the seriousness of the problem. 'Praying for mild weather' was the government energy policy, a risky policy at best, and a disaster for an administration whose credibility was at an all-time low.[73]

Freeman's conspiratorial views were significant because of the role he was to play in development of Carter's first National Energy Plan (NEP). The Carter administration also had available the results of still another major energy study commissioned by the Twentieth Century Fund and released in January 1977, just as Carter took office. The Fund's study, dismissed by liberals as an industry response to the energy crisis, advocated federal price incentives for domestic oil and gas production, development of oil and gas resources on Alaska's North Slope and the OCS, and support for nuclear and coal technology.[74]

Among the numerous theories of energy policy during the Carter years were those propounded by Amory Lovins. In a treatise called *Soft Energy Paths*, Lovins rejected prevailing energy policy approaches, arguing that governments and technocrats were captives of energy supply system mentality when, in fact, the future lay in viewing energy as a pattern of demand. The demand for energy, Lovins argued, could be met far more efficiently, at lower social cost, and with far less environmental stress through energy efficiency and renewable energy technology.[75]

Carter had strong views on energy policy. In an address to the nation on April 18, 1977, Carter defined the energy problem in dramatic terms:

The energy crisis has not yet overwhelmed us, but it will if we do not act quickly. It is a problem we will not be able to solve in the next few years, and it is likely to get progressively worse through the rest of this century...Our decision about energy will test the character of the American people and the ability of the President and the Congress to govern this nation. This difficult effort will be the 'moral equivalent of war,' except that we will be uniting our efforts to build and not to destroy.[76]

The general command for war's moral equivalent was assigned to James Schlesinger, a Harvard-trained doctor of economics, veteran of Nixon's OMB, former secretary of defense, former director of Central Intelligence, and former chairman of the AEC. Upon his appointment, Schlesinger established an Energy Policy Planning Office in the Old Executive Office Building, across from the White House, as a separate and distinct entity from the congressionally chartered FEA. John O'Leary had been appointed by Carter to head FEA, but Schlesinger's presence in Carter's inner council signaled to Washington's political establishment that the energy policy action would be at the White House.

In January 1977 Schlesinger assembled a small staff of trusted aides—economists, lawyers, former bureaucrats—under the supervision of Alvin Alm and gave them three months to produce a national energy plan. Schlesinger, who was to dominate U.S. energy policymaking for the first three years of the Carter administration, subscribed to the prevailing 1970s view of limited global energy resources and of OPEC dominance over the oil market. However, unlike many energy analysts of the time, Schlesinger had an instinctive faith in America's ability to solve problems like the energy crisis by developing and using new technology. Like his social-democratic counterparts in Europe, he also believed in a benevolent relationship between government and industry. This public/private partnership, if properly motivated, Schlesinger believed, could assure the successful resolution of grave public policy issues. He did not have much faith in Congress, and was impatient with public participation in federal policy development processes.[77]

The first National Energy Plan

With a presidential mandate as potent as the "moral equivalent of war," it was unsurprising that Schlesinger and his staff viewed their work in historic terms. In the NEP that they crafted within the president's prescribed ninety days, Schlesinger and staff defined a world divided into three energy eras: the nineteenth century transition from wood and windmills to coal, the post-Second World War transition from coal to oil and gas, and the late twentieth century transition from hydrocarbons to non-fossil fuel technology.

The last transition, according to NEP's authors, could not be successfully ushered in without first attacking the short-term, fundamental problem of rapidly increasing oil imports and the related problem of oil and gas prices which were, in the United States, far below the cost of replacement. No aspect of NEP, however, was to prove more provocative, than the intervention, probably at Schlesinger's behest, of the Central Intelligence Agency (CIA).

A few days before NEP's unveiling, the administration made public a review of international energy conditions that had been undertaken by the intelligence community. The CIA report argued that, within a decade, OPEC would not only be the marginal producer of oil for the Western world, but also for the Soviet Union and its satellites. This, the CIA argued, would come about because USSR production was expected to peak in the 1980s and OPEC production would be needed thereafter to meet Warsaw Pact oil requirements. The implications of the intelligence report were that the Soviet Union's future oil requirements would profoundly shape its Middle Eastern policy and would add a new dimension to the cold war.[78]

With NEP's unveiling, the government of the United States had transformed a temporary, six-month embargo of oil shipments by a group of Arab producers intent on sending a sharp diplomatic signal to the United States into a social, economic and cold war crusade. Carter described the crusade in his memoirs as "this struggle for a national energy policy...an exhausting fight involving almost every federal agency, all state and local governments, every member of Congress, dozens of interest groups, and hundreds of billions of dollars."[79]

Actually, nothing resembling an energy crisis existed in the United States in 1977. Carter was motivated to precipitous action by a chronic winter fuel shortage in New England. Problems with fuel deliveries during Northeast winters were recurrent throughout the 1970s, and remain so today, among other reasons because of the region's singular dependence on fuel oil for heating. But because of its political clout and the emotional appeal raised by the prospect of the proverbial elderly couple possibly freezing in some rural hamlet, the region has historically succeeded in turning its local vulnerabilities into national crises.

In government, as in the mass media, crises are absorbing. They give new meaning and fresh purpose to government agencies that become involved in them. Bureaucracies receive greater benefits (larger budgets, more clout, greater public interest) from grave national circumstances than from routine duties. And so, Schlesinger and his staff seized the center of Washington's obsessions and portrayed for the media and Congress a fatal, bleak future that could only be brightened by concerted and sweeping government action.

NEP would, according to Schlesinger, be deemed a success if it achieved seven quantitative goals. These were:

1. Reduction of national energy demand growth to two percent annually;
2. Reduction of gasoline consumption by ten percent below 1977 levels;
3. Reduction of oil imports to 6 MMB/D from projected 1980 levels of 16 MMB/D;
4. Establishment of a one billion-barrel strategic oil reserve;
5. Increase of coal production to one billion tons per year;
6. Increase in energy efficiency for ninety percent of all new homes and buildings; and
7. Use of solar energy in more than 2.5 million homes.

These goals were actually relatively modest compared to those that had been proposed by President Ford. The difference was in the means of achieving them. NEP assumed, for example, that the achievement of the generally desirable conservation goals of EPCA legislation could not be left to regulation. It advocated, therefore, financial penalties for auto manufacturers that would not meet EPCA's fuel efficiency standards. Furthermore, NEP posited that even with regulation and criminal penalties, the achievement of overriding national goals could not be entrusted entirely to the private sector.[80] The effort required, rather, extensive management and ongoing oversight by the federal government, and most especially by the new DOE that Carter had proposed within a month of assuming office.

NEP reflected both policy and moral goals. It was the intent of Carter, as it had been of the New Dealers, to use energy policy as a means to a social end. The plan contained a sweeping combination of tax incentives and federal subsidies for preferred fuels and technologies: more coal, less natural gas and oil, more ethanol and solar power. It proposed regulations to mandate energy conservation in automobiles, buildings and homes. With NEP, electric utilities, wrote Carter in his memoirs, "could no longer encourage waste of energy with their distorted rate structures." At the philosophical core of NEP was the belief that human behavior could be molded through moral suasion (lower thermostat setting), style (sweaters) and pain (taxes).

To carry out the NEP, Carter submitted five energy bills to Congress in April 1977. In August 1977, the Congressional Office of Technology Assessment (OTA) issued a detailed review of Carter's plan at the request of the chairmen of House committees on Science and Technology and on Interior and Insular Affairs. OTA considered NEP's analysis of the "world energy crisis...accurate." NEP's correctness lay, the OTA said, among other things, in the diagnosis that "the dominant world problem, which the United States shares, is the long-run *prospect of running out of oil and natural gas* (emphasis added)." The panel also noted that NEP did not "discuss the alternative of allowing prices for energy to rise to the level at which supply and demand are balanced," and went on to suggest, in the typically ambiguous energy economics of the 1970s, that "excessive imports could be discouraged by imposing a tariff. Revenues from both tax and tariff could then be used to redress inequities."[81]

The Carter bills were debated in Congress for over a year and finally enacted on October 15, 1978. The congressional debate was relatively non-controversial on proposals related to conservation and renewable technology. Extended battles were fought, however, on oil and gas price decontrols and energy taxes. Carter proposed to continue price controls on most domestic oil except for oil produced from stripper wells. As to natural gas, Carter's proposal was to subject all new gas sold in the United States to a price ceiling.[82]

Oil and gas price decontrols had been considered and largely legislated by Congress during the Nixon and Ford administrations. Carter was either misinformed about the EPCA authority he already possessed, or sought a more explicit congressional consent. Congressional and special interests' divisions on the issue were territorial and predictable. The Southwest energy-producing regions were in favor of decontrol as were the energy industries and the U.S. Chamber of Commerce. The Northeast was opposed to decontrol, as were consumer advocates and the AFL-CIO. The political alignments were consistent with the policy presumption of t. time, which posited that oil and gas price decontrol meant de facto higher prices to consumers and windfall profits for industry.

The National Energy Act

On November 9, Carter signed into law the National Energy Act of 1978, a massive legislative package comprising: The National Energy Conservation Policy Act (NECPA), the Powerplant and Industrial Fuel Use Act (PIFUA), the Public Utilities Regulatory Policy Act (PURPA), the Energy Tax Act, and the Natural Gas Policy Act (NGPA). The merits of the legislation notwithstanding, this was an impressive achievement under any circumstances, all the more so because the bills had been enacted without Republican support and in a mid-term election year.

NECPA authorized utility-managed conservation programs for homes, weatherization assistance for low-income f milies, solar energy and conservation loan programs, conservation grants to schools and hospitals, and directed DOE to issue efficiency standards for thirteen categories of home appliances. NECPA also provided funds to finance the establishment and operation of energy offices in all fifty states and U.S. territories. These offices were and remain the distributors of federal energy assistance funds to state institutions and local communities.

PIFUA prohibited the use of oil and gas in new electric generation plants and in new industrial plants. It remained on the books until 1992 when Congress finally recognized the counter-productivity of banning the use of abundant natural gas by utilities required to meet stringent new clean air standards. PIFUA did, however, assist in moving the United States away from use of oil in applications for which there were alternatives. By 1985, oil use in the U.S. economy had essentially been concentrated in the transportation sector and as a feedstock for the chemical and plastics industry. The single, notable exception remained New England's use of oil for heating.

PURPA provided voluntary standards for electric utility rate designs, banned rates that favored large electricity consumers, supported co-generation,[83] and promoted public intervention in rate proceedings before state and federal utility commissions. Under PURPA, utilities were required to purchase power at avoided cost from electricity generators who used (mainly) renewable resources. The concept of avoided cost was sufficiently vague in the legislation as to be very liberally interpreted by rate setters in state proceedings. Over time, the costs avoided proved prohibitively burdensome to consumers, but PURPA provided the foundation for the subsequent restructuring of the electric utility industry.

The Energy Tax Act provided tax incentives to homeowners who insulated their homes or installed solar water heating systems and penalized automobiles classified as gas guzzlers. The latter tax continues in force to date, but the insulation tax credit was eventually repealed because it proved costly as well as ineffectual as an energy conservation stimulant.

The NGPA, by far the most controversial of the legislative components, extended wellhead price controls to intrastate markets while allowing for phased, partial decontrol of new, high-cost gas. The NGPA produced a nightmarish regulatory regime, created incentives to produce higher cost gas while stifling production of low-cost gas, and reconfirmed the political mythology that natural gas was a limited, precious resource in need of federal safeguards. The NGPA proved costly to residential, commercial, and industrial consumers, and the economic damage it caused was not contained until a decade later, when Congress enacted the Natural Gas Wellhead Decontrol Act of 1989.

The Department of Energy

The newly created DOE was entrusted with implementation of this monumental legislative package. In its wisdom, Congress created DOE not merely as a successor to ERDA, the Federal Power Commission, and the FEA. Congress also forced upon DOE the responsibility—held previously by AEC and later by ERDA—to manage the nation's entire nuclear weapons design and production complex. By so doing, Carter and Congress created a permanently schizophrenic organization with incompatible military and civilian obligations.

As will be discussed later in greater detail, DOE is overseen by numerous committees of Congress whose interests range from coal gasification and liquefaction to the superconductor supercollider, from the Yucca Mountain nuclear waste repository to energy welfare services for the poor and from the Strategic Petroleum Reserve (SPR) to the Nevada nuclear weapons test site. The breadth of DOE's mission has proven fertile ground for congressionally designated R&D demonstration projects of dubious technological value. From its inception, DOE has attracted powerful constituencies of business, professional societies, and private interest groups that force a division of budgetary spoils as a condition precedent to the pursuit of policy in the national interest.

DOE was Carter's and Congress' final answer to the oil embargo of 1972–73. It was a manifestation of the ambiguity felt by the American people and their government about energy and its role in society. DOE was directed to ensure adequate supplies of conventional energy. But it was also mandated to lead the United States into a new era of fuels and technology that would be clean, inexhaustible and, most importantly, free of OPEC control. The mission of DOE was, in short, impossible.

The congressional energy policy wars over, Carter and Schlesinger probably assumed that 1979 would be a year devoted to consolidation of gains, organization and management of the complex new DOE and freedom from energy preoccupations. But it was not to be.

The second oil crisis

The Iranian revolution moved inexorably to crisis in November 1978. Unrest in Iranian oil fields shut down production and reduced supply to the international market by 3 MMB/D. Output was not restored until six months later, in April 1979. Oil prices rose eighty-two percent from near $13 per barrel in the fall of 1978 to over $23 per barrel in spring 1979.[84] The disruption's effects were initially felt in California, where lines began to form at gasoline stations in early 1979. The shortages moved east, as did the violence. Americans were seen nightly on television, incensed by shortages of gasoline to which they thought themselves entitled, often assaulting one another in a senseless scramble to top off their fuel tanks.

The second U.S. energy crisis found the Carter administration in a state of confusion. At the time of the Iranian disruption, United States was importing approximately 750,000 barrels of oil from Iran, or barely four percent of U.S. consumption. Schlesinger could not convincingly explain to his president or to members of Congress how such a relatively small volume of oil could wreak havoc on the U.S. supply system. Neither Schlesinger nor Congress seemed able to view the oil market as the global, integrated enterprise it had become. In such an enterprise, a disruption anywhere in the system will affect everyone in the system, regardless of a particular nation's level of import dependence from a specific source.

In April 1979, Carter once again addressed the nation on the subject of energy.[85] He proposed a combination of new and recycled initiatives, including the creation of an Energy Security Trust Fund financed by receipts from a windfall profits tax. He also proposed the construction of regional petroleum reserves for Hawaii and the Northeast. His proposals were clarified and made specific in the National Energy Plan II (NEP II) that he submitted to Congress in May 1979.

The second National Energy Plan

NEP II was crafted in the same environment of crisis that had brought forth the earlier Nixon, Ford, and Carter plans. NEP was shaped by policymakers under siege—from within by a president frustrated by events he could not control and from without by Congress interested only in reducing constituents' gasoline costs. It was unsurprising, under the circumstances, that the plan would err on the side of overreaction. NEP II proposed a virtual mobilization of the federal government to wage war on an enemy it could not clearly define. The plan proposed far-reaching initiatives that seemed no less urgent for having been tried and tested, time and again, previously.

On energy conservation: NEP II proposed pricing of fuels at their replacement costs, a tax credit for investments in conservation, a regulatory regime to reduce energy consumption in new buildings and in automobiles, conservation grants to low-income groups, schools and hospitals, and new federal investments in R&D of energy efficient technology.

For the petroleum sector: The plan called for complete but phased decontrol of prices by 1981; tax incentives for production of oil from new wells, marginal wells, and wells using enhanced oil recovery; a windfall profits tax "to prevent excessive revenues from flowing to producers in the wake of decontrol;"[86] commercial-scale demonstration of oil shale technology financed with windfall profits tax; a one billion barrel strategic oil reserve; multilateral bank financing of oil exploration and production in developing countries, and accelerated development of technology for extraction of heavy oil and tar sands fluids.

To increase availability of natural gas: NEP II proposed to stimulate production through "a more stable and predictable"[87] regulation, phased deregulation of prices for high cost gas (usually found below fifteen thousand feet), displacement of "foreign" oil used in industry and utilities with "surplus gas", increased utilization of the natural gas supplies of Alaska, Canada and Mexico, and accelerated technology development and tax incentives for production of unconventional gas such as tight sands, Devonian shale, coal bed, and geo-pressurized methane.

For coal: The plan proposed nothing less than a requirement that it be used exclusively in all new electric and industrial plants, but also called for intensified R&D of emissions control technology, coal liquefaction, and gasification and magnetohydrodynamics technology.

For nuclear: NEP II called for a national nuclear waste site, streamlined procedures to site and license nuclear plants, R&D to improve light water reactors, lower costs for uranium enrichment services, continued research on breeder reactors and research to demonstrate the scientific feasibility for fusion "in the mid-1980s."[88]

For the renewable energy industry: The industry in 1979 was just beginning to surface, and the plan called for tax credits and other financial incentives to increase penetration of solar technology; R&D and "product support" for renewable technologies with potential to displace oil, and tax incentives and loan guarantees for geothermal resources development.[89]

The authors of NEP II estimated that these proposals would result in savings of "over 1 million barrels of oil per day" by 1985, incremental to the 2.5 to 3.0 MMB/D of oil demand reductions expected from implementation of the 1978 National Energy Act.[90] Congress, however, was not prepared to deal with a proposal as sweeping as NEP II. Its members were besieged by constituents about scarce gasoline supplies and high prices, and they were trying to make sense of the first nuclear accident in U.S. history: a reactor at the Three Mile Island power plant had been critically disabled in March 1979.

In July 1979, buffeted by the continuing effects of the second oil crisis in a decade and humbled by the taking of American hostages in Teheran, Carter retreated to Camp David to ponder his presidency. He consulted with myriad experts, political figures and ordinary citizens during the ten days of his self-imposed exile. He returned to the White House on July 14, and on the following day he delivered the now notorious sermon on the national malaise. He also announced a dramatic cabinet shake-up.

Carter fired Schlesinger and replaced him with Charles Duncan, the deputy secretary of defense and a former Coca-Cola executive. John Sawhill was asked to return from exile at New York University to assume the post of deputy DOE secretary. Former Massachusetts Institute of Technology professor John Deutch, already at DOE as director of energy research, was elevated to the position of undersecretary. Even with these changes, morale at the department, then in the midst of the latest fuel crisis in the Northeast, remained low. It soon became evident, internally because of visible conflicts among the decision-makers and externally as reported by the national media, that the three new senior officials at the helm were incompatible with one another. DOE, barely two years old, was already developing a reputation as the sick department of the cabinet.[91]

It was not until mid-1980 that Congress began work on NEP II by enacting the windfall profits tax and creating the Synthetic Fuels Corporation (SFC). The SFC, led by Sawhill for a brief period at the outset, soon came to represent a kind of federal energy folly. The SFC provided investments and loan guarantees for plants that would produce liquid and gaseous fuels from coal and shale. During the seven years that it was in operation, the industry that became associated with the SFC received unstinting congressional support even as one uneconomic project followed another, justified by the ever-elusive standard of energy security. As had been the case with similar programs since FDR, SFC produced not a single cost-effective barrel of fuel but managed to rack up federal debt obligations of over $2 billion.[92]

As a final act, the Carter administration produced a stand-by gasoline rationing plan as required by a provision of EPCA. Congress rejected the first plan submitted by Carter in March 1979 on the grounds that rural and urban states were treated unequally. A second plan was drafted after the Iranian crisis but was held in camera at the DOE. The second plan resulted in the printing of nearly five billion gasoline rationing coupons at a cost of $12 million.[93] The coupons—the currency of the next crisis—were found and destroyed by the incoming Reagan administration.

REAGAN I : LAISSEZ FAIRE, BUT FOR SECURITY

It remains a mystery of the American political process that the election of a new president, any president, seems to renew hope, lift the spirit, and raise fresh expectations. The 1980 election of Ronald Reagan lifted the pall of depression under which the collective national consciousness had labored during the last two years of the Carter presidency. Everywhere, that is, except in the DOE that Reagan had slated for extinction.

"The policy of this Administration," wrote the members of Reagan's CEA in their first report to Congress, "is to remove the inconsistency, inefficiencies, and uncertainty caused by inherited policy, and thereafter to facilitate the operation of market forces as the guiding and disciplining constraints shaping investment, production, and consumption decisions in the energy sector."[94] The policy was put into effect with lightning speed. Acting under the authority of EPCA, which had set a schedule of September 30, 1981, for full decontrol of petroleum prices, Reagan issued an executive order to liberate the oil market from federal price controls on January 28, 1981. The White House announcement was measured in tone. "Ending price controls," Reagan declared, "is a positive first step towards a balanced energy program, a program free of arbitrary and counter-productive constraints, one designed to promote prudent conservation and vigorous domestic production."[95]

The effect of this action on the oil sector was, in policy terms, almost immediate. U.S. oil production, which had been on a downward spiral since 1973, began to see a reversal in August 1981. Oil well drilling activity jumped from a total of 1,789 wells completed in January 1981 to 4,581 in December of the same year. Crude oil imports, which had reached 6.3 MMB/D in January 1980, dropped to 3.8 MMB/D in December 1981.[96] Shortages disappeared. Average oil prices rose briefly to $31 per barrel,[97] then began a five-year downward spiral that culminated in the 1985–86 price collapse.

The marketplace took charge of oil policy, as Reagan had intended. OPEC's decade of decisions to extract maximum rents from Western oil consumers served, finally, to stimulate investment in oil exploration and production outside the Persian Gulf. The relatively high oil prices of the 1970s brought forth oil production on the North Slope of Alaska, in the British and Norwegian fields of the North Sea, and in Mexico. Non-OPEC production surged from 14 MMB/D in 1976 to 23 MMB/D in 1985.[98]

High oil prices also induced conservation and fuel switching in the United States and throughout the industrialized world. U.S. oil consumption, which had peaked at nearly 19 MMB/D in 1978, fell to 15 MMB/D in 1982.[99] Other industrialized countries experienced similar changes in consumption patterns. Oil consumption in countries of the Organization for Economic Cooperation and Development (OECD) was reduced from 42 MMB/D in 1979 to 34 MMB/D in 1982.[100] OPEC output fell from nearly 31 MMB/D in 1979 to 17.5 MMB/D in 1983.[101]

In March 1983, OPEC for the first time in its short and tumultuous history was forced to adopt oil production quotas for its members in a desperate attempt to bring world supply and demand into equilibrium. However, OPEC members had no experience with disciplined and coordinated production and proved unable to refrain from widespread cheating in a scramble to maintain market share. It was not until December 1985, with oil prices tumbling towards $9 per barrel that OPEC finally absorbed the full dimensions of market fundamentals.

The dramatic reversal of fortunes between oil producers and consumers in the first half of the 1980s provided fresh proof on old evidence of the complex role that oil policy plays in modern economies. But the 1985–86 collapse of oil prices further underscored the permanent state of tension inherent in U.S. oil and energy policy.

U.S. energy plans before the 1980s had not accounted for the effects of volatility in oil prices. During the period from 1972 to 1982, real world oil prices had increased from $10 to $39 per barrel, peaking in 1980 at $46 per barrel.[102] This increase and the expectation that oil prices would continue to rise had been instrumental in securing a twenty-six percent reduction in U.S. energy use during that period.[103] High oil prices had furthermore induced substantial changes in investment and consumer behavior—better energy management, changes in purchasing decisions, greater awareness of energy's social cost.[104] How would low or, more importantly, uncertain oil prices affect the U.S. energy economy? And how, if at all, would the unpredictability of oil markets influence energy policy?

On the supply side of the equation, the ramifications of the oil price collapse seemed clearer. It was apparent to analysts, though not necessarily to the Reagan administration, that OPEC decisions profoundly affected the U.S. energy economy whether oil prices rose or fell. How would America's newly deregulated oil sector fare in a chaotic international market under unsteady cartel influence? The United States is, after all, concurrently one of the world's largest oil consumers and one of the major oil producers.

The great dichotomy of the U.S. energy economy, perhaps unique among nations, is that a federal policy to foster economically efficient, market-priced oil consumption is antithetical to U.S. oil production. U.S. oil production is dominated by high-cost marginal wells pumping on average thirteen barrels of oil per day. By contrast, production per well in Saudi Arabia is nearly seven thousand barrels per day and in Iran close to nine thousand barrels.[105] Similar disparities exist in regard to finding and lifting costs: $13 per barrel in the United States and less than $5 per barrel in the Middle East.[106]

In sum, the economic and political forces that emerged during Reagan's presidency were the opposite of those prevailing during the previous three administrations: disarray in OPEC, unexpectedly low oil prices and a worldwide glut of oil supplies. The Republican response to these conditions was predictable. Reagan opposed the Windfall Profits Act, supported broader and more rapid leasing of OCS tracts for oil and gas exploration and production, and advocated access to the energy resources of Alaska's Arctic National Wildlife Refuge (ANWR).[107] Congress would have none of it.

Congress needed income from the Windfall Profits Tax to continue financing the expensive Synthetic Fuels Corporation. In the first three years of collection, the tax yielded nearly $53 billion,[108] which were earmarked in support of the $88 billion Congress had authorized for the synfuels effort. At the same time, the evolution of the environmental movement into a political force recast the energy producer/consumer coalitions in Congress. As a consequence, the debate on ANWR and OCS brought together strange new bedfellows. The energy-producing state of Colorado, for example, was represented in the Senate by the environmentalist Timothy Wirth who took up the anti-ANWR banner. Similarly, most of California's congressional delegation opposed ANWR development and OCS leasing, notwithstanding the fact that California —America's largest oil consumer—absorbed the bulk of Alaska's oil production.

On the domestic front

James Edwards, former governor of South Carolina—a dentist and committed political conservative—was the first energy secretary of the Reagan administration. He carried to the Forrestal building (DOE Headquarters) an intense dislike for the regulatory and policy functions that had defined DOE in the public's mind during the Carter years. Edwards knew that DOE comprised much more than the two thousand lawyers of the Economic Regulatory Administration (the energy price control bureau), because in South Carolina, at Savannah River, DOE operated one of its largest nuclear defense facilities. Edward's views of DOE had been shaped by his regular contact with staff and officials of the Savannah River complex.

In a classic reenactment of the shoot-the-messenger cliché, Edwards began surgery on DOE by dismantling the three hundred-strong policy office career staff. It should be parenthetically noted that political officials of newly installed administrations frequently settle scores with their defeated but no longer reachable political opponents by punishing the career civil servants who staff the agencies and departments over which they assume control. Edwards and his advisers were especially vindictive on this score, acting on the dubious assumption that the career civil servants at DOE had been Carter's willing accomplices.

Edwards' next targets were the offices established by Schlesinger to represent the secretary of energy in the ten federal regions around the nation. Next, Edwards attacked the Economic Regulatory Administration and set the course for its dismemberment. In his short tenure at DOE, Edwards saw no need to scrutinize the organizational components of DOE responsible for defense functions. These elements and the political appointees who managed them were at the core of the environmental, health, and safety debacle that came more fully to light during Reagan's second term in office.

Although policy is usually associated with the presidents that promulgate it, in reality it has an institutional context as well as a history. The history of DOE, with its roots in the nuclear age, is especially burdensome to latter-day cabinet secretaries. DOE's national defense functions far exceed in staff, budget, and sheer policy weight the responsibilities it carries out in the civilian energy area. DOE comprises a nationwide structure created by the Manhattan Project, later expanded by AEC, to design, test, build and maintain all nuclear weapons in the U.S. arsenal. Three national research laboratories are dedicated to this enterprise—Lawrence Livermore, Los Alamos, and Sandia. Over 100,000 specialized workers at plants in ten states handle the production of weapons.[109]

Other institutions—owned by DOE but managed by private contractors or university consortia—straddle the defense and civilian R&D functions. These include the national laboratories of Argonne, Brookhaven, Oak Ridge, Idaho, and Lawrence Berkeley. Still others are mandated to carry R&D of more conventional energy technologies. They include the Pittsburgh and Morgantown Energy Technology Centers for coal, the renewable energy laboratory in Colorado, and the National Institute for Petroleum Research in Oklahoma.

DOE has on its payroll one of the world's largest rosters of theoretical physicists. They conduct research into the fundamental structure of matter at DOE-owned centers such as the Stanford Linear Accelerator in California and the Fermi National Accelerator in Chicago. DOE is the sole U.S. agency—public or private—responsible for research on nuclear fusion. This work is carried out at DOE's Princeton Plasma Physics Laboratory. DOE is also solely responsible for the design, construction, and related waste management of all nuclear reactors for navy ships and submarines. DOE builds propulsion systems for NASA satellites, enriches uranium to fuel civilian reactors, conducts research on virtually all energy transformation and conservation technologies, sells electric power from federal installations, manages the nation's SPR, and provides financial support to weatherize low-income homes.[110]

DOE's institutional culture has been shaped less by its cabinet secretaries than by the personalities who forged its origins. In the history of DOE live the ghosts of J. Robert Oppenheimer, the first director of Los Alamos National Laboratory; Nobel laureates Enrico Fermi, Edward Teller, and Emilio Segre; and Admiral Hyman Rickover, father of the nuclear navy.

The politically invisible community of men and women who staff DOE's operations include thousands of workers who have over the years jeopardized their health and well-being in order to fulfill the nation's need for ever more perfect weapons. These workers operate the nation's oldest and least reliable nuclear reactors. Others labor at research reactors that produce medical isotopes. Many are assigned to build, as the law requires, a permanent nuclear waste repository whose safety, by congressional dictum, must be guaranteed for ten thousand years.[111] Many hundreds manage the environmental cleanup of sites contaminated by the cold war mission of the AEC and by the arms build-up of the Reagan administration.

Edwards moved on in 1982 and was replaced by Donald Hodel, who distinguished himself by practicing an enlightened form of public administration. He restored the morale and productivity that had been destroyed by Edwards' short, vicious reign. Among Hodel's priorities was the rehabilitation of DOE's policy office, which reassumed its duties of energy policy planning.

The National Energy Policy Plans

The Department of Energy Organization Act passed by Congress during the Carter administration called for the biennial preparation of

National Energy Plans. For Reagan officials, plans had connotations of leftist approaches to economic management, and so the statutory requirement was met by the preparation and submittal to Congress of what came to be known as National Energy Policy Plans (NEPP). A total of three NEPPs were crafted during the Reagan administration, the first in July 1981.

The 1981 NEPP offered the first opportunity for the Reagan administration to present a comprehensive statement of its energy policy views. The views offered were a radical departure from the prevailing public and private wisdom of the 1970s. They rejected theories of natural resource limits, distanced the federal government from the day-to-day management of the energy economy, and minimized the value of energy policy analysis based on long-term projections of supply and demand. NEPP declared that:

> Consumption of energy is not the sole determinant of a strong economy; we could be consuming primary energy resources at any level and have a weak economy, a less satisfied people, a huge bureaucracy, a damaged environment, and continuing apprehension about our position as the leader of the free world.[112]

The first NEPP, barely twenty-four pages in length, proclaimed the Reagan administration's intent to rely on market decisions as the "means of charting the Nation's energy path," in preference to "government dictates or on a combination of subsidies and regulation." On petroleum and coal, the plan promised accelerated exploratory leasing on federal lands. On natural gas, it demurred, indicating that the administration would assess options for future policy. On nuclear policy, it committed to "reversing past Federal government excesses" preventing plant licensing. For the electric utility sector a review was announced of "licensing activities, fuel use stipulations, and environmental restrictions, with an emphasis on streamlining procedures, eliminating costly delays and uncertainties, and rescinding ineffective and unnecessary regulations."[113]

SFC was also addressed in the 1981 NEPP. In the absence of congressional support to abolish it, the administration announced a restructuring of SFC so that private investment would be greater than federal outlays and federal guarantees would be extended to SFC loans rather than to the price of fuels produced by synfuel plants. "Decontrol of conventional fuel prices," NEPP stated, "revitalization of the economy, and removal of regulatory uncertainties, will improve the growth climate for synthetic fuels." On renewable energy the administration was more categorical. It took the position that the planned elimination of subsidies for conventional fuels would "enhance the competitive position of renewables," but retained support for existing federal tax credits for renewable technology. NEPP also announced that DOE would thenceforth concentrate on long-range R&D, thereby encouraging "the private sector to take greater responsibility for developing and marketing renewable systems" in the near term.[114]

As for energy security, the Reagan administration declared its adherence to six fundamental principles:[115]

1. Primary reliance on market forces to determine the price and allocation of energy supplies, even during an emergency.
2. Rapid growth in the government's SPR and simultaneous removal of factors that have discouraged private firms from building up their own emergency oil stockpiles.
3. Development of criteria and mechanisms for making SPR available for use in case of emergencies.
4. Encouragement to manufacturers and utilities to stress dual-fuel capability for plants and equipment, so that they could switch readily to the most widely available fuel during a disruption.
5. Advanced planning to permit domestic energy producers to increase output and delivery above optimum levels during a disruption without economic penalties.
6. International coordination of emergency responses.

To underscore the importance it attached to the SPR, the administration pledged to fill the reserve as rapidly as possible, aiming for 750 million barrels in storage by 1989. The oil stockpiling approach, NEPP indicated, "is contrary to past government policies that attempted to manage any oil shortage by intervening in the marketplace."[116]

The second NEPP

By 1983, the ideological edges of the Reagan administration had been softened by the experience of governing. Departments and agencies had begun to come to terms with their natural constituencies and with the leadership of congressional committees—of the other political party—who controlled the purse strings. The second Reagan NEPP, released in October 1983, was less categorical than the first. It adopted the slogan of fostering "an adequate supply of energy at reasonable cost." Recognizing that judgments were bound to vary as to what constituted "adequate" and "reasonable," NEPP-2 authors argued that what in the end was required involved "a flexible energy system that avoids undue dependence on any single source of supply, foreign or domestic, and thereby contributes to our national security."[117]

The mild language of NEPP-2 was intentional. The administration could afford a reprieve in the energy policy battles because it had carried out most of its initial agenda. Crude oil price and allocation controls had been removed. A substantial number of Carter energy regulations had been rescinded. Congress had enacted an administration-backed Nuclear Waste Policy Act in 1982. R&D priorities had been realigned to the maximum extent permitted by congressional appropriators. What remained of interest to the administration were, as noted in NEPP-2, two legislative initiatives. The first was the removal of federal price controls on the wellhead price of natural gas. The second was the reform of the nuclear licensing and regulatory process. Congress was not, however, disposed to proceed with either.[118]

Congressional concerns were, rather, focused on the budgetary side of federal energy matters, where Reagan and Hodel were achieving notable successes. Hodel was redirecting federal energy R&D funds to more Republican areas of interest. DOE's nuclear research budget was raised to $1.5 billion per year. The energy conservation budget was reduced from $1 billion per year in 1980 to less than $400 million and the renewable energy budget to less than $200 million from a Carter era high of over $800 million per year.[119]

These budgetary realignments were politically satisfying, but as usual, made little difference to the energy marketplace. Not a single new nuclear power plant was commissioned during Reagan's two terms in office.[120] Nor did the energy economy suffer particularly from reduced federal expenditures in conservation. The link between federal R&D investments and the performance of the energy sector is, in any case, tenuous at best. The federal R&D budget is more precisely a battleground for special interests—the spoils of political victory. Republican administrations increase DOE's fossil fuel and nuclear budgets and, with some notable exceptions, reduce those for conservation and renewable energy. Democratic administrations reverse the order.

Reviewing Reagan's first-term energy policy accomplishments, Hodel told the National Press Club[121] on June 14, 1984 that "the U.S. is better off than it was before Reagan came to office." He noted that U.S. oil consumption was down ten percent from 1980, oil imports were down thirty-three percent and that only three percent of U.S. oil imports came from Persian Gulf sources. Using a stunningly inept metaphor, Hodel warned, however, that "the world (oil) market is like a swimming pool, and we are all in it together. Some are not as close to the drain, but if somebody pulls the plug, we will all go down the drain."[122]

Hodel decried attempts by the House Energy Committee to re-control natural gas prices and defended the Reagan administration policy of entrusting the private sector rather than the federal government with applied research and commercialization of energy technologies. He confirmed that the SFC was "moribund" because of fundamental disagreements between Congress and the Reagan administration, but was gratified by the progress that had been made in filling the SPR to 400 million barrels. On the matter of the continuing existence of DOE, Hodel thought that it should be merged with the "Department of Commerce or the Department of Interior." But, he concluded, "Congress will not support the idea."[123]

Reagan's first term in office concluded with the departure of Hodel, who assumed the helm at the Interior Department. John Herrington replaced him.

The third NEPP

By 1985, the year in which the final Reagan NEPP was completed, the energy policy world—public as well as private—was dormant. There were no issues demanding federal attention, at least not within the civilian aspects of DOE's policy portfolio. There were few if any energy policy approaches that had not been thoroughly debated in the previous decade. Furthermore, there were few initiatives that the policy staff could propose to the secretary of energy, which met the strictly constructionist Reagan test of market reliance.

Herrington's advisers were nevertheless required to create a conceptual framework for NEPP-3, and they finally settled on the idea of "America's Energy Triad." "A healthy energy future for the United States," the latest NEPP declared on behalf of Herrington, "will require a balanced mix of resources overall, but for the next decade or two it will find three supporting elements pivotal and indispensable...conservation, coal, and nuclear power."[124] This triad of resources, Herrington stated, would provide "energy stability in price and supply, energy strength (through) a balanced and diversified mix," and "energy security in an uncertain world."[125]

NEPP-3 was a confusing document. It presented the resource triad as pivotal but called for a diversified mix of fuels as necessary to achieve the amorphous notion of energy strength. It aimed for "price and supply and stability" but declined to discuss how this could be achieved by a policy of exclusive reliance on markets. The presentation of a triad of energy resources itself seemed to contradict faith in the ability of the private sector to make economic choices.

Herrington viewed the federal role in energy conservation as providing a "technological base that allows industry to make informed decisions regarding further development," meaning that government would pursue fundamental research in technology but leave applied research to the market. Unlike the limited government role he saw for conservation, for coal he supported both fundamental research as well as technology R&D, pursued at federal laboratories to the stage of proof-of-concept. Under congressional pressure he subsequently went further, accepting the concept that the federal government would actually construct coal plants to demonstrate a new generation of clean coal technology. Herrington considered nuclear power second only in importance to coal in its ability to reduce "U.S. dependence on imported petroleum," a concept fundamentally at odds with actual U.S. fuel consumption patterns.[126]

NEPP-3 did little to advance an informed discourse on national energy policy. It reflected, rather, the uninformed mentality of an energy secretary—an attorney by training—lacking grounding in the fundamentals of energy policy data, analysis and history. It was submitted to Congress in spring 1985 and quickly forgotten.

On the international front

Energy policy frequently inspires obsessive presidential behavior. Nixon, Ford, and Carter were consumed by the energy crises of the 1970s. In the 1980s, a Russian natural gas pipeline became Reagan's object of distress.

The issue arose in 1981 when several European governments led by West Germany's signed agreements with the Soviet Union to finance the construction of a 3,600-mile pipeline that would carry natural gas from Siberia's Taz peninsula to ten countries in Western Europe.[127] The Yamal pipeline, as it came to be known, was designed to quadruple Soviet gas sales to Western Europe from 24 billion cubic meters (BCM) in 1980 to between 90 BCM and 105 BCM in 1990.[128] Such a level of sales was projected to raise West German and French dependence on Soviet gas to thirty percent of their total gas imports, and Italy's to fifty percent.[129]

The West German government of Helmut Schmidt viewed the Russian gas deal as a practical expression of *Ostpolitik*, or "opening to the East." He considered it an extension to the commercial sector of the U.S.-inspired policy of political détente. It was, of course, merely a coincidence that the deal also represented a business bonanza worth $15 billion to West German, British, French, and Italian suppliers of large-diameter pipe, compressor stations, and construction equipment. [130]

The Reagan administration viewed the deal in geopolitical terms—as providing aid, comfort and precious foreign exchange earnings to the enemy. From an energy policy point of view, Reagan judged it a misguided European effort to substitute for reliance on OPEC oil a more dangerous dependence on Soviet gas. In testimony before Congress, Richard Perle, assistant secretary of defense for international security policy, expressed the administration's concerns in stark, implacable cold war terms:

> We believe that the increasing dependence of our European allies on Soviet energy, and especially natural gas, will weaken the (Western) alliance politically and militarily, shifting an already adverse military balance still further in the direction of a Soviet advantage and threatening the unity and purpose on which our collective security ultimately depends. [131]

Perle's fatal view of the Yamal project echoed that of many political figures of the time. In opening remarks during Senate hearings on the issue,[132] Banking Committee chairman Jake Garn declared, "If President Brezhnev (of the USSR) and Helmut Schmidt (of West Germany) sign that agreement, it could mean a major foreign policy defeat for the United States, in a battle that we did not begin to fight until the victor was already carrying off the spoils."

For his part, Pennsylvania Congressman James Nelligan feared "...the impact that this [Yamal project] is going to have on my child, and the future generation of children in America."[133] Nelligan thought, not without some political self-interest, that the Europeans should have considered American coal a much more desirable alternative to Russian gas. Some in the analytical community supported the political view of the pipeline, albeit with more nuanced language. Anthony Cordesman, a fellow at the Woodrow Wilson Center, wrote that "...the financing of this pipeline will make our NATO allies vulnerable to Soviet political and economic pressure, and make them even more vulnerable in a crisis of war."[134]

Reagan needed no encouragement. At the 1981 Ottawa summit of the Group of Seven (G-7), he urged the Europeans to restrict imports of Soviet natural gas and offered to assist the allies in finding alternatives.[135] The allies rejected the American position on grounds that no serious alternative to Soviet gas existed for them. In a brilliant display of rhetorical sophistry, Chancellor Schmidt argued that the Yamal deal actually increased Soviet dependence on Western hard currency rather than Western dependence on Soviet energy.[136] Clearly, U.S. and European views on the matter seemed unlikely to be bridged, especially given the barely disguised contempt in which conservative Reagan was held by social-democratic Schmidt.[137]

Political events played into Reagan's predispositions when in December 1981 martial law was declared in Poland. Reagan retaliated by imposing economic sanctions on the Soviet Union. He suspended issuance by the U.S. Department of Commerce of licenses for export of oil and gas equipment to the USSR.[138] The suspension on licenses was subsequently expanded to include a ban on oil and gas equipment by European subsidiaries[139] of American companies.[140]

The extension of the export ban to U.S. overseas subsidiaries caused a furor in European capitals, at the U.S. Chamber of Commerce and, incomprehensibly—given its previous pronouncements to the contrary—in Congress. The West German government served notice that "the U.S. measures...are unacceptable under international law because of their extraterritorial aspects," and warned that "there is now a considerable risk of the conflict [between the United States and Europe] escalating."[141] The U.S. Chamber of Commerce warned the president: "the unprecedented blanket prohibition on U.S. subsidiaries and control of previously licensed U.S. technology pose serious questions concerning the present direction of U.S. international economic policy."[142] Rhode Island Senator Claiborn Pell reflected the view of many of his senatorial colleagues when he stated that "the President's decision to expand sanctions on the sale of oil and gas related equipment...has only succeeded in driving a serious wedge between the United States and our most critical allies."[143]

Against near-universal European opposition and against the advice of Secretary of State Alexander Haig, Reagan kept the sanctions in place through the acrimonious G-7 Summit at Versailles in May 1982. By October, however, facing the possibility that deployment in Europe of U.S. Pershing missiles would be derailed, Reagan was forced to reconsider. First, however, he fired Haig and named George Shultz to replace him. Schultz successfully negotiated a face-saving agreement with the allies who provided vague assurances that they would manage trade with the Soviets on more normal commercial terms. With the agreement in hand, and on a personal plea from British Prime Minister Margaret Thatcher,[144] Reagan lifted the sanctions.

The Yamal pipeline was nevertheless eventually built with subsidized Western European loans.[145] Soviet gas began flowing in the late 1980s. None of the predictions put forth by either side in the Yamal debate proved correct. The Soviet Union did not become stronger, as feared by Reagan, as a result of hard currency earnings from gas sales to the West. Soviet gas turned out, after all, not to be so critical or so cost effective to Western Europe once the North Sea's Troll field was brought under production. What the Yamal crisis demonstrated was how conveniently energy security policy can serve other political objectives. As was the case with Iran during Eisenhower's administration, no American interests were actually threatened by the sale of Russian gas to European consumers, but Yamal perfectly served Reagan's cold war purposes, as other energy security considerations were to serve the entire purpose of energy policy in his second term.

REAGAN II:
THE ENERGY SECURITY REPORT

Serious policy analysis was resumed at DOE with the 1986 appointment of William Martin as deputy secretary of energy. Martin brought to his job respected credentials in energy policy formulation as well as international experience. He had served at the International Energy Agency in Paris, and had more recently been the executive director of the National Security Council. His appointment revitalized DOE's policy office. Almost immediately upon assuming office, Martin undertook a comprehensive review of U.S. energy policy.

Martin's energy policy assessment effort reached for inspiration to the historic Paley report, rather than to the Carter-era energy plans. This was due partially to Martin's belief in the power of analysis to stimulate policy action, but it was also a more prudent political path to take in light of White House aversion to any form of policy activism at DOE.

"Those who think that all virtue is to be found in their own party principles," wrote Aristotle in *Politics*, "push matters to extremes." Reagan's party principles decreed that the markets would determine energy policy.

But the markets were effectively devastating the U.S. oil and gas industry in the wake of the 1986 price collapse. The effects were cascading to the banking, real estate, and service sectors that sustain the oil patch in Texas, Louisiana, Oklahoma, Colorado, and other energy-producing states. Low energy prices were also influencing consumer behavior, slowing conservation gains achieved in the previous decade.[146]

Although the collapse of oil prices in 1986 stimulated assessment of U.S. energy conditions, Martin was also responding to recurrent criticism in the media, from Congress, and from the National Governors Association, that the Reagan administration lacked a veritable energy policy. No progress had been made, for example, on a coherent plan to decontrol the natural gas market. Legislation to decontrol natural gas prices had been initially proposed by the administration in 1983, and partial decontrol of wellhead prices was achieved in 1985. But comprehensive decontrol remained elusive.[147] There was, as well, a great deal of debate about the future structure of the electric utility industry. Reagan's CEA—rather than DOE —had dabbled with this issue for several years without surfacing specific legislative proposals.

Martin assigned to the policy office the responsibility to produce the elements that would eventually combine into "Energy Security: A Report To The President Of The United States." The policy staff saw the effort as an opportunity to put forth for public debate a number of policy initiatives that had remained unattended during Reagan's first six years in office. Three issues specifically took center stage early in the analytical process. The first was oil policy and the ramifications of the 1986 price collapse: was U.S. security potentially threatened by a probable, significant drop in domestic production, and, if so, what could be done about it? Second, what role should market forces play in the electricity sector, and could the conditions that created the 1970-1980 rate shocks be addressed by regulatory reform? Lastly, could Congress be persuaded that decontrol of natural gas production would enhance the natural gas market without harming consumer interests?

These issues were not new, but Martin believed that because market conditions were never static, neither could federal policy afford to be. In the case of energy, Reagan policy was not only static but, by design, invisible. Martin had no illusions that he would succeed in securing executive branch or legislative action on initiatives he might propose. He was, after all sandwiched between the policy indifference of Energy Secretary John Herrington and White House involvement in the Iran-Contra affair.[148]

Special interest pressure, never far from any policy development process, was felt as soon as Martin's effort became public. The oil industry immediately sought relief from the drop in oil prices by lobbying for the repeatedly proposed and always rejected fee on imported oil. The industry would have settled for any policy that would have set a floor price on domestically produced oil. Less desirable, from the industry's viewpoint, but always appreciated were tax credits for exploratory drilling and higher depletion allowances. As expected, natural gas producers supported wellhead decontrols in line with administration thinking. The gas industry was less enthusiastic about reform of natural gas transportation regulation, however. The electric utility industry, for its part, wanted no part of federal reform of any part of this sector.[149]

When the analyses for the Energy Security report were completed, Martin invited representatives of key federal agencies to review drafts of the report. He refused to transmit the report to other agencies for fear of premature leaks to the media but allowed agency representatives to read the document, in draft, in a DOE conference room. The agencies objected strenuously to the arrangement, denouncing it as a breach of policy review protocol. Martin, however, held firm and the agencies acquiesced.

As expected, most departmental representatives were vocal in their insistence that no new policy on energy was necessary. OMB warned that the mere presentation of policy options in any administration report was dangerous because it would encourage interventionist mischief from Congress. The national security agencies, on the other hand, welcomed the initiative, specifically offering support for a proposed enlargement of the SPR. The social agencies also welcomed the Martin initiative because it provided a rare opportunity to argue for increases in their budgets. [150] Still, the Troika[151] agencies—OMB, Treasury, and the CEA—could not be moved from their opposition. The only recourse left to Martin was to force the issue, at cabinet level, in the Economic Policy Council (EPC).[152]

For the EPC meeting, which was attended by the president, Martin had charts prepared to illustrate key issues of particular importance. One such chart showed a comparison of Soviet and U.S. oil production, with the former represented by red oil derricks becoming larger over time and the latter shown as shrinking blue derricks. Reagan's cold warrior heart was chilled by the demonstrable (but entirely misleading) Soviet superiority in oil production. But, perhaps remembering the Yamal debacle, he demurred.[153]

The Energy Security report was issued in late March 1987 without interagency clearance. The report comprehensively analyzed conditions in the energy sector, as well as the cost and benefit of remedial action. It made a precedent-setting case for consideration of federal policy on alternative transportation fuels. It began to define the case for reform of wholesale electricity generation markets. In sum, the Energy Security report served the purpose of revitalizing the energy policy debate and to also set the stage for action by the succeeding administration.

A postscript of note to the Energy Security report was the action taken in December 1987 by a group of independent oil producers acting as a National Energy Security Committee. As documented by Wilfrid Kohl in *After the Oil Price Collapse,*[154] the group petitioned the Department of Commerce for a finding, under Section 232 of the Trade Expansion Act, that oil imports impaired the security of the United States. In response, and displaying keen bureaucratic acumen, the Commerce Department issued a finding that "petroleum imports *threaten* to impair the national security. (emphasis added)"[155]

Reagan agreed with the finding, but announced in January 1989 that "no action to adjust oil imports...need be taken."[156]

NOTES AND COMMENTS

1. There are many theories on the question of what precipitated the formation of OPEC in 1960. I argue that Eisenhower's imposition of mandatory oil imports control was perhaps the key factor behind Venezuela's initiative to call a meeting of oil exporters in 1959. John G. Clark, on the other hand, argues in *The Political Economy Of World Energy* (University of North Carolina Press, 1990) that the formation of OPEC was precipitated by a reduction of crude posted prices by multinational oil companies, acting unilaterally and without consultation of Middle Eastern governments. My view is that price disputes among the parties involved had historically been the rule rather than the exception. The imposition of trade controls by the United States, in contrast, was an unprecedented political step that threatened the very foundation of Venezuela's relations with the United States. Venezuela's response to the threat—the move to create OPEC—was in line with the stakes involved.

2. My judgments on the significance of federal R&D budgets for the economy at large concern applied research and do not extend to basic research. It is inarguable that the private sector is unlikely to invest in particle accelerators or in the development of fusion energy. The payoff of basic research is too imprecise and too long-term for the average corporation or business enterprise. Applied research is another matter. It is questionable, for example, whether it is the duty of the federal government to develop the next generation of coal burning technology. Coal accounts for nearly sixty percent of electricity generation primary energy. Is it not in the interest of the coal industry to assure its own future by investing in technology for its future? Similarly on conservation technology: is it the responsibility of the federal government to develop more energy efficient doors, windows and light bulbs? Or is it in the interest of industries to improve products for an evolving, energy-conscious, environmentally aware consumer?

REFERENCES

[1] Arthur M. Schlesinger, Jr., *The Coming of the New Deal: The Age of Roosevelt* (Boston: Houghton Mifflin Company, 1958), p. 350.

[2] David McCullough, *Truman*, (New York: Simon & Schuster, 1992), p. 537.

[3] Ibid., p. 538.

[4] C. Goodwin, *Energy Policy in Perspective*, ed., C. Goodwin (Washington, DC: Brookings Institution, 1981), pp. 64-69.

[5] Ibid., p. 71.

[6] Ibid., p. 68.

[7] McCollough, op. cit., p.526.

[8] Goodwin, op. cit., p.195.

[9] Ibid., p. 197.

[10] Ibid., p.115.

[11] Ibid., p.115.

[12] Ibid., p. 116.

[13] Ibid., p.119.

[14] Ibid., p. 126.

[15] Ibid., p. 126.

[16] C. Goodwin, "The Truman Administration: Toward a National Energy Policy," in *Energy Policy in Perspective*, ed., C. Goodwin. (Washington, DC: Brookings Institution, 1981), p. 37.

[17] Ibid., p.38.

[18] Goodwin, op. cit., p. 147.

[19] Goodwin, op. cit., p. 153.

[20] Goodwin, op. cit., p. 160.

[21] Goodwin, op. cit., p. 162.

[22] DOE, EIA, *The Potential for Coal Liquefaction: Supporting Analysis for the National Energy Strategy*, SR/NES/90-07. Washington, DC, January, 1991.

[23] Martin Greenberger, *Caught Unawares: The Energy Decade in Retrospect*, (Cambridge, MA: Ballinger Publishing Company, 1983), pp. 39-40.

[24] Henry R. Linden, *World Oil*, Illinois Institute of Technology Press, Chicago, 1987.

[25] W. Barber, "The Eisenhower Energy Policy: Reluctant Intervention," *Energy Policy in Perspective*, ed., C. Goodwin. (Washington, DC: Brookings Institution, 1981).

[26] Ibid., p. 247.

[27] D. Bohi and D. Montgomery, *Oil Prices, Energy Security, and Import Policy*, (Washington, DC: Resources for the Future, 1982).

[28] Ibid., p. 255.

[29] FEA, *Project Independence: A Summary*, Washington, DC, 1974.

[30] Douglas R. Bohi and Milton Russell, *Limiting Oil Imports: An Economic History and Analysis,* RFF/John Hopkins University Press, Washington, DC, 1978.

[31] Greenberger, op. cit., p. xxi.

[32] W. Barber, "Studied Inaction in the Kennedy Years," in *Energy Policy in Perspective,* ed., C. Goodwin. (Washington, DC: Brookings Institution, 1981), pp. 324-330.

[33] Ibid., p. 330.

[34] Ibid., p. 332.

[35] Ibid.

[36] Greenberger, op. cit., pp. 39-43, quote on p. 42.

[37] J. Cochrane, "Energy Policy in the Johnson Administration: Logical Order Versus Economic Pluralism," in *Energy Policy in Perspective,* ed., C. Goodwin. (Washington, DC: Brookings Institution, 1981), p. 348.

[38] Ibid.

[39] Greenberger, op. cit., pp. 45-48.

[40] *Executive Energy Messages.* Printed at the Request of Henry M. Jackson, chairman, Committee on Interior and Insular Affairs, United States Senate, Pursuant to S. Res.

[41] Ibid.

[42] Ibid.

[43] Ibid.

[44] Ibid.

[45] Ibid.

[46] Ibid.

[47] Ibid.

[48] Ibid.

[49] Ibid.

[50] Ibid.

[51] Ibid.

[52] DOE, *Strategic Petroleum Reserve: Analysis of Size Options* DOE//IE-0016. February 1990.

[53] *Executive Energy Messages,* op. cit.

[54] Charles K. Ebinger, *The Critical Link: Energy and National Security in the 1980s: A Report of the Energy, Natural Resources and Security Studies Division* (Cambridge, MA: Ballinger Publishing Co., 1983).

[55] D. Bohi, "Searching For Consensus on Energy Security Policy," in *Making National Energy Policy,* ed., H. Landsberg. (Washington, DC: Resources for the Future, 1993).

[56] *Executive Energy Messages,* op. cit.

[57] Ibid.

[58] Ibid.

[59] Goodwin, op. cit.

60 *Executive Energy Messages*, op. cit.

61 Ibid.

62 Ibid.

63 Ibid.

64 Ibid.

65 Ibid.

66 Ibid.

67 N. Marchi, "The Ford Administration: Energy as a Political Good," in *Energy Policy in Perspective*, ed., C. Goodwin. (Washington, DC: Brookings Institution, 1981).

68 Ibid.

69 Goodwin, op. cit.

70 Marchi, op. cit.

71 Charles T. Unseld, et al, editors, "Study of Nuclear and Other Energy Stems" by the Committee on Nuclear and Alternative Energy Systems of the National Research Council, published in collected form by the National Academy of Science, Washington DC, 1979.

72 Morris A Adelman, et al, "A Time to Choose America's Energy Future", Ford Foundation Energy Policy Project, Institute of Contemporary Studies, San Francisco, 1975.

73 S. David Freeman, *Energy, The New Era*, (New York, NY; Walker Publishing Company, 1974) p. 4.

74 Twentieth Century Fund, Task Force on United States Energy Policy, "Providing for Energy," with background paper by Richard B. Mancke, McGraw-Hill, New York, 1977.

75 Amory Lovins, "Soft energy paths: towards a durable peace," Friends of the Earth International, San Francisco, publishers, distributed by Ballinger Publishing Co., Cambridge, MA. 1977.

76 Jimmy Carter, *Keeping Faith: Memoirs of a President*, p. 91. (New York, NY: Bantam Books, 1982).

77 Cochrane, op. cit.

78 Ibid.

79 Carter, op. cit., p.123.

80 Cochrane, op. cit., p. 61.

81 DOE, Office of Technology Assessment, *Analysis of the Proposed National Energy Plan*, August 1977.

82 Cochrane, op. cit., p. 572.

83 Co-generation is the concurrent generation of electricity and production of steam

84 DOE, op. cit.

85 S. Yager, "The Energy Battles of 1979," in *Energy Policy in Perspective*, ed., C. Goodwin. (Washington, DC: Brookings Institution, 1981).

86 DOE *National Energy Plan II*, A Report to the Congress, Required by Title VIII of DOE Organization Act (Public Law 95-91). Washington, DC, 1979, p. 10.

[87] Ibid., p. 11.

[88] Ibid., pp. 13-14.

[89] Ibid.

[90] Ibid.

[91] The author joined DOE in 1979 as special assistant to Secretary Charles Duncan.

[92] OMB estimate provided at author's request, January 1994.

[93] Franklin Tugwell, *The Energy Crisis and the American Political Economy*. (Stanford, CA: Stanford University Press, 1988), p.1.

[94] *Economic Report of the President*, transmitted to the Congress, February 1982, together with the Annual Report of the CEA. Washington, DC, 1982, p. 156.

[95] DOE, *United States Energy Policy 1980-1988*, Washington, DC, October 1988, p. 1.

[96] *Economic Report of the President*, op. cit., pp. 157-158.

[97] DOE, EIA, *Annual Energy Review 1992*. Washington, DC, June 1993.

[98] Ibid.

[99] Ibid.

[100] DOE, *United States Energy Policy*, op. cit.

[101] Cambridge Energy Research Associates (CERA) and Arthur Andersen Worldwide Organization, *World Oil Trends*, 1991 edition (Cambridge, MA: CERA, 1991).

[102] Applied Energy Services, Inc. and Energy and Environmental Analysis, Inc., *The Projected Impact of Lower Oil Prices on U.S. Energy Conservation*, prepared for DOE, Office of Policy, Planning & Analysis, DOE/PE/77029-H1. Washington, DC, January 1988.

[103] Ibid.

[104] DOE, Office of Policy, Planning & Analysis and Office of Conservation & Renewable Energy, *Energy Conservation Trends: Understanding the Factors that Affect Conservation Gains in the U.S. Economy*, DOE/PE-0092. Washington, DC, September 1989.

[105] DOE, *Energy Security: A Report to the President of the United States*, DOE/S0057. Washington, DC, March 1987.

[106] Ibid.

[107] DOE, *United States Energy Policy*, op. cit.

[108] Tugwell, op. cit., p. 159.

[109] Vito Stagliano, "A Study of the Field Structure of the Department of Energy" Draft Report (prepared for Energy Secretary Charles Duncan). Washington, DC, January 1981.

[110] Ibid.

[111] Nuclear Waste Policy Act of 1982, as amended in 1987.

[112] DOE, *The National Energy Policy Plan: Securing America's Energy Future*, A Report to the Congress Required by Title VIII of DOE Organization Act (Public Law 95-91), DOE/S-0008, July 1981.

[113] Ibid.

[114] Ibid.

[115] Ibid.

[116] Ibid.

[117] DOE, *The National Energy Policy Plan*, A Report to the Congress Required by Title VIII of the Department of Energy Organization Act (Public Law 95-91), DOE/S-0014/1, October 1983.

[118] Ibid., pp. 2-4.

[119] DOE. Budget Submissions: 1980, 81-84.

[120] DOE, EIA, *World Nuclear Capacity and Fuel Cycle Requirements 1993*, DOE/EIA-0436(93), November 1993.

[121] Bureau of National Affairs, "Reagan's Energy Policy Has Worked, Hodel Says, But U.S. Cannot Afford Complacency," *Daily Report for Executives*, June 18, 1984, p. A-13.

[122] Ibid.

[123] Ibid.

[124] DOE, *The National Energy Policy Plan*, A Report to the Congress Required by Title VIII of the Department of Energy Organization Act (Public Law 95-91), DOE/S-0040, 1985.

[125] Ibid., pp. 2-6.

[126] Ibid., pp. 13-20, quote on p. 18.

[127] M. Karr and R.W. Robinson, Jr., "Soviet Gas: Risk or Reward," *Washington Quarterly*, Autumn 1981,

[128] U.S. Senate, "Proposed Trans-Siberian Natural Pipeline," Hearing Before the Committee on Banking, Housing and Urban Affairs, United States Senate, 97th Congress, 1st session, November 12, 1981.

[129] Ibid.

[130] Karr and Robinson, op. cit.

[131] U.S. Senate, op. cit., November 12, 1981.

[132] Ibid.

[133] Ibid.

[134] Ibid.

[135] Myer Rashish, "East-West Economic Relations," *American Enterprise Institute Economist*, April 1982.

[136] William F. Martin, at the time, special assistant to the undersecretary of state for Economic Affairs and participated in the Ottawa Summit at staff level. Personal communications to Stagliano, May 1994.

[137] Ibid.

[138] "White House Statement on U.S. Measures Taken Against the Soviet Union," *Weekly Compilation of Presidential Documents*, Vol. 17, No. 53, December 29, 1981.

[139] Companies affected were Manufacturing Associates of General Electric: John Brown Co. of U.K.: A.E.G. Kanis of West Germany; Nuovo Pignone of Italy; and GE licensee Alsthom Atlantique of France.

[140] U.S. Senate, Committee on Foreign Relations, Subcommittee on International Economic Policy, Hearings on Economic Relations with the Soviet Union, 97th Congress, 2nd session, July 30, 1982. Washington, DC, 1982.

[141] Peter Hermes, ambassador from the Federal Republic of Germany, Memorandum transmitted to Senator Charles McC. Mathias dated July 29, 1982; and *Hearings on Economic Relations with the Soviet Union*, before the Subcommittee on International Economic Policy, Committee on Foreign Relations, 97th Congress, 2nd session, July 29, 1982. Washington, DC, 1982.

[142] Richard Lesher, president, U.S. Chamber of Commerce, Letter to President Ronald Reagan, February 5, 1982.

[143] Claiborne Pell, Statement before U.S. Senate Subcommittee on International Economic Policy, Committee on Foreign Relations, *Economic Relations with the Soviet Union*, 97th Congress, 2nd session. Washington, DC, August 12, 1982.

[144] Martin, op. cit.

[145] U.S. Congress, *Soviet Pipeline Sanctions: The European Perspective*, Hearing before the Joint Economic Committee on September 22, 1982, 97th Congress, 2nd session. Washington, DC, 1983.

[146] DOE, *Energy Conservation_Trends*, op. cit.

[147] DOE, *United States Energy Policy*, op. cit., p. xiv.

[148] Martin communication with the Policy staff, of which the author was then a member.

[149] Author's direct knowledge, op. cit.

[150] Ibid.

[151] The term "Troika" came into use during the Reagan administration to denote cabinet agencies whose positions essentially controlled final policymaking decisions within the cabinet and usually, but not always, in the White House. The term was abandoned during the Clinton administration.

[152] The author was present in these discussions.

[153] Martin, op. cit. and Scott Campbell, director of Policy, DOE, 1986-1987, Personal communications to Stagliano, May-June 1994.

[154] Wilfrid Kohl, "Oil and U.S. National Security," in *After the Oil Price Collapse*, ed., W. Kohl. (Baltimore, MD: The Johns Hopkins University Press, 1991), p. 151.

[155] Ibid., p. 152, italics added.

[156] Ibid.

CHAPTER TWO

THE SEARCH FOR
POLICY CONSENSUS

THE ADMIRAL AND THE ADVISERS

The call came on January 11, 1989, from Craig Fuller, the president-elect's chief of staff. Fuller asked James D. Watkins, admiral, U.S. Navy (Retired) and former chief of naval operations, to consider the position of secretary of energy in the administration of George H. W. Bush. Watkins met with Bush the following day and without hesitation accepted from his new commander in chief the charge of "cleaning-up the mess at Energy."[1] The White House announced the admiral's selection on January 13.

The "mess at Energy" had begun to come to light during Reagan's second term in office. Though admitting to the existence of problem areas, Reagan officials had played down the extent to which the nation's nuclear weapons complex, DOE's core element, had been allowed to deteriorate. "The environmental problems we are finding now at (DOE) facilities," Energy Secretary Herrington had noted in 1985, "are, for the most part, legacies from the past…practices conducted in a different atmosphere and under different standards than today's."[2]

The practices characterized by Herrington as "different" amounted in actuality to a self-declared exemption by DOE from national environmental, health, and safety laws. The "legacies from the past" were found by later investigations to involve, among other things, dangerously lax operation of DOE's nuclear reactors, especially those at Savannah River in South Carolina; widespread violations of worker safety regulations, especially at the Rocky Flats plant in Colorado; and inability to ensure the physical integrity of tanks holding the most toxic liquid waste known to man, at Hanford Reservation in the state of Washington.

Virtually all sites in the nationwide nuclear weapons complex were contaminated by hazardous materials. Conditions in the complex amounted, in sum, to what Brookings' Bruce L. R. Smith termed an "environmental disaster."[3] For more than forty years after the Manhattan Project, the nuclear weapons complex had been veiled in secrecy—prudent stewardship of federal staff and plant sacrificed in the name of national security.

Watkins was generally aware of conditions at the nuclear weapons complex from his many years of service in Admiral Rickover's nuclear navy command. He had pursued a graduate degree in mechanical engineering, specializing in nuclear power systems, requiring courses of studies at Oak Ridge National Laboratory and at other DOE nuclear research centers. He had thus been exposed to institutions, factories, and laboratories that design, build, test, and maintain the U.S. nuclear arsenal. Watkins had followed the evolution of the nuclear weapons complex throughout his subsequent naval career, particularly in the early 1960s, when he had served with Rickover at AEC. And he had continued to be aware, in his words, of "falling safety practices" in the complex and of "less attentive oversight by the Department of Energy,"[4] from his vantage point as chief of naval operations (CNO) from 1982 to 1986.

He was not, however, prepared for the conditions he actually found. Within three months of assuming office, having encountered a pattern of operational conduct seemingly immune to acceptable safety practices, as well as institutionally indifferent to secretarial oversight, Watkins was forced to take the unprecedented step of shutting down the entire complex. In June 1989, to Watkins' great distress, Americans also witnessed, for the first time in history, an unprecedented raid by a team of federal environmental inspectors on the DOE-owned Rocky Flats plant.

Bush's choice of Watkins appeared fortuitous on personal as well as professional grounds. During World War II, after ditching his plane in the sea, Bush had been rescued by a submarine crew and had a special fondness for submariners. Watkins had captained a nuclear submarine in mid-career. As vice president, Bush and his wife, Barbara, had been frequent visitors to the Navy Yard's historic Tingey House, the official residence of the CNO during Watkins' incumbency in that post. Watkins and his wife, Sheila, had regularly attended the annual Christmas party at the vice president's Naval Observatory residence. In June 1988, when the AIDS Commission report was issued, it was then-Vice President Bush who had been first to publicly support the report's findings—had indeed called commission Chairman Watkins to thank him for the effort. Words of appreciation were not received from Ronald Reagan until well after he left office, and then only at the urging of Senator Howard Baker.[5]

Watkins' confirmation to office was within the jurisdiction of the Senate Committee on Energy and Natural Resources, whose chairman J. Bennett Johnston of Louisiana had been vocal in his contempt for Reagan energy policies. Speaking at the highly publicized Conference on International Energy Security in May 1988, Johnston had derided Reagan policy as the "pursuit of free market purity." He had also offered a prognosis of things to come: "We will have a new energy policy. The only question is whether the new energy policy will be forced upon us by more embargoes, shortages, and national travail, or whether we will do it the easy way." He had sent a warning to the future White House occupant as well. "We cannot expect," he said, "and should not want the next Administration to present us with a campaign-created solution" to the energy problems faced by the nation.[6]

Johnston opened Watkin's confirmation hearing on February 22, 1989, by bluntly reminding Watkins that the first priority for the new secretary of energy will be to restore "the credibility of the Department's nuclear weapons protection complex." Johnston went on to declare that his other concerns included the management of nuclear waste, reform of DOE's uranium enrichment enterprise, development of advanced nuclear reactors and a broader mission for DOE's national laboratories. Oil policy was also on Johnston's mind. He told Watkins of his intention to introduce legislation imposing a fee on imported oil because, he said, "way too much oil is imported from the Middle East."[7]

Virtually all other members of the committee, Republicans as well as Democrats, echoed Johnston's concern about the poor state of the nuclear weapons complex. The senators also were of one mind on the need for DOE to be truthful and forthcoming about environmental, health, and safety practices at the complex. Senator James McClure of Idaho, warned that, although the Bush administration had inherited, not created the problems of the nuclear weapons complex, "Admiral Watkins will be the man in the hot seat, charged with getting the situation effectively under control."[8]

Senator Howard Metzenbaum of Ohio picked up the refrain: "For years we were told that the national defense necessitates that nuclear weapons production be cloaked in secrecy, outside of public and expert scrutiny. Now we see that the approach has produced the opposite effect, leaving the nation with a bill of over $100 billion in clean-up costs."[9] On a more practical level,

Senator Jeff Bingaman of New Mexico offered to help secure from Congress "the resources needed to correct our past neglect of this complex."[10]

In his opening statement Watkins reiterated the president's campaign pledge of new directions for the nation's energy policy: a policy that "cleans up the problems of the past and gives incentives America needs to build a future that is *energy-independent,* (emphasis added) healthy and safe." He promised to put in place at DOE a management team "that understands how to motivate people, how to achieve and reward excellence, and how to reject and deal firmly, fairly and swiftly with incompetence." He concluded by offering to the committee a preview of what he would set out to accomplish. "We need to develop over the next few years an integrated energy strategy which can encapsulate seemingly intractable issues under one integrated set of actions that the majority of Americans will judge as both fair and sensible."[11]

There were, of course, other views on what the newly elected president and just-designated energy secretary should do on energy. Illinois Institute of Technology Professor Henry Linden hoped that the new administration would dismiss forecasts of inevitable shortages and high energy prices. "A firm commitment to least-cost energy supply and utilization options," Linden advised in January 1989, "is the only winning strategy for both government and private investment."[12] But Linden was in the minority. The oil price collapse of 1986 had reinvigorated the energy policy community. Between 1987 and 1989, over two dozen energy policy proposals were put forth by a variety of public and private organizations, individuals and groups ranging from the General Accounting Office to the New England Energy Policy Council.[13]

These plans and proposals, however varied in their motivation and objectives, mined common ground in seeking government intervention to foster greater energy efficiency and conservation. Such intervention was seen as justified because of government failure to internalize—through taxes and regulation—the full or social cost of fuels in the otherwise abnormally low consumer price of energy. The abnormality of U.S. energy price policy was deemed especially pronounced when compared to energy prices in Western Europe and Japan.

Watkins had no preconceptions about energy policy and, except for the instinctive conservatism of a military man, he professed no particular ideology. He believed, however, that the general public was ill-prepared—by education and by the media—to debate intelligently issues of science and technology. He was devoted to consensus-building processes. In his view, few issues of public policy were in greater need of informed debate and national consensus than those associated with energy. He was not predisposed to particular policy proposals, but was sufficiently Republican not to want Carter era plans developed by in-house specialists.[14]

Above all, Watkins wanted a public policy process that would be viewed as an extension of how an administration should wish to govern: open and accountable to the public, ethical and competent. For that, he needed the explicit engagement of the president himself. Without a presidential mandate his actions could be viewed as self-serving, something he abhorred.[15]

Watkins was sworn in as the nation's sixth secretary of energy on March 9, 1989, by the chief justice of the United States in the presence of the president. At the ceremony, which was held at the DOE headquarters building, Bush took the opportunity to reassure the department's employees that their professional future was assured. "To the 16,000 men and women of the Department of Energy from Juneau to Georgia," the president declared, "and your 130,000 contract co-workers, I want to tell you how much I admire you—your professionalism, your loyalty, and your tremendous technical expertise." And, he continued, in a rejection of previous Republican Party proposals to do away with DOE, "this Department is here to stay."[16]

"It is a great honor," Watkins stated, after taking his oath of office, "for me to appear before you today as your new Secretary of Energy. It is also a great personal honor to have been asked to serve in this capacity by a President who has such in-depth, personal knowledge of this nation's energy needs and resources." Watkins pledged his commitment to the new administration's agenda, referring specifically to a budget message Bush had recently transmitted to Congress, in which the President had described energy security, safety and environmental protection as coequal national priorities.[17]

The traditional budget message, presented by the president to a joint session of Congress on February 9, 1989, had subsequently been published by the White House under the title *Building a Better America*, and disseminated to the public and to federal agencies to make known the president's priorities. It was from this document that DOE policy staff had learned of the Bush administration's intent to pursue very specific, and in some cases very un-Republican, energy sector initiatives.[18]

In *Building a Better America*, the president was quoted as having definitive positions on most issues of interest to DOE. On alternative fuels:

> "The time has obviously come for the government to do all it can to accelerate the use of ethanol and methanol; establish a 'clean fuel standard' and require that fuel sold in areas that exceed federal standards for carbon monoxide contain at least 3% oxygen by weight; get EPA to aggressively pursue greater use of alcohol blends; [set the] goal [to] produce 2.5 billion gallons of ethanol annually by 1990."

On coal: "I don't think you can look at the future of this country without saying that coal is going to be vital; continue [the] $2.5 billion Clean Coal Technology program." On conservation: "I will personally emphasize the importance of conservation and new technologies as means for reducing oil imports." On natural gas: "What we need, then, is a major effort to exploit this great resource." On nuclear energy: "I believe we can safely use nuclear power."[19]

The administration's agenda and the president's position seemed unequivocal also in regard to oil and gas policy: "We should provide more stability to the industry by reducing the cost of domestic exploration and production for both oil and gas—with the objective of saving marginal wells, stimulating exploration, and encouraging enhanced oil and gas recovery."

To that end, the president intended to propose:

- a 10% credit against alternative minimum tax obligations for the first ten million dollars invested in exploration and a 5% credit for investments beyond ten million
- expansion of the R&D tax credit to include enhanced recovery techniques

- elimination of 80% of intangible drilling costs as an alternative minimum tax preference for independent producers
- repeal of the Transfer Rule prohibiting independent producers from using percentage depletion on acquired properties
- OCS leasing but delayed drilling in environmentally sensitive areas
- opening of the ANWR for exploration and development
- full decontrol of natural gas wellhead prices, and encouragement of greater competition in natural gas transportation.[20]

"I know—from conviction and personal experience," the president stated in *Building a Better America*, "that a strong domestic oil industry is vital to our national security." The president also declared his intent to increase the fill rate for the SPR and achieve 750 million barrels of stored oil by 1993 and press U.S. allies to maintain comparable reserves. He also declared his opposition to the imposition of any federal fees or tariffs on imported oil.[21]

Given the specificity of the energy proposals in *Building a Better America*, the policy mandate provided to incoming Secretary Watkins seemed uncommonly clear. And yet, he had announced at his confirmation hearing before the Senate Energy and Natural Resources Committee his intent to undertake the development of a comprehensive, integrated energy strategy. For the DOE policy staff, the question was: How would—how could—the Watkins strategy differ from the already published policy positions of the president in whose cabinet he would serve?

The Congressman

W. Henson Moore had served twelve years in Congress as representative of the 6th District of Louisiana before appearing on Bush's short list of candidates for energy secretary. He had built a personal portfolio of expertise on energy matters by serving for eight years on the powerful House Ways and Means Committee, three years on the Energy and Commerce Committee, and two years on the Budget Committee. After his senatorial campaign defeat of 1987, he had been offered the directorship of TVA by the Reagan administration, but had declined in favor of a partnership in the law firm of Sutherland, Asbill & Brennan.

The selection of Watkins as Bush's energy secretary was a profound disappointment for Moore. In the two months between Bush's election and the choice of Watkins, Moore's candidacy for the energy post had remained viable while the names of other candidates were floated and discarded. He had received strong support from most elements of the energy industry, especially from the Mid-Continent Oil and Gas Association. Other trade associations had joined the campaign to secure the energy post for him, along with several of Moore's former congressional colleagues.[22]

Moore's Republican credentials were impeccable. He had been a lifelong successful Republican in the populist Democratic stronghold of Louisiana. As vice president, Bush had made three campaign trips to Louisiana to support Moore's bid for the Senate. Moore, in turn had assisted Bush's presidential campaign by providing his list of political contributors and by writing op-ed pieces, published by most of Louisiana's newspapers, urging his state's majority Democratic voters to favor Bush over Michael Dukakis in 1988.[23]

Watkins' selection placed Moore in a quandary. He was urged by Fuller at the White House to consider the deputy secretary position. But he was counseled by his circle of political friends to shun a position with no statutorily defined responsibilities. In the end, he acceded to a request from Lee Atwater, the president's former campaign chairman and newly selected leader of the Republican National Committee, to, the very least, give Watkins a hearing.[24]

Watkins and Moore met for the first time at the president-elect's Connecticut avenue transition office in downtown Washington, in mid-January 1989. The meeting lasted four hours. "You probably feel about former congressmen," Moore told Watkins at their first encounter, "as I feel about former admirals."[25] Moore had no expectations that he and Watkins could work together. But his opening salvo produced a laugh, and the two proceeded to explore common ground. Two additional meetings, including a lengthy session at Watkins' Georgetown residence, proved necessary to convince Moore that he would have substantive responsibility, as well as meaningful authority, if he joined Watkins at DOE.[26]

Conscious of his limited knowledge of civilian energy matters and, more importantly, of the workings of committees of Congress with jurisdiction over DOE's non-defense portfolio, Watkins offered to Moore broad oversight of DOE's civilian energy functions. These included the offices of Energy Research, Fossil Fuels, Conservation and Renewable Energy, Policy and International Affairs, the EIA, Congressional and Intergovernmental Affairs, the Economic Regulatory Administration, and Procurement and Contracting. As a final accommodation, Watkins and the president agreed to announce Moore's selection at the White House. They thus sealed what both referred to as a "full partnership" that remained stable and true during their joint stewardship of DOE.[27]

It was during pre-confirmation, courtesy visits to key members of Congress that Watkins and Moore found themselves in agreement on the need to craft a national energy strategy. They settled on the terminology of "strategy" in preference to "plan," because they envisioned it, in somewhat military terms, as a set of specific proposals (tactics) to achieve defined strategic objectives. The strategy in other words was not to be merely a declaration of broad policy principles, as had been the case with the Reagan plans, but a blueprint for action.[28]

Moore used his Senate confirmation hearing on April 5, 1989, to expand on the ideas introduced previously by Watkins' confirmation testimony. "Essential," he stated in his opening statement, "…is the need to develop a long range strategy that will enable the nation to utilize all our available fuels." He argued that the full range of fuels and energy technologies would in the future be necessary to power America's growing economy. "In working towards a national energy consensus," he concluded, "we need to assure that our policies recognize and address competing regional priorities and economic interests across the nation."[29]

In the members of the Senate Committee on Energy and Natural Resources, Watkins and Moore found uncommonly bipartisan interest in fresh initiatives on energy policy. They found greater skepticism on the House side, from John Dingell, the redoubtable chairman of the Committee on Energy and Commerce, who had been through the energy policy wars as far back as the Carter administration. But neither Dingell, nor Philip Sharp, chairman of the Subcommittee on Energy and Power, offered any discouragement.

Had the legislators queried the senior ranks of Bush's White House, however, they would have discovered, notwithstanding the explicit policy agenda outlined in *Building a Better America*, profound antipathy to the very idea that the president's political capital should be spent on a public policy issue as unpromising as energy.[30] Chief among the antagonists was John Sununu, the White House chief of staff. As governor of New Hampshire, Sununu had come to be known as a champion of nuclear energy. He had given unstinting support to the construction of the Seabrook nuclear power plant. He saw federal energy policy exclusively in political terms. "Politics of energy is *[sic]* real," he declared in a speech delivered in Washington six months before the 1988 presidential election. "It is easy to gather political points," he went on, "by saying 'no.' It is very difficult to say 'yes' [to energy policy initiatives] without political cost."[31]

Watkins and Moore did not know, at the outset of their tenure at DOE, the position that Sununu would take on matters related to DOE. Nor did they think it necessary to seek *a priori* approval from the chief of staff to carry out what they saw as one of DOE's fundamental missions. Watkins assumed that the cabinet and White House staff would respect his prerogatives on matters within his statutory purview. Moore, for his part, was confident that he could manage the political aspects of energy policy development at least as well as the president's White House advisers. Moore felt that he understood the energy community very well. He had, after all, represented in Congress one of the country's principal energy-producing states.[32]

As they assumed control of DOE, Watkins and Moore saw the possibility of transforming a backwater, unpopular department into a well-managed center of activist national policy. Their expectations were not without foundation. Watkins had recently prevailed in the effort to produce a national policy on AIDS, notwithstanding a White House hostile to the issue. Moore had survived the populist politics of Louisiana and those—perhaps more demanding because of their national implications—of the House Ways and Means Committee. Could energy policy be more divisive than AIDS? Could it be more complex than the tax code? They thought not.[33]

As a first step, though, it was necessary to recruit reliable leadership for the DOE policy office. They needed someone who could rebuild a staff that, except for the short tenure of William Martin, had been marginalized by the Reagan Energy Department appointees of the previous eight years. Moore had just the person in mind.

The counsel

Moore began his recruitment drive for Linda G. Stuntz in February 1989. What he offered was, however, not exactly irresistible: the leadership of a small staff and office without political rank and the promise of a central role in the development of a national energy strategy. Stuntz, who was at the time practicing law at Jones Day Reavis & Pogue, aspired rather to a commissioner's chair at the Federal Energy Regulatory Commission (FERC), successor to the Federal Power Commission. At the very least, she wanted to be nominated to a position requiring Senate confirmation. Twice she declined Moore's offer to join the administration.[34]

Stuntz finally succumbed to the collective persuasive powers of Moore, Watkins and DOE Chief of Staff Polly Gault in March 1989. She was offered the title of deputy undersecretary and was promised an assistant secretaryship as soon as one became available. Most important, she was assured by Watkins that she would have the authority necessary to develop and integrate the policy mission of DOE's various assistant secretaries. Knowing of Stuntz's two young children, the admiral also promised (implausibly) that, on most days, she would be home by 6 p.m.[35]

Stuntz was not entirely convinced of the need for a national energy strategy. She could not quite isolate the specific problems that an "integrated strategy," as Watkins referred to it, would actually resolve. She was familiar, if unimpressed, with the country's previous energy policy plans from her two-year tenure as minority counsel and staff director of the House Committee on Energy and Commerce. She had, furthermore, served for a previous five years as associate minority counsel for the House Subcommittee on Fossil and Synthetic Fuels and knew all about DOE's record of technology development experience.[36]

She understood energy issues as distinct elements of policy, requiring specific legislative or regulatory fixes, affecting discrete constituencies in measurable economic terms. She had no practical knowledge of policy development processes in the executive branch and assumed Watkins and Moore had the power to do what they proposed to do with relatively unencumbered freedom to act on issues within their bureaucratic fiefdom.[37]

She sensed early on that Watkins was focused on the process by which the strategy would emerge, and that Moore was fixed on the product. Moore spoke often of wanting to produce "the most important energy policy ever done." She was wary about the ambitious scope of the effort thrust upon her. As to her position in the political landscape of the Bush administration, she did not perhaps fully appreciate the implications of having been selected by Watkins and Moore for a position normally reserved as a White House political plum. She was in fact to wait until May 1989 for White House clearance of her appointment.[38]

To her staff at DOE, Stuntz presented herself as a free market, economic conservative. Her thinking had been shaped by the disastrous oil price and allocation controls of the 1970s, by the perverse effects of natural gas regulation, by the economic distortions induced by the Fuel Use Act and by the waste of public resources that had defined the federal synthetic fuels effort. She was particularly skeptical of government ability to influence technological innovation in the marketplace.[39]

Her first months in office were marked by a crash course in the political landscape of the Bush administration. The unpredictable ideological bent of the Bush White House surfaced early in the bureaucratic struggle to develop the administration's proposals to amend the Clean Air Act (CAA) of 1970. As more fully explained later, the first skirmishes on the CAA initiative pitted DOE against EPA on the issue of how much federal intervention would be necessary to achieve ambient air quality standards. The historically interventionist DOE was placed in the position of arguing market principles and economic efficiency to EPA's penchant for prescriptive regulation. Interestingly, DOE emerged from the debate as a spoiler of EPA's initiative, even as it carried the burden of arguing what should have been argued by the economic stewards at CEA and OMB. But in the process, Stuntz earned a seat at Domestic Policy Adviser Roger Porter's table for the entire period in which the CAA were debated at the White House and in Congress.

Like most political appointees, Stuntz had reservations about career members of her staff who appeared to be less than wholly committed to the agenda of DOE's new leadership. She also remained concerned about her ability to prevail with her political colleagues at DOE, the assistant secretaries who manage the congressionally protected program offices. She was not sure how to respond to Moore's tendency to raise very high public expectations for the energy strategy—expectations that were beginning to be interpreted by energy industries as promises of federal budgetary largesse. Also, she did not possess the history of warfare in the trenches of the AIDS Commission that united (and concurrently separated from all others) Watkins' personal staff.[40]

Stuntz's credibility and stature grew with her tenure at DOE, along with the leadership's confidence in her ability. During her four-year term she was given multiple difficult assignments. She served for several months concurrently as head of the Policy Office and as acting assistant secretary for Fossil Energy, and subsequently as head of the Combined Policy and International Affairs Office. In the end, she fulfilled her highest expectations by being nominated, and confirmed by the Senate, to the post of deputy energy secretary—the first woman and youngest official in DOE history to serve in that position. First, though, she had to find her way through the bureaucratic and political maze created by the men of the Troika—Nicholas Brady of Treasury, Richard Darman of the Office of Management, and Budget and Michael Boskin of the Council of Economic Advisers—for the national energy strategy and for all domestic policy initiatives of the Bush Administration.

The economic adviser

It was initially unclear to Richard Schmalensee why the country needed another energy plan. As one of Bush's appointees to the three-member CEA, he became involved in the administration's internal debate on the energy strategy early in the process. In a division of labor with council chairman Michael Boskin, Schmalensee assumed responsibility for energy policy matters, though Boskin reserved the right to intervene on issues of tax policy. Schmalensee, a distinguished economist with uncommon dedication to prudent public policy, displayed no pronounced political coloration and was therefore able to view policy issues on the merits. In interagency meetings on the strategy, he often reminded his colleagues that while most policies do not threaten the republic, they should nevertheless be resisted when potentially harmful to the economy.[41]

The energy strategy advocated by Watkins and Moore appeared to Schmalensee to be a nearly impossible task: too many options, too many alternatives and too vast an agenda to reconcile in a single, integrated edifice of policy.[42] His skepticism about the strategy grew in proportion to Watkins' pursuit of a publicly derived policy consensus. Rather, he would have concentrated the effort on an intelligent characterization of key issues and on careful analysis of where markets were distorted or unresponsive. He viewed the AIDS Commission model as inappropriate to the making of energy policy. In the case of the AIDS process, Schmalensee saw an effort at public education, a raising of the collective consciousness and a campaign against prejudice. In energy, the objective was less a matter of defining common goals than in making difficult choices. He viewed the energy strategy, if one were to be developed, as the means to carry out the policy agenda for which presidents are elected. Policy, in his view, did not equal the sum total of special interests.[43]

From the perspective of the White House, the energy strategy process undertaken by Watkins rapidly became a matter of damage control. Schmalensee thought, as did Boskin, that Watkins' approach would raise expectations of widespread government intervention in the energy sector. In that event, the administration would be forced to respond in the negative. And the matter would not end there because it would be virtually certain that the Democrats in Congress would use any public dissatisfaction with policy to bait the president.[44]

White House distrust of Watkins and Moore deepened after the president's announcement of the National Energy Strategy (NES) in July 1989. The announcement, unsupported by CEA, created the impression that Watkins would not play by Troika's (unspoken but assumed) rules. Boskin and Schmalensee agreed that the energy strategy development process had to be prevented from becoming a vehicle for undesirable policy and politics.[45] Consequently, Schmalensee and his two staff assistants, Douglas Holtz-Eakin and Howard Gruenspecht, kept close watch on activities, analyses, and proposals emanating from DOE. Schmalensee also established a regular communication channel with Linda Stuntz. He frequently served as arbiter of the chronic contest of wills among DOE, Treasury, and OMB, but took positions on the strategy—especially on regulatory proposals—that were non-doctrinaire and typically apolitical.

Boskin's communications with Watkins were rare and nearly always unsuccessful. Watkins could not speak in Boskin's economic vocabulary, and Boskin appeared unwilling to entertain the idea that a former military officer could pursue economically efficient policy.

Schmalensee and Boskin came, in the end, to believe that Watkins stood for no particular policy at all, except that which the public consultation process might somehow manage to broadly define. Watkins was, in their view, too enthralled by the idea that reasonable men and women would somehow find the policy and political center.[46]

Schmalensee and Boskin were only partially correct in their assessment of Watkins. Watkins avoided taking nonnegotiable positions and remained neutral on policy not because he lacked conviction, but because he wanted to preserve the president's prerogative to make final decisions. Watkins believed—as perhaps few senior officials did in the Bush administration—that the consequences of policy are reaped by the president and not by cabinet secretaries. He was therefore unequivocally committed to his duty to protect the president's options.[47]

The CEA and others viewed Watkins' deference to the president as rather naive. After all, everyone took positions on policy. Sununu and Darman had emerged from the 1989 budget negotiations with Congress as proponents of policy that the president had previously opposed but was now forced to accept.[48] Yet, the historical record was rife with examples of aggressive cabinet officers foisting energy policy of dubious value on wary presidents. Ickes had done it to Roosevelt and Truman, and Schlesinger, most recently, to Carter.

Neither Schmalensee nor Boskin undertook to directly discover the reasoning behind Watkins' approach to the energy strategy effort. Effective and open communications were in any case not the norm among Bush's cabinet members. Schmalensee recalls no direct discussions on the strategy between himself and Brady at Treasury or Darman at OMB. He also recalls that Brady, who demanded a great deal of deference, was usually unpredictable as to the policy positions he would ultimately support and would not share his thinking in advance with other cabinet members. As for Darman, one was from time to time given the privilege of his views, but in the manner of the specially anointed giving guidance to the mortals.[49] Sununu, for his part, did not customarily solicit views beyond the Troika members.[50]

The director of OMB

"To appreciate Richard Darman's Dickensian dimensions," wrote Charles Kolb in *White House Daze,* "one need only meet him in person.[51]" Aloof in his demeanor to those he considered his inferiors, helpful to those with credible political connections and acquiescent to those who exercised real power, Darman was a technocrat in the tradition of Asian bureaucratic mandarins, self-preservation taking precedence over situational political interests. His iconography comprised children's metaphors for the most part: ducks for taxes and Sesame Street's Cookie Monster as allegory for the budget deficit.

In cabinet meetings Darman played solely to John Sununu. Uninterested in energy policy, or in any protracted policy development process, he delegated to OMB Associate Director Robert Grady the task of watching over the energy strategy effort. He would nevertheless attend EPC meetings in which the strategy was on the agenda, contributing to the NES debate a form of body language and nasal sounds indicating disagreement with the speaker (Moore or Watkins), followed by comments to indicate insider knowledge on the ultimate decision, that would remain, nonetheless, unshared. Darman and Sununu could often be seen passing notes to one another during EPC meetings on the strategy, but would neither publicly clarify their positions nor clue their audience to their own or the president's thinking.[52]

Grady could not pay much attention to the early stages of NES development because of the demanding role he assumed in crafting the president's CAA amendments. As a consequence, OMB was represented in the interagency NES process by career staff of middle rank, who were interpreting the will of higher ups with little explicit guidance. With Grady too busy and Darman inaccessible, OMB staff—typically averse to new initiatives except those that might reduce budget requirements—were free to intervene at will in a process they instinctively distrusted.

OMB staff could, however, be counted upon to expertly read the currents of White House influence. These currents suggested displeasure with NES at the very apex of intergovernmental power: the chief of staff, the CEA chairman and the Treasury secretary. The prevailing winds seemed to indicate therefore that the strategy's development should be obstructed rather than helped along.

The cabinet and EPC secretaries

David Bates remained at his post as cabinet secretary barely a year. He was to be the only White House official to support Watkins openly in the quest for NES. Bates was succeeded by Ede Holiday in spring of 1990. Her arrival at the White House spelled trouble for Watkins. Holiday, who had served as general counsel at the Treasury Department, was a protégé of Treasury Secretary Brady.

As cabinet secretary, Holiday was not only in a position to serve Brady's interests and facilitate communications with Sununu, but she also controlled the schedule, if not the agenda itself, of both EPC and the Domestic Policy Council (DPC). From Treasury, she brought Richard Porter to the position of DPC executive secretary and Olin Wethington to the equivalent position for EPC. Former White House aide Charles Kolb thought that Holiday "had scarcely a word to say about (the) substance" of issues.[53] But her position and those of Wethington and Porter provided a gatekeeping function that proved fully effective in containing Watkins.

Mid-level White House staffers have from time immemorial believed themselves wiser than cabinet secretaries, if for no other reason than their proximity to the Oval Office. They can take aggressive stands on issues because they are generally immune from public scrutiny or, in all but rare cases, from congressional accountability. They may or may not know the subjects they attend to in the course of their White House staff duties, as in the case of Olin Wethington, an attorney, who had no background in energy matters. Over the nearly two years of the energy strategy effort, Wethington was permitted to edit technical documents, hold sway on issues of policy quite as an equal to Watkins and Moore, and clear DOE documents directed to the EPC cabinet and the president.

The authority given to Wethington by Holiday and Brady represented for Watkins, in his words, "the equivalent of inexperienced army captains deciding strategy for battle-scarred generals."[54] Wethington was, in fact, deciding nothing. Rather, he transmitted communications that Holiday and Brady had neither the courtesy nor the good sense to relay directly to Watkins. Wethington faithfully discharged the duties assigned to him by Brady who, in due course, rewarded him with the position of assistant Treasury secretary for international affairs.

Others near the center

FERC was represented in the NES process by William Scherman, its general counsel. Scherman could speak authoritatively on NES issues because he had the full confidence of FERC Chairman Martin Allday. FERC was understandably sensitive about a number of proposals that surfaced in the NES' development. Key among these were proposals to amend the Public Utility Holding Company Act (PUHCA), repeal sections of the Public Utilities Regulatory Policy Act (PURPA), require open access to the electric transmission system, reform licensing of certain hydropower plants, restructure natural gas pipeline transportation and possible abolish the FERC itself. Scherman played a skillful and subtle role in protecting FERC interests without infringing upon executive branch prerogatives.

National Security Adviser Brent Scowcroft provided Watkins the most consistent and forceful support, especially during periods of unusually obstructive EPC behavior. Eric Melby, the National Security Council's (NSC) director of International Economic Affairs, stayed close to the NES development debate and frequently intervened to upset Wethington's more egregious abuses of the interagency process. Melby was especially instrumental in transferring from EPC to NSC consideration of the decision to draw down the SPR during the Iraqi war. The SPR decision, as more fully explained later, was strongly opposed by Brady.

THE WHITE HOUSE
RELUCTANTLY AGREES

The initial encounters between Watkins' senior aides and DOE's career policy staff were less than promising. The staff welcomed the prospect of an activist secretary in pursuit of new policy initiatives, but was puzzled by Watkins' disinterest in allowing the policy staff to undertake internally the effort necessary to produce the NES. The situation was not helped by the fact that Watkins' personal staff was unversed in the vocabulary of energy policy, displayed little interest in energy policy history and precedent and would not shed much light on the secretary's expectations of the role that the policy staff would be expected to play.

Early in his tenure the admiral, as Watkins liked to be called, declared his intent to pursue an extensive public consultation process as a prelude to the development of NES. The career staff of the policy office considered such consultations as little more than political window dressing. The staff's frame of reference had been defined by the experience of drafting energy plans in-house, forwarding them to OMB for clearance, presiding over *pro forma* public hearings (as required by the DOE Organization Act), and finally transmitting the plans to Congress.

This process had been in place since 1978. National Energy Policy Plans had been compiled every two years, with the exception of 1987 when the Energy Security Report[55] was submitted to Congress in lieu of a plan. The staff, in short, thought that it had mastered the energy policy process and could respond to any thematic variation required by a new secretary. The staff viewed public hearings as counterproductive. Such hearings had in the past attracted generalists without technical knowledge, representatives of special interests with narrow agendas to promote, state or local politicians seeking federal aid of one form or another, and members of the energy industry seeking subsidies. These views were anathema to Watkins.

As explained to the policy staff by Watkins' counselor, Nancy Wolicki, during the course of a meeting in April 1989, the admiral had no interest in a strategy developed internally by DOE bureaucrats. He considered public hearings and consultations to be essential steps in educating the American people on the difficult choices inherent in energy policymaking. And he wanted DOE to obtain knowledge and advice from external, independent sources as a means of counteracting internal professional prejudice and predispositions. Only through this approach—which, according to Wolicki, had worked successfully for the AIDS Commission—would the admiral be able to realize his objective of building a national consensus for NES.

As a consequence, the policy staff remained generally aloof from the public hearings, until eventually requested by Watkins to make sense of the hearing record and draft an interim report on initial findings. The staff at the outset concentrated on defining the analytical structure that the strategy was likely to require. In any case, Watkins made no demands on the policy staff while he awaited the all-important signal from the White House to proceed. Moreover, other matters came to the fore that were to substantially influence energy policy considerations within DOE, as well as relations between DOE's leadership and other key players in the Bush administration.

The Clean Air Act Amendments

Efforts to revise the CAA of 1970 preoccupied the Bush administration for nearly a year beginning in February 1989. The Clean Air Act Amendments (CAAA) that were eventually proposed by the administration evolved from intense interagency debate that frequently pitted DOE against EPA.

DOE was concerned about the impact that EPA-proposed acid rain provisions—a reduction in sulfur dioxide emissions of ten million tons per year—would have on the electricity generation sector. EPA's first set of proposals lacked an assessment of costs and did not distinguish between utilities that had invested in emission controls and those that had not. Secondly, the proposals seemed to DOE to presage a profound shift in the coal market from Eastern high sulfur coal to Western low sulfur coal, with little EPA appreciation of the resulting regional dislocations. Generally, DOE policy staff thought CAAA would likely engender significant and inequitably distributed electricity rate shocks at a time when the industry had just emerged from the nuclear plant over-investment debacle of the 1970s and early 1980s.

DOE's concerns turned to alarm when, in the design of CAAA's proposed mobile sources vehicles provisions, EPA unveiled a scheme to mandate the use of methanol as the transportation fuel of choice to combat ozone and carbon monoxide pollution. The use of methanol for purposes of meeting air quality standards had captured the imagination of William Rosenberg, assistant EPA administrator for Air and Radiation. The proposed mandate also had the strong support of Bush's White House counsel and long-time aide, C. Boyden Gray. Gray believed that methanol use in transportation could address two critical national problems, energy security and clean air, and assumed that DOE saw both issues as he did.

DOE's analyses of methanol led to conclusions different than those reached by Gray. The potentially positive aspects of an alternative transportation fuel were not, in DOE's view, sufficient to merit a mandate from the government of the United States. To mandate a fuel into America's vast transportation market meant mandating its production, its distribution and probably its price to consumers. After all, if the federal government were to decree the use of a specific fuel, it meant that consumers would have to bear whatever the cost of making it available. Furthermore, a mandate would essentially close competition to other, perhaps equally viable, alternative fuels and fuel-using technology. DOE policy staff was surprised that this EPA proposal was being given serious consideration by an administration professing adherence to market principles and disappointed that the body of research DOE had painstakingly accumulated on the issue was not being used as a basis for sound policy formulation.

DOE policy staff had for several years, in spite of Reagan policy to the contrary, advocated government intervention—but not mandates—to encourage the introduction of alternative transportation fuels. Studies of the costs and benefits of such fuels and related issues of technology, environmental impacts and energy security had led the staff to be extremely cautious about the scope of federal policy. Prudence dictated that policymakers tread lightly into advocacy of change for a one hundred-year-old system then comprising 175 million vehicles, two hundred thousand fuel distribution outlets, nearly two hundred fuel refineries and thousands of miles of fuel delivery pipelines. But the real reason for caution was knowledge of the potential source of low-cost, large-scale methanol supplies.

Methanol, generally produced from natural gas, had emerged from DOE studies as the lowest cost alternative to oil. The policy staff had learned, however, that methanol could be produced at lowest cost not in the United States, Europe, Asia or Latin America, but in the Persian Gulf. The factors that led to this perverse conclusion were plain. The large-scale production of oil in the Middle East was necessarily accompanied by large-scale production of associated gas. In the United States, such gas was either re-injected into oil wells to enhance production, or separated and sold as liquid petroleum gas (LPG). In the Middle East, oil production did not require re-injection of the gas, and little demand existed for LPG. As a consequence, associated gas from Mid-Eastern oil production was flared into the atmosphere.

DOE staff reasoned that if the U.S. government mandated methanol as a required transportation fuel, Persian Gulf producers would use their essentially cost-free associated gas to produce the world's least cost methanol for the American market. They would have a clear cost advantage because nowhere else in the world was there a likelihood of duplicating Persian Gulf oil production capacity and, by extension, the production of associated gas.[56]

It was, under the circumstances, not unreasonable to conclude that a government-directed market for methanol would have the effect of trading a troublesome dependence on oil for a doubly troublesome dependence on a single oil alternative. A federally mandated methanol market would, moreover, create parallel fuel demand rather than fuel competition. And, even if other producers were eventually to enter the methanol market, Persian Gulf producers could be expected, according to DOE studies, to establish a commanding market position.[57]

The policy staff, furthermore, was convinced that a government fuel mandate would impede rather than encourage technological innovation. The staff had envisioned a policy that would foster vigorous experimentation and development of new vehicle propulsion systems in an evolutionary break with the internal combustion engine. In sum, DOE wanted entry into the market of the widest possible range of fuels and technology—compressed natural gas, propane, ethanol, electricity, fuel cells, and hybrids. DOE and EPA positions were consequently irreconcilable.

CEA Chairman Michael Boskin was asked by the president to arbitrate the dispute between DOE and EPA. The case for DOE was presented by Moore and a senior DOE policy analyst.[58] DOE made the case on free market terms aimed at what were assumed to be Boskin's and the administration's predispositions. Rosenberg made the case for EPA, in the presence of Boyden Gray. The debate turned especially heated between Moore and Gray, each seeming to misunderstand the other's motives while both claiming to know the president's mind on the issue. In the end, Boskin accepted the DOE position as more in tune with the administration's market reliance philosophy than EPA's proposal.

The DOE victory proved pyrrhic. After the CAAA debate, Gray made a point of involving himself on a more or less permanent basis in the affairs of DOE, particularly in the national energy strategy process. This was unprecedented for a White House counsel. His involvement complicated the decision-making process on NES because he would intervene at unpredictable moments and form unexpected coalitions with other cabinet members. EPA for its part, politically spent after the CAAA battle, fought DOE on most aspects of NES, especially and counter-intuitively, on global climate change policy. Indeed, the agency abdicated to DOE the struggle to forge a policy on climate change during the Bush administration while concurrently voicing dissatisfaction with the policy that emerged.

The clean air debate offered a lesson in White House decision-making, a display (unappreciated at the time) of the tensions among neo-Reaganites and Bush pragmatists. It also offered a preview of Bush's approach to domestic policy matters (*e.g.,* heavy reliance on a limited number of cabinet and sub-cabinet officials, with only end-state presidential involvement). Stuntz and the policy staff learned also that Bush administration policy would in the end be shaped on the merits of each case, but that final decisions were as likely to depend on the personal standing of the cabinet advocates within the White House power structure as on analytical rigor.

Gratified by the role they had played in the clean air debate and by the analytical support they had received from the policy office, Watkins and Moore turned to the business of building bureaucratic momentum for NES. They still lacked a White House mandate, but felt confident in their ability to eventually persuade the president of the desirability of undertaking the administration's second major domestic policy initiative after the clean air act reforms.

Internal organization of NES effort

Watkins gave the policy office charge of the NES effort on May 12, 1989. "I view the development of the NES as a Department-wide effort, however," Watkins stated, "and expect the active participation of all Departmental elements."[59] Linda Stuntz was singled out as the official whom Watkins would hold responsible for the successful completion of NES. She accepted the charge with some misgivings as to the authority she would have to ensure the cooperation of DOE's resource-rich but statutorily independent assistant secretaries. But she was assured by both Watkins and Moore that she would receive the backing necessary for the job.

As a first task, Stuntz directed the policy staff to develop a preliminary outline of the analytical, data, and modeling requirements that would be needed to complete the strategy. Concurrently she ordered a review of more than forty policy plans submitted to DOE by interest groups seeking early influence on the NES project. On June 2, 1989, a DOE-exclusive NES Development Committee (NESDC) was established by Stuntz, made up of representatives from virtually all organizational elements of DOE. The NESDC was to facilitate intra-departmental communications, conduct, and peer-review NES analyses, as well as maintain liaison with DOE's broad and diverse constituency. NESDC remained active until the completion of NES, meeting on a weekly basis and acting as a counterweight, albeit a modest one, to what became the oppressive oversight of the EPC.[60]

Stuntz then turned her attention to energy models. A DOE-wide consensus rapidly emerged that the EIA models had sub-optimal forecasting capability for energy demand and for renewable energy supply. EIA Administrator Calvin Kent was fully aware of the models' shortcomings. He was also aware that various DOE organizational elements used non-EIA models to conduct analyses of particular energy issues.

Stuntz and Kent agreed in June 1989 to construct a "comprehensive model of the energy system of the United States"—the National Energy Modeling System, or NEMS. NEMS was to "simulate the complex interactions that take place between the various sectors of the energy market, the economy in general, and the environment." Responsibility for NEMS development rested with EIA, but it was understood that EIA would work closely with the Policy Office and also seek the advice and counsel of the National Academy of Sciences.[61]

Stuntz next commissioned a series of studies from DOE's national laboratories. These were intended to ensure substantive involvement of the considerable talent available there. Although Stuntz believed that the laboratories had institutional biases, she and the policy staff also recognized that the laboratories would be able to weigh the claims and counterclaims of policy advocates with greater objectivity than could DOE's competing program offices. The policy staff also felt that on politically volatile issues like global climate change, laboratory researchers would be better insulated from external pressures than would career bureaucrats. The studies' scope and the laboratories involved were:

- *Conservation and Energy Efficiency:* Determination of the further technical and economic potential for energy efficiency and conservation on a sector by sector basis and for the NES time frame (1990-2030). Direction of the study was assigned to Oak Ridge National Laboratory, with the participation of Lawrence Berkeley, Pacific Northwest, and Argonne National laboratories.

- *Global Climate Change:* Assessment of global climate change science, scope of uncertainty, and design of tools to integrate climate and energy models capable of testing optimal energy and emission paths. Direction of the study was given to Lawrence

Livermore Laboratory, with the participation of Brookhaven, Pacific Northwest, Oak Ridge and Argonne.

- *Renewable Energy:* Boundary analysis of the technical and economic potential for renewable energy technology and estimated timing of systems deployment into the various sectors of the energy economy. Direction of the study was assigned to the Solar Energy Research Institute (SERI),[62] with Sandia, Oak Ridge and Los Alamos participating.

- *Technology Transfer:* Analysis of options to accelerate transfer of technology from DOE laboratories to the private sector. The analysis was to include: (a) an assessment of technology transfer success and failure rates, under the direction of Los Alamos, with assistance from Pacific Northwest, Lawrence Livermore, Lawrence Berkeley, Sandia, SERI, Brookhaven and Argonne; (b) an assessment of technology transfer potential to less developed countries, under the direction of Lawrence Berkeley, with assistance from SERI, Sandia and Oak Ridge laboratories; and (c) an evaluation of transfer mechanisms, under the direction of Pacific Northwest, with Oak Ridge and SERI laboratories.

Agreement with the laboratories on the analyses to be undertaken was reached during the course of a two-day meeting in June, 1989. The laboratories were also promised a consultative role throughout the NES development process.[63] Indeed, a National Laboratory Advisory Committee on NES was formally constituted on October 25, 1989.[64]

By July 1989, internal preparations for NES were essentially complete. What remained elusive was the presidential mandate that Watkins thought essential to obtain. Cabinet Secretary David Bates rescued Watkins from the untenable possibility of pursuing the development of NES without the president's endorsement.[65] Acting on a plea by Watkins, Bates succeeded in inserting a formal announcement of NES in a speech that the president was scheduled to deliver on the occasion of the signing of the Natural Gas Wellhead Decontrol Act of 1989.

White House announcement of the National Energy Strategy

"And so today," the president declared on July 26, 1989, in the Rose Garden, "I want to make this announcement that I'm directing Jim Watkins to take the lead in developing a comprehensive national energy strategy. We cannot and will not wait for the next energy crisis to force us to respond. And so I've asked Jim to craft this strategy in close consultation with the Cabinet, leading members of the United States Congress, and then with our cities and our States. Our task—our bipartisan task—is to build the national consensus necessary to support this strategy and to make this strategy a living and dynamic document, responsive to new knowledge and new ideas and to global, environmental, and international change.[66]

Later conversations between Bates and Watkins[67] indicated that the announcement of the NES had been opposed by OMB, CEA, and the Treasury Department. Indeed, the president's conditioned charge to Watkins suggested that, though it was defeated in the first battle to take control of the process, the Troika would be a force for the duration of the NES development war. As the president ordered, Watkins could develop the strategy only by working with the cabinet—and the cabinet was organized in such a manner as to force energy policy decisions into the purview of EPC. EPC was, of course, controlled by Treasury Secretary Brady, CEA Chairman Boskin, and OMB Director Darman.

Brady had learned of the president's decision to endorse the development of NES several days before the White House announcement. On July 21, 1989, five days before the president's speech, Deputy Secretary Moore had received the draft of a memorandum from Brady to EPC members[68] proposing terms under which NES was to be developed. The contents of the memorandum had not been discussed in advance with Watkins—as cabinet protocol would have required—and it made pointed reference to the fact that the administration, not DOE, would develop NES. "To develop a National Energy Strategy," Brady declared in the memo, "I am establishing an Economic Policy Council Working Group on Energy Policy." He went on to direct the Working Group to produce an interim NES report for review by EPC by March 1990, and a final document by December 1990.[69]

The Brady memorandum was received at DOE in the spirit in which it was sent. It was considered insulting, the more so because it had actually reached DOE by fax from the White House Office of Cabinet Affairs and not directly from Brady's Treasury office. Third-party communications between Brady and Watkins remained the norm throughout the NES process. Brady acted through Cabinet Secretary Ede Holiday, who replaced Bates soon after the NES announcement and, on day-to-day matters, via EPC Executive Secretary Olin Wethington. Not once in the twenty-two months of NES deliberations, did Brady find it necessary to speak directly with his counterpart at DOE. [70]

The details of the role that EPC would play in the development of NES were argued by proxy in late July by Linda Stuntz on behalf of Watkins and Lehman Li, representing Brady. In the end, DOE was forced to accept the cabinet oversight that the president himself had stipulated in the White House announcement. The EPC Working Group on NES was formally established on July 26, 1989, and, in a conciliatory gesture by Brady, Henson Moore was named to its chair. On August 4, 1989, Moore issued invitations to the agencies that were to participate in the Working Group to name a representative holding not less than assistant secretary rank. Two months later, on October 11, 1989, the Working Group held its first meeting.[71]

Twenty-four federal departments, agencies and commissions sought and obtained representation on the Working Group, a greater number by far than the customary membership of EPC.[72] The paucity of domestic policy initiatives during the Bush administration led departments and agencies to seek opportunities to advance their agenda in any forum they could find. The CAA deliberations had offered one such possibility, albeit of short duration and, in any case, tightly controlled by OMB and EPA. NES, launched with a presidential mandate of cabinet involvement, looked especially inviting to the federal establishment. Experienced Washington operatives knew that policy processes with high visibility could frequently be exploited for advantage, even if the subject were removed from a particular agency's statutory confines.

Most members of the Working Group had little to contribute to the analytical work that was carried out during the two-year NES effort, except to provide comments to documents generated by DOE. They viewed their role, as their predecessors had in similar circumstances during previous administrations, as invitees to a process they could exploit at no cost. They saw their duty as mainly to ensure that NES would not infringe on the prerogatives of their agencies while searching for opportunity to advance pet projects the administration would not have otherwise considered. The Department of Health and Human Services, for example, sought through the NES process to secure an increase in its budget to aid low-income households with their energy bills. The Defense Department sought a fuel reserve dedicated to the military. The Transportation Department was interested in greater financial support for its high-speed rail initiative. Not surprisingly, the environmental agencies saw NES as a vehicle to press a very reluctant administration into a more activist policy on global climate change.

A few members of the Working Group were there to obstruct considerations of initiatives they opposed, which might nonetheless win administration support. The Nuclear Regulatory Commission feared long-standing efforts to reform the nuclear plant licensing process, for example, and FERC opposed proposals to deregulate the licensing of the smallest hydropower plants. Other agencies sought cover for politically explosive issues, such as the Department of Transportation's fear of political pressure for higher automotive fuel economic standards. Treasury wanted no consideration of new tax preferences for any industry and the Interior Department, which supported the exploration and development of ANWR, wanted to avoid reform of policies on federal royalties.

The management of the Working Group proved awkward and time-consuming for DOE policy staff. DOE's political leadership, however, accepted the arrangement as necessary and the staff could do no less. "Men cooperate after different fashions," wrote Marcus Aurelius in *Meditations*, "and even those cooperate abundantly who find fault with what happens and those who try to oppose it and hinder it."[73]

Notification of Congress

On the afternoon of the White House announcement on the NES, Watkins appeared before the Senate Energy and Natural Resources Committee. The NES, he stated, "will serve as a blueprint for energy policy and government program decisions. It will contain specific short-term, mid-term, and long-term recommendations. This strategy will chart our course, set our pace, and provide mileposts by which to evaluate our progress in providing the energy our economy needs, while protecting the Nation's health, safety and environment."

He promised the committee that NES would not reflect his private views or those of the special interests. "Rather," he said, "it will be developed from the consensus of views we receive throughout the [development] process."[74]

THE VOICE OF THE PEOPLE

"The secretary of energy in the Bush cabinet is doing something rather unusual for a politician," wrote *The Economist* in the fall of 1989, "Admiral Watkins is going around the country, listening. Just listening."[75] The public hearings that impressed the British magazine began on August 1, 1989, in Washington, DC. Others, in the first series, were held in Tulsa, Oklahoma, Boise, Idaho, Seattle, Washington and Louisville, Kentucky. Watkins described the initial hearings as "fact finding in nature." He assigned broad themes to the hearings: What should NES priorities be? How can environmental and energy objectives be optimally achieved? What should be DOE's R&D agenda? What do state governments and the private sector expect from the federal government in terms of energy policy leadership?[76]

The hearings were aimed at soliciting the broadest possible range of views. Panels of witnesses were selected to provide political and special interest balance. On the first day of hearings, for example, Watkins heard from a state senator from Louisiana, a vice president of the Worldwatch Institute, the president of a natural gas company, a former FERC commissioner, and the chief economist of a major oil company. Testimony was eventually heard from the vast majority of public and private organizations with interest in energy and environmental policy.[77] Reporting on the hearings, the *New York Times*[78] saw NES as "a tacit acknowledgment by the Administration that the Energy Department is to have a much bigger role in setting priorities and policies for energy development in the 1990s than it did in the 1980s." The trade press, however, was not impressed. The *Oil Daily* of August 3, 1989, commented after the first hearing, "there clearly are few new pieces of information that haven't been examined in some minute detail during the latter years of the Reagan administration."[79]

A total of eighteen public hearings were held from August 1, 1989, through August 27, 1990. They were conducted in three rounds. The first set of five broached general topics. The second set of ten was more thematic, seeking debate on such matters as the domestic energy resource base, national security, industrial productivity at home and abroad, energy regulation and tax policy, and environmental consequences of energy use. The final hearings were held in the summer of 1990 after publication of the NES Interim Report. These last focused on such issues as the public health effects of energy fuel cycles, energy pricing as a tool to achieve environmental objectives, and integration of policies on energy, the environment and the economy.

DOE records indicate 379 witnesses from forty-three states testified at the NES hearings. An additional one thousand individuals submitted statements for the record. In all, over twenty thousand pages of testimony were collected, organized for access by subject and site and made available to the public in specially designated reading rooms at fourteen nationwide DOE offices.[80]

The Troika agencies opposed the hearings. They feared, correctly as it turned out, that the hearings would surface support for more interventionist policies than the administration was likely to tolerate. To Watkins, the hearings revealed, in his words, the heterogeneous nature of American society. "I say we have five nations," he noted in a post-mortem interview, "Northeast, Southeast, the Midwest, the Northwest and the Southwest. They are totally different cultures. One section loves hydro, the other hates it. Some love coal, others hate it. Most dislike nuclear waste, but they love clean power."[81] As the *New York Times* summarized, during a single full day of testimony the environmentalists promoted conservation, the natural gas industry requested new tax breaks, the oil industry thought ANWR should be opened to development, and the solar and nuclear industries sought more federal funds for research and development of their respective technologies.[82]

The hearings demonstrated that a consensus on non-objectionable policy could easily be forged. In principle, everyone supported energy conservation, and no American could be found who opposed solar power. On more difficult choices—nuclear power, coal use, energy taxes, and the means by which energy objectives should be achieved—no consensus was forthcoming. However, NES public hearings produced a record of opinion that was remarkably consistent with previous professional surveys and polls. In a 1985 study of public opinion on energy issues, Olsen *et al.* found that "overall, the public believes that the solution to the energy problem lies equally in more energy production and more energy conservation."[83] This was the concluding message of NES public hearings once extremist views were discarded.

The Troika agencies dismissed the hearings as media events, their value inherently suspect because private views were not subjected to public accountability. For Watkins, the hearings justified his plan to educate, to be tolerant of views distant from his own, and to bring the policy process into the public arena. The media covered the hearings extensively, and the analytical community took them seriously enough to provide carefully crafted testimony as well as scholarly analysis. Members of Congress and governors eagerly accepted invitations to participate in the hearings, as did numerous Bush administration officials. The hearings also raised to exceptional visibility the public expectations of change in energy policy that Watkins sought.

The raising of public expectations was the Troika agencies' worst fear. The Troika leaders, acting in concert with Sununu, had in fact succeeded in obscuring from public view the commitments that had been made by Bush in his agenda for *Building a Better America*. In the first year, the administration had pursued none of the energy initiatives it had announced in its first budget message. Congress, for its part, had acted on the long-simmering natural gas wellhead decontrol legislation but on no other energy initiative. Watkins saw in the public expectations voiced by witnesses at NES hearings the key to making the administration true to itself.

THE INTERIM REPORT

In November 1989, the DOE policy office began drafting a progress report on the NES development process. The objective of what came to be known as the "Interim Report on the National Energy Strategy: A Compilation of Public Comments" was to "draw from the hearings process the key issues of public concern, present them in a logical and reasoned framework, and provide the basis for a 5-month period [April through September 1990] of public debate and consensus building."[84]

Drafted on a template of five chapters that aimed at concurrently informing the reader of the status of the energy economy and reporting on the findings of the public consultation process, the Interim Report urged, in its preface, the following course of action:[85]

- *Increase Efficiency of Energy Use:* Higher efficiency of energy use, where cost-effective, can help reduce energy costs to consumers, reduce energy demand, balance environmental concerns with economic development and enhance energy security.
- *Secure Future Energy Supplies:* Even with advances in energy efficiency, our nation will likely need more energy in the future. All energy sectors will need to contribute to our future energy mix and to the achievement of our energy security, environmental, and economic goals.
- *Respect the Environment:* All energy options for the future must be sensitive to our environment—local and global. Energy and environmental goals can and must be achieved in mutually beneficial ways. Advanced technology and improved energy use practices can help us produce adequate supplies of affordable energy while maintaining the quality of our environment.
- *Fortify Foundations:* Underlying all of the above is an essential foundation of human, technological, and entrepreneurial resources, without which no comprehensive strategy would be successful. This

foundation comprises basic science and research, education and technology transfer.

The words in the preface of the Interim Report were the result of numerous drafting compromises between DOE and EPC reviewers. The preface became the political part of the report, a measure of the Bush cabinet's inability to agree on any substantive area of energy policy except in highly generalized terms. The preface proved embarrassing to DOE policy staff because it failed utterly to convey the rather complex message embedded in the Interim Report.

The drafters of the substantive portions of the Interim Report, under the direction of DOE's Robert Marlay, faithfully summarized the public record, using citations from testimony at the hearings to outline issues raised, obstacles to progress, and options to consider in development of new policy. The report addressed Watkins' desire to use the record of the public hearings as a starting point for narrowing policy options. His plan was to construct a final strategy on consensus views that reflected the political center.

As a follow-up to the Interim Report, Watkins envisaged the publication by DOE of a series of analytical papers that would without prejudice address the advantages and disadvantages of the policy options raised in the public hearing process. He thought DOE analyses would marginalize the policy positions of extremists on the right and left of the political spectrum. As a sign of further good faith, he intended to release DOE analyses for public comment between April and July 1990. A final series of public hearings would follow. Thus would be perfected the policy proposals that would ultimately constitute the NES Final Report.[86]

Watkins' plan had no support whatsoever from EPC. The EPC Working Group reviewed a draft of the Interim Report in February 1990 and attacked it as inconsistent with administration policy. "There is a blurring of the lines between public comments, DOE policy, and administration policy," declared most of the reviewers. "Administration views should not be treated like other [public] views," said the usually single-minded Troika. To drive the message home, the Working Group actually caucused without DOE representatives and agreed to transmit via OMB the blunt message that the

Interim Report should present "…only the most basic, innocuous, and necessary statements."[87]

The EPC Working Group held three meetings in March to resolve interdepartmental differences on the content of the Interim Report. EPC's micromanagement of NES' first visible product especially irked Stuntz. In a memorandum to Deputy Secretary Moore on the eve of the final EPC meeting, she complained, "Some agencies, especially Treasury, CEA and OMB, have difficulty accepting parts of the report that characterize issues in a manner that is inconsistent with their view of Administration policy."[88]

Matters were actually worse. EPC Working group members had assumed the position, in Stuntz's words, "that they are entitled to veto the [Interim] report if their views are not fully and explicitly adopted."[89] CEA and OMB were especially aggressive in protecting the administration from what appeared to them as the accusatory voice of public opinion. Staff from those two agencies went so far as to redraft the entire chapter on petroleum. Their objective was to interpret public comments in such a way as to support the administration's view that rising oil imports were not, *per se,* a problem.[90]

Late in the drafting stage, DOE staff further unnerved the Working Group by recommending that the Interim Report be used to announce an initial set of initiatives to indicate that, on some issues the administration had heard the message of the public hearings. The proposal and the initiatives had been pressed upon Stuntz by the restless assistant secretaries in charge of DOE's program elements, who had argued that the slow pace of NES development needed to be punctuated by action. The assistant secretaries, detached from the EPC processes on NES, thought that the Interim Report initiatives would likely become administration policy sooner or later anyway.

Reluctantly, Stuntz agreed to place before EPC a set of seven initiatives, which she and the policy staff believed might gain support. The seven so-called "action items" were rather modest proposals for federal support of policy areas so well-developed as to be deemed self-evident. They included initiatives in integrated resource planning, energy efficiency programs for electric utilities, capacity enhancements at federal hydropower facilities, streamlined procedures for transfer of technology from DOE laboratories to the private sector, involvement of DOE researchers in math and science curricula development efforts in local school districts and common sense pollution prevention and waste minimization efforts at DOE facilities.[91]

The EPC disagrees

DOE staff considered these initiatives to be politically harmless, *de minimis* components of any credible energy strategy. They had been culled from a more aggressive list of proposals submitted by DOE's assistant secretaries. Although wary of EPC reactions, Stuntz saw no disadvantage to the adoption of these proposals. She came to accept Assistant Energy Secretary Michael Davis' argument that the Interim Report would be better received by Congress and the general public if it contained something more than a compilation of opinions. The action items, Davis insisted, could not but raise the credibility of the administration with friends and foes alike.

With the action items, the DOE staff thought the initiative could actually be seized from the EPC Working Group. But the action items were also intended to give practical expression to Watkins' personal conclusions about the hearings. His key conclusion, eventually relegated by the Troika editors to the very end of the Interim Report's preface was, "The loudest single message [from the hearings] was to increase energy efficiency in every sector of energy use. Energy efficiency was seen as a way to reduce pollution, reduce dependence on imports, and reduce the cost of energy."[92]

The EPC Working Group saw things differently. It vehemently rejected the action items proposal as premature and inopportune. The Troika representatives opposed, on principle, any linkage between public testimony and administration policy. They viewed the DOE proposal as a transparent effort to short-circuit the process that had been established by the president and cabinet for NES development, and as further evidence of DOE's instinctive policy activism. As a consequence, the initiatives were shelved.

Moore tried to be conciliatory during the final March 16, 1990, meeting of the Working Group to review the Interim Report draft. "Needless to say," he declared, "some views expressed by some of the witnesses heard in the NES development process do not coincide with our own views of the same issues, nor with Administration policy." But, he went on, "one of the main reasons we're developing the NES is because this divergence of views needs to be reconciled."[93]

The EPC audience was unyielding. The final draft of the Interim Report was so sanitized as to leave no doubt that the administration would not be linked to the public debate that the report purported to present.[94] The five-page preface to the report received special scrutiny by Troika staff that, by rendering sterile the preface's message, assumed that readers would pay little attention to the rest of the report. The preface was the only document presented to EPC cabinet members who met on March 21, 1990, in the historic White House Roosevelt Room, to formally approve the NES Interim Report.[95]

Watkins set aside the just completed interagency battle when he appeared at the March 21 cabinet meeting. He declared his commitment to be a team player, cooperative and loyal to the president, but holding to his vision of how NES should be crafted. "I'm here today," he said, "to obtain your support to release an Interim Report on the development of the NES. This report is not a draft Energy Strategy and does not represent Administration policy."[96] He summarized the contribution that he believed NES would make to the energy policy debate by stating, "Congress will get a better picture, and be more responsive to our collective needs if we can show that we're neither supply-siders nor demand-siders. Governors will know what our agenda is, and where the limits are of our ability to do something about a range of problems, and private interests will get a clearer signal of what can and what cannot be expected."[97]

He concluded with a plea to his cabinet colleagues to "work cooperatively on this or the President won't get the best advice he's entitled to."[98] The Interim Report was released to the public on April 2, 1990.

THE COMPLEX
U.S. ENERGY ECONOMY

The Interim Report was an amalgam of program and policy proposals culled from the public hearing process and of energy sector data and analysis compiled by DOE staff. Watkins and Moore believed that the hearings would generate new information about the energy sector that DOE staff might have ignored or overlooked, either through lack of motivation or out of sheer bureaucratic inertia. They feared being co-opted by the institutional habits of the career officials on whom they nonetheless had to depend for NES' development.

It was due to Stuntz's foresight that policy staff had focused its attention on the analytical foundation of NES while Watkins and Moore pursued their public hearings. The staff had assembled comprehensive profiles of energy use in the key sectors of the economy as a means of testing whether or not the innumerable proposals put forth by participants in the hearing had actual merit. These profiles proved useful in placing the public hearings results in some context. They served also to present and explain in the Interim Report the fundamental structure of the U.S. energy economy and the need—or not—to take corrective action.[99]

Structure and trends of the U.S. energy economy

In 1988, the baseline year for NES, the United States consumed slightly over eighty quadrillion British thermal units (Btu)[100]of energy to power an economy with a gross national product (GNP) of $4.8 trillion. Roughly one-third of this energy was used in the industrial sector, another third in the transportation sector and the remainder in commercial and residential buildings. Between 1973 and 1988, energy use had increased by 8% while economic output had expanded by 47%. During the same period, twenty million homes had been added to the national stock and fifty million vehicles to the national fleet.[101] These data indicated to analysts familiar with the unique structure of the U.S. economy that consumption of energy per unit of economic output—a crude measure of energy efficiency—was moving in a positive direction.

However, liberal critics of U.S. energy policy during the 1980s were vocal in their view that the American people were among the world's most wasteful energy consumers. These critics usually pointed to lower energy consumption in Japan and Western Europe as proof of higher (more ethical) energy efficiency achievements outside the United States. DOE policy analysts did not subscribe to this view of the domestic and international energy sector.

DOE policy studies conducted during the 1980s provided a different understanding of the differences in energy consumption among industrialized nations. Japan, for example, used less energy because its typical household lived in less than one-half the residential space of the average American family, used proportionately smaller and fewer household appliances and rarely air-conditioned or centrally heated living space. These conditions were not due to personal choice or to more ethical behavior, but to absolute constraints in collectively available physical space. Furthermore, the use of less energy was not synonymous with being more efficient. In Europe, it was discovered that energy consumption had historically tracked American patterns, notwithstanding substantially higher taxes—and prices—for all energy.[102]

With this baseline of energy consumption as a given, the NES public hearings inspired a wealth of future energy scenarios.[103] Projections of energy demand requirements ranged absurdly wide. In *Energy for a Sustainable World*, Goldemberg et al. offered the prognosis of a 50% reduction in 1988 primary energy consumption by the year 2020 if aggressive energy conservation policies were pursued.[104] At the other extreme, EPA projected a near doubling of 1988 energy requirements by 2025, as part of its "Policy Options for Stabilizing Global Climate Change."[105] Interestingly, the majority of projections offered as reference cases for NES fell within a fairly narrow range of estimates. This indicated, as Watkins suspected, there indeed existed a political as well as an analytical energy policy center.

Energy use in transportation

At the core of American anxiety about energy has traditionally lain the specter of shortages in liquid fuels for transportation. Two-thirds of all petroleum used in the U.S. economy is in the form of refined products to power cars, trucks, buses, airplanes, trains, and ships. The transportation sector is 97% dependent on petroleum for its energy requirements with the totality of that dependence being fuel inflexible (*e.g.,* devoid of the option to switch from one fuel to another). Four-fifths of all U.S. passenger traffic and one-fourth of the entire freight traffic moves on highways. Americans use about 125 billion gallons of gasoline every year, and the transportation sector alone requires more oil than is produced domestically.[106]

Americans remain concerned about the transportation sector's energy requirements because, in addition to creating reliance on politically unstable Persian Gulf oil suppliers, vehicles are also a major source of air pollution and contribute to global warming. Throughout the 1970s and 1980s, federal fuel efficiency standards for automobiles and light duty trucks known by the regulatory acronym CAFE (Corporate Average Fuel Efficiency), had been the sole instrument of government policy to affect oil demand in transportation. CAFE standards for automobiles, set by the Transportation Department's National Highway Traffic Safety Administration (NHTSA) had risen from 13 miles per gallon in the early 1970s to 27.5 miles per gallon in 1986. There they remained.

It was not surprising therefore that witnesses at NES public hearings would focus on higher CAFE standards as an essential element of policy for the transportation sector. Other proposals included the imposition of higher taxes on gasoline, taxes and fees on fuel-guzzling cars, rebates for purchases of highly fuel-efficient cars, carbon taxes for all vehicles, and government acquisition and removal from circulation of older, inefficient cars.[107]

Some NES witnesses supported a more radical solution to vehicles' linkage to oil: alternative fuels and technology. The problem, however —understood by most analysts and fully addressed in DOE's own extended study of the subject[108]—was cost. No market-priced alternative fuel was cost-competitive with gasoline. No higher-priced alternative fuels would enter the market until vehicles were manufactured (and purchased by consumers) to use these fuels. And such vehicles were unlikely to enter the market without compelling reasons for their use. Only two rationales could be found to compel change in the petroleum-dominated transportation sector: national security and environmental quality. Action on either or both could only be instigated by federal policy. But views differed widely—in the executive branch, in Congress, among analysts and in the general public— as to how these externalities (in economic parlance) could be internalized in the social cost of energy.

Energy use in homes

Two-thirds of all American households reside in single-family homes, with the remainder in apartments, multi-family dwellings or motor homes.[109] These living patterns have important implications for how residential energy is used in the United States. Unlike Europeans and Japanese, who in far larger numbers reside in apartment buildings, Americans retain personal control of how, and how much, they use energy in their homes. Economists assume rational economic behavior by consumers, but in the energy sector, to the factor of rationality must be added factors of personal preference. Households of the elderly and the very young, for example, require warmer winter environments than could be tolerated by other age groups. Similarly, individuals find comfort at varying levels of air conditioning in the summer. The economics of energy use, though important, do not solely determine consumers' decision-making.

In the period between Nixon's first energy crisis and Bush's NES, the number of U.S. households had increased by 33%, while energy use per household had fallen by a third.[110] Consumers had reacted to higher energy prices and to the availability of a wide array of new energy efficient products —double glazed windows, high efficiency heat pumps, energy efficient refrigerators—by becoming more prudent energy consumers. By 1990, however, consumers' energy behavior had changed radically. EIA surveys showed typical households setting winter thermostats one full degree higher at the end of the 1980s than they had at the beginning of the decade and a

40% increase in the number of households operating their air conditioning systems throughout the summer.[111]

Energy prices affect consumer behavior in distinct ways. DOE data indicate that annual energy expenditures by urban consumers averaged about 10% of gross income. But expenditures are between 15% and 25% of pre-tax income for individuals with income in the lowest quartile. For the highest income consumers, energy expenditures represent less than 7% of pre-tax income.[112] These so-called distributional effects are important considerations in the choice of energy policy by any administration.

The NES public hearing record provided few practical proposals to achieve improvements in energy conservation in the residential sector. Many witnesses felt that relatively low U.S. energy prices would always discourage conservation investments. Others believed that human beings act in the same manner as businesses: a short-term outlook that precludes investments in energy efficient products that have payoffs too far into the future. The general view was that only government incentives would make it economically worthwhile for consumers to invest in energy conservation measures and practices.[113]

Energy in commercial buildings

In the two decades between 1970 and 1990, the U.S. economy underwent a profound shift in the composition of its GNP, from heavy industry to services. The service economy, in turn, shifted energy consumption from the direct use of fossil fuels to their indirect use as electricity. In 1990, 70% of the energy used in the commercial sector was in the form of electricity.[114] Generation and transmission losses, reaching as high as 50% of the primary energy used in generation, make electricity use relatively inefficient and, in the case of fossil fueled plants, environmentally problematic. Clearly, however, the convenience of electricity and the fact that it cannot be replaced in many applications makes alternatives difficult to imagine. From an energy policy point of view, public debate was less about whether more or less electricity should be used than about the technology and fuels that generate it.

DOE analyses indicated that higher primary energy transformation losses incurred in the economy's shift to services were offset by substantial improvements in energy management of commercial buildings. In the ten years prior to NES, office buildings, stores, warehouses, restaurants, and other buildings had been equipped with more efficient heating and cooling systems, high efficiency lighting, computerized thermostats, and other energy saving systems. DOE calculated that had 1970s energy consumption trends continued, the commercial sector would in 1990 have required about 50% more energy than was actually the case.[115]

Beyond measures already taken—building and equipment efficiency standards—few options were identified in the public hearings that would substantially alter the energy profile of the commercial sector. NES witnesses were hesitant to admit that the efficiency of energy use in buildings was more likely to be achieved by action of states and cities than by federal intervention, but the fact was inescapable that local rather than national authorities set and enforce building standards. These jurisdictions also control the retail electricity rates paid by their consumers.

Energy in industry

Unlike transportation, the industrial sector uses every available fuel and has great flexibility to shift from one fuel to another. In industry, market forces determine patterns of energy consumption to a far greater degree than does federal policy. Changes in the average price of fuels engender shifts in industrial fuel use as well as investments in conservation or in more efficient equipment. A few industries account for the bulk of this sector's energy consumption. Petroleum refining, chemicals production, primary metals mining and manufacturing, and pulp and paper production are dominant. Because of the substantial energy costs they bear, these industries have the economic incentive to adopt energy efficient technology and processes.[116]

Structural changes in American industry, especially pronounced in the early 1980s, had the effect of reducing energy consumption from a high of twenty-five quadrillion BTUs in 1979 to a historic low of slightly more than nineteen quads in 1990.[117] Throughout the period, the industrial sector was affected by a near shut down of rust-belt manufacturing, closing of energy-intensive steel and iron plants, and reduced output from the auto manufacturing sector, which was under siege from foreign manufacturers.

NES public hearings provided no particularly innovative proposals to increase energy efficiency in the industrial sector. Some witnesses thought the high cost of capital hampered investment in new or more efficient equipment, while others thought that low energy costs acted as a disincentive to efficiency investments. Most witnesses at the hearings supported expedited transfer of new technology from laboratory to industry, and agreed that federal tax incentives to accelerate turnover of capital stock were the effective means to significant energy savings.[118]

In sum, the public hearing record held no surprises for DOE policy staff. The problem areas identified by the witnesses were well-known. The proposed solutions ranged from the obvious—governmental tax incentives—to the laissez faire.[119] Still, the hearing record provided the instrument by which Watkins and Moore could place before the American people the essential facts about the U.S. energy economy.

As French poet diplomat Paul Claudel once remarked, "It is not enough to know. It is necessary to understand."[120]

The fuels

Notwithstanding William Paley's hope that the United States would eventually adopt a holistic view of energy, the NES public hearing record indicated that Americans understood energy in terms of specific fuel use. Fuels—their production, transformation, transportation, distribution, taxation—were transparent in a manner that no systemic discussion of energy could provide. Except, that is, where electricity was concerned.

Americans tend to judge issues surrounding electricity either in personal terms of availability and cost, or, abstractly, as a social choice between desirable and undesirable technology. They oppose on principle the siting in their neighborhood of any power plant. They are especially antagonistic to nuclear power on grounds of safety and in visceral fear of radiation. They oppose new construction of coal plants because of concern about air quality and acid rain depositions. Many oppose hydropower because of its impact on fish and on the flow of rivers. Others oppose construction through their counties and towns of pipelines needed to carry natural gas, the cleanest of all fossil fuels, to power generating stations. Most agree that more power should be generated from renewable resources such as sun and wind, though the majority have neither seen such systems in actual operation nor understand the inherent engineering limitations of their use.

Petroleum. Americans have been concerned about petroleum supplies at least since the Second World War. The United States contains 4% of the world's proven oil reserves but consumes on average 30% of the world's average daily production. In 1990, the United States consumed 17.2 MMB/D of oil but produced only 9.2 MMB/D. Imports in 1990 reached an average of 7.1 MMB/D, up from a modest 4.3 MMB/D in 1985, but below the historic high of 8.6 MMB/D reached in 1977.[121]

The downward spiral in U.S. domestic oil production actually began in the 1970s, moderated only by discovery and production of the giant Prudhoe Bay field in Alaska. Incrementally lower market prices for oil, following the price collapse of 1986, accelerated abandonment of marginal wells, reduced exploration and development activity, and generally depressed the domestic oil sector. During the NES process, independent oil drillers and producers without access to overseas fields sought access to U.S. frontier areas. These areas comprise the federally designated wilderness areas in the lower forty-eight states and Alaska and the federally controlled OCS on the Atlantic, Pacific, and Alaskan coasts. In Alaska alone, 160 million acres of land are off-limits to exploration and production of hydrocarbons.[122]

Vast areas of the OCS were closed to oil and gas production by a series of moratoria enacted by Congress or decreed by presidents beginning in the early 1980s. Congress voted a moratorium on leasing of 736,00 acres in four Northern California basins in 1982. By 1990 the moratoria were extended to eighty-four million acres offshore California, New England, the Gulf of Mexico coast of Florida, the Mid-Atlantic and Alaska's North Aleutian Basin.[123]

EIA estimates that economically recoverable oil resources from undiscovered fields range between 27.8 and 35.2 billion barrels in the lower forty-eight states alone. An additional 8.4 to 14.5 billion barrels are potentially recoverable off the Atlantic and Pacific coasts. A further 16 billion barrels are estimated to be potentially recoverable on- and offshore Alaska.[124]

The issue for the United States is, in the end, a choice between foregoing development of domestic oil supplies because the risk of environmental degradation is determined to be too great, and accepting increasing reliance on oil imports. Each option implies consequences that cannot be explained away. The liberal community insisted at NES public hearings that reliance on imported oil could be addressed by federally imposed regulation of consumption. This could only mean higher fuel efficiency standards for automobiles.

The historical data indicated that the combination of fuel efficiency standards and higher gasoline prices had succeeded only in moderating the rate of growth of oil consumption, not the structural demand for oil. On the political right, the proposal was to provide access to the resources of the OCS and Alaska. To the contrary, DOE estimates indicated that the potentially largest Alaska field, the coastal plain of the ANWR, might add at most 500,000 barrels per day to domestic supply, hardly sufficient to offset the decline in all other fields, including Alaska's North Slope, and the projected increase in demand.

In the NES process, liberal and conservative policy proponents were unwilling to find common ground on the very element of petroleum policy that had traditionally been their field of battle: the relatively low price of crude oil. In the liberal economic view, an increase (through taxation) in the consumer price of oil was acceptable as a deterrent to higher consumption, but an increase in the producer price of oil was unacceptable on grounds of unearned profitability. This policy position might have had merit if it were possible to assume that while oil demand decreased, domestic oil production could be maintained in a steady state. The irreversible downward slide in domestic production and concomitant increase in imported oil was resolved by liberal witnesses in proposals to increase the consumer price of oil at a level equivalent to the value of some security externality. In sum, liberals were willing to resolve the causes of oil consumption and their effects on domestic production and national security solely by increasing consumer costs.

Conservative economists, for their part, opposed non-market increases in energy prices for both consumers and producers as economically inefficient.

They professed concern about the effects on national security of a market price policy for oil, which were, of course, increased reliance on politically volatile sources of imported oil, politico-military entanglements in the Middle East, and, on the home front, the economic burden of maintaining a strategic reserve. In sum, conservatives were unwilling to address the causes of their energy security concerns but were willing to risk possibly more costly consequences.

Then there were the facts. The oil shocks of 1973 and 1979 notwithstanding, oil prices have had a history of remarkable stability. In 1968, refiners could acquire petroleum at an average $10.09 per barrel. In 1989 the price was $16.47, hardly a notable rise given the far greater increase in wages, disposable income, and the increased cost of other goods and services in the same twenty-year period. Consumers had derived great economic benefits from this price history. In 1980, after the last oil shock, U.S. retail gasoline prices exclusive of taxes averaged $1.03 per gallon. By 1989, gasoline could be purchased at 75.6 ¢ per gallon, or at 99.0 ¢ with taxes.[125] By contrast, consumers in Italy were paying $3.71 (tax included) for a gallon of gasoline; in France, they were paying $2.96; in England, $2.43; and in Germany, $2.10.[126] Interestingly, the dramatically higher European consumer prices had produced no better results than those obtained in the United States in the previous ten years in terms of consumption trends or energy security.

In sum, the debate engendered by NES public hearings left the nation no more united about the direction of its oil policy than had the previous forty years of policy trial and error. There was, however, a robust consensus on what *not* to do—no price controls, no import controls, and no floor or ceiling prices for domestic oil. This understanding would, in the end, protect the American public from the policy adventurism of the 1970s.

Natural Gas. No fuel represents more starkly the political dynamics of the American energy economy than does natural gas. Three states— Texas, Louisiana, and Oklahoma—produce 75% of the natural gas used in the United States. The natural gas market, however, is controlled by the states that consume it. In 1990—at the time these issues were under study—natural gas accounted for 26% of total U.S. primary energy use. It supplied 48% of the energy used in residential and commercial buildings, 35% of industrial and 12% of electricity generation requirements.[127]

Abundant, reasonably priced, and environmentally benign natural gas has nonetheless accumulated a history of federal and state regulatory turmoil. States have always limited its availability through production rationing regulations and have controlled intrastate sales. The federal government has controlled the wellhead price of natural gas and its interstate transportation. Consuming states have regulated sales of natural gas by setting variable rates at which it could be sold to residential, commercial, and industrial consumers.

The Natural Gas Policy Act (NGPA) of 1978 came to represent congressional confusion about the market for this fuel. Conscious of consumer dependence on natural gas for cooking and heating, Congress was loath to allow markets to signal supply requirements and set price. As a consequence, Congress legislated a formula in NGPA that resulted in the creation of a dual gas market that for years operated either under conditions of shortages or excess supply. Furthermore, for over ten years, under the Powerplant and Industrial Use Act of 1978, Congress prohibited the use of this fuel by industry and electric utilities. It was not until January 1993—with the full effects of the Natural Gas Wellhead Decontrol Act of 1989—that federal meddling in natural gas wholesale pricing came to an end.[128]

The natural gas resource base of the United States is estimated to be in the range of 1,200 trillion cubic feet, recoverable with fairly conventional technology. Nearly 600 trillion cubic feet are deemed recoverable at less than $3 per thousand cubic feet.[129] With U.S. consumption in the range of twenty trillion cubic feet per year, witnesses at NES public hearings agreed that the supply of natural gas—deemed in the previous decade to have been very limited—could no longer be viewed as a constraint to expansion of its use.

Natural gas prices were another matter. In 1968, residential consumers paid $1.04 for a thousand cubic feet (MCF) of gas. Utilities could obtain the same volume for 22 cents. By 1983 prices had risen to $6.06 per MCF for residential customers and to $3.58 per MCF for utilities. In 1990, they averaged $5.60 per MCF and $2.40 per MCF respectively. These were retail prices. At the wellhead, the price rise had been far less dramatic. In 1968, due to then-existing price controls, the price of natural gas to producers was a nominal 16 cents per MCF or about 50 cents in 1990 dollars. A run-up in price was experienced in 1981–1983 due to the continuing distortions of the

NGPA, but by 1989, wellhead prices were at \$1.56 per MCF, hardly sufficient to secure new investments in production.[130]

Also of concern to NES witnesses was the future direction of federal regulation of interstate natural gas transportation. In 1977, FERC inherited from the Federal Power Commission jurisdiction over the natural gas market and in 1985 began to reform interstate transportation rates with Order 380. The order allowed a local gas distributor who was supplied by more than one pipeline to purchase from the pipeline offering the lowest cost, and therefore, for the first time in history, jeopardized the ability of pipelines to unconditionally recover their gas acquisition costs.

In 1986, FERC issued Order 436, proposing a voluntary open access transportation program. Pipelines that accepted the order's conditions received blanket authorization to transport gas they owned, provided they would also transport, on a first-come/first-serve basis, gas owned by others. Order 436 was challenged by the industry but was essentially reaffirmed by the courts. It was followed by Order 500, which clarified means by which pipelines could recover costs incurred in disputes over take-or-pay provisions of contracts.[131]

There the matter rested at the beginning of NES. The natural gas transportation industry was not entirely happy with FERC's reforms. And FERC sought further decontrol of the transportation market through unbundling of services provided by pipelines and local distribution companies. Reform proposals were heatedly debated during the NES public hearing process, with industry divided over whether DOE should seek a legislative fix to interstate transportation rules and rates, or whether it was preferable to leave the issue to FERC. A legislative proposal was eventually submitted by DOE but Congress could not find the votes to enact it. In 1991, FERC issued Order 636, which brought unprecedented competition in the delivery of natural gas to American consumers.

The deregulation of the natural gas market, already well along at the time of NES public hearings, did not deter witnesses from seeking new federal interventions. Some industry representatives sought preservation of federal subsidies for production of gas from unconventional sources such as coal-bed methane, tight sands, and Devonian shale. These subsidies, economically unjustifiable given the abundance of low-cost conventional natural gas, affected private interests spanning the states of the entire Appalachian coal-bed methane basin, Midwestern states with large Devonian shale deposits, and western and southwestern states with tight gas formations, and were therefore protected by a strong congressional coalition.

Other witnesses recommended government incentives to induce gas use in nontraditional markets such as transportation. The natural gas industry was especially aggressive in seeking some form of government sanction for use of compressed natural gas in vehicles, notwithstanding the high cost of converting vehicles to operate on such a fuel and the cost of constructing a new national network of fueling stations. Many witnesses recommended changes in tax policy to allow higher deductions for intangible drilling costs and depletion allowances for natural gas producers.[132]

Policy staff took a dim view of proposals to subsidize an industry whose prospects were being brightened by enactment of CAAA, and an even dimmer view of the clamor for continuation of subsidies for unconventional gas. In the end, it found itself in the minority, even within the ranks of the presumably market-driven Troika, and the natural gas industry joined the long list of other energy industries with entitlement to federal tax dollars.

Electricity. Like no part of the energy economy, electricity links virtually all Americans. The generation, dispatch, and use of electricity comprise a vast public and private enterprise created to provide consumers their most convenient form of energy. The United States has the world's largest electric utility industry. More than 3,000[133] utilities manage more than 10,000 power plants and dispatch power via nearly 140,000 miles of transmission lines and nearly 500,000 miles of local distribution lines. No industry serves more customers, nor serves customers more constantly. The industry has assets of over $550 billion and annual revenues above $160 billion.[134]

Electricity could potentially displace all other forms of useful energy. Inherently flexible, it can power automobiles; heat, light, and cool homes and buildings, and drive industrial motors and other equipment. All fuels can be (and are) used to generate electricity, their choice normally dependent on cost, efficiency of the technology that transforms them, and reliability of source. However, electricity reaches consumers through a market system that blurs the connection between the fuels and technology that generates power and the useful power itself. For this reason—and because of the statutorily complex regulation of electricity generation, dispatch and distribution—informed public debate on electricity policy is difficult to conduct.

In 1990, slightly over thirty quads of energy were used to deliver slightly less than ten quads of useful power to consumers.[135] Energy losses, due to the relatively low efficiency of conversion technology and to the transmission of power over distances, were slightly less than twenty quads. Fuel use in the generation of electricity in 1989 comprised coal, 53% of the total; nuclear, 20%; hydro, geothermal and other renewables, 12%; natural gas, 9%; and petroleum, less than 1%.[136]

At the start of the energy strategy debate, the retail price of electricity to American residential consumers was 7.0 ¢ per kilowatt-hour (kWh), down 3.0 ¢ per kWh from the price paid by residential customers in 1960. For commercial customers, the price was 6.6 ¢ per kWh and for industry it was 4.3 ¢ per kWh.[137] In other words, Americans in 1989 enjoyed the lowest electricity prices in the industrialized world.

NES public hearings did not dwell on the benefits, which for over one hundred years the nation had enjoyed from the construction of an uncommonly reliable electricity sector. The debate, rather, focused on proposals, initially put forth in the 1987 "Energy Security Report to the President," to break up the monopoly power most electric utilities exercise in their service area in exchange for state-regulated reliability of service.

The enactment of PURPA of 1978 launched the first substantive effort to reform regulation of electric utilities since passage of PUHCA in 1935. PURPA introduced the concept that electricity could be generated by nonregulated industries if they bore the investment risks normally assumed by a utility's ratepayers. PURPA had won congressional favor as a result of a decade of poor economic and technical performance by traditional utility generators. Electric utilities' cost overruns on construction of excess coal and nuclear generating capacity in the 1960s, consented to by their state public utility commissions (PUCs), had reached disastrous proportions in the 1970s. Poor management of power plant construction had been compounded by high interest rates, inflation of capital costs, and an increasing inability to raise financing in capital markets.[138]

To address ratepayer discontent, Congress enacted PURPA to open the door to non-utility construction of power plants, especially plants that co-generated heat for industrial processes and electricity for local markets. Congress also directed utilities to purchase PURPA-generated power, and state PUCs ruled that such purchases be at a cost equal to a utility's avoided cost of new capacity additions. By the time of NES, a total of 496 co-generation facilities had been built with installed capacity of 16,500 megawatts of power—the equivalent of sixteen typical baseload power plants.[139] PURPA plant owners received PUC-approved long-term contracts for their power output at rates substantially above their marginal costs. That PURPA plants were no more economic than the utility plants they replaced would not become apparent until much later when the contractual arrangements between PURPA plant owners and utilities became, like investment in nuclear plants, stranded investments in the equation of state restructuring efforts.

To its supporters, PURPA proved the feasibility of competition in the wholesale generation market and offered a view of what the competition could be like if congressionally dictated limitations[140] on PURPA facilities were eliminated. But it also raised new issues of federal and state regulatory oversight, especially when a PURPA facility served multiple jurisdictions. There was also the matter of ensuring to PURPA facilities access to the transmission system that remained a monopoly.

Witnesses at NES public hearings were, as expected, divided in their advocacy of change in the wholesale power market. Traditional utilities argued that reliability of service would be compromised by greater reliance on independent power producers who were not tied to local ratepayers by obligations to serve. Independent producers responded by noting that their obligations to investors were no less binding than those of utilities to rate-payers. Still others argued that full competition in the wholesale generation market would eliminate altogether the need for federal and state regulation.[141]

Many NES witnesses focused on the responsibility of regulators to treat investments in electricity conservation on a par with those in new capacity. From the hearings emerged a consensus to institutionalize so-called integrated resource planning processes that would allow supply and demand options to be objectively weighed for their costs and benefits. Some witnesses argued for the full internalization of environmental and security costs in the rates paid by electricity consumers. Others recommended greater caution in federally imposed environmental burdens on the electric utility industry.[142]

Environmental protection, as related to the power sector, was a recurrent topic of discussion at the hearings. The liberal community insisted that future electricity demand could be met with aggressive conservation efforts and new investments in renewable fuels and technology. Conservatives argued that continued reliance on diverse electricity-generating fuels and technology would best serve the economic and security needs of the nation. Neither side gave ground on specific issues. Would the liberal community support a revitalization of nuclear energy technology, given its emissions benefits? Would the conservative community support conservation investments embedded in electricity rates? Would the large federal-private investment in a new generation of coal burning technology begin to satisfy the concern of environmentalists for global climate change? Would the fossil fuel industries support increases in federal conservation and renewable energy investments to equal those in nuclear, coal and oil technology R&D?[143]

Watkins' policy—middle-ground on electricity issues—emerged as rather broad, but consistent with his own view that the nation could not afford to eliminate any fuel or technology option. It was, in any case, too early in the process to exclude any reasonable policy option, but not too early to detect where the special interests would coalesce or divide.

THE COST OF POLICY

Energy policy rests on a foundation of price, behavior, and technology. Since the Second World War, governments have succeeded in manipulating each of these elements in turn, but have seldom been able to optimize the complex interaction among the three. Governments can affect the price of energy and shape consumer behavior by a combination of exhortation, regulation, and taxation.

As for technology, presidents and Congresses since the New Deal have sought to remake the transformation and use of energy through public investments in research, development, and demonstration (RD&D) projects. With notable exceptions, they have failed. Energy technology typically enters the marketplace when it reaches a stage of cost competitiveness. Technologies that are uneconomic are either abandoned or kept alive by the federal government for reasons of national security, or environmental considerations, or to satisfy political constituencies. The energy crises of the 1970s engendered explosive interest in a wide array of energy technologies that could, among other things, reduce what were seen as America's permanent vulnerabilities to uncertain oil supplies. Congress responded by appropriating funds for virtually any energy technology that showed promise.

With the creation of DOE in 1977, a new venue was made available to Congress for the making of energy policy by budgetary means. Over time, the DOE budget was carved into fiefdoms for congressional committees and subcommittees that exercised oversight of DOE activities by, among other things, financing and protecting R&D and programs of special interest to members. These programs in turn invariably acquire a constituency of public and private supporters who then work to secure an annual flow of funds as a form of entitlement to the federal budget. It becomes ultimately inevitable that the energy policy of different administrations be judged by the level of budgetary support they propose to provide to each of DOE's myriad R&D endeavors.

And so it was that a substantial number of participants in the NES public hearing process voiced their view of policy in terms of the budgetary support that the Bush administration was likely to accord to DOE's research programs. Witnesses variously castigated and praised budget decisions on nuclear, coal, oil, gas, solar, wind, fusion, hydrogen, conservation and other DOE programs. Witnesses erroneously but conveniently assumed that federal funding for a particular energy technology would actually determine that technology's future in the marketplace.

It thus became clear to Watkins that the NES process would not be complete without a review of the R&D priorities of DOE. Policy staff was consequently assigned the additional task of factoring into the NES process a reconciliation of budgetary and policy priorities.

Federal investments in energy technology R&D have historically been substantial and diversified. The results, however, have seldom been commensurate with expectations. Furthermore, there has been a pronounced tendency to continue to invest in certain technologies long after the research has demonstrated the futility of making them economically viable. The more expensive components of DOE's R&D portfolio represent investments, essentially without returns, that the private sector is deemed unable to underwrite, but that should nonetheless be made by the federal government in the national interest.[144]

Indicative of the large-scale, long-term energy research projects managed by DOE are those in coal liquefaction and coal gasification and in what came to be known in the Reagan administration as the Clean Coal Technology (CCT) program. These programs have been aimed at deriving liquid fuels for transportation so as to contribute to a reduction in oil imports and at creating alternatives to natural gas for power generation, heating and cooking as a means of increasing the natural gas resource base. CCT, jointly financed by the federal government and the U.S. electric utility industry, but without the participation of the presumably self-interested coal industry, has sought to engineer environmentally more benign coal combustion technology. Cumulative expenditures for coal research amounted to over $11 billion in the decade of 1980 and 1990 alone. Economically viable fuels and technology have not yet reached developmental maturity sufficient to penetrate the marketplace.[145]

For the oil sector, DOE research has focused on enhanced oil recovery (EOR), a means to prolong the life of marginal wells and to access the estimated three hundred billion barrels of oil left in reservoirs by conventional extraction. Cumulative federal expenditures in fiscal years 1980 to 1990 were $250 million, a fraction of comparable private industry investments. Federal tax credits for EOR, however, totaled $1.36 billion in the same period.[146]

Federal natural gas research has sought to improve secondary recovery of gas from producing wells, develop geologic atlases of gas resources, develop hydraulic fracturing technology to release gas from subterranean formations, and produce unconventional gas from Devonian shale, coal-bed methane, and tight sand basins. Expenditures from 1980 to 1990 were $250 million and federal tax credits totaled a $2.4 billion in the same period.[147]

Renewable energy research has also received substantial federal support. R&D on photovoltaics (PV) has focused on reducing the cost of PV systems, which convert sunlight directly into electricity. Expenditures from 1980 to 1990 were $900 million. For biofuels, research has been aimed at perfecting technology and reducing the cost of converting biomass into liquid fuels such as ethanol, methanol, and biodiesel. federal support totaled $390 million from 1980 to 1990, exclusive of tax credits for ethanol production, which amounted to $600 million. Ethanol production would not be possible without structural subsidies to make ethanol use economic. The subsidies— protected by a powerful congressional caucus and actually used by less than two dozen ethanol producers in the Midwest—amount to a permanent federal entitlement.[148]

Solar buildings research, carried out at DOE since the Carter administration, has been aimed at perfecting technology for water heating, space heating and cooling, and PV systems for building-specific power generation. Expenditures from 1980 to 1990 were $625 million, exclusive of tax credits of $1.8 billion. Similarly, solar thermal power plant research has aimed to reduce cost and improve reliability of systems that indirectly convert sunlight into electric power. Expenditures in 1980 to 1990 were $880 million. DOE research on wind-driven technology has focused on reliability of wind turbines and aerodynamics of propellers. Expenditures from 1980 to 1990 were $470 million. Geothermal R&D has aimed to develop technology to find and evaluate geothermal sources, reduce the cost of drilling wells to the source, and efficiently convert geothermal heat to electricity. Expenditures in 1980 to 1990 were $980 million.[149]

Nuclear technology was, of course, developed by the federal government. At the time of NES, DOE nuclear research involved development of an advanced liquid metal reactor—a so-called fast breeder technology that could also be used to "burn" long-lived actinides in spent uranium fuel. Expenditures in 1980 to 1990 were $950 million. Federal expenditures on breeder reactor research from 1948 to 1990 were $7.3 billion. Similarly, DOE has financed virtually all research on magnetic fusion to demonstrate the feasibility of sustaining a fusion reaction within a viable containment structure and demonstrate the commercial application of a technology that in effect duplicates the sun's power system. Federal expenditures from inception to 1990 totaled $6.1 billion, still with no end-state technology in sight.[150]

Opinions have always differed as to the connection between the expenditure of federal funds on discrete energy technologies and their relative success in the marketplace. The debate on these issues was particularly heated in the Bush administration because a number of senior members of the cabinet believed, whether from professional experience or ideology, that government intervention in the private sector typically did more harm than good. The fact that many advisers to the president were also likely to display favoritism to one energy technology or another, did not diminish the fundamental question of whether or not the U.S. taxpayers were getting their money's worth from DOE investments in R&D.

NOTES AND COMMENTS

1. References attributed to personal communications with Admiral James Watkins result from numerous conversations that took place between the admiral and the author, beginning in March 1994 and extending through February 2001. Secretary Watkins was given an opportunity to review all references to himself in Chapter 2 and provide comments at his discretion. To the extent possible and, if consistent with the record, his comments were incorporated in the final version of Chapter 2.

2. References attributed to personal communications with Congressman W. Henson Moore result from numerous conversations and exchanges of messages and notes, which took place in the period from March 1994 to January 2001. Mr. Moore was given an opportunity to review all references to himself in Chapter 2 and provide comments at his discretion. To the extent consistent with the record, his comments were incorporated in the final version of Chapter 2.

3. References attributed to personal communications with Secretary Linda Stuntz result from numerous conversations that took place in the period between March 1994 and February 2001. Ms. Stuntz was given an opportunity to review all references to herself in Chapter 2 and provide comments at her discretion. To the extent consistent with the record, her comments were incorporated in the text and are reflected in the final version of Chapter 2.

4. References attributed to personal communications with Professor Richard Schmalensee result from conversations that took place specifically on March 14, 1994, in Cambridge, Massachusetts. Professor Schmalensee was given an opportunity to review all references to himself in Chapter 2 and provide comments at his discretion. No comments were provided.

5. Summary of the Action Items proposed by DOE for the Interim Report on the NES.

Integrated Resource Planning (IRP): DOE proposed to expand this well-established program by intensifying data collection and analysis and disseminating this information to States, fostering the use of IRP by the federal power marketing administrations and by TVA, and by requesting that FERC adopt IRP processes in ratemaking procedures.

Enhanced Energy Efficiency: DOE proposed to use the purchasing power of the federal government—the nation's largest consumer of electricity—to foster more energy efficient and environmentally benign practices by utilities, independent power producers, and providers of energy services to federal agencies. The program would have required federal contractors to purchase the lowest cost but least polluting electricity from vendors throughout the nation and to consider cost-effective energy demand reduction options on a par with power supply options. The proposal also targeted federally subsidized housing, recommending a partnership between states and the Department of Housing and Urban Development to train local housing authorities in energy-saving measures, integrate energy efficiency requirements in the rental structure of public housing, consider energy efficiency investments in housing repossessed by DOE, and promote energy-efficient mortgage programs to make housing more affordable to the poor.

Increased Use of Renewable Resources: First, a coordinated federal and state effort to increase hydropower capacity at existing dams—based on estimates by the Electric Power Research Institute and the Army Corps of Engineers—that an increment of sixteen thousand megawatts of power could be obtained by upgrading turbines and adding variable speed generators. Secondly, a collaborative R&D development program between DOE and the Department of Agriculture to use farm and forest products for the manufacture of liquid fuels.

Streamlined Technology Transfer: This initiative sought to promote stronger ties between American business and federal research laboratories in order to accelerate the transfer of research results to the private sector. It also recommended a new export promotion program to help U.S. firms sell efficient and environmentally superior energy technologies to developing nations.

Mathematics, Science and Engineering Education: This proposal would have committed federal agencies to join a nationwide effort to improve the teaching of science and technical subjects.

The program was also intended to encourage the interest of minority and female students in technological and scientific subjects—areas in which most non-white/non-male members of the general population were underrepresented. The initiative would have required DOE's national laboratories to open their doors to students and teachers and provide hands-on experience that might inspire the pursuit of scientific and technical careers. The laboratory staff would have also been directed to seek involvement with local school boards, public and private colleges and universities, and to assist in improving mathematics and science curricula.

Pollution Prevention and Waste Minimization: This initiative would have recognized the duty of DOE to more explicitly collaborate with EPA on environmental, health and safety at DOE installations. It also recognized that the energy sector, and DOE itself, was responsible for a high proportion of the nation's pollution and waste problems. The proposal would have resulted in a joint DOE-EPA program of research on less polluting technologies and on processes to minimize or eliminate the generation of wastes from energy production.

REFERENCES

[1] James D. Watkins, admiral, U.S. Navy (Retired). Personal communication, March 1, 1994.

[2] *National Journal,* November 16, 1985.

[3] Bruce L.R. Smith, *The Advisers: Scientists in the Policy Process.* (Washington, DC: Brookings Institution, 1992), p. 113.

[4] Watkins, op. cit.

[5] Ibid.

[6] J. Bennett Johnston, "Future Energy Concerns." Speech delivered before the Conference on International Energy Security, Washington, DC, May 24, 1988.

[7] J. Bennett Johnston. Opening statement in the Hearing before the Committee on Energy and Natural Resources, United States Senate, 101st Congress, 1st session, February 22, 1989.

[8] James McClure. Opening statement in the Hearing before the Committee on Energy and Natural Resources, United States Senate, 101st Congress, 1st session, February 22, 1989.

[9] Howard Metzenbaum. Opening statement in the Hearing before the Committee on Energy and Natural Resources, United States Senate, 101st Congress, 1st session, February 22, 1989.

[10] Jeffrey Bingaman. Opening statement in the hearing before the Committee on Energy and Natural Resources, United States Senate, 101st Congress, 1st session, February 22, 1989.

[11] James D. Watkins. Opening statement in the hearing before the Committee on Energy and Natural Resources, United States Senate, 101st Congress, 1st session, February 22, 1989.

[12] Henry R. Linden, "An Energy Agenda for a New Administration," *Public Utilities Fortnightly,* January 5, 1989.

[13] GAO: *Energy Issues,* WorldWatch Institute*: Blueprint for the Environment-Energy Recommendations;* National Governors Association*, Comprehensive National Energy Policy (1989)*; United States Energy Association, *U.S. Energy 1989;* New England Energy Policy Council, *Power to Share: A Plan for Increasing New England's Competitiveness Through Energy Efficiency;* Northwest Power Planning Council, *Northwest Conservation and Electric Power Plan;* State of New Jersey, *Energy Master Plan;* State of New York: *Energy Plan.*

[14] Watkins, Personal communication, op. cit.

[15] Ibid.

[16] Presidential Remarks: Swearing in of Secretary Watkins, DOE, Thursday, March 9, 1989. Faxed from David Q. Bates, assistant to the president and secretary to the cabinet to Polly Gault, DOE, March 7, 1989.

[17] Remarks by Admiral James D. Watkins, U.S. Navy (Retired), the swearing in ceremony as secretary of energy, Forrestal Building, Washington, DC, March 9, 1989.

[18] Office of the Press Secretary, the White House, "President Bush's Agenda: Building a Better America," February 9, 1989.

[19] Ibid.

[20] Ibid.

[21] Ibid.

[22] W. Henson Moore. Personal communication, March 19, 1994.

[23] Ibid.

[24] Ibid.

[25] Ibid.

[26] Ibid.

[27] Ibid., and Watkins, Personal communication, op. cit.

[28] Ibid.

[29] W. Henson Moore. Statement in hearing before the Committee on Energy and Natural Resources, United States Senate, 101st Congress, 1st session, on the nomination of W. Henson Moore to be deputy secretary of energy, April 5, 1989.

[30] Richard L. Schmalensee (then member of the CEA). Personal communication, March 14, 1994.

[31] John H. Sununu, "A Governor's Perspective: The Emerging U.S. Energy Crisis." Keynote speech delivered before the Conference on International Energy Security, Washington, DC, May 24, 1988.

[32] Watkins and Moore, Personal communications, op. cit.

[33] Ibid.

[34] Linda G. Stuntz. Personal communication, March 11, 1994, and January 30, 2001.

[35] Ibid.

[36] Linda G. Stuntz. Personal communications, February 8, 2001.

[37] Ibid.

[38] Ibid. and Moore, Personal communication, op. cit.

[39] Stuntz, op.cit., February 8, 2001.

[40] Ibid.

[41] Schmalensee, Personal communication, op. cit.

[42] Ibid.

[43] Ibid.

[44] Ibid.

[45] Ibid.

[46] Ibid.

[47] Watkins, Personal communication, op. cit., and February 1, 2001.

[48] White House-congressional negotiations on the Budget Reconciliation Act of 1989. Sununu and Darman agreed to a federal tax increase that violated the president's campaign pledge of no new taxes.

[49] Schmalensee, Personal communication, op. cit.

[50] Watkins. Personal communication, February 1, 2001.

[51] Charles Kolb, *White House Daze: The Unmaking of Domestic Policy in the Bush Years*, (New York, NY: Free Press, 1994), p. 52.

[52] Ibid.

[53] Charles Kolb, *White House Daze: The Unmaking of Domestic Policy in the Bush Years*. (New York: The Free Press, 1994), p. 260.

[54] Watkins: Personal communications, op. cit. and on February 1, 2001.

[55] DOE, *Energy Security: A Report to the President of the United States*, Washington, DC, 1987.

[56] DOE Office of Policy, Planning and Analysis, Office of Policy Integration, *Assessment of Costs and Benefits of Flexible and Alternative Fuel Use in the U.S. Transportation Sector, Technical Report Three: Methanol Production and Transportation Costs*. Washington, DC, November 1989.

[57] Ibid.

[58] The policy analyst in question was the author. Hence the absence of citations/references in this section and in all sections related to alternative transportation fuels, the studies of which were also directed by the author.

[59] James D. Watkins, admiral, U.S. Navy (Retired), Memorandum for DOE secretarial and staff officers, Subject: NES, May 12, 1989.

[60] DOE, "National Energy Strategy Development—Status Report," July 3, 1989.

[61] Minutes of meeting of June 26 and NEMS summary outline

[62] SERI has been renamed the National Renewable Energy Laboratory.

[63] DOE, Mimeo record of the "DOE National Energy Strategy Meeting National Laboratories." Meeting held in Washington, DC, July 27-28, 1989.

[64] DOE, Office of Policy, Planning and Analysis, "National Energy Strategy: General Overview, August through October 1989," no date.

[65] Watkins, Personal communication, op. cit.

[66] The White House, Office of the Press Secretary, "Remarks by the President at the Natural Gas Bill Signing Ceremony," July 26, 1989.

[67] Watkins, Personal communication, op. cit.

[68] EPC members were: the vice president, the secretaries of state, defense, interior, agriculture, commerce, transportation, energy, the OMB director, the U.S. trade representative, the chairman of the CEA, the EPA administrator, the National Security adviser, and the assistant to the president for economic and domestic policy.

[69] Nicholas F. Brady, chairman *pro tempore*, EPC, draft memorandum to members of EPC; Subject: Energy Policy, circa July 21, 1989.

[70] Watkins, Personal communication, op. cit.

[71] W. Henson Moore, deputy secretary of energy, Letter to the Honor Manuel Lujan, Jr., secretary of the interior et al., August 4, 1989, and DOE, "National Energy Strategy: General Overview," op. cit.

[72] EPC, Mimeo of Economic Policy Council Working Group of the National Energy Strategy, current membership, June 1990.

[73] Marcus Aurelius, *The Meditations*, translated by George Long, (Garden City, NY: Doubleday Dolphin, 1968), p.66.

[74] James D. Watkins, admiral, U.S. Navy (Retired), "Statement of Admiral James D. Watkins, secretary of energy, before the Committee on Energy and Natural Resources, United States Senate," U.S. Congress, 101st Congress, 1st session, July 26, 1989.

[75] "American Survey: In Pursuit of Power," *The Economist*, October 1989, pp. 9-10.

[76] DOE, Office of the Press Secretary, "Admiral Watkins Announces Hearings on National Energy Strategy," July 26, 1989.

[77] "Watkins Wants Broad Views for Strategy," *Inside Energy/with Federal Lands*, July 31, 1989, pp. 1-3.

[78] Keith Schneider, "Energy Planning to Plan," *The New York Times*, August 6, 1989, p. E4.

[79] *The Oil Daily*, August 3, 1989, Washington DC, p. 1.

[80] DOE, *Interim Report: National Energy Strategy, a Compilation of Public Comments*, DOE/S-0066P, April 1990, and DOE, *National Energy Strategy, Technical Annex 2, Integrated Analysis_Supporting the National Energy Strategy: Methodology, Assumptions and Results*, First Edition, DOE/S-0086P, February 1991.

[81] Dr. Benjamin Franklin Cooling, DOE historian, Interview of James D. Watkins, admiral, U.S. Navy (Retired), June 8, 1993.

[82] Schneider, op. cit.

[83] Marvin E. Olsen, et al., "Public Opinion Versus Governmental Policy on National Energy Issues," in Richard G. Braungart and Margaret M. Braungart, eds., *Research in Political Sociology*, Volume 1. (Greenwich, CT: JAI Press, Inc., 1972), pp. 189-210.

[84] Linda G. Stuntz, DOE, deputy undersecretary, Policy, Planning and Analysis; Memorandum to assistant secretaries PE office directors; Subject: NES, November 29, 1989.

[85] Linda G. Stuntz, DOE, deputy undersecretary, Policy, Planning and Analysis; Memorandum for assistant secretaries, PE office directors; Subject: NES, December 15, 1989.

[86] Linda G. Stuntz, DOE, deputy director, Office of Policy, Planning and Analysis; Memorandum for assistant secretaries, PE office directors; Subject: NES, January 3, 1990.

[87] "Over-Arching Concerns: Economic Policy Council Review" (2/28/90), Attachment 4 to Robert G. Marlay, DOE, director, NES Staff, Policy, Planning and Analysis; Memorandum for NES/DC representatives, NES Interim Report writing teams, PE office directors; Subject: Review of Draft NES Interim Report, March 8, 1990.

[88] Linda G. Stuntz, Memorandum for the deputy secretary, Subject: Today's meeting of the EPC Working Group on the NES; undated, likely sent on March 15, 1990.

[89] Ibid.

[90] Ibid.

[91] [DOE], "Interim Report on the Development of a National Energy Strategy: Action Items", Working Draft (3/7/90), April 1990.

[92] DOE, *Interim Report*, op. cit., p. 4.

[93] W. Henson Moore, DOE, deputy secretary, "Deputy Secretary's Talking Points," for EPC Working Group on the NES, Review Meeting of 16 March 1990.

[94] "Preface" to *Interim Report*. Attachment to W. Henson Moore, DOE, deputy secretary, March 15, 1990. Mark-up by hand of final revisions demanded by CEA/OMB/Treasury.

[95] Olin Wethington, Memorandum for EPC; Subject: Meeting on NES, March 15, 1990.

[96] James D. Watkins, admiral, U.S. Navy (Retired), "Secretary Watkins' Talking Points," for EPC cabinet meeting on the NES, March 21, 1990, 3:00 p.m., Roosevelt Room, White House.

[97] Ibid.

[98] Ibid.

[99] DOE, *Interim Report*, op. cit., pp. 42-126.

[100] Quadrillion Btu commonly measure energy in the large U.S. economy. Quad is often used as a shorthand. One quad equals the energy available from roughly 500,000 barrels of oil per day over a full year.

[101] DOE, Office of Policy, Planning and Analysis, Office of Conservation and Renewable Energy, *Energy Conservation Trends: Understanding the Factors that Affect Conservation Gains in the U.S. Economy*, DOE/PE-0092, September 1989.

[102] Ibid., p. 14.

[103] DOE, *Interim Report*, op. cit., p. 11.

[104] J. Goldemberg, T.B. Johansson, A.K.N. Reddy and H.R. Williams, *Energy for a Sustainable World*, (New Delhi, India: Wiley Eastern Limited Publishers, 1988).

[105] EPA, "Policy Options for Stabilizing Global Climate," D. Leshof and A. Tirpak, editors. Draft Report to Congress, Washington, DC, 1989.

[106] Ibid., pp. 12-19.

[107] DOE, *Interim Report*, op. cit., p. 15.

[108] DOE, *Assessment of Costs and Benefits of Flexible and Alternative Fuel Use*, op. cit.

[109] DOE, *Interim Report*, op. cit., p. 20.

[110] Ibid.

[111] Ibid.

[112] DOE and Bureau of Labor Statistics. U.S. Energy: Uses, Costs and Sources. Compilation of data, no date.

[113] DOE, *Interim Report*, op. cit., p. 22.

[114] Ibid., p. 26.

[115] DOE, *Energy Conservation Trends*, op. cit.

[116] Ibid., p. 32.

[117] DOE, *Energy Conservation Trends*, op. cit.

[118] DOE, *Interim Report*, op. cit., pp. 34-35.

[119] Ibid., p. 23.

[120] Paul Claudel, *Le Soulier du Satin*, (Paris, France: Editions Gallimard, 1953), p. 175.

[121] Ibid., p. 42.

[122] EIA, *The Domestic Oil and Gas Recoverable Resource Base: Supporting Analysis for the National Energy Strategy.* (Washington, DC, 1990)

[123] Ibid.

[124] Ibid.

[125] EIA, Office of Energy Markets and End Use, *Annual Energy Review 1992*, DOE/EIA-0384(92), June 1993, pp. 163-165.

[126] International Energy Agency, Gasoline Prices and Taxes in OECD Countries, Third Quarter 1988.

[127] DOE, Office of Policy, Planning and Analysis, Office of Electricity and Natural Gas Policy, "Gas Sector Profile: The National Energy Strategy," October 1989.

[128] DOE, *Interim Report*, op. cit., pp. 57-58.

[129] DOE, "Gas Sector Profile," op. cit.

[130] EIA, *Annual Energy Review 1992*, op. cit., pp. 187-189.

[131] DOE, "Gas Sector Profile," op. cit.

[132] DOE, *Interim Report*, op. cit., pp. 60-61.

[133] In 1989 there were 220 investor-owned utilities, six federal utilities, one thousand electric cooperatives, and two thousand municipal utilities, collectively with 690 gigawatts of installed generating capacity. (Source: Lawrence Berkeley Laboratory, "The U.S. Electric

Utility Industry Is Large and Complex, Summary Report for the National Energy Strategy," undated.

[134] Ibid.

[135] EIA, *Annual Energy Review 1992*, op. cit., p. 213.

[136] DOE, *National Energy Strategy, Technical Annex 2*, op. cit., p. 11.

[137] EIA, *Annual Energy Review 1992*, op. cit., p. 233.

[138] Pfeffer, Lindsay & Associates, Inc., *Emerging Policy Issues in PURPA Implementation*, DOE/PE70404-H1. Prepared for DOE under Contract No. PEAC01-83-PE-70404. Washington, DC, March 1986.

[139] Ibid, p.3.14.

[140] PURPA facilities were statutorily limited as to fuel and technology used and to cogeneration projects.

[141] DOE, *Interim Report*, op. cit., pp. 113-114.

[142] Ibid., pp. 121-122.

[143] Ibid., pp. 121-123.

[144] Hazel R. O'Leary, secretary of energy, Letter to the Honorable J. Bennett Johnston, Committee on Appropriations, U.S. Senate, with undated enclosure titled, "List of Technologies" (50 pages plus appendices), June 15, 1993.

[145] Ibid.

[146] Ibid.

[147] Ibid.

[148] Ibid.

[149] Ibid.

[150] Ibid.

CHAPTER THREE

THE ECONOMIC POLICY COUNCIL
TAKES CONTROL

FROM PUBLIC HEARING RECORD TO POLICY OPTIONS

The Interim Report on NES was made public on April 2, 1990.

DOE described it as "a baseline for development and analysis of energy options," but warned, in Watkins' words, "the hardest (policy) choices lie ahead."[1] Carefully crafted caveats—that the report should be viewed only as a compilation of public comments and not as administration policy—were generally ignored by the national media, which as if by design focused on the issues most likely to irritate the Troika agencies.

The Chicago Tribune: "The Bush Administration said it is serious about energy conservation and environmental issues, which it suggested were given short shrift under former President Ronald Reagan."[2] *USA Today*, in a headline: "Energy chief wants 20% hike in efficiency."[3] *The Christian Science Monitor*: "Secretary of Energy James Watkins—conducting an 18-month study of America's energy policy—is searching for ways the U.S. can avoid empty gas tanks, cold homes, and shuttered factories."[4] *The Dallas Morning News*: "The Bush Administration stepped toward a national energy policy that would encourage efficiency and rely less heavily on market forces to determine the nation's energy mix."[5] *CNN-TV*: "The Watkins agenda recalls conservation ideas spawned during the Carter Administration but abandoned in the Reagan era."[6]

The Troika agencies were disturbed by the media's apparent conclusion that the Bush administration would set aside market policies in favor of government intervention in the energy sector. Their staff were eager to conclude that some sort of DOE "spin" had been responsible for the media's message. Staff exchanges in the following days produced from the Troika vows of far greater future scrutiny of NES development process and products. The Troika staff warned that NES would not obtain the approval of EPC unless DOE demonstrated strict adherence to the president's original direction to continue what he had referred to in the NES announcement as the "successful policy of market reliance."[7]

Concerns about the evolution of NES were not, however, relayed directly to Watkins by any of his cabinet colleagues and certainly not by the Troika leaders.[8] He in any case believed that the merits of what he sought to accomplish would become evident at the completion of NES and in due course earn the support of the cabinet. He believed he had the explicit support of the president to continue to build political and public support for the strategy, and would do so regardless of Troika insistence to the contrary.[9] Watkins was not a member of Bush's inner circle of advisers, and it was not in his nature to cultivate personal relationships for the purpose of advancing his department's agenda. By the same token, the inner circle of advisers showed no inclination to understand Watkins' objectives or motives. As a consequence, NES development turned into a far greater bureaucratic ordeal than seemed necessary to the staff in the trenches.

The SEAB review

Bruised by the latest skirmish with the Troika, but convinced he was on the right path, Watkins sought counteractive support for his vision of NES from his most prestigious counselors, the members of the Secretary of Energy Advisory Board (SEAB). He had revitalized SEAB in early 1990 and had assured its new members that their advice and counsel would be heard. As one of its first tasks, Watkins asked the reconstituted SEAB to review and comment on the NES *Interim Report*. Four subgroups were rapidly constituted to respond to this charge, and on May 2, 1990, SEAB provided ten pages of commentary on both the Interim Report and the future scope of NES.

The SEAB subgroup on energy efficiency provided the most disappointing advice. Politically naive and removed from the mainstream of serious policy research, the advice of the subgroup was also in some respects a throwback to concepts of energy sector management that had long since proved unviable. Representative portions of the subgroup's report are reproduced below in the language used by the advisers. NES, the subgroup advised, should be aimed at the following elements.[10]

Creating Constancy of Purpose. Political considerations lead to a distortion in the allocation of resources for energy related-problems. This is particularly true in the area of energy efficiency, where time scales for improvement are long. Lacking constancy of purpose and direction, promising lines of inquiry never reach fruition. There are scientific opportunities that could pay large dividends in a more stable, predictable, and supportive environment.

Changing Public Behavior. It is vital to get people to use less energy. One way to accomplish this is by increasing the price of energy. Another is to change social norms by motivating and instilling in the public a sense of social responsibility. Americans must start to think about the long-term implications of near-term actions, to ensure that they, their children, and future generations can maintain their standards of living.

Assuming a World Leadership Role. To maintain leadership of the free world, the United States must move quickly to steer a new course relative to energy efficiency before the rest of the world adopts our old methods. If developing countries continue their present course—more or less mimicking our profligate use of energy—it will exacerbate shortages and environmental problems worldwide.

Reflecting the True Social Cost of Non-Renewable Energy. We have had a national policy for decades of systematically under-pricing non-renewable energy. The four consequences of this policy are:

- energy-using technologies are not efficient enough, and unless corrected, more efficient technologies with somewhat higher prices but lower social costs will continue to be underutilized
- energy-intensive parts of contemporary U.S. society and their associated technologies are over utilized, overemphasized, and overdeveloped relative to the less energy-intensive parts of society
- developing countries, where the rate of energy growth is the most rapid, are making commitments right now to energy and transportation infrastructures that are inefficient and that will put them on a path of economic development that is inconsistent with the world's and their long-term economic and environmental benefits [sic]

- new emerging technologies that make more efficient use of energy or that improve activities in the non-energy-intensive sector are not being pursued, such as new ceramic materials.[11]

Tending towards social engineering, simplistic in its assessment of how markets absorb technology, statist in its view of economic management, the sweeping advice of SEAB's energy efficiency subgroup was judged by DOE policy staff to result in further reducing the already narrow policy common ground between Watkins and the EPC. Watkins, however, welcomed the report, gratified by the apparently perfect congruence of views between the public and the SEAB.

Watkins had breathed new life into SEAB in order to counteract what Brookings' Bruce L. R. Smith called the "technocratic logic" of DOE staff. In *The Advisers: Scientists in the Policy Process*, Smith wrote that Watkins had turned to SEAB for help with NES in order to "bridge...popular aspirations and the complex technical dimensions of energy policy."[12] The advice of the SEAB subgroup on conservation appeared, at first glance, to do just that, and Watkins welcomed it all the more, precisely because it differed from the in-house, "technocratic" view of the energy sector.

DOE staff's judgment of the SEAB conservation report did find support from Stuntz and Moore who had questions of their own about both the political and analytical usefulness of the advice provided. What, for example, could one make of SEAB's declaration that "to maintain leadership of the free world, the United States must steer a new course relative to energy efficiency"? Did U.S. international leadership really depend on the ratio of energy consumption to gross national product? And what of the idea of "encouraging economic activity that favors lowered energy use"? Were SEAB members actually advocating a degree of economic micro- management that would force the government to choose, say, between unfavorable tax treatment of investments in energy-intensive aluminum plants and favorable treatment of investments in low-energy shoe factories?

To Stuntz, the SEAB advice seemed incompatible not only with well-established analytical findings but also with the mainstream of public hearing comments.[13]

The second SEAB subgroup, on future energy supplies, summarized its recommendations in what it called "principles" to be observed in crafting the final strategy. The principles, in their original, awkward sequence, possibly reflecting too rapid a search for consensus, declared:

- the Nation's economic and social development should not be constrained by an inadequate supply of reasonably priced energy
- all energy supply operations should be conducted in ways that optimize benefit-cost ratios with respect to improvement of human health and protection of the environment
- dependence on foreign sources of oil should be kept below a threshold level determined by a balance among cost, national security, and international relations
- aggressive steps should be taken to convert select energy systems to domestically abundant fuels: coal, gas, uranium
- a comprehensive program to educate the public about energy supply and its social/environmental implications should be established
- conservation measures deemed to be cost-effective should be initiated immediately."[14]

The first two of the subgroup's principles seemed sensible enough, if not self-evident in practice. The rest were more problematic. How, for example, would an administration determine the optimal threshold of dependence on foreign oil? Would equal weight be given to cost, security and international relations, and would oil imports at, say, 30% of national consumption provide greater socioeconomic security than would imports at 50%? What "aggressive steps," short of a declaration of national emergency, could a president take to "convert" energy systems to domestic fuel use? How could the federal government ensure that all cost-effective conservation measures are undertaken "immediately" except by decreeing, mandating or financing them?[15]

The third of the SEAB subgroups dealt with environmental issues. The group provided very practical guidance not only on environmental matters but also on how NES might be constructed and defended through the interagency process. The group's key points were:

- consider the full social cost of energy production and use options. To the extent that the NES relies on market forces to produce efficient solutions, options to capture full social cost in market prices (e.g., taxes) must be considered
- present a full array of policy options for debate, including the use of prices and taxes
- enlarge through basic research the range of technological options available to meet energy, economic, and environmental needs
- specify how and when scientific uncertainties can be resolved by research, especially for issues where uncertainty complicates policy development (lest) research be seen as an excuse for delaying action."[16]

Stuntz had no hesitation in accepting this advice even as she realized the difficulty of carrying it out. Certainly DOE wanted to keep a full array of options under consideration until the president made his final decisions, but she was already under pressure from the Troika to eliminate all options that were deemed inconsistent with administration policy. The policy staff supported the concept of social costing of energy, though social-costing analytical methods were not as self-evident as SEAB members seemed to suggest. Otherwise, the advice was sound as well as pointed: SEAB's reference to "scientific uncertainty excusing inaction" perfectly described the administration's position on global climate change.

The SEAB's fourth subgroup provided advice on R&D policy, science and mathematics education, and technology transfer. Their noncontroversial advice was essentially followed in the crafting of the final NES. SEAB concluded its report by urging Watkins to "harness the public's energy and support."[17] Watkins needed no encouragement on that score.

THE TROIKA TAKES CONTROL

Watkins saw the SEAB report as a vindication of his approach to NES, notwithstanding the inability of DOE staff to persuade their intergovernmental counterparts to see the SEAB advice as valuable political capital. In the end, the SEAB report served mainly to complicate the highly contentious negotiations then underway between Linda Stuntz and the Troika leadership on the structure and scope of the NES analysis. Consistent with SEAB advice, Watkins had directed the policy office to analyze each of the options raised in the public hearing process, which numbered well over five hundred. The Troika dismissed the idea as not only undesirable but infeasible. An intense two-week consolidation effort finally resulted in reducing the options to a more manageable roster of sixty.[18] These still represented a formidable analytical assignment, but Watkins would allow no further reductions in the scope of the analysis.

The Troika agencies strongly opposed the sixty-options analysis plan presented by DOE at a May 23, 1990, meeting of the EPC Working Group.[19] They insisted that the analysis had to be more tightly bound to focus on critical elements of administration policy, rather than on comprehensive treatment of what had been gleaned from the public hearings. They insisted furthermore on establishing at the outset of the analytical process a clean break between the public dialogue and the eventual administration-sanctioned energy strategy. Treasury warned that it would "very likely oppose any energy strategy that looks like the current list of options."[20] The CEA, for its part, indicated that the scope of the analysis remained daunting and that the DOE list of "options remained heavily weighted toward distortionary command and control policies."[21]

Troika displeasure was actually even more pronounced than indicated in staff memoranda. Schmalensee and Boskin had in fact concluded by May 1990 that NES was becoming a vehicle for undesirable policy, a project that would end up embarrassing the president. They felt that by placing the public hearing results at the center of the energy debate, Watkins was virtually relinquishing the administration's right to set policy. It looked to

Schmalensee as if the admiral's absorption with public opinion reflected the absence of an agenda—ideological, philosophical, personal, or political—with which to drive the process.[22]

Admonitions to DOE that the NES process was flawed had, Schmalensee believed, gone unheeded, and it was time for a stronger signal from the White House. As a consequence, CEA leaders urged John Sununu, the White House chief of staff to meet with Watkins and provide un-ambiguous guidance on what would henceforth be expected from him.[23]

John Sununu takes issue

Watkins and Moore met with Sununu on June 8, 1990. Neither was aware that CEA leadership had orchestrated the meeting. Although Watkins was aware of interagency staff grumbling over the NES public hearing process, he refused to believe that his cabinet colleagues would fail to understand the rationale behind the hearings, which was to nurture political support for the eventual policies that the president would promulgate. For the meeting of June 8, he had received no warning from either Boskin or Schmalensee that NES development issues were being raised to Sununu's level. DOE leaders saw the meeting, rather, as an opportunity to brief Sununu on the political rationale for NES, which Watkins believed was fully understood by the president, and on its analytical underpinnings.[24]

In preparation for the meeting, Stuntz had directed the policy staff to prepare a one-page summary of the issues that DOE intended to address analytically—a schema that would present a highly aggregated synthesis of critical policy areas to be incorporated in NES and the essential elements of contemplated policy responses. The one-page schema used by Watkins in his meeting with Sununu (Table 3-1) distilled the scope of policy action primarily to the transportation and electric utility sectors of the economy.

	ELECTRICITY	TRANSPORTATION
Supply	1. Develop new technologies: nuclear, clean coal, renewables, natural gas. 2. Remove barriers to efficient markets: (a) regulatory reform of nuclear licensing, power plant construction, transmission and generation pricing, (b) statutory reform of PURPA, PUHCA, FPA NGA.*	1. Alternative fuel introduction: (a) via regulation (mandated markets) or (b) research and development 2. Increase domestic production of petroleum through tax incentives, access to federal lands, federal research and development.
Demand	1. Market disincentives to consumption+ 2. Reduce barriers to efficient demand side investments 3. Regulatory actions: (a) efficiency standards, (b) building codes 4. Develop/demonstrate new technology (R&D)	1. Market disincentives to adoption 2. Infrastructure/behavioral changes 3. Regulatory actions (e.g., CAFE) 4. Develop/demonstrate new technology

(*)Public Utilities Regulatory Policy Act, Public Utilities Holding Company Act, Federal Power Act, Natural Gas Act. (+) e.g., disincentives to use of efficient products and alternative fuels.

TABLE 3-1: NES ANALYTICAL FRAMEWORK

These two sectors seemed to embody most of the constraints surfaced by the NES process, as well as the opportunities for change that NES would eventually address. The choice of transportation was obvious. By 1990, fully two-thirds of petroleum consumed daily in the United States was used for transportation and, consequently, no successful oil policy could be crafted that did not come to terms with this sector's inflexible energy requirements. As to the electricity sector, its fuels, technology, and institutions reflected the world that EPC thought ripe for reform, comprising multiple layers of state and federal regulation and holding the key to advances in environmental quality and economic efficiency.

The analytical framework was intended to appeal to Sununu's logic, but the elements of the framework that listed remedies for structural or market failures could not help but reveal the strategy options that would be seen as provocative by the admiral's White House audience. Watkins and Moore told Sununu, in the presence of Boskin and Schmalensee, that in the next phase of NES development they proposed to analyze all reasonable options, examine their costs and benefits and quantify their impacts on energy, the environment, and the economy. DOE staff would then subject the analyses to professional peer review and public scrutiny without foreclosing any option that the president might be likely to consider. They concluded by expressing their intent to engage political stakeholders like governors and members of Congress in final NES deliberation, but would ensure adherence to the administration's principle of market reliance in the analyses and ultimate policy recommendations.[25]

Sununu showed himself entirely unreceptive. He dismissed the public consultation process as irrelevant to White House decision-making and told Watkins that the media visibility of NES was not desirable because it served the interests of the president's critics. He declared that, as a matter of fact, a new energy policy might not be necessary at all, among other reasons because the president was enjoying high popularity ratings and needed no fresh domestic initiatives. If the NES effort were to be made useful to the president, Sununu added, it should be argued internally, without publicity, and within the bounds of what the administration was likely to support. Public controversy about NES would, he added, serve mainly to attract congressional mischief. In a final display of personal pique, Sununu closed the meeting by directing Watkins to return to the White House only with some options for the president's consideration and not with a strategy.[26]

Watkins was taken aback by Sununu's apparent hostility. In a post-mortem with his staff he expressed disbelief that his motives and the plan he was pursuing could be so fundamentally distrusted by the White House chief of staff. He felt he had no choice but to accept Sununu's directive to submit to the president a strategy's components (options) rather than the strategy itself. He was not, however, prepared to allow Sununu and the Troika to choose the options that were or were not to be eventually placed on the decision table. He was willing to tolerate the fractious interagency NES process, but was adamant in maintaining the broadest set of policy options culled from the public hearings, even if some of these were supported only by DOE.[27]

For their part, Schmalensee and Boskin came away from the Sununu meeting believing they had gotten the message across to Watkins that the NES debate should be brought into internal administration deliberation. Schmalensee hoped to use the NES process as a means to recast the energy policy debate in what he considered to be more subtle terms than those adopted by Watkins. He wanted to raise the intellectual level of debate above that achieved by the public opinions published in the Interim Report. What was meant by energy security? To what extent did energy regulation impede economic efficiency? Could energy and environmental objectives be attained by means other than federal command and control strategies? What role should government play in the development and dissemination of technology?[28]

This approach—a kind Socratic discourse—was fundamentally incompatible with the pragmatic agenda that Watkins and Moore had set for themselves in assuming responsibility for DOE. Watkins and Moore had committed to policy and cultural change, not intellectual discourse. They believed that bureaucracies are mobilized and government made to do useful work by the crafting of detailed plans, implemented with unambiguous tactics and clear objectives. Policy was not, for them, a bounding of public issues or a definitional exercise, but the instrument of action. They ascribed the White House reaction to NES to the detachment afforded officials who, unlike those responsible for actually managing the daily affairs of departments and agencies, were not accountable to Congress or to public and private constituencies.[29]

The policy staff saw the conflict between DOE's leadership and the White House as a repetition of the process that had emasculated the Energy Security Report of former Deputy Secretary William Martin in the waning days of the Reagan administration. The staffs of the Troika agencies responsible for the passive outcome of the Energy Security Report were the same individuals who were now micro-managing NES development, and the Bush-appointed agency heads appeared to take the same positions on energy policy as had their Reagan predecessors. The policy staff feared that, as with the Martin effort, a costly investment would be made to analyze and defend sweeping new policy initiatives only to reap a treatise without consequence.

The NES analytical structure

Negotiations between the Troika agencies and Stuntz on the organization and scope of the NES analysis continued for most of June 1990. During that time, the Treasury Department succeeded in eliminating from consideration all options related to fiscal incentives for the oil and gas industry, arguing that tax credits had already been provided in the Fiscal Year 1990 Omnibus Budget Reconciliation Act (OBRA).[30] Also eliminated at Troika insistence were options related to energy taxes, on the grounds that any tax increase would constitute a violation of the president's campaign pledge not to impose new burdens. For its part, OMB insisted on adding to the list the option of phasing out public subsidies to federal power administrations, even though Congress proscribed DOE from delving into this issue.[31] The NSC, in turn, requested that DOE examine the option of encouraging oil and gas development outside the Persian Gulf.

Stuntz reached agreement with the Troika on the analysis framework at the end of June. The NES analysis was organized into three major topical categories—electricity policy, energy security policy, and environmental policy. For each of the study categories a policy analysis charter was devised that bound the scope of work, identified the policy options to be considered, and provided both subject-specific and general guidance on analytical assumptions and methodology. The EPC Working Group then created a subgroup for each of the three study categories, with authority to oversee the respective analysis.

The analytical charters were detailed and bore the unmistakable imprimatur of the Troika. Stuntz had reserved for DOE the right to independently analyze options not included in the interagency roster, accepting the risk that the cabinet might never consider such options. Indeed, the members of the Working Group assumed that non-EPC-sanctioned policy initiatives would, by definition, fail EPC scrutiny. The language of the charters illustrates the precision of the guidance as well as the manner in which EPC characterized the issues. The three charters were given the same preamble, followed by the specific guidance to each of the subgroups:[32]

> *Preamble:* "The study activities proposed...draw their mandate from direction provided by the Economic Policy Council. The analytical goal is to identify market inefficiencies and security and environmental vulnerabilities: non-competitive markets (not stemming from government policy); market inefficiencies (resulting from government regulation); strong externalities or spillover effects (environmental, security, economic); distorted or ineffective market signals (stemming from government policy, R&D investments, or information). Where market inefficiencies, failures and vulnerabilities are identified, their impact should be, to the maximum possible extent, quantitatively analyzed."[33]

The assignment given to the Electricity Working Group comprised distinct demand and supply analyses, recognizing that the issues would coalesce on matters of price, investment preferences and regulatory choice. The analytical charter defined barriers to efficient decision-making in the electricity sector as being:[34]

- Regulatory: forcing utilities to make profit-reducing investments in energy efficiency rather than providing regulatory incentives to make such investments economically desirable

- Institutional: inability to address differences in the economic interests of various actors in the energy market, such as the differences between landlords' and renters' interest in the purchase of energy efficient equipment
- Fiscal: allowing utilities to *expense* efficiency investments outside their rate base but not to *amortize* them as in the case of investments in new generation plants
- Economic: selling electricity from Federal hydropower plants at below market rates while advocating energy conservation as a national policy.[35]

To address these barriers, the Electricity Working Group would analyze a range of remedies that included reform of utility pricing policies and decoupling of utility sales from profits; competitive bidding for new electricity capacity or for demand-reduction instruments, and improved energy efficiency standards for commercial and residential buildings and for energy-using equipment in those buildings. It was recognized that barriers and solutions to efficient and environmentally benign utility services would eventually have to be addressed within some form of institutionalized process at state level, rate-making proceedings.

On the supply side, EPC narrowed the policy options to reform of PUHCA, reform of state and federal regulation of access by wholesale generators of electricity to the transmission system, and reform of regulations that govern the licensing and relicensing of hydropower facilities. To this initial roster was later added reform of nuclear plant licensing. None of these reform proposals presented ideological or political problems for the Bush administration. The issue was whether the reforms could be carried out administratively, which would involve a process controlled by the executive branch, or legislatively, in which case the outcome would be substantially more uncertain.

The Energy Security Working Group assignment was more complex, though couched in terminology that veiled the ideological divisions among EPC members. The Troika agreed to the scope of this work with great reluctance and only on the insistence of NSC and the departments of Defense and State. Within this policy area were lodged the most volatile issues of the NES: oil price policy and security externalities, automotive fuel efficiency standards, alternative transportation fuels, and dependence on insecure supplies of oil. In the background—and notwithstanding Treasury's declared opposition—remained the issues of taxes on energy and reform of energy tax policy.[36]

The Energy Security Working Group was charged with examining options related to both demand and supply of oil and gas. On the demand side, the remedies to be considered were externalities not reflected in fuel prices, economic and regulatory disincentives to conservation of fuels, energy codes and standards, and government disincentives to private sector investment in energy technology research and development. These issues represented administration policy pre-dispositions, even if they were not entirely consistent with the Troika's definition of market failures that justified government action.

The energy security analyses comprised:

- economic or fiscal disincentives to investments in domestic hydrocarbon exploration and development
- access to federal lands in Alaska and on the OCS, especially areas that had been leased but later denied production rights by congressional or presidential moratoria
- technical and economic barriers to alternative fuel use
- regulatory inefficiencies in natural gas transportation markets
- vulnerability to energy supply interruptions and potential response measures
- regulatory barriers to siting and construction of energy plants.[37]

Surprisingly, the Environment Working Group was given a broader charter than DOE had come to expect from EPC. The group was directed to undertake four major studies that would attempt to concurrently integrate the environmental implications of the other groups' analyses while providing an estimate of NES' combined impacts on environmental quality. The group was also permitted to delve into global climate change policy, a highly contentious issue for the Bush administration. The four studies to be undertaken by the group were defined as follows.[38]

assumption was made at staff level and entirely for purpose of analytical consistency with the facts.

Nuclear power assumptions. The NES reference case assumed that no new nuclear power plants would be built and that no existing plants would receive an extension of their operating life. This was based on the proposition that new nuclear plant orders were unlikely without regulatory changes and absent a radical turnaround in public attitudes about nuclear technology. The assumption proved correct in regard to new plant construction, but the Nuclear Regulatory Commission (NRC) eventually granted extension of operating licenses.

U.S. and world oil resources assumptions. The NES reference case was based on the assumption that world oil resources were sufficiently vast to permit the United States to import large volumes with only moderate (direct) impact on world oil prices. More explicit assumptions were made on U.S. domestic resources, which were estimated to be in the range of 80 billion barrels of oil. Estimates of U.S. oil reserves were (and are) subject to widely different interpretations depending on assumptions of oil prices and lifting technology. DOE data indicated that about 300 billion barrels of oil remained in U.S. reservoirs after exhaustion of conventional lifting methods. This oil could constitute a recoverable reserve if policy options were considered that would subsidize production or federally supported development of new lifting technology.

Natural gas resources assumptions. The NES reference case assumed that natural gas resources capable of being produced at $5 per million Btu[41] or less were in the range of 500 to 900 trillion cubic feet, although previous DOE studies had estimated the economically recoverable resource base at over 1,200 trillion cubic feet. Differences in resource estimates could be explained by the assumptions used in calculating market prices for natural gas—the higher the prices assumed, the larger the recoverable resource. Yet, the underlying assumption of resource limitations inherent in the statistics used for NES reflected lingering perceptions of historical (especially congressional) views of natural gas as a scarce fossil fuel.

Computation of economic costs and benefits. Reference case assumptions were supplemented by guidance from OMB on methodology to be used in estimating net economic benefits for each of the options to be analyzed for NES. OMB required calculation of national benefits, computation of economic costs, and summary national benefit/cost ratios.[42]

OMB methodology for calculation of national benefits required a precise analytical sequence—derivation of microeconomic benefits of a policy option by estimates of changes in producer and consumer surplus and derivation of macroeconomic benefits of a policy change by estimates of short- and long-run changes in GNP. Where appropriate, benefits were to be weighted by probability of occurrence, estimated by year of occurrence and computed on the basis of constant dollars. Estimates of benefits were to be discounted at a prescribed 10% rate.

The negotiations with the Troika agencies on the scope and methodology of NES analysis were thus concluded a year from the White House announcement of NES development. Stuntz had managed to reach agreement with the president's political establishment in spite of her leaders' worsening relations with the Troika and while under pressure from DOE assistant secretaries to free the DOE from what they considered unprecedented intrusion of the EPC in their programmatic prerogatives. In the process, Stuntz also confronted her staff's suspicion that Troika support for NES had been won at the price of virtual DOE surrender of authority.

Upon reflection, DOE policy staff was forced to admit that the Troika-imposed guidance, assumptions and methodology were, on the whole, not only reasonable but also necessary to sound analysis. Those of the career staff who had come to consider NES as an exercise in political posturing now saw it as a challenge to their professional capabilities. After all, why would the Troika insist on detailed analytical instructions except to ensure a defensible NES outcome? Under the circumstances, Stuntz suggested, the best way for DOE to prevail was to demonstrate a fuller understanding of the issues than could be expected from the Troika staff.

Acceptance of the challenge did not, however, mean compliant behavior. In a recurrence of behavior that political leaders have always found difficult to control, the policy staff would without hesitation carry out the analysis as prescribed, but it would also make the interagency process as difficult for the Troika as it was possible to do. In the tradition of career civil servants, DOE policy analysts would become unbending advocates of their department's positions. In the interagency battleground created by EPC they would protect what they saw as their historic bureaucratic turf and seek to settle old scores with counterparts in other agencies.[43]

The policy staff was especially committed to a last-ditch defense of options it considered—not without great presumption—nonnegotiable if, in their view, the final NES were to gain public and congressional confidence. These included: higher fuel efficiency standards for automobiles, alternative transportation fuels, tax incentives for the oil and gas industry, tax subsidies for renewable energy systems and for efficiency investments, and new federal efficiency standards for commercial lighting and electric motors.

DOE staff, who knew that these options would remain to the end the Troika's greatest irritants, was especially keen to outmaneuver OMB, whose staff had thwarted every major initiative of DOE's policy office in the previous five years, and Treasury, whose staff under Brady had grown especially arrogant.

E PLURIBUS OPTIONS UNUM POLICY

Like many of his predecessors, Watkins sought for NES a unifying principle that would make sense to politicians, experts, and ordinary people. Schlesinger, under Carter, had conceived a "third age of energy," moving humanity from the limitations of fossil fuels to a new age of technology. Watkins strove for a policy fulcrum on which to balance the great diversity of America's energy interests. He thought such a balance could be achieved if the public could be made to understand that every policy choice, even the most benign, carried inherent and multi-dimensional advantages and disadvantages.

Watkins believed that too much government emphasis on energy supplies would erode public interest in conservation, and the obverse—that overemphatic concentration on energy conservation would lead people to ignore the far more difficult decisions to expand the supply of energy. He believed in technology, but wanted an investment in science education as well, so that Americans could make informed decisions about the benefits and risks of the technology they chose. He wanted to reflect, in the philosophical underpinnings of his energy strategy, the nation's regional diversity, spirit of technological innovation, and sense of economic risk-taking. He thought, in sum, that one could best assess the value of a particular policy option by seeing it as part of the broader policy landscape.[44]

Americans expect political leaders to be visionaries and the policies they promulgate to reflect American values. In the field of energy, however, national values are often in conflict with local interests, and political contradictions therefore abound. Resource-rich states, unsurprisingly, want more energy consumed at prices that will sustain their income. For consumers, the very expectation of growth-oriented markets for energy tends to instigate behavior to curb the use of fuels for reasons of environmental protection, trade, or security, or for myriad social goals. Resource-poor states, unsurprisingly, seek energy at reasonable cost, hedge their dependence by diversifying suppliers, and insist on government protection from producers' behavior that they deem inimical to their interests.

Examples of national divisions on energy policy abound. The heavily oil-dependent Northeast has historically objected to any federal action (import curbs or fees, higher taxes) that would make oil more expensive, even though higher-priced oil might provide the economic incentive needed to reduce the region's dependence upon it. The environmentally sensitive citizens of the West Coast are served, in part, by federally subsidized hydropower, but are concurrently impatient with their utilities' slow progress in achieving energy conservation that is rendered uneconomic by those same subsidies. Americans are frustrated by slow progress in the introduction of renewable fuels and technology, but are angered by any undue upward trend in the price of conventional fuels, which is a precondition to the advent of alternatives.

In the development of NES, Watkins noted that advocates of conservation did not frequently allow much room in the debate for energy supply requirements. Protectors of the environment who, for the best of reasons, objected to most of the energy sources then in use would not often be willing to concede that renewable resources alone could not meet future supply requirements. Watkins was willing to accept objections to certain energy choices but expected that reasonable men and women would, in the end, reach a modicum of common understanding on the essentials: more conservation—even perhaps uneconomic conservation—but in the context of ensuring the availability of reasonably priced long-term supplies. More renewable energy—even heavily subsidized systems—but with an understanding of the need for other fuels and systems. In short, balance.

To the jaded DOE staff, some of whom had been working on energy matters since the Nixon administration, policy balance was entirely in the eye of the political beholder. Analytically, balance was achieved when energy models showed equilibrium in projections of supply and demand. The public hearings witnesses had shown precious little inclination to treat supply and demand issues with reasonableness about the relative place of each in the broader equation of energy. Similarly, EPC had shown itself more ready to withdraw from the demand side of the energy marketplace than do so from the supply side. In short, a lack of balance.

There was a substantial degree of supply and demand balance among the sixty options, and variations thereof, assigned for study to the staff groups organized, as earlier noted, under the EPC-sanctioned headings of energy security, electricity regulation, and environmental quality. To these, Watkins added what he called foundations: issues of basic and fundamental science, applied research, and scientific literacy and education. The options and the summary results of their analysis are discussed below.

For ease of access by the political leadership, each option analysis, once completed, was reduced to a two-page summary. These summaries—never made public, as initially intended by Watkins—are the data source for the presentation that follows.[45]

Energy security policy options

Twenty-five policy options were analyzed under the heading of energy security, although the definition of "security" was subject to wide-ranging interpretation throughout the NES development process. Free market advocates saw energy security as a matter of reducing the national economy's vulnerability to oil market disruptions and price shocks. Environmentalists saw it as reduced consumption of oil. Producers saw it as higher domestic production of fossil fuels. Deputy Secretary Moore saw it as reduced reliance on Persian Gulf oil suppliers. Stuntz considered energy security a much-abused concept that in the past had served to justify harmful, or at best counterproductive, government involvement in the oil sector. Watkins came to understand energy security as lower intensity of oil use in the economy and reduced reliance on oil imports.[46] These definitional shadings made it convenient for the EPC study groups to broach the subject with intentional ambiguity.

Most of the energy security policy options examined for NES represented the ancient battle-axes of energy policy analysts immemorial. Had DOE staff been less taken with EPC intergovernmental battles, it might have pondered the meaning of rehashing in 1990 a good many of the same policies examined by predecessor analysts in every administration since the end of the Second World War. History, however, was not on the staff's mind at the time, nor on the mind of the political leadership, and so the policy options seemed freshly minted.

One of the key energy security options was a variable oil import fee that would create a nominal oil price floor of $20 or $25 per barrel beginning in 1991 and ending in 1994. The $20 per barrel floor would reduce net U.S. petroleum demand in 1995 by an insignificant 80,000 barrels per day; the $25 floor by 370,000 barrels per day. The $25 floor price had a net present value of plus $7.3 billion if world oil prices were assumed to change in response to imposition of the fee, and minus $1.4 billion if assumed to remain unchanged. Macroeconomic losses were estimated to be $32.8 billion for the $20 floor and $150.4 billion for the $25 floor.

A second set of energy security options included access to oil and gas resources of the OCS and the ANWR and development of unexploited resources on Alaska's North Slope. OCS access would be allowed to tracts taken off-limits by congressional and presidential leasing moratoria covering the Eastern Gulf of Mexico, the coast off Washington and Oregon, most of the coast of California, Alaska's North Aleutian Basin, and part of the Mid-Atlantic coast. Interior Department estimates indicated a 95% probability of finding at least 800 million barrels of oil in OCS areas closed by the moratoria and a 5% probability of finding 7.5 billion barrels.

The ANWR option would have allowed exploration and development on the 1.5 million-acre coastal plain of the 19-million-acre reserve. The

Interior Department estimated a 95% probability of finding at least 600 million barrels of oil below the ANWR coastal plain and a 5% probability of finding 9.2 billion barrels. Net economic benefits from ANWR production, for the mean reserve base of 3.2 billion barrels, were estimated at $23.5 billion. ANWR became the rallying option for the environmental community, which mobilized to defeat access to what it called (with near total disregard of the facts), America's Serengeti.

The Alaska North Slope option addressed difficulties in the development of discovered but non-producing fields at West Sak, Point Thomson, Seal Island/North Star, Gwydyr Bay, and Sandpiper Island. Reserves in these fields were estimated by industry to range between 850 million and 1.1 billion barrels, but their exploitation was mired in a web of regulatory red tape controlled separately by the Corps of Engineers, EPA, Fish and Wildlife Service, Bureau of Land Management, Minerals Management Service, and the National Marine Fisheries Service. The option was directed at resolving these overlapping federal jurisdictions, but EPC staffs of every persuasion believed it highly unlikely that these bureaucracies could be made to cooperate.

Five policy options were considered for reforming the natural gas sector.

- First, streamlining the certification process for construction of new pipelines, legislatively by amending the Natural Gas Act of 1938 or administratively by making FERC the sole agency responsible for NEPA (National Environmental Policy Act) compliance.
- Second, deregulation of gas pipeline sales rates when the pipeline did not possess market power.
- Third, reform of interstate gas pipeline rate design and removal of regulatory impediments to open pipeline access by third parties.
- Fourth, elimination of DOE regulations on imports and exports of natural gas.

The reforms were estimated to increase natural gas consumption over the 1991 to 2030 period by 41 trillion cubic feet. The NES projections proved conservative to a fault: By the year 2000, natural gas consumption and prices reached levels that the analysts of 1990 had not expected until 2030.

Variable taxes were considered for the purpose of obtaining $1.3 billion in yearly revenue by 1995 to finance expansion of the SPR from 600 million to one billion barrels by 2005. The estimated per barrel tax required to meet those objectives was: 41 cents if imposed on crude imports only, 32 cents if imposed on imported crude and products, 20 cents if imposed on domestic and imported crude and on imported products, and 1 cent per gallon if imposed on domestic gasoline sales. DOE staff became a strong advocate of the "one cent" solution, in preference to the always problematic federal budget for the SPR, but the Troika could not be convinced to support the option, even in light of strong, bipartisan congressional backing.

Options related to automotive fuel efficiency and energy conservation in transportation were few but among the most politically controversial. Beyond the baseline option of simply increasing the average 27.5 miles-per-gallon fuel economy standard then in place, options considered for NES included a reform of the CAFE provisions of EPCA. Numerous studies undertaken in the previous decade had shown the domestic industry to have carried a disproportionate regulatory burden compared to foreign manufacturers in the achievement of higher U.S. auto fuel efficiency. This was because U.S. manufacturers found their market among buyers of mid-sized to larger vehicles. Foreign manufacturers sold overwhelmingly small cars that easily met CAFE standards, in contrast with domestic mid-sized and larger cars, which had to undergo a virtual transformation in design.

Among the proposals made by DOE to reform the CAFE law were the elimination of imported and domestic distinctions in manufacturers' fleets; allowing averaging and trading of CAFE credits among manufacturers; replacing criminal conduct provisions of the law with a non-compliance fee for civil penalties, and alternative forms of standards based on interior volume, size, and weight of vehicles or annual percentage increases. A second option was the accelerated scrappage of older vehicles. The proposal was to engage state and local governments and the private sector in programs that offered a variable bounty for vehicles of designated model years, in order to permanently retire them from the national fleet. The cost of the program was estimated to be a relatively modest $1.5 to $2.1 billion for scrappage of two million vehicles. The benefits were deemed to be more environmental than economic, especially for regions such as southern California, where air quality standards were difficult to meet by other means.

EPC wanted no part of CAFE reform. After lengthy debates involving Secretary Sam Skinner at Transportation, the head of the NHTSA, and Chief of Staff Sununu, the issue was remanded to the National Academy of Sciences for study. Vehicle scrappage programs were deemed to be the responsibility of state and local governments and of EPA, which could, if they wished, devise regulatory incentives to encourage adoption of car scrappage programs in conjunction with state plans for Clean Air Act compliance. The CAFE reform battle eventually moved to Congress, attracting passionate adherents as varied as Senators Bryant of Nevada and Gore of Tennessee, who saw higher fuel economy standards as the only means of substantially mitigating U.S. reliance on oil.

For alternative transportation fuels, a number of options were considered, including a government mandate to ensure market penetration of non-oil fuels and technology. The options remained under active consideration in spite of the strong opposition of Troika members. Government mandates were also anathema to Stuntz, but she could tolerate their use in the case of alternative transportation fuels because few other viable options were available to credibly address the growth in U.S. oil consumption. Based on a requirement that most U.S. commercial vehicle fleets be incrementally replaced by fuel flexible vehicles, it was estimated that NES alternative fuel options would reduce U.S. oil consumption by 700,000 barrels per day in 2005 and by between 1.6 and 2.4 MMB/D in 2010.

A mandate to convert commercial fleets to alternative fuel use was eventually enacted in the Energy Policy Act of 1992 after long and arduous debate. The mandate was universally ignored by the industry in the ensuing years because it was virtually unenforced by the unexpectedly *laissez-faire* Clinton administration.

Oil and gas production options outside the Persian Gulf were assessed at the request of NSC with the aim of stimulating U.S. investments in oil provinces removed from OPEC control. A carrot-and-stick approach would be used to encourage investment in nations that had historically barred foreign access to their hydrocarbon production sectors. The constitution of Mexico, for example, prohibited foreign ownership of hydrocarbon resources and

Venezuelan law precluded equity participation by foreign firms in the oil production sector. On the horizon, one could perceive rich investment possibilities in the republics of the former Soviet Union. The option proposed the use of trade negotiations and bilateral consultations as the means to open opportunities in nations then closed to U.S. private investment.

Although the Troika consistently opposed their consideration, various options to tax gasoline remained on the NES development agenda. The economic and social welfare impacts of gasoline taxes had been comprehensively documented in the 1987 Energy Security Report. DOE had estimated that a 10 cent-per-gallon tax on gasoline and diesel fuel would reduce oil imports by up to 250,000 barrels per day; a 25 cent-per-gallon tax would reduce imports by up to 615,000 barrels per day in five years. Macroeconomic losses for the 10 cent-per-gallon tax were estimated at $9 billion in 1990, dropping to $7 billion in 1995. Equivalent losses for the 25-cent tax were $21 billion in 1990 and $16 billion in 1995.

For NES, the staff examined the effects of a $1-per-gallon gasoline tax, an option widely advocated by environmental activists as well as numerous members of Congress, and even the General Accounting Office. Effects of the option were derived by modeling a phase-in of the tax over a four-year period. The results were very significant: oil savings of one million barrels per day by 2000 and federal revenues totaling $600 billion over ten years. The macroeconomic losses of imposing the tax, however, were a staggering $570 billion, which represented an economic cost so high as to actually be capable of inducing a recession.

Electricity sector policy options

Unlike the energy security options, NES electricity sector reforms were intended to break new policy ground. As expected, the proposals also attracted the attention of powerful constituencies, in and out of government. Internally, the interests of statutorily protected agencies like the Securities and Exchange Commission and FERC were threatened by plans to reform the fundamental laws under which they oversaw the governance and operation of electric utilities. Also involved were the antitrust division of the

Justice Department and the Federal Trade Commission. These agencies were not accustomed to participation in executive branch policy planning and thus reacted to NES deliberations with defensive caution. Still, a strong consensus soon emerged on the electricity sector reforms that EPC would pursue, even as the industry itself remained divided and consequently ineffective in influencing the decision-making process.

One of the principal reforms on the NES agenda was a proposal to amend the Public Utilities Holding Company Act (PUHCA) of 1935 with the aim of introducing competition in the power generation market. The amendments would create a new class of producers—exempt wholesale generators (EWGs)—free from most PUHCA requirements and therefore able to make broader and more diversified investments, beyond utility confines, at home and abroad.

The debate on reform of PUHCA remained intense throughout the NES process, if simplistic in retrospect. Utilities took the position that non-utility power producers were likely to build highly leveraged, low-capital-cost projects that would rely for energy exclusively on high-cost natural gas. Utilities believed that, as with PURPA, they would in the end be required by regulators to buy power from independent generators, even if they could produce it cheaper themselves, and that PUHCA reform would lead inexorably to non-utility generators selling electricity directly to native load, retail customers.[47]

State regulators took the position that PUHCA reform could erode their authority and possibly lead to corporate restructuring designed to evade state regulation, with the consequence that consumers would be less protected.[48] Proponents of reform, including some utilities that broke ranks with their industry counterparts,[49] argued that competition would shift investment risks from ratepayers to private investors, improve operating efficiency, and reduce costs. They suggested that consumer interests could be protected through a combination of market forces and regulation, and that issues of service reliability were a technical and not a policy problem.[50]

The second of the regulatory reforms of NES was access to the electric transmission system. This option would ensure that independent power producers (IPPs) and EWGs would have non-discriminatory access to a transmission system largely owned by vertically integrated utilities. A heated interagency debate that was skillfully managed by FERC general counsel Scherman resulted in a recommendation to EPC that in preference to legislative action, FERC would be mandated to devise a regulatory regime for transmission access. FERC did so, four years later, in Orders 888 and 889, but on the basis of new authority granted by Congress in the Energy Policy Act of 1992.

The phase-out of federal subsidies to some electricity sales was, as earlier noted, of special interest to OMB. This option affected the 25% of utility customers benefiting from special rates for power generated at federal installations and sold by federal power marketing administrations (PMAs). Federal PMA rates could be as much as 50% lower than comparable rates for investor-owned utilities, thereby contributing to market distortions in several extended U.S. regions. Among the reasons for substantially lower federal power rates was the fact that PMAs, such as Bonneville Power Authority (BPA), which served the Pacific Northwest, had through 1989 repaid barely $15 million of the $1.14 billion it owed to the U.S. Treasury.

Similarly, municipal utilities and rural electric cooperatives, which together serve about 22% of American households, are exempted from federal income tax and can borrow funds from the Federal Rural Electrification Administration at a government-guaranteed rate of 5%. Most egregious to OMB was the case of TVA, which continued, after 60 years of existence, to borrow capital at subsidized rates from Treasury's Federal Financing Bank, paid no federal income tax, was exempt from regulation, and additionally received annual appropriations from Congress to finance its operations.

OMB estimated that these federal electric subsidies cost the Treasury about $500 million per year. The PMAs were thought to be the most costly, with estimated losses to the Treasury of $15 billion over the life of their outstanding federal loans.[51] EPC, whose members were fully aware of the political storm that would ensue from any effort to reverse the status quo, in the end agreed to pursue in nonspecific terms the placement of federally subsidized utilities on a business footing, with a phase-out of rate subsidies and amortization of outstanding loans. The debate and the analysis proved in the end futile. Congress would have none of it.

On nuclear matters, much was expected from Watkins by the then-moribund nuclear industry. Although it could not reverse the negative public view of nuclear technology, DOE was required to address nuclear issues because of its statutory responsibility to manage civilian and defense nuclear waste. Reforms contemplated in the NES process involved the then-protracted and costly licensing of plants by the NRC and the development of a new generation of reactors, with inherently safe features, that could simplify the licensing process.

The state of play on nuclear waste in 1990 was that the Nuclear Waste Policy Act of 1982 had imposed on DOE the requirement to build a monitored, retrievable storage facility in New Mexico capable of receiving spent nuclear fuel by 1998, and to study the feasibility of establishing a permanent repository either at Yucca Mountain, Nevada, or at a second, non-specified site in another region of the country. Both congressional mandates had been stalled by successful legal challenges by state authorities, and consequently DOE saw no possibility of fulfilling its statutory responsibilities until and unless federal legislation was enacted to override local opposition. Eventually, the Energy Policy Act of 1992 established Yucca Mountain as the sole site to be considered for the permanent repository, but could do little to reduce the legal options of the state of Nevada to oppose the repository, even though the site itself is entirely on federal lands.

The licensing issue had also been fought and lost in the courts. An effort by NRC to streamline the licensing process by reducing the number of public hearings it was required to hold before issuing an operating license had been derailed by the U.S. Court of Appeals for the District of Columbia. The court had determined that nuclear licensing reform was a congressional and not an NRC prerogative. NES therefore would propose legislation to provide for a single comprehensive hearing designed to lead to the issuance of a combined construction and operating license for future nuclear plant projects. This indeed was achieved as one of the provisions of the Energy Policy Act of 1992.

Somewhat less intractable, coal policy issues engendered no less controversy in the NES process. Although by 1989 nearly $2 billion in federal funds had been invested in development and demonstration of so-called clean coal technology (CCT), it became the mission of Robert

Gentile, DOE assistant secretary for fossil energy, to secure additional support for CCT in the guise of regulatory incentives. Gentile argued that utilities' instinctive risk-aversion, as it was perceived in 1990, would delay deployment of these operationally untested technologies. He consequently proposed a series of incentives that state regulators could consider in decisions related to CCT, including rolling prudence reviews to prevent cost disallowances for less than fully successful CCT projects, exemptions from the regulatory "used and useful" criterion so as not to disadvantage CCTs for their lack of commercial operating experience, incentive rates of return to utilities willing to accept a CCT, and simplified siting and project approval procedures. Gentile's agenda proved entirely disingenuous in practice because state commissions were not about to cede their regulatory powers in order to commercialize the deployment of a federally-developed new fossil technology.

Renewable energy was to be supported in NES through the adoption of a federal tax incentive designed to provide a 2 cent-per-kWh credit against income to any producer that generated electricity from photovoltaics, solar thermal, wind, geothermal, or biomass systems. What distinguished this proposal from previous federal support for these technologies was the provision that the subsidy would be paid only for actual production of power, rather than for merely making an investment in a plant. The program was estimated to cost $1.77 billion for the first five years and $17.3 billion over a thirty-year period, substantially more than the $80 million cost of the then-existing renewable tax credit. The tax incentive was thought capable of stimulating construction of 19 gigawatts of new renewable energy capacity in 2000, 28 gigawatts in 2010, and 88 gigawatts in 2030. The Troika objected to the high cost of the option and killed it.

Reform of the Public Utility Regulatory Policy Act (PURPA) was also to be addressed by NES: first, by removal of the statutory 80-megawatt limitation on the capacity of plants that qualified as small power producers (provided that competitive bidding was used by states to acquire this new capacity); and second, by a relaxation of the co-firing limit of 75% renewable/25% fossil fuels by qualifying facilities, to allow for a 50-50 ratio—but, again, only in cases of plants procured under competitive bidding procedures. The option was eventually implemented, but all of PURPA became irrelevant as the electric power industry moved to a restructured world beginning in the mid-1990s.

Other "soft" options considered in the NES process included a change in federal taxation of utilities' efficiency rebates to consumers, new and more demanding lighting efficiency standards and equipment labeling, first-in-history federal energy efficiency standards for buildings, and the establishment of a $300-million revolving fund for investments in energy efficiency in federal buildings. The latter proposal was intended to address the generally deplorable record of federal agencies in becoming more energy efficient. The fund would provide extra-budgetary financing of efficiency investments estimated to have payback periods of two to five years. With such paybacks, the fund could be re-capitalized by about $100 million per year, and result in federal energy consumption savings of 5% per year after full operation.

Environmental policy options

NES was intended to produce environmentally benign energy policy. Indeed, no other objective was deemed feasible in the political landscape of 1990. But the achievement of desirable environmental goals was complicated, internally, by the Bush administration's all too recent, politically wrenching experience with the CAAA and, externally, by expectations that NES would serve as the instrument of choice for policy on global climate change.

DOE had by 1990 emerged as a key federal player in climate change research in part due to distrust of EPA by both the Reagan and Bush white house. This did not sit well with EPA, which, despite the opportunities provided by NES, nevertheless hoped that DOE would not succeed where EPA had failed. DOE succeeded in placing climate change policy options before EPC, even as the Bush administration came to view climate change policy as inescapable. By the same token, NES also focused on reform of environmental regulations deemed burdensome to energy industries as well as ineffective in protecting the environment. The environmental community saw in the very consideration of these options a DOE bias in favor of its traditional energy constituency and attacked NES as inimical to the environment.

Among the more contentious NES environmental remedies was a proposal to impose a tax on carbon emissions, ranging from $35 to $135 per ton of carbon emitted. This proposal was justified analytically on the premise that consumer prices did not reflect the full social costs of carbon emissions. The "social cost" concept had not acquired currency in the Bush administration, whose policy on global climate change was based on a "no-regrets" approach. No regrets meant that environmental action could be taken under existing laws that would coincidentally reduce greenhouse gas emissions. Under the approach, the administration supported such initiatives as tree planting programs, known to be effective carbon sinks, and strict adherence to the Montreal Protocol on ozone-depleting chemicals.

The NES Working Group estimated that a $135 per ton carbon tax would be necessary to stabilize U.S. greenhouse gas emissions in the year 2000 at approximately 1990 levels. Such a tax was estimated to have a net present value of minus $2.2 billion, if world oil prices were assumed to change in response to the tax, and of minus $4.0 billion if they were not. The $135 per ton tax would have by 2000 reduced net greenhouse gas emissions by 9.4%, primary energy consumption by 7.2 quads, oil consumption by 900,000 barrels per day, and coal consumption by 160 million tons per year. Treasury revenue would have been $200 billion annually, but GNP would have suffered a staggering 1.2% reduction in growth in 2000. Needless to say, the tax was rejected by the administration. (The tax resurfaced early in the Clinton administration, whose presumed greater commitment to mitigation of climate change was insufficient to impose it.)

To reduce uncertainties in the science of global climate change, NES analysts focused on four areas of scientific inquiry:

- definition of sources and sinks of greenhouse gases, which would affect future concentrations of these gases
- analyses of the effects of clouds, which were known to influence strongly the magnitude and trend of climate change
- analyses of the effects of oceans, which were known to influence the timing and patterns of climate change
- studies of polar ice sheets, which were known to affect sea levels.

Additional research was also deemed important to address uncertainties about the actual effectiveness of individual or collective policy options in averting climate change. Incremental investments needed to address these uncertainties—estimated to add $100 million to the over $1 billion per year global climate change federal research budget of 1990—were readily adopted by EPC.

Research and development policy options

Grouped under the favored Watkins term of "foundations," options were considered that would realign federal R&D priorities and reverse the physical deterioration of the national research laboratories. Consideration of these options was also motivated by the congressional habit of financing scientific and technological research based on political rather than scientific criteria. Congressional earmarking of funds for favored projects had by 1990 become common. Watkins believed that if congressional committees saw R&D spending within a strategic context, they would be less prone to politicize the DOE budget.

The differences of view between Congress and the executive branch were significant and affected most areas of the DOE research budget. Congress had insisted on greater support for coal technology R&D than either Reagan or Bush had been willing to accept. Congressional appropriators had, for example, inexplicably kept alive magneto-hydrodynamics research that both administrations had consistently zeroed out of their proposed budgets. Similar battles had occurred on R&D for renewables, conservation, and nuclear technology. The two sides had only agreed in the end to finance what they were finally able to negotiate by frequently raiding the operating and discretionary budgets of the national laboratories.

The laboratories became pawns, constrained on one side by congressional earmarkings of otherwise reduced R&D budgets, and on the other by pressure from Watkins to forego their historical exemption, and come into compliance with federal environmental, occupational, safety, health, and labor laws. As a consequence the laboratories had been forced to divert increasing proportions of their discretionary budgets away from basic research and into congressionally sanctioned demonstration projects of dubious value. Their operating budgets had been essentially taken over (or so they claimed) by OSHA[52] compliance requirements.

The laboratories had entered the NES development process with hopes of remedying their financial plight. They reasoned that the very public NES process would expose the nation to their capabilities and perhaps inspire greater financial support by the administration and by Congress. They were to be disappointed on most counts, but the research policy debate engendered by NES shed sufficient light on the plight of the national laboratories as to draw the attention of the congressional authorizing committees. These took protective steps on behalf of the laboratories as part of later deliberations on the Energy Policy Act of 1992.

The research issues examined for NES included a wide-ranging assessment of DOE basic research capabilities. Five initiatives were considered under the general heading of revitalizing the two dozen research laboratories involved. First was a proposal for the federal government to establish national priorities for energy science; second, a proposal to establish a program of industrial research to stimulate private sector investment in basic (as opposed to applied) science; next, a proposal to obtain international partners for high-cost research projects such as the superconductor supercollider, the liquid metal reactor, and the integral fusion reactor. A further proposal was aimed at strengthening collaboration between DOE laboratories and universities; still another would offset declining federal budget resources by creating federal/state/private partnerships to co-finance state-of-the-art research centers in various regions of the country.

Research cost-sharing was high on OMB's agenda. Under the then highly constrained federal budget, federal R&D investments could be expanded only if a larger share of costs would be borne by the private sector. The proposal was to apply to a greater number of DOE research projects the co-financing criteria successfully used for the CCT program. The CCT effort had involved private support in excess of 50% of program cost, to which was attributed both the technical relevance and timeliness of the program. The issue for NES analysts was whether similar private investment could be secured for basic research projects.

Federal technology transfer also preoccupied NES analysts who were charged with examining how the National Competitiveness Technology Transfer Act of 1989 could be most effectively carried out. It was proposed that DOE focus its technology transfer capabilities on four areas of presumed high interest to the private sector: intelligence gathering for foreign and domestic markets, technical assistance, independent (federal) validation and testing of private research results, and brokering—bringing innovators into contact with parties who could further develop their ideas. The specific elements of this option remained sketchy throughout the NES development process, among other reasons because the Commerce Department insisted that it, not DOE, had principal responsibility for federal technology transfer activities. Also questionable was the intent to use the intelligence community for what amounted to industrial spying.

Of special interest to CEA was the NES option to improve the performance of the dozen federal agencies involved in promotion of U.S. merchandise exports. With the specific aim of increasing the U.S. share of a projected $1.6 trillion (1990-2010) worldwide market for energy equipment and technology, the idea was to create a Commercial Opportunities Initiative (COI) under the direction of EPC. COI would aggressively identify trade opportunities, assist U.S. manufacturers and exporters in breaking through bureaucratic barriers, and coordinate U.S. trade promotion functions. It was estimated that a mere 5% increase in the U.S. share of the world energy technology market would increase the value of exports by $100 billion and create fifty thousand new jobs.

The Troika options

It was clear to DOE's policy staff that the Troika agencies deemed critical to the eventual success of NES only those policy options related to regulatory reform. These included reform of PUHCA, PURPA, natural gas pipeline transportation, and nuclear licensing. OMB had hopes, but no great expectations, of restructuring the debt of federal hydropower administrations, and Sununu was keen on nuclear licensing reform. As for the remaining, DOE-driven NES options, the Troika considered them inconsequential.

Notably absent from the building blocks of NES were many of the standard components of previous energy policy plans. No one, for example, seriously contemplated a new synthetic fuel effort. Oil price or import controls of any kind were clearly no longer imaginable, and federally dictated fuel and technology choices were also—mostly—out of bounds.

By the same token, NES, like its predecessors, was to be built on the promise of technological opportunity, which was seen as more reassuring as well as politically more acceptable, than alternatives such as higher energy taxes or more stringent regulations. The EPC Working Group would have subscribed to the idea that policy was founded on price, technology, and behavior, but would have defined these terms in radically different ways than had their 1970s predecessors. To the EPC of 1990, the price of energy would be determined exclusively by the market, and technology would remain the engine of improvement of the energy system, regardless of the federal role in its development and deployment. Furthermore, government would hold sacrosanct the right of consumers to behave in their own best interests.

Energy security policy did not dominate the NES debate nearly as it had the energy debates of the previous two decades. CEA generally, and Schmalensee in particular, never permitted NES deliberators to forget the lessons of the past. This meant constant reminders that commonly accepted measures of energy security were not only costly but futile. Security, in Schmalensee's view, would not be achieved by reducing U.S. oil imports by 10% or 50% or even 90% because the United States could not be reasonably insulated from the international oil market, whatever the import level.

THE INTER-LABORATORY WHITE PAPERS

Admiral Watkins had very high regard for the intellectual capabilities of DOE's national laboratories. He sought advice from the laboratories on a broad range of issues, but especially when controversies raged over public policy issues such as the notorious cold fusion case, nuclear safety, the superconducting supercollider—and NES. The laboratories never failed to respond, and they did so again in mid-1990 by transmitting to DOE the white papers, commissioned at the outset of the NES effort, on the subjects of global climate change, renewable energy and energy conservation potential, and technology transfer.

Five white papers were produced by men and women voluntarily drawn together by the hope of translating years of research into national policy. More than one hundred individuals were involved in the effort. They worked with great diligence and speed, with very limited financial resources, setting aside traditional rivalries, and conscious of needing to provide advice that would withstand intense political scrutiny. Their diligence proved futile.

The white papers were characterized by the Troika staff as minimally useful to the NES deliberation process because, although devoid in the main of self-serving policy recommendations, they presented evidence to bolster government initiative in policy areas that held little interest for the Bush administration. Advice from respected institutions could not however be peremptorily dismissed, and so ways were found by Troika staffs to ascribe fatal analytical flaws to the white papers. "In sum, to be useful for the NES," wrote an OMB staff member about one of the papers, "the fundamental assumptions and approach...need to be redone along the lines of a conventional market-based study."[53] In truth, DOE had not requested a market-based study from the national laboratories. Rather, it had requested their best collective wisdom on issues with which the laboratories were thoroughly familiar.

The reaction of DOE's leadership to the white papers was muted, among other reasons because Watkins and Moore were not quite sure how the white papers could be used to gain EPC support for NES. Watkins continued to refrain from taking hard positions on specific NES options. He was not wedded to a particular policy on energy conservation or renewable energy. He was keen on improving the process of technology transfer from DOE laboratories to industry, but had no preconceptions about how this should be done. His views were much clearer on global climate change, and they were also in the public record.

In testimony before the Senate Committee on Energy and Natural Resources in 1989, he had articulated six principles he thought should be applied to the threat of global climate change. These principles—in fact the sum total of Bush administration policy on the subject—governed his thinking throughout his tenure at DOE. The principles represented a balanced response to a difficult public policy issue: prudent action coupled with further research. The Troika heads agreed with the Watkins policy in principle but sought to carry out only those aspects of it that required research, as opposed to those requiring other forms of government intervention.

The team of laboratory researchers charged with examining the issue thought enough about the soundness of the principles to quote them back to Watkins as an excellent basis for policy in the white paper on global climate change. The principles were:[54]

1. Take aggressive action on those issues on which scientific consensus exists.
2. Assess the state of the science on issues where no scientific consensus exists, and identify areas for further inquiry.
3. Where scientific uncertainty exists, move forward with those measures that make sense on other grounds, *e.g.,* efficiency and reduction of chlorofluorocarbons (CFCs).
4. Consider the costs and benefits of any response measures suggested.
5. Link responses to scientific and technical information.
6. Determine how to share technological responses with developing countries.

Watkins' prudent response to the potential for climate change was not shared by a number of key members of DOE's congressional oversight committees. In 1989, then-Senators Timothy Wirth and Albert Gore had introduced sweeping legislation to establish a national energy policy to reduce global warming. The bill, later known as the Energy Policy Act of 1990, had gathered a total of forty-one cosponsors and had passed the Senate in August 1990.[55] The Bush administration had opposed the legislation as overly prescriptive and economically damaging.[56]

But congressional interest had intensified, among other reasons because, in the wake of congressional failure to adopt climate change legislation as part of the CAAA of 1990, Gore and Wirth saw NES as the next best vehicle for action on the issue. Watkins was wary of this congressional activism, fearing that climate change would overwhelm the policy balance he sought in the NES.

The inter-laboratory advice seemed to vindicate the general thrust of administration policy on climate change without excusing the administration's penchant for downplaying the need for more deliberate action. The global climate change white paper was especially nuanced in its presentation of scientific uncertainty, its caution about prematurely sweeping new policy initiatives and its call for action that made sense for greenhouse gas mitigation as well as for other environmental protection reasons. The paper's cautious conclusions irritated the liberal community while its agenda for action irritated the Troika agencies. Watkins, again in the line of fire between internal watchdogs and external critics, acknowledged the advice and temporarily kept his peace.

The white papers, which are summarized below, were never published as appendices to NES. They were distributed for review and comment within the analytical community, but did not receive the public visibility expected by those who crafted them.

The global climate change white paper

Michael MacCracken of Lawrence Livermore National Laboratory led a thirty-member team[57] from nine national laboratories responsible for the white paper on global climate change. Also involved in the effort were two non-laboratory researchers: Norman Rosenberg of Resources for the Future and Gary Yohe of Wesleyan University. Titled *Energy and Climate Change*, the paper sought, in MacCracken's words, "to provide an overview of scientific understanding of the potential chemical, climatic, and environmental effects of continuing emissions of carbon dioxide and other...trace gases."[58] MacCracken and his team appreciated the distinction between climate change science and climate change policy. They respected the wishes of DOE's policy staff to refrain from prematurely making policy recommendations and concentrated instead on comprehensively addressing the nature, scope, and scientific foundation of a very complex issue.

MacCracken and his team were careful in their statements of what could and could not be concluded about potential changes in earth's climate from the state of knowledge of 1990. They could state categorically that "...The atmospheric concentrations of carbon dioxide and other gases have been increasing as a result of energy generation, transportation, and industrial, agricultural, and other societal activities."[59] It is certain, they said, that the climate is warmed by these greenhouse gases. "The greenhouse question," they declared, "is not whether atmospheric composition is a primary determinant of the global average temperature and climate but, rather, how large and how fast the changes will be as atmospheric composition is altered."[60]

The team agreed that significant gaps in knowledge existed, for example, to "satisfactorily explain the relative importance of oceanic and biospheric carbon reservoirs and the interactions of chemistry and climate on atmospheric concentrations."[61] Lest these conclusions lead to facile calls for action, the authors of *Energy and Climate Change* warned, "modeling studies suggest that natural processes may not be sufficient to reduce the atmospheric concentrations *unless releases from human activities are reduced by 50 to 80% or more* (emphasis added)."[62]

The last point was especially important as a message to the environmental and mainly Democratic political community that was active in promoting policy initiatives aimed at stabilizing greenhouse gas emissions in the year 2000 at 1990 levels. DOE policy staff read the MacCracken report as indicating that stabilization policies could prove politically satisfying but scientifically irrelevant. In other words, those who had become convinced that the earth was literally at risk from this latest environmental threat could not reasonably accept a solution—stabilization—that would be the medical equivalent of prescribing a permanent splint for a broken leg.

MacCracken's team was equally explicit about the limitations inherent in addressing the climate change issue as a matter of national policy. "Although the U.S. must contribute to moderation or mitigation of the greenhouse issue," the researchers noted, "there is neither a U.S. solution nor a single technological adjustment or control measure that could readily and economically limit the increase in the concentrations of carbon dioxide and other trace species."[63] But they suggested that for NES purposes, "economically attractive actions to slow the rate of emissions could provide time for the development of new technology and make easier the adaptation to change."[64] The team concluded *Energy and Climate Change* with the old policy maxim that "choosing to do nothing is just as much a choice as choosing to do something."

The energy efficiency white paper

The inter-laboratory white paper on energy conservation, titled *Energy Efficiency: How Far Can We Go?*, was produced by a twenty-four-member team from five national laboratories, under the collective leadership of Roger Carlsmith of Oak Ridge, James McMahon of Lawrence Berkeley, William Chandler of Pacific Northwest, and Danilo Santini of Argonne.[65] The paper, concise and rather limited in scope, comprised essentially a study of two scenarios of future efficiency gains. In the first "where we are headed" scenario were posited business-as-usual assumptions about population and economic growth and fuel prices that produced results essentially similar to those of EIA's *Annual Energy Outlook* projections. Scenario results indicated that U.S. primary energy consumption would reach 102 quadrillion Btu in 2010, with market-driven energy efficiency improvements of about 12% from an 1988 baseline.[66]

In the second scenario, the team modeled the gains that would be possible to obtain from aggressive installation of new energy efficiency technology. They constructed a "cost-effective efficiency" scenario resulting in 2010 primary energy consumption reaching 88 quadrillion Btu, embedding in the economy energy efficiency improvements of 14% above the first scenario.[67] The researchers acknowledge the "remarkable progress in efficient energy use" made by the United States since the first oil crisis, noting that between 1973 and 1988, U.S. energy use had "increased only 8% while gross national product had increased 46%."[68]

The DOE policy office accepted the energy efficiency white paper at face value and in marked contrast to the advice that had previously been received by SEAB. The paper confirmed, if further confirmation were needed, that American consumers could buy a great deal of efficiency provided they were willing, as in energy supply, to pay the price. The white paper underscored the policy office's historical concern with the inadequacy of energy efficiency data and models and was explicit about the inherent uncertainty of estimating technology adoption and performance in projections of future energy prices.

In a chapter titled "Closing the Efficiency Gap," Carlsmith *et al.* posed the question: if energy efficiency is so great, why do we continue to be inefficient? The answer they offered was that a combination of structural and behavioral barriers prevented efficient decision-making.[69] Structural barriers were conditions beyond the control of individuals, including distortions in fuel prices and uncertainty about future energy prices, limited access to capital, unpredictability in government fiscal and regulatory policy, and inefficiently designed and inconsistently enforced codes and standards. Behavioral barriers, associated with decision-making by energy end-users, included variable attitudes about conservation, perceptions that investments in conservation were riskier than other energy investments, inadequate or inaccurate information about energy efficiency technology, and benefits and misdirected government policy and incentives.[70]

"There is ample evidence," the researchers noted, "that we are not even close to fundamental limits in energy efficiency."[71] DOE staff thought this thesis was theoretically true. However, in the context of particular economic conditions at specific points in time, real limits existed because of investment choices that individuals were willing to make. In other words, the average consumer had difficulty investing in technology and processes that did not pay immediate dividends, but rather would reduce their energy costs in the long term. One could have argued, as easily, that the nation was not even close to fundamental limits in energy supply. Both limits were a function of the price one was willing to pay.

Carlsmith *et al.* concluded their paper with a rather disappointing policy mantra. "Environmental problems, the needs of developing nations, and resource depletion," they stated, "make it increasingly imperative that we use energy as efficiently as possible."[72] One could accept environmental quality as a compelling rationale for energy efficiency, but it was difficult to see how greater U.S. conservation could help meet the needs of developing countries. As to the resource depletion argument, it appeared to DOE staff that even experienced researchers found it difficult to make a case for energy efficiency without resorting to the rather emotional terminology of depletion that continued to infect the language of energy policy.

In the view of DOE's policy staff, nothing harmed the cause of energy efficiency policy more than casting it in the social vocabulary of moral behavior. It was DOE's intent, rather, to persuade NES policymakers to consider energy efficiency policy in hard economic and business terms. The policy staff wanted to divorce energy policy from social policy, from foreign aid policy and from welfare policy, because only by so doing were utilities, bankers, builders and consumers likely to see energy conservation as investment rather than charity.

The white paper on renewable energy

Thomas Bath, of the Solar Energy Research Institute (SERI),[73] led a team of thirty-seven analysts from five laboratories[74] in a nine-month effort to complete the white paper titled: *The Potential of Renewable Energy*. The paper comprised presentations of the renewable energy resource base, the stage of technology development and cost, barriers to deployment of new technology, projections of renewables' share of national primary energy, and R&D requirements. Bath *et al.* constructed three scenarios to indicate the degree of penetration of renewable energy technology into the national energy equation. The scenarios were inconsistent with those used in the other white papers and with DOE forecast assumptions, making it difficult to use the white paper results in an analytically comparable manner.

The researchers made clear, what is typically unclear to the average American, that renewable energy accounted for 8% (or 7 of 82 quads) of total primary energy supply in 1988. The 7 quads, in turn, were contributed by hydropower (46%), biomass (47%), geothermal (4%), and wind, alcohol fuels, solar thermal, and photovoltaics (3%).[75]

The researchers estimated that in a "business as usual scenario" of no new policy or R&D initiatives, renewables would account for 15% (or 22 of 144 quads) of total energy supply in 2030. Under a second scenario called "research, development and demonstration intensification," the renewable share of total energy would rise to 28%. This, however, would require sustained federal R&D expenditures of $3 billion per year over two decades. A third scenario, called "National Premium," based on the imposition of a variable tax on fossil fuels, would increase the economic "competitiveness" sufficiently to ensure a 22% share of total energy for renewables.[76]

The authors of the white paper on renewables made the case for federal support not by offering the prospect of research breakthroughs that would make this technology cost-competitive with other forms of useful energy, but by appealing to what they called "national values."[77] They argued that renewable technology should be judged on non-quantifiable attributes of benign environmental quality, energy security, and potential domestic and international economic usefulness. They assumed furthermore that the environmental, security, and economic values of renewable energy systems could not, in fact, be calculated.

On the question of environmental national values, the researchers wrote that "comparing a strict market appraisal of the cost of renewable systems with other systems does not adequately reflect the environmental costs that can be avoided with renewables."[78] Such a position, carried to its logical conclusion, would lead analysts to conclude that no energy system can be compared with another. Actually, resource economics theory and practice were a well-established discipline at the time NES was under development. From Freeman was available *The Measurement of Environmental and Resource Values: Theory and Practice*,[79] and from Maler, *Environmental Economics*.[80] Smith and Krutillo had long since issued *Technical Change, Relative Prices and Environmental Resource Evaluation*.[81] And Kopp and Smith had edited *Valuing Natural Assets: The Economics of Natural Resources Damage Assessment*.[82]

The issue of security was addressed in an awkward manner as well. "Replacing imported oil with domestic renewable resources," the group declared, "obviously contributes to national security."[83] Developing countries, the researchers noted, would benefit from locally produced renewable fuels because they could devote to economic development the foreign exchange resources they previously expended on purchasing foreign oil. "Greater (fuel) competition should," the group thought, "reduce the likelihood that OPEC or any other group of producers would be able to restrain supplies and drive prices up."[84] It was difficult to know what to make of such advice. It was not at all obvious to DOE staff that domestic renewable resources could enhance energy security, as promised by the authors of the report. Nor was the connection self-evident between domestic support of renewable energy technology and the foreign exchange needs of developing countries. As to the group's theory of OPEC behavior, DOE staff could only assume a lapse of memory on the prevailing wisdom of a past decade.

The economic values posited by the group were also oddly defined. "The foremost advantage," the group declared, "is that all energy prices should be lower as renewable (or any other) energy enters the market."[85] Actually it was *not* self-evident that the entry of new, higher-priced energy sources into the market tended to lower prices. There was, for example, no evidence to suggest that the entry of ethanol in the transportation fuel market had lowered gasoline prices. Nor had wind systems or solar or geothermal systems lowered the price of electricity even when these resources and systems were federally subsidized.

In sum, the inter-laboratory white paper on renewable energy, while containing some useful data on system performance and cost, proved disappointing as independent advice with which to convince the skeptical, market-oriented members of EPC to support new policy initiatives in this area. Stuntz pondered, after the fact, the advisability of entrusting this analysis to an institution—SERI—whose sole purpose was the advocacy of the subject under study.

The white papers on technology transfer

DOE considers itself first and foremost a research organization, devoted to finding scientific and technological answers to national problems. This comes as a surprise to many officials who occupy the thin, upper political ranks of the department for short periods of time. Public perceptions of DOE were shaped by its oil market regulatory mission of the 1970s and by its nuclear waste management mission of the 1980s. Between those two unpopular policy brackets exist three dozen specialized and multi-purpose centers of basic and applied research staffed by nearly fifty thousand of some of America's best scientists.

Congress has been tinkering with the role and mission of DOE's laboratories since they were created in the mid-1940s. The specialized research of the nuclear weapons laboratories notwithstanding, Congress has recurrently sought ways to transfer to the economy at large the ideas and technical innovations incubated at DOE research facilities.

In 1974, Congress passed the Non-nuclear Energy Research and Development Act that, among other things, allowed DOE to waive government ownership of rights to research when private individuals or companies sought to commercialize DOE-developed inventions. Broader technology transfer legislation was enacted in 1980. The Bayh-Dole Act allowed small business and nonprofit government contractors to retain title to patents developed at DOE expense, without obtaining government approval, and the Stevenson-Wydler Act, also enacted in 1980, subsequently amended by the Federal Technology Transfer Act of 1986, made technology transfer a congressionally-mandated mission of DOE laboratories. The law further required that government agencies devote 0.5% of their R&D funds to technology transfer functions and directed federal laboratories to actively manage their technology transfer activities.

Congressional intent is not always sufficient to spur effective action, and so it was that Watkins came to believe that DOE's technology transfer mission needed revitalization. The issue was analyzed during NES development by three separate laboratory groups who produced papers on the nature of the transfer process itself, the actual experience of DOE's key laboratories, and the potential benefits of transferring DOE technology to developing nations.

The white paper on the technology transfer process

A team of six researchers from three laboratories[86] examined technology transfer processes at DOE laboratories and at other federal and state research institutions. They concluded that successful processes had certain characteristics in common that included: personal interaction to break bureaucratic inertia, a designated champion capable of guiding commercial development once the transfer is effected, a short time span to minimize loss of information between the technology's exit from the laboratory and its commercialization, customized processes that differentiate the handling of technologies at different levels of development—the less developed the technology, the more complex the process of transfer—and recurrent evaluation of results.[87]

The researchers examined program-specific and institutional processes at DOE, NASA, (which has one of the oldest and most comprehensive technology spin-off programs in government), the National Institute of Standards and Technology (whose name was changed from Bureau of Standards precisely to underscore its technology transfer mission), and the Gas Research Institute. They concluded that programs aimed at transferring information required substantially different approaches than programs to transfer licenses or products, or spin-offs of actual companies.

The white paper on technology transfer at DOE laboratories

Ronald Barks of Los Alamos National Laboratory was commissioned to conduct a quantitative survey of the technology transfer history and experience of DOE laboratories from 1977 to 1989.[88] Barks contacted eighteen of the laboratories, sixteen of which provided inventories of 564 technology transfers. The survey produced 129 case studies, including eighty-four case studies of the transfers considered most successful and forty-five of cases considered least successful. Interestingly, the three nuclear weapons laboratories—Lawrence Livermore, Sandia and Los Alamos—accounted for 374 of the transfers surveyed.[89]

Barks analyzed the survey results by constructing a chi-squared contingency table and provided the following key conclusions:[90]

- The greater the level of effort invested in technology transfer and the greater the variety of mechanisms used, the higher the probability of success.
- For successful transfer cases, planned transfers outnumbered unplanned transfers by 3.2 to 1.
- Manufacturing businesses were the primary recipients of DOE technology; energy production businesses came second.
- Information was the primary form of technology transfer from DOE laboratories, followed by process software, patents, and products.
- The most successful transfer efforts were classified as 60% technology "push," which is recognized by industry as most risky, and 40% as market "pull."
- The two most common stages at which technology was transferred were "proof of concept" and "process development."
- Sixty-five percent of all transfers required one to five years to complete, 24% took more than five years, and 6.2% took less than one year.

Barks' survey and analysis, though admittedly incomplete and subject to a great many qualifiers, indicated that technology transfer at DOE laboratories could be expanded only with substantial, long-term effort. Some laboratories were less willing than others to invest in such an effort, believing it the responsibility of potential users to seek knowledge and information at the laboratories. In short, most laboratories wanted to be left to their research but would respond to customers if asked. Other laboratories were more enthusiastic about expanding their technology transfer activities, believing that if nothing else they would likely receive greater budgetary support from DOE and Congress. In the end, Watkins concluded the laboratories would not act aggressively on this issue without constant pressure from DOE's political leadership.

The white paper on technology transfer to developing countries

Mark Levine of Lawrence Berkeley Laboratory led a thirteen member team from seven laboratories[91] that compiled *Energy Technology for Developing Countries*. The report argued that the United States should be concerned about the energy policies and choices of developing nations because these would have consequences for U.S. interests in the international oil market, on global climate change, and in emerging markets for American technology.

The researchers noted that commercial—as opposed to indigenous—energy consumption in developing countries rose from 16% of world consumption in 1970 to 25% in 1988. Third World energy use, they noted, was highly inefficient: typically high electricity losses, outmoded technology in industry, poorly maintained buildings, and power-consuming equipment and high and unsustainable use of biomass in rural areas, in the absence of commercial energy availability. The researchers stated that although financial institutions like the World Bank provided energy sector loans and grants on the order of $10 billion per year, developing countries were not paying sufficient attention to energy efficiency or to nonconventional technologies that might be economically and environmentally more appropriate to their needs.[92]

Levine and his colleagues recommended that DOE mount a major research, development, and technology transfer effort to meet the specialized needs of developing nations. The recommendations included adaptation of U.S. equipment to withstand typical developing world conditions—poor maintenance practices, development of power systems that could operate economically on non-fossil fuels, in-country demonstration of innovative energy technology, and technical assistance to enhance institutional capabilities in energy planning and management.[93]

Although Levine *et al.* acknowledged that DOE already invested in technology transfer programs aimed at developing countries through the government-wide Committee on Renewable Energy Commerce and Trade, or through bilateral arrangements, they sought a significant expansion of these efforts. The researchers recognized also that very substantial barriers existed to effective technology transfer overseas, including poorly developed policymaking institutions prone to government command and control practices, subsidized prices for energy, lack of foreign exchange currency to purchase new technology, and a poor record of technology management.[94]

DOE policy staff was skeptical of the proposals submitted by Levine's group because they would assign to a fundamentally domestic agency matters more appropriately handled by the foreign policy and foreign aid establishment. True, DOE had an office of international affairs, but its mission was to manage DOE's membership in the International Energy Agency and the International Atomic Energy Agency. The office also negotiated and oversaw research and development agreements with other industrial countries, financed on an equal basis by the governments involved. It would have required substantial new resources to expand DOE's mission to include aid to more than 130 developing nations.

In sum, the inter-laboratory white papers provided advice of uneven quality and feasibility that, however, represented a fulfillment of a commitment by Watkins, Moore, and Stuntz to hear the voice of all who had something of substance to contribute. The policy staff was mildly disappointed by the results, given a long history of professional interaction with the laboratories, believing the white papers to be not entirely representative of the best that the laboratories could do. There were mitigating factors, however: the very short time allowed for completion of the reports, lack of financial support from DOE and, perhaps most of all, the inexperience of the researchers involved in processes that translate technical advice into national policy.

The white papers were most useful in that they raised no unexpected or unforeseen issues, thereby indirectly providing support to the analytical foundation of NES. The global climate change paper, perhaps the most sophisticated of the five, was especially persuasive in sanctioning approaches that reasonable leaders—other than over-interventionist liberals and blatantly laissez-faire conservatives—could agree to pursue. A centrist, bipartisan Congress eventually adopted in the Energy Policy Act of 1992 the majority of the proposals embedded in the climate change white paper, in the process marginalizing the policy extremism of Senators Wirth and Gore on the left and *messieurs* Sununu and Brady on the right.

THE ADVICE
OF CENTRAL INTELLIGENCE

As earlier noted, Schlesinger was the first secretary of energy to invest energy policy with the trappings of exaggerated gravity bestowed by a finding of the intelligence community. Probably unaware of his antecedent's controversial act, Watkins sought what in the trade is known as a national intelligence estimate (NIE) for NES. NIEs are developed under the direction of the CIA, with the participation of staffs from the entire intelligence community. NIEs are usually classified at levels of "secret" or higher, depending on the subject matter. NIE 3-90, titled "The Global Energy Environment into the Next Century," was completed, as the label indicates, in March 1990. Watkins was so well satisfied by the effort that he requested a nonclassified version of the NIE so that the findings could be more widely circulated. Because NIEs cannot, in fact be declassified, he was in June 1990 provided with an "Intelligence Community View" of worldwide energy conditions and projections, including geopolitical judgments on energy policy.[95]

The intelligence community's world energy outlook was summarized in four paragraphs, reproduced verbatim below.

- Oil will remain the dominant energy fuel. Oil prices will rise but will not repeat the dramatic price swings of the last two decades.
- Heavy reliance on Persian Gulf oil will continue, rising to about 30% of total world supply in 2000, as compared with 18% in 1985.

- Supplies will be adequate to meet increasing demand. The major oil disruptions of the 1970s are unlikely to be repeated in part because of the rising financial stake of Persian Gulf producers in Western economies.
- Environmental concerns will increasingly shape national policies in the decade ahead, but—because of long lead-times—these policies will have little impact on world energy markets before the year 2000.

The community's key findings were supported by less than two pages of additional text. The authors thought that moderate growth in energy consumption and in oil and energy prices would be experienced in the decade of the 1990s and that environmental concerns and new technology would begin to reshape world energy markets toward the end of the decade. They estimated that the Persian Gulf would supply about one-third of the world's oil by 2000 when consumption would rise by about 7 MMB/D—presumably from 1989 levels, though the intelligence community baseline was not specified in the transmittal to DOE.[96]

A finding of special interest to DOE indicated that "...projected energy trends are adequate to support economic growth...but will also imply a reduction in surplus oil production capacity, a key element of energy security."[97] Watkins was soon to learn how important a role surplus production capacity was to play in confronting the economic consequences of the Iraqi war. But in June of 1990 neither he nor the policy staff appreciated the full dimensions of this issue.

"U.S. oil imports," the community advised, "are expected to rise sharply over the decade [of the 1990s], and the U.S. oil and gas import bill could roughly double from 1 to 2% of GNP by the year 2000." The rise in U.S. oil imports could, the community concluded, "erode U.S. energy security."[98] These findings were appreciated by Deputy Secretary Moore who considered nearly irresponsible the position of CEA that oil import levels and costs were of no particular significance to the economy.

The community's further—rather conventional—view was that worldwide population growth, industrialization, and urbanization would drive demand for more energy and that by the year 2000, developing nations and former communist countries might account for 50% of total world energy consumption. All of these factors and trends, the community concluded, "will make efforts to curb global pollution and carbon dioxide emissions increasingly difficult."[99] In sum, the opinion of the intelligence community, however wide of the mark its projections of future energy demand proved to be, constituted broad support for the DOE and NSC view of the energy world, but carried little political weight within EPC.

Taking stock

By the end of July 1990, Stuntz believed that a coherent puzzle might emerge from the myriad NES component elements. Within DOE she held undisputed domain over policy. Her relations with Watkins and Moore were excellent, as was her interaction with Richard Schmalensee, a key member of the Troika. Unlike many of her predecessors, she had earned the loyalty as well as the respect of the policy staff by sheer weight of knowledge. She continued to be wary, with reason, about the policy staff's own agenda, but was confident of their ability to protect her interests and the interests of the secretary in the interagency process.[100]

Deputy Secretary Moore also seemed satisfied with matters as they stood in mid-1990. As a former congressman with highly tuned political instincts, he was gratified by the breadth of the consultations that had taken place for NES. He saw the NES process as populist, democratic and inclusive. NES was generating national attention to an important policymaking task and concurrently providing documented expressions of the public will that, if not always congenial, could do no harm to the expected future interactions between DOE and Congress.[101]

Moore regularly sought appropriate and legal means to provide access to the NES development process for key constituencies. He established an informal industry roundtable, with membership from virtually all energy-related trade groups in the Washington area, in order to essentially preview the lobbying effort that would take place when NES would reach its legislative stage. He met regularly with this group, exchanging views on subjects of common interest, exploring reactions to what the administration might stand for on particular issues, offering status reports on NES and an opportunity to comment on the results of the options analyses. He scrupulously avoided any commitments on substance and never sought to influence NES analyses on behalf of constituent groups.

Moore also sought greater visibility—and potential future benefit—for DOE in the senior councils of the Bush administration by actively participating in the so-called Deputies' Group. The group, made up of the cabinet's deputy secretaries, met weekly to consider and offer judgment on any policy manner destined for cabinet consideration. He thought the Deputies' Group might prove useful during prospective final deliberations on NES, but the group never became involved.

With what appeared to be a wide range of external advice in hand, DOE policy staff was in late July about to turn its entire attention to the task of analyzing NES options. Then, suddenly and unexpectedly, the Middle East erupted in conflict over nothing more—and nothing less— than the price of oil. On August 2, 1990, Saddam Hussein of Iraq launched his army to the rape of Kuwait.

NOTES AND COMMENTS

1. Commenting on his relations with the cabinet, Secretary Watkins provided the following retrospective to Dr. Benjamin Franklin Cooling, chief historian, Department of Energy, On June 8, 1993:

> I had support from Reilly (Environmental Protection Agency), support from Skinner, who was then Secretary of Transportation; I had support from Bob Mosbacher, who was Secretary of Commerce; I had no support from the Defense Department, but they weren't that heavily involved (in the NES). Jim Baker, Secretary of State, had excluded himself from all oil and gas matters and basically stayed out of the energy business altogether. So, Secretary of Treasury Nick Brady, Chief of Staff John Sununu, Director of OMB Dick Darman, and Roger Porter, Domestic Policy Adviser to the President, were the primary naysayers

It should be noted that the support of Transportation Secretary Skinner was secured by an agreement to eliminate from NES consideration proposals aimed at ensuring higher fuel efficiency (CAFE) standards for automobiles. CAFE standards are established by the National Highway Traffic Safety Administration, an agency of the Transportation Department. Watkins did not recall, in the Cooling interview, that Mosbacher was also recused from energy policy decisions because of his previous private holdings in energy companies.

2. Secretary Watkins reviewed the contents of the initial drafts of this chapter on June 15-17th 1994, and reviewed more advanced drafts again from January 19 to February 28, 2001. He confirmed the accuracy of the views and statements attributed to him, with clarifications as to his interactions with EPC and with OMB, that were subsequently, in part, incorporated in the text. Secretary Watkins felt that, from the

retrospective of February 2001, the interagency battles at staff level were in the end inconsequential to the final crafting of NES. Secretary Watkins was requested to specifically attest to the accuracy of the exchange which took place during the course of the June 8, 1990, meeting with White House Chief of Staff John Sununu, which he did.

3. Deputy Secretary Linda Stuntz reviewed the contents of chapter 2 in May and June 1994 and on June 17 attested to the accuracy of the views attributed to her, with some clarifications which were subsequently incorporated in the text. She reviewed more advanced drafts of the chapter in the period between January 19 and February 28, 2001, and provided additional comments that were, to the extent possible, incorporated in the final version of the text.

4. Deputy Secretary W. Henson Moore initially reviewed the contents of chapter 2 in June 1994 and attested on June 13 to the accuracy of the views attributed to him, with some clarifications which were, to the extent possible, subsequently incorporated in the text. He reviewed more advanced drafts of the chapter in the period between January 19 and February 2001, and provided further, minor comments, which were incorporated in the final version of the text.

5. The Interim Report policy initiatives were proposed and championed principally by C. Michael Davis, assistant secretary for Conservation and Renewable Energy, but also by the policy staff. Linda Stuntz doubted the wisdom of proposing the initiatives, but loyally (if reluctantly) sought EPC approval once they were adopted by Watkins.

6. Analysis of energy security policy options was carried out under the joint direction of David Doane and Carmen Difiglio. The environmental analysis group was led by Edward (Ted) Williams and his deputy, David Moses. Analysis of electricity policy options was directed initially by David Meyer and subsequently by Kevin Kelly. The research and development policy options analysis was carried out under the leadership of Robert Marlay. Cherry Langenfeld led the team

responsible for technology transfer issues. Abraham Haspel oversaw economic analysis and all NES modeling. These individuals were all senior officers in the DOE Office of Policy, Planning and Analysis.

7. Researchers (and affiliations) who contributed to the inter-laboratory white paper, "Energy and Climate Change"

Eugene Aronson	Sandia National Laboratories
David Barns	Battelle Pacific Northwest Laboratory
Sumner Barr	Los Alamos National Laboratory
Cary Bloyd	Argonne National Laboratory
Dale Bruns	Idaho National Engineering Laboratory
Robert Cushman	Oak Ridge National Laboratory
Roy Darwin	Battelle Pacific Northwest Laboratory
Donald DeAngelis	Oak Ridge National Laboratory
Michael Edenburn	Sandia National Laboratories
Jae Edmonds	Battelle Pacific Northwest Laboratory
William Emanuel	Oak Ridge National Laboratory
Dennis Engi	Sandia National Laboratories
Michael Farrell	Oak Ridge National Laboratory
Jeremy Hales	Battelle Pacific Northwest Laboratory
Edward Hillsman	Oak Ridge National Laboratory
Carolyn Hunsaker	Oak Ridge National Laboratory
Anthony King	Oak Ridge National Laboratory
Albert Liebetrau	Battelle Pacific Northwest Laboratory
Michael MacCracken	Lawrence Livermore National Laboratory
Bernard Manowitz	Brookhaven National Laboratory
Gregg Marland	Oak Ridge National Laboratory
Sean McDonald	Battelle Pacific Northwest Laboratory
Joyce Penner	Lawrence Livermore National Laboratory
Steve Rayner	Oak Ridge National Laboratory
Norman Rosenberg	Resources for the Future
Michael Scott	Battelle Pacific Northwest Laboratory
Meyer Steinberg	Brookhaven National Laboratory
Walter Westman	Lawrence Berkeley Laboratory
Donald Wuebbles	Lawrence Livermore National Laboratory
Gary Yohe	Wesleyan University, Sigma Xi.

8. Researchers (and affiliations) who contributed to the inter-laboratory white paper, *Energy Efficiency: How Far Can We Go?*

J. U. Anderson	Idaho National Engineering Laboratory
D. Belzer	Pacific Northwest Laboratory
M. A. Brown	Oak Ridge National Laboratory
R. S. Carlsmith	Oak Ridge National Laboratory
P. Chan	Lawrence Berkeley Laboratory
W. U. Changer	Pacific Northwest Laboratory
J. Eto	Lawrence Berkeley Laboratory
E. Fleischman	Idaho National Engineering Laboratory
B. Garrett-Price	Pacific Northwest Laboratory
E. Hirst	Oak Ridge National Laboratory
L. Johnson	Argonne National Laboratory
J. Koomey	Lawrence Berkeley Laboratory
J. E. McMcMahon	Lawrence Berkeley Laboratory
M. Miller-Mintz	Argonne National Laboratory
D. B. Perman	Lawrence Berkeley Laboratory
A. :M. Perry	Oak Ridge National Laboratory
J. Rajan	Argonne National Laboratory
D. J. Santini	Argonne National Laboratory
S. M. Sorensen	Idaho National Engineering Laboratory
K. H. Vaughan	Oak Ridge National Laboratory
A. Vyas	Argonne National Laboratory
J. Weyand	Idaho National Engineering Laboratory
K. H. Zimmerman	Oak Ridge National Laboratory

9. Researchers (and affiliations) who contributed to the inter-laboratory white paper, The Potential of Renewable Energy

Richard Benson	Los Alamos National Laboratory
Michael Berger	Los Alamos National Laboratory
Desikan Bharathan	Solar Energy Research Institute
Eldon Boes	Sandia National Laboratories
Donald Brown	Los Alamos National Laboratory
Stanley Bull	Solar Energy Research Institute
Lynn Coles	Solar Energy Research Institute

Henry Dodd	Sandia National Laboratories
Virgil Dugan	Sandia National Laboratories
Robert Drake	Los Alamos National Laboratory
William Fulkerson	Oak Ridge National Laboratory
Bimleshwar Gupta	Solar Energy Research Institute
William Hoagland	Solar Energy Research Institute
Susan Hock	Solar Energy Research Institute
David Hudson	Solar Energy Research Institute
William Marshall	Sandia National Laboratories
Robert McConnell	Solar Energy Research Institute
Marty Murphy	Solar Energy Research Institute
Robert Noun	Solar Energy Research Institute
Jack Ranney	Oak Ridge National Laboratory
Joel Renner	Idaho National Engineering Laboratory
Carol Riordan	Solar Energy Research Institute
Tom Rizy	Oak Ridge National Laboratory
Fred Roach	Los Alamos National Laboratory
Donald Schueler	Sandia National Laboratories
Walter Short	Solar Energy Research Institute
Garold Sommers	Idaho National Engineering Laboratory
Don Stevens	Solar Energy Research Institute
Susan Stiger	Idaho National Engineering Laboratory
Tom Surek	Solar Energy Research Institute
Blair Swezey	Solar Energy Research Institute
Robert Thresher	Solar Energy Research Institute
Robert VanHook	Oak Ridge National Laboratory
Carl Wallace	Solar Energy Research Institute
Lynn Wright	Oak Ridge National Laboratory
Federica Zangrando	Solar Energy Research Institute
Kenneth Zweibel	Solar Energy Research Institute

10. Researchers (and affiliations) who contributed to the inter-laboratory white paper, Energy Technology for Developing Countries

Bill Buehring	Argonne National Laboratory
Dick Cirillo	Argonne National Laboratory
Duane Deonigi	Battelle Pacific Northwest Laboratory
Bill Fulkerson	Oak Ridge National Laboratory
Don Grether	Lawrence Berkeley Laboratory
Wayne Hardie	Los Alamos National Laboratory
Gary Jones	Sandi National Laboratory
Mark Levine	Lawrence Berkeley Laboratory
Steve Meyers	Lawrence Berkeley Laboratory
Bob Noun	Solar Energy Research Institute
Jayant Sathaye	Lawrence Berkeley Laboratory
Carole Szpunar	Argonne National Laboratory
Tom Wilbanks	Oak Ridge National Laboratory

REFERENCES AND CITATIONS

[1] DOE NEWS, "First Phase Completed in Development of National Energy Strategy," April 2, 1990.

[2] Associated Press appearing in *The Chicago Tribune*, April 3, 1990, p. 9.

[3] Timothy A. Worth, *USA Today*, April 3, 1990.

[4] John Dillin, *The Christian Science Monitor*, April 3, 1990, p. 1.

[5] Anne Reifenberg, *The Dallas Morning News*, April 3, 1990.

[6] CNN-TV, *The World Today*, April 2, 1990, 6:00 p.m.

[7] Telephonic communication from Todd Buckholtz, deputy executive secretary of EPC to Stagliano, April 4, 1990.

[8] Post-mortem assessment of release of the Interim Report by Stuntz, Moore, Gault and Stagliano.

[9] Personal communications from Admiral Watkins to the author, March 1994, December 2000, January 2001.

[10] DOE, SEAB, "Summary of Discussion on Interim Report, National Energy Strategy," May 2, 1990.

[11] Ibid.

[12] Bruce L.R. Smith, *The Advisers: Scientists in the Policy Process*. (Washington, DC: Brookings Institution, 1992), p. 117.

[13] Post-mortem discussions of SEAB report between Stagliano, Marley, Stuntz, Moore and Peter Saba, the counselor to Moore, in the week following receipt of the report.

[14] DOE, SEAB, op. cit.

[15] Post-mortem discussions of SEAB reports by Stuntz et al.

[16] Ibid.

[17] Ibid.

[18] DOE, "National Energy Strategy Draft List of Candidate NES Options and Points of Contact," December 21, 1990.

[19] Linda G. Stuntz, DOE, deputy undersecretary, Policy, Planning and Analysis, Memorandum for Economic Policy Council, NES Sub-Group Staff, Subject: NES, May 17, 1990.

[20] Ray Squitieri (U.S. Treasury Department), Memorandum to Bob Marlay (DOE), June 1, 1990.

[21] Richard Schmalensee, CEA, Executive Office of the President, Memorandum for the Honorable Linda G. Stuntz, deputy-under secretary, Policy, Planning and Analysis, DOE, Subject: Comments on the Materials Distributed at the EPC NES Staff Meeting, Washington, DC, June 5, 1990.

[22] Richard L. Schmalensee. Personal communication, March 14, 1994.

[23] Ibid

[24] James D. Watkins, admiral, U.S. Navy (Retired). Personal communication, March 1, 1994.

[25] James D. Watkins, admiral, U.S. Navy (Retired), Talking Points, "Meeting with Gov. Sununu on NES," June 8, 1990.

[26] Personal communications with Watkins and Schmalensee, op. cit., and W. Henson Moore. Personal communication, March 19, 1994.

[27] James D. Watkins, admiral (U.S. Navy, Retired). Debriefing with Linda G. Stuntz and Stagliano after meeting with Governor Sununu.

[28] Schmalensee, Personal communication, op. cit.

[29] Watkins and Moore, Personal communications, op. cit.

[30] OBRA '90 contained the following energy tax preferences: Extension of the 10% tax credit for investments in solar, geothermal and ocean thermal projects; modification of intangible drilling costs; amortization treatment for purposes of Alternative Minimum Tax obligations, from ten year to five years; extension of the 20% research tax credit; extension of Section 29 tax credits for unconventional gas production; and other minor adjustments to the tax code.

[31] In 1986, at OMB's request, DOE policy office launched a study of federal subsidies to PMAs with a view to restructuring the federal debt carried by the PMAs at interest below market rates. Members of Congress from the Pacific Northwest, which is served by the BPA, succeeded in introducing language in a bill of appropriations of funds barring DOE from acting upon or studying this issue. The Congress, for good measure, drastically reduced the analytical budget of DOE's policy office, as a signal that PMA issues should be off-limits for policy reform purposes.

[32] Linda G. Stuntz, deputy undersecretary, Policy, Planning and Analysis, DOE. Memorandum for: EPC Working Group on the National Energy Strategy, Subject: NES, with three attachments, July 3, 1990; and Linda G. Stuntz, deputy undersecretary, Policy, Planning and Analysis. Memorandum for EPC Working Group, Subject: NES Analytical Plan, with attachment, July 9, 1990.

[33] Ibid.

[34] Stuntz, attachment to July 3, 1990, memorandum, op. cit.

[35] Ibid.

[36] Stuntz, attachment to July 9, 1990, memorandum, op. cit.

[37] Ibid.

[38] Stuntz, attachment to July 3, 1990, memorandum, op. cit.

[39] Ibid.

[40] OPEC recaptured control of the petroleum market in 2000, as predicted by NES, in the wake of Clinton administration policy inaction on the oil supply and demand front.

[41] Btu: British thermal unit, a common measure of the heat content of hydrocarbons.

[42] OMB, Executive Office of the President, Circular No. A-94, Revised, to the heads of executive departments and establishments, Subject: Discount rates to be used in evaluating time-distributed costs and benefits, March 27, 1972, with 2-page addendum dated July 17, 1990.

[43] Communications between the author and DOE staff under his supervision.

[44] Watkins, Personal communication, op. cit.

[45] DOE, "National Energy Strategy Option Papers." Draft papers, dated between November 1990 to January 1991.

[46] Personal communications—Watkins to Stagliano.

[47] DOE, NES Option Papers, Amendment to the Public Utility Holding Company Act (PUHCA), December 3, 1990.

[48] Ibid.

[49] For a list of the coalitions that supported and opposed PUHCA reform, and for an in-depth treatise of PUHCA reform, see *Analysis of Options to Amend the Public Utility Holding Company Act of 1935: National Energy Strategy: Technical Annex 1*, DOE/S-0084P. Washington, DC, DOE, First edition, 1991/1992.

[50] DOE, NES Option Papers, PUHCA, op. cit.

[51] Because of congressional prohibitions on the issue, all data on PMAs was generated by OMB and transmitted to DOE on the presumption that the estimates would be neither questioned nor recalculated by DOE policy staff.

[52] OSHA: Federal Occupational Safety & Health Administration

[53] Ken Glozer, deputy associate director for NRES Special Studies, Executive Office of the President, OMB, Memorandum for Linda Stuntz, deputy undersecretary for Policy, Planning and Analysis, DOE, Subject: Comments on the Energy Efficiency Laboratory White Paper, June 20, 1990.

[54] Lawrence Livermore National Laboratory, Chair, *Energy and Climate Change: Report of the DOE Multi-Laboratory Climate Change Committee.* (Chelsea, Michigan: Lewis Publishers, 1990), p. 144.

[55] U.S. Congress, legislative calendar, 101st Congress, Committee on Energy and Natural Resources, United States Senate, December 31, 1990.

[56] Linda G. Stuntz, Testimony before the Senate Energy and Natural Resources Committee on S. 234, National Energy Policy Act of 1990, April 5, 1990.

[57] See note 7 for list of participating researchers.

[58] *Energy and Climate Change*, op. cit., p. v.

[59] Ibid., p. ix.

[60] Ibid., p. 6.

[61] Ibid., p. ix.

[62] Ibid., emphasis added.

[63] Ibid., p. x.

[64] Ibid., p. 145.

[65] See note 8 for complete list of researchers.

[66] Oak Ridge National Laboratory (ORNL), *Energy Efficiency: How Far Can We Go?*, ORNL/TM-11441. Prepared under contract DE-AC05-84OR21400 for the U.S. DOE, Office of Policy, Planning and Analysis. (Oak Ridge, TN: ORNL, January 1990), p. 2.

[67] Ibid.

[68] Ibid., p. 3.

[69] Ibid., p. 25.

[70] Ibid.

[71] Ibid., p. 38.

[72] Ibid.

[73] Later renamed National Renewable Energy Laboratory.

[74] See note 9 for list of participating researchers.

[75] Solar Energy Research Institute, et al. *The Potential of Renewable Energy: An Inter-laboratory White Paper*, SERI/TP-260-3674, DE90000322. Prepared under contract DE-AC02-83CH10093 for DOE, Office of Policy, Planning and Analysis, March 1990, p. viii.

[76] Ibid., pp. ix and 35.

[77] Ibid., p. 30.

[78] Ibid., p. 31.

[79] A. Myrick Freeman, *The Measurement of Environmental and Resource Values: Theory and Practice*, RFF/Johns Hopkins University Press, 1983.

[80] V. Kerry Smith & John Krutillo, *Technical Change: Relative Prices and Environmental Resource Evaluation*, RFF/Johns Hopkins University Press, 1974.

[81] Raymond Kopp & V. Kerry Smith, *Valuing Natural Assets: The Economics of Natural Resources Damage Assessment*, RFF/Johns Hopkins University Press, 1983.

[82] SERI: *The Potential of Renewable Energy*, OpCit.

[83] Ibid.

[84] Ibid.

[85] Ibid.

[86] D.E. Deonigi, N. L. Moore, S. A. Smith, and R. L. Watts of Pacific Northwest Laboratory; M. A. Brown of Oak Ridge National Laboratory; and R. J. Noun of Solar Energy Research Institute.

[87] Pacific Northwest Laboratory, team leader, *The Technology Transfer Process: Background for the U.S. National Energy Strategy*, PNL-SA-17482. Prepared under contract DE-AC06-76RLO 1830 for DOE, January 1990, p. iv.

[88] Los Alamos National Laboratory, et al., "Analysis of Technology Transfer in the DOE Laboratories," final draft form. Los Alamos, NM, December 22,1989.

[89] Ibid., Executive Summary, p. 1.

[90] Ibid., pp. 2-5.

[91] See note 10 for list of participating researchers.

[92] Lawrence Berkeley Laboratory et al., *Energy Technology for Developing Countries: Issues for the U.S. National Energy Strategy*, LBL-28407, UC-400. Prepared under contract DE-AC03-76SF00098 for DOE, December 1989, pp. 1-3.

[93] Ibid., pp. 3-4.

[94] Ibid., p. 3.

[95] National Intelligence Council, Office of the Director of Central Intelligence, "Intelligence Community View: The World Energy Outlook". Mimeo, June 5, 1990.

[96] Ibid., p. 2.

[97] Ibid., p. 2.

[98] Ibid., pp. 2, 3.

[99] Ibid., p. 3.

[100] Personal communications. Stuntz to Stagliano, weekly status review of NES development.

[101] Personal communications. Ex post facto evaluation of the NES process, in discussions between Moore and Stagliano that took place over several years from 1994 onward.

CHAPTER FOUR

SADDAM HUSSEIN LENDS A HAND

THE U.S. OIL EMBARGO OF 1990

The 1990 occupation of Kuwait by the armed forces of Iraq gave purpose to the politically sterile administration of George Bush. Within the administration, one could sense from the early hours of the crisis that the president would seize the opportunity to display the talent and experience of a lifetime in the single field of policy he could truly call his own. The administration was galvanized by the Iraqi aggression, leaving little doubt that the United States would come to the aid of Kuwait, one of the Persian Gulf's most reactionary states. The irony of Bush's concern for the fate of the emirate was not lost on those willing to recall that the distinctly anti-American oil embargo of 1973 had been orchestrated in the city of Kuwait.

T. E. Lawrence thought, "Arabs believe in persons, not in institutions."[1] If so, one might wonder at the political psychology of a people who throughout their history have allowed themselves to be governed mostly by autocratic rulers. "Arab conflict proneness," the otherwise sympathetic Raphael Patai states in *The Arab Mind*, "is nowhere fraught with more dire consequences for the Arab nations than in the political arena."[2] The attempted destruction of Kuwait was merely the latest example of Arab statesmanship by violence.

Fate could not have provided to George Bush a more perfect enemy than Saddam Hussein. As chronicled by Sandra Mackay in *Passion and Politics*, Saddam's despotic political life began in 1959, at age twenty-two, when he participated in the unsuccessful attempt to assassinate Iraq's President Qasim. He escaped capture and returned briefly to life as a cadet at the Baghdad Military Academy, where a poor academic performance subsequently forced him to leave without credentials. This "shame" was later corrected by his self-appointment to the rank of lieutenant general in 1976 and field marshal in 1979.[3]

Saddam Hussein executed twenty-one members of his own ruling Revolutionary Command Council when he took absolute control of Iraq in 1979. He proceeded to acquire the title of "Butcher of Baghdad" for the brutality with which he oppressed Kurds and other minorities opposed to his rule. All this notwithstanding, he surfaced for a brief moment as an Arab folk hero, praised on Baghdad radio as "...the perfume of Iraq, its dates, its estuary of the two rivers, its coast and waters, its sword, its shield, the eagle whose grandeur dazzles the heavens."[4]

In *The Commanders*, Bob Woodward portrays the Bush administration in the early days of the Iraqi crisis as ready for action but initially unfocused. He describes the first post-invasion meeting of the National Security Council (NSC), on the morning of August 2, as follows: White House Chief of Staff Sununu suggests that the administration "...ought to try to stop Iraq from selling Kuwaiti oil on the open market and gaining an immediate benefit from the invasion."[5] To which, Defense Secretary Cheney replies that "...the marketing of oil could normally not be stopped with economic and political pressure."[6] Energy Secretary Watkins then proposes that, because Iraqi oil moved through pipelines in Saudi Arabia and Turkey, these "might present interesting opportunities as targets."[7]

The first post-invasion meeting at the White House took place in the Cabinet Room at 8:05 am on August 2 with the president presiding. Present at the meeting, though not a member of NSC, was Secretary Watkins, accompanied by Assistant Secretary John Easton.[8] Watkins was asked to address the energy implications of a possible strategy by Saddam to propel his army into northern Saudi Arabia. Such a push would dramatically change the world's petroleum supply equation because of the extensive production and refining capacity in the region.

Woodward's attribution to Watkins of the suggestion that the United States might consider attacking oil pipelines in Saudi Arabia to punish Iraq was entirely without foundation,[9] but indicative of what became recurrent attempts by unnamed White House officials to denigrate Watkin's reputation.

NSC had been closely monitoring events in the Persian Gulf since July 21, when satellite imagery indicated the presence of thirty thousand Iraqi troops at Kuwait's border.[10] The show of force had been insufficient for Saddam to obtain guarantees from Kuwait and the United Arab Emirates, at a meeting of OPEC ministers held in Geneva on July 27, to refrain from cheating on their oil production quotas. On July 30, U.S. satellite imagery showed that Iraq's forces at Kuwait's border had been increased to a credibly intimidating 100,000 heavily armored troops.[11]

At DOE, the Energy Emergency Management Team (EEMT), a staff group responsible for responding to energy-related crises of any kind, at home and abroad, was activated at 7:00 a.m. on August 2, 1990, six hours after Iraq's army crossed the Kuwaiti border. The EEMT's first task was to provide to DOE's leadership a factual assessment in real time of the invasion's energy implications. The salient points of the initial assessment, summarized below, were transmitted to Watkins and Moore on August 2, in the form of briefing material for the NSC meeting with the president later that morning.[12]

The Oil Situation Prior To August 1, 1990. During the first five months of 1990, U.S. petroleum imports from Iraq averaged 610,000 barrels per day (B/D), representing 8% of U.S. net imports and 3.6% of U.S. consumption. In the same period, the U.S. imported 120,000 B/D of oil from Kuwait. Prior to the invasion, oil consumption in the world's market economies was projected to be in the range of 51.8 to 52.5 million B/D and OPEC production was projected to range between 24.4 and 25.6 million B/D. Net OPEC exports were estimated at 20.2 to 21.4 million B/D. Persian Gulf oil production was projected to be 15.9 to 17.1 million B/D, including 2.6 million B/D of within-region consumption. Net exports from the Gulf region were estimated at 13.4 to 14.5 million B/D. Excess world production capacity was estimated at 5.0 million B/D, with 1.0 to 1.5 million B/D of that capacity outside the Persian Gulf.

Oil Situation on August 2, 1990. Kuwait production losses could total 1.55 million B/D. Exports from Iraq were likely to be disrupted at a level of 3.50 million B/D. Several means would be available to offset a disruption of this size:

- use of worldwide excess production capacity of 4.0 million B/D, exclusive of Iraq/Kuwait, including 1.0 to 1.5 million B/D outside the Persian Gulf
- release into the market of U.S. strategic reserves of 589 million barrels
- a coordinated drawdown of government controlled stocks in member states of the International Energy Agency (IEA), totaling over one billion barrels[13]

- switching from oil to other fuels, especially in electricity generation and industry where installed fuel-switching capacity exceeded 0.5 million B/D
- use of world commercial stocks of 391.9 million barrels, or 92.0 million barrels above minimum operating inventory

Pursuant to this assessment, DOE issued a statement to the media on the afternoon of August 2, 1990, indicating that "...uncertainties in the Middle East pose no immediate threat to the supply of petroleum products for American consumers, nor do they *necessitate* (emphasis added) increases in prices for American consumers."[14] On the same day, the White House issued an executive order freezing Iraqi and Kuwaiti assets in the United States and embargoing imports and exports of goods and services from both states. The executive order became effective at 5:01 am, EST, August 2, 1990.[15]

The executive order had been issued without DOE concurrence. DOE consequently sought clarification from the Treasury Department as to the effect of the order on the 40 million barrels of Iraqi and Kuwaiti oil that DOE estimated to be in tankers on the high seas. DOE pointed out that exclusion from the embargo of ship-loaded oil would provide a highly desirable near-term supply cushion to the market. Initially averse to making exceptions, the Treasury Department finally agreed to permit the importation of oil on the high seas, which had been purchased by contract before August 2, but under three conditions:[16]

1. The oil was loaded prior to the effective date of the embargo (05:01 hours, EDT, August 2, 1990), intended for ultimate delivery to the U.S.;
2. The bill of lading was issued prior to the embargo's effective date, and
3. Provided that any balance not yet paid to Iraq or Kuwait for the shipment be paid into a blocked account in the U.S.

With this clarification settled, the Treasury Department on August 3, 1990—barely thirty-five hours after Kuwait's invasion—issued rules to carry out the president's executive order.[17] By August 8, the first squadron of American fighter jets was in Saudi Arabia.[18] The Bush administration proved, in sum, exceptionally agile in its military and diplomatic response to the invasion of Kuwait. It would prove less skillful in responding to the domestic consequences of its Gulf war policy.

The role of the DOE

Deputy Secretary Moore was in charge of DOE for most of the month of August. Watkins was at his cabin in Canada, but in close touch with events in Washington. Among Moore's immediate tasks was the need to enhance the previously correct but cool working relations between DOE and NSC so that DOE could claim a seat in a cabinet council in which power and influence were newly realigned by the Iraqi assault. Not formally a member of NSC, Watkins had found few occasions to interact with Scowcroft, in whose domain the policy action now resided. Moore seized the opportunity presented by his participation in White House meetings on the Iraqi crisis to ensure a substantive role for DOE in all NSC deliberations on Iraq. As a consequence, DOE's views on the energy implications of the crisis were regularly brought to the attention of Scowcroft who ensured that Moore's (and DOE's) concerns were heard.[19]

Moore attended his first NSC meeting on August 3, 1990. He provided a summary of oil market conditions as well as a list of steps he thought NSC should consider in the wake of the President's oil embargo. These next steps were intended to consolidate and make effective the initial, unilateral actions taken by the U.S. government. The DOE recommendations were:

- Secure a multilateral (United Nations) embargo of Iraqi oil
- request that Saudi Arabia and Turkey shut down the two critical pipelines by which Iraq exported most of its oil
- encourage increased production from countries with excess capacity
- draw down and sell crude oil held in the SPR
- reduce oil consumption through conservation and fuel switching.[20]

The issue of whether or not the United States should proceed with the use of its strategic oil stocks did not represent a consensus view within DOE.

Policy chief Linda Stuntz recommended the use of the SPR as soon as it became clear that the president would impose an oil embargo. She argued that the embargo's elimination from the market of roughly 4.3 million barrels of oil—the combined Iraqi and Kuwaiti production—represented the largest disruption of the international oil market in the previous thirty-five years.[21] If the SPR would not be brought to bear under these circumstances, she asked, when would it then be used?

John Easton, assistant energy secretary for International Affairs, initially opposed the SPR drawdown proposal on the grounds that no actual disruption of U.S. imports had yet occurred. Moore was ambivalent about an immediate recommendation to the president to employ what effectively constituted the most potent weapon in the market economies' oil emergency arsenal. He decided, in the end, that there was no harm in placing the SPR on the table as an option for NSC to consider, without necessarily making it—as the law requires—a direct recommendation from the secretary of energy to the president.

In any case, Moore's immediate task—one that would have implications for the NES—was to ensure that the cabinet fully appreciated the energy policy implications of the new status quo in the Persian Gulf. The key judgments on the new reality, drafted by EEMT staff and presented by Moore to NSC, were contained in this text:

> While the market is nervous and prices have moved upward, there is sufficient excess oil production capacity both in the Gulf and elsewhere to more than offset any continuing loss of Kuwaiti oil production. If that excess capacity can be mobilized, there will be little or no lasting effect on world oil prices. However, Iraq will almost surely view any offsetting production increases in the region as contrary to its national interests. With massive military build-ups in striking distance, chances are that the other major Middle Eastern oil producers, especially Saudi Arabia and the United Arab Emirates, will be hesitant to make use of their excess capacity.

The long-term implications of such a scenario are very significant. Iraq would be in a position to achieve through military threats what OPEC has been notoriously unable to accomplish voluntarily. Production could be held in check and world crude oil prices could rise substantially above pre-war levels. Indeed, from Iraq's point of view, having eliminated serious overproduction problems within OPEC, the only remaining constraint would be non-OPEC supply, e.g. the ability of non-OPEC producers to react to higher oil prices by developing new sources of supply. This is a much-feared force that has driven earlier OPEC production from some 31 million B/D in 1979 to some 16 million B/D just a few years later.

Whether Iraq would or would not use its power to raise crude oil prices is an open question. Since OPEC's inception Iraq has been one of the price hawks and it is known to have recently advocated a target price of $25 per barrel. Indeed, the last ministerial OPEC meeting, held under the threat of force, had already brought on a realignment of quotas aimed at raising prices.[22]

DOE staff were especially concerned about the behavior of Saudi Arabia, Iran, and the United Arab Emirates, which together accounted for most of the world's excess production capacity. Would these nations use the U.S.-United Nations (UN) embargo and Iraqi threats as cover to raise the posted price of OPEC oil? Would they once again reap from a political crisis in their own region the unearned income they had realized from the two previous major oil disruptions? Or would they risk the opprobrium of Arab radicals—cheerleaders of Saddam's "conquest"—by bringing excess production capacity on-line and thereby moderate the embargo's impact on Western economies?

The answer to these questions was bound to shape the energy security posture that the Bush administration would adopt for the Iraqi crisis and for the NES. The impact of events in the Persian Gulf on NES was foremost on the minds of DOE policy staff. The staff recognized from the outset that the

United States was going to experience a variation of the 1973 and 1979 energy crises, with all the political repercussions associated with those events. The question was whether the federal establishment—the executive branch and Congress—had fully absorbed the lessons of the 1970s about managing convulsions in the oil market.

Gearing up for war

By the end of the first week of the Iraqi crisis DOE was essentially on a war footing. As a first priority, Moore directed Easton to intensify consultations with other members of the IEA for the dual purpose of coordinating response measures and preparing the ground for a possible drawdown of strategic stocks held by member-states. Second, he requested from EIA Administrator Cal Kent a daily report on all aspects of the oil market, including size and movement of commercial stocks of gasoline, fuel oil, and especially propane—the chronically problematic winter heating fuel. Third, he directed Stuntz to design policy response measures that would be viewed as interim steps to the eventual use of the SPR.

Moore also directed DOE General Counsel Stephen Wakefield to review existing statutory authority to manage energy crises. Not incidentally, Wakefield discovered in the process that authority to draw down the SPR would expire in September 1990unless reauthorized by Congress. Finally, EEMT was directed to devise and conduct a series of tests simulating oil market disruption scenarios of increasing severity, including one simulating a shutdown of Saudi Arabia's entire oil production. The Saudi worst-case scenario was by no means alarmist because until late August it was not at all clear that the Iraqi military drive would end at the Kuwaiti border.

On August 6, spot market crude prices reached \$28.73 per barrel, and regular, unleaded gasoline sold for \$1.18 per gallon.[23] This provoked charges of price gouging in the press and a strong reaction from Congressman John Dingell, chairman of the House Energy and Commerce Committee. In a letter to Janet Steiger, chair of the Federal Trade Commission, Dingell demanded a "description of what the (Commission) considers to be price gouging and what sanctions or penalties are companies or individuals subject to for violating these policies."[24] From Watkins, Dingell concurrently requested, on an ongoing basis, "a detailed assessment of the current supply and demand for crude oil and refined petroleum products."[25]

The White House was prepared for the reactions of the general public and Congress. On the day that Dingell dispatched his letter, the White House announced that the Justice Department would "closely examine the causes of the increases that have occurred in the wake of the Iraqi invasion of Kuwait."[26] This was a surprising declaration from an administration that had repeatedly affirmed its devotion to market-driven economic policies, but the declaration went further. "We will look closely," the announcement stated, "for any indication that these increases may be the result of anti-competitive activity," which, if discovered, "will be met with vigorous antitrust prosecution."[27] The announcement quoted Moore as stating that while markets may be forgiven for reacting to uncertainty about future supplies, "the fact remains that oil stocks, at home and abroad, are at record high levels."[28] Transportation Secretary Sam Skinner also weighed in to "urge all transportation related companies not to overreact to events in the Middle East. I trust that they will act responsibly."[29]

The message was unambiguously received by the oil industry. On August 8, Chevron Chairman Kenneth Derr sent a wire to the president with assurances that his company "will and is exercising restraint in passing on sharply higher raw-material costs to its customers."[30] Similar declarations from other major oil companies followed. American Petroleum Institute President Charles DiBona, however, complained privately to Moore that the administration's jawboning was unwarranted.[31]

Immediate Response Measures

DOE policy staff approached with considerable trepidation the assignment by Moore to design measures aimed at mitigating the effects of the U.S.-imposed oil embargo. Many staff members had experienced the energy crisis of 1979—a few, the one of 1973—and knew that federal management of oil supply disruptions had a history of aggravating rather than improving conditions in the market. The staff assumed that the administration would not under any circumstances consider price controls as was done in 1973, even though statutory authority to do so remained available.[32] There seemed also to be no question of imposing gasoline rationing programs, such as those of 1979. Clearly the most effective response to the disruption was to allow oil prices to rise as necessary to induce a market-clearing demand response.

It was not, however, in the nature of DOE's leadership to defer entirely to markets the management of a crisis that reached unequivocally into the statutory domain of the secretary of energy. It was also not in the nature of Congress to permit a secretary of energy to remain unresponsive to consumer complaints about fuel price increases that seemed inconsistent with government assurances of adequate oil supplies. Moore and Stuntz, who were attuned to congressional currents, knew that most members of Congress would have little tolerance for sharp rises in fuel prices and that political pressure would mount for vigorous intervention.

The relatively sharp rise in the price of gasoline in early August was especially troublesome because it represented the most visible—in the wallet—domestic manifestation of Bush's Iraqi policy. Congress had made itself heard on the issue within hours of the oil embargo's declaration. Among many others, Representative Tom Tauke of Iowa, member of the House Energy and Commerce Committee, dispatched a letter to Watkins on August 3 warning: "The citizens of Iowa paid dearly during last winter, when propane prices tripled in December 1989. We cannot afford a repeat of those price increases for petroleum products such as gasoline."[33]

Thus, with the historical record as a warning and responsiveness to political direction as duty, the policy staff proceeded to craft a first set of measures that would above all do no harm, be viewed as evenhanded in their effects on supply and demand, and gain the approval of the ideologically vigilant EPC. Dubbed "immediate energy measures" and announced on August 15, 1990, after not too rough a treatment by EPC, the proposals seemed to satisfy Watkins' and Moore's activist mood. The measures were, however, immediately labeled as entirely inadequate by Washington's newly energized environmental community and ridiculed by the White House staff.

The immediate energy measures consisted of what Watkins termed common-sense steps that, however undramatically, were meant to raise public awareness about a market disruption of extraordinary size and unknown duration. At White House insistence, the measures could not be made to in any way appear alarmist, and could not be seen as imposing anything resembling federal requirements upon unwilling participants. The measures were as follows.[34]

Supply measures. To increase the availability of domestic supplies, DOE proposed to activate the modest excess production capacity available in the United States and facilitate fuel switching. First was a proposal to arbitrate a three-year-old regulatory conflict preventing the start of production of 75,000 B/D of oil from the Point Arguelo fields, operated by the Chevron Corporation off the Santa Barbara Coast in California. This matter pitted the county of Santa Barbara, which insisted that the oil be brought ashore by pipeline, against Chevron, which sought the cheaper solution of shipping the oil by tanker. Second was a request to oil producers in Alaska to "surge" production by 50,000 to 100,000 B/D. Third, the managers of the DOE-owned Naval Petroleum Reserve were directed to increase production by 5,000 B/D.

Next, a request was sent by DOE to state energy regulators in Texas, New Mexico, Kansas, Alabama, and Mississippi to raise allowable oil production from certain fields (such as Austin Chalk in Texas) by 20,000 B/D to 100,000 B/D. Finally, regulatory obstacles imposed by the Fuel Use Act were administratively removed, so that fuel switching by electric utilities and industry could proceed without government impedance. DOE estimated that switching from oil to natural gas wherever pipeline connections were available could produce immediate oil savings of 100,000 B/D or more. Finally, DOE sought surge production of ethanol which could be blended with gasoline and potentially offset an additional 10,000 B/D of oil.

DOE staff thought that modest but meaningful increases in domestic oil supplies could be rapidly achieved, as indeed they were but not entirely as foreseen. In a mid-August letter to Watkins, the chairman of the Board of Supervisors of Santa Barbara County declared that transportation by tanker of Point Arguello oil would not be allowed, and that the oil could reach on-shore refineries only if transported by pipeline.[35] Arbitration by DOE General Counsel Wakefield proved futile. Thus spoke California, America's largest consumer of oil.

On the positive side, ARCO Corporation notified Watkins on August 22, that Alaska North Slope production would be increased by 226,000 B/D for a ninety-day period.[36] On August 30, the Railroad Commission of Texas—the state's oil and gas production regulators—voted to increase allowable production by 20,000 B/D to 30,000 B/D.[37] None of the other oil producing states took action to increase allowable production, nor were they urged to do so by their delegations in Congress, who were clamoring for action on rising prices. Naval Petroleum Reserve production, however modest, was increased without incident.

Conservation measures. On the conservation front, DOE recommended maintenance of proper vehicle tire pressure, which could result in savings of up to 100,000 B/D; compliance with posted speed limits, which could result in savings of 50,000 B/D; the greater use of the more efficient of the multiple vehicles owned by American households, which could save up to 40,000 B/D; and higher levels of car- and van-pooling and use of public transit, with projected savings of at least 90,000 B/D. Watkins also vowed to seek greater conservation within the federal government, with possible oil savings of 10,000 B/D.

The Iraqi embargo provided the unexpected opportunity to test long-held theories of the crisis behavior of consumers towards energy conservation. The DOE conservation message was disseminated nationwide by radio and television with the assistance of the Advertising Council. As later reported by the General Accounting Office, DOE received $36.6 million worth of public service media announcements in the fourth quarter of 1990.[38] This not inconsequential investment produced very modest results—results indeed so meager that policy staff was forced to conclude that DOE's models contained serious flaws in assumptions of consumer response to voluntary conservation efforts.

DOE engineers could fairly precisely calculate the difference in fuel consumption of vehicles traveling at 55 or 60 miles per hour and its analysts could access data indicating that over half of American households owned two vehicles, one of which was on average 5 miles per gallon more efficient than the other. DOE could calculate that if just 20% of households would shift to driving the more efficient of the two vehicles, a minimum of 40,000 B/D of oil could be saved. DOE staff knew, as well, that improperly inflated tires negatively affected vehicles' fuel consumption and that correction of this all too typical condition could result in very substantial reductions of gasoline consumption. But this theoretical knowledge and these data could not account for what, in the end, would be individual consumer decisions and behavior.

Although the results of the conservation campaign proved disappointing, the experimentation provided fresh knowledge that would prove useful in the later debate on NES. Would the imposition of a gasoline tax on the order of the price increases engendered by the Iraqi crisis produce similar reductions in consumption? What effects would higher gasoline prices have on car- and van-pooling and use of public transit? The international dimensions of the embargo also provided lessons. The new evidence suggested that European nations—whose oil-disruption obligations to the IEA were equivalent to the imposition of mostly voluntary conservation measures—were far less burdened than nations that had paid the cost of strategic fuel stocks.

The immediate supply and demand measures were estimated to mitigate 455,000 B/D[39] of equivalent oil imports by December 1990. In Watkins' mind, these projected savings would help offset pre-war U.S. imports of Iraqi oil (610,000 B/D on average in the first five months of 1990) and Kuwaiti oil (120,000 B/D in the same period).[40] Watkins would not dwell on the well-known fact that the international oil market did not, in a crisis, allocate disrupted volumes in proportion to pre-disruption levels. Rather, he needed a target figure against which to plan a response and the pre-invasion oil import volumes from Kuwait and Iraq served the purpose.

On August 23, 1990, spot market prices for West Texas intermediate crude oil reached $31.67 per barrel.[41] In the congressional clamor that followed, Watkins turned again to policy staff for new initiatives to mitigate the consequences of the oil market disruption. Staff responded with a second set of proposals derived from the policy options under consideration for NES, with the understanding that these initiatives could preempt significant aspects of NES and that EPC would not take kindly to the effort. The available policy choices, however, were finite.

Unlike the generally non-intrusive, immediate measures that had been crafted entirely by the policy office, the development of medium-term initiatives brought the involvement of other DOE organizational elements. Assistant Secretary Davis, frustrated by the slow pace of NES development—and under fire from his special interests constituency for his failure to remedy the Reagan record on renewable energy and energy conservation—was especially keen on joining the quest for new policy initiatives that were likely to receive high public visibility.

The new measures were negotiated over a two-week period with the members of the Troika agencies, under the frequently obstructionist oversight of EPC Executive Secretary Olin Wethington. The proposals were then submitted to what became a fractious meeting of the cabinet on September 5, 1990. The cabinet finally agreed on fourteen initiatives. Some were new, others were variations of the immediate measures, and still others were a reiteration of administration proposals previously rejected by Congress. The "Administration's Medium Term Energy Measures"[42] that were announced on September 13 were grouped under the headings of energy efficiency, fuel switching, oil back-out and alternative fuels, and petroleum supply options. They were estimated to collectively reduce U.S. "reliance on oil imports" by 725,000 B/D over the period extending to December 1991. In summary form, the measures were:

- energy efficiency measures to encourage consumer use of lower octane gasoline
- tune-up and replacement of oil-burning equipment
- better and more energy efficient driving techniques
- electricity conservation
- industrial oil conservation
- federal government reduction in energy consumption.

Fuel switching, alternative fuels, and oil back-out measures included expedited approval by FERC of natural gas pipeline construction projects, minimization of oil-generated electricity, accelerated conversion of the federal fleet to alternative fuels, and expedited permitting of waste-to-energy plants. To increase supplies, the measures were to expedite issuance of federal permits for production of discovered but undeveloped fields around Alaska's Beaufort Sea, increase production of heavy oil in California,[43] provide tax incentives for domestic oil and gas exploration and production, and permit exploration of Alaska's ANWR.

EPC considered but rejected a number of other proposals. Three of these were proposed changes in tax policy (strongly opposed by the Treasury Department), aimed at increasing the percentage depletion allowance for oil producers using enhanced recovery methods; restructuring of federal tax treatment of renewable energy projects; and a ruling by the Internal Revenue Service to treat investments in energy conservation as tax free rebates from utilities to customers.

The Troika agencies opposed the tax proposals as too costly. Treasury calculated federal revenue losses from the tax measures at upward of $3 billion over five years—an estimate challenged by DOE as inflated, but impervious to change because Treasury's Office of Tax Policy could not be made to reveal the basis of its calculations. The Troika labeled the tax proposals a departure from the administration's market orientation on energy, which would lead to pressure for comparable incentives for other industries. Additionally, White House staff judged the tax initiatives as politically inadvisable because they would provide special benefits to energy businesses at a time when the general public was experiencing significantly higher fuel prices.[44]

Actually, the vast majority of the medium term measures, including those rejected by EPC, would have had little effect on the international oil market during the initial months of the Iraqi crisis. Proposals such as the tax credit for renewable energy, even if approved, would not—could not—alter the petroleum equation because renewable sources other than hydropower were insignificant to U.S. electricity generation. Similarly, taxation (or not) of utility rebates for conservation was a legitimate electricity policy matter but would not have affected the oil market.

However, EPC was castigated by the environmental community as ideologically biased because of what it *did* approve. Waste-to-energy plants, which EPC favored, would also have no impact on the oil market, and the ANWR policy was also of questionable value. As Schmalensee noted, "A decision to seek development of ANWR will not increase domestic production for 10-12 years and could detract attention from other measures."[45] EPC bias was especially evident in the disparity between the exhortatory nature of the conservation measures it supported and the backing (enforceable by regulation) provided to the supply measures. To further exacerbate political reactions to the measures, White House staff leaked to the media word of the dissentions within the Cabinet. "Some department (of Energy) officials hoped for a high-profile announcement of major energy conservation measures," reported the *Wall Street Journal,* "but the White House limited them to minor measures and refused to give the announcement a presidential push."[46]

The measures' results

The effects of DOE's immediate and medium-term measures were evaluated by EIA a few months after the end of the Iraqi war. EIA summarized its findings in a memorandum to the secretary as follows: "During the recent Gulf crisis, U.S. petroleum demand was 790,000 B/D below the level previously anticipated, while domestic crude oil and natural gas liquids production was 370,000 barrels per day above pre-crisis expectations."[47] Were these results connected to the response measures? The analytically interesting aspects of the results could be found in EIA's supporting analysis.

EIA estimated that 390,000 B/D of reduced demand was attributable to mild winter (1990/91) weather and slower economic activity. Higher oil prices caused demand reductions equal to 480,000 B/D. Between 80,000 B/D and 180,000 B/D of the demand reductions were offset by consumers' oil products stockpiling and by increased military demand. And, EIA concluded, "as much as 100,000 B/D in lower demand can be explained by unanticipated consumer behavior, including responses to the DOE short- and medium-term measures."[48]

The Strategic Petroleum Reserve (SPR) debate

By the end of August, it seemed apparent to analysts in and out of government that no policy initiative short of a drawdown of the SPR was likely to have a serious impact on the continually rising price of oil. The Troika staffs agreed with this view but refused to concede that the SPR should be used for the express purpose of mitigating the market price of oil. The Troika would consider a SPR drawdown only if it were demonstrated that the market was threatened by further actual physical shortages of oil—a position equivalent to the economic sophistry that had been practiced, disastrously, by the Nixon and Carter administrations.

Troika staffs knew that in the international oil market of 1990 it was impossible to demonstrate physical supply shortages except by the upward movement of prices. Visible shortages, such as rationed sales at gasoline stations, were a thing of the past. Troika staff insisted, in classic Catch-22 reasoning, that the upward movement of prices was a demonstration that the markets were working smoothly; in that case, releasing strategic stocks aimed at dampening prices would amount to unwarranted government intervention in the market. All of this was true, except for the political implications of government inaction as the consumer price index rose with the inflationary effect of sharply higher oil prices.

Stuntz believed that, the Troika position notwithstanding, the cabinet and the president could not long ignore the impact of rising fuel prices on congressional and public support for the administration's Iraqi policy. Consequently, she directed the policy staff to draft a formal recommendation from the secretary of energy to the president on a drawdown of strategic stocks to be carried out in coordination with IEA allies. The recommendation was based on DOE's judgment that a net supply shortfall of 2.4 million B/D of oil would become fully evident in the market in the third and fourth calendar quarters of 1990.

The net shortfall of supplies was derived from the calculations shown in Table 4-1.[49]

Although production increases were eventually greater than the levels indicated in DOE's estimates, DOE was acting on data available in August 1990 as to sustainable surge production. The probability that the entire volume of oil disrupted by the embargo would be covered by incremental production at some point in time, did not, in DOE's view, alter the supply shortfall internalized through sharply higher prices by the market in the wake of the embargo. Future incremental production was uncertain, of course, but it would not in any case alter near-term or spot market contracts.

Gross disruption size:	4.3 million barrels/day (MMB/D)
Plus incremental military demand:	0.2 MMB/D
Gross disruption size:	**4.5 MMB/D**
Less increased production from:	
Saudi Arabia	1.2 MMB/D
United Arab Emirates	0.2 "
Venezuela	0.2 "
Iran	0.2 "
United States	0.1 "
All others	0.2 "
Net disruption size	**2.4 MMB/D**

TABLE 4-1: NET SHORTFALL OF SUPPLIES (AUGUST, 1990)

Data subsequently published by the EIA supported *ex post facto* the analysis used by the DOE policy office to justify its first recommendation for SPR drawdown. In calculating the difference between supply losses and surge production gains during the August-December 1990 period, EIA derived the following worldwide petroleum balance:[50]

- August: 2.150 million barrels net loss
- September: 3.372 million barrels net loss
- October: 0.722 million barrel net loss
- November: 0.070 million barrels net gain
- December: 0.440 million barrels net gain

As can be seen, it was not until November that new production was finally sufficient to offset the embargo's full supply loss, and then only to redress current requirements. While cumulative loss of supply from August to October could not, of course, be made up, it was this cumulative loss that accounted for the market's oil price rise in the first ninety days of the embargo, and it was this cumulative loss that the SPR proposal was intended to offset.

Stuntz believed that the SPR recommendation would be viewed by the cabinet as the logical next step in the process of responding to the crisis. Her intent was to signal to the market the willingness of the United States to employ an instrument that many observers thought would never be used. She based her thinking on well-established opinion in the analytical community. Douglas Bohi of Resources for the Future and William Quandt of Brookings had concluded in the mid-1980s that "there is little to lose and potentially much to gain from a modest drawdown of the reserve early in a disruption."[51] The DOE SPR proposal stated:

"The Department recommends a coordinated IEA draw down of 400,000 B/D for the U.S. and of 800,000 B/D by all other IEA countries, for a total of 1.2 million B/D, beginning on October 1, 1990. The draw-down recommendation is based on the assumption that the balance of the net supply shortfall of 2.4 MMB/D can be met by supply and demand measures being undertaken by the U.S. and other IEA countries, and by market-induced fuel switching and reduction in consumption. Total U.S. SPR use at the end of the fourth quarter would be a maximum of 40 million barrels, which would leave 93% of the SPR (550 million barrels) still available. A drawdown rate of 400,000 B/D can be sustained for four years. The proposed coordinated draw down of strategic stocks would have the following effects: the inflation rate would decrease by up to 20%, GNP losses would decrease by about 25%; total economic losses would be reduced by 20%."[52]

The SPR proposal was actually put forth without a firm commitment from IEA members. Watkins knew from the results of initial consultations undertaken by Easton that IEA would not publicly commit to the use of strategic oil stocks without a pre-determined U.S. decision. He knew also, from interagency staff discussions, that the White House, which was committed to multilateral diplomacy in the Persian Gulf, would insist on multi-lateral action on all other matters, including a consensus agreement from the IEA member-states. Frustrated by this circular logic, Watkins decided to move ahead with the SPR proposal, secure a firm U.S. decision, and later seek the agreement of the IEA.[53]

Opponents of the proposal argued that too-early a use of the SPR might discourage OPEC members with excess capacity from increasing production. Stuntz initially accepted the legitimacy of this position, but felt it weighed insufficiently against the near certainty of domestic economic damage. She rejected the argument entirely once the Saudis committed to the deployment of U.S. troops. At that point it was inconceivable that the Saudis would refuse to bring on-line the totality of their excess capacity.[54]

The national media strongly favored the use of SPR oil. Wrote the *Boston Globe* on August 11, 1990: "Bush's refusal to tap the (SPR) reserves is virtually the only aspect of his handling of the Persian Gulf crisis so far to come in for heavy criticism, and reveals the pro-market thinking of his top aides White House Chief of Staff John Sununu and Budget Director Richard Darman."[55] Editorialized the *Los Angeles Times* of August 13, 1990: "Since Iraq invaded Kuwait on Aug. 2, the department (of energy) has been criticized for its initial unwillingness to release strategic oil reserves to restrain oil price hikes."[56] Concluded the *Washington Times* of August 17, 1990: "Here is how President Bush could yet emerge as the Jimmy Carter of the 1990s: let an oil shock run through the American economy, not to mention the rest of the West. Under no circumstances use this country's Strategic Petroleum Reserve. Blame the oil companies!"[57]

Stuntz felt that in her SPR recommendation to Watkins she was acting prudently as well as in the mainstream of expert opinion. She was convinced that a failure to use the SPR would prove politically unforgivable for the administration. She believed, as well, that it was DOE's duty to do everything in its power to protect the domestic flank of a president otherwise preoccupied with the foreign policy aspects of the crisis. She was fully aware of overwhelming congressional support for an SPR drawdown and knew that even some major oil companies wanted the SPR used, if for no other reason than to escape the spotlight in which they found themselves, through no fault of their own. Her arguments seemed unimpeachable—except to the Troika.[58]

BUREAUCRATIC INERTIA AT THE INTERNATIONAL ENERGY AGENCY (IEA)

Watkins' five-month battle to use the U.S. strategic oil reserve as a countermeasure to the 1990 embargo of Iraqi and Kuwaiti oil was fought on two fronts—primarily, of course, within the senior ranks of the Bush administration, and collaterally at the Secretariat of the IEA in Paris. By the U.S. treaty of accession to the agency and by the terms of IEA's long-established energy emergency and oil-sharing agreements, Watkins was required to consult the twenty-one members of IEA

IEA was created from the energy policy chaos of 1974[59] as the industrialized countries' institutional counterpart to OPEC. Cynics have since charged that IEA came into being as a balm to the wounded vanity of Secretary of State Henry Kissinger, who was briefly nudged from center stage by Treasury Secretary William Simon, Nixon's energy czar.[60] The purpose of IEA was "to take common effective measures to meet oil supply emergencies by developing self-sufficiency in oil supplies, restraining demand, and allocating available oil among (member) countries on an equitable basis."[61] Because energy emergencies were unlikely to be frequent, the architects of the IEA also charged it with "undertaking long-term cooperative efforts on conservation of energy, on accelerated development of alternative sources of energy, on research and development in the energy field."[62]

From the very beginning, IEA assumed a highly formalistic structure. Under its first two executive directors—Ulf Lantzke of Norway and Helga

Steeg of Germany—the IEA was shaped to deliberate rather than to act. A history of the agency, commissioned by Steeg to commemorate the 20th anniversary of its founding and written by Richard Scott, its first legal counsel, devotes 412 pages to an examination of the rules and regulations that govern the internal workings of the agency and a mere eight pages to its major accomplishments.[63]

In the forward to *The IEA History: Origins and Structure*, Steeg notes that industrialized countries had not, at the time of the first energy crisis, devised "a workable system for responding to serious disruptions in oil supply and their organizational arrangements for co-operation could not enable them to cope effectively with the institutional implications of those situations."[64] Scott, for his part, views the energy crises of 1973 and 1979 as comeuppance. The industrialized countries had, he states, "accepted for some years the short-term luxury of growing oil import dependence...(and were therefore)...largely responsible for the very predicament in which they suddenly found themselves."[65]

In 1990, as during most of the previous decade, DOE policy staff viewed IEA as anachronistic, an organization whose reason for being had long been overtaken by events. Bohi and Quandt[66] saw the IEA paradox as early as 1984, when they wrote: "The usefulness of the oil-sharing agreement [the IEA's core responsibility] is reduced because the market works better today than it did before, with fewer rigidities to hinder the redistribution of oil supplies." DOE's policy staff judged IEA to be statist in its view of energy policy and accustomed to seeing the energy sector as the sum total of mostly government-controlled monopolies.

John Easton arrived in Paris on August 8, 1990, with instructions from Moore to lay the groundwork for IEA-wide measures to respond to the Iraqi crisis, and for a coordinated drawdown of strategic stocks. With a meeting of the IEA Governing Board scheduled for August 9th, the Secretariat was drafting, as it usually did in advance, the communiqué that would be issued by the board after its meeting. Easton, accompanied by the State Department's William Ramsey, found the Secretariat pondering reasons to refrain from action. A bland communiqué had been drafted to indicate that IEA was cognizant of events in the Persian Gulf, would monitor the situation closely, and would take appropriate steps as necessary.[67]

Steeg responded to Easton's and Ramsey's insistence for a more substantive expression of concern, as well as a declaration of intent to use strategic stocks, with charges of overreaction. Wishing to proceed with completion of the draft communiqué without further interruptions from the Americans, Steeg decided to caucus in secret with like-minded European delegates. Easton and Ramsey discovered the caucus room by chance and barged in. They made it clear that the United States would not accept a typically anemic communiqué from the IEA. Unless U.S. concerns were addressed, they warned, the U.S. would act unilaterally in response to the crisis, possibly with an uncoordinated drawdown of the SPR.[68]

Easton's bluff succeeded in awakening the IEA Secretariat from its cultivated detachment. Consequently, a more muscular communiqué was drafted that, while short of U.S. expectations, demonstrated a modicum of awareness of conditions in the marketplace. Issued on August 9, the communiqué declared: "The present oil supply situation is such that, given the availability of supplies at sea, the high level of company and government controlled stocks, as well as the possibility of higher output from oil producers, sufficient oil supplies are currently available to compensate for the loss of Iraqi and Kuwaiti crude and product to the market. Therefore, there is no need for recourse to the IEA emergency response system at this time. Companies should show restraint by avoiding abnormal spot market purchases or other undesirable purchases of oil during the period of this supply disruption. Consumers, in their own interests, should (adopt) a sound buying attitude and refrain from abnormal purchases."[69]

The communiqué was not entirely accurate in its estimates of the oil supplies available to the market and presumptuous in its recommended responses. IEA did not know on August 9, 1990—nor did anyone else, for that matter—that "sufficient oil supplies" were available to "compensate for the loss of Iraqi and Kuwaiti crude." And the pronouncement that companies should avoid "abnormal spot market purchases," and consumers should display a "sound buying attitude" could only be regarded as bureaucratic paternalism of the kind that European governments feel entitled to practice, but that Americans could never tolerate.

The opportunism of Japan

IEA's *laissez-faire* position was not without consequence. The government of Japan took advantage of what it interpreted as the IEA-sanctioned view that no supply problems existed by moving aggressively to increase its oil imports.

Japan's oil policy diverged from the policy of its IEA partners throughout the Iraqi crisis until its government was jolted, as will be seen, by a message from Bush. The divergence is illustrated by Table 4-2[70], which is compiled from EIA data. The difference between Japan's oil demand trends and those of the United States became increasingly more significant as the supply disruption of 1990 played itself out.

1989-1990 PETROLEUM DEMAND
(millions of barrels)

	July	August	September	October
Japan 1989	3.27	3.27	3.32	3.40
Japan 1990	3.57	3.74	3.68	3.57
USA 1989	16.5	17.4	16.8	17.3
USA 1990	16.9	17.9	16.4	16.4

TABLE 4-2: JAPANESE AND U.S. PETROLEUM DEMAND, 1989-1990

European demand patterns in Europe followed those of the United States, with Japan the only IEA member to increase its imports of oil following the declaration of the U.S-UN embargo. Japan's oil import increases in September and October were especially egregious because they took place during the market's tightest supply period. The increases aggravated the most severe monthly net supply loss of the entire Iraqi crisis, which reached 3.372 million barrels in September. Japan would, however, pay a price for its hoarding behavior when, three months later, the value of its stocks tumbled in line with the market price of oil.

The IEA promises to meet again

The IEA Governing Board met repeatedly between August 9, 1990 and January 28, 1991, to consider, and finally ratify what were mainly U.S. initiatives on the crisis. It was not until January 11, 1991, that IEA finally concurred with a coordinated drawdown of strategic stocks. Even then, the actual agreement was reached outside IEA's institutional structure, on the basis of a decision orchestrated by the United States directly with Germany and Japan and without IEA Governing Board involvement."[71]

When it finally arrived, Watkins publicly welcomed IEA's rubber stamp of U.S. policy, but DOE policy staff denounced the IEA consultative process as sclerotic and inimical to U.S. interests. Of IEA's twenty-one members, only three held actual stocks of oil but all demanded the right to decide on their use. The Secretariat itself acted in support of a delay in the use of strategic stocks rather than in the more appropriate role of neutral analyst. In violation of accepted protocol, Steeg herself actually traveled to Washington DC in October 1990 to argue publicly against the need to drawdown strategic stocks at a seminar, with high visibility, organized by Wilfrid Kohl at Johns Hopkins University's School of Advanced International Studies.[72]

Crises do not lend themselves to the type of extended consultations and consensus-building processes required by IEA. Because of its size and drawdown capacity, the U.S. SPR is the only strategic stock capable of making a difference to a highly disrupted oil market. Except for Germany, the Europeans have avoided the great expense of holding strategic oil stocks, and received therefore what is referred to in the trade as an economic free ride from the U.S. investment. The European contribution to a market disruption is largely based on exhortatory conservation efforts that, as was learned from U.S. experience during the Iraqi crisis, are no substitute for liquid oil supplies.

In truth, the battle on the IEA front was merely an extension of the one on the domestic front; the differences of opinion in IEA quite as deep as those in the cabinet. The opposition from the United Kingdom, Europe's paramount oil producer, was understandable. Germany, Italy and Spain, whose total dependence on imported oil exposed their economies to the highest vulnerability, were incomprehensibly passive, as was Japan. The U.S. Troika read these signals from key Western allies as a confirmation of its wisdom in refraining from use of the SPR.

THE TREASURY SECRETARY MISREADS THE MARKET

Although discussed on a number of occasions by EPC, the SPR drawdown proposal was not formally considered by the cabinet until September 21, 1990, at a meeting of the NSC chaired by the president. The SPR proposal provoked a heated exchange between Watkins and Brady who, unusually agitated, pulled from his coat pocket a paper napkin on which he had that morning scribbled spot and futures prices for oil traded on the New York Mercantile Exchange (NYMEX). The numbers indicated a trend that Brady interpreted as market confidence in administration policy, which he said also proved that a drawdown of the SPR was unnecessary.[73]

Futures prices were trending lower than spot prices, Brady stated, because the market was unconcerned about future supply. Given this mark of confidence, he concluded, the administration should not act to confuse market conditions by insisting on a theoretical supply shortage that could only be rectified by sale of SPR oil. Watkins, an engineer by training, had no ready response to Brady's view of market behavior. In briefing Watkins for the meeting, the policy staff had failed to anticipate Brady's argument against the SPR proposal, however implausible it might have seemed that the United States Treasury secretary could misread market signals.[74]

The market that gave Brady confidence was in a state known as *backwardation:* oil traders were willing to pay a premium for immediate supplies and encourage sales of current stocks because the availability of future supplies was too uncertain. The market had shifted from its usual state of *contango*[75] on the day following the White House announcement of the embargo.

Spot and futures prices had risen—in tandem mostly, but higher for immediate deliveries—from $20.57 per barrel (spot) and $20.69 per barrel (futures) on July 31, to $28.73 (spot) and $28.05 (futures) by August 6, to $31.10 (spot) and $30.91 (futures) by August 24.[76]

Traders were internalizing, in futures prices, the probability that the embargoed oil would likely be made up by excess production capacity. Saudi Arabia, the critical player, had ambiguously signaled its intent to increase production, subject to OPEC concurrence, but had concurrently notified its customers to expect reduced shipments in September.[77] It was not clear to traders how much worldwide excess production capacity would eventually be brought online, or when.

In the mean time, refineries were drawing down commercial inventories and therefore required resupply. Concurrently, strategic stocks were being held in abeyance in both Europe and the United States. The market was acting rationally by bidding up spot prices and hedging futures prices. Brady's argument, by contrast, was that lower futures prices were indicative of traders' *un*concern for future supplies.

At the cabinet meeting, Brady did not discuss the inflationary effects of the sharply higher oil prices or their distributional effects, arguing instead that interventions in the oil market should be as rare as interventions in the currency markets. He was convinced that market conditions in general were stable and that no government intervention was warranted either on energy or on monetary policy.[78] No one present at the meeting challenged Brady's assessment of the market. Although he personally favored a drawdown of the SPR, Schmalensee, reflecting the position of CEA chairman Boskin, opposed the SPR proposal. OMB's Darman backed Brady, as did Sununu. Transportation Secretary Samuel Skinner supported Watkins. Deputy Secretary of State Lawrence Eagleberger—substituting regularly on matters of energy policy for the permanently recused James Baker—also backed Watkins. All others present remained silent. [79]

With a solid nay vote from the Troika, Watkins was denied any possibility of prevailing.[80] To secure a favorable decision on the SPR he would have needed the support of at least one member of the Troika. Schmalensee, particularly, would have been in a position to turn the tide. But Watkins had declined to lobby his colleagues in advance of the meeting and Schmalensee was under no other obligation than to carry out Boskin's charge. Nor was the matter allowed to end in the cabinet room. Sununu and Darman proceeded to humiliate Watkins publicly by telling the *Wall Street Journal* that DOE was "too eager to act."[81]

Strategic Petroleum Reserve policy

At the time that the Iraqi events took place, United States policy on the use of the SPR could not have been clearer. Formulated in 1984 as a result of an interagency review ordered by the Reagan administration and recommunicated to Congress in 1988 by outgoing Energy Secretary Herrington,[82] the policy was spelled out in terms unlikely to be misinterpreted: "Recognizing the need to calm the markets quickly, the Administration's basic policy is to *use the SPR early and in large volumes* (emphasis added) in response to a major supply disruption."

The policy had also been adopted by IEA in July 1984. A "stock draw could be particularly effective in the initial disruption stages, when the danger may be greatest of markets over-reacting," the IEA Governing Board had stated in a communiqué issued immediately after its commitment to adhere to a policy of early and massive release of strategic stocks in the case of a serious oil supply disruption.[83] Most importantly, the Bush administration itself had embraced the policy barely five months prior to the Iraqi crisis, by the very individuals who in August 1990 declined to implement it.

The EPC Council undertook a comprehensive review of SPR policy in the fall of 1989 in order to determine whether the administration should accede to congressional intent to enlarge the SPR to one billion barrels. The analysis was carried out by an interagency staff group, directed by Guy Caruso of DOE, acting under the oversight of DOE's policy office. In order to answer the question of what constituted an acceptable size for the SPR, the analysts calculated the probability of future oil disruptions, posited likely degrees of severity and duration of disruptions, and modeled various means of employing American and allied strategic oil stocks to mitigate the disruptions' economic consequences.

The staff group concluded its analysis and reported to the cabinet: "The net economic benefits to be gained by the United States and other countries would likely be maximized by a coordinated early release of stocks. This fact is recognized by most IEA countries, and many of the larger economies (e.g., Germany and Japan) now view early draw down of stocks as the first line of defense against severe oil supply disruptions—as opposed to their previously held position of holding stocks for use as a measure of last resort."[84]

These judgments—arrived at by no less than twelve federal agencies[85]including the Troika—were formally approved without dissent by Brady's EPC in January 1990 as part of the Bush administration decision to fill the SPR to a maximum of 750 million barrels.[86] The policy was soon after communicated to Congress by the testimony of Deputy Secretary Moore before the Senate Energy and Natural Resources Committee.[87]

This history notwithstanding, in the fall of 1990, facing the most serious oil supply disruption in 35 years, both the administration and IEA nonetheless declined to carry out a policy they had unequivocally endorsed.

Daniel Yergin, the emeritus founder of Cambridge Energy Research Associates, spoke about this issue to the Council on Foreign Relations in April 1990 with uncommon insight: "The declared (SPR) policy is one of 'early release.' But some believe that, in real life, there would be a fractious and angry policy debate involving the 'early releasers' in conflict with the 'doubters,' who question the reality of a crisis and suspect oil company manipulation, and the 'hoarders,' who uncertain as to what is ahead, want to hold unto the oil in the reserve. The result might well be indecision, delay, and confusion, with the result that the SPR would be used too late to be effective, if used at all."[88]

In real life, no cabinet member reminded Brady of the consequences of his advice to the president. The two other Troika leaders did not offer estimates of the probable cost to the economy of allowing oil prices to rise unimpeded. The members of the cabinet representing the social agencies did not provide advice on the disproportionate burden carried by the nation's low-income citizens. The foreign policy agencies made no mention of the impact that higher energy prices were having on developing nations. The international trade agency did not offer estimates of the embargo-induced wealth that would be transferred to Arab nations whose very existence the U.S. government was willing to protect with American lives. Was this knowledge available?

Ironically, a task force of Brady's own Treasury Department, named the Oil Price Impact Study Group, had actually calculated these domestic and international costs and had presented its findings to the National Security Council on August 29.[89] The group had modeled the Iraqi oil embargo's effect on the economies of the United States, Eastern Europe, and selected countries in and around the Persian Gulf. The classified results were unambiguous: each one million B/D of SPR oil released into the market would reduce the market price of oil by $4 to $8 per barrel and the retail price of gasoline by eight to fifteen cents per gallon; increase gross national product by 0.4 to 0.7%; reduce the unemployment rate by 0.15 to 0.25% and the inflation rate by 0.6 to 1.0%; and provide total economic gains of $3 to $5 billion.[90]

It was not until the war was over that the president's economic advisers acknowledged the role played by the 1990 oil price spike in the recession that was to plague the Bush administration until the elections of 1992. "The spike-up in the price of oil and in interest rates," Darman told Congress in April 1991, "is what tipped us into recession."[91] CEA chairman Boskin confirmed in July that the "oil price shock" had severely affected the burgeoning recession of 1990.[92] Brady, for his part, admitted nothing, including the very existence of the recession.

In a 1990 *New York Times Magazine* profile of Bush's cabinet, William Safire wrote that Nicholas Brady was to "George Bush what Harry Hopkins was to F.D.R., a trustworthy repository of confidences."[93] The analogy was entirely apt. Hopkins had advised Eisenhower to impose the 1959 mandatory oil import quotas that were to cost American consumers $5 billion per year until revoked in 1973. Brady's 1990 advice to Bush to forego the use of the SPR, and thereby mitigate the inflationary pressures of sharply higher oil prices, may have carried an even higher cost—the 1992 recession that contributed to the demise of the Bush Administration.

CONGRESSIONAL NERVES

During international crises, congressional frustrations rise because its members are unreconciled to the limited role the Constitution has assigned to them. Senators and representatives want debate and deliberations, but crises, by their very nature, require execution rather than discussion of policy. Military and diplomatic initiatives of great consequence would be virtually paralyzed if subjected to the infinite shadings of congressional opinion. Members of Congress know this to be true, but are compelled nevertheless to enter the fray. Wars inspire Congressional activism, along with fears about the handling of the crisis, hopes that the circumstances will enhance the prospects of opportunistic legislation and dismay about the always insufficient degree to which Congress is consulted by the president. And so it was during the Iraqi crisis.

Alaskan senator Frank Murkowski struck the first congressional blow by introducing his National Energy Security Act on August 3, 1990. The act aimed to establish a ceiling of 50% of U.S. consumption for imports of crude oil and refined products. The legislation called for the president to submit to Congress an "Energy Production and Security Action Plan" when the ceiling was found to have been breached for six consecutive months in any given year. In a virtual throwback to 1970 energy policy, the president's plan that Murkowski sought would contain specific proposals to reduce imports below the prescribed level, including "production incentives such as oil import fees, royalty reductions, and tax incentives."[94]

Legislative proposals are by tradition based on congressional findings. The findings for the Murkowski bill were instructive for their Lazarus-like resurrection of words, phrases, and concepts of another era, illustrating how little progress had been made in congressional thinking about the ever-elusive notion of energy security. The National Energy Security Act found that:

> "The United States is the leader of the free world with responsibility to promote economic and political security. The exercise of traditional responsibilities in foreign policy

requires that the United States be free of the risk of energy blackmail in times of shortages. The level of U. S. oil security is directly related to the level of domestic production of oil, natural gas liquids, and natural gas. The ability of the U.S. to exercise its free will and to carry out its responsibilities as leader of the free world could be jeopardized by an excessive dependence on foreign oil imports. Increasing dependence on foreign oil imports has and continues to impose severe risks to the lives of United States service men and women and unacceptable costs to the national defense."[95]

Murkowski's legislative prose was matched by the rhetoric of his bill's cosponsors. The *Congressional Record* of August 3 virtually brimmed with senatorial angst. Senator Lloyd Bentsen of Texas told his colleagues that "...the events of the last 48 hours have underscored what I have been saying for years: the United States is slipping inexorably into excessive dependence on foreign oil...we simply must stop this downward spiral into the abyss of energy dependence." Senator James McClure of Idaho expanded the debate by stating: "...[i]t is clear from our growing dependence on foreign oil that our economy and national security is increasingly at risk...this Nation and the other nations of the industrialized world are threatened by developments in the Persian Gulf...these events underscore once again the fragility of the economies of the Western World and the marginal supply of energy that fuels it."[96]

Perhaps unintentionally, but with identical purpose, the senators' words echoed the seemingly immutable terms by which the United States has historically debated oil questions. The terminology of oil import dependence as a measure of national security has remained essentially unchanged since World War II, though in more recent times voiced with the added urgency of oil crisis experience. Consider the following.

President Carter in 1979. "Our excessive dependence on OPEC has already taken a tremendous toll on our economy and our people...On the battlefield of energy we can win for our Nation a new confidence, and we can seize control again of our common destiny...Beginning this moment, this Nation will never use more foreign oil than we did in 1977—never."[97]

President Ford in 1975. "Americans are no longer in full control of their own national destiny, when that destiny depends on uncertain foreign fuel at high prices fixed by others. Higher energy costs compound both inflation and recession, and dependence on others for future energy supplies is intolerable to our national security."[98]

President Nixon in 1974. "[T]he energy crisis itself came suddenly, borne by a tragic war in the Middle East. It was a blow to American pride and prosperity, but it may well turn out to be a fortunate turning point in our history. We learned, at a stage short of the truly critical, that we had allowed ourselves to become overly dependent upon foreign supplies of a vital good. We saw that the acts of foreign rulers, even far short of military action, could plunge us into an authentic crisis. The Arab oil embargo will temporarily close some gasoline stations, but it has opened our eyes to the shortsighted policy we had been pursuing."[99]

Also seemingly immutable was the road that Congress would travel in responding to the first energy crisis of the 1990s. On August 4, the Senate unexpectedly enacted a bill on global climate change.[100] The bill, introduced by Senator Wirth of Colorado in February 1989, had been vehemently opposed by the Bush administration and previously given little chance of passage. It was now the Senate's first, if dubious, post-Gulf crisis achievement. More to the point was the action taken by the House of Representatives on the same day, which by a margin of 281 to 82 voted to ban drilling for oil and gas off the coast of North Carolina.[101]

Congressional confusion about energy security was matched by congressional reaction to higher gasoline prices. The following excerpts from a letter written to Watkins on August 6 by Senator Jeff Bingaman of New Mexico illustrate the tone of congressional correspondence received by DOE throughout the Iraqi crisis.

"There is strong public outrage over the dramatic increase in gasoline prices since the Iraqi invasion of Kuwait," the Senator stated. "It appears that these price increases are based more on greed than on legitimate market forces. I ask that you investigate these unwarranted price hikes immediately and report back as to what corrective action is needed."[102]

Hearings by the House of Representatives

Congressional hearings on the energy dimensions of the Iraqi crisis began on August 7 in the House of Representatives, organized by Philip Sharp, chairman of the Energy and Power Subcommittee, and John Dingell, chairman of the Subcommittee on Oversight and Investigations. Sharp's key objective for the hearings was to build congressional pressure for a rapid draw-down of the SPR. Dingell was more concerned with the behavior of the oil industry.

The DOE sent three officials to testify at the August 7 hearing: John Easton, because he was the assistant secretary responsible for international affairs and energy emergencies; Robert Gentile, because he was the assistant secretary responsible for the SPR; and Calvin Kent, because as the administrator of EIA he was expected to provide objective data.

Easton began his testimony by summarizing conditions in the oil market, indicating that consultations on the crisis were ongoing with North Atlantic Treaty Organization (NATO) and IEA allies, and assuring Chairman Sharp that the administration and DOE had the situation well in hand. Sharp would have none of it. He pressed Easton on the nature and forcefulness of consultations with U.S. allies, implying that the consultations were being carried out at low bureaucratic levels with little engagement by senior administration officials. He next castigated DOE for issuing media releases indicating broad availability of excess production capacity without specifying that the capacity was located in the now more-dangerous-than-ever Persian Gulf.

Finally, he bore down on the matter of when the administration would use the SPR:[103]

Mr. Sharp: "[M]y concern simply is that there is a high risk of damage to the economy through delay. Early action does not bring anything like those kinds of risks to us. And so whatever fumbling or mistake could possibly occur through early draw down [of the SPR] is I think less likely to be a problem for the U.S. Government and the U.S. citizens than is the delay in trying to take action."[104]

Mr. Easton: "[W]e are prepared to use the Strategic Petroleum Reserve to address a severe energy supply interruption and [sic] that we will coordinate that with our allies. And we feel strongly that ...this needs to be done in concert with our allies and needs to be done if the threshold of the statute is met, and that is [we make a finding that there exists] a severe energy supply interruption."[105]

Mr. Sharp: "So you don't think we have met the test of the statute?"[106]

Mr. Easton: "We have not yet taken a position on that...we are prepared to use it (the SPR) if the conditions of the statute are met."[107]

Mr. Sharp: "What do you mean, *if the provisions of the statute are met?* You mean to tell me when the U.S. Government and the Europeans and the Japanese are able to stop several million barrels of oil, potentially, from coming into the market [as a result of the embargo] we have not disrupted this international market?"[108]

Mr. Easton: "[W]e are still trying to assess the effectiveness of how much oil has been removed from the world market."[109]

The provisions of the statute that were the subject of the Sharp-Easton debate were those contained in section 161 of the Energy Policy and Conservation Act. The statute specifies that the SPR may not be used unless and until the president determines that a 'severe energy supply disruption (a) is, or is likely to be of significant scope and duration, and of an emergency nature; (b) may cause major adverse impacts on national safety or the national economy; and (c) results, or is likely to result, from an interruption in the supply of imported petroleum products, or from sabotage or an act of God.'"[110]

As far as Sharp was concerned, the oil embargo had created the conditions necessary to trigger a release of the SPR and he was not reassured by what he considered to be Easton's legalistic quibbling about whether or not the statute's requirements were literally met. Easton had no choice but to be vague about administration intent on the SPR because he had been given no other guidance. His personal instincts told him the administration was unlikely to resort to the SPR, but he did not want to create a furor by conceding such a possibility at the hearing.[111]

Easton's seemingly bureaucratic language succeeded only in frustrating Sharp and his subcommittee members. Sharp left no doubt about where he stood on the SPR issue in the statement concluding his questioning of Easton.

"The Department has got to seize on this [the SPR] in the same way in which this Administration has seized on its desire in very difficult circumstances to make a difference in the Middle East," Sharp said. "Well, we have the tool. For the first time in 15 years we have the tool to make a difference and I hope we won't botch it by waiting too late, until we have absorbed an enormous hit in our economy."[112]

On August 14, it was the turn of energy conservation advocates to press for legislative action. Senator Richard Bryant of Nevada introduced his Motor Vehicle Fuel Efficiency Act, calling for an increase in fuel efficiency (CAFE) standards for automobiles and light trucks of 20% from 1990 levels in 1995 and 40% in 2001. The legislation, fiercely opposed by the Bush administration,[113] proved politically irresistible. The bill provided the means for members of Congress who were unwilling on environmental grounds to support the development of oil resources in Alaska or on the Outer Continental Shelf to demonstrate concern for U.S. reliance on oil imports by politically risk-free regulation. The Bryant bill reached the Senate floor on September 14 with not less than 68 cosponsors.[114]

The DOE resisted further requests for congressional appearances during the remaining days of August, but by early September Congress could no longer be put off. Easton testified before the House Committee on Government Operations—a panel not usually concerned with energy matters but anxious to delve into the present crisis—on September 5. He delivered a simple, reassuring message that, unlike the one delivered to Sharp, now contained unequivocal language on U.S. determination to use the SPR when warranted. He told the committee that supplies were ample and commercial stocks high. He said that excess production capacity had been brought on line and was expected to fully offset the loss of supply induced by the embargo. With a bow to its oversight prerogatives, Easton also assured the committee that energy conservation measures would be aggressively implemented in the federal government itself.[115]

EIA administrator Calvin Kent testified before the House Subcommittee on Energy and Power on September 10. He delivered dispassionate testimony on what the available data showed about market conditions and made it clear that he would not "explain or defend any proposed policies of the Administration or those suggested by Congress."[116] Kent stated that gasoline inventories were at their lowest level since 1988, fuel oil stocks were above normal, jet fuel stocks were decreasing due to higher military demand, and propane stocks were on the increase. He warned, however, that unless higher oil prices were allowed to induce conservation, problems could develop with gasoline, kerojet and propane stocks.[117]

Kent concluded his testimony by stating that the oil situation was under control and would remain manageable assuming no change in the military situation in the Middle East and assuming no abnormal winter weather. The subcommittee was not persuaded. Chairman Sharp decried DOE's tendency to underestimate what could go wrong and asked Kent to take back the message that DOE should "move more aggressively in terms of conservation, (and) take action on the Strategic Petroleum Reserve, if only at a modest level, in order to help make sure that system works and oil is out in the marketplace."[118]

A Joint Session of Congress

On September 11, the president addressed a joint session of Congress. In the speech—later remembered for its coining of the "new world order" terminology—the president insisted that "vital (U.S.) economic risks" were at stake in Iraq's destruction of Kuwait and laid out the energy dimensions of the crisis:[119]

> "Oil-producing nations are already replacing lost Iraqi and Kuwaiti output. More than half of what was lost has been made up. If producers, including the United States, continue steps to expand oil and gas production, we can stabilize prices and guarantee against hardship. Additionally, we and several of our allies always have the option to extract oil from our strategic petroleum reserves if conditions warrant. As I've pointed out before, conservation efforts are

essential to keep our energy needs as low as possible. And we must then take advantage of our energy sources across the board: coal, natural gas, hydro, and nuclear. Our failure to do these things has made us more dependent on foreign oil than ever before. Finally, let no one even contemplate profiteering from this crisis. We will not have it."

The president's declarations were largely disconnected from the actions of his EPC. The EPC had ridiculed the conservation components of DOE's response measures even as the president now found energy conservation to be "essential." EPC had berated DOE for response measures unrelated to oil consumption, but the president was now promoting coal, hydro, and nuclear fuels. The Troika agencies had lectured DOE about the dangers of building energy policy on the unreliable ground of oil import levels, but the president was announcing to the nation his concern about our being "more dependent on foreign oil than ever before." And, witnessed by the nation and the world, a Republican president was warning of dire consequences for profiteers, notwithstanding his senior advisers' refusal to consider the only tool (the SPR) capable of mitigating the profiteers' very source of temptation.

DOE staff had not been asked to write or review the energy-related text of the president's speech, which had been drafted at the White House without the involvement of the department most affected by its message. Had Stuntz been consulted, she would have discarded much of the language used by the president. The fact was that conditions in the oil market were not quite as portrayed by the president. Guarantees against hardship could not be issued by any agency in the executive branch, prices could not be stabilized by the measures adopted by the Bush administration, and the remaining declarations missed by far the mark of credible energy policy.

A single hearing in the Senate

The greatest deliberative body in the world held a single hearing on energy during the eight months of the Persian Gulf Crisis. Senator J. Bennett

Johnston, the chairman of the Committee on Energy and Natural Resources, opened the hearing on September 13 by welcoming Watkins as the star witness and Moore in the supporting role.

"The Middle East crisis highlights our strategic and economic vulnerability," Johnston stated in opening the hearing, "(because) we have allowed ourselves to become subject to the whims of the Persian Gulf dictators."[120] He continued: "The crisis raises the serious issue of where we will replace the oil lost to the embargo. I worry that the Administration may have based its policy decisions to date on overly optimistic estimates of the world's ability to offset the shortfall."[121]

Johnston was unusually measured in his statements on the SPR. "As stated, the policy is to relieve shortfalls, not merely suppress prices," he said, "...[T]he SPR is our best and perhaps only meaningful weapon to offset a crude shortfall. If necessary it should be used, but it should be used thoughtfully."[122]

The chairman's prudent approach to the SPR was not shared by a number of his colleagues, as exemplified by the position of Idaho senator James McClure. After first comparing the Kuwaiti invasion with a recent California earthquake—"just a warning of the 'Big One' that is yet to come"—McClure went on to say: "there is one thing that we must not do and that is to use the Strategic Petroleum Reserve to manage or manipulate the price of oil, as some are now urging. The reserve must be preserved for the purpose for which it was originally intended, that of responding to severe interruptions of oil supplies and to avoid physical shortages."[123]

Other committee members were preoccupied less by the SPR per se than by rising fuel prices. North Dakota senator Kent Conrad stated: "[N]o American should be subject to price gouging by those who control the retail price of gas, but states like North Dakota are particularly vulnerable to unjustified increases in the price of petroleum products."[124] Alabama Senator Howard Heflin echoed these sentiments: "[M]any of my constituents...have complained bitterly about escalating gas prices at the pump."[125] Senator Conrad Burns said, "[I]n my state of Montana—although we don't get a drop of oil from the Middle East—prices at the retail pump are among the highest in the United States."[126]

A number of the senators focused their remarks on energy policy's past failures and future opportunities. Senator Jay Rockefeller of West Virginia blamed the Bush administration for having discarded federal programs on energy conservation, renewable energy, and fossil fuel research. He also implied that the "oil industry mega-mergers" of the previous decade, which had not in his view been properly scrutinized by federal regulators for possible antitrust violations, were partially responsible for present conditions.[127]

In turn, Kentucky Senator Mitch McConnel decried the consequences of America's reliance on low-cost energy, noting: "While it has fueled unprecedented economic growth, it has also provided a disincentive to conserve."[128] Senator Don Nickles of Oklahoma held the opposite political ground. "We must be wary of calls for a return to the command and control regulation of the 1970s," he said, warning against any attempts to resurrect the Synfuels Corporation, legislate new windfall profit taxes, or dramatically increase the fuel economy of vehicles.[129]

When he was finally allowed to speak, Watkins summarized the energy situation in reassuring but not entirely persuasive terms. He told the committee that the complete effects of the oil embargo would not be fully felt in the United States until late September "because the oil in transit lifted from Iraq and Kuwait prior to the embargo takes, on the average, 45 days (to reach) the United States."[130] He then committed to the use of the SPR, but only in collaboration with IEA members, and "should the situation warrant it." He went on to review the status of available stocks of various fuels, and then brought the committee's attention to the immediate measures earlier announced by the administration and to the medium-term measures that were to be announced imminently.[131]

Watkins concluded his testimony by turning tables on the need for action, placing in the lap of Congress the responsibility for further steps needed to manage the crisis. He called for enactment of tax incentives for domestic oil and gas production, citing proposals made two years earlier by the Bush administration but ignored by Congress,[132] and asked that Congress permit the development of oil and gas resources in the Arctic National Wildlife Refuge. He next sought clarification by legislation of an EPA decision deemed to discourage fuel switching by coal-burning utilities. He closed his opening statement with a request for legislation to eliminate a rather obscure limitation imposed by PURPA on the type of fuel that could be used by independent generators.[133]

During the subsequent question-and-answer period Watkins went on record with a number of positions he would later regret. He told Senator Conrad Burns, who declared the SPR insufficient to affect the retail prices of oil,[134] that the SPR was "a cherished reserve that has a finite life and we do not want to misuse it."[135] He assured Murkowski that the National Energy Security Act the senator had introduced in early August had a great deal of merit and was "very consistent with the National Energy Strategy."[136] He also deflected Senator Conrad's insistent demand that the administration pay closer attention to price gouging and profiteering.[137]

The questioning continued with Moore in the witness chair after Watkins' early departure from the hearing. Perhaps the most revealing line of inquiry, indicating profound confusion about the workings of the spot and futures markets, was pursued by Senator Bingaman. The following exchange ensued:[138]

> **Senator Bingaman:** "It seems very simple to me that people who would benefit from the price of oil going up could get in the futures market and bid it up and then see that translated into the spot market and then see that translated into the price of gas and then say, well, we have no control over it, this is the free market at work."
>
> **Mr. Moore:** "I would agree with your basic premise. There is no question that the price of oil today that you are seeing, whatever it is today, in the $31 range, has nothing to do with supply and demand. It is strictly a psychological price, and the spot market is being driven up by anticipation of shortages of oil."

Back to the House

Congressmen Sharp and Dingell held the last of their Gulf crisis hearings on September 27, two days after the White House had finally agreed to a test drawdown of the SPR (as will be discussed later). In his opening remarks, Dingell quoted from a letter he had sent to the White House the previous day.

"Mr. President," Dingell's letter stated, "you must take steps to deal with the domestic economic effects of the Iraq situation. In addition, you must prepare for the possibility that the Iraq situation will worsen. The single biggest step you could take to mitigate the economic effects of the Iraq situation is coordinated draw down of strategic oil stocks in the United States and (sic) our allies, such as Japan and Germany."[139]

Watkins, again accompanied by Moore, largely repeated the testimony he had previously given to the Senate. He told Sharp and Dingell that oil prices would remain volatile for the foreseeable future. He said that worldwide excess crude oil production capacity was available to offset the embargoed oil, but noted that the production capacity that had been brought online was "insufficient to fully offset the 4.3 million B/D lost."[140] Having provided the assurance that the administration was, if necessary, prepared to use strategic stocks, he turned his attention to the ongoing work on the NES.

Watkins told the committee that in the NES development process, as in the more recent experience of crafting response measures for the embargo, he had come to realize that the nation accorded a very low priority to energy matters. "The view that our energy objectives are negotiable while all other national goals are critical," he stated, "needs to be radically changed. We will do our part in redressing the public policy balance, as we move towards completion of the NES."[141]

In response to questions on the SPR, Watkins made the best of his NSC defeat by talking about administration consideration of a limited SPR test drawdown. He suggested that such a test—of about five million barrels—would be unlikely to affect the market, would in fact hardly stress the SPR system at all, but would be reassuring. When pressed by the committee on what he considered to be a demanding test of the system, he offered the figure of fifteen million barrels.[142]

The hearing concluded with exhortations from the members of Congress for more aggressive action by the administration and reassurances by Watkins that everything possible was being done to manage the crisis. Watkins would not discuss the position he had taken within the cabinet on the SPR and would not express doubt about the wisdom of the president's decision to refrain from using the SPR. He defended NSC's decision on the SPR and refused to comment on the dissension within the cabinet's ranks. Throughout his tenure, Watkins never took issue publicly with administration decisions with which he disagreed. Loyalty to the president was, in his view, a prerequisite for service in the Cabinet.[143]

THE STRATEGIC PETROLEUM RESERVE DRAWDOWNS

The initial administration decision on the SPR could not be allowed to stand. It would have amounted to an admission that the United States and other nations had made a terrible mistake in basing their oil security policies of the last decade on the power of strategic stocks to protect their economies from harm. Watkins, as the cabinet officer responsible for execution of the SPR statute, felt it was his duty to keep the SPR option in the forefront of administration deliberations, regardless of the number of setbacks. He determined that, at minimum, he needed to convince the president to support a drawdown of the SPR in some form. He settled on a test of the system, as an interim step to what he called "full deployment."[144]

In continuing to press for the use of the SPR, Watkins had the unswerving support of DOE's policy staff. The staff had been stunned by NSC's rebuff, not only because of Brady's erroneous reasoning, but because with each passing day the rationale for early and massive release of strategic stocks was becoming less compelling. The staff was also puzzled by the contradictions in administration behavior—forceful and effective internationally, reactionary on the home front. The staff assumed that the SPR decision reflected personal animosities rather than meritorious deliberations and that the president would eventually reverse the SPR decision.

DOE staff welcomed Watkins' pursuit of a test drawdown also because questions had been raised about the operational readiness of the SPR.

A lengthy article published by the *Wall Street Journal* in early September, later placed in the congressional record by Congressman Sharp,[145] raised questions about the engineering soundness of the SPR, the quality of the oil stored in its caverns, and the fairness of the process by which the oil would be sold. "Two-thirds of petroleum reserve oil is the wrong kind for many U.S. refineries," the article claimed. "At one site, certain pipes have corroded and ruptured. Another $90 million facility may collapse inward as soon as oil is withdrawn," the writers declared. "If the SPR is opened, anyone with enough money will be able to buy its oil, including speculators who could hoard it. "[146]

The charges were outrageous. John Bartholomew, the director of the SPR office, responded to them in a letter to *Journal* editors dispatched by DOE on September 11, 1990. The DOE letter stated that the SPR held low-sulfur sweet and high-sulfur sour petroleum in approximately the same proportion as the quality of oil imported into the United States. It pointed out that the corroded pipes found by the *Journal* reporters had been used to carry brine when the storage sites were initially built and were never intended to carry oil lifted from the reserve. Bartholomew dismissed the notion of caverns collapsing after drawdown, and would not dignify with an answer the charge that speculators would buy and hoard SPR oil.[147]

Of greater concern to DOE than the SPR's operational readiness was the question of statutory authority to conduct a large-scale test drawdown. The authority seemed at best murky, and Watkins therefore thought it prudent to seek a clearer congressional mandate. He obtained it on September 13, in conjunction with reauthorization of the Energy Policy and Conservation Act (EPCA) legislation that governs all aspects of SPR management. The EPCA amendments of 1990 authorized a test draw-down of the SPR of up to five million barrels. The figure was arbitrary but the authority was clear. With EPCA's amendments, Congress also defied the administration's threat of a veto by authorizing an increase in the size of the SPR to one billion barrels, 250 million barrels above the level supported by the president.

The test draw

On September 21, NYMEX spot prices for West Texas Intermediate (WTI) reached above $35 per barrel and on the 24th rose to $39.05 per barrel, in direct defiance of Secretary Brady's earlier prediction that prices were headed downward.[148] At the White House, correspondence from Congress and the public objecting to the apparently unstoppable rise in oil prices intensified in volume as well as tone. As a consequence, the previously untuned White House domestic political antennae finally began to pick up the full dimensions of public discontent with the price of fuels.

It was thus that on September 25, after persistent urging by Watkins, the president announced his decision to proceed with a test sale of SPR oil, even though "no justification existed for the recent run-up in oil and gasoline prices."[149] In the same announcement, Press Secretary Marlin Fitzwater also promised that the president would take "additional steps to stabilize energy prices."[150]

The SPR test sale was conducted on schedule, beginning on September 28th. The system performed precisely as designed. There were no delays in the bidding process and in the award of contracts. The pumps, as expected, lifted the oil from the salt caverns in which it was stored and the pipelines transported the oil without leakage. The caverns did not collapse. There was no evidence of speculative or hoarding behavior. In sum, the system that had cost $19.7 billion[151] to build and the career staff who managed it had performed flawlessly.

The president requested a status report on the SPR test drawdown on October 29, 1990, in a radio message from Air Force One that asked: "How did the SPR test draw down work? Is all functioning well? Did we take bids?"[152] The president's message puzzled Watkins because he had been forwarding regular reports on the test to the White House since mid-October. (Fig. 4-1) The reports had been sent to the president in care of Sununu, as cabinet protocol required, who had apparently not forwarded any of them to the president.[153]

Memorandum For The President (October 31, 1990)
Subject: Strategic Petroleum Reserve Draw down

The Strategic Petroleum Reserve test draw down is functioning well. Initially, 40 bids were received from 33 offerors. Of the 33 offerors, 11 contracts were awarded for 3.925 million barrels of crude oil. The first delivery took place on October 19. Two additional deliveries took place on October 29, with remaining deliveries scheduled for the month of November. We did not receive reasonable offers for the remaining 1.075 million barrels, as there appeared to be a surplus of sour crude at the time of the sale.

James D. Watkins

FIG. 4-1: MEMORANDUM, WATKINS TO PRESIDENT BUSH, OCTOBER 31, 1990

The market was not impressed by the test, however, probably because traders could tell the difference between a real drawdown and a *test* drawdown of the SPR. Spot market prices rose to $39.53 per barrel on September 28 and, after a short plateau reached $41.07 per barrel—the highest level of the Iraqi crisis—on October 11, 1990.[154] The additional measures to combat the rise in oil prices, promised by Marlin Fitzwater in his announcement of the test draw, never materialized because they never existed.

Conditions in the oil market finally proved intolerable for the Senate Republican leader. On October 10, Robert Dole wrote to the president that, notwithstanding the leadership demonstrated internationally by the administration, policy initiatives were needed on the domestic front to alleviate the suffering of American consumers. He defined his position in blunt terms: "In August, I wrote to urge that you use the Strategic Petroleum Reserve to ease the burden on the United States. We have committed 150,000 young Americans and billions of dollars to confront the evils of Saddam Hussein. The United States is paying the price for a free world where aggression will not be tolerated. Asking our economy to shoulder the additional burden of unnecessarily high oil prices is not required."[155]

In conjunction with the air war

In late November, Watkins traveled to the Middle East to obtain first-hand knowledge of the oil production system in key Gulf nations. He met in Saudi Arabia with Hisham Nazer, the petroleum minister. The two agreed to establish a back channel[156] communications system they code named *Blackgold,* which would relay to DOE daily and actual oil production data from Saudi Arabia. The communication arrangements were established to provide to the U.S. government the means to respond to expected, future, unsubstantiated rumors about the war's effect on Saudi production facilities.

Oil market analysts throughout the Iraqi crisis closely monitored Saudi production facilities. Their uninterrupted operation was deemed to be the sole guarantor of relative stability in the international oil market. Reports of problems in the Saudi system usually increased market volatility, regardless of their veracity. Watkins was planning ahead to the probability of actual hostilities and the probability that Iraq's army had targeted Saudi production facilities. He reasoned that in a shooting war Iraq would have an interest in denying oil income to the Saudis to revenge the loss of income suffered by the Iraqis as a result of the UN embargo.

Watkins initiated his final campaign to obtain support for a coordinated SPR drawdown in mid-October. He directed the Energy Emergency Management Team (EEMT) to conduct a series of exercises simulating market conditions during an actual war. He invited the participation in the exercises of senior officials from the Defense Department, NSC, the Central Intelligence Agency and, in one case, the Commodities Futures Trading Commission and the New York Mercantile Exchange. Separate exercises were conducted with members of the oil industry and congressional staff. The exercises kept EEMT staff on full alert, attuned to worldwide events that could in any way disturb the equilibrium achieved by the markets. Skip Wright, the deputy assistant secretary for energy emergencies directed the EEMT and designed and conducted the exercises.

On November 29, just before his departure for Saudi Arabia, Watkins sent a confidential letter to Scowcroft summarizing the results of the exercises. The letter stated: "Although oil market fundamentals of supply and demand have improved steadily since August, the exercises raised concerns about the impact of hostilities on market psychology. Increased military requirements during hostilities can be met even under current market conditions. Nevertheless, experts at the exercises indicated that panic buying and hoarding could drive crude oil prices substantially higher. In order to reassure the market, I would propose that we announce as an element of our contingency plans, intentions to offer for sale a large quantity of Strategic Petroleum Reserve Oil (in coordination with stock draw by our IEA partners) in the event of outbreak of hostilities."[157]

Watkins' proposal was held in abeyance by Scowcroft throughout December. The DOE policy staff thought—erroneously, as it turned out—that the opportunity for effective use of the SPR was by now lost. A prediction issued by Illinois Institute of Technology Professor Henry Linden at a well-publicized conference in late September, seemed to seal the SPR debate.

"[N]o government bureaucrat will ever want to take the risk of releasing oil from the SPR," Linden stated, "when it is so much safer to keep it in reserve for what might be a rainier day."[158] In the event, the career bureaucrats wanted action. It was the political leadership that was averse to risk.

Then, unexpectedly, and without further cabinet consultations, the president accepted Watkins' SPR drawdown proposal on January 4, 1991. Related decisions were taken simultaneously. To secure the collaboration of two key allies, NSC drafted, and the president cabled identical messages to Japanese Prime Minister Toshiki Kaifu and German Chancellor Helmut Kohl on January 8. The presidential messages stated, in part: "In the event of hostilities, there is likely to be a strong reaction in oil markets, reinforced by the probability of temporary loss of some oil from the Gulf. I have asked my officials to work with their colleagues to reach immediate IEA agreement on coordinated action. For our part, I will make available, in the event of hostilities, up to 1.5 million barrels a day of oil for one month. I am requesting that Japan make available a proportionate amount. I am making a similar request to Helmut Kohl."[159]

Kohl and Kaifu responded affirmatively to the request and instructed their delegates to the IEA Governing Board, which met on January 11, to finalize arrangements for a coordinated drawdown of 2.5 million B/D, for a initial period of thirty days.[160] The board, as expected, raised no objections. IEA Executive Secretary Steeg was not consulted.

The announcement

The first-ever drawdown of the SPR was announced by the White House at 6:00 a.m. on January 17, 1991, in conjunction with the start of the air war against Iraq. The United States offered for sale 33.75 million barrels of sweet crude for an initial thirty-day contract period. Coming in the wake of what was immediately billed as the highly successful bombing campaign against Iraq, the effect of the SPR sale on the market was instantaneous. Within hours on the morning of the 17th, the price of oil on the NYMEX dropped to levels not seen since the pre-embargo days of July 1990. Major U.S. newspapers headlined the impact of the SPR on January 18.

Wrote *The Los Angeles Times*: "Crude plunges $10.56 a barrel in Record Fall: The Movement Defies Predictions. The record-breaking free fall on the New York Mercantile Exchange caught traders, government officials and oil industry executives by surprise."[161] Added *The Washington Times*: "An Oil Glut: Opened Reserves, Success of Attacks Steady Oil Market: within hours of the outbreak of hostilities in the Persian Gulf, major oil companies froze gasoline prices. It took two energy crises to do it, but the globe appears ready to cope with all but the most catastrophic oil consequences of the Gulf War."[162] Concluded *The Washington Post*: "The price dropped so fast, in fact, that it immediately triggered the NYMEX's new price-limit rules. Although most analysts had expected that 'circuit breaker' to get its first test in a rising market after the outbreak of war, instead it was triggered as prices tumbled within seconds of the 9:45 a.m. opening."[163]

Traders signed contracts for a total of only 17 million barrels of SPR oil. All deliveries were completed on schedule by March 31 and receipts from the sale totaled $300 million.[164] The per-barrel price paid by traders was roughly equal to the initial price paid by the government to obtain the oil for the

SPR—no government profits and no taxpayer losses. The SPR performed to its precise physical specifications. Congress and DOE rejoiced in the results. The Troika greeted the event in silence. Watkins heard, much later, from the President. In mid-April, Watkins received back from cabinet Secretary Ede Holiday a memorandum he had forwarded to the president on April 11, 1991, containing a summary of the results of the SPR drawdown. The memorandum was stamped: "The President Has Seen." On the right margin, in Bush's handwriting, was the single word: "interesting."[165]

Of profiteers and gougers

In November 1990 and in response to a request by Deputy Secretary Henson Moore, the Energy Information Administration (EIA) released a report on oil prices and oil companies' profits in the three months following Kuwait's invasion. The report contained an analysis of financial data publicly reported by energy industries and summarized the embargo-induced movement of oil acquisition costs and consumer prices for various oil products in the U.S. and in selected other countries.

To the question of who benefited from the increase in oil prices that resulted from the invasion of Kuwait, EIA replied with the following conclusions.

> "The third quarter (1990) profits data clearly indicate that oil producers benefited most from the price increases. The division of these upstream economic gains is roughly proportionate to the division of world oil production. Eighty percent of world oil production is foreign-owned with the bulk of this share being owned by foreign oil producing countries. The U.S. major petroleum companies own less than 14% of the world's oil production. U.S. independents and royalty owners own approximately 6%. *The biggest beneficiaries of the increase in the price of crude oil were foreign governments who owned the oil.*" (emphasis added).[166]

As would be expected, the highly diverse petroleum industry was not uniformly affected by conditions created by the 1990 oil embargo. It should also be parenthetically noted that the embargo was imposed by the United States and not by the oil-producing countries of the Persian Gulf. The effects of the embargo on the various elements of the oil industry were documented, also by the IEA, in the quarterly publication *U.S. Energy Industry Financial Developments: 1990 Third Quarter.* In summary, the EIA found the following.

Major oil and gas companies. The upstream (production) operations benefited substantially from the higher oil prices while their downstream (refining and retail sales) generally suffered. Net income for major petroleum companies rose 2% in the third quarter of 1990 compared to the third quarter of 1989. Income from their domestic production operations rose 90%, while income from their overseas exploration and production activities rose by 47%. The majors' domestic and foreign refining/marketing operations reported declines in income ranging from 42% to 33%. Income from chemical operations declined 50%.[167]

Independent oil and gas producers. The sharp rise in the price of oil during the six months of the Iraqi crisis resulted in a 476% increase (third quarter 1990 *vis* third quarter 1989) in income for independents with no increase in downstream operations such as refining and product retailing.[168]

Independent refiners and marketers. In contrast to the major integrated companies, these independent operators reported increases in net income from third quarter '89 to the same quarter of 1990 of 129%.[169]

Oil field companies. Previously depressed because of a year-long decline in U.S. oil production, these companies, which supply goods and services to producers, saw their income rise by 96% in the third quarter of 1990 compared to year earlier earnings.[170]

Were consumers charged excessive prices for gasoline at the pump? EIA found that retail gasoline prices had risen sharply in the first week following imposition of the embargo but less than the increase in crude oil prices or in wholesale gasoline prices. Crude oil prices rose from about $17.00 per barrel in late July to over $40.00 per barrel in October. Retail unleaded gasoline prices rose $5.90 per barrel between third quarter 1989 and third quarter

1990, while spot prices for unleaded gasoline rose $11.72 per barrel in the same period.[171]

Throughout the crisis period, retail gasoline prices rose less than would have been the case without the psychological restraint imposed by the Bush administration's jawboning and threat of antitrust investigations. Ironically, EIA concluded in its two reports on the subject that, "while major oil companies were being denounced for price gouging, independent retail gasoline station owners were accusing the majors of excessive price restraint for not raising their retail gasoline prices in line with crude oil price increases."[172]

How did American consumers fare in comparison to their counterparts in Europe and Asia? As Table 4-3 illustrates, American consumers fared better than did all other consumers in industrialized countries. The table, compiled from EIA data, shows retail gasoline price, pre- and post-embargo, and the percent change for selected countries. The prices shown are exclusive of taxes and duties. The data indicate that retail prices rose least in the United States and most in France.[173]

Country	Price on 7/30/90	Price on 9/17/90	%Change
Belgium	1.18	1.67	41.9
France	0.88	1.35	54.1
Germany	1.05	1.49	42.5
Italy	1.10	1.52	38.4
Japan	1.69	2.19	29.6
U.S.A.	0.82	1.01	23.3

TABLE 4-3: RETAIL PRICES FOR MOTOR GASOLINE ($/GALLON), 1990. *Source: U.S. Energy Information Administration*

The price effects of the embargo were, in sum, evenly distributed among the nations involved. The United States fared better than most of its allies, by all accounts because the oil industry heeded the president's call to exercise restraint. Similar calls were not issued in Europe or in Japan. It is difficult to explain, on the basis of the available data, the vociferous congressional charges of price gouging heard throughout the Iraqi crisis period.

Not all Americans decried the Iraqi crisis' rise in oil prices. There was at least one voice to remind Congress, perhaps in vain, of how the oil industry is affected, over time, by cycles of boom and bust. "I did not hear (my colleagues in the Senate) speaking when the price of oil went from $25 to $9.25 (per barrel) in 1986," said Senator Don Nickles of Oklahoma at the opening of the September 13 hearing of the Senate Energy Committee. "I did not hear (my) colleagues speaking up when we had the number of active rigs in this country falling from 4,000 to less than 1,000," he went on, and "we did not hear...when the number of independents were basically decimated in the states of Louisiana, Oklahoma and Texas."[174]

A POSTSCRIPT IN RIYADH

Deliberations on the SPR did not end with the Desert Storm drawdown. There was unfinished business with Congress.

In 1988, Congress had directed DOE[175] to explore means other than federal budget appropriations to finance the expansion of the SPR. The mandate had come about as a result of profound differences in spending priorities between congressional authorizing and appropriation committees.

The appropriation committees had succeeded in annually reducing the SPR budget through the decade of the 1980s and consequently slowing the rate at which DOE could purchase oil for the SPR. From a high of 336,000 B/D in 1981, the SPR fill rate had dropped to 40,000 B/D in 1990.[176] The SPR account had simply become too tempting a target for congressional appropriators seeking funds for other favorite programs because the SPR budget was perceived as benefiting only Texas and Louisiana. As a consequence, with the power of the Federal purse beyond their reach, the authorizing committees—the Senate's Energy and Natural Resources, and the House's Energy and Commerce—had sought alternatives.

The Bush administration found it politically opportune to pursue alternative SPR financing arrangements in the Summer of 1991, in the wake of a determined effort on the part of Energy and Power Subcommittee Chairman Sharp to require U.S. oil importers to contribute 1% of their imports, in cash or in-kind, to the SPR. Sharp's Strategic Petroleum Reserve Enhancement Act, which the administration viewed as a new tax, also provided authority to draw down the SPR in response to supply disruptions as well as significant oil price increase. The initiative reflected Sharp's unhappiness with SPR policy during the Iraqi war and his impatience with DOE's slow pace in seeking alternative ways of acquiring SPR oil. Although the administration strongly opposed Sharp's legislation and had threatened to veto it if enacted, [177] Sharp had nonetheless made his point that the administration needed to explore alternative means of acquiring SPR oil.

An appointment in Riyadh

John Easton arrived in Riyadh on Friday evening, July 26, 1991,[178] with instructions from the NSC to seek to acquire from the Saudis 100 to 180 million barrels of oil for the SPR, at a cost substantially below the market price of oil. His schedule called for an initial meeting with Saudi Oil Minister Hisham Nazer on Saturday, July 27. He could remain in the Saudi capital for several days if the first meeting opened the door to detailed negotiations.

Preparations for the meeting with Nazer had taken several weeks. NSC and DOE staff had argued a variety of negotiating tactics, all aimed at securing Saudi oil for the SPR at a cost not far above the Saudi cost of production. This SPR-filling option had been given the misleading term "leasing" because, although by law the U.S. government needed to have full control of the oil for an indefinite period of time, the lessor could be promised a return on investment when the leased oil was sold as part of an SPR drawdown. The lessor could theorize about a possible end-of-lease balloon payment, but no actual figure could be attached to such a payment, given the variability of conditions that could exist in the event of a future drawdown.

In reality, Easton was directed to make the case that the United States should not alone shoulder the burden of filling and maintaining a strategic reserve because stability in the oil market was everyone's concern. Could oil market stability also be the concern of producers, such as Saudi Arabia, who stood to gain from the price increases of a disrupted oil market? Yes, Easton was told to argue, because Saudi Arabia had on several occasions expressed the view that a stable oil market was a force for peace and stability. In any case, Easton would not be seeking oil entirely cost-free to the United States. In fact, if the Saudis would negotiate a deal, they could look forward to a substantial upfront payment for the leased oil at a time when the Saudis claimed to be strapped for cash.

In 1991, the SPR account was unusually flush. DOE had in hand nearly $900 million dollars in cash. It had acquired $315 million from the Desert Storm drawdown sale and $123 million from the test sale in September 1990. Additionally, Congress had provided $196 million in advance appropriations for fiscal year 1992 and DOE retained, unspent, $244 million in funds appropriated by Congress in fiscal years 1990 and 1991.[179] This cash reserve allowed for unusual flexibility in the financial arrangements that could be negotiated with potential oil lessors.

Easton was to begin negotiations by requesting that the Saudis provide oil to the SPR at a cost to the United States equal to the cost of storage. The Troika assumed that the Saudis would reject the opening bid, but would know that the United States would negotiate further. Upon formal rejection of the opening bid, Easton was authorized to offer incrementally higher prices up to a per-barrel cost that would in all cases be lower than the market price of oil. DOE policy staff had calculated the actual cost of Saudi oil was about $3 per barrel, including lifting and transportation costs. The staff had estimated the average replacement cost for Saudi oil to be a maximum of $10 per barrel and the opportunity cost in the range of $18, including all producer and consumer taxes, royalties, transportation, insurance and related costs.[180]

Nazer received Easton in his ostentatious office on the top floor of the Petroleum Ministry building in Riyadh at 1:00 p.m. on Saturday.

Surprisingly, he met with the U.S. delegation alone. The delegation included Easton, DOE's associate undersecretary[181], and David Dunford, the U.S. Embassy's *charge d'affaires* in Riyadh. The absence of aides on Nazer's side was troubling to the visitors. It meant that either Nazer had extraordinary powers to make a deal and keep it confidential—even from the Saudi bureaucracy—or he was there to merely relay a decision, already made and probably negative, from the king.

Easton presented the U.S. offer by faithfully following the script of the negotiating strategy approved by NSC. The strategy called for a review—a reminder—of the excellent relations between the two countries, most recently manifested in the defeat of Saddam Hussein, and then a presentation by Easton of the initial elements of the deal he now placed before Nazer. "An arrangement between the United States and the Kingdom to fill the United States Strategic Petroleum Reserve," Easton began, "would further strengthen security and economic relations."[182]

Nazer was not impressed by the proposal. He responded by decrying the awful state of Saudi finances in the wake of the Iraqi war. He said that the kingdom was shouldering the greater proportion of the war's costs, including payment of obligations to the United States, financial support to allies such as Egypt and Syria, and the payment of other bills presented by the UN. As an aside, Nazer remarked that the Saudi kingdom had become responsible for financing U.S. forces in Saudi Arabia, which were, he noted, the "world's most expensive army." "Also the most effective," Easton shot back, appalled by the rudeness of the remark.[183]

Nazer went on to explain that Saudi law required Aramco, the kingdom's oil producer, to pay taxes and royalties to the state treasury immediately upon the lifting of the oil, and no exceptions could be made to these payments regardless of the ultimate disposition of the oil. War-related commitments, he went on, demanded that the kingdom sell immediately all the oil it could produce, rather than store it. Also, and most importantly, he said, a U.S.-Saudi deal on strategic stocks was likely to be viewed by other nations as collusion aimed at fixing future oil prices.[184]

Nazer then wondered whether there were other proposals aside from the one presented. He had read in the media, he said, that the United States might agree to other arrangements.

Easton replied that he was authorized to negotiate an agreement that would be consistent with U.S. law, but starting from the proposal already presented. He noted that there were some—not many—non-negotiable elements in the U.S. proposal, such as unconditional presidential authority over all the oil stored in the SPR. Beyond that, Easton stated that he was ready to negotiate the details of a government-to-government, but not a commercial arrangement, for Saudi oil.

Nazer responded that he, of course, would discuss the proposal with the king, since he possessed no authority to sell Saudi oil below market price. Easton emphasized that under discussion was not a commercial deal but a security arrangement between two governments. Nazer thought that his ministry might be interested in discussing storage of commercial stocks of oil in SPR caverns, but only if the kingdom retained complete access to these stocks and was able to draw them down and refill them at will. Easton replied that such an arrangement might be feasible, but not in lieu of the U.S. proposal. The SPR, Easton stated, could not be used for commercial storage because, once stored, SPR oil could only be withdrawn by authority of the president, and because the SPR system was not engineered for repeated fills and withdrawals.

The discussions ended at 3:30 p.m. The U.S. delegation was invited to the minister's house for lunch where the conversation turned to social topics selected, however, with guile. Nazer noted that he loved to visit the United States—California, especially—where he lived as a graduate student, and where he and his family spent their annual vacations. He noted that when in the United States, he received on a nearly constant basis, a variety of requests for help from Americans in need. He did his best to help these people, he said, but wished he could do more.

The visiting Americans drew from these remarks the conclusion that Nazer considered the SPR proposal one more request for aid, albeit it from the financially strapped government of the United States.

Easton remained impeccably polite throughout the lengthy discussion at lunch, but once free of the arrogant and patronizing Nazer he gave vent to his dismay at this encounter. How could one respond to a privileged Saudi official with the temerity to decry the cost of the U.S. military? Only a few months previously the "costly" American army had secured the oil minister's personal future and, probably also the very existence of his government and his nation.[185] Nazer, who had an excessive amount of the typical Arab sense of self pride, had seemed unable to imagine that the pride of his audience might be affronted by anecdotes depicting Americans as beggars. In sum, Nazer was bemoaning the conditions of a country whose oil wealth had been increased by the recent war to visitors whose country had emerged from the war in an economic recession.

Saudi war benefits

Aside from having ensured the survival of its monarchy, the U.S.-led confrontation of Iraq had produced a financial windfall for the Saudi state. Saudi production had surged by 3.0 million B/D in the aftermath of the August 1990 embargo, reaching maximum sustainable capacity of 8.5 million B/D in early September. For all of 1990, Saudi oil exports had averaged 4.76 million B/D, nearly doubling to $45 billion its 1989 income of $24 billion. In 1991, Saudi oil exports had increased an additional 50% to 6.6 million B/D, with commensurate increases in income.[186]

The OPEC-sanctioned production quota of eight million B/D obtained by the Saudi government in August 1990 had never been rescinded. Saudi oil exports had remained above six million B/D and were commanding prices higher than those paid in the pre-war period, mainly because of U.S. support for continuation of the embargo of Iraqi oil. Saudi oil income had tripled during the Iraqi war, not merely in the critical period of August 1990 to February 1991, but for a full year thereafter. Saudi oil had sold on the international market at prices ranging from $28 per barrel to $41 per barrel for a total of seven months and thereafter at more than $21 per barrel. Such prices had not been seen since 1980. In sum, the Iraqi war had been highly profitable for the Saudis—the third massive transfer of unearned wealth in as many decades from Western economies to the Persian Gulf.[187]

U.S. interagency estimates of the Iraqi war's cost to the United States ranged from $40 to $60 billion in total.[188] The Saudi government had contributed slightly less than $14 billion to defray a part of the U.S. costs for the war.[189] Nazer's lament about the cost of U.S. troops was therefore aberrant. To the extent they were real, the financial difficulties of the Saudi government—which presumably prevented the SPR oil storage/leasing deal of July 1991—were due rather to the cost of the structural subsidies with which the House of Saud purchases the loyalty of its subjects.

The final response

There were no further meetings with Nazer in Riyadh. Easton met with him in Boston a month later to receive his formal reply that the U.S. offer was not acceptable to the kingdom. Furthermore, Nazer said, the Kingdom was not interested in further negotiations on the subject.[190]

Watkins took the response in stride. Moore thought that the Saudis' peremptory reaction was probably due to the negotiating constraints that had been imposed by the Troika. NSC staff, privately agreeing with Moore, subsequently cabled to the Saudi foreign ministry a reassuring message that the aborted SPR negotiations would not affect bilateral relations between the two countries.[191]

It is conceivable that the SPR negotiations might have produced different results had the U.S. delegation been given different negotiating authority, but Nazer's apparent lack of engagement, coupled with his attitude that Americans were making unreasonable demands on what he considered Saudi largesse to the war effort, seemed to preclude a successful deal. Richard Murphy, a former ambassador to Riyadh, had suggested to Easton prior to the start of negotiations that a government-to-government SPR agreement between the United States and Saudi Arabia could be concluded by no one else but the president and the king. This venue, however, the president would not pursue.[192]

NOTES AND COMMENTS

1. The eyewitness tone in the account of events related in chapter four is due to the role that the author was assigned by the leadership of the DOE during the period of the Iraqi crisis. Formally appointed by Watkins to the (career service) position of associate deputy undersecretary for policy analysis, Stagliano served as one of two deputies to policy chief Linda Stuntz. The other deputy, Mark Kerrigan, was a political appointee. During the period in question, Stagliano was directly involved in, or fully privy to virtually all departmental deliberations on the energy aspects of Iraqi war policy, directed the development of the short- and medium-term response measures and the SPR drawdown proposals. He served, further, on the Executive Committee of the Energy Emergency Management Team. He was responsible for the preparation of staff papers and briefing books related to the secretary of energy's participation in cabinet meetings, and had authority to represent the Department in negotiations with the White House Office of Cabinet Affairs.

2. Major world oil supply interruptions: (Source: Interagency Working Group, Strategic Petroleum Reserve Analysis of Size Options, Department of Energy, February 1990)

Date	Event	Disruption Size (million B/D)	World Oil Consumption (million B/D)
Mar.'51-Oct.'54	Iranian oil nationalized	0.7	13.2
Nov.'56-Mar.'57	Suez war	2.0	17.5
Dec.'66-Mar.'67	Syrian transit fee dispute	0.7	34.3
Jun.'67-Aug.'67	Six day war	2.0	40.0
Jul.'67-Oct.'68	Nigeria civil war	0.5	40.1
May'70-Jan.'71	Libyan price dispute	1.3	48.0
Apr.'71-Aug.'71	Algeria nationalization	0.6	50.2
Mar.'73-May'73	Lebanese conflict	0.5	58.2
Oct.'73-Mar.'74	Arab-Israeli war	1.6	58.2
Apr.'76-May'76	Lebanon civil war	0.3	60.2
May 1977	Damaged Saudi fields	0.7	62.1
Nov.'78-Apr.'79	Iranian revolution	3.7	65.1
Oct.'80-Jan.'81	Iran-Iraq war	3.0	60.4
Jul.'88-Nov.'89	U.K. Piper Alpha explosion	0.3	49.8
Dec.'88-Mar.'89	U.K. Fulmer accident	0.2	51.6
Apr.'89-Jun.89	U.K. Cormorant explosion	0.5	51.6
Aug.'90-Feb.'91	Iraqi-Kuwait war	4.3	61.0

3. California heavy oil initiative: This proposal, contained in the response measures the DOE pursued during the Iraqi war, comprised two aspects of policy. The first was related to production, the second to marketing. Production of California's large heavy oil resources required injection of steam into wells in order to ensure a minimum flow rate for the high viscosity/low porosity oil. In 1985, application was made to FERC for construction of the Kern-Mojave pipeline that would transport Wyoming natural gas to California's San Joaquin Valley—the center of heavy oil production. The lower-cost natural gas was intended to replace electric power for production of steam for injection. FERC authorized the Kern-Mojave pipeline in 1989, but subject to an environmental permit from the U.S. Forestry Service because the pipeline was to traverse a small portion of the Wasatch Catch Forest in Utah. The Forest Service held up the pipeline's permit for over two years until publicly embarrassed by the DOE during the Iraqi War. The marketing aspects

of the issue were related to captive markets. California refineries blended cheap heavy oil with more expensive Alaska North Slope light crude and reaped higher-than-usual profit margins because, without a market outside the state, California heavy oil producers had to be content with prices for their oil essentially set by the refiners. A market for heavy crude existed in countries of the Pacific Rim, but the Commerce Department refused for four years to issue an export permit to California heavy oil producers on the grounds that Congress had intended the ban on exports of Alaskan oil to also apply to California heavy oil. DOE attacked the position of Commerce and finally prevailed in 1992 when Commerce issued the first export licensing, but only for a maximum of twenty-five thousand B/D.

4. IEA was created as a forum for coordination of the petroleum and energy policies of members of the Organization for Economic Cooperation and Development (OECD). IEA mission and functions were designed by an OECD-sponsored Energy Coordinating Group, which drew plans for the creation of the agency in the six months following the 1973-1974 oil embargo. The IEA was launched in Brussels, Belgium, on September 21, 1974, by the representatives of 12 nations: The United States, Japan, Canada, United Kingdom, Federal Republic of Germany, Belgium, the Netherlands, Luxemburg, Italy, Ireland, Denmark, and Norway. Other European nations joined in subsequent years, with France joining last in 1991 to raise the total membership to twenty-one countries. The Brussels plan was entitled: "Agreement on an International Energy Program." The program established a mechanism by which IEA member-states would manage oil emergencies by spreading the burden of a supply shortfall. It was envisioned that the shortfall might be caused by selective embargoes against one or more member states (as happened in the Arab oil embargo of 1973) or by a temporary supply disruption affecting all consuming nations. The Governing Board is the highest decision-making body of the IEA. Countries are represented on the board usually at ministerial level. A number of committees oversee subject-specific areas of IEA's mandate. They include: Standing Groups on Long-Term Cooperation, on Emergency Questions, on the Oil Market and on Relations with Producer

and other Consumer Countries. A Management Committee coordinates the activities of the standing groups.

5. Bush administration tax incentives for the oil and gas industry: With the first budget submitted to Congress by the Bush administration in 1989, the president proposed, but Congress declined to enact: (a) a temporary tax credit for exploratory drilling expenditures, (b) a temporary tax credit for new enhanced oil recovery (EOR) projects, (c) elimination of the transfer rule, (d) an increase in the percentage depletion net income limitation, and (e) increased deductions—for alternative minimum tax purposes—of exploratory intangible drilling costs. These were the tax incentives mentioned by Secretary Watkins in his September 1990 testimony before the Senate Energy and Natural Resources Committee and the House Subcommittee on Energy and Power. The DOE policy office attempted, unsuccessfully, to expand the president's tax credit for enhanced oil recovery projects, as part of the mid-term response measures to the Iraqi oil embargo, arguing that the originally proposed credit, by its size and its temporary nature, was insufficient to encourage substantial new EOR investments. The two temporary tax credits proposed by the administration were designed to be phased out when oil prices reached $21 per barrel during a full calendar year. They were estimated to induce increased production of between 172,000 and 196,000 B/D of oil. Treasury estimated the cost of the credits at a maximum of $462 million per year if wellhead prices averaged $18 per barrel, and a median of $101 million per year if wellhead prices averaged $25 barrel.

Notwithstanding the president's support for these proposals, DOE policy staff discovered during the course of preparing testimony for Secretary Watkins in the Iraqi war period, that the Treasury Department had never submitted legislation to Congress to implement the tax measures, and had not notified the White House of this fact. The Treasury Department refused to provide an explanation for the record of its failure to implement the president's proposal, when requested to do so by DOE in conjunction with Watkins' testimony on the subject before Congress, in September 1990.

For the National Energy Strategy (NES), the DOE policy office also recommended a substantial reform of the Alternative Minimum Tax requirements for independent producers. The Troika opposed it and it was dropped from the final NES. Congress subsequently voted it into law as part of the Energy Policy Act of 1992. Treasury recommended that the president veto the Energy Policy Act because it contained this tax provision and a few lesser ones, but the president discarded the advice and signed the bill in October 1992.

REFERENCES

[1] T.E. Lawrence, *Seven Pillars of Wisdom: A Triumph*. Originally published in a private edition by the George Doran Publishing Company in 1926. (New York: Anchor Books, Doubleday, July 1991), p. 25.

[2] Raphael Patai, *The Arab Mind*. Revised edition. (New York: Charles Scribner's Sons, 1983), p. 221.

[3] Sandra Mackey, *Passion and Politics: The Turbulent World of the Arabs*, (Plume/Penguin Books USA, 1994), pp. 322-332.

[4] Ibid., p. 338.

[5] Bob Woodward, *The Commanders*. (New York: Simon & Schuster, 1991), p. 226.

[6] Ibid.

[7] Ibid., p. 227.

[8] DOE, "Revised Schedule for Secretary James D. Watkins" Date: Thursday, August 2, 1990: 7:45 am: Meet Joe Bullock (official driver); 8:00-10:00 AM: "The White House: National Security Council Meeting with the President."

[9] Summary minutes of NSC Meeting of August 2 1990, George H.W. Bush Presidential Library, Houston, TX.: No reference whatsoever to statements by Secretary Watkins on the subject of potential pipeline targets in Saudi Arabia. Also personal communications from Admiral Watkins to Stagliano: "I would under no circumstances presume to recommend potential military targets in a meeting of the NSC since such recommendations would be entirely beyond my statutory purview."

[10] Deborah Amos, *Lines in the Sand: Desert Storm and the Remaking of the Arab World*. (New York, NY: Simon & Schuster, 1992), p.34.

[11] Ibid., p. 36.

[12] DOE, Energy Emergency Management Team (EEMT), Situation Analysis Report as of August 2, 1990. Unclassified. Mimeo. Washington, DC.

[13] IEA estimates of strategic stocks held by member countries in August 1990 were as follows (in millions of barrels): U.S.: 590; Japan: 212; Germany: 196; Netherlands: 17; Denmark: 14; Italy: 6; Sweden and Austria: 2 each, for an IEA total of 1.039 billion barrels.

[14] DOE, Office of the Press Secretary, "DOE Says U.S. Petroleum Supplies Adequate for Immediate Future Despite Middle East Turmoil", *DOE NEWS*, August 2, 1990.

[15] Executive order blocking Iraqi government property and prohibiting transactions with Iraq. Issued by the White House, Office of Press Secretary, August 2, 1990.

[16] Charles Schotta, U.S. Department of the Treasury, Eastern European, Soviet, and Middle Eastern Affairs. Fax message to Thad Grundy, DOE, Subject: Oil Imported from Kuwait and Iraq, August 3, 1990.

[17] U.S. Department of the Treasury, "The Treasury Department Today Announced the Following Actions: (1) Oil Contracts Entered Into Prior to August 2, 1990, and en route to the United States...", *TREASURY NEWS*, August 3, 1990.

[18] Amos, op. cit., p. 37.

[19] W. Henson Moore. Personal communication, March 10, 1994.

[20] W. Henson Moore, deputy secretary, DOE, Talking Points, "National Security Council Meeting, August 3, 1990." Mimeo.

[21] For a chronology of world oil supply disruptions from 1951 to 1989, see note two of notes and comments section of chapter 4.

[22] Moore, NSC Meeting August 3, 1990, op. cit., Addendum titled "Acquiescing to the Status Quo".

[23] DOE, Energy Emergency Management Team, Situation Analysis Report as of August 6, 1990. Unclassified. Mimeo. Washington, DC.

[24] John D. Dingell, chairman, Committee on Energy and Commerce, U.S. House of Representatives, Letter to the Honorable Janet D. Steiger, chairman, Federal Trade Commission, August 6, 1990.

[25] John D. Dingell, chairman, Committee on Energy and Commerce, U.S. House of Representatives, Letter to the Honorable James D. Watkins, secretary, DOE, August 6, 1990.

[26] DOE, Office of the Press Secretary, "The Departments of Energy, Justice and Transportation Express Concern with Gasoline Price Increases", *DOE NEWS*, August 6,1990.

[27] Ibid.

[28] Ibid.

[29] Ibid.

[30] Chevron Corporation, Press release, Chevron Chairman Responds to President Bush's Middle East Action, August 8, 1990.

[31] Personal communication, Moore to Stagliano, on the day of the phone call from DiBona.

[32] Section 101(b) of the Defense Production Act authorizes the secretary of energy to "control the general distribution of oil in the civilian market."

[33] Tom Tauke, member of Congress, Letter to the Honorable James Watkins, secretary, DOE, August 3, 1990, paragraph 1.

[34] DOE, Department of Energy—Action Items, August 20, 1990.

[35] Thomas A. Rogers, chairman, Board of Supervisors, County of Santa Barbara, CA, Letter to Secretary of Energy Admiral James D. Watkins, U.S. Navy (Retired), August 14, 1990.

[36] ARCO internal correspondence from R.E. Wycoff to Mr. L.M. Cook (chairman), Subject: Response to Bob Mosbacher, August 21, 1990.

[37] DOE, Office of the Press Secretary, Note to Editors, *DOE NEWS*, August 31, 1990.

[38] GAO, *International Energy Agency: Response to the Oil Supply Disruption Caused by the Persian Gulf Crisis*, GAO/NSLAD-92-93. Washington, DC, National Security and International Affairs Division, January 1992.

[39] DOE, U.S. Energy Immediate Measures Initiatives. Mimeo, no date.

[40] EIA, Iraq/Kuwait Fact Sheet. Mimeo, July 1990.

[41] EIA, "Energy Situation Analysis: Persian Gulf - September 20, 1990." Washington, DC, p. 2 (Spot Crude Oil and Spot Unleaded Gasoline Prices (7/30-present).

[42] DOE, Administration's Medium Term Energy Measures. Mimeo, September 13, 1990.

[43] For background on this initiate, see note three in notes and comments section of chapter 4.

[44] EPC, Draft Memorandum for [The President], Subject: Medium Term Measures to Mitigate the Energy Effects of the Middle East Situation (with mark-up of changes by Linda G. Stuntz). Mimeo, September 7, 1990.

[45] Richard Schmalensee, member, CEA, Executive Office of the President, Memorandum to Linda Stuntz, Subject: ANWR, etc., September 6, 1990.

[46] *Wall Street Journal*, "Washington Wire," September 24, 1990, p. A1.

[47] Calvin A. Kent, administrator, EIA, Memorandum to the secretary, deputy secretary, undersecretary, Subject: Analysis of Recent Changes in Domestic Petroleum Demand and Supply, June 21, 1991.

[48] Ibid.

[49] DOE. Mitigating the Energy Effects of the Iraqi Situation: Measures for the Medium Term, Section IV. Other Measures: Limited SPR Drawn-down. DOE classified document finalized on August 31, 1990.

[50] EIA, *Petroleum Prices and Profits in the 90 Days Following the Invasion of Kuwait*, SR/OA/90-01. Washington, DC, November 1990, Table 1-3 in Appendix A, p. 3.

[51] Douglas R. Bohi and William B. Quandt, *Energy Security in the 1980s: Economic and Political Perspectives*. (Washington, DC: Brookings Institution, 1984), p. 22.

[52] DOE, Mitigating the Energy Effects, Section IV, op. cit.

[53] The author was directly involved in all of these deliberations.

[54] The author was directly involved in all of these deliberations.

[55] *Boston Globe*, Editorial Page, August 11, 1990.

[56] *Los Angeles Times*, Editorial Page, August 13, 1990.

[57] *Washington Times*, Editorial Page, August 17, 1990.

[58] Personal communications: Stuntz to Stagliano.

[59] For further details on the founding of the IEA, see note four in the notes and comments section of chapter 4.

[60] C. Goodwin., op. cit.

[61] Richard Scott, *IEA: The First 20 Years, Volume One, Origins and Structure.* (Paris: OECD/IEA, 1994), p. 359.

[62] Ibid.

[63] Ibid.

[64] Ibid., p. 11.

[65] Ibid., p. 19.

[66] Bohi and Quandt, op. cit., p. 25.

[67] John Easton. Personal communication.

[68] Ibid.

[69] IEA. Governing Board Conclusions on Implications of the Iraqi Aggression Against Kuwait. Mimeo, August 9, 1990.

[70] EIA, Graphic table of Japanese and U.S. Petroleum Demand, 1989-1990.

[71] IEA, Press release. Statement by Mrs. Helga Steeg, executive director of IEA, Paris, January 17, 1991.

[72] School of Advanced International Studies (SAIS), Johns Hopkins University, *Energy Papers, International Energy and Environment Program: Annual Report, 1990-1991 and Conference Summary: "After the Gulf War: Implications for U.S. Energy and Foreign Policies."* (Washington, DC: SAIS), October 10 seminar, p. 4.

[73] EIA, "Energy Situation Analysis Report: Persian Gulf, September 21, 1990." Washington, DC.

[74] Personal communications, Watkins to Stagliano

[75] A commodity market is in a state of *Contango* when forward prices are higher than current prices.

[76] EIA, "Energy Situation Analysis Report: Persian Gulf, September 10, 1990." Washington, DC.

[77] Mark Potts, *Washington Post*, August 16, 1990.

[78] *Wall Street Journal*, "Washington Wire," September 26, 1990, p. A1.

[79] Personal communications, Watkins to Stagliano

[80] Schmalensee position related directly to author. Assessment of meeting and vote count relayed by Watkins to DOE senior staff during a post-mortem on the EPC meeting, within the hour after conclusion of the meeting.

[81] *Wall Street Journal*, "Washington Wire," September 24, 1990, p. A1.

[82] DOE, *United States Energy Policy 1980-1988*. Washington, DC, October 1988, p. 134.

[83] Energy Security Analysis, Inc. *The Crude Oil Market: After the Iraq Crisis*, Washington, DC, January 1991, p. A1-19.

[84] DOE, chair, Interagency Working Group, SPR: Analysis of Size Options, DOE/IE-0016. Washington, DC, February 1990.

[85] Participants in the interagency study were: DOE, State, Treasury, Defense, Interior, Commerce, OMB, CIA, CEA, NSC, and Federal Emergency Management Agency.

[86] DOE, Strategic Petroleum Reserve Option Paper [for the EPC meeting of February 1990]. Mimeo, no date.

[87] Vito Stagliano, (signed by Linda G. Stuntz, deputy-under secretary), Summary Memorandum to the deputy secretary, Issue: March 20, 1990 Testimony on SPR before Senate Energy Committee, April 12, 1990.

[88] Daniel Yergin, Joseph Stanislaw, and Dennis Eklof, *The U.S. Strategic Petroleum Reserve: Margin of Security*. (Cambridge, MA: Cambridge Energy Research Associates, Inc., 1990).

[89] Charles Schotta, U.S. Department of the Treasury, Memorandum for Oil Price Impact Study Group, Subject: Study Plan, Schedule, and Weekend Logistics, August 10, 1990.

[90] U.S. Department of Treasury, *Potential Impacts of a Disruption/Mitigating Economic Impacts of Drawing the Strategic Petroleum Research*. Classified Confidential/NOFORN, subsequently declassified and transmitted to Congress to be included in the record of hearings conducted by the House Energy and Power Subcommittee.

[91] Philip R. Sharp, chairman, Energy and Power Subcommittee, Committee on Energy and Commerce, U.S. House of Representatives, "How Bush Made the Recession Worse", *Washington Post*, December 29, 1991.

[92] Ibid.

[93] William Safire, "Bush's Cabinet: Who's Up," *New York Times Magazine*, March 25, 1990, p. 63.

[94] U.S. Senate, S. 2884: *National Energy Security Act of 1990*, proposed to the U.S. Senate, 101st Congress, 2nd Session by Senator Frank Murkowski.

[95] Congressional Record, U.S. Senate, August 3, 1990, pp. S 11828-11833.

[96] Ibid.

[97] U.S. Senate, Committee on Interior and Insular Affairs, *Executive Energy Messages*. Printed by the Request of Henry M. Jackson, pursuant to S. Res. 45, A National Fuels and Energy Policy Study: Energy and National Goals, Address to the Nation (July 15, 1979): Presidential Documents, Week ending Friday, July 20, 1979. Washington DC, 1979.

[98] U.S. Senate, Committee on Interior and Insular Affairs, *Executive Energy Messages*. Printed by the Request of Henry M. Jackson, pursuant to S. Res. 45, A National Fuels and Energy Policy Study: Address by the President on Live Television and Radio, January 23, 1974. Washington DC, 1975, p. 171.

[99] Ibid., *Proposals to Deal with the Energy Crisis*, Message to the Congress of the United States, January 23, 1974, p. 133.

[100] U.S. Senate, Committee on Energy and Natural Resources, *Legislative Calendar, 101st Congress 1989-1990: Calendar*, S. PRT. 101-146. Washington DC, December 31, 1990, p. 21.

[101] Ibid.

[102] Jeff Bingaman, United States senator, Letter to the Honorable James D. Watkins, secretary of energy, Washington, DC, August 6, 1990.

[103] U.S. House of Representatives, Committee on Energy and Commerce, *Energy Impact of the Persian Gulf Crisis*, Serial No. 101-209. Joint Hearings, 101st Congress, 2nd session, August 7, September 10 and 27, 1990. Washington DC, 1991, pp. 53-65.

[104] Ibid., p. 59.

[105] Ibid., p. 60.

[106] Ibid.

[107] Ibid.

[108] Ibid.

[109] Ibid.

[110] *The Energy Policy and Conservation Act of 1975*, signed into law by President Gerald Ford on December 22, 195, Sec. 161 (d) and Sec. 3(8).

[111] The author was directly involved in preparations for the hearing and privy to Easton's thinking.

[112] Ibid., p. 69.

[113] OMB, Executive Office of the President, Statement of administration policy: S. 1224, *Motor Vehicle Fuel Efficiency Act of 1990*, September 10, 1990.

[114] Richard Bryant, United States senator, et al., Letter to "Dear Colleague," Washington DC, August 14, 1990.

[115] John J. Easton, Jr., assistant secretary, International Affairs and Energy Emergencies, DOE, Statement before the Committee on Government Operations, U.S. House of Representatives, September 5, 1990.

[116] Calvin A. Kent, administrator, EIA, Testimony before the subcommittee on Energy and Power, Committee on Energy and Commerce, U.S. House of Representatives, September 10, 1990.

[117] Ibid.

[118] U.S. House of Representatives, *Energy Impact of the Persian Gulf Crisis* Hearing Record, op. cit., p. 185.

[119] The White House, Office of the Press Secretary, Remarks by the president to the Joint Session of Congress, September 11, 1990.

[120] U.S. Senate Committee on Energy and Natural Resources, *Implications of the Middle Eastern Crisis for Near-Term and Mid-Term Oil Supply*, S. Hearing. 101-1120. Hearing

before the Committee on Energy and Natural Resources, United States Senate, 101st Congress, 2nd session, September 13, 1990, p. 1.

[121] Ibid.

[122] Ibid., p. 2.

[123] Ibid., p. 6.

[124] Ibid., p. 4.

[125] Ibid.

[126] Ibid., p. 7.

[127] Ibid., pp. 4-5.

[128] Ibid., p. 9.

[129] Ibid., p. 7.

[130] Ibid., p. 9.

[131] Ibid., p. 11.

[132] For further details on the president's tax proposals, see note five in notes and comments section of chapter 4.

[133] U.S. Senate, *Implications of the Middle Eastern Crisis Hearing Record*, op. cit., p. 16.

[134] Ibid., p. 44.

[135] Ibid., pp. 45.

[136] Ibid., p. 48.

[137] Ibid., pp. 45-47.

[138] Ibid., pp. 50-51.

[139] U.S. House of Representatives, *Energy Impact of the Persian Gulf Crisis* Hearing Record, p. 204.

[140] DOE, Summary of the Testimony of Admiral James D. Watkins, September 27, 1990.

[141] Ibid.

[142] U.S. House of Representatives, *Energy Impact of the Persian Gulf Crisis* Hearing Record, op. cit., pp. 225-233 and 301-302.

[143] The author participated in preparations for the hearing and was privy to Watkins' thinking.

[144] James D. Watkins, admiral, U.S. Navy (Retired). Personal communication, March 1, 1994.

[145] U.S. House of Representatives, *Energy Impact of the Persian Gulf Crisis* Hearing Record, op. cit., pp. 311-314.

[146] Caleb Solomon and Rose Gutfeld, "No Panacea: Petroleum Reserve Has Lots of Oil, But Using It Could Be a Challenge," *New York Times*, September 5, 1990, p. A1.

[147] John W. Bartholomew, director, SPR, DOE, Letter to Mr. Daniel Henninger, deputy editor, Editorial Page, *Wall Street Journal*, September 11, 1990.

[148] EIA, *Petroleum Prices and Profits*, op. cit., p. B-10.

[149] Associated Press, Bush-Oil, September 26, 1990.

[150] Associated Press, Bush-Oil, September 26, 1990.

[151] DOE, SPR Analysis of Size Options, op cit., Table II-2.

[152] Radio message received from Air Force One by DOE Communications Center on 29 October 1990, addressed to "Jim Watkins."

[153] James D. Watkins, admiral U.S. Navy (Retired), secretary of energy, Memoranda for the Honorable John Sununu, chief of staff to the president and the Honorable Brent Scowcroft, assistant to the president for national security affairs, Subject: SPR Test Sale-90, Situation Reports 1-6, various dates October 1990.

[154] EIA, *Petroleum Prices and Profits*, op. cit., p. B-11.

[155] Bob Dole, Office of the Republican Leader, U.S. Senate, Letter to the president, October 10, 1990.

[156] Normally, communications between the U.S. and other governments are carried out through diplomatic channels handled by the State Department and its overseas embassies. We judged these channels too slow and cumbersome for the purposes described in the text.

[157] James D. Watkins, admiral, U.S. Navy (Retired), secretary of energy, Letter to Honorable Brent Scowcroft, assistant to the president for national security affairs, November 29, 1990. Classified Confidential.

[158] H.R. Linden, "Energy, Economic and Social Progress, and the Environment: Inseparable Issues in Resource Allocation, *International Journal of Energy, Environment, Economics*, vol. 1, no. 1, 1991, pp. 1-12. (Paper presented at the Illinois Institute of Technology Centennial Conference on Science, Technology and Allocation of Global Resources, September 27, 1990.)

[159] James D. Watkins, admiral, U.S. Navy (Retired), secretary of energy, Memorandum for the Honorable John H. Sununu, chief of staff to the president, the Honorable Brent Scowcroft, assistant to the president for national security affairs, the Honorable Nicholas Brady, secretary of the treasury, Subject: SPR Drawdown, with attachments including texts of presidential messages to Kohl and Kaifu, January 29, 1991.

[160] Personal communications, Melby to Stagliano, based on cable traffic accessible to Melby.

[161] *Los Angeles Times*, "Crude Plunges $10.56 a Barrel in Record Fall", by Patrick Lee and Robert A. Rosenblatt, January 18, 1991.

[162] *Washington Times*, "An Oil Glut: Opened reserves, success of attacks steady oil market", by Ronald A. Taylor, August 18, 1991.

[163] *Washington Post*, "Price of Oil Plunges By $10.56 a Barrel: Major Companies to Lower Gas Prices:, by Mark Potts, January 18, 1991.

[164] SPR Office internal documents and reports to the secretary of energy.

[165] Memorandum for the president, from James Watkins: Summary Results of SPR Drawdown, April 11, 1991.

[166] EIA, "Petroleum Prices and Profits in the 90 Days Following the Invasion of Kuwait," November 20, 1990.

[167] EIA, "U.S. Energy Industry Financial Developments, 1990 Third Quarter." Washington DC, November 1990, p. 2.

[168] Ibid.

[169] Ibid.

[170] Ibid.

[171] Ibid., p. 7.

[172] Ibid., p. 8.

[173] DOE, EIA, "Energy Situation Analysis Report – Persian Gulf, September 21, 1990: Comparative Recent International Retail Prices for Motor Gasoline and Heating Oil, Excluding Taxes and Duties."

[174] U.S. Senate, *Implications of the Middle Eastern Crisis* Hearing Record, op. cit., p. 54.

[175] Public Law 101-46 required DOE to study alternative financing methods for the SPR and report back to Congress by February 1, 1990. DOE responded with a report proposing, inter alia, oil leasing arrangements with major international oil producers.

[176] DOE, SPR Analysis of Size Options, Table II-2, op. cit.

[177] W. Henson Moore, deputy secretary of Energy, Letter to the Honorable Philip R. Sharp, chairman, Subcommittee on Energy and Power, Committee on Energy and Commerce, U.S. House of Representatives, July 23, 1991.

[178] Official itinerary of John Easton and Vito Stagliano. Travel plans held confidential by DOE in order to reduce press speculation.

[179] DOE, "Strategic Petroleum Reserve Option Paper," presented to the NSC. Mimeo, June 5, 1991.

[180] Howard Borgstorm (DOE) through Rick Furiga, DOE, Note to Vito Stagliano, Subject: SPR Financing Negotiating Approach, July 23, 1991.

[181] The DOE associate undersecretary was the author.

[182] John J. Easton, Jr., assistant secretary for International Affairs and Energy Emergencies, DOE, Memorandum for deputy secretary, Subject: SPR Partnership with Saudi Arabia, with Confidential attachment, June 26, 1991.

[183] The author was present at the meeting between Nazer and Easton.

[184] Eugene J. McAllister, European Bureau and John Kelly, Near East Bureau, U.S. Department of State, Memorandum to Frank Zoellick, undersecretary of state for Economic Affairs, Subject: Meeting with Ambassador Chas. Freeman, with attachment

summarizing report of meeting cabled by J. Easton and V. Stagliano from Riyadh, August 2, 1991.

[185] Conversations between Stagliano and Easton after the meeting with Nazer.

[186] Embassy of the United States of America, Riyadh, Saudi Arabia, "1991 Oil Survey," July 1991.

[187] Ibid.

[188] DOE, "Strategic Petroleum Reserve Option Paper," op. cit.

[189] Brent Scowcroft, the White House, Letter to the Honorable Philip R. Sharp, chairman, Subcommittee on Energy and Power, Committee on Energy and Commerce, U.S. House of Representatives, November 27, 1991.

[190] The author was also present at the Boston meeting with Nazer.

[191] Post-mortem assessment of the SPR negotiations involving Moore, Easton and Stagliano.

[192] Post-mortem assessments of the negotiations with Nazer among Watkins, Moore, Melby, Easton and Stagliano.

CHAPTER FIVE

THE NATIONAL ENERGY STRATEGY
EMERGES (SCATHED)

THE OPTIONS OF DISCORD

"Few words," former Undersecretary of the Interior Cordell Moore once noted, "so innocently incorporate into their basic meaning as much simplifying illusion as does the word 'policy'."[1]

In theory, the making of national policy seeks to redress social ills, remedy economic inefficiencies, provide prudent access to natural resources, and generally transform a multiplicity of special interests into some common good. Policy, however, is made by men and women whose deliberations are driven by political passion and human frailty. Policymaking embraces the maker's relative skill in the exercise of power, personal standing in the hierarchy of authority and the need to temper the highly desirable with the politically feasible.

The Bush administration's NES took final shape during the politico-military lull between Operation Desert Shield—the protection of Saudi Arabia—and Desert Storm, the liberation of Kuwait. DOE leadership turned its full attention to the NES final act in October 1990, conscious of the fact that the cabinet and the president had already shown disinclination to support what seemed to many in the cabinet to be the far too broad energy policy agenda advocated by DOE. Energy Secretary Watkins had no allies among the Troika leaders and held no favor with White House staff. The president was preoccupied with Iraq.

By mid-October, analysis was completed of the policy options that would be the building blocks of NES. Consistent with Sununu's June 1989 direction to Watkins to define options but avoid premature policy recommendations, DOE staff on October 26 dispatched to the member agencies of the EPC Working Group briefing books containing summary analyses for sixty-seven NES options.[2] On the advice of EPC Executive Secretary Olin Wethington, Stuntz concurrently requested that the agencies take a position on each of the options and communicate their vote to DOE no later than October 30, 1990.[3]

The majority of the agencies responded to Stuntz's request by simply checking off the columns for or against each of the options; a few also provided rationale and explanations for their positions. The critical agencies—those most likely to dominate EPC's deliberations—used the polling process to communicate to DOE and to each other the rationale they would use to oppose options that in their view did not meet the criteria established in the original EPC guidance. The formal poll of Troika positions produced no surprises, but did indicate the degree of available negotiability for options, or variations of options, that were viewed as inadequately justifying a market failure.

Agencies' initial positions on NES options

Alan Hubbard, executive director of the Vice President's Council on Competitiveness, communicated strong support for efforts to "remove unnecessary government-imposed burdens on nuclear energy, natural gas transportation, hydro-electric licensing, and electric generation and transmission." Hubbard indicated that policies were already in place to ensure reduced vulnerability to oil supply disruptions and to safeguard environmental quality, citing "the market mechanism for oil, the tax structure on oil and oil products, and the existing and new environmental [CAAA] regulation of energy production and use that are quite stringent."

Hubbard indicated that the council strongly opposed options dealing with automotive fuel efficiency. "We are very concerned," he wrote, "that any effort to suggest a regulatory increase in the [CAFE] standard, or to modify existing [CAFE] legislation, will erode the support we were able to generate on the Hill for the President's opposition" to previous legislative proposals on this issue." Hubbard reminded DOE that, during the Reagan administration, a "Task Force on Regulatory Relief, chaired by then-Vice President Bush [had] developed a proposal to repeal CAFE because of its adverse effects on American industry."[4]

Sidney Jones, assistant secretary for economic policy, transmitted the Treasury Department positions. Treasury opposed fifteen of the sixty-seven options, including a variable fee on imported oil, higher gas taxes on gas guzzling cars and rebates to gas sippers, tax incentives for mass transit, tax and regulatory incentives for alternative transportation fuels, tax production credits for renewable energy, energy efficiency standards for buildings and new equipment, and a tax on the carbon content of fuels. Jones also indicated opposition to the option of seeking to prescribe energy impact assessments in environmental rule makings. Treasury considered new efficiency standards for energy-using equipment as "a significant new Federal regulatory intervention that restricts consumer and business choice." Jones stated that Treasury could not support options requiring that buildings financed with federal funds should meet more stringent energy efficiency standards than privately financed buildings and recommended that technical assistance be provided instead.[5]

Timothy Deal, NSC senior director for international economic affairs, responded to the poll by indicating that NSC would not take a position on individual options. He proposed, instead, that to meet national security objectives, the United States should adopt four key policy goals: (1) reduce the role of oil in the energy supply mix, (2) increase energy diversity and efficiency in all sectors of the economy, but particularly in transportation, (3) remove market barriers to the development of non-oil energy resources, and (4) improve mechanisms, nationally and internationally, to respond to energy supply disruptions.

"The interdependence of most energy markets," he concluded, "and particularly that of oil, demonstrates that the U.S. is unlikely to be able to carry out any energy strategy in isolation of events occurring outside the U.S."[6]

NRC, commenting only on NES options related to its statutory mandate, suggested that legislation proposed by DOE to standardize nuclear reactor design and licensing would not be desirable. NRC agreed with DOE's proposal to seek a comprehensive, congressionally mandated solution to the nuclear waste problem and supported the "concept of developing a model energy facility siting program." It opposed the option of requiring energy impact analysis in environmental regulations but supported a proposal to eliminate "state regulation of radio-nuclide emissions for licensing facilities which are already regulated under the Atomic Energy Act."[7]

Richard Schmalensee provided CEA's' positions. CEA opposed all the options opposed by Treasury, but went further. It opposed any form of motor fuel taxes, including a proposed tax to finance the SPR, a position more categorical than that adopted by Treasury, which had indicated a willingness to consider a higher gasoline tax in the future.[8] CEA also opposed the option providing access by independent generators of electricity to the transmission grid. This position, oddly inconsistent with CEA support for electric utility reform, was later clarified by Schmalensee to mean that CEA supported regulatory rather than legislative means to transmission access. The CEA also opposed creation of a revolving fund to finance investments for energy efficiency in federal buildings.[9]

In a memorandum from Robert Grady, OMB declined to take formal positions on NES options, warning DOE instead to balance any new federal expenditures with offsetting reductions in existing programs, consistent with the requirement imposed by the recently enacted Omnibus Budget Reconciliation Act (OBRA). "All new proposals affecting the budget," he stated, "must be scored by Treasury and OMB using very specific rules legislated in the OBRA." He stressed that it was DOE's sole responsibility to identify federal budget reductions that would be used to offset the cost of any and all new NES initiatives.[10]

The Department of Transportation's (DOT) Jeffrey Shane, assistant secretary for policy, wrote: "The analyses (of NES options) do not provide a basis for determining that there is a national energy security problem. Thus, positive positions with respect to any of the transportation-related options are difficult to defend." Shane indicated that DOT opposed all options related to the CAFE law, arguing that the recently enacted CAAA was expected to have a significant effect on motor fuel economy. DOT also opposed all options related to alternative transportation fuels and energy taxes. On the latter, Shane wrote, "the implications of these taxes extend far beyond considerations of energy policy," and should be debated instead as tax policy. [11]

Richard Stewart, the Department of Justice (DOJ) assistant attorney general, indicated opposition to four NES options. On natural gas pipeline construction, he objected to the proposal to make the FERC solely responsible for builders' compliance with National Environmental Policy Act (NEPA) requirements. He declared the DOJ "unpersuaded" by the need to require unbundling of natural gas transportation services and opposed the option to impose a carbon tax, because "the environmental variable of interest is emissions of all GHGs [greenhouse gases], not CO_2 [carbon dioxide] alone." A piecemeal CO_2-only policy, he added, "could be ineffective or even counterproductive." He concluded by stating that DOJ opposed the energy impact assessments in environmental rule makings because it "would unduly interfere with regulatory deadlines and could set an undesirable precedent for other issues."[12]

Chief of staff Scott Farrow communicated positions for the White House Council on Environmental Quality (CEQ). He indicated that eight of the NES options presented a problem for the CEQ. Opposition was declared for a variable oil import fee. Qualified support was indicated for access to ANWR but only if "explicitly balanced with significant policies directed at the demand for energy." CEQ supported some tax credits proposed by DOE for alternative fuels, believing that federal efforts should be concentrated on development of the fuels and not the infrastructure that used them. Reform of hydropower licensing was supported but not if FERC were to become the sole agency responsible for the permitting process. Support was expressed for electricity generation technology R&D, beyond continuation of the then existing clean coal technology program. Carbon taxes, CEQ thought, should remain under consideration.[13]

With Secretary Mosbacher permanently recused from decisions on energy matters, the Department of Commerce (DOC) responded to the NES poll with surprisingly independent, in some cases astoundingly un-Republican positions. DOC—alone among departments—supported reform of the CAFE law and a high gas guzzler tax without corresponding rebates for gas sippers. DOC also supported tax incentives for users of mass transit, provided that states and cities added local incentives and a graduated tax on motor fuels (initially ten cents rising to fifty cents) if a "valuation of the externalities of the use of motor fuels could be calculated and then applied as a tax such that the private cost of motor fuel equaled its social cost." DOC offered qualified support for the various options on alternative transportation fuels, the tax to finance the SPR, hydropower licensing reform, new efficiency standards for appliances and equipment, voluntary standards for buildings, mortgage financing based on energy efficiency ratings of homes, and a federal fund for energy efficiency investments.[14]

Views of the Secretary of Energy Advisory Board

Members of SEAB were also given an opportunity to express their views on the NES options. The DOE policy office received comments from a number of SEAB members during the last week of October 1990, the most extensive of which are summarized below.

Susan Wiltshire thought the DOE analysis was overly focused on the automobile. What about air transport? she asked, or high speed rail transport and innovative systems of public transportation? She recommended that a small "task group immediately undertake a strategic analysis of the whole question of energy use by the four sectors identified in the *Interim Report*: transportation, residential, commercial, industrial."[15]

Harry Mandil indicated that NES needed to establish national energy goals compelling enough to remain unchanged over time, even as the means to achieve them might undergo revision. The goals that he proposed be adopted for NES included: availability, at all times, of sufficient energy and electricity at reasonable cost; minimization of damage to the environment; a permanent campaign of public information about energy technology risk and benefit; the pursuit of energy efficiency and renewable energy; and the conservation of "irreplaceable resources such as oil, gas and coal, which have taken millions of years to form."[16]

John Landis forwarded fourteen suggestions to improve NES. He questioned the validity of a number of assumptions in DOE's models and suggested that the electricity sector model results appeared to under-estimate the "significant economic impacts of cleaning up the combustion of coal." He thought that eventually the energy supply would be "dominated by renewables, but their potential during the next few decades cannot be quantified unless subjected individually to a thorough and comprehensive system analysis." He wanted a more positive message on nuclear power. He recommended that environmental options be classified not as concerns or as efforts to address global warming but as "emission reduction possibilities, dispersion techniques and ameliorative measures." He argued that NES options should have included a greater number of recommendations made by SEAB in recent years, "particularly in the areas of nuclear power, solar energy and geophysics."[17]

John McTague provided a six-page critique of the options dealing with auto fuel efficiency, alternative transportation fuels, fuel taxes, and related effects on global climate change. He was especially dissatisfied with DOE's analysis of CAFE because it "did not reflect adequately the significant differences of opinion on technical opportunities and costs, or the effects of such requirements on U.S. competitiveness and product costs." McTague favored higher fuel taxes as a more efficient means of improving auto fuel efficiency. On global climate change, he supported "CFC [chlorofluorocarbon] phase-out, reforestation, consumer education," or any approach that encouraged action through market forces rather than by additional government regulation[18]

Warren Washington thought that "the options on the environment seem(ed) quite well written and consistent with the new IPCC [UN Intergovernmental Panel on Climate Change] report." He suggested more precise language to describe the state of knowledge on greenhouse gases. "We are certain of the following:" he recommended that DOE state in NES, "[that] Emissions resulting from human activities are substantially increasing the atmospheric concentrations of the greenhouse gases—carbon dioxide, methane, chlorofluorocarbons [CFCs], and nitrous oxide. These increases will enhance the greenhouse effect, resulting on average in an additional warming of the Earth's surface."[19]

Glenn Paulson wrote that he was "extremely dissatisfied both by the options presented and by the analyses behind them, except for the section on integrated resource planning." He believed DOE analysts had failed to appreciate the "huge" potential for energy savings in the structure of the economy, especially in the industrial sector. As to options concerned with renewable technology, he believed that the DOE options did not "adequately recognize the potential of the sun, especially for passive solar" systems.[20]

Robert Fri provided a four-page commentary. "Although analysis of the individual options is a necessary evil," he wrote, "I think that the document (the NES) will rise or fall on the overall strategy that is put forth. The right approach, it seems to me, is to design a strategy that balances energy, environmental and economic factors. Without concentration on these tradeoffs, one gets merely another energy plan that quickly dissolves into an argument about imports, supply, and conservation." Fri thought that environmental issues should be an integral part of the analysis of all options rather than separate elements of the strategy and that some NES environmental policy options were, "red flags in the face of the environmentalists: an energy impact statement, no less!" He recommended an assessment of "environmental costing" of electricity generation and suggested that global climate change research should extend to the topic of climate change adaptation. He concluded by reiterating that good policy required above all a "strategic vision."[21]

The vision thing

DOE policy staff had been pondering the matter of a "strategic vision" for a number of months, anticipating that the cabinet would find it difficult to debate the merits of a national policy by arguing the technical details of the policy options. But the weight of opinion among EPC agencies and political signals from the White House seemed to suggest that the president preferred to deal with an omnibus package of proposals that allowed him to exercise the equivalent of a line-item veto. The president was known to be disdainful of what he called the "vision thing" on any policy matter, and the direction that had been given to Watkins by Sununu also seemed to reinforce the idea of option-by-option decision-making.

The Troika members soon came to the conclusion that in the forthcoming cabinet meetings on NES it would prove impractical to debate the policy options in the absence of an agreed policy framework. They, however, could not agree on the scope of such a framework—how it should be structured, what it should contain, and whether it should be crafted as the equivalent of a draft national energy strategy. For Stuntz, a draft strategy paper implied that policy choices had been made when in fact they had not. DOE staff understood the need for a framework paper, but suspected that the Troika would frame the debate in terms favorable only to the policy options they supported. The staff believed that, framework or not, the options at risk were always likely to be those supported by DOE.

A FRAMEWORK FOR DECISIONS

Watkins did not seem particularly bothered by the absence of a strategic framework by which to consider NES policy options. He conceived the final NES as analogous to a scale balanced by the equal weight of reasonable energy supply options and common sense energy demand policies. He believed that NES would be rejected by the public as well as by Congress if perceived as tilting too far in either the direction of conservation or production. In his thinking, the value of individual policy options was less important than their cumulative effect on the scale.[22]

Although always loyal to Watkins' concept of policy balance, Deputy Secretary Moore saw the critical NES decisions mainly in the sphere of a credible federal response to domestic oil production, oil import dependence, and related vulnerabilities. His experience in Congress, especially during the Carter administration, had instilled in him a profound skepticism on matters of tax policy, federal alternative fuels programs, and government mandates for what he called "the commanding of conservation." He supported energy efficiency initiatives such as new efficiency standards for light bulbs because it made sense to have a single national standard rather than multiple, incompatible state standards. He opposed energy standards for Federal buildings and housing because Housing and Urban Development Secretary Jack Kemp had warned him that the cost of this option would have the perverse consequence of eroding already tight budgets for low income housing.[23]

Stuntz thought the energy sector too diverse and too complex to capture in a single, unifying strategic vision. She could conceive of a clearly articulated strategy for the reform of the electric utility sector, a separate and distinct strategy for oil and energy security, a natural gas transportation and distribution strategy, and one for energy efficiency in end use sectors. Each of these strategies would be based on distinct laws and regulations that, in the end, had little common ground. She believed that any strategic vision capable of encompassing the multiplicity of NES policy elements would be either too general to be meaningful or likely to be viewed by the Troika as smacking of government central planning.[24]

The matter of a strategic vision for NES was in the end forced by Wethington who, on his own initiative and without consultations with DOE, proceeded to draft a document he titled "Framework Paper: The National Energy Strategy." Wethington faxed his paper to Stuntz on October 30 and subsequently telephoned to reassure her that the document was merely "illustrative."[25] There followed a virtual battle of wills for control of what amounted to definition of terms of the debate on NES. Stuntz and Wethington exchanged numerous policy framework papers in the following two weeks, some drafted by DOE, others by individual agencies or coalitions of departments opportunistically taking advantage of DOE's apparent loss of control. The exchange came finally to an end on November 15—the deadline that Cabinet Secretary Ede Holiday had set for completion of all papers and documents to be transmitted to EPC, in advance of its first meeting on NES.

The paper transmitted to EPC members on November 16, called "A Framework for Consideration of Options," did not contain anything resembling a strategic vision. Rather, the paper defined the NES debate by the four key areas of policy to be considered by the cabinet. It presented a concise statement of fact about each of the policy areas in question, provided a summary list of relevant policy options, and showed the results of the October poll of the agencies by indicating where a general consensus of support existed for each of the options. The structure, data, and terminology of the paper had required virtual verbatim clearance from the Troika leaders. The essential parts of the paper—reproduced below in the form sent to EPC—are instructive for the conceptual terms of reference by which the Troika wanted the cabinet to decide national energy policy generally and NES options specifically.

NATIONAL ENERGY STRATEGY: FRAMEWORK FOR CONSIDERATION OF OPTIONS[26]

I. *Energy Security: Reducing Dependence on Unreliable Suppliers.*

Issue: To what extent, and by what means, should the U.S. seek to reverse or slow the trend towards increased dependence on insecure energy supplies?

Discussion: Energy security impacts national security to the extent our dependence, or that of our allies, on foreign energy sources limits flexibility in directing economic and foreign policy. Oil supplies present the largest uncertainty, and transportation reliance on oil represents our most important vulnerability. Whether self-sufficient or totally dependent, the U.S. economy is sensitive to disruptions in internationally traded energy. Oil and the efficiency of its use means disturbances anywhere resonate everywhere. Secure supplies of energy are essential to U.S. prosperity. The concentration of 65 percent of the world's known oil reserves in the Persian Gulf means we must continue to ensure reliable access to competitively priced oil, and have the capability to respond to any major supply disruption.

Energy security and security of supplies are not necessarily interchangeable concepts. Notwithstanding the U.S.' probable, continuing reliance on suppliers from unstable regions of the world, energy security could be enhanced by policies aimed at increasing world-wide excess production capacity, fuel switching capacity, and trade in alternatives to oil, especially natural gas, as well as expanded use of nuclear and other non-oil fuels.

U.S. imports of oil are forecast to rise substantially over the next decade and beyond. In 1989, U.S. oil imports rose to 41 percent of domestic consumption, up from 27 percent in 1985. By 2000, the Department of Energy estimates that imported oil will account for 67 percent of U.S. consumption. By 2030, imports could approach 82 percent of domestic consumption.

The Department of Energy projects U.S. oil imports will rise from 7.2 million barrels per day (MMb/d) in 1989 to 11.2 MMb/d in 2000. A recent National Intelligence Estimate (NIE) forecasts a doubling of the U.S. oil and gas bill from 1 to 2 percent of GNP [Gross National Product] by 2000. During this period, according to the NIE, the Persian Gulf states will supply a greater percentage of total world oil supply— rising from 18% in 1985 to 30 percent in 2000. U.S. domestic production of oil has declined over the past decade, from 8.6 MMb/d in 1980 to 7.2 MMb/d in 1990. Domestic production is expected to further decline to 5.6 MMb/d in 2000 and 3.6 MMb/d in 2030.

The link between oil and transportation is unlikely to be substantially affected by any combination of economically viable policies before the turn of the century. But growth in demand could be dampened through conservation and alternative fuels measures. The U.S. has a Strategic Petroleum Reserve [SPR]currently holding 590 million barrels of oil, with a potential increase to 1 billion barrels. Congress has also authorized the creation, on a pilot basis, of one or more petroleum product reserves in various geographic areas of the country. Other OECD nations hold strategic and other government-controlled stocks of about 500 MMb.

Options for Increasing Energy Security: The available government options[27] for lessening U.S. dependence on insecure supplies of oil fall into five broad categories of measures to:

1. *Increase domestic production:* Provide Federal tax incentives to domestic oil and gas producers, impose a variable oil import fee, permit access to new development areas (OCS, ANS, ANWR), and streamline environmental permitting and regulatory requirements.

2. *Improve efficiency of oil and natural gas markets:* reform permitting process for pipeline construction, deregulate pipeline sales rates, reform pipeline rate design, improve nondiscriminatory access to pipeline transportation, deregulate oil pipelines.

3. *Increase efficiency of oil use:* reform CAFE law/increase CAFE standards, revise guzzler/sipper tax, impose higher energy taxes, initiate Federal programs to scrap older cars, remove disincentives to mass transit use/ride sharing.

4. *Promote production and use of alternative fuels:* Provide CAFE incentives to manufacturers of alternative fuel vehicles, Federal incentives for production of alternative fuels and tax incentives for alternative fuels infrastructure development, extend the ethanol production tax credit.

5. *Reduce vulnerability to oil market disruptions:* Impose a petroleum tax to finance expansion of SPR, lease the Naval Petroleum Reserve to finance SPR, foster international measures to increase diversity/reliability of supply.

II. *Electricity: Enhancing Efficiency of Electricity Markets.*
Issue: To what extent, and by what means, should the Federal Government seek reform of the statutory and regulatory regime that governs electricity generation, transportation and use?

Discussion: The electric utility industry is one of the most highly regulated sectors of the U.S. economy, at Federal, State and local levels. Investment choices by the utility industry affect a wide range of fuels, technologies and environmental impacts. Electricity demand growth tracked GNP growth between 1973 and 1986 while total U.S. energy consumption remained flat. In 1970, electricity accounted for 24 percent of primary energy consumption, 36 percent in 1990. By 2010, electricity is projected to account for 41 percent of total energy consumption. This creates a strong national interest in efficiency of electricity supply and consumption choices. Under very conservative assumptions, the U.S. will likely need to build a minimum of 200 GW of new capacity between 1990 and 2010. Who, with what technology and fuels, and with what environmental consequences, will build what capacity, will to a large degree depend on the regulatory regime that governs these decisions.

Current regulations impede construction of new hydroelectric and nuclear capacity. The 1990 Clean Air Act will likely push utility choices further toward natural gas, at least until a new generation of clean coal technologies can be brought on line. Renewable energy, mostly hydropower, but also including some biomass, geothermal, wind and solar thermal will show modest growth, from the current 103 GW of installed capacity to 142 GW in 2010.

On the supply side, Federal statutes such as PUHCA, PURPA, and the Federal Power Act and Federal regulation of nuclear, hydropower, and transmission access exist in tandem with substantial State regulatory requirements. Competition among wholesale electricity producers, on a regional or inter-regional scale, was not considered feasible when PUHCA legislation was passed. Since the enactment in 1978 of PURPA, limited competition has emerged, suggesting that broader competition may be feasible, practical, and beneficial.

On the demand side, wide ranging experimentation is taking place at State and local levels to increase efficiency and reduce consumption. The demarcation line between Federal and non-Federal responsibility for electricity demand policies is unclear. Factors that influence demand choices include technology, price, tax policy and consumer behavior. Integrated Resource Planning (IRP) is the process increasingly used by public utilities commissions to determine the cost effectiveness and desirability of new investments in electricity supply additions and demand reductions.

The emerging competitive market in electricity generation is also affected by the generation and transmission pricing practices of Federally created agencies, including the five Power Marketing Administrations and the Tennessee Valley Authority. These agencies can act as laboratories for policy experimentation and set national trends in areas such as rate design, transmission access, environmentally sensitive operation of facilities, and IRP.

Options For Enhancing Efficiency of Electricity Markets. The available government options to improve the economic performance of the electric utility industry, diversify fuels and technology options and to increase end-use efficiency fall into the following three broad categories:

1. *Increase supply competition:* Amend PUHCA, reform PURPA by removing cap on project size and relaxing co-firing limits, ensure access of wholesale generators to the transmission system, eliminate subsidies to Federal electricity generation.

2. *Increase fuel and technology diversity:* Provide regulatory incentives to clean coal technology systems, tax incentives for renewable energy production, incentives to municipal solid-waste-to-energy plants,

reform hydropower licensing and increase Federal hydro capacity, reform nuclear power plant licensing and nuclear waste legislation to ensure construction of repositories.

3. *Enhance and assure efficiency investments:* Federally support State IRP processes, remove taxation of utilities' rebates to customers for efficiency investments, increase efficiency standards for appliances and equipment, tighten Federal building efficiency standards, provide incentives for mortgages on energy efficient housing, establish a fund for Federal efficiency investments, finance investments to increase energy efficiency of public housing.

III. *Environment: Balancing Energy and Environmental Objectives.*

Issue: To what extent, and by what means, can the Nation's commitment to a cleaner and safer environment be reconciled with the need for adequate supplies of energy at reasonable cost?

Discussion: Growing international concern regarding the potential for global climate change is forcing many nations to consider measures to reduce greenhouse gas emissions, in particular carbon dioxide (CO_2). The U.S. accounts for 23 percent of global CO_2 emissions, primarily through fossil fuel combustion. In the U.S., 38% of CO_2 emissions comes from electricity generation and 30 percent comes from transportation. U.S. emissions of CO_2 are projected to grow by 85 percent from current levels by the year 2030.

Energy-related activities also contribute significantly to air pollution. Electric utilities (mostly coal-fired) produce approximately two-thirds of total national sulfur dioxide (SO_2) emissions. Other pollutants that contribute to urban air pollution—nitrogen oxides (NO_x), carbon monoxide (CO) and volatile organic compounds (VOCs)—result primarily from the transportation and energy supply sectors. For example, 40 percent of U.S. emissions of NO_x comes from transportation use. In addition, electric power plants, petroleum refineries, coal and uranium mines and some oil wells discharge a wide range of contaminants directly to surface waters. About 20% of all point sources discharge to surface waters in the U.S. are energy related.

The NES Working Group not only assessed the environmental effects from energy, but also analyzed the impact of environmental regulation on the cost of energy supply. Costs of environmental compliance to the Nation are growing and will be greater than $100 billion per year by the year 2000. A significant portion of these costs is associated with energy supply and use, in particular for air pollution controls.

If fully implemented, many of the NES options would augment existing measures and significantly reduce the rate of growth in greenhouse gases, especially carbon dioxide. The 1990 Clean Air Act will limit, and in many cases reduce from current levels, the major air pollutants from power plants, transportation use and energy using industries. Many of the NES options and existing R&D programs, such as the development of alternative fuels for transportation, clean coal technologies, and energy efficiency improvements, would further reduce air and water pollutants and waste from projected levels.

Options have been proposed to reduce costs to the energy sector while maintaining environmental quality. These options do not constitute new Administration priorities, but alternative means and processes for implementing current policy, would utilize market-oriented approaches and greater regulatory flexibility to achieve environmental compliance.

Options For Balancing Energy and Environmental Goals:

1. Adopt the NES options as a key element of the U.S. strategy for addressing global climate change (GCC) concerns
2. Enhance scientific and economic research to reduce uncertainties associated with GCC
3. Impose taxes on the carbon content of fuels as a means to reduce carbon dioxide emissions.
4. Streamline Federal and State environmental processes for siting and permitting energy facilities, and require energy impact statements for major environmental rule makings.
5. Widely deploy emissions-trading and other market-based mechanisms in implementing the Clean Air Act and other environmental protection programs.

6. Adopt regulatory changes or legislation to encourage industries to minimize waste through the use of technology.
7. Ensure that State regulation of radio-nuclides reflects added health and safety needs, and does not discriminate among sources.

IV. *Science and Technology: RD&D, Technology Transfer, Education.*
Issue: To what extent should Federal Research, Development & Demonstration (RD&D) priorities be realigned, and by what means should research results be transferred to the private sector, in order to sustain NES and other economic and environmental objectives? How should the Federal government contribute to improving science and math education?

Discussion: Federal investments in energy research, development and demonstration are indicators of the relative priorities that the Administration attaches to fuels and technologies. DOE manages the majority of these investments aimed at improving cost, efficiency and environmental effects of a wide range of energy production, transformation, and end-use technologies. DOE also manages programs to transfer research results from Federal laboratories and research centers to the private sector, and to other nations. All DOE national laboratories and most of DOE's program elements manage technology transfer activities.

The development and management of energy technologies require a skilled work force that is unlikely to emerge, without Federal, State and private support. Although this is particularly true in a number of demanding areas, such as nuclear fusion and fission, advanced renewable technologies, and in promising areas such as fuel cells and hydrogen applications, it applies generally to all areas of energy technology research, development and application.

Options for Science and Technology RD&D and Education:
1. Invest in maintenance of basic research capabilities at national laboratories
2. Redirect applied R&D priorities to match NES objectives
3. Reform national technology transfer services
4. Federally support export of energy technologies

5. Expand Federal math and science education initiatives.

NES options comprise proposals for conforming RD&D priorities to NES options. Specific budget proposals to carry out the realignments needed to support NES implementation will be negotiated through the normal budget process.

Reluctantly admitted

The framework paper distilled a vast amount of analytical detail and provided to members of the cabinet a concise decision-making tool. Left to its own devices, DOE's policy staff, as with the staff of any department pressing a particular agenda, would have most likely produced a less objective paper. The interagency process, however frustrating, had after all served the purpose of viewing policy problems from a national rather than a departmental perspective. Stuntz and her staff had been particularly well served by Schmalensee, who had guided the drafting of the paper with patience and care, less as the representative of an agency seeking dominion than as an official ensuring the integrity of a national policy making process.

The framework paper was distributed to the members of EPC on November 15, 1990. It was perhaps a measure of the paper's lack of bias that, unlike most other documents or reports of internal discussions related to NES, it was never leaked to the media. EPC was now ready to render its verdict on a strategy most of its members did not want.

ECONOMIC POLICY COUNCIL
DELIBERATIONS

"By its very nature," Undersecretary Cordell Moore had gone on to say, "policy only needs to be formulated when there are complex, uncertain alternatives so difficult to analyze and resolve that it is almost impossible to settle on a single, definite course."[28]

The Bush administration's EPC met on November 19, 1990, in the White House's historic Roosevelt Room to begin the process of determining for the nation a new course on energy.[29] A total of six cabinet meetings would be required to reach decisions on all elements of NES. The president presided over the last two of the meetings; Secretary of the Treasury Nicholas Brady, the chairman *pro tempore* of the council, chaired the rest.

The EPC meeting of November 19, 1990

Watkins launched the cabinet's NES debate by reminding the members of the council that the president had directed him to develop NES as a bipartisan task and to forge a national consensus to support it. He noted that energy markets were not free, citing the extensive federal and state regulation of the electric utility sector and of natural gas transportation and distribution. He pointed out that outside the United States, governments rather than private companies controlled the oil sector, and everywhere governments imposed environmental regulation of the energy production and consumption cycle. He then clarified the terms by which the policy should be debated by summarizing the results of the modeling that had been used to assess the impact of various combinations of NES options.

The first model results were those for the "no further action base case." The base case incorporated economic growth assumptions provided by the Troika and embodied all then-current law and regulation, including the just-enacted amendments to the Clean Air Act. The base case assumed only market-driven improvements in technology and gains in energy efficiency. The results for the no further action base case, derived from DOE's Fossil2 integration model, showed that in the absence of further policy intervention, U.S. primary energy consumption would increase by a very significant 60 quads in the period from 1990 to 2030.[30]

Watkins next presented Fossil2 model results, in graphic form, for NES policy options supported by EPC in the October poll of agency positions. The "NES consensus case" showed no change from the base case in terms of projected year 2030 U.S. primary energy consumption. The consensus case did, however, show variations from the base case in terms of relative fuel shares—a significant reduction in coal use, a drastic reduction in nuclear use, a slight decline in oil and gas use, no change in renewable energy use.[31]

Watkins then presented the model results for all sixty-seven policy options. The "all EPC options case" showed primary energy consumption dropping by ten quads in 2030, from the base case of 140 quads. It also showed very substantial shifts in fuel shares, including a notable but modest reduction in oil use, unchanged levels of natural gas use, a dramatic reduction in coal use, a significant increase in nuclear generation and a substantial increase in renewable energy capacity.[32]

Watkins completed his presentation with a summary assessment of how each of the cases examined met—or failed to meet—the president's declared objectives for NES. The president's objectives, Watkins reminded the council, were energy at reasonable prices, a safer and healthier environment, a strong economy, and reduced dependence on unreliable oil suppliers. The no-further-action case, Watkins stated, would fail the president's criteria because it would increase energy costs and encourage heavier reliance on coal, with concomitant increase of CO_2 emissions by up to eighty-five percent in 2030. A no-further-action policy, he said, would impede the efficient functioning of the energy marketplace and likely result in oil imports exceeding sixty-five percent of domestic consumption in 2000 and eighty percent in 2030.[33]

The consensus case, Watkins continued, would reduce energy costs to consumers somewhat and decrease reliance on coal, but would still result in a 65% increase in CO_2 emissions by 2030. The consensus case would enhance competition in the natural gas and electricity markets, but provide negligible improvement in oil import dependence. The all-options case, Watkins continued, would raise consumer energy costs because of the impact of the tax options, would lower coal and oil use, and would increase reliance on nuclear and renewable technology. Importantly, he said, only with the all-options case could CO_2 emissions be stabilized at 1990 levels after 2015, though economic growth would be slightly lower, again because of the tax options. Still, he concluded, an all-options NES would increase competition among fuels, foster technological innovation, reduce oil imports by 10% below base case levels in 2010 and substantially increase transportation fuel flexibility.[34]

EPC members accepted the Fossil2 model results without objections. Brady, Boskin, and Darman suggested that it would be fruitful to focus the EPC discussion initially on questions of overriding policy concerns. One such concern was the wide range of opinions held by EPC members about the meaning of energy security. Because agencies' opinions on the topic tended to determine their position on options related to oil production, consumption and imports, the Troika leaders thought it opportune to devote a full meeting of EPC to the subject and seek a common understanding of the concept.

A second concern was Sununu's view that the interagency working group had given insufficient weight to technology R&D issues. Consequently, DOE was directed to analyze a new set of options that would be entitled "enhanced R&D" and provide a quantitative assessment of what could be accomplished in the energy sector with higher levels of federal and private investment in targeted R&D.[35]

Next on the EPC agenda was the elimination of options that did not, according to the Troika leaders, merit further consideration. Among these were the tax credits for oil production of domestic oil, non-conventional fuels, and ethanol. Tax credits for these fuels—at more modest levels than proposed in NES—had been enacted in OBRA 1990 and, Brady posited, needed no further consideration. After a brief discussion, Watkins reluctantly agreed to forego further consideration of these options, but reminded his colleagues that in the absence of further tax credits, the administration would then be forced to base its domestic oil policy solely on the highly controversial options of access to ANWR and the OCS.[36] EPC members accepted the trade-off without further debate.

The Troika leaders then proposed eliminating from further considerations all tax options—variable oil import fee, gasoline and diesel taxes, taxes on oil to fill the SPR and carbon taxes. They argued that the president's campaign pledge not to impose new taxes effectively precluded EPC from recommending to the president options that violated his own pledge. Watkins objected, reminding the council—Darman and Sununu in particular—that the pledge had already been violated by the administration's agreement to raise taxes in order to obtain congressional backing for OBRA.

EPA's Reilly supported Watkins as did State's Eagleberger. The tax options thus remained on the NES active list.[37]

The second EPC meeting on NES

EPC was scheduled to meet again on November 28, 1990.[38] During the nine days available between the first and second EPC meeting, DOE policy staff worked virtually without pause to craft and obtain interagency clearance for the energy security framework paper requested by the council. A separate staff group was directed to produce the new enhanced R&D option commissioned by EPC at Sununu's direction.

The development of the energy security paper sparked the attention of White House staff, that had previously remained in the background of EPC deliberations on NES. Two senior members of the White House Office of Policy Development, Larry Lindsey[39] and Teresa Gorman, joined the energy security debate both to support Stuntz and to ensure consideration of the domestic dimensions of energy security. Lindsey suggested that greater emphasis be placed in NES on technology solutions to energy security vulnerabilities, as an alternative to more interventionist regulatory means. Gorman sought consideration of how the notably domestic U.S. oil and gas industry—independent producers, especially—would fare in the NES debate, and what electoral ramifications might result for the president. These considerations, already if not explicitly internalized in the thinking of DOE staff, became an additional policy denominator with the intervention of Gorman and Lindsey, and to some degree complicated the conceptual framework of the energy security paper. [40]

A framework paper on energy security eventually emerged from the interagency process that sought to be all things to all advocates. The paper comprised a recitation of facts about domestic and international oil production and related consequences. The paper did not seek to force the issue of how the United States might either come to terms with the erosion of its domestic oil production or seek aggressive diplomatic or trade relief from the politically volatile producers that accounted for its vulnerability.

Key elements of the energy security paper that was transmitted to EPC are reproduced below in the language (and tense) of the original memorandum.

FRAMEWORK FOR CONSIDERATION OF ENERGY SECURITY OPTIONS.[41]

Middle East nations are the world's low cost oil producers. The average cost of production in the Middle East is $2.25 per barrel, in the U.S. $4.10 per barrel and in the North Sea $4.54 per barrel.[42] Persian Gulf states hold two-thirds of the world's proven oil reserves and can produce more oil per well and over a longer time frame than any other producer. Average daily per well crude oil production is 13 barrels in the U.S., 7000 barrels in Saudi Arabia and nearly 9000 barrels in Iran. Given geologic and cost advantages, exclusive reliance on market forces will result in increasing dependence by the U.S. and its allies on Persian Gulf suppliers who may or may not be potentially unreliable.

In the United States, oil use is concentrated in the transportation sector. Of the 17 million barrels per day used in the U.S. in 1990, 11.4 million went to transportation, 3.8 million b/d were used in industry as feed stocks, nearly 1 million b/d were used for residential heating, mainly in New England, nearly 0.5 million b/d were used in the commercial sector and 0.7 million b/d were used by utilities, mainly for peak power electricity generation.

Oil use in all but the transportation sector is likely to be affected by the increased fuel competition that will be fostered by a number of NES options. Also, the natural gas market can be expected to undergo substantial expansion as a result of the effects of the Clean Air Act Amendments. The Canadian Free Trade agreement will foster expanded use of natural gas especially in the Northeast, where residential and commercial oil use is four times higher than in the rest of the Nation. Industrial fuel use, except for feed stock requirements, is a function of price competition between oil and gas.

Fuel competition in the transportation sector is more difficult to achieve. No fuel is likely to emerge in the near term that would be cost-competitive with gasoline. Largely as a consequence of projected higher transportation oil demand, U.S. oil imports are forecast to rise from 7.2 million b/d in 1989 to 11.2 million b/d in 2000. Persian Gulf producers will meet most of the increase. The issue to be resolved is the following: To what extent and by what means can the linkage between domestic requirements for petroleum and dependence on potentially insecure suppliers be altered?

Unpalatable means to uncertain ends

The energy security options proposed to EPC by Watkins were deemed by the Troika to fall variously in the categories of cosmetic, uneconomic, politically infeasible, or undesirable policy. For the energy security framework paper, these options were grouped in four categories comprising international, domestic, supply, and demand considerations.[43]

First among the options was a proposal to increase the strategic stocks held by the United States and other members of the International Energy Agency (IEA). In 1990, the U.S. SPR held 590 million barrels of oil, constituting the largest reserve of emergency stocks in the world. Only Germany and Japan held stocks of significance, while the other eighteen members of IEA expected to respond to a major oil supply disruption with demand restraint measures of imprecise scope and effect. DOE's policy office took the position that the costs and benefits of supply disruption management were inequitably distributed among IEA members, and that the IEA treaty should consequently be revised.

The second option represented a proposal by the NSC to stimulate non-Persian Gulf oil production. "The stability of the world oil market," declared the energy security paper, "is directly affected by the availability of excess production capacity and the market share of OPEC oil." Opportunities for expansion of this capacity were deemed to be substantial in the (then) Soviet Union, Venezuela and Mexico. In a reversal of the Reagan administration's 1980s opposition to Western investment in the Soviet energy sector, the NSC now recommended an infusion of Western capital and technology to reverse the deterioration of the Soviet oil sector. Equally implausibly, DOE also recommended trade negotiations with Mexico and Venezuela to remove their constitutional ban against foreign investment in their oil industry."[44]

A third group of options was designed to foster the use of alternatives to oil in less developed countries (LDCs). Oil demand in LDCs was projected to grow at twice the rate of demand in market economies. It was recognized that LDC economies were highly vulnerable to sharp increases in oil prices, among other reasons because the intensity of their oil use was high, their fuel switching capacity minimal, and foreign exchange assets with which to purchase dollar-denominated oil, limited. The proposal was to redirect part of the foreign aid provided to LDCs by IEA member nations to (non-specified) programs aimed at reducing LDC oil use intensity.[45]

The fourth proposal focused on increasing domestic oil production. Excluding interventions such as floor prices or import tariffs, the policy options likely to increase domestic production included the opening of ANWR, suspension of some leasing moratoria on the OCS, reform of regulations hampering new production on Alaska's North Slope, and advanced technology for recovery of oil left in reservoirs by conventional lifting methods. DOE recommended the adoption of all four of these options but with a preference for imposition of environmental regulations more stringent than those contained in then current law, as a condition for granting access to ANWR and OCS.[46]

The fifth proposal dealt with domestic oil demand. Notwithstanding the vehement opposition of the Vice President's Council on Competitiveness, DOE policy staff continued to insist to Watkins that the credibility of NES would be compromised without some commitment to higher CAFE standards. The staff argued that no other option considered in the interagency process was found to compare with the power of CAFE to reduce domestic oil consumption. Passenger autos and light duty trucks accounted for 11 MMB/D of transportation oil consumption and therefore, represented the ideal target of opportunity for conservation. Other oil use in transportation—2.7 MMB/D used in freight and inter-city commerce and 1.3 MMB/D used by aircraft—presented extremely limited conservation possibilities.

The Troika was willing to concede in theory that higher CAFE standards could be set at cost-effective levels, but the economics of CAFE were invariably connected to the projected future price of oil and therefore subject to a wide range of uncertainty. This uncertainty was the intellectual basis of the Troika's opposition to higher CAFE standards, which, they noted, would be set by regulators typically unconcerned with economic efficiency. Nonetheless, DOE staff inserted CAFE reform into the energy security framework paper, but went further. Also added to the paper was the proposition that oil conservation could be even more certainly achieved by an incremental gasoline tax, capped at $1 per gallon in the year 2000, and imposed in conjunction with higher CAFE standards.[47]

The most sweeping DOE proposals were on alternative transportation fuels. "The U.S. vehicle fleet of over 170 million cars is difficult to transform," the energy security paper noted. The fleet would be modestly transformed by the effects of the CAAA, which called for test use of alternative fuels in ozone non-attainment areas and for introduction of gasolines "reformulated" or "oxygenated" by the same additives (ethanol, methanol) that could also serve as alternative fuels. However, DOE staff argued, CAAA effects would not translate into structural changes in transportation oil use. Such a change was also unlikely to be accomplished by reliance on market forces because alternatives to oil required a concurrent and coordinated transformation of vehicles, fuel refining and distribution, retail sales, environmental control of new substances, and consumer education and acceptance. Therefore, DOE staff recommended an alternative fuels policy initially requiring that commercial vehicle fleets—the most controllable element of transportation—become fuel flexible. The program would cost $5.0 billion if the alternative fuel were compressed natural gas and $0.8 billion if methanol.[48]

The energy security paper admitted that the proposed mandate for alternative transportation fuels represented a high level of economic risk as well as possibly counterproductive government intervention. However, the widespread use of such fuels also represented the only demonstrable means of effectively breaking the transportation sector's inflexible linkage to oil. Conservation, the paper argued—either by higher taxes or higher CAFE standards—would, of course, reduce oil consumption, but only alternative fuels could ensure the emergence of competition in both fuels and technology in a sector of the economy notably devoid of both.[49]

In sum, the energy security paper drafted for the second EPC meeting re-argued the merits of policy options representing DOE's core agenda. The paper reflected the limitations of an interagency policy development process geared to the achievement of common ideological denominators rather than strategic thinking. It reflected, as well, the Bush administration's internal *realpolitik* of November 1990, meaning that the president's principal advisers were deeply divided in their assessment of the political costs and benefits of NES.

The divisions were not trivial. An energy policy constructed in the context of Iraq's destruction of Kuwait could be justified on entirely different political terms than a policy constructed to justify a domestic Republican agenda. Furthermore, an energy policy constructed in the absence of Persian Gulf turmoil, might comprise options—such as the dissolution of OPEC—that would be unthinkable in the context of the deployment of one-half million American soldiers on the territory of OPEC's swing producer.

Externalities

There was one more item to consider for the second EPC meeting on NES—a report by a task force of analysts charged, at the outset of the NES process, with determining whether the market price of oil reflected its true social cost. The task force, chaired by DOE chief economist Abraham Haspel, had identified five possible sources of externality:

- frictional or cyclical GNP losses resulting from changes in oil prices
- inflationary losses that accompany increases in oil prices
- monopsony price effects that result from the relationship between additional domestic consumption of imports and the world price of oil
- terms-of-trade effects that result from transfers of wealth to exporting countries as prices increase
- the financing of government strategic stocks and military operations associated with oil.

The task force had estimated that, for a given number of oil market disruptions occurring over a thirty-year period, the SPR would "leave expected present value losses of between $4.3 billion and $93.6 billion." These losses amounted to an externality value ranging between 12¢ and $1.56 per barrel of oil, depending on the year of occurrence of the disruption.[50]

Troika staffs would not agree to these externality values. OMB staff insisted that the tools available to measure residual economic losses from the use of the SPR were too crude to be dependable. Treasury's staff agreed with OMB. CEA analysts admitted the probable existence of an externality but would not endorse the range of values resulting from DOE's modeling efforts. The task force report was consequently withheld from consideration by EPC and shelved.

Results of the second EPC meeting

EPC met for two hours on November 28. The cabinet members could not agree on reforming the CAFE law. They diverged on means to stimulate greater consumer use of mass transit, ride sharing, and car- and van-pooling. The Troika agencies remained opposed to federally mandated alternative transportation fuels. A consensus could not be reached on efficiency standards for electric motors, lights, and buildings. Treasury and OMB opposed a production tax credit for renewable energy and the fund for federal energy efficiency investment. DOE, Interior, Commerce, Agriculture and Housing & Urban Development would not support the phase-out of subsidies to federally marketed electricity. Treasury opposed the tax-free treatment of utility rebates, and agreement could not be reached on the size and scope of new R&D investments.[51]

Virtual unanimity was, however, achieved on all other NES options, including highly controversial issues such as access to ANWR and the OCS. The reforms proposed for the electric utility and natural gas transportation industries carried virtually without opposition, following only cursory discussion by the cabinet. Among the conservation options adopted by EPC at its second meeting were policies to accelerate the scrapping of older cars;

improvement of energy efficiency in low-income housing; financial incentives for mortgages that financed energy efficiency homes, and greater energy efficiency investments in public housing.[52]

The EPC decisions of November 28 were leaked to the media over the following several days by the anonymous "reliable sources" on which the Washington media depends for its influence. The leaks engendered a feeding frenzy in the press and a call-in campaign to DOE, overwhelmingly in opposition to the decisions. On December 5th alone, a campaign orchestrated by the Greenpeace organization resulted in 568 telephone calls to DOE over a five-hour period.[53]

The third meeting of the EPC

For Watkins, the losses seemed to be mounting. In the first two EPC meetings he had been outvoted on each of the issues he believed to be critical to a balanced NES. Within the administration, he was now isolated by the Troika, distrusted by Sununu, and trapped within the EPC process, but he was far from defeated.

As tactical defense for the third EPC meeting, Watkins turned for support to the only still-neutral power center within the Bush administration: On December 6th, he dispatched a letter to Secretary of State James Baker, seeking support for the kind of NES he thought the remaining EPC process should produce. "I know you have recused yourself from being involved in matters dealing with oil and gas issues," Watkins wrote, "but I need help from State in the final stages of preparing the National Energy Strategy."[54]

DOE staff, meanwhile, completed the "enhanced R & D" option paper requested by Sununu. The paper was drafted by Robert Marlay, head of DOE's technology policy office. Entitled "Potentially High Payoff Technologies for Reducing U.S. Oil Vulnerability," the paper was a paean to the Troika's aversion to regulatory means for oil displacement and conservation ends. The paper recommended increased federal investments in selected technologies deemed critical to reducing U.S. oil use intensity. Federal selection of preferred energy technology was not new, of course. As noted in chapter 1, virtually all U.S. energy plans since the New Deal have contained a commitment to support government-favored energy technologies. The surprise in the case of NES was the Troika's acceptance of federal choices they would otherwise decry as unwarranted intervention in the marketplace.

The paper identified ten "high payoff technologies" capable of displacing or substituting oil use in the U.S. economy. The technologies included advanced systems for oil recovery, for transportation fuels from biomass, next generation aeronautics systems, electric vehicles, high speed and magnetic levitation (Maglev) rail systems, hyper-efficient industrial processes, intelligent vehicles and highway systems, telecommuting, and non-electric advanced vehicle propulsion systems.[55]

To make the government-centric selection process palatable to the less flexible market reliance advocates on the EPC, Marley's paper also called for new technology development initiatives to be jointly financed with industry. However, the paper argued, industry was likely to need a financial carrot in order to absorb the risk of investing its resources in pursuit of federally prescribed technology development objectives. Consequently, a 40% increase in the federal R&D tax credit was proposed, coupled with a further tax credit for first-of-a-kind technology. Finally, the option paper recommended the establishment of federal prizes and awards for R&D programs that exceeded contractual goals.[56]

Wethington distributed the R&D option paper to EPC members on December 10. The Wethington package also included, for the first time, DOE's initial draft of a summary NES. Policy staff had proceeded to draft the sixteen-page summary, notwithstanding the numerous critical issues still pending at EPC that would affect the final outcome. The staff acted, as did Stuntz and Watkins, as if all EPC decisions were advisory and assumed the president's final choices would be fairly close to DOE's recommendations. R&D strategy was to be the focus of debate for the third EPC meeting on NES, scheduled for December 12, 1990, once again in the Roosevelt Room.[57]

The draft strategy paper

Titled, "A National Strategy: Setting the Course on Energy," the DOE paper opened with a *pro forma* tribute to the market policies of the Reagan and Bush administrations, which it noted, had "substantially improved the ability of the U.S. economy to withstand disruptions in the world oil markets." The proposed NES, the paper stated, recognized, however, "that all energy markets are influenced by political or regulatory interventions designed to achieve other objectives, often in the areas of environmental quality and National security." To remind EPC of the long and public consultative process which had been undertaken by DOE in order to arrive at the present decision-making point, and to underscore the nature of the forces at play in the energy sector, the DOE paper concluded its introductory section as follows:[58]

> The NES, developed in concert with the American people, charts a course for reduced vulnerability to oil disruptions, a more efficient and technologically diverse electricity sector, an unconstrained natural gas industry, enhanced environmental quality, and availability of ample supplies of reasonably priced energy to fuel a growing economy. It has been shaped by consideration of the role that petroleum plays in the security of the U.S. and other nations; by the influence that regulation in the electricity sector exerts on technology choices, economic efficiency and environmental quality; and by the promise of science and technology.

The DOE paper played heavily on the Iraqi crisis. It noted: "Between August 1, 1990 (the date of Kuwait's invasion by Iraq) and December 1, 1990, U.S. consumers paid $21 billion more to oil producers—$8 billion to foreign producers—than would have been the case without the Iraqi crisis. Worldwide, $83 billion were transferred from oil consumers to oil producers in the same period."[59]

The paper presented various options to lessen U.S. reliance on imports—taxes, tariffs, subsidies for synthetic fuels or smaller cars, fuel economy standards, etc.—but rejected most of these as resulting in "unacceptable GNP losses and unemployment increases."[60]

"Energy independence," the paper declared, "is neither an achievable or a useful goal. First, the U.S. is concurrently a large producer and consumer of oil, so that whatever the direction of international oil price fluctuations, some part of our economy is negatively affected. Second, an increase in the world price of oil, brought about by any event, anywhere, would raise the price of U.S. oil, and the price of oil to our allies and trading partners, regardless of the degree of import dependence."[61]

Nevertheless, the paper noted, economic vulnerability to supply disruptions remains a matter of national concern, which should be addressed by reducing the intensity of oil use (barrels per day per dollar of GNP) in the American economy. "Real improvement in U.S. energy security," the paper stated, "requires efforts on two fronts: (1) support the environmentally responsible development of oil production capacity around the world, including the U.S., and increase strategic reserves; and (2) reduce the use of oil in the U.S. economy through increased efficiency and fuel switching, and by broader use of alternative fuels to decrease the transportation sector's near total reliance on petroleum."[62]

The strategy paper faithfully reflected the policy line that Watkins had come to accept. He believed, for example, that although oil import levels did not define U.S. energy security, it was inherently better policy to encourage greater domestic oil production than to accept higher levels of oil imports. He believed that the oil and gas resources of ANWR and of the OCS were there to be used, and that these regions could absorb energy extraction with due regard to environmental protection. Watkins also believed that his energy strategy could not gain the credibility essential to ensure its long-term acceptance without attention to oil conservation. For that reason, and in the face of clear opposition by the majority of EPC members, he insisted on including in the draft strategy paper, and making explicit, his support for the full panoply of NES options, including those earlier rejected by EPC.[63]

The paper contained sections on electricity policy, science, technology, and environmental quality. The text reflected the consensus already established within the ranks of EPC, but, as in the case of energy security options, continued to advocate conservation initiatives rejected by the council. Watkins and Stuntz wanted EPC to be clear as to exactly what they did and did not support. The efficiency options in question were consequently restated in language far more explicit than had been used in previous interagency communications:[64]

- Eliminate taxation of utility efficiency rebates
- Require Integrated Resource Planning (IRP) from federal power producers, increase assistance to states for IRP
- Extend appliance standards and labeling to commercial lighting and other equipment
- Assist states in promulgating and implementing improved building standards
- Encourage more widespread use of mortgage incentives for energy efficient housing
- Create a self-financing fund for federal efficiency investments
- Increase home weatherization under existing low-income energy assistance programs
- Improve the energy management of federally funded public housing

A Blowup in EPC

The council gathered again in the Roosevelt Room on December 12. The room was crowded to capacity. The meeting, nominally under the chairmanship of Secretary Brady, was summarily taken over by Chief of Staff Sununu. The DOE strategy paper, circulated two days earlier, had prompted speculation among White House Staff that the meeting was likely to be explosive. Stuntz had been warned by her White House contacts that the DOE paper had incensed Sununu, who had interpreted the paper's explicit advocacy of options previously rejected by the Troika as tantamount to disloyalty to the administration.[65]

Watkins began the meeting by ignoring the undercurrent of turmoil around him. He told the council that the NES package should be forwarded to the president along with DOE's draft strategy paper. In his view, the NES proposed by DOE was fully responsive to the president's charter and, not incidentally, to the energy implications of the Persian Gulf war. The proposals provided to the president the means to exercise leadership on energy policy and defuse congressional criticism of the administration's anemic domestic policy agenda. Watkins then summarized what the DOE-recommended compendium of options would contribute to energy security and economic growth and rested his case.[66]

Sununu wasted no time in entering the fray. He declared the draft strategy unacceptable because it was inconsistent with the administration's commitment to market policies. He dismissed the estimates of energy and oil savings projected by DOE as a result of conservation and alternative fuels, questioning the "intelligence" of basing public policy on model results. He rejected, in particular, options related to higher standards for CAFE, appliances, and other equipment, as gross interference in the free market. He concluded by declaring that unless the strategy were recast to eliminate new regulatory interventions, it was unlikely that the administration would actually release an NES at all.[67]

In what appeared to Watkins as an orchestrated attack, CEA Chairman Boskin followed Sununu's outburst by comparing the draft strategy paper to President Carter's first National Energy Plan. Boskin focused his attack on the options related to alternative transportation fuels, casting them in the mold of Carter's discredited Synthetic Fuels Corporation. OMB Director Darman, in turn, argued that DOE's proposals were simply too costly to be absorbed in a tight federal budget. No members of the council defended the proposed strategy.[68]

Watkins responded by reminding his critics of the guidance provided by Sununu himself at the outset of the NES development process, which was for DOE to submit to the White House a full range of options from which the president would choose. He reiterated the view that the president would not be well served by advice lacking in balance or by advice that had been screened for its ideological purity. He insisted that the NES proposal be forwarded to the president along with the positions of the council.[69]

News of the contentious third meeting of the EPC was not long in reaching the media. "At a stormy White House Session Wednesday," reported the Knight-Ridder Service on December 15, "Bush's top economic aides threatened to freeze the entire National Energy Strategy, which Watkins has spent 18 months preparing, until the energy conservation proposals are dropped."[70] On December 17, the *Los Angeles Times* editorialized, "The Energy Department was reportedly told that the White House doesn't even want (efficiency) standards as an option that President Bush would consider when he puts together a new energy policy."[71]

And on December 20, the ABC *World News Tonight* led its broadcast with the NES story. "No one knows," ABC reported, "which options the President will choose, but sources say a major battle is underway. On one side is Energy Secretary Watkins, who says no plan can work without a serious commitment to energy savings. Against him are White House aides John Sununu and Michael Boskin, who say Watkins' efficiency measures will mean heavy regulation and will not save much oil."[72]

Negative media coverage of the third EPC meeting continued throughout the month of December, even as public comments from unnamed White House officials became more biting. Most damaging to both Watkins and the president were comments quoted in the *National Journal* edition of December 22. "Energy Secretary James Watkins' occupational future seems clouded," the article stated, quoting a Bush adviser who thought that Watkins was "incompetent and not a very smart man."[73] The article caught the attention of the president, who telephoned Watkins. Watkins assured the president that the media speculations did not originate at DOE and there was no truth to rumors of his departure from the cabinet. The president then asked whether Watkins knew the source of the stories, to which Watkins replied that he was certain they originated in the White House but could not prove it. The president assured Watkins that if the identity of the anonymous White House aide could be discovered, the person "would be history."[74]

The stage was thus set for the cabinet's first meeting with the president on the scope and content of NES. The meeting was scheduled for December 21, 1990, providing to Brady, EPC chairman, a nine-day window of opportunity either to repair the polarization created by the last council meeting or admit defeat in the process of seeking a cabinet consensus on energy policy. Stuntz thought it unlikely that the EPC leadership would leave it to the president to arbitrate the differences between the Troika and Watkins. Always rather tentative on domestic policy matters, the president was known to dislike policy battles among cabinet members. In the event, Brady was having second thoughts.

THE PRESIDENT'S BRIEFING

Continuing his reflections on the nature of policy, Undersecretary Cordell Moore had written: "The illusory qualities of the word 'policy' have merit, however, for once the compromising, hedging judgments have been made, choosing, chances are, not one but several somewhat indefinite and conflicting courses, it is comforting to be able to describe them by a word implying such wisdom, certainty and singleness of purpose." [75]

"Singleness of purpose" perfectly described the mood of Watkins, Stuntz, and Henson Moore in the final days of 1990. The NES development process had been too long, the mental and physical effort expended too great, the institutional belief in the policy proposals too visceral to allow for a derailment of purpose by the president's men. Watkins' refusal to yield on options unpalatable to EPC had placed Brady in a quandary. Although the checkmating of Watkins had underscored the power of the Troika, it had also shown Brady incapable of arbitrating differences among EPC members.

As a consequence, the EPC—having become a debating society rather than a policy-making body—was about to refer the most contentious elements of NES to the Oval Office. In Washington's environment, this meant that Brady would be transferring to the president virtually all of the political fallout from the policy choices that would eventually be made.

Upon further reflection, Brady proposed that EPC meet in advance of the meeting with the president to seek a way out of the deadlock. Brady's conciliatory meeting took place on December 17. Sununu, Darman, and Boskin did not participate, but were represented, respectively, by Ede Holiday, Robert Grady, and Richard Schmalensee. Brady conducted the meeting in a manner intended to soothe Watkins' agitated state. He actively sought areas of common ground, invited the involvement of second tier cabinet officials capable of negotiating differences that the principals could not, and searched for face-saving compromises for all concerned.[76]

After some discussion, OMB's Grady was charged with the task of negotiating a resolution of outstanding differences on options opposed by what was, after all, a minority of EPC members. These included the proposal to lease to the private sector the Naval Petroleum Reserves and use the resulting revenue to finance expansion of the SPR, the deregulation of oil pipelines, the reform of hydropower licensing, creation of a public corporation to assume control of nuclear waste management, efficiency standards for electricity-using equipment, energy efficiency standards for buildings, the fund for federal efficiency investments and the energy impact analysis of environmental rule-makings.[77]

Satisfied that the negotiations to be undertaken by Grady would be fair, Watkins offered an olive branch in the form of two major concessions. Having consulted with Transportation Secretary Skinner prior to the December 17 meeting, Watkins recommended that EPC defer the issue of CAFE in all its aspects, by entrusting the matter to the National Research Council.[78] The Council would undertake a comprehensive study of CAFE and report back to the administration one year later its view of the technological, economic, safety and environmental potential to improve the CAFE law.[79] Watkins also agreed to forego further debate on virtually all options related to imposition of new taxes on energy.

These compromises thus reached with unexpected comity left EPC—and Brady—with a more manageable list of non-consensus issues to argue with the president.[80]

Before the meeting's adjournment, Watkins also presented to OMB estimates of NES' budgetary impacts. The five-year cost of NES—including the consensus options but excluding the renewable energy tax credit and the enhanced R&D proposals—came to $2 billion. Five-year revenues (including federal income from new OCS and ANWR leases and from leasing of the Naval Petroleum Reserve) were estimated to total $3.4 billion. Under those assumptions, income exceeded expenditures and the resulting NES would consequently meet OBRA rules.

The outlay-to-revenue equation changed substantially, however, when the renewable energy tax credit was added—$2.7 billion over five years—and also the cost of new investments totaling $1.2 billion over five years to support the enhanced R&D initiatives. With these items included, NES would carry a cost of $7.4 billion against revenues of $3.4 billion.[81] If the president were to support Watkins on the renewable and R&D investments, budgetary means would therefore need to be found to offset the resulting revenue losses. In the spirit of the moment, Grady chose not to make an issue of these budget implications until the president's final decisions were known.

Thus concluded the fourth meeting of the EPC. Watkins returned to DOE in good spirits and reported to Stuntz and the policy staff that the process was back on track. He felt that the forthcoming session with the president would provide the best opportunity to press DOE's agenda on the remaining non-consensus options, assuming progress could be expected on matters referred to Grady for resolution. He directed the staff to offer no further compromises to EPC and Troika staffs, but to collaborate with Grady in good faith.[82]

Briefing papers for the president

EPC was scheduled to meet with the president on December 21. In preparation, fresh briefing material needed to be drafted, reflecting the status of decisions on what were ongoing negotiations among EPC members. For DOE policy staff, the preparatory tasks included redrafting "A National Strategy: Setting the Course on Energy," negotiating with Grady on options he was attempting to resolve, and developing talking points for Watkins' first defense of NES before the president of the United States.

The process of redrafting the summary strategy paper was facilitated by the vigorous intervention of the State Department, in response to Watkins' plea to Baker, and newly aggressive involvement by NSC's Eric Melby. In the early stages of the NES development process, Melby had frequently clashed with Wethington. He was now resolved that EPC should not be allowed to dictate the terms of debate for the energy security aspects of NES.

With the full backing of Scowcroft and complete collaboration from State and Defense, Melby proceeded to reformulate all sections of the summary strategy document dealing with oil policy and related security considerations. Melby further insisted (since the issue was under the authority of NSC) that members of EPC would not be permitted to alter, or provide clearance for, text submitted by the foreign policy and security agencies. The text on which the foreign policy community eventually agreed was blunt and, Watkins thought, probably closer to the president's thinking than language previously fostered by EPC.[83]

"For seventeen years," the summary strategy paper, as revised by NSC, finally read, "American Administrations have sought to balance the economic and environmental benefits of increasing reliance on imported oil against the foreign policy and military costs of dealing with threats to the free flow of oil, in particularly from the Persian Gulf. Although the probabilities of events such as the current Gulf crisis are quite small at any time, when one occurs it shows conclusively the high cost of supply disruptions and military intervention." Referring to the historical objective of energy independence as "elusive," rather than "undesirable"—the preferred Troika term—the NSC-cleared strategy paper went on to state that "no feasible combination of domestic or foreign energy policy options can fully relieve us of the risk of oil dependency in the next two decades." Indeed, the paper declared, "America's and the world's oil dependency on Middle East suppliers is likely to grow, and as the current crisis demonstrates, with major implications for our foreign, economic and defense policies."[84]

Stuntz marveled at the ability of the national security apparatus to reaffirm concepts and terminology previously rejected by the Troika in documents headed for the president's desk. DOE had been repeatedly castigated by the Troika for using Melby's energy security vocabulary. Here now was the combined might of the foreign policy establishment insisting that "market forces do not give adequate consideration to the objectives of environmental quality and national security."[85] Unfortunately, the robust language of NSC could not be translated into any further policy action than already agreed to by EPC. The options remained therefore what they were, but Stuntz thought that Melby's vigorously argued security case might very well convince the president to support the markedly interventionist options on which EPC had failed to agree.[86]

The national security agencies' view of the energy world was not, of course, free of self-serving political implications. The foreign policy activism now assigned to NES by NSC promised a great deal more than could possibly be delivered. The United States, according to text supplied by State, would "secure and maintain unrestricted flows of oil from all major producing regions." The United States would also "reduce underlying tensions that threaten major world oil producing regions."[87] These appeared to DOE staff to be highly charged and most likely unachievable foreign policy objectives. The historical record indicated that diplomatic aggressiveness on energy policy seldom withstood the test of time and, in any case, always stayed clear of the source of the security problem, which was membership in the OPEC cartel by the major Persian Gulf producers. Were the national security agencies using NES as the means to merely send Saddam Hussein another message?

NSC motives did not matter to Watkins. NSC was providing the language and terminology he needed to make the case that the strategy he was proposing was responsive to serious energy security concerns. The intervention of the foreign policy, security, and intelligence establishment proved that these concerns were not merely DOE's opinion of what constituted a threat to national security. Watkins could therefore argue to the president that the security aspects of NES, presented in the summary strategy paper, represented judgments rendered by no less an authority on the subject than the National Security Council of the United States.[88]

For the policy staff, the latest clash of concepts presented further evidence of the unresolved tensions between those who have historically argued energy policy on national security grounds and those who have opted for economic reasoning. In each administration since Nixon's, advocates for the two points of view have prevailed—or not—by seeking the heart rather than the mind of the presidents they served. It would likely be no different in the case of George H.W. Bush. Would the president be convinced to support DOE's version of energy policy by the thrilling language of energy security or would he settle for the unexciting but more cautious, even if more prudent vision of the free market economists?

Grady reduces the disagreements

Robert Grady's effort to bridge the differences between DOE and the Troika on key conservation and oil displacement options of NES could not be completed in the short period of time between the fence-mending meeting of EPC on December 17 and the meeting scheduled with the president on December 21. He succeeded, however, in narrowing differences in the scope of some options and moving a few others into the consensus column. His efforts also resulted in a more precise description of what each of the non-consensus options proposed to do.

The rewording of the contentious options, included in the summary strategy draft forwarded to the president by Wethington on December 20, spelled out the policy proposals in terms that left no doubt as to intent. The briefing package itself was structured in a manner designed to focus the president's attention on the following key options:[89]

1. *Remove the (statutory) cap on fuel efficiency (CAFE) incentives to manufacturers of alternative fuel vehicles by amending the Alternative Motor Fuels Act (AMFA) of 1988; expand alternative fuel use in all commercial light and heavy duty vehicle fleets, including Federal fleets; require the sale of non-petroleum fuels.*

    Supporting documentation to the president's briefing papers provided further detail on the meaning of the option's component parts. The president could turn to an appendix of his briefing package and read that the existing AMFA credit in question was capped at 600,000 vehicles per year per manufacturer. The removal of this cap was expected to increase the manufacture of so-called flexible fueled vehicles because automakers could use the resulting credits for the purpose of complying with CAFE standards. Second, the information in the appendix indicated that legislation would be proposed requiring commercial fleets composed of ten or more vehicles to become fuel flexible by the year 2000. The final component of the option involved a legislated requirement that refiners and petroleum and products importers commit five percent of their annual sales to non-petroleum fuels in 2000, rising to ten percent of sales by 2005.

The briefing package informed the president that the option would involve investments of $5 to $7 billion in infrastructure costs and would raise the average price of vehicles by $275 if fuel flexibility was achieved with methanol and by $800 if achieved by compressed natural gas. The option was estimated to reduce oil demand by 1.0 MMB/D in 2005, rising to between 1.9 and 2.7 MMB/D in 2010.

2. *Reform hydropower licensing in order to reduce uncertainty and cost; deregulate licensing of small dams; expand capacity at existing Federal and non-Federal dams.*

This licensing reform, the president was told, aimed at rationalizing a process that typically required five or more years to complete because of the multiple and duplicative regulatory requirements imposed on hydropower licensees by numerous federal agencies.

The proposal was to amend the Federal Power Act in order to vest in FERC the authority to conduct a single, comprehensive review of the licensing process accommodating all National Environmental Policy Act conditions. The option further called for FERC to delegate to state jurisdiction the licensing of projects with capacity of five megawatts or less and called for new federal investments to increase generating capacity at existing federal hydropower plants.

3. *Phase out federal power subsidies.*

The president was informed that federal policy historically had provided lower electricity prices and preferential treatment to utilities and customers served by the five federal power marketing administrations (PMAs)—Bonneville, Western, Southwestern, Southeastern and Alaskan.

The policy had allowed PMAs to sell power at prices below the government's cost of generating it, thereby encouraging consumption and discouraging conservation. The subsidy was disguised in the lower-than-market rates charged by Treasury on loans that originally financed the construction of federal hydropower projects. OMB estimated the cost of subsidy at $500 million per year, or $15 billion over the life of the outstanding loans. The president was told that previous efforts to eliminate this subsidy had encountered unbending congressional opposition, especially by members of Congress from the Northwest, a region in which the Bonneville PMA was the dominant electric power provider.

4. ***Transform the renewable energy tax credit into a production tax credit.***
    The president was advised that this option represented a shift in federal policy to link tax credits directly to energy production, as opposed to the traditional investment tax credit that benefited investors regardless of energy produced.

    The proposal was to offer a credit of up to two cents per kilowatt-hour to producers of electricity generated from new (as opposed to previously built) renewable energy sources. Electricity could be generated by wind, solar thermal, photovoltaic, geothermal, and biomass systems. The credit would be allowed only for the first seven years of system operation, but the rate would be lower than two cents per kWh after the first five years.

    The credit was estimated to induce investment in 1.4 quads of new renewable capacity by the year 2000 and 2.2 quads by the year 2010, at an estimated federal cost of $1.8 billion[90] over five years and $17.3 billion over the twenty-year life of the program.

5. ***Eliminate taxation of utility efficiency rebates.***
    The Internal Revenue Service (IRS) had determined that electric utilities' rebates to customer, of part of the cost of purchasing conservation equipment resulted in taxable income to the customers. DOE opposed the IRS determination on the grounds that rebate payments were not made by the equipment seller and could not therefore be viewed as discounts on the price of the equipment. Nor were the utilities' rebates conditioned on the purchase of electricity and thus could not be viewed as discounted power purchases.

    The proposal was to consider an exemption from federal taxation of utilities' efficiency rebates to customers. This could be accomplished administratively by a Treasury Department rule or legislatively through a tax code amendment. The cost of the rebate was estimated to be in the range of $400 million over five years, a theoretical cost since the IRS had not yet begun to collect the tax and the treasury could not therefore lose what it did not have.

6. *Extend appliance standards to lighting, require efficiency labeling for lighting fixtures.*

The president was asked to support legislation to provide DOE with authority to set efficiency standards for residential, commercial, and industrial lamps.

The proposal was justified by the fact that federal efficiency standards were already set for thirteen categories of residential appliances and for fluorescent lighting systems. Furthermore, other components of commercial lighting systems (fixtures and controls) and other categories of equipment (commercial space conditioners, electric motors) were required by law to carry labels indicating energy performance. The savings from lighting efficiency standards were estimated to be potentially significant because lighting accounted for sixteen percent of total electricity demand and five percent of total energy demand.

The president's meeting

As a result of Grady's arbitration effort, only six issues separated Watkins from a solid consensus of the cabinet on NES. He viewed these issues less in terms of their policy significance than for the political consequences that could be expected from their absence. He believed also that the Troika had exaggerated the importance of these options to the administration's market-reliance image and that the president would come to see it.[91]

In the Cabinet Room, four days before Christmas 1990, Watkins did not wish to engender a repetition of previous arguments with Sununu, Boskin, Darman, and Brady. His opening statement to the president was brief, non-argumentative, and focused on the consensus achieved rather than on remaining, unresolved issues. He provided a summary of what he called the "outcomes of DOE's NES package," which included the six non-consensus options, by stating that the strategy advocated by DOE would:[92]

- reduce vulnerability to future oil shocks
- reduce oil imports to less than 50% of U.S. consumption
- engage U.S. foreign policy in efforts to address unstable energy supplies
- deregulate, diversify, and improve technology of the electric utility sector
- challenge the scientific community to convert research results into products
- balance energy production with environmental protection
- secure adequate energy supplies at reasonable cost

Turning to others around the cabinet table, the president asked for comments on the package presented by Watkins and on the non-consensus options.

Vice President Quayle stated his opposition to any further regulation of the economy, citing specifically the new efficiency standards proposed for buildings and lighting systems. Brady stated that he could not support the costly renewable energy tax credit and would not recommend what amounted to a retraction of the IRS rule on the taxation of efficiency rebates. Boskin agreed with the vice president on the regulatory options and also objected strenuously to the alternative fuels proposals. EPA's Reilly thought that the alternative fuels proposals were desirable but should be made consistent with related requirements of the recently enacted CAAA.[93]

Boyden Gray, the president's counsel, defended federal support for alternative fuels and vehicles. Sununu, less aggressive than in the previous EPC meeting, continued to oppose all remaining non-consensus options. However, during the course of the debate on alternative fuels, he realized that a link could be forged between his support for nuclear power and alternative energy sources for transportation. He told the president that a stronger case could be made for the NES nuclear options if the need for more generation capacity were to be justified on the basis of projected increases in electricity demand from future electric vehicles.[94]

The meeting with the president lasted slightly less than one hour. It was noteworthy for its ordinariness, absence of substantive debate, and its focus on what would eventually be judged as issues tangential to the long-term implications of NES. The president withheld judgment and decision on all outstanding options, but indicated that a second meeting of the cabinet would likely be necessary before NES could be finalized. He promised to study the briefing papers provided to him by EPC over the holidays and suggested, before leaving the cabinet room, that further negotiations among the EPC members might very well narrow the remaining differences on the non-consensus options.[95]

THE PRESIDENT'S CHOICE

The second cabinet meeting with the president took place on, January 8, 1991. The week previous to the meeting had been marked by two unexpected controversies. The first of these concerned Sununu's request that Watkins more closely link NES' nuclear power options to electric vehicles' likely higher demand for electric power. Analysis of the issue by DOE policy staff could not be made to justify Sununu's theory. Watkins had consequently sent a memorandum to the chief of staff on January 4, with the following conclusions: "A recent study by the Electric Power Research Institute [EPRI] estimates that available off-peak power in the United States is adequate to support recharging of about 130 million electric commuter vehicles. DOE estimates that the number of electric or hybrid vehicles that might reasonably be in use by the year 2010 is in the range of 12 million vehicles." [96]

The chief of staff was not pleased with the DOE response. Sununu tended to think, as Ralph Cavanaugh of the Natural Resources Defense Council succinctly noted, that he had "a technical mastery of all subjects."[97] Sununu consequently recruited to his nuclear power support effort the president's science adviser, D. Allan Bromley, who shared Sununu's obsession for nuclear technology. Bromley had remained indifferent to energy policy throughout the eighteen months of NES development, but on January 7, the day before the scheduled second and final cabinet meeting with the president, Bromley distributed to the Troika agencies a memorandum to underscore what he considered to be the administration's unequivocal support for nuclear power. He furthermore insisted that his views be accommodated in the text of the NES briefing papers that were to be sent to the president.

The Bromley memo, forwarded directly to Sununu[98] rather than, as protocol would have required, to Watkins, sought revisions in two NES option papers. Bromley demanded that the list of ten critical technologies defined in the enhanced R&D option paper be modified to show displacement of imported oil achievable first and foremost by "advanced design nuclear energy plants," and a federal commitment to "expanded R&D aimed at second-generation, passively-safe reactors."[99] The justification provided by Bromley was that nuclear technology had "large economic and environmental advantages in meeting the Nation's increasing demand for electricity." Without the nuclear option, he wrote, "oil use for electricity generation is projected to increase to over 2 million barrels/day by the year 2000." As a consequence, Bromley concluded: "Vigorous research and development of advanced reactors designs is needed to assure that our plants are the safest, most reliable and most efficient possible. Second generation nuclear technologies resulting from this research and development could provide, according to conservative projections, 140 GW of new capacity by 2030." [100]

The Bromley text was faxed to DOE by Wethington without comment and passed on to the policy staff. The staff read the Bromley note and thought it absurd at best, at worst a bad joke. The staff had no references for the projections cited by Bromley. DOE projections—already accepted by EPC—had never indicated a rise to 2 MMB/D of oil consumption for electricity generation. As to the 140 gigawatts of new nuclear capacity that Bromley thought probable by 2030, the staff considered the number not only illusory in theory but a practical impossibility as well. To reach Bromley's projected nuclear capacity it meant that at least one hundred new nuclear power plants would need to be built in thirty years, on a crash construction program of unprecedented proportions that would see licensing, on average, of not less than three new plants per year.

The staff relayed these misgivings to Watkins, who dismissed the Bromley memo as inopportune and ill-advised. Sununu, however, would not let the matter rest.[101]. At the January 8 cabinet meeting with the president, Sununu strongly endorsed the Bromley initiative and directed Watkins—with no objections from any other member of the cabinet and silent assent by the President—to fully accommodate Bromley's recommendations.[102]

The cabinet meeting then proceeded—awkwardly—to a discussion of the non-consensus options. The president indicated a generally favorable disposition toward the alternative fuels option, provided that the fleet requirements did not overly burden small businesses and provided also that the provision for sales of non-oil fuels by refiners be dropped. The president also agreed with the vice president and the Troika leaders that if the CAFE issue were opened for debate in the Congress, its eventual outcome, including heavy-handed new regulation, could not be contained.[103]

The decision on alternative fuels, a stunning reversal for Boskin, was seen by the cabinet as entirely due to the influence of Boyden Gray rather than to any analytical arguments advanced by DOE. The president further noted that he tended to side with the treasury secretary on the high cost of the renewable energy tax credit and indicated that if the credit could be made less costly, he might reconsider. Brady suggested that the alternative lay in a simple extension of the 10% investment tax credit for renewable projects. Sununu interjected that if the renewable tax credit were to remain under consideration, then it should be redesigned to ensure the highest possible level of federal support for geothermal resources.[104]

The president went on to say that he had not yet reached a conclusion on the tax-free treatment of utility rebates, but Treasury's view on cost would weigh heavily on this matter also. He expressed skepticism about the value of new regulatory initiatives such as the proposed standards for lighting and motors. He agreed, in principle, with the phase out of federal power subsidies and the reform of hydropower licensing, but recognized the political difficulties of carrying them out.

In closing, he suggested that Brady and Watkins work together on further refinement of the renewable energy tax credit, the utility rebates and the revised alternative fuel options.[105]

Final maneuvers

On January 10, Watkins dispatched a memorandum to Secretary Brady and a second to the president, seeking resolution of outstanding issues and warning, once again, against settling on a strategy that lacked balance.

To Brady he offered compromises on the alternative transportation fuel option and on the renewable energy tax credit, but not on utility rebates, because he was confident that the president would in the end support the latter. On alternative fuels, Watkins reminded Brady that the DOE option requiring fleets of ten or more vehicles to become progressively fuel-flexible had been designed to be consistent with a similar provision of the CAAA. The CAAA provision applied to approximately twenty-six metropolitan areas classified as being in non-attainment of ozone pollution standards. Watkins suggested that, in deference to Reilly at EPA, the ten-vehicle requirement be maintained for the non-attainment areas. In the rest of the nation, the requirement would be extended to fleets of twenty vehicles or more.[106]

On the renewable energy tax credit, Watkins offered a more modest proposal estimated to cost $671 million over five years, or one-third the original proposal. DOE staff had reached the conclusion that the tax credit was in great jeopardy because of its high cost and that it was prudent to scale it back in the hope that Congress would enlarge it. The staff reluctantly added geothermal energy to the sources qualified for the credit, as Sununu had dictated, notwithstanding the well-known economics of renewable energy, which showed that geothermal power was the most cost-competitive of renewable resources and least in need of subsidy.[107]

Watkins' memorandum to the president summarized the ongoing discussions with Brady and went on to underscore the importance of political perception about the final NES. "Conservation and renewable energy provisions," Watkins wrote, "principally embodied in the five non-consensus options within the package I placed before the EPC, are critical to achieving political consensus that would, in turn, allow desired energy security outcomes, for example, opening ANWR. Were we not to include reasonable, cost-effective measures in these 'balancing' areas up-front in your strategy, the Congress would surely adopt their own." As to the timing of the NES' release, Watkins reminded the president that Security Advisor Scowcroft had, in the last cabinet meeting, expressed concern "about the consequences of releasing an anemic or unbalanced NES at a time when war is imminent or underway in the Middle East."[108]

The president makes it (nearly) final

Final decisions on NES were held in abeyance during most of January 1991 as the air war against Iraq unfolded with the first bombardment of January 17. DOE policy staff celebrated the hard-fought drawdown of the Strategic Petroleum Reserve that, within hours of the announced sale, had been instrumental in lowering world oil prices to pre-war levels. The celebration was muted, however, in expectation of the president's not entirely supportive final decisions on NES. It was difficult actually for the staff to imagine the president dealing concurrently with battlefield reports and NES options.

Watkins was summoned to the White House by Sununu on January 31 to receive word of the president's final decisions on NES. He was told that the president had decided against the proposed appliance standards, the tax-free treatment of utility rebates, and the renewable energy tax credit. On the renewable energy option, the president had decided on a simple one-year extension of the investment tax credit. Disappointed by this news, Watkins requested that the decisions not be made public until he could appeal to the president for reconsideration.[109]

On the following day, Watkins dispatched two memoranda to the White House. "The decision to extend by one year the current 10% investment tax credit for solar and geothermal (projects) will be of little political value to the President," Watkins wrote to Sununu, "and will make no significant difference to investors. In fact, the decision rewards the Democratic members of Congress who have extended this credit for 10 years over the Administration's opposition."[110] On the rejected utility rebates option Watkins was even more blunt. "This is the pivotal conservation initiative in the National Energy Strategy," he told Sununu. "It is a powerful tool for gaining immediate acceptance of the NES as a balanced strategy." As to the political dimensions of the option, Watkins declared that Senator Steve Symms had "already introduced S. 83 (a bill) which will do this anyway, and it will pass overwhelmingly."[111]

In the separate memorandum to the president, Watkins reiterated the arguments used with Sununu, but more emphatically. "Mr. President," the memorandum stated, "I regard the utility efficiency rebate issue as a critical symbol of whether you are serious about conservation in the NES. Without it, I have little with which to parry the charge (that) the Strategy is unbalanced." Watkins then reminded the president of the consequences of eliminating from NES both the renewable tax credit and the efficiency rebate options. "Taking into account your decision on both issues," the memorandum stated, "our analysis indicates that (projected) renewable electricity production is cut in half, electricity demand reduction is halved, and carbon emissions are significantly increased."[112]

In one final attempt to change the President's mind, Watkins appealed to Secretary of State Baker. "I am very worried," Watkins wrote on February 7, "that this (NES) could be a loser, instead of a big winner for the President...Any help you can give me would be greatly appreciated."[113]

These efforts proved futile. The president remained apparently unconvinced by Watkins' evaluation of the NES' political fall out. Schmalensee would later reveal that he and Boskin would have reconsidered their opposition to at least the lighting efficiency standards had Watkins sought their help.[114] Schmalensee did intervene on the issue of tax treatment of utility rebates by offering a compromise, accepted by DOE and the Troika, by which the rebates would be tax-free if provided by utilities in the form of reduced monthly billings for electricity consumption. Cash payments to consumers would remain subject to tax.[115]

THE SUM OF ITS UNEQUAL PARTS

The Washington special interests community, on which the media often depends for an understanding of complex technical issues, rendered judgment on NES long before it actually existed.

"There is no vision," declared WorldWatch Institute's senior energy analyst in mid-December 1990, "there is simply a long list of options."[116] And Public Citizen, a group not previously known for its energy policy expertise, was quoted by no less an authority than the *New York Times*, as believing that the (still unwritten NES) was "a politically expedient response to the Persian Gulf crisis that lacks any long-term vision and will result in continued energy waste and environmental destruction."[117]

DOE policy staff transformed NES options into a comprehensive statement of policy in early 1991. The first, complete version of NES was distributed for interagency review on January 29, 1991. The draft was marked 6:06 a.m., meaning that the staff had labored during the previous night in order to meet the completion deadline established by Stuntz. The first paragraph of NES read:

> The National Energy Strategy lays the foundation for a more efficient, less vulnerable, and environmentally sustainable energy economy. It defines diplomatic, commercial, regulatory, and technological policy tools that will substantially diversify U.S. sources of energy supplies, and offer more flexibility and efficiency in the way energy is transformed and used. Specifically, it will spur more efficiency and competition throughout the energy sector, expand the fuel and technology choices available to the Nation, improve U.S. research and development know-how, and extend to international energy policy the leadership the United States exercises in economic, security, and environmental policy.[118]

The draft NES was organized along the same topics used in the Interim Report of 1990. The four major sections were increasing energy and economic efficiency, securing future energy supplies, enhancing environmental quality and fortifying foundations. Energy's end uses in the electric utility sector and in the residential, commercial, industrial, and transportation sectors were discussed in the first section. Fuels and related technology, including research and development initiatives, followed. The environmental quality section addressed energy-related pollutants and emissions. Under the heading of fortifying foundations were grouped the topics of basic and fundamental research, technology transfer, and education. Goals, and the means to achieve them, were presented at the forefront of each chapter.[119]

Following distribution of the NES' first draft, DOE staff braced for the predictable interagency editorial onslaught. Each of the member agencies of EPC responded to the draft, many providing several pages of critiques, editorial comments and, as expected, mutually contradictory advice. In some cases, the agencies seemed to be unaware of previous White House deliberations, castigating DOE for decisions actually made by the president.

The White House Council on Environmental Quality: "We applaud the considerable work you have done...toward a balanced and evolving National Energy Strategy. But as you are well aware, the Strategy will receive substantial criticism from Congress and the public for not having easily identifiable 'big ticket' efficiency measures such as CAFE, energy taxes such as the 'gas guzzler,' or a more comprehensive alternative fuels package."[120]

Council of Economic Advisers: "Overall, this is a very good document that shows the fruits of these long months of work...A discussion is needed (however) explaining and justifying the objectives of the NES. We suggest: 'The objectives established by President Bush are: continuation of the successful policy of market reliance; and achieving balance between (*sic*) our increasing need for energy at reasonable prices and our commitment to a cleaner, healthier environment, our determination to maintain an economy second to none, and our goal to reduce dependence by ourselves and our friends and allies on potentially unreliable energy suppliers.'"[121]

Department of the Treasury: "The new report is much clearer than the interim report, the option papers, and other earlier material. It makes its case well, and is, in most places, well written. What we find lacking is a clear statement of the role of markets and the importance of market reliance. Without such a statement, the document, taken as a whole, may be interpreted as the first step toward an U.S. industrial policy for energy. Although DOE may not have intended to propose an industrial policy, the present document may be interpreted by interventionists on Capitol Hill and elsewhere as supporting that approach."[122]

National Security Council: "The draft is not very inspiring and merits substantial rewriting. It should not highlight Iraq's invasion of Kuwait. Doing so suggests the NES has new proposals to prevent such an event in the future. The President should not be tied to the 50% (oil) import number. The U.S. already is the leader in international energy policy through its leadership in the IEA. Remove reference to reducing underlying tensions (in the politically volatile Middle East). This is a foreign policy and national security issue; the NES can do nothing about it".[123]

Office of Management and Budget: "The document includes some very positive points (but) parts of the text claim that we must take a new approach on energy—implying the past decade was a serious mistake and rejecting the President's guidance that we are to continue the successful policy of market reliance. This needs to be dropped, in our view."[124]

Department of Justice: "We applaud the advocacy in the NES of market-based incentives for addressing environmental externalities. The NES will give added momentum to the current reformation of American environmental law: the transition from technology-based command-and-control strategies to performance based market mechanisms. But the NES does itself a disservice by emphasizing only the cost savings advantages of market incentives. The NES ought to advertise the environmental advantage of performance-based market incentives as well.[125]

Department of the Interior: "The discussion of oil supply does not adequately present the economic dimensions of domestic oil production. Despite the current (Iraqi) crisis, basing recommendations for NES oil supply options strictly on the quantity of oil produced, ignoring the economic benefits of domestic oil production, leaves those options open to a variety of criticisms. Such a concentration on the quantity of production rather than on the economics would be appropriate for a centrally planned economy".[126]

Fourteen days in February

Draft followed draft as the DOE policy office attempted to accommodate a virtually uninterrupted stream of comments, revisions, and suggested and demanded changes to the NES document—by now 250 pages in length—during the first two weeks of February 1991. The White House had meanwhile determined that NES would be released to the public on February 20, meaning that a camera-ready text had to be transmitted to the Government Printing Office no later than the evening of February 14. The deadline was met.

DOE general counsel Steve Wakefield began drafting legislation to enable implementation of NES immediately after the conclusion of the cabinet's decision-making process. The legislation would be submitted to Congress concurrently with NES. Following normal interagency clearance, the legislative proposal was forwarded to the White House for final approval. The approval was withheld until the afternoon of February 19, one day before the NES' scheduled release. Watkins, summoned to the White House for what he believed were final preparations for the president's NES news conference on the following day, was instead told that the purpose of the meeting was altogether different.

Acting at the urging of the Vice President's Council on Competitiveness, the president informed Watkins that he had decided to add to the NES legislative proposals a provision to abolish FERC. The commission would be transformed into a federal energy administration under the purview of the secretary of energy. Watkins was surprised by the decision, pleased by the president's wish to expand the powers of DOE, but wary of congressional reaction. He knew that House Energy and Commerce Committee chairman John Dingell, historically diligent in safeguarding the autonomy of FERC, would fiercely oppose the proposal.

Watkins expressed these concerns to the president, as well as the opinion that FERC Chairman Martin Allday would also be unhappy with the decision. The president accepted the concerns as reasonable, but felt that the move would dramatize Republicans' commitment to a less regulated economy. He then proceeded to telephone Chairman Allday, who had been kept in the dark on White House deliberations about the future of the commission he headed, and informed him of the decision. Allday responded that he opposed the decision as ill-advised but would go along if the president insisted on it. The president did. The NES legislative proposal was thus revised during the evening of February 19 to reflect the proposal to abolish FERC.[127]

THE ANNOUNCEMENT

NES was released by the White House on February 20, 1991. In a cramped auditorium of the Old Executive Office Building, the president presided over a ceremony also attended by members of Congress who would become critical to the enactment of legislation enabling implementation of the Strategy. The president acknowledged the presence in the auditorium's first row of Congressmen John Dingell, Norman Lent, Philip Sharp and Carlos Moorehead [128] and of Senators Malcom Wallop and J. Bennett Johnston.

From the cabinet ranks, the president identified Watkins, Moore, and Stuntz of Energy; Clayton Yeutter of Agriculture; Skinner of Transportation, and Lujan from Interior. Council of Environmental Quality (CEQ) Chairman Deland was acknowledged as well, but misidentified by the president as representing the CEA. Hank Habicht, EPA's deputy administrator was present, as was James Edwards, Reagan's first energy secretary.[129] The rest of the audience, which filled the auditorium to spillover capacity, represented Washington's special interest community.

"I want to thank Admiral Watkins," the president said, "and also acknowledge and thank the efforts of so many. We now have, thanks to all, a carefully balanced energy strategy, and it is designed to diversify America's sources of energy. It's designed to encourage efficiency and conservation, spur competition throughout the energy sector, give Americans greater choices among fuels, and enhance U.S. research and development in new technology."[130]

Watkins followed the president to the podium. "The NES is a strategy," he stated, "that for the first time in our history lays a comprehensive foundation for a cleaner, more efficient and more secure energy future." Watkins went on to praise the idea of balance and shared responsibility, and then, with the aid of large and colorful charts, he provided some specifics as to what could be expected from full implementation of the strategy.

NES, he said, will, "decrease the U.S. economy's demand for oil by 3.4 million barrels a day while increasing domestic production by 3.8 million barrels a day by the year 2010. It will also result in the increased availability of electricity produced from renewable sources and could increase the use of alternative transportation fuels and technology by up to 3 million barrels per day in 2010."[131]

Watkins then described the long, public process he had pursued in the development of NES, citing the public hearings, number of witnesses, and the involvement of state and local officials. He noted that the president—uncommonly prescient—had commissioned NES a full year before Iraq's invasion of Kuwait. He reminded the audience that "we know from experience that we can neither solely produce nor conserve our way to a secure, environmentally sound and affordable energy future."[132]

Watkins concluded by declaring that the NES will "protect the pocketbooks of U.S. consumers, the jobs of U.S. workers, and the global environment. The NES demonstrates that environmental, economic and energy objectives can be brought into balance."[133] There were, of course, other views as to what NES represented and what it would accomplish. These views—from Congress, the media and the myriad special interest groups—proved harsh.

The snap judgment

Notwithstanding the intensity of the debate on petroleum and energy security issues, NES' innovation lay in two essential aspects.

First, policymakers avoided the historical pitfall of transforming the politically volatile issue of oil import dependence into a clarion call for government intervention to control imports or raise taxes. NES did adopt the half measure of federally promoted introduction of alternative transportation fuels, but the measure was significantly less draconian than the oil substitution proposals that had been adopted as policy by Nixon, Ford, and Carter in the previous decade.

Second, the crafters of NES proposed a leap of faith into a future energy economy by endorsing the reform of regulation governing the generation and dispatch of electricity. Amending PUHCA, to allow unencumbered competitors to traditional utilities, represented a step no previous administration had been willing to take. It would prove to be a step of profound significance, engendering a restructuring of the electric utility industry by federal and state initiatives with consequences far more complex than ever envisaged by the NES designers.

Neither of these two elements of innovation received much attention from the public and the media when NES was finally published. *TIME* magazine captured the consensus reaction in an article it titled "The Energy Mess." "The President is expected to unveil a national energy policy," *TIME* advised, "that will favor increased use of natural gas and nuclear power and stepped-up oil exploration...but the plan is almost certain to ignore any significant steps to promote conservation...the program is expected to shun the two most effective means to put the brakes on fuel consumption: a hike in the gas tax and a higher federal fuel efficiency standard for U.S. autos." *TIME* placed the blame for the shortcomings of the NES on what it called the three big gunners of the White House: Budget Director Richard Darman, White House Chief of staff John Sununu, and Michael Boskin, chairman of the Council of Economic Advisers.[134]

Editors of the national daily newspapers echoed TIME's refrain. "Energy strategy stresses reliance on domestic fuel," the *Washington Times* headlined.[135] "Bush Unveils Energy Strategy Emphasizing Fossil, Nuclear Power Production," declared the *Washington Post.*[136] "Bush Asserts Need for Foreign Oil," concluded the *New York Times.*[137]

Columnist David Broder of the *Washington Post* rendered perhaps the most balanced judgment. "The policy proposal assembled by Secretary of Energy James D. Watkins and his aides," Broder wrote on February 24, "is the product of a serious intellectual and political effort sustained over 18 months. Despite predictable potshots and cheap shots from some environmental and consumer spokesmen, it has not been dismissed as 'dead on arrival' on Capital Hill." After castigating the president's men for trivializing Watkins' efforts and enjoying "petty bureaucratic victories," Broder concluded, "But the report could also have been a real spur to action had the President chosen to use it in that fashion. Instead, as it emerged, the National Energy Strategy is heavy on analysis, but short on motivating power. One has to wonder if that is really what the President wanted."[138]

On February 20, fresh from the news conference announcing his NES, Watkins was ebullient. Before leaving his office for home that day, he sent a note to the president. "On behalf of all who have worked so hard on developing your National Energy Strategy," Watkins wrote, "I want to thank you for your wonderful and supportive statement today. We continue to serve you with great pride and the highest respect for your leadership."[139]

The president thus set his energy policy proposals on the legislative table. It was now up to Congress to dispose of the policy initiatives that had preoccupied the executive branch for nearly two years, and make them law. Congress turned in earnest to consideration of NES on the very afternoon of its release by the White House.

NOTES AND COMMENTS

1. *Note One:* The sixty-seven policy options of the National Energy Strategy were the following:

Exploration and development tax credit, 2. 27.5% depletion allowance for EOR, 3. Tax credit for stripper well production, 4. Nonconventional fuels tax credit (sec. 29), 5. Oil import fee, 6. Allow access to restricted OCS, 7. Allow access to ANWR, 8. Accelerate Alaskan North Slope development, 9. Gas pipeline construction without federal certification, 10. Coordinated NEPA review for gas pipeline construction, 11. Deregulate pipeline sales rates, 12. Reform pipeline rate design, 13. Improve pipeline transportation, 14. Eliminate DOE import/export regulation, 15. Increase CAFE standards, 16. Reform CAFE law, 17. Accelerate scrappage of older cars, 18. Revise gas guzzler/gas sipper tax, 19. Stimulate commuter HOV use, 20. Motor fuels taxes: ten to fifty cents per gallon, 21. BTU tax, 22. Ad Valorem tax, 23. Carbon tax, 24. Low-income home efficiency, 25. Extend/modify ethanol tax credit, 26. Production incentive for long-term alternative fuels, 27. Larger federal alternative fuel vehicle fleet, 28. CAFE incentive for alternative fuel vehicles, 29. Alternative fuel vehicle production, 30. Alternative fuel infrastructure, 31. Petroleum taxes to pay for SPR, 32. Using NPR receipts to finance SPR, 33. Oil pipeline deregulation, 34. Reform PUHCA, 35. Transmission access for wholesalers, 36. Hydropower regulatory reform, 37. Facilitate expansion of nuclear power, 38. Nuclear waste—comprehensive solution, 39. Nuclear waste—alternative to federal management, 40. Accelerate introduction of innovative electric technologies, 41. Encourage clean coal in electric utilities, 42. Renewable energy production incentive, 43. Municipal solid waste to energy, 44. Reform PURPA—remove size cap, 45. Reform PURPA—relax co-firing limits, 46. Promote Integrated Resource Planning,, 47. Appliance and equipment standards, 48. Building energy efficiency standards, 49. Mortgage financing incentives, 50. Fund for federal efficiency investments, 51. Improve the efficiency of public housing, 52. Global climate change—integrate NES, 53. Added global climate change research, 54. Reduce economic and societal costs of environmental regulation, 55. Energy impact assessments for environmental rule makings, 56. Modified New Source Review applicability, 57. Emission trading for environmental compliance, 58. Managing environmental impacts of energy systems, 59. Encourage waste minimization in industry, 60. Dual regulation of radionuclide, 61. Realign federal R&D priorities, 62. DOE basic research capabilities, 63. Leverage NES-related R&D resources, 64. Reform the national technology transfer service, 65. Spur the export of energy technologies, 66. Math-science education initiative, 67. Implementation strategy for National Education Goal # 4.

2. *Note Two:* The National Research Council issued *Automotive Fuel Economy: How Far Should We Go ?* on April 9, 1992. The report was compiled by a "Committee on Fuel Economy of Automobiles and Light Trucks," appointed by the council. The committee's conclusions are summarized in the following paragraph from the executive summary of their report:

> The charge to the committee was to estimate "practical achievable" fuel economy levels in various size classes of new passenger cars and light trucks using gasoline and diesel fuel. Any such determination of practically achievable fuel economy levels, however, necessarily involves balancing an array of societal benefits and costs, while keeping in mind where the costs and benefits fall. Such judgments must include a complex manifold of considerations, such as the financial costs to consumers and manufacturers, the impact on employment and competitiveness, the trade-off of fuel economy with occupant safety and environmental goals, and the benefits to our national and economic security or reduced dependence on petroleum. *In the committee's view, the determination of the practically achievable levels of fuel*

economy is appropriately the domain of the political process, not this committee. (Emphasis added)

The committee was chaired by Richard A. Meserve and had the following members: Gary L. Casey, W. Robert Epperly, Theodore H. Geballe, David L. Greene, John H. Johnson, Maryann N. Keller, Charles D. Kolstad, Leroy H. Lindgren, G. Murray Mackay, M. Eugene Merchant, David L. Morrison, Phillip S. Myers, Daniel Roos, Patricia F. Waller, Joseph D. Walter.

3. *Note Three:* The legislative proposal submitted to the 102nd Congress by the Bush administration for the purpose of carrying out provisions of NES that could not be implemented under then-existing statutory authority was titled the National Energy Strategy Act and given the designation of H.R. 1301 by the Clerk of the House of Representatives. The bill, reluctantly cosponsored by Dingell, Lent, and Moorehead, was introduced on March 6, 1991. Title IV of the bill described the creation of a Natural Gas and Electricity Administration within the DOE and abolishment of FERC. The bill was referred to the Committees on: Energy and Commerce, Interior and Insular Affairs, Armed Services, Merchant Marine and Fisheries, Science-Space-Transportation, Government Operations, Judiciary, Public Works and Transportation, and Ways and Means. All of these committees and others would claim jurisdiction over NES legislation. They would produce various bills of their own or amendments to others' bills.

    Eventually, Dingell and Sharp would produce H.R. 776, which would become the legislative vehicle of choice—in the House and in the Senate—to reach a consensus for the Energy Policy Act of 1992. (Ref: H.R. 1301, pp. 22-26).

REFERENCES

[1] Robert B. Krueger, *The United States and International Oil: A Report for the Federal Energy Administration on U.S. Firms and Government Policy.* (New York: Praeger Publishers, 1975), p. 83.

[2] See note one of chapter five for a complete list of final options considered by EPC and the president.

[3] Linda G. Stuntz, deputy undersecretary, Policy, Planning and Analysis, DOE, Memorandum for EPC Working Group Members on NES, Subject: NES, October 26, 1990.

[4] Allan Hubbard, executive director, Council on Competitiveness, Office of the Vice President, Memorandum for Admiral Watkins, Subject: NES Options that Raise Regulatory Issues, October 31, 1990.

[5] Sidney L. Jones, assistant secretary for Economic Policy, Department of the Treasury, Memorandum for Olin Wethington, director, EPC, Subject: NES Option, December 4, 1990.

[6] Timothy E. Deal, special assistant to the president and senior director for International Economic Affairs, NSC, Memorandum for the Honorable W. Henson Moore, deputy secretary, DOE, Subject: NES Options, October 31, 1990.

[7] Harold R. Denton, director, Office of Governmental and Public Affairs, NRC, Letter to the Honorable Linda G. Stuntz, deputy undersecretary, Policy, Planning and Analysis, DOE, October 30, 1990.

[8] Sidney Jones, Department of the Treasury, Memorandum to Linda G. Stuntz, DOE, Subject: NES: Voting on Options, Notes on Treasury Votes, No. 20, October 31, 1990.

[9] Richard Schmalensee, CEA, Executive Office of the President, Memorandum for Olin Wethington, EPC and Linda Stuntz, DOE, Subject: Second Round of NES voting, December 4, 1990.

[10] Robert E. Grady, OMB, Executive Office of the President, Memorandum for Linda G. Stuntz, Subject: Comments on the NES Options Papers, October 30, 1990.

[11] Jeffrey N. Shane, assistant secretary for Policy and International Affairs, U.S. Department of Transportation, Letter to the Honorable Linda G. Stuntz, deputy undersecretary, Office of Policy, Planning and Analysis, DOE, November 1, 1990.

[12] Dick Stewart, assistant attorney general, U.S. Department of Justice, Memorandum to Olin L. Wethington, executive secretary, EPC and Linda G. Stuntz, deputy undersecretary of Energy, Subject: Votes on NES Options, December 3, 1990.

[13] Scott Farrow, Council on Environmental Quality, Agency Position on NES Options with attachment, December 3, 1990.

[14] Frederick W. Volcansek, U.S. Department of Commerce, Agency Positions on NES Options, November 30, 1990.

[15] Susan Wiltshire, Memorandum to Robert M. Simon, Subject: Additional Comment on NES, October 31, 1990.

[16] Harry Mandil, Letter with enclosure to Admiral James D. Watkins, U.S. Navy (Retired), secretary of energy, October 26, 1990.

[17] John W. Landis, Letter to Admiral James D. Watkins, secretary of energy, DOE, October 31, 1990.

[18] John P. McTague, vice president, Technical Affairs, Ford Motor Company, Letter to Robert M. Simon, SEAB, DOE, October 31, 1990.

[19] Warren M. Washington, director, Climate & Global Dynamics Division, National Center for Atmospheric Research, Letter and attachment to Dr. Robert M. Simon, SEAB, DOE, October 24, 1990.

[20] Glenn Paulson, Ph.D., research professor and member of SEAB, Memorandum to Robert E. Simon, Ph.D., executive secretary, SEAB, Re: NES, November 2, 1990.

[21] Bob Fri, Memorandum to Bob Simon, Subject: NES Comments, October 22, 1990

[22] Verbal communications by the admiral to Stuntz and Stagliano, subsequently reconfirmed, verbally in January 2001.

[23] Verbal communications by Moore to Stagliano after Moore's tenure at DOE, subsequently confirmed in writing on February 13, 2001.

[24] Internal DOE discussions involving the leadership identified in the text and various members of the policy staff, including the author, which took place between October 30 and November 14, 1990.

[25] Olin L. Wethington, executive secretary to EPC, the White House, fax to Linda Stuntz, DOE, Draft "Framework Paper: NES" (with handwritten notation by Stuntz), October 30, 1990.

[26] Olin L. Wethington, executive secretary, Transmittal sheet from the White House Office of Cabinet Affairs, Staffing Memorandum with "NES Framework for Consideration of Options," November 15, 1990.

[27] The Fossil2 Model was used by the policy staff for all NES scenarios presented to EPC and the president.

[28] Robert Krueger, *The United States and International Oil*, op. cit., p. 83.

[29] Olin L. Wethington, executive secretary, EPC, the White House, Memorandum for EPC, Subject: EPC Meeting, NES, November 19, 1990 at 2:00 P.M., November 15, 1990.

[30] Secretary of energy's briefing materials and graphics in a package titled "A Process for Finalizing the National Energy Strategy," distributed to the cabinet by the White House Office of Cabinet Affairs on November 19, 1990.

[31] Ibid., graphic titled "Primary Energy Consumption by Fuel: NES 'Consensus' Case".

[32] Ibid., graphic titled "Primary Energy Consumption by Fuel: NES 'All EPC Options' Case".

[33] Ibid., chart titled "Meeting the President's Objectives".

[34] Ibid.

[35] Post-mortem discussions of the cabinet meeting among Watkins, Moore, Stuntz, Gault and Stagliano, on the afternoon of November 19, 1990, and directions to staff.

[36] Ibid.

[37] Ibid.

[38] Olin L. Wethington, executive secretary, EPC, the White House, Memorandum for EPC, Subject: EPC Meeting, NES, November 28, 1990, at 2:00 P.M., November 26, 1990.

[39] Lindsey was subsequently appointed a governor of the Federal Reserve.

[40] Vito Stagliano, DOE, Memorandum for Mr. Grady, OMB et al., Subject: Draft Framework for Consideration of NES Energy Security Options, November 23, 1990.

[41] DOE: "NES: Framework for Consideration of Energy Security Options," November 23, 1990.

[42] 1990 U.S. Dollars.

[43] Ibid.

[44] Ibid.

[45] Ibid.

[46] Ibid.

[47] Ibid.

[48] Ibid.

[49] Ibid.

[50] Abraham Haspel, chief economist, Office of Economic Policy Analysis, DOE: "Report of the NES Oil Externality Subgroup", DOE Memorandum, October 12, 1990.

[51] Post-mortem briefing of DOE staff by Secretary Watkins and, separately, by EPC Executive Director Olin Wethington, to summarize decisions taken by EPC at its meeting of November 28, 1990.

[52] Memorandum with attachment for EPC, Subject: NES EPC Meeting, Wednesday, December 12, 1990, Appendix II, Non-Consensus Options to "A National Strategy: Setting the Course on Energy," distributed December 10, 1990.

[53] Larry Gresham, DOE, Office of Public Affairs, "Notes for the Record," December 6, 1990, compilation of telephonic records for December 5, 1990.

[54] James D. Watkins, admiral, U.S. Navy (Retired), secretary, DOE, Letter to the Honorable James A. Baker, III, secretary of state, December 6, 1990.

[55] Wethington, Memorandum with attachment, December 10, 1990, op. cit., Appendix B: Enhanced R&D, Potentially High Payoff Technologies for Reducing U.S. Oil Vulnerability.

[56] Ibid.

[57] Wethington, Memorandum with attachment, December 10, 1990, op. cit.

[58] Ibid., "Strategy" section dated December 9, 1990.

[59] Ibid.

[60] Ibid.

[61] Ibid.

[62] Ibid.

[63] Ibid.

[64] Ibid.

[65] Telephonic message from Teresa Gorman to Linda Stuntz, December 11, 1990.

[66] James D. Watkins, admiral, U.S. Navy (Retired), secretary, DOE, Talking Points for the third EPC principals meeting, December 12, 1990.

[67] Post-mortem briefing to Undersecretary Stuntz and Policy staff by Secretary Watkins in the hour following conclusion of the EPC meeting.

[68] Ibid.

[69] Ibid.

[70] Robert A. Rankin, "Top White House Aides Attack Energy Conservation Measures," *Kansas City Star*, December 15, 1990, p. A3.

[71] *Los Angeles Times*, "Why Not Go the Extra Mile?," December 17, 1990, p. B4.

[72] Radio TV Reports, Inc., *ABC World News Tonight*, December 20, 1990, 6:30 P.M.

[73] National Journal: White House Notebook, "A Cabinet Member Gets the Boot", Vol. 22, No. 51, p. 3098, Washington DC, December 22, 1990.

[74] James D. Watkins, admiral, U.S. Navy (Retired). Personal communications.

[75] Kruger, op. cit., p. 83.

[76] Post-mortem report by Watkins to the staff, Stuntz, Moore and Gault, subsequently verified in phone conversations between Gault and Grady.

[77] Admiral James D. Watkins, Briefing book for December 17, 1990 EPC meeting, Tab NES Options.

[78] Ibid.

[79] The National Research Council accepted the charge in April 1991, appointed a Committee on Fuel Economy of Automobiles and Light Trucks, which began deliberations in May 1991, and submitted its final report to the Department of Transportation on April 9, 1992. See note two of chapter five for a summary of NRC's findings.

[80] Watkins, Briefing book for December 17, 1990 EPC meeting, op. cit.

[81] Watkins, Briefing book for December 17, 1990 EPC meeting, op. cit., Tab marked Budget Impacts.

[82] Post-mortem strategy meeting with staff by Secretary Watkins, December 17, 1990.

[83] Communications involving Watkins, Stuntz, Melby and Stagliano on December 22-23, 1990.

[84] Olin L. Wethington, executive secretary, EPC, the White House, Memorandum with briefing package for EPC, Subject: EPC Meeting on the NES, December 21, 1990, "A National Strategy Setting the Course on Energy," December 20, 1990.

[85] Ibid.

[86] Stuntz and Stagliano review of Melby text and strategy discussions of December 18-19, 1990.

[87] Ibid.

[88] Discussions among Stuntz, Moore, Watkins and Stagliano on December 20, in preparation for the EPC meeting with the president on December 21.

[89] Ibid.

[90] Treasury's Office of Tax Policy insisted that the cost of the credit was actually $2.2 billion, but declined, as usual, to provide a basis for its estimate. In a remarkable break from Troika solidarity, Schmalensee agreed to use the lower DOE estimate in the president's briefing book, because of Treasury's refusal to divulge the basis of its higher estimates even to the CEA.

[91] Exchange of views during the secretary's preparatory briefing by the staff on December 20, 1990.

[92] James D. Watkins, admiral, U.S. Navy (Retired) secretary of energy, Briefing and Talking Points for December 21, cabinet meeting, December 21, 1990.

[93] Post-mortem discussion of the Dec. 21, 1990, EPC meeting with the president, among Watkins, Moore, Stuntz, Gault and Stagliano.

[94] Ibid.

[95] Ibid.

[96] James D. Watkins, admiral, U.S. Navy (Retired), secretary of energy, Memorandum for the Honorable John H. Sununu, chief of staff to the president, Subject: Electric Vehicles Impact on Generation Capacity, January 4, 1991.

[97] John W. Mashek, "Watkins, Sununu Square Off in Debate on Energy Policy," *Boston Globe*, January 6, 1991.

[98] D. Allan Bromley, the White House, Memorandum with attachments for John H. Sununu, Subject: Nuclear Energy R&D in NES, January 7, 1991.

[99] Ibid.

[100] Ibid.

[101] The incident became notorious enough to inspire a Hollywood film, named *Naked Gun 2-1/2*, featuring Bromley and Sununu as characters in a plot to hijack the NES.

[102] Post-mortem meeting with DOE Policy staff by Secretary Watkins, January 8, 1991.

[103] Ibid.

[104] Ibid.

[105] Ibid.

[106] James D. Watkins, admiral, U.S. Navy (Retired), secretary of energy, Letter with attachment (titled Memorandum for the secretary, Subject: EPC Meeting of January 8, 1991) to the Honorable Nicholas Brady, secretary of the treasury, January 10, 1991.

[107] Ibid.

[108] James D. Watkins, admiral, U.S. Navy (Retired), secretary of energy, Letter to the president, the White House (copied to John Sununu), January 10, 1991.

[109] Watkins summary report to the staff following the January 31 meeting with Chief of Staff John Sununu.

[110] James D. Watkins, admiral, U.S. Navy (Retired), secretary of energy, Memorandum with attachments for the Honorable John H. Sununu, chief of staff to the president, Subject: NES:Follow-up on Our Meeting on Thursday, January 31, 1991, February 1, 1991.

[111] Ibid.

[112] James D. Watkins, admiral, U.S. Navy (Retired), secretary of energy, Memorandum for the president, Subject: NES, February 1, 1991.

[113] James D. Watkins, admiral, U.S. Navy (Retired), secretary of energy, Letter to the Honorable James A. Baker,III, secretary of state, February 7, 1991.

[114] Richard L. Schmalensee, Cambridge, MA. Personal communication, Spring 1994.

[115] Adam Jaffee, CEA, Executive Office of the President, Memorandum for Abe Haspel, DOE, Ray Squitieri, Treasury, Subject: Possible compromise on the tax treatment of utility efficiency rebates, February 5, 1991.

[116] Associated Press article carried by the *Dallas Morning News*, quoting Christopher Flavin, December 11, 1990.

[117] Robert D. Hershey, Jr., *New York Times*, December 22, 1990.

[118] DOE, "A National Strategy: How We Expect to Produce and Use Energy in the Future, Executive Summary, Working Draft, January 29, 1991, 6:06 a.m.

[119] Ibid.

[120] Scott Farrow, Council on Environmental Quality, Executive Office of the President, Memorandum to Olin Wethington, EPC and Linda Stuntz, DOE, through Michael Deland, chairman, Subject: Comments on Draft NES of January 29, 1991, January 31, 1991.

[121] Richard Schmalensee, CEA, Executive Office of the President, Memorandum for Linda Stuntz, DOE and Olin Wethington, EPC, Subject: Draft NES Report, January 31, 1991.

[122] Sidney L. Jones, assistant secretary for Economic Policy, Department of the Treasury, Memorandum for Linda Stuntz and Olin L. Wethington, Subject: Comments on NES January 29 Draft, fax dated January 31, 1991.

[123] Eric Melby, NSC, Memorandum for Olin Wethington, executive secretary, EPC and Linda Stuntz, deputy undersecretary for Policy, Planning and Analysis, DOE, Subject: Comments on January 29 Draft of NES, February 1, 1991.

[124] Gary Bennethum, OMB, Note for Linda Stuntz, Subject: OMB Comments on Draft NES, February 1, 1991.

[125] Paul T. Denis, counselor to the assistant attorney general, Memorandum to Olin Wethington, executive secretary, EPC and Linda Stuntz, deputy undersecretary, DOE, RE: NES Report, January 31, 1991.

[126] Ed Cassidy, Office of the Secretary, Department of the Interior, Memorandum to Olin Wethington Subject: Comments on NES Report, faxed January 31, 1991.

[127] See note three at end of chapter five for details. Post-mortem briefing to Linda Stuntz, W. Henson Moore and Policy staff following his meeting with the president.

[128] Dingell and Lent were, respectively, chairman and ranking minority member of the House Energy and Commerce Committee. Sharp and Moorehead were, respectively, chairman and ranking minority member of the House Subcommittee on Energy and Power. Johnston and Wallop were, respectively, chairman and ranking minority member of the Senate Energy and Natural Resources Committee.

[129] Office of the Press Secretary, the White House, Remarks by the president at energy policy briefing, February 20, 1990.

[130] Ibid.

[131] *DOE NEWS*, "President Releases National Energy Strategy," February 20, 1991.

[132] Ibid.

[133] Ibid.

[134] Richard Lacayo, "The Energy Mess," *Time*, February 18, 1991.

[135] Richard A. Taylor, "Energy Strategy Stresses Reliance on Domestic Fuel", *Washington Times*, February 18, 1991, p. A3.

[136] Thomas W. Lippman, "Bush Unveils Energy Strategy Emphasizing Fossil, Nuclear Power Production," *Washington Post*, February 21, 1991, p. A5.

[137] Matthew L. Wald, "Bush Asserts Need for Foreign Oil", *New York Times*, February 21, 1991, p. D1.

[138] David S. Broder, "Bush's Energy Priorities," *Washington Post*, February 24, 1991, p. B7.

[139] James D. Watkins, admiral, U.S. Navy (Retired), secretary of energy, Letter to the president, the White House, February 20, 1991.

CHAPTER SIX

CONGRESS WANTS TO KNOW

THE RESTLESS COMMITTEES

The civilian and military statutory responsibilities of the DOE are overseen by a broad array of congressional panels. In 1990, Senate oversight was divided among fifteen committees and twenty-four subcommittees. In the House of Representatives, twenty-one committees, and an astounding forty-seven subcommittees had jurisdiction over DOE's affairs.[1] The majority of committees exercised oversight by their scrutiny of DOE's patchwork budget, holding a single hearing during the annual appropriations process.

Departmental responsibilities in theory reflect programmatic and operational priorities established by the authorizing committees, which consider themselves the policy-making panels of Congress. In practice, congressional intent is given weight by the power of the purse, which is controlled by the appropriations committees. Congressional appropriators find it frequently irresistible to provide policy direction in the process of establishing annual spending limits, especially when authorizing committees are idle. This was the case throughout the decade of the 1980s when, in the absence of legislative debate on policy, energy sector priorities were fixed by budget choice. With the advent of NES, the authorizing committees reclaimed center stage.

Two committees in particular would play critical roles in the development and enactment of legislation giving to the strategy the mantle of statutory legitimacy: the Senate Energy and Natural Resources Committee, chaired by J. Bennett Johnston of Louisiana, and the House Committee on Energy and Commerce chaired by John Dingell of Michigan.

The DOE oversight committees had been starved for attention by the executive branch during the decade of Reagan *laissez-faire* energy policy. During the period some skirmishes—but no major battles—were fought between the appropriations committees and the White House over proposals, repeatedly put forth by OMB, to diminish or eliminate the myriad research, development, and demonstration projects by which DOE's special interest community is served. OMB would annually submit to Congress budgets containing drastic reductions in federal support for programs in energy conservation, renewable and fossil energy research, and block grants to states for local energy activities; the committees would annually declare the OMB budgets "dead on arrival" and proceed to restore financial support for long-standing and, in the committees' view, essential DOE programs.

Beyond the budget process, the Reagan and Bush administrations had succeeded in denying opportunities for congressional activism on energy by studiously avoiding energy policy initiatives requiring legislative action. The single notable exception of the 1980s had been the legislative proposal to decontrol natural gas wellhead prices submitted to Congress by Reagan in 1987, enacted two years later and, as previously noted, signed into law by Bush in July 1989. It was thus unsurprising that NES should open the floodgates of Congressional activism on energy policy.

In the eighteen months during which NES was under development, seventy-eight energy bills were introduced in the 101st Congress. Among these were four bills dealing with access to the ANWR and the OCS; seventeen to address energy conservation and efficiency issues; two dealing with electricity policy; nine with energy emergency preparedness; twenty-eight with fossil fuels policy; fifteen with global climate change, six with nuclear power, and two with renewable energy.[2]

Senators Albert Gore, Howard Metzenbaum, and Richard Bryan were the principal congressional activists on automotive fuel economy.[3] In 1989, Gore introduced a bill to increase CAFE standards by an unprecedented—technically infeasible—65% above the 1989 level of 27.5 miles per gallon by the year 2000. Also in 1989, Metzenbaum introduced legislation to increase the standards to 34 miles per gallon by 1996 and to establish higher financial penalties for non-complying automobile manufacturers.

In early 1990 Bryan introduced a bill to raise CAFE standards on average by 20% over the 1995-2000 period and by 40% after 2000.[4] (He initially introduced it in the form of an amendment to the Clean Air Act legislation then under debate in Congress and, when defeated, as an independent measure.) The Bryan bill, considered the most moderate of the CAFE proposals, gathered strong support during the final congressional session of 1990. The Bush administration, worried about the measure's likely enactment, threatened a veto of the legislation in the text of a strongly worded letter transmitted jointly by the secretaries of transportation and energy to the senate majority leader on September 13, 1990. EPA Administrator Reilly raised additional objections to the bill by a letter of September 24. A cloture vote, taken in the Senate on September 24, failed to kill the measure. Consequently the Senate adopted the Bryan bill on a vote of 57-42. The Bryan bill was introduced in the House by then-Congresswoman Barbara Boxer of California, referred to the Energy and Commerce Committee, and there bottled by Dingell to prevent further action.[5]

During the same period, Senators George Mitchell and John Kerry, and Congressmen Dennis Hertel, Leon Panetta,[6] Walter Jones, and Gerry Studds pursued legislation to prevent further development of oil and gas resources of the OCS. Their various proposals—eventually incorporated into the Omnibus Budget Reconciliation Act (OBRA) of 1990—reauthorized the Coastal Zone Management Act, expanded the authority of states to intervene in OCS leasing procedures on grounds of protection of the coastal environment, broadened the areas that states could include in their coastal zones management programs, and established fees to recover the cost of state appeals to federal coastal zone management decisions.[7]

Between 1989 and 1990, bills were also introduced in Congress to provide tax incentives and various other subsidies for domestic production of oil and natural gas, solar and geothermal power generation, ethanol production, and production of non-conventional fossil fuels. Other bills were proposed to increase the federal excise tax on gasoline and diesel fuel and the "gas guzzler" tax on automobiles. The majority of these bills were disposed of in OBRA '90 (which also notoriously codified President Bush's violation of his campaign pledge against new taxes).

OBRA increased motor fuel taxes by 5¢ per gallon, imposed a new 2.5¢ per gallon tax on fuels used in rail transportation, reduced the federal ethanol subsidy from 60¢ per gallon (of gasohol) to 54¢ per gallon, and doubled the "gas guzzler" tax. OBRA extended the tax subsidy for non-conventional fuels (coal seam methane, tight sands gas) for two years, adopted a 15% tax credit for enhanced oil recovery, increased from 50% to 100% the net income limitation for oil and gas depletion, increased the percentage depletion allowance on marginal production of oil and gas, established new deductions for computation of the alternative minimum tax, and extended the business tax credit for solar and geothermal properties.[8]

Global climate change was a topic of great interest to the 101st Congress. Senators Timothy Wirth and Albert Gore sought legislation that would force the Bush administration into a more active stance on the issue. The political debate centered on whether greenhouse gas reduction targets should be immediately adopted, as advocated by Gore and Wirth, or whether further research should be undertaken to reduce the scientific uncertainty of climate change theory. The bill that eventually emerged from the Senate called for the adoption of voluntary measures to stabilize CO_2 and other greenhouse gases and for a study of the feasibility of reducing CO_2 emissions by 20% from 1988 levels in 2005.[9] Enacted by the Senate in August 1990, the bill subsequently died in the House, but many of its provisions would be resurrected for inclusion in NES legislation.[10]

Representative Philip Sharp, chairman of the House Subcommittee on Energy and Power, led the 1990 effort to remove the eighty-megawatt size limitation contained in PURPA for solar, wind, and geothermal power production facilities. In the Senate, Senators Wirth and Pete Domenici pursued a similar measure. The Sharp bill was signed into law in November 1990. The issue was revisited during consideration of NES legislation, which contained proposals to further amend PURPA so as to relax co-firing limits and allow both fossil and non-fossil fuel use in PURPA facilities.[11]

Also enacted in the 101st Congress, prior to completion of NES, were bills to extend federal financial support for state energy conservation programs,[12] authorize an increase in the size of the SPR to one billion barrels, test the feasibility of creating strategic reserves for refined oil products, expand the DOE program of research and development of hydrogen fuels, increase financial liability for oil spills on land and water, and require double hulls on ocean-going oil tankers. The single most important energy legislative achievement of the 101st Congress—perhaps the single most important legislative achievement overall—was, of course, the enactment of amendments to the Clean Air Act of 1970.[13]

Various congressional committees conducted hearings during the 101st Congress on numerous energy policy issues that would eventually find their way into the legislative debate on NES. Senator Johnston himself was at work on a comprehensive energy bill that would rival the Bush administration's enabling legislation for NES.

In sum, by early 1991, DOE oversight committees were fully ready to engage the Bush administration in debate on energy policy. The debate commenced in earnest on the day that the White House released the NES.

BIPARTISANSHIP IN THE SENATE

The Honorable J. Bennett Johnston gaveled the Senate Energy and Natural Resources (SENR) Committee to order at 9:40 a.m., on February 21, 1991, to begin congressional scrutiny on the NES, which had been formally transmitted to Congress by the White House the previous day. The witnesses seated at the table of the committee's hearing room, in the Dirksen building, were Energy Secretary James Watkins, Deputy Secretary W. Henson Moore, and Linda Stuntz, the deputy undersecretary.

"Yesterday's announcement of the NES was the culmination of some 18 months of hearings and study and work by the Department of Energy," the chairman stated. "Secretary Watkins and his staff are to be commended for their dedication to this effort to define a national energy policy. Secretary Watkins also deserves commendation for elevating the importance of energy policy within the administration."[14]

DOE leaders—who had heard no such words of praise from the president they served, nor from the senior staff of the White House, nor from most of their cabinet colleagues—were being celebrated by the Democratic chairman of the most important energy committee in Congress. Over the many hours of the hearing's duration they would hear further accolades, some words of regret about the shortcomings of NES—pointedly directed at the White House rather than at DOE's leadership—and strong declarations of commitment on the part of committee members to work with DOE leaders in crafting comprehensive energy legislation.

Watkins could not have hoped for a more congenial congressional forum. The SENR committee could claim a history as old as the Republic, tracing its roots to the small group of senators who first deliberated on Thomas Jefferson's purchase of the vast Louisiana territory from Napoleon Bonaparte. Johnston's immediate predecessor, Scoop Jackson, the Democrat who had given his party its conservative credo, had steered to passage virtually all of the energy legislation proposed by Nixon, Ford, and Carter. "Perhaps more than any other standing Committee of the Senate," wrote James McClure, the committee's former minority leader, "the Energy and Natural Resources Committee has a history—indeed a habit—of being bipartisan in nature."[15]

The latest evidence of bipartisanship had been provided on February 5, 1991, by Johnston and Malcom Wallop, the committee's ranking Republican, who had jointly introduced Senate Bill 341—The National Energy Security Act of 1991. S.341 contained not only the full range of recommendations proposed in NES but also the majority of policy options that had been rejected by the Bush White House. Unsurprisingly, Watkins saw the 285-page Wallop-Johnston bill as the vehicle that would carry his hopes for a balanced, comprehensive energy policy to a bipartisan congressional majority.[16]

"We look forward to continuing our very close working relationship with Admiral Watkins and his staff," Johnston continued, in his opening statement at the February 21 hearing, "and be assured we intend to move quickly with this legislation."[17]

Johnston then recognized Senator Jeff Bingaman of New Mexico, who, less sanguine about the NES, decried the failure of the Bush administration to set targets for "net (oil) imports, domestic production, and end-use consumption." The NES, he said, "purports to provide a road map to a more secure and cleaner energy future, but it is difficult to know whether we have the right road map when we don't know what the destination is."[18]

Other senators entered into the record their initial reactions to NES, their words revealing, in the frequency of allusion to the angst that has haunted the American debate on energy policy since the fateful first oil embargo of 1973.

Senate voices

Senator Richard Shelby of Alabama: "Although we have had warning signals in the past, the current conflict in the Gulf has made us painfully aware that we must not delay to explore ways to reduce our dependence on foreign oil! One of the greatest tasks facing Congress is the passage of bipartisan legislation for an energy policy to aid in securing our Nation's future. Sacrifices will be required from all sides."[19]

Senator Malcom Wallop of Wyoming: "As the Congress moves toward enacting a national energy policy, we will blend many of the Administration's proposals with our own. We must revive the idea of 'National Interest." Let us recognize that unless we act now to provide for our future, the energy we need won't be there when we want it. We must develop an energy policy that takes all reasonable steps to promote domestic energy production. We face a choice. We can act to assure our well being, or we can instead do nothing and consign our future and our treasure to the good will of foreign producers."[20]

Senator Paul Wellstone of Minnesota: "I am a little bit disappointed insofar as I do not see the emphasis on energy conservation and clean energy alternatives, an emphasis that I think many Americans were waiting for. I think that people in our country do not want to see us so dependent upon Middle Eastern oil. We are all for reducing that dependency."[21]

Senator Pete Domenici of New Mexico: "We ought to think a little bit for just a few minutes, maybe three minutes, on how we got here. In 1976 and thereafter we had the luxury of trying to fashion an energy policy with the prospect of ever escalating oil prices. We could fashion a bad policy in a market place that would bail us out. We saw remarkable conservation over the next decade. Senator McClure, Senator Johnston, (myself) and five or six others saw the peril of low oil prices and what they would do and what their effect would be. That is why we created a Synthetic Fuels Corporation. It is gone now, but it was an institution which at least some of us envisioned as carrying us through this inevitable decline in (oil) prices."[22]

Senator Timothy Wirth of Colorado: "I think it is very clear that behind all this (energy) debate is the obligation we have to 550,000 young

Americans in the Persian Gulf. It is clear that we are in the Persian Gulf for two reasons. One is a concern about Saddam Hussein's weaponry. And the other is a concern about oil. We have the obligation to take on the second one right here."[23]

Senator Conrad Burns of Montana: "If there was one sin that was committed in the 1980s, it was that we completely, through probably no fault of our own, and maybe (because) we did not realize how fragile it was, but we completely destroyed the infrastructure to search for and drill and lift petroleum. And now we are having a hard time amassing venture capital to go into high risk areas so that we can get our dependency away from foreign sources."[24]

Senator Don Nickles of Oklahoma: "We spent the better part of 10 years trying to undo a lot of the damage that was done and a lot of the mistakes that were done during the Carter administration. The Carter administration passed a windfall profits tax (and) we repealed it. We repealed the Synthetic Fuels Corporation and we finally did repeal the Fuel Use Act. We also repealed the Emergency Allocations Act. So I think it is important as we work on energy strategy for the 1990s that we not repeat the mistakes of the past."[25]

Senator Kent Conrad of North Dakota: "Admiral Watkins, you have done a superb job in putting together an overall strategy. I wish more of it had been preserved in the bureaucratic conflict that always ensues when one comes forward with an initiative. There are two areas where I think we can do better. If we are going to have a comprehensive policy that can sell, we have to do more on the conservation side. The second area would be our coal resources, we cannot cut back on clean coal technology."[26]

Senator Daniel Akaka of Hawaii: "Unfortunately, the energy plan falls short of what this country needs. The problem with our country is that we are addicted to cheap oil. Unfortunately, our addiction is linked to the supplies from the very dangerous neighborhood of the Middle East. Our servicemen and women are now preparing for a ground offensive against Iraq. They are about to find out just how dangerous the Middle East can be."[27]

Senator Larry Craig of Idaho: "Many have found it to their rhetorical advantage to talk about our presence in the Persian Gulf being that of an oil presence or a need for oil. I think we are there because of the power that an abundance of energy in a given area can bring, and therefore, the misuse of that power. This Nation has been a wealthy Nation historically because we have had an abundance of energy. Any policy that denies us an abundance of energy denies us the wealth of this Nation."[28]

Senator Mark Hatfield of Oregon: "Unfortunately the administration has chosen to focus on production of new oil resources and nuclear energy enhancement, charting a dangerous course for this nation over the long term. The assumption that nuclear power will take care of our electrical needs now or in the future is misplaced. These proposals (the NES) only address the symptoms of our energy problems, not the cause—our dependence on oil."[29]

Senator Wendell Ford of Kentucky: "When it comes to foreign affairs, the President is a tail-kicking, name taking kind of guy. Domestic policy (is) another matter entirely. In his home arena, this Rambo bears a strong resemblance to Casper Milquetoast. He is unable or unwilling to take a tough stand. Never has this split personality been more evident than when the administration released its new national energy strategy. Bush can't or won't summon moral courage to stand against gas-guzzling automobiles, to ask Americans to pay a price for wasteful energy practices, to spend money on alternative energy sources, or even to encourage the development of a more efficient light bulb."[30]

A separate reality

For well over an hour on the opening day of congressional hearings on NES, Watkins, Moore, and Stuntz sat silently as senator after senator offered praise with the same breath that decried the strategy's shortcomings.

Some senators seemed only vaguely acquainted with the contents of the NES, which had, after all, been transmitted to Congress less than twenty-four hours prior to the hearing. Still, for a significant number of senators the terms of reference on energy policy had remained frozen in time, their words and concepts seemingly lifted from the congressional record of 1973 and 1978. Oil, and the nation's dependence on it, elicited as always, the visceral reaction formed in the frustrated fury of history's oil embargoes. True, the ground offensive in the Iraqi war was imminent and the senators could be forgiven for rhetorically linking the NES to (as Akaka put it) the dangerous Middle East, but it was remarkable nonetheless how wide the chasm had become between the senators' view of oil and energy security and that of the analytical community at large.

The SENR's frame of reference was profoundly different from the intellectual framework of economic efficiency within which NES had evolved. Schmalensee's carefully nuanced language on the meaning, and relatively modest importance, of U.S. reliance on oil imports was nowhere reflected in the imagery and rhetoric of senators speaking to the nation on February 21, 1991. Yet, the SENR's memory spanned the entire history of U.S. energy policymaking. True, the spectrum of opinion held by committee members had broadened over time to add the voices of environmental activists to those of the historic conservationists, but on the issue of energy security, the new members seemed to have adopted the very same oil taboos of their more tenured colleagues. Liberals differed from conservatives only in how, not whether, oil import dependency should be remedied by federal intervention.

The SENR was held together as well by an element of pathos. Among its members were many who had believed passionately—had indeed struggled mightily to enact energy legislation proposed by Nixon, Ford, and Carter, only to see their efforts reversed by Reagan. The newer committee members—Wirth, Wellstone, Akaka, and Gore, generally outside the mainstream of traditionally pro-development committee thinking—were brash and demanding, but lacked the experience that had concurrently traumatized and invigorated the committee and the Congress during the energy policy heyday of the 1970s. The young Turks on the committee were impatient with warnings of the need for prudence in the making of energy policy, they carried no memory of battle for legislation that in practice would prove utterly misguided.

Watkins among the believers

In his testimony, Watkins declined to take the bait offered by the senators' repeated references to White House rejection of options the committee thought should have been included in NES. On that score, he remained faithful to his president. He approached the hearing as a duty to brief Congress on the dimensions of the strategy he had crafted and not as a political debate. He used large, colorful charts to illustrate the key points he wished to fix in the committee's collective mind. Before turning to the details of his presentation of NES, he praised the legislative efforts already underway in Congress.

"Your bill," he told Johnston and Wallop, "has so many elements of compatibility with ours. There is a bill (also) coming up in the House signed by thirty members that will be very compatible," he noted in reference to legislation by Philip Sharp and John Dingell.[31]

Watkins was blunt on the key findings of NES, especially concerning U.S. dependence on oil imports. "The reality is the United States and the rest of the world will continue to rely on oil for the foreseeable future," he stated, "and Persian Gulf producers will remain critical players in the world oil market." In response to this condition, Watkins told the committee, the "National Energy Strategy attacks the challenge of increasing energy security in a balanced way by reducing our need for oil by 3.4 million barrels a day by the year 2010 and increasing domestic supplies of oil by 3.8 million barrels a day by the year 2010."[32]

As to how these objectives were to be met, Watkins stated, "On the demand side, the aim of the NES is to introduce alternative fuels and technology and increase the efficiency of all of our vehicles. We do this by using alternative fuels in fleet vehicles; second, by accelerating research and development on electric, gas turbine, and fuel cells propulsion systems and on high efficiency conventional engines; third, by intensifying R&D on more efficient industrial processes and aircraft bodies and engines, and fourth, by scrapping older cars and by wider use of intelligent vehicle-highway systems. On the supply side, the aim is to use superior production technology and environmental safeguards to increase domestic production, including advanced R&D for enhanced oil recovery technologies, access to a discrete portion of the coastal plain of the Arctic National Wildlife Refuge, and access to certain portions of the Outer Continental Shelf."[33]

Watkins then departed from his text and from Bush administration rhetoric to offer his view of how oil imports should be seen. He noted that NES projections showed import levels rising to 65% of domestic consumption in less than twenty years, and noted, "imports, themselves, are hardly the villain. It is those elements of imports that come from unstable and unreliable regions (that are problematic). So I do not want to run down imports. We have good imports from Venezuela. We have them from the Brent Fields in the U.K., and so forth."[34]

Watkins' characterization of imports as either good or evil, depending on source was of course anathema to Bush's Troika, but the SENR members understood him perfectly, accepting the distinction intuitively. To many of the senators, the economic proposition that cheap Persian Gulf oil was good for the country represented merely the inability of free market advocates to understand the underlying national security dangers of such a position. In any case, and unlike the Troika, few if any of the senators believed that economic efficiency should be the sole or even the principal objective of energy policy.

Troika agencies' staffs would later complain to Stuntz that Watkins had in his testimony departed from approved Bush policy on oil imports, insisting that Watkins should have disabused the senators of their outdated notions of energy security. Troika staffs, however, seldom if ever testify before committees of Congress and are never publicly held accountable for what they say. In any case, with the start of hearings on NES, DOE leadership had ceased worrying about Troika opinion.[35]

Watkins next turned to the NES' vaguely defined notion of encouraging oil production outside the politically volatile Middle East and presented it as a rich opportunity for foreign policy activism. He told the committee that "undeveloped world (oil) resources could be as high as one trillion barrels outside the Persian Gulf," but their exploitation was hampered by institutional and trade barriers, insufficient indigenous investment capital, and lack of access to technology. The administration, Watkins promised, would pursue diplomatic and trade initiatives to foster development of these resources in the Western Hemisphere, Eastern Europe and elsewhere.[36]

On energy conservation, Watkins invited the committees' attention to the "very significant menu of efficiency items" presented in the NES report, and noted that the president's fiscal year 1992 budget (which had just been transmitted to Congress) included "$903 million for NES-related research and development, an increase of $227 million or 34% over that which we would have come forth with had we not published the National Energy Strategy." Anxious to make a strong case for the energy conservation aspects of NES, Watkins further told the committee that the administration's energy efficiency proposals encompassed initiatives to increase competition (and therefore efficiency) in electricity generation, reform (and render more efficient) the licensing of hydropower and nuclear plants, and extensively reform (and therefore make more efficient) the natural gas regulatory system.[37]

Watkins next offered a response to the critical comments heard in Congress and in the special interest community, about the administration's treatment of fuel economy (CAFE) standards for automobiles. "Forced higher CAFE standards," he said, "only reduce oil consumption if Americans buy smaller cars and if they drive smart." Higher CAFE standards, he insisted, would still leave the transportation sector entirely dependent on oil. Furthermore, he stated, the Department of Transportation had come to accept the view that safety would be "severely jeopardized by going immediately to a 40-mile per gallon objective," as suggested by Senator Gore. By contrast, Watkins declared, "The NES would break transportation's total oil dependence by providing fuel and technology choice [and] diversification of fuels; dramatically reduce emissions from cars and trucks, [and] preserve American technological leadership."[38]

Watkins went on to discuss the environmental, educational, and technology transfer elements of NES, and the totality of economic benefits that American consumers could expect from full implementation of the strategy. He concluded by reiterating the quantitative achievements that could be expected in 2010 from the sum total of NES recommendations, and offered, as a final thought: "So these are powerful ideas for America that we think will be implemented through the shared responsibilities of Government, science, industry, and the American people."[39]

SENR members reacted to Watkins' testimony by ignoring the inconsistencies and resuming the dramatic rhetoric beloved of senators conscious of having the media's undivided attention. Chairman Johnston was especially adept at voicing the thinking of the committee's venerable old guard.

"This is the third energy crisis since I have been on this committee," he stated. "In those 18 years, things have only gotten worse—production has gone down, consumption has gone up, we have half a million people in the Gulf. I think we have to ask ourselves, how did we have such a triumph of ignorance as a country, such a colossal failure of will?" Energy policy, the chairman said, was an area "where philosophy ripens into religious dogma. The producers—those people who want to develop ANWR, nuclear power, et cetera—are regarded by many as being greedy, obscene profiteers, environmentally polluting gas guzzlers, and otherwise nasty people. Those who want to develop the soft path, conservation, alternative fuels, are regarded as soft-headed, sentimental, job destroying, big Government regulators."[40]

The challenge, the chairman declared, was to develop a policy that would somehow find common ground among producers and conservationists: "So I am pleading with my colleagues, I am pleading with this administration: let us come in with a balanced package. Let us lower our voices. This scarlet rhetoric that I keep reading, is not serving the national interest."

To the audience beyond the hearing room, the chairman said, "I ask the great newspapers of this country, I ask the great environmental groups, I ask the producing groups, to let us work together, reason together, give a little. Even if you do not believe it is right, much of America believes it is right."[41]

On that note, Johnston gaveled the hearing closed at 1:15 p.m.

Sowing political oats

The chairman's plea for reasonable compromise would be utterly ignored by the White House and the special interest groups during the many months of NES debate, but Johnston would prove more than equal to the task of steering his energy bill through perilous congressional waters. He proved in fact untiring in his search for common ground among apparently irreconcilable antagonists and in safeguarding his energy bill from parliamentary ruin.

The SENR proceeded with its methodical examination of each of the NES proposals and of proposals presented in the Johnston-Wallop bill during the three months following the February 21 inaugural hearing. On February 26 the committee examined conservation and renewable energy issues. DOE Assistant Secretary J. Michael Davis, testifying for DOE, paid lip service to the administration's decisions on efficiency standards and tax credits and then unmistakably threw his support to the more expansive energy conservation and renewable energy proposals contained in the Johnston-Wallop bill.[42]

Hydropower licensing reform was next on the committee's agenda. On the afternoon of February 26, three administration witnesses testified on the subject: G. Edward Dickey spoke on behalf of the Army Corps of Engineers, Kevin Kelly spoke for DOE, and Dennis B. Underwood, for the Bureau of Reclamation.

Dickey reminded the committee that since 1938 the Corps had, as intended by Congress, developed hydropower resources to the point of becoming the largest producer of hydroelectricity in the United States The Corps operated seventy-five stations generating 21,000 megawatts of power for the national grid. Kelly told the committee that FERC's licensing procedures (which, as NES proposed, should be reformed) hampered further development of U.S. hydropower resources. Underwood told the committee that although he recognized the validity of NES proposals to upgrade the fifty-two aging power plants operated by the Bureau, he was unable to promise action by the Bureau because funding was a major constraint.[43]

On February 28, the committee held hearings on CAFE standards. Jerry Ralph Curry, administrator of the National Highway Traffic Safety Administration (NHTSA), the Transportation Department agency responsible for the CAFE law, was the sole administration witness. "Congress can go down one of two roads in CAFE policy," Chairman Johnston stated in his opening statement for the hearing. "It can, on the one hand, simply pick a number that sounds tough and say, 'do it.' Or it can undertake the difficult process of evaluating these policy choices and determining the new CAFE standard after an explicit and well-informed debate."[44]

Curry, a protégé of Sununu, focused his testimony on the need for his agency to concentrate its regulatory powers on vehicle safety rather than on fuel efficiency. He justified inaction on fuel economy regulation by stating that "the principal shortcoming of the CAFE program has always been that it affects only the supply side of the automobile industry. It can encourage the manufacturers to produce fuel efficient vehicles, but it does nothing to persuade the public to buy the right types and mix of vehicles."[45]

Curry's testimony was followed by that of Steven E. Plotkin of the Congressional Office of Technology Assessment, and of K.G. Duleep, a private sector expert on the technology aspects of fuel economy. Both witnesses assured the committee that higher fuel economy standards could be achieved with then-available technology without compromising safety or downsizing vehicles.[46]

On March 5, the committee dealt with nuclear issues. The witness for the administration was William Young, DOE's assistant secretary for nuclear energy. The committee moved quickly past Young's sanguine view of a robust nuclear future and his overly optimistic projections for the development and licensing of advanced reactor designs. It heard opposing views on nuclear power plant licensing reform from the Union of Concerned Scientists, whose witness objected to NES proposals to reduce the number of public hearings required in the licensing process. Utility industry executives provided other views that were supportive of NES.[47]

The committee took up natural gas regulatory reforms on March 7. William Scherman, FERC's general counsel, and Stephen Wakefield, DOE general counsel, were the executive branch witnesses. "The main objective of the administration's (NES enabling) legislation," Wakefield stated, "is to remove regulation that is unnecessary to protect the consumer. If someone is willing to take the risk to build facilities, it should be the investors and the lenders, not the regulators, who assess whether that is a good idea. If consenting adults can agree on a commercial transaction, whether it is for transportation or sale of natural gas, they should be able to structure their own deal without the imposition of the regulator's view."

Wakefield went on to explain the rationale for the sweeping reforms contained in the administration's NES legislative proposals dealing with the natural gas sector. He concluded his testimony by reiterating the president's decision to abolish FERC and create, in its stead, a natural gas and electricity administration fully incorporated into DOE.[48]

Speaking, as customary, for FERC staff and not for the commission, Scherman assured the committee that NES proposals were a logical extension of FERC decisions toward "greater reliance on market forces in its regulation of the gas industry."

The differences in the terminology used by Scherman, the consummate regulator, and Wakefield, the Republican political appointee, were subtle but striking. Regulation, according to Wakefield, should not be used as a tool to protect competitors. Where markets are competitive, Scherman would reply, the FERC should "seek to allow them to operate" without "unwarranted government intervention." For Wakefield, the current system of natural gas regulation needed "a major overhaul, not just tinkering around the edges or asking people at FERC to work harder." For Scherman, the NES proposals would "build upon FERC's recent progress to foster a competitive gas industry."[49]

Johnston was not amused by both subtle and obvious differences in FERC and DOE views. He told Wakefield that the NES legislative process would be too arduous on substance to allow for further complicating factors such as the administration's insistence on abolishing FERC. By the same token, he warned Scherman that FERC's hope for greater authority over National Environmental Policy Act review processes—for both hydropower and natural gas pipeline construction—was misplaced because it was politically not doable.[50]

The SENR held further hearings on March 11 concerning oil and gas development provisions. The administration witnesses were Robert Gentile, DOE's assistant secretary for fossil energy, and Barry Williamson, director of Interior's Minerals Management Service. Gentile, as instructed, provided support for the enhanced oil recovery proposals of NES. The committee deemed him less than credible because in the two years of his incumbency as head of DOE's fossil energy office, he had devoted his efforts almost entirely to increasing the size of coal research programs while minimizing resources and attention to R&D for oil and natural gas. Williamson, for his part, underscored the need for further OCS leasing and assured the committee that oil and gas production on the OCS could be carried out with due protection for the environment.[51]

On March 12, the SENR took up the highly contentious issue of ANWR. Watkins, accompanied by Henson Moore, returned to the committee's familiar hearing room. "The history of oil and the history of energy policy in this country since the embargo in 1973," chairman Johnston declared in his opening statement for the hearing, "has been a history of grandiose plans, extravagant rhetoric, and very little follow through. We remember President Nixon with Project Independence when he said literally that we were not going to use any more imported oil, zero, zip. President Ford came in shortly thereafter and adopted Project Independence, which was meant not to get us off all imported oil, but most imported oil. And the history ever since has been these extravagant claims and no action."[52]

"The energy strategy proposes three critical initiatives to enhance domestic oil production," Watkins told the committee during the course of his second appearance to defend NES. "An aggressive R&D program to develop and use advanced technology for oil recovery, access to discrete portions of the Outer Continental Shelf, and access to a small fraction of the coastal plain of ANWR."[53]

The size of the ANWR area in question, Watkins assured the committee, was minuscule—about 13,000 acres representing "less than 1% of the 1.5 million acre coastal plain." The coastal plain itself represented less than 10% of the nineteen million-acre ANWR.[54] The long-term value of ANWR development, Watkins claimed, lay in keeping oil production investments and jobs in the U.S., improving the balance of trade by "reducing the level and cost of future U.S. oil imports," and contributing to energy security by "reducing our dependence on oil imported from insecure sources."[55]

Two witnesses from the Department of the Interior then joined Watkins and Moore at the witness table. David O'Neil, the assistant secretary for lands and minerals management, told the committee that his department felt it was "time we moved forward on opening the Coastal Plain on behalf of the American people in a sound environmental manner."[56] More critical was the statement of John Turner, director of the U.S. Fish and Wildlife

Service. "We have been conducting extensive biological studies for many years on refuge wildlife and fisheries resources and their habitat," Turner stated, "and I am convinced that we know enough to do a good job in opening ANWR while offering good biological protection."[57]

Other witnesses would, of course, strongly oppose the proposal to develop ANWR, but the administration's testimony was unusually well scripted. Watkins and O'Neil confined their testimony and subsequent answers to the senators' questions to the economic and energy security aspects of the issue. They left it to Turner, the scientist and trustee of a large portion of the national biological resources, to confirm, indeed certify, that ANWR's oil could be lifted from the ground and transported to market with manageable environmental consequences.

The SENR hearings continued without pause. On March 14, Linda Stuntz testified on the electricity policy provisions of NES. On March 18, CEA's Richard Schmalensee testified on the abstruse topic of how EPA regulators should address the matter of new sources of pollution resulting from otherwise benign engineering changes in existing power plants. On March 19, Robert Gentile returned to the committee room to testify on coal and coal technology. On the same day, Reid Detchon, DOE's deputy assistant secretary for conservation, testified on the issue of energy efficiency standards for houses and buildings. Finally, on March 21, George Helland, DOE's deputy assistant secretary for export assistance, testified on NES-sanctioned technology transfer from federal research laboratories to the private sector.[58]

The SENR committee record

The hearings produced a voluminous record of proceedings for the SENR, later enlarged by the printed record of answers to questions posed by the senators during and after the hearings. The committee, as part of the NES legislative record, eventually published three volumes, containing more than twelve hundred pages of documentation supplied by DOE, other agencies, and other witnesses. DOE policy staff replied to more than five hundred questions posed by the senators and supplied several hundred pages of documents containing the various options analyses undertaken during NES' preparation.[59]

In the months following the initial hearings on NES, Johnston and Wallop never wavered from their pledge of bipartisanship. In April 1991, in an act of unprecedented courtesy, they invited Stuntz and Moore to participate in the process known as legislative mark-up, which translated the record of hearings, the lobbyist's bids for preference, and the senators' extensive list of favored amendments to the Johnston-Wallop bill, into the legislation that would eventually reach the Senate floor. The two senators encouraged a close working relationship between SENR committee staff and DOE policy office throughout the process. They received in response the unstinting support of Watkins, Moore and Stuntz, even when this support incurred the displeasure of White House staff.

CHAIRMAN SHARP TAKES THE TORCH

Unlike his counterpart in the Senate, John Dingell, the chairman of the House Committee on Energy and Commerce, did not usually reserve for himself the policymaking leadership on matters of energy, preferring a subtler role as *eminence grise*. The yeoman's labor on energy policy was customarily undertaken by Philip Sharp of Indiana, chairman of the Subcommittee on Energy and Power. A former aide to senator Vance Hartke, credentialed as a Ph.D. in government from Georgetown University, briefly a professor of political science at Ball State University, Sharp had won his first election to Congress in 1974, at the age of 32.[60] He had risen to the chairmanship of his subcommittee by sheer intellect and effective leadership.

The subcommittee chaired by Sharp was composed of thirteen Democrats and seven Republicans during the 101st Congress. Carlos Moorhead was the ranking Republican, but he was not known as an activist. DOE policy staff knew Sharp as a thoughtful and diligent legislator, knowledgeable—unlike many of his colleagues—about the technical and regulatory arcana of the energy field and not particularly partisan in his approach to issues that rose to prominence within the realm of his subcommittee. He had gained the affection of DOE policy staff most recently for his sponsorship and management to enactment of the Alternative Motor Fuels Act of 1988.

Sharp opened his subcommittee's deliberations on NES on the morning of February 20, 1991, several hours before the White House's release of NES. "This morning," he said in his opening statement, "we will begin consideration of proposals for a comprehensive energy policy for our country. The war in the Middle East has been a painful reminder that the United States and, indeed, the world are dependent for an important portion of their oil on the unstable area of the Middle East." He went on to say that American prosperity hinged on ample supplies of reasonably priced energy—terminology adopted by the drafters of NES—and then outlined the two major concerns that would drive his panel's deliberations.

"We are dependent for between 40 and 45% of our oil from the world market," he said, "with the Middle East being the key source of oil in the world market. That dependence, regrettably, is expected to grow unless we take further action. We have the long-term problem of sorting out our environmental and our energy needs. We know that we have to prevent the pollution and the poisoning of our land, water, and our air, indeed, the poisoning of ourselves and the generations to come. Much of our pollution, of course, is generated from the production, distribution, and the use of energy."[61]

Dramatic language, extreme choices—but effective political rhetoric on the day a Republican president was scheduled to make public a new policy on energy, which had already been pegged by the special interest community as anti-conservation and anti-environment. Sharp had additional surprises. The first panel of witnesses included Daniel Yergin, author and chairman of Cambridge Energy Research Associates (CERA), John Gibbons, head of the Congressional Office of Technology Assessment, and Charles Curtis, former chairman of FERC.

"Well, why do we consider, why do we concern ourselves with energy policy?" Yergin, the first witness, asked rhetorically: [62]

One is economic. During the First World War, French Premier George Clemenceau referred to oil as the "blood of the earth." Well, certainly, energy is the basis of our economy, and disruptions threaten our economy and the economic well being of Americans. The second is the strategic significance of energy and oil. One important aspect of the Second World War and one that has not been given a great deal of attention was that it was in certain ways an oil war. And if we had not won that oil war, it is questionable whether we would have won the overall war.

"The third reason is that we are now in what we might call the third wave of environmentalism. This is far-reaching and pervasive in our society. A very strong focus of energy industries is not to seek to harness energy policies to environmental objectives."

As to the elements of a new energy policy, Yergin recommended, "some starting points: promote the use of natural gas, re-ignite conservation efforts, slow the decline in U.S. oil production, pursue a diversified program of research and development, and develop more consistency in government policies."[63]

For DOE policy staff listening to Yergin in the packed committee room, the language of war seemed extraordinary. The Troika and EPC would have considered extreme Yergin's terminology of oil as the *casus belli* of WWII. And what to make of Yergin's contention that energy industries sought to divorce energy from environmental policies? One would normally expect all industries, not merely energy industries, to resist new legislative and regulatory burdens, but the effectiveness of industry resistance was rather poor, considering the vast amount of environmental law that had been imposed by Congress since 1970. As to "starting points," the policy staff thought that NES met or surpassed Yergin's recommendations.

Gibbons was next to testify. To Yergin's five starting points, Gibbons added a "few principles." The first of these was that energy systems change slowly and therefore require long-term planning. The second was that energy supply and use are "inextricably global in nature." The third principle was that "energy itself is not an end. It is not a goal. It is subsidiary and derivative from broader national goals." In conclusion, Gibbon stated that, in devising energy strategies, "three overriding goals—economy, environment, security—need to be attended."[64]

Congressional witnesses are fond of reducing complex policy to a few points or a number of principles, because generalities couched as precepts avoid the necessity of putting forth specific proposals. Gibbons' generalities were especially remarkable because they were uttered by the leader of an agency devoted to understanding the role of technology in society. Terminology, such as the global nature of energy and the linkages among economic, environmental and security concerns—borrowed in any case directly from NES—added little of consequence to the debate. The question before the policymakers of 1991 was not *whether* policy should serve economic, environmental and security interests, but *how*.

Curtis, the third speaker, avoided Yergin's and Gibbons' penchant for precepts and formulas. He spoke, instead in the vocabulary of experience in making rather than preaching policy. "The first and foremost lesson of the past," Curtis told the subcommittee members, "is that attempts to impose governmental policies that run against market forces, except as short-term transitional devices, are doomed to failure and high cost. And the second most important lesson is that Congress dissipates its energies in attempting to speak comprehensively on energy policy. All things do not have equal weight. All things are not equally important."[65]

The second Sharp hearing

Sharp's subcommittee met again on February 27. The second hearing was devoted to "oil and natural gas policy goals," as Sharp noted in his opening statement. The witnesses for the hearing were organized into two panels. The first included North Dakota Governor George Sinner, speaking on behalf of the National Governors Association; former Deputy Secretary of Energy William Martin; Texas Railroad Commission Chairman Robert Krueger, and Arlon Tussing, president of ARTA, Inc.[66]

Sinner told the subcommittee that NES looked "awfully good," but had some shortcomings. Among the latter he mentioned CAFE, calling the administration's decision to study it "indecisive." He thought the strategy would be of little or no help to small oil and gas producers, because only the major oil companies would benefit from drilling in the ANWR and on the OCS. The NES emphasis on research he believed laudable but the results uncertain. He suggested that the way for Congress to proceed was to pull together all the stakeholders—producers, consumers, environmental interests, economic competition interests, and national security interests—in a manner more coherent than the administration had been able to do. He declared virtually inescapable the need to set a "floor price for oil and gas" and to "come to grips with the gluttonous (energy) market in the United States" by putting "some conservation in place."[67]

Martin, the next witness, commended Watkins in general terms, but felt the international aspects of NES were rather weak. He suggested that U.S. energy policy should be constructed on the basis of global, not merely American vulnerability to oil price shocks. He believed that U.S. oil imports were headed to levels of fourteen million barrels per day, implying worldwide reliance on OPEC oil for forty million barrels per day. "Some advocates of market reliance will say well, yes, that's fine," Martin noted, "we can get some cheap oil from OPEC. But is forty million barrels a day a prudent level? The answer is absolutely not."[68]

"Oil, to be clear, is the umbilical cord that serves as the lifeline to industrial nations," Kruger declared in his testimony. "And in my judgment if oil is worth dying for in the Middle East it is worth drilling for in America." Proceeding to lay out the depressed state of the domestic oil industry and the related slide in crude production, Krueger called for a "stable floor price for oil," achievable through the imposition of a fee on imported oil. "You have the power," he told the subcommittee, "to bring stability to prices, the necessary supplies to our consumers, and in the process, in my judgment, to bring peace and stability to the Middle East."[69]

Tussing, the last panel member, would have none of the arguments presented by his fellow panelists. "Real war in the Middle East has vastly revived the nostalgia of the 1970s energy consciousness and the yearning for a coherent national energy policy," he told the subcommittee. "Before

Congress yields to this yearning it ought to take a hard, cold look at the energy policies of the 1970s." Berating Congress for the "megabucks" channeled into "white elephants like the fast breeder reactor, synthetic oil and gas," Krueger urged the subcommittee to avoid "a new crusade for energy independence."[70]

The second panel of witnesses of February 27 brought together Robinson West, president of Petroleum Finance Co., William Chandler, a senior scientist of the Battelle Memorial Institute, Daniel Sperling,[71] director of the University of California-Davis' Institute of Transportation Studies and Adam Sieminski, a vice president of NatWest USA. West declared U.S. energy policy unique in the industrialized world in at least two aspects: discouragement of energy production and encouragement of consumption and fragmentation of energy policymaking authority in the federal government. Chandler stated that transportation sector fuel efficiency was key to solving the problem of oil dependence. The higher fuel efficiency, he said, could be achieved equally effectively by regulation or taxation. Sperling argued that alternative transportation fuels should be "considered central to U.S. energy policy." Sieminski recommended higher gasoline taxes and a return to nuclear power.[72]

The return of the Admiral

Watkins testified before the Energy & Power subcommittee on February 28. Sharp welcomed the admiral, again accompanied by Moore and Stuntz, with restrained praise intended to draw a distinction between the laudable NES development process and the less laudable results. "Those of us who have been involved in this issue know that (the NES) is a formidable effort;" Sharp stated in his opening remarks, "it's very difficult politically; it's very difficult substantively; and it's an endurance record that only a few people can appreciate." Others on the subcommittee were less inclined to praise. Representative Al Swift of Washington: "This energy policy, as it is finally presented, has got right-wing economists' fingerprints all over it."

Representative Mike Synar of Oklahoma: "In critical areas, the goals of this strategy are simply not responsive to the national needs." Representative

Tom McMillan of Maryland: "There are not sufficient measures in this strategy to reduce or mitigate this country's reliance on this oil addiction." Representative Edward Markey of Massachusetts: "As far as the public and the Congress are concerned, the national energy strategy's imbalance is as bad politics as it is bad policy."[73]

Watkins was by now immune to predictable criticism by liberal Democratic legislators. He had developed rhetoric unyielding in its defense of NES process and product. He told the subcommittee:[74]

"In this strategy, you will find an attack on the regulatory system, which is at the heart, in many cases, of not being able to have a free flow of energy in this country. I think that this (NES) database that has been developed is second to none. There is nothing like it in the world. You will see some outcomes here this morning in my presentation that defy those that say that we are not interested in efficiency and conservation. About one third of the 100 initiatives here (in the NES), put into action form, are dedicated to efficiency and conservation."[75]

"We have accomplished our mission and laid a foundation for the future. On the historic perspective, never before has there been a strategy compiled to reach the objectives of energy security, environmental quality, and affordable energy."[76]

Watkins continued his testimony in the briefing style he had adopted for the Senate hearings. He provided a summary, with visual aids, of the main components of NES, the recommended courses of action and projected results. Midway through his presentation he felt compelled to return to congressional criticism of his efforts. "The debates within the Administration," he granted, "are just as tough as they are going to be here on the Hill. We would like to think that people would respect our ability to disagree."[77] Then, with barely disguised disdain, "I am not a politician. I was an admiral in the Navy. I don't know anything about politics. I was called in here to do a job, to clean up a mess, and that is what I am trying to do. I hope that is the spirit of cooperation that we can expect out of this committee."[78]

Watkins concluded his testimony by requesting that the entire text of the NES' executive summary be placed in the hearing record. Sharp asked Watkins if he were willing to share data and analyses compiled for NES. Watkins agreed to do so, but asked for reciprocity. "We would like to see some of the analyses that some of the experts here and others have," he said, "because I think it is time to compare analytic work and not snipe at each other on how bad the other's analysis is."[79]

Watkins' prickly demeanor had its effect on the subcommittee members. The congressmen thereafter spoke in more respectful tones, the usually lengthy prologues to their questions filled with declarations of admiration and praise.

Representative Gerry Studds of Massachusetts: "I am one of your great fans. I think your service to the country after your service in the Navy has been remarkable."[80] Representative Richard Lehman of California: "I certainly appreciate your excellent presentation this morning. I think you have been very candid with us. I think your goals are commendable and credible."[81] Representative Michael Oxley of Ohio: "Mr. Secretary, first of all I want to compliment you and Henson Moore, and particularly Linda Stuntz, who probably knows more about energy policy than anybody in this town."[82]

The hearing lasted three hours. Subcommittee members subsequently requested from DOE answers to several dozen questions. DOE policy staff replied to the questions with nearly one hundred pages of text and data that became part of the hearing record.[83]

A feverish pace

The hearings before Sharp's subcommittee continued unabated in March and April of 1991. On March 7, witnesses discussed utility issues. On March 13, the topic was oil consumption by cars and light duty trucks. On March 20 the subcommittee returned to electricity regulation.[84] In April, Sharp devoted no less than three hearings to the combined topics of CAFE and alternative fuels. Forty witnesses testified at the three hearings, including Linda Stuntz. In the process, nine distinct bills were introduced by members of the House of Representatives. The bills contained various, and variously astute, proposals to "strengthen" the alternative fuels provisions of NES or fill NES' "void" on CAFE standards. On the two topics alone, the hearing record eventually comprised over one thousand printed pages.[85]

In May 1991, Sharp proceeded to draft a comprehensive bill that was eventually presented to the House of Representatives as H.R. 776, the Comprehensive National Energy Policy Act (CONEPA) of 1991. On the Senate side, the Johnston-Wallop initial legislative proposal was modified and relabeled S. 1220, the National Energy Security Act of 1991. The two bills, with many common and some diverging provisions, made their separate way through the mark-up process in the spring and summer of 1991. Watkins placed DOE policy staff at the disposal of the two committees for any assistance or analysis they might require. Stuntz, gratified by the intensity and breadth of congressional attention to NES, paid close attention to the committees' needs. She thought the odds were in favor of obtaining from the 101st Congress the first significant energy legislation since the Energy Policy and Conservation Act of 1975. [86] Then, in mid-1991, the bipartisan illusion was shattered by unexpected political attacks from two members of the House of Representatives.

THE POLITICAL DIMENSIONS OF POLICYMAKING

Members of Congress frequently profess to be shocked, by the political dimensions of policies proposed by a president of the other party. And yet, if policies were not in fact a reflection of political persuasion, it would be difficult to justify voting candidates in and out of office. But the obvious is seldom a deterrent to political play. The bipartisanship that in 1990 briefly bound the congressional committees on energy was the exception rather than the rule of the 101st Congress. Peripheral committees felt no compunction about exploiting the controversy now surrounding the Bush administration's energy policy, especially in view of the considerable public attention generated by the release of NES.

Two House committees, in the summer and fall of 1991, undertook efforts—ultimately futile because transparently partisan—to discredit the NES development process and results.

The Wyden storm

Congressman Ron Wyden of Oregon chaired the obscure Subcommittee on Regulation, Business Opportunities and Energy of the House Committee on Small Business. In September 1990, Wyden engaged the congressional General Accounting Office (GAO) to "provide information on the process the Department of Energy (DOE) has used in developing the National Energy Strategy (NES) and evaluate the analyses and assumptions supporting the NES."[87]

GAO began its investigation of the NES development process by collecting opinions—rather than data—from DOE policy staff. Inconsistent impressions gathered during the staff interviews led GAO investigators to conclude that the NES process had been manipulated for political advantage and that the analytical foundation of the strategy was less defensible than DOE claimed. Consequently, the investigators requested that DOE make available to GAO what amounted to the entire record of documentation compiled on NES from inception in mid-1989 to December 1990. GAO was particularly interested in the papers that had been drafted for the EPC decision-making process on the NES. DOE coincidentally received the request from GAO during the period when the policy staff was involved in the final Cabinet deliberations on the strategy.[88]

Stuntz considered the GAO request unreasonable to the extent that it sought documentation related to cabinet deliberations. She agreed to provide non-sensitive background information on NES processes and products, but felt that papers prepared for the cabinet and the president required a measure of confidentiality, at least until all decisions on NES had been finalized. DOE general counsel Stephen Wakefield, in full agreement with Stuntz's position, therefore dispatched a letter to his counterpart at GAO on December 14, writing, "Under well-established principles, the

President is entitled to 'consultative privacy' in the formation, receipt, and consideration of advice" from his senior advisers.[89]

The claim of executive privilege infuriated both GAO and Wyden. In a three-page letter to the president, Wyden charged that "DOE's arbitrary restrictions (on providing information to GAO) have effectively thwarted Congressional oversight of this important project." Accepting GAO's anecdotal view that NES documentation was being withheld because it contained flawed data and analysis, Wyden advised the president that NES policy options "now before you and the cabinet are so tainted and biased as to preclude any reasonable opportunity to build the coalition necessary to pass a broad-visioned, comprehensive energy package."[90]

The White House office of legislative affairs responded to Wyden noncommittedly and referred the matter back to DOE.[91] A formal response was dispatched by DOE's Henson Moore on January 25, 1991. "The Department," Moore wrote, "has provided the General Accounting Office with some 700 pages of background documents. I have no doubt that these materials should afford an ample basis for the General Accounting Office representatives to understand how the Department has gone about its task of framing the matters ultimately presented to the President for decision."[92]

GAO issued its report on February 21, 1991, not coincidentally on the day following the White House's formal release of NES. In its transmittal letter to Wyden, GAO wrote "The Executive Secretary of the White House Economic Policy Council (EPC), on the advice of the White House Counsel, declined to speak with us regarding the internal EPC and White House processes for examining options under consideration for the NES. As a result, we are unable at this time to provide complete information on the final stages of the strategy's development." The report expressed grudging praise for "the unprecedented effort by DOE to solicit the nation's views on energy policy" and concluded that "while it is unclear to what extent public participation may have shaped DOE's strategy, we believe that the NES should ultimately be judged on its content."[93]

DOE heard nothing more from Wyden until June 1991 when the subcommittee chairman issued an invitation for DOE to provide a witness for a hearing scheduled for July 8.[94] Wyden began the hearing by distributing an opening statement drafted in the form of a press release. "For the last year," the statement read, "the Subcommittee has been working with the General Accounting Office to determine whether the conclusions and decisions reached by the President in the National Energy Strategy were reasonably and adequately supported by scientific analysis and data compiled by the Department of Energy. Today, the General Accounting Office will report on its very disturbing findings."[95]

These "very disturbing findings" were delivered by a GAO associate director, who summarized the agency's concerns as follows:[96]

- In developing NES, there was less public participation than DOE originally intended
- The administration included the estimated impacts of the CAAA of 1990 in projecting the overall impacts of NES and, as a result, energy and environmental benefits from implementing NES are unclear and may be overstated
- A key macroeconomic assumption used in the NES analysis, namely, rate of growth in GNP, is significantly higher than projected by the CEA in its most recent report to the president
- The administration's approach of depending to a large extent on R&D and the dissemination of information on energy-efficient technologies may not be as effective as projected if current low oil prices continue
- The models DOE used in performing NES analyses are imprecise because of the complicated nature of the problems addressed, and this inherent imprecision is magnified when forecasting over the forty year horizon in the NES

The DOE witness, one of Stuntz's deputies,[97] responded to the GAO's critique by reiterating the facts of the NES public hearing process: eighteen hearings, 499 formal witnesses including twenty-eight members of Congress and eight governors, over twenty-nine thousand pages of written material, issuance of the Interim Report which, in turn, generated further public reactions, public access to summary analyses of policy options and publication of technical annexes to NES.

The DOE witness went on to dismiss the matter of GNP growth rates as a non-issue because projections of GNP rates were normally subject to revision by CEA on a regular basis, and those used in the NES modeling effort had been the latest available at the time. The DOE witness dismissed the charge of over-reliance on R&D and information dissemination for achievement of NES objectives as an unfair characterization of NES policy instruments, which also comprised regulatory reform proposals (for electricity generation and natural gas pipelines), and government mandates (for use of alternative transportation fuels). As to models being imprecise? Models were thus by definition.[98]

Wolpe's unicorn hunt

A more serious effort to undermine the credibility of NES was undertaken by Representative Howard Wolpe of Michigan who chaired the Subcommittee on Investigations and Oversight of the House Committee on Science, Space & Technology. Unlike Wyden's subcommittee, Wolpe's had legitimate jurisdiction over DOE's science and technology portfolio. More importantly, like other investigative congressional panels, Wolpe's subcommittee also had the power to force full disclosure of any and all internal DOE documents related to NES. With a well-trained staff at his disposal, Wolpe also did not need external assistance from agencies like GAO in order to pursue his quarry.

Wolpe's initial information requests to DOE in March 1991, were both sweeping and oddly, indeed peculiarly, focused on aspects of NES dealing with industrial energy policy. He demanded "all documents received, generated, or reviewed which include, but are not limited to, memoranda, letters, notes, reports, computer information, studies, records of oral communication, or any information or other description; whether preliminary, draft, or in final form; *and whether signed or unsigned* [emphasis added]," relating to industrial energy use, waste recycling and waste use as feed stock.[99] For DOE's policy staff, well accustomed to capricious congressional information requests, the Wolpe search seemed particularly abstruse. The reply would require a large investment of staff time, digging through the files of several offices, copying and collating hundreds of pages of documents of little practical value—signed and unsigned, no less—on a subject of tangential significance to the purpose of NES.

However, it soon became clear that Wolpe's document search of March was only the beginning of his quest to obtain virtually all of the documentary record of the NES development process, including all of the papers drafted for the EPC. On May 6, he sought the complete NES files of the EIA and those of the assistant secretary for conservation and renewable energy.[100] On the same day, he wrote to deputy secretary Moore that the information forwarded to him by DOE in response to his March requests was incomplete and that DOE's claim of executive privilege for documents related to the EPC process was unacceptable.[101]

Wolpe's demands for documents increased in direct proportion to DOE's reluctance to provide them. Letters of explanation, implied threats of serious consequences for non-compliance and partial submissions of additional documents by DOE continued for the next three months. Still, Wolpe would not be satisfied. Finally, on August 1, 1991, at a specially convened meeting of his subcommittee, Wolpe requested authority to issue a subpoena to the secretary of energy to produce all the documentation deemed necessary by investigators of the NES process.[102] The motion carried and Wolpe was given power to issue the subpoena. After consultations with the White House, Watkins saw no choice but to comply.

Throughout the test of wills, the purpose of Wolpe's investigation remained unclear to DOE's policy staff. It was difficult to understand why an investigation, as opposed to a normal hearing, was deemed necessary in order to scrutinize the NES development effort. Nor was it clear why a subcommittee of Congress believed it necessary to examine the cabinet's decision-making process rather than the results of that process.

Finally, on October 2, Wolpe wrote to Watkins requesting that five specifically named DOE officials—both political and career appointees—be made available to testify[103] at a hearing scheduled for October 16, and that these same officials, and others, be ready for interviews by subcommittee staff in advance of the hearing.[104] The interviews took place during the week of October 7-11, 1991. The questions posed by the congressional investigators shed no light on the purpose of Wolpe's undertaking: How did

DOE ensure against technological optimism in its analytical effort? What was EIA's role in ensuring consistency of technology data? What were the key differences among the models used for NES analyses? What technologies were included in the nuclear inputs to the NES? How were rates of market penetration calculated for renewable technologies? Which electric utilities were consulted for advice on matters of integrated resource planning and demand side management? Were the cost and performance values of nuclear, fossil and renewable technologies consistent?[105]

Chairman Wolpe resolved the mystery of the subcommittee's investigation in his opening statement at the hearing of October 16. Secretary Watkins, declared Wolpe, "attempted to sell the [National Energy] strategy as a flawless product of extensive public participation, state-of-the-art computer modeling, expert analysis, and innovative public policy. In my judgment, that is not really what has resulted. In fact it is hard to argue that we have a strategy at all."[106]

To which the subcommittee's ranking Republican member, Robert Walker of Pennsylvania, replied, "You say in your statement, Mr. Chairman [Wolpe], that you hope the Administration will not misinterpret today's hearing as a political attack. I hope that that's the case, as well, except the Administration—I think—has some reason to be somewhat cautious when it appears as though the Investigations & Oversight Subcommittee has drawn its conclusions before the hearing."[107]

The hearing proved anticlimactic. The congressmen's questions were synchronized with the distribution to the witnesses of documents from the record, theatrically intended to build the proverbial case for the prosecution—one of deceit and manipulation of a national policy development process. Typical exchanges:[108]

Mr. Wolpe: If you will turn to page two of the exhibit, you will find a glossary of NES terms. It indicates that the NES has three over-arching goals: economic strength, environmental quality, and economic security. The Department [of Energy's] goals make no reference to the continuation of the successful policy of market reliance, however, as referred to in the President's speeches of July 1989. Was this simply an oversight?

DOE witness: Oh, I think that the market reliance was a starting point. It did not need to be repeated.

Mr. Wolpe: It's my understanding that in NES parlance, the "troika" refers to the Office of Management and Budget, the Council of Economic Advisers, and the Treasury Department. Is that correct?

DOE witness: It's not NES parlance. Those agencies have been referred to as troika for a very long time, and not for the purpose of the NES.

Mr. Wolpe: Did the failure to include market reliance in the Department's NES goals subsequently cause any friction with the troika?

DOE witness: The Department did not fail to include market reliance as its operating principle and I don't think that was a particular source of irritation with the three agencies. No, sir.

Other members of the panel pursued similarly impressionistic lines of questioning, some wishing to point out flaws in the NES analytical process, others in the deliberative process. Distinctions between the interests of Republican and Democratic members became indistinguishable:[109]

Congressman Boehlert of New York: How rigorous was the modeling used as you addressed the subject of increasing CAFE standards?

DOE witness: I believe, actually, that we maintain the only comprehensive model on fuel efficiency in the Federal Government. It's operated for us at Oak Ridge National Laboratory. It's our model, but it's also used, for instance, by the Office of Technology Assessment in Congress, and by most people who do research on fuel efficiency issues.

Mr. Boehlert: This rigorous modeling, was that used in terms of developing the NES strategy?

DOE witness: Yes, but it's not very difficult to model what cost and technology potential is. People will continue to argue on the assumptions, as in every other modeling effort.

Wolpe had surprisingly few questions for the two senior political appointees of DOE whom he had called to testify. It was late in the hearing when Linda Stuntz and Calvin Kent were finally allowed at the witness table. Stuntz defended NES processes and results in a very brief statement in which she also reminded Wolpe: "There have been some 50 Congressional hearings on NES-related issues since publication of the NES. This subcommittee's extensive review joins the reviews of the NES process, models, and analysis by the General Accounting Office, the Congressional Research Service, the Office of Technology Assessment, and the National Academies of Sciences and Engineering."[110]

Wolpe wanted to know why an administration devoted to keeping the government out of the energy markets "proposes to give General Electric and Westinghouse millions of dollars to help them develop their particular products [nuclear reactors]." Stuntz replied that the answer lay in how one defined the role of Government in R&D. "What we did in the NES," she added, "was to look for those areas where the private sector may have insufficient incentive to pursue R&D objectives that we as a government and in the public interest think need to be pursued."[111]

EIA administrator Kent was the last to testify. He told Wolpe that EIA's role in the NES process had been limited to modeling and analysis and that, as prescribed in EIA's congressional charter, the agency played no role in the policymaking process.[112] Wolpe asked a few superficial questions, then moved on to closing remarks. "I would indicate," he said, "that I am glad that the Department intends to continue the NES process. I am sure that all of you have learned a great deal from this experience that will be put to good use in the future. I would also indicate that today's hearing is not a one-shot exercise for this subcommittee, either. We intend to follow the NES process very closely in the future."[113]

Actually, it became after all, a one-shot exercise. The Science Committee under whose jurisdiction Wolpe had pursued his inquiry thought the hearing pointless and declined to include the hearing's transcript in the record of the committee's deliberations on NES. Wolpe had succeeded only in belaboring the conduct of a policy development process that the president had the right to organize in any way he pleased. On a procedural level, the hearing, and the eight months of contentious preparations for it, came to be viewed by the policy staff as abuse of power by an overzealous member of Congress. The staff considered the hearing as an attempt by a congressional committee chairman to exploit career officials' obligation to respond honestly to congressional inquiries, for the purpose of entrapping the officials' political supervisors. Wolpe's exercise was dangerous as precedent for seeking explanations of policy not from those appointed to that responsibility by an elected president, but from civil service staff who by regulation and tradition is expected to serve duly appointed policymakers.

Wolpe's hearing, like Wyden's, produced little of value to the drafters of energy legislation who were laboring in the House and Senate in the fall of 1991 to build coalitions sufficient to ensure a majority vote. Both hearings were unusual for their leaders' insistence that differences of views on procedures by which federal policy is developed can be used to discredit the final product. The hearings' political purpose was transparent. No congressional interest had been evident, for example, in how public participation and cabinet deliberations had been accommodated during development of the Carter administration's first and second National Energy Plans. Indeed, as noted in earlier chapters, then-Secretary Schlesinger held no public hearings whatsoever for the first energy plan. He had "ensured" public participation by publishing an address in the Federal Register, to which interested parties could write, if they wished.

Congressional capriciousness bothered Watkins. He recalled that the CAAA proposed by Bush in 1989, which had sparked intense interest and debate, had instigated no congressional hearings on policy development process, analytical rigor or cabinet deliberations. Similarly, National Transportation Policy, completed and published by Bush's Department of Transportation in February 1990, which involved potentially hundreds of billions of dollars in federal expenditures for highways, public transit, railroads and the air transport system, had similarly inspired no investigative fervor from Congress. Clearly, he concluded, few public policy issues had the power to motivate congressional passions quite like energy.

THE COMMITTEES CRAFT COMPETING BILLS

Johnston in the Senate and Sharp in the House undertook the arduous task of crafting energy legislation with due respect for the distinct political and jurisdictional differences embodied in their respective committees. The two leaders understood that, to be successful, a bill would need to capture and hold the support of the White House and therefore reflect the critical elements of NES. In order to attract a majority of members of Congress, however, such a bill also had to contain provisions that were likely to court a presidential veto.

Because its political and ideological divisions were more predictable, SENR was able to move ahead more rapidly than its House counterpart. The House Energy and Commerce Committee needed more time in which to build a coalition because the ideological spectrum of its members' interests was broader and more volatile

The Senate bill

SENR leaders Johnston and Wallop completed mark-up of S. 1220, the National Energy Security Act (NESA) of 1991, in record time. Johnston brought the bill to a formal vote by his committee on March 23, 1991 and prevailed on a vote of seventeen yeas and three nays. The opponents were Senators Dale Bumpers of Arkansas, Bill Bradley of New Jersey and Paul Wellstone of Minnesota.[114]

The NESA contained fourteen titles in addition to the usual findings and definitions. It incorporated virtually all proposals put forth by NES[115] and a few key provisions opposed by the Bush administration. The purposes given to NESA by the committee, expressed in the very first title of the bill, reflected the senators' tenacity of belief in an energy world shaped by political rather than economic forces. The terminology and conceptual framework were a mix of current knowledge, data and analysis and of unreconciled regret about government's historical failure to ensure energy security. With NESA, SENR members signaled to the White House that the Troika's faith in markets could not bring full deliverance. The stated purpose of their legislation was the following.[116]

1. Slow the nation's increasing dependence on imported oil over the short term, and in the long term significantly reduce that dependence;
2. Reduce the consumption of oil in the transportation sector and encourage development and use of alternative energy sources, particularly for transportation;
3. Encourage development and deployment of renewable energy sources in the United States and on an international basis in lesser-developed countries;
4. Streamline the hydropower licensing process and encourage hydroelectric development at federal dams;
5. Encourage more efficient use of energy throughout the economy, including improvements in the industrial, commercial and residential sectors, increasing energy efficiency in Federal energy management and encouraging more efficient energy use by electric utilities;
6. Provide for oil and gas exploration, production and development in the ANWR in Alaska in an environmentally sound manner;
7. Encourage the production and use of nuclear power by providing for the commercialization of advanced nuclear reactor technologies and improving the nuclear reactor licensing process;
8. Enhance the competitive position of the federal uranium enrichment enterprise;
9. Encourage increased utilization of natural gas and other domestic energy resources to displace imported oil and meet domestic energy demand in a manner consistent with environmental values;
10. Encourage development of domestic energy resources on the OCS;
11. Establish priorities for federal energy research, development, demonstration, and commercialization of technology;
12. Encourage enhanced oil and gas recovery from known and producing domestic reserves;

13. Enhance the role of coal and clean coal technology in meeting the nation's energy needs;
14. Foster competition in the electric utility industry; and
15. Provide enhanced oil security protection through the SPR.

The analytical community had actually abandoned the energy security concepts contained in the Senate bill ten years earlier. It had been argued in NES, and in responses to questions submitted for the record by DOE and by other private and public commentators, that U.S. demand could not be satisfied in the foreseeable future, if ever, without reliance on oil imports. Furthermore, all previous efforts to decrease U.S. dependence on such imports had proved to be costly failures.

Similarly, the senators' belief that particular fuels and technologies were worthy of special government attention seemed, anachronistically, a throwback to Nixon's Project Independence. Why, for example, should the use of natural gas, an abundant and cost-competitive fuel, require encouragement of use by the Senate of the United States? And why should government concern itself with commercialization of advanced nuclear reactors?

The role of government was not, however, central to the deliberations of the SENR. Johnston and Wallop sought a bill with measures that would attract sufficient votes from the left and right of the political spectrum to offset the likely loss of support from those who would find certain of the bill's provisions to be unacceptable under any circumstances. One such provision was the proposal to allow access to the oil and gas resources of ANWR, the single most offensive feature of the bill as far as the environmental community was concerned. To reduce the political cost of making ANWR palatable, the two senators offered at least two measures deemed likely to seduce the liberal constituency of the Senate.[117]

The first of the inducements, cleverly placed in Title I of NESA, called for the appointment of a director of climate protection in the higher ranks of DOE's organizational structure. The director would carry out the research program advocated by Wirth and Gore, on the feasibility of reducing U.S. emissions of greenhouse gases by up to 20% by the year 2000. The second tactical provision was contained in Title III. Here Johnston offered a formula for increasing CAFE standards for automobiles and light duty trucks. He proposed, in deference to Dingell, that CAFE standards remain at the 1990 level of 27.5 miles per gallon until 1995. Thereafter the standards would be increased by rule of the secretary of transportation, on a percentage rather than a numerical basis for all manufacturers and for all vehicles in two phases between 1996 and 2001, and in 2002 and thereafter.[118]

As part of his automobile efficiency lure, Johnston added provisions to increase the "gas-guzzler" tax, and programs to scrap older, fuel-inefficient vehicles. On the supply side, he adopted, notably against personal conviction, surprisingly sweeping federal mandates for the introduction of alternative fuels and technology into private and public vehicle fleets. He supplemented these mandated measures with extensive research and development investments in electric and hybrid vehicles and with tax and regulatory incentives for manufacturers, purchasers and operators of any vehicles and fuel distribution systems that were not oil based.[119]

On renewable energy systems, NESA proposed federally subsidized loans to developers of electricity generation plants using solar, wind and biomass energy, increased federal R&D investments to reduce the cost of most renewable energy technologies and expanded government efforts to export such technology. The bill fell short of proposing new tax credits or production subsidies. For hydropower, NESA recommended a streamlined licensing process with FERC as the lead agency for all National Environmental Policy Act reviews.[120]

Title VI of NESA addressed energy efficiency in a manner generally consistent with Bush administration proposals. It called for promulgation of model federal building standards to be used as seen fit by states but with financial incentives to motivate their adoption; efficiency ratings but no standards for lighting fixtures and for commercial cooling and heating equipment; new but voluntary energy efficiency standards for industry; and requirements that energy efficiency investments in federal buildings be undertaken by dates certain. Utility regulators were directed to conduct formal proceedings to ensure that investments in energy efficiency and conservation were treated on the same basis as investments in new generation capacity.[121]

The nuclear licensing reform provisions of NESA reflected Bush administration proposals as well. The bill called for the issuance of a combined construction and operating license to builders of new plants and constrained the intervention of third parties in the proceedings. On other nuclear-related matters, the bill called for the U.S. uranium enrichment enterprise, operated by DOE, to be transformed into a public corporation managed on a private business basis. The bill proposed no new initiatives on the matter of nuclear waste management, notwithstanding Watkins' plea for Congress to override the determined opposition of the state of Nevada to the study of Yucca Mountain as the site of a permanent repository.[122]

The transportation of natural gas by pipelines from wellhead to burner tip was comprehensively addressed in NESA. FERC was given clearer authority, as with hydropower licensing, to streamline and expedite permitting procedures for pipeline construction, abandon old rate structures and establish new ones for interstate transport of gas, unbundle services provided by common carrier pipelines and protect local distribution companies from common carriers' bypass powers. FERC authority was, however, curtailed in terms of influencing state regulation of local gas companies and eliminated altogether in regard to sales of natural gas as fuel for vehicles.[123]

The Johnston-Wallop bill was surprisingly hesitant on OCS oil and gas development leasing. The bill ignored past leasing policy and current moratoria on leasing and created, instead, a new federal fund, financed through royalty income of the Department of the Interior, to be used for assistance to coastal states. Almost as an afterthought, the legislation called for a report from the president with "recommendations and findings regarding the availability of areas of the OCS for oil and gas leasing, development and production."[124]

NESA called for reform of PUHCA to promote greater competition in the generation of electric power and allowed access to the transmission grid by independent power producers. The reform would create a class of electric producers known as exempt wholesale generators (EWGs), meaning companies exempt from regulation by the Securities and Exchange Commission. Other provisions in this title were directed at preventing self-dealing by utilities that established subsidiary EWGs and allowing access to the financial records of EWGs by state utility regulators.[125]

The remaining sections of the Johnston-Wallop bill provided the typical confectionery store of federal projects and programs of support for the pet fuels and technologies of a large number of senators. Funds were authorized for research on natural gas, oil shale (Eastern and Western), renewable energy, electric heating and cooling, tar sands, high efficiency heat engines and sundry other, generally uneconomic technologies residing in DOE laboratories since the Truman administration. The SENR devoted an entire title to coal research, requiring DOE to continue the fifty year-old federal investment in processes and technologies such as underground coal gasification, use of low-rank coal, magneto-hydrodynamics and even coal-fired locomotives, whose economic non-viability had been repeatedly demonstrated.[126]

NESA was, with notable exceptions, aligned with NES. It was deemed, therefore, highly suspect by the liberal special interest community and their representatives in the Senate. Environmental advocates were not prepared, as Johnston hoped, to trade ANWR for CAFE. Nor were they likely to support the nuclear licensing regulatory reforms. Objections were also immediately raised to the hydropower licensing reforms, which were in any case also opposed by Dingell, who had adopted "free-flowing rivers" as his environmental protection motto. Johnston and Wallop expected the reactions, seeing NESA as their initial bid; they were willing to engage in the time-honored political horse-trading.

The House bill

In the House, Sharp's subcommittee labored for eight months (from February to October 1991) to craft H.R. 776, CONEPA. H.R. 776 was an amalgam of twenty-one separate bills, modified and unified through an extended series of topical hearings conducted by the subcommittee between January and September 1991. The bill emerged from the subcommittee on October 31, 1991, backed by a vote of twenty-one in favor and one opposed. After a further six months of deliberations, amendments and substitutions, the bill was approved by the full Energy and Commerce Committee, by a vote of forty-two to one, on March 11, 1992. Representative Henry Waxman of California was the bill's sole opponent.[127]

The final version of Sharp's legislative effort was generally compatible with the Johnston-Wallop bill, but differed profoundly in many aspects. The similarities and differences could be gleaned from the report issued by the committee at the completion of its drafting task. The committee, the report stated, endeavored to reduce the nation's vulnerability to the economic devastation of oil price shocks by reducing demand, developing domestic alternatives to imported oil and by filling the SPR and making it more usable. Secondly, the report said, the committee had exposed "hidden energy costs" by assigning the costs of a fuel or a program to the beneficiaries rather than to the taxpayers in general. Thirdly, the committee had incorporated environmental considerations in energy policy deliberations at the outset, rather than focusing on after-the-fact cleanup.[128]

On the specifics, CONEPA differed from its Senate-drafted counterpart in several critical aspects. CONEPA contained neither ANWR nor CAFE provisions. On energy efficiency, however, the bill directed the promulgation of new efficiency standards for lights, electric motors, showerheads and heating and cooling equipment for commercial buildings. Its natural gas provisions reflected the concerns of northeastern legislators that FERC, in its ratemaking, not discriminate against imports of Canadian supplies on which the region might in the future depend. On nuclear waste, CONEPA called for statutory means to "prevent the State of Nevada from procedurally blocking site characterization work" at Yucca Mountain.[129]

The House bill adopted the production tax credit initially proposed by DOE but rejected by the Troika, called for expansion of the SPR to one billion barrels financed by contributions from oil importers and refiners. Finally, the subcommittee rejected the Senate proposal to streamline hydropower licensing and instead gave additional authority to the federal fisheries services to prescribe fishways and collect from licensees the full cost of regulation.[130]

In sum, the House bill was both more interventionist on some issues—and less so on others—than the White House and the Senate thought desirable. It was deemed unlikely to gain favor in the Senate unless the disparities on SPR, ANWR and CAFE could somehow be rationalized either through negotiations or by means of a showdown vote. Watkins and Stuntz believed that Dingell might compromise on SPR and ANWR, but would under no circumstances do so on CAFE. Henson Moore thought the House SPR provision could not be allowed to remain in the final bill. The White House issued immediate warnings that the SPR provisions of the House bill and CAFE provisions of the Senate bill would doom the chances of enacting comprehensive legislation during the Bush administration, but few members of Congress believed it.[131]

OTHER AND DISSENTING VIEWS

Under the terms of an agreement reached by Dingell and the Speaker of the House, H.R. 776 was sequentially referred to eight committees claiming jurisdiction over its various provisions once the bill emerged from the Energy and Commerce Committee. The panels, which were directed to complete their review in the period between March 11 and May 5, 1992, comprised the committees on the Judiciary, on Foreign Affairs, on Government Operations, on Interior and Insular Affairs, on Merchant Marine and Fisheries, on Public Works and Transportation, on Science, Space and Technology, and, most importantly, the tax-writing Committee on Ways and Means.[132]

Most of the referral committees responded to H.R. 776 by proposing marginal amendments to some provisions or taking issue with one committee presuming to intrude on the jurisdictional prerogatives of another. Two of the referral committees, however, adopted extensive amendments that substantially altered the moderate, consensus-built achievement of the Sharp-Dingell bill. The two most radical proposals came from the committees on Interior and Insular Affairs and on Space, Science & Technology—both chaired by Californians.

Energy as the enemy within

"The Committee [on Interior and Insular Affairs] takes the view," its chairman, George Miller declared, "that the undeniable desire rising largely from the citizenry itself to protect other values such as environmental preservation and human health and safety will continue to overwhelm any energy policy that gives these values short shrift." Miller's answer to H.R. 776 was a substitute bill, sixteen titles in length that he offered as an "amendment" to the Sharp-Dingell bill and named the "Energy development and Environmental Protection Act (EDEPA)."[133]

EDEPA's biases against energy production were not subtle. In its very first title, it rejected reform of nuclear plant licensing and prohibited NRC from renewing the licensing of plants beyond forty years of age. It transferred from NRC to states the authority to regulate low-level radioactive waste. It barred any leasing or pre-leasing planning activity by the Department of the Interior for OCS areas in Oregon, Washington, California, the entire Atlantic Coast and off Florida, until January 2002. It barred access to ANWR for any development purpose and placed off-limits to oil exploration most of Alaska's coastal waters. It directed the Interior Department to assess market conditions before issuing oil, gas and coal production leases on federal lands. It directed utility customers of PMAs to conduct "a balanced electric power planning process which considers both demand and supply options."[134]

The Miller bill provided federal subsidies to the energy systems of U.S. commonwealth and trust territories and geothermal power production (mainly Californian). It prohibited construction of any new hydropower dam in national parks, provided to the Interior Department virtual veto power over FERC re-licensing of any hydropower dam, subscribed to the establishment of a uranium enrichment corporation but withheld the financial assets needed to ensure eventual privatization. The bill strengthened federal law to protect whistleblowers in nuclear civilian and defense industries and directed EPA to reissue standards on health and safety for nuclear waste repositories, which had been rejected by the courts. The bill was silent on CAFE and on energy supply options, indicating for the latter that domestic needs for hydrocarbons could be met by simply "reworking" existing wells and mines.[135]

"The energy history of this Nation," Miller concluded in his report to the House, "is replete with examples of failed extraction, generation, transmission and waste disposal projects whose common defect was an attitude of exclusion; the public was to be ignored and potential hazards and technical defects were to be glossed over and covered up. These self-defeating practices must come to an end in favor of an open and accountable process."[136]

There were, of course, dissenting views to Miller's proposals provided by the Republican members of the committee, who issued a twenty-five-page rebuttal referring to Miller's bill as "the disarming of our nation in the field of energy." The Republicans objected to Miller's rejection of nuclear licensing reform and thought that state regulation of low-level radioactive material would "disrupt and balkanize established national uniform standards on critical nuclear issues." The minority report ridiculed Miller's proposal to privatize a uranium enrichment enterprise "saddled from the outset with no real assets, no working capital, an unproven technology, no meaningful track record of performance, not a dime of profits allowed to be put towards future research and development, a bonanza of government regulation, special deals for unions, etc." The minority objected in variously mild and insistent ways to virtually all other aspects of Miller's deliberations and generally decried the ensuing legislative product.[137]

The administration responded to the Miller amendments with a ten-page letter from the Secretary of the Interior. "The Administration is strongly opposed to many of the provisions in this legislation," Secretary Manuel Lujan wrote. He added, "From the perspective of this Department, this bill is so seriously flawed that I would have to recommend to the President that he veto it if it were passed."[138]

Policy equals jurisdiction

George Brown, Miller's fellow Californian, chaired the Committee on Science, Space and Technology. Brown saw in H.R. 776 a vehicle concurrently to expand his committee's jurisdiction over DOE's R&D portfolio and the means to bring home valuable federal subsidies. He persuaded his committee to add to the Sharp-Dingell bill no less than eight additional titles devoted to taxpayer financed technology demonstration projects.

Brown proposed extensive new federal investments for development of electric vehicles and related fueling infrastructure as well as R&D projects for all other alternative fuels and technology. He sought as well, federal support for research on conventional vehicles with the aim of reducing emissions and finding substitutes for crude oil. Virtually all of the R&D projects advocated by Brown were designed to serve almost exclusively the interests of California. In early 1992, California had committed itself by state law to forcing electric and other non-conventional vehicles into its marketplace, in a desperate attempt to clean up what was (and remains) the worst air quality in the nation. In short, Brown sought to shift to the federal purse most or all of California's cost of complying with the CAAA of 1990.[139]

Under the general rubric of energy efficiency, Brown sought to authorize the broadest array of RD&D activities at DOE since the Carter administration. He sought investments in technologies for gas and electric heating and cooling, pulp and paper, low-emission/low-energy buildings, electric drives, steel and aluminum casting, renewable energy generators, high efficiency heat engines, nuclear reactors, fusion energy, coal combustion, fuel cells and efficient electric energy systems in general.[140]

To support "energy and economic growth," Brown authorized a "national critical advanced materials initiative" as well as a "national critical advanced *manufacturing technologies* [emphasis added] initiative." He recommended the establishment of an "energy efficient pollution prevention program," and a federal office to audit such a program. He established anti-free-trade requirements to use domestic products in the demonstration projects and directed DOE to pursue its RD&D activities on the basis of cost-shared joint ventures with private industry.[141]

The sixteen Republican members of Brown's committee filed dissenting views. They noted, "The $5 billion of additional spending in this proposed legislation can only come from three places: other discretionary domestic and/or defense cuts, which have already been overwhelmingly rejected by this House; new taxes, which is perhaps the real agenda, or outright deficit spending, increasing our $400 billion of annual red ink even more." In conclusion, the dissenters wrote, "To succeed, the Science Committee must set real energy R&D and program priorities. This requires making hard choices. H.R. 776 does not."[142]

Watkins objected strenuously to Brown's legislative micromanagement of DOE's R&D portfolio. The amendments proposed by the Science Committee, Watkins wrote, "are overly prescriptive of research and development components and phasing, call for large numbers of costly programs to demonstrate technologies that are well beyond demonstration requirements, and establish energy R&D targets and objectives that are inconsistent with the National Energy Strategy and with market conditions."[143]

One-upmanship

Walter Jones of North Carolina, a state anxious to avoid oil and gas drilling off its shores, chaired the House Committee on Merchant Marine & Fisheries. The committee examined H.R. 776 during the first week of May 1992 and reported back a fifty-two-page amendment to the bill. The committee declared its opposition to reform of the NEPA review process by which FERC would have broader authority to permit and license natural gas pipelines. Secondly, the committee banned leasing on the OCS until 2000 and established a fund, in the Treasury, which would provide block grants to states for coastal resources management. Next, in deference to its Louisiana and Texas members, the panel authorized $151 million for a five-year study to assess "the adequacy of available physical oceanographic, ecological, and socioeconomic information" for the central and Western Gulf of Mexico and offshore Alaska.[144]

The committee went on to direct the treasury secretary to establish a global climate change response fund, as "the mechanism for United States contributions to assist global efforts in adapting and responding to climate change." Finally, the committee added a provision to deny U.S. port privileges, even under emergency circumstances, to any vessel[145] "in transit from a foreign nation to a foreign nation that is transporting plutonium."[146]

In response, the committee Republican minority declared, "It is with a deep sense of sadness that we must strongly oppose the enactment of Title

XX (the Jones committee proposal) of H.R. 776. This section will cripple our nation's energy policy, endanger our national security, and make us far more vulnerable to foreign energy producers."[147]

The administration did not bother reacting to the Jones committee amendments. DOE and OMB concluded that the funding requirements, essentially in violation of the pay-as-you-go provisions of OBRA, would doom the effort to failure either in the Ways and Means Committee or on the House floor. Many of the provisions adopted by the committee were in any case similar to those of the Interior and Insular Affairs Committee, against whose Democratic members the administration would concentrate its fire.

The real field of battle

For the White House, the most objectionable provision of H.R. 776 was the proposal, crafted by Sharp, requiring importers and refiners of crude oil and natural gas liquids to provide in-kind or cash payments to fill the SPR to one billion barrels. The provision had become a rallying cry for the oil industry and OMB had labeled it a tax, "pure and simple." Henson Moore and Watkins, believing—incorrectly, as it turned out—that the oil industry's backing would be crucial to secure final passage of the energy bill, sought a venue to kill the measure early and definitively. They found it in the Committee on Ways and Means, chaired by the redoubtable Dan Rostenkowski of Illinois.

In a letter to Rostenkowski and to Ways & Means ranking minority member Bill Archer of Texas, Watkins declared the SPR provision "inordinately expensive and economically inefficient." He added: "The Department of Energy would strongly recommend that the President veto any bill containing the proposals."[148] Treasury Secretary Brady weighed in with a similarly unambiguous veto threat. "The greatest burden from this provision," Brady wrote on April 28, "will be felt by those who have to pay—the American public. The incidence of this burden will be similar to a simple tax on oil. Our economy does not need an additional drag at this time."[149]

The Ways and Means Committee met on April 29 and 30. As one of their first acts, they voted to strike the SPR provision from H.R. 776.[150]

They then proceeded to adopt alternative minimum tax relief for independent oil and gas producers, establish a contribution by nuclear utilities to a decontamination and decommissioning fund for the uranium enrichment corporation, raise to sixty dollars per month the tax-free benefit that employers could provide to employees using public transit, permanently extend the federal tax credit for qualified solar and geothermal production facilities, provide a tax credit for the purchase of alternative fuel vehicles and reduce the tax imposed on utilities to finance the nuclear decommissioning trust fund.[151]

The committee thus provided all that Watkins could hope for and more. The stage was now set for the decisive battle on the House floor. The Senate had, in the meantime, passed its version of the Wallop-Johnston energy bill.

BY A PERSUASIVE MARGIN

The leadership of the Senate Energy Committee labored throughout 1991 to enlist a majority of senators in support of NESA. Johnston's legislative strategy was to force consideration of the bill in its entirety by prohibiting the selection of favored provisions. Only under these terms could he and Wallop hope to forge the grand compromise by which liberal senators would swallow ANWR and the conservatives accede to CAFE.

Johnston's strategy was derailed by OMB on October 31, 1991, when Richard Darman transmitted to the Senate and made public the White House's formal statement of policy on NESA. "The Administration," Darman declared, "strongly supports Senate passage of S. 1220, but will not support it if certain provisions are included in the final bill. In particular, the President's senior advisers would recommend a veto if the bill includes amendments which mandate Corporate Average Fuel Economy (CAFE) levels that would jeopardize the safety of American car buyers, risk American jobs, or impose unacceptable costs on consumers and manufacturers. Furthermore, if the provisions of S. 1220 concerning ANWR development are deleted, the President's senior advisers would recommend a veto."[152]

On November 1, under a filibuster threat from within and the presidential veto outstanding, the Senate rejected the Johnston-Wallop bill. It would take the following two months for the senators to redraft NESA by, among other things, dropping from the bill the two provisions—CAFE and ANWR—which stood in the way of Senate passage. With the revisions, Senate opposition was substantially diluted and floor debate was consequently scheduled for February 5, 1992. Under the terms of an agreement reached by Johnson with Senate majority leader George Mitchell, senators would be allowed to introduce a total of forty-one amendments to the NESA in the three initial days of debate.[153]

On the day before commencement of Senate floor action on NESA, Watkins dispatched a letter to Johnston and Wallop to, as he put it, "share with you the Administration's position on several key issues."[154] The letter stated that the administration remained committed to "the environmentally responsible development of a small portion of the Arctic National Wildlife Refuge," warned against Senate adoption of a proposal to "establish a voluntary certification and registry scheme for greenhouse gas reductions," declared opposition to an amendment proposed by Senator Jeffords of Vermont to "mandate that 10% of America's fuel supply be alternative or replacement fuels," signaled unwillingness to accept changes in the nuclear licensing reform provisions of NESA and urged unwavering support for the reform of PUHCA.[155]

The Senate acts

The Senate debated NESA for three consecutive days on February 5 to 7, 1992. On the first day it adopted by voice vote thirty-nine noncontroversial, mainly technical amendments and rejected the Jeffords alternative fuel proposal on a vote of fifty-seven to thirty-nine.[156] On the second day it defeated an amendment by Senator Bob Graham of Florida requiring separate NRC hearings for construction and operation of nuclear power plants and took up a proposal by Gore to require stabilization of carbon dioxide emissions at 1990 levels by the year 2000.[157]

On the third day, Gore withdrew his proposal due to lack of support and the Senate proceeded to adopt thirteen other amendments. These included a number of senatorial pet projects such as a Domenici proposal to conduct research on solar-powered vehicles, a McCain proposal to subject Congress to energy efficiency building codes, a Dole proposal to establish a DOE energy research center in Kansas and a Glenn proposal to apply energy efficiency codes to federal government contractors.[158]

Debate on the Senate bill was resumed on February 18, at which time Senator Frank Murkowski of Alaska was permitted to introduce an amendment restoring to the Senate bill the provision allowing development of ANWR's hydrocarbon resources. The amendment was defeated. Thirty other amendments were debated and disposed of before the Senate could move to a final vote on the bill.[159] The final vote came on February 19, 1992. The Senate passed the NESA by a margin of ninety-four yeas to four nays.[160]

The action moves to the House

The House bill, H.R. 776, had not yet emerged from Sharp's energy and power subcommittee on the day that the Senate secured passage of NESA. The referral of the bill to multiple committees of jurisdiction further delayed House floor action on the bill until late May 1992.

On May 20 OMB forwarded to the Speaker of the House its habitual Statement of Administration Policy on H.R. 776. The effects of the administration's penchant for repeated veto threats were undermined by the successful management of the Senate bill, notwithstanding the defeat of Administration-supported ANWR and other provisions. With the House, OMB displayed less demanding requirements, albeit entirely focused on the interests of the oil and gas industry. "H.R. 776, as reported by the House Energy and Commerce Committee and amended by the Committee on Ways and Means," Darman wrote in his policy statement, "provides a good bipartisan basis for the development of an acceptable bill in conference." The Administration, Darman went on, "strongly supports amendments to provide relief from the alternative minimum tax for independent oil and gas producers."[161]

Watkins and Stuntz were amused by the declaration of strong administration support for the alternative minimum tax (AMT) provisions of the pending legislation. Three months earlier, Darman and Brady had told them that such support was budgetarily and politically impossible. Watkins, suspecting that his two cabinet colleagues were signaling personal predilections rather than administration policy, had sought the president's intervention. "I understand that the Administration will not advance a proposal for AMT relief for the depressed oil and gas industry," Watkins had written in February to the president. He added with barely disguised sarcasm, "Instead, Administration representatives will 'wink and nod' when others propose AMT relief. I must tell you that I think this is a serious mistake."[162] The president had agreed, dispatching a hand-written note from aboard Air Force One: "Jim—your February 27 memo was very helpful. Brady will tell [Senator] Nickles we want to correct the AMT inequity."[163]

Also on May 20, the House leadership heard from Watkins and from NRC Chairman Ivan Selin on nuclear matters. Both objected to the nuclear licensing reform provisions that had emerged from Miller's Interior and Insular Affairs Committee. Watkins declared his support for a substitute [to Miller's] amendment, crafted by Congressmen Barton and Clement, which in his view, "would ensure fair and direct access by the public in raising concerns about plant safety while providing a predictable process that is necessary for investment in new nuclear plants."[164]

House floor action on H.R. 776 commenced on the afternoon of May 20. After adopting a number of peripheral measures by voice vote, the House passed an amendment by Congressman Atkins of Massachusetts to establish performance standards for faucets, water closets and urinals, measures whose relevance to energy policy was obvious only to the sponsors. The House then defeated an amendment by Congressman Jontz of Indiana, which would have required the secretary of energy to promulgate a program of octane substitution by forcing the use of ethanol in all gasolines.

Next, and in a major victory for Watkins, the House rejected Miller's nuclear licensing provisions and adopted in their stead the Clement-Barton amendment. In its final action of the day, and in the first defeat of an administration position, the House adopted an amendment by represent-ative Markey of Massachusetts prohibiting states from using their long-established production rationing regulations for the purpose of influencing natural gas prices.[165]

The House was to take up the Rostenkowski amendment on the SPR on May 21. The issue would involve a confrontation between one of the most powerful committee chairmen in Congress and Sharp, the author of H.R. 776. Watkins dispatched a letter to Speaker Foley on the morning of May 21 indicating support for Rostenkowski's amendment. "This obligation," Watkins wrote, "is tantamount to an oil import fee and a tax on domestically produced oil and natural gas liquids. I and the President's other senior advisers would recommend that he veto any bill containing SPR provisions such as these."[166]

The House postponed consideration of the SPR issue until its very last day of deliberations on the energy bill. On May 21, it instead adopted an amendment sponsored by Dingell, reinstating a provision that had been stricken from the bill by Miller's committee to ensure federal pre-emption of state authority over siting of the Yucca Mountain nuclear waste repository. This was another major victory for Watkins and the near total defeat of Miller's effort to transform the energy bill into ill-conceived environmental legislation. By voice vote the House next rejected the special interest projects and budget authorization proposed by Brown's Science Committee.[167] The House then adjourned. It would reconvene on May 27 and complete action on the CONEPA.

The fruits of tenacity

"On Wednesday, May 27, 1992," Watkins wrote to the president after a day-long vigil, "the House completed floor action on the energy bill and approved it by a margin of 381-37. This action marks a critical milestone in the effort you launched almost three years ago to develop and implement a National Energy Strategy."[168] Watkins went on to underscore for the president key victories—some of dubious value—embodied in the House's rejection of Sharp's "Strategic Petroleum Reserve Tax" and of the majority of measures that the administration had earlier found objectionable. "We did not have the votes in the House to address sweeping Outer Continental

Shelf moratoria," Watkins confessed, "nor are we pleased with the Miller hydropower licensing provisions." The bill, he concluded, "generally vindicates your efforts to pursue this important domestic initiative."[169]

The White House reacted cautiously to the energy bill's passage. "Although pleased with the progress," the White House press secretary stated, "the President noted that the House bill needlessly locks up some of America's best prospects for domestic oil and natural gas production and restricts state pro-rationing authority. While there is much work to be done, the President believes this bill forms a welcome bipartisan basis for moving to conference [to reconcile differences with the Senate bill]"[170] The President reacted to Watkins with slightly more fervor: "Jim: Well Done !! Real Progress—thanks. GB"[171]

DOE issued a press release of its own on May 27, stating, "This achievement is in large part due to the extraordinary bipartisan leadership provided by Mr. Dingell and Mr. Lent, Mr. Sharp and Mr. Moorehead, Senator Johnson and Senator Wallop, and other dedicated members of Congress. Their efforts have been translated into sustainable, long-term policy that will positively affect every aspect of energy production, transportation and use. This quest for comprehensive energy legislation has demonstrated that complex national problems can be addressed; that government can work constructively and that the national interest can be served when the Administration and Congress share common goals."[172]

Compromise within sight

Reconciliation of the differences between the House and Senate bills would prove more arduous than expected. The conference committee representing the two chambers labored throughout the summer and fall of 1992 to construct a final legislative package capable of winning a majority of votes in both the House and Senate. Some members sought opportunities to force consideration of new measures disguised as clarifications of elements of the bills. Senator Jay Rockefeller of West Virginia sought a federal bailout of an under-funded health benefit plan for miners in his state.[173] Other senators, spearhead by Senator Bill Bradley of New Jersey, sought to reduce the AMT benefits adopted by the House.[174]

Conference committee negotiations came to an end in September. A compromise bill with the title of Energy Policy Act (EPAct) was reported back to the two chambers for final debate and vote. The House enacted the bill in late September. The Senate, after a long and bitter debate over the provision to override the state of Nevada's obstruction of the Yucca Mountain repository studies, enacted the bill with an overwhelming margin on October 8, 1992. What remained was for the president to formally sign the bill into law; normally a simple matter, but not in this case.

A POSTSCRIPT IN LAFAYETTE

EPAct became law on October 24, 1992. The setting was a makeshift stage built for the occasion and set before a drilling rig in Louisiana. On the stage were six roughnecks from the rig, enlisted as props at the last moment, and Energy Secretary Watkins. It was a warm Saturday in the Fall and it was dusk by the time the president arrived.

The remoteness of the site, the absence of national media coverage and the general lack of political attention provided to the event reminded Watkins of how well the president's domestic policy advisers had succeeded to the very end in marginalizing NES. Surprisingly, given the general disarray of the president's re-election campaign, White House political strategists had found the time to discover buried deep in EPAct a number of revenue-raising provisions that would, in the campaign's political calculus, be seen as a further violation of the president's 1988 pledge not to raise new taxes.[175] In the opinion of the campaign staff, the discovery had made the EPAct unworthy of significant presidential attention.

Watkins had forwarded proposals for a signing ceremony to the White House on October 8, indicating, "The passage of H.R. 776 is a major domestic agenda victory for the President. The Administration should make every effort to highlight this accomplishment to the American people."[176]

To that end, Watkins had recommended that the president sign the legislation in a location outside the capital with concurrent ceremonies, linked by teleconferencing, in Washington, DC, the Midwest, the oil patch and the West Coast.[177]

At the White House, in the Fall of 1992, political and policy decisions were made by former Secretary of State, now Chief of Staff James Baker. Baker had been brought to the White House by the president to take over from Samuel Skinner, who was the successor to Sununu. Sununu had been forced from office for abuse of power. Baker's White House reign was ambiguous because he had found it difficult to disengage from the State Department and, rumor had it, was unwilling to re-engage in an electoral campaign that seemed already lost. Baker had delegated day-to-day management of the White House to Robert Zoellick, his long-time aide, who in early October had received Watkins' memorandum on the signing ceremony.

Apparently, Zoellick could see no political or policy significance to EPAct, letting it be known that in the final days of the electoral campaign, the president should distance himself from the Democratic Congress and therefore from legislation enacted by it. Like his predecessors, Zoellick had not found it necessary to inform Watkins of the conclusion he had reached on EPAct, nor had he found useful to consult Watkins on alternative arrangements for the signing ceremony. Rather, word of Zoellick's thinking had reached Watkins through Henson Moore, who had left DOE in mid-1992 to briefly serve as deputy White House chief of staff.

On October 21, still without a decision as to time and place for the signing ceremony, Watkins sent a second memorandum to Zoellick. "I am astonished," he said, "to learn that the signing ceremony is being deliberately downplayed by the White House staff by limiting the attendance of Members of Congress and scheduling it at a time to receive the least amount of public attention. The amount of criticism which would result from such a low class handling of this bill would be great."[178]

Watkins' urgings proved futile. The White House set the signing ceremony for Saturday, October 24 at 5:08 pm, to conclude by 5:15 pm. The site chosen for the event, without consultations with the leadership of DOE, was an oil-drilling rig in Maurice, Louisiana, outside Lafayette.[179] Invitations to the chairmen and ranking members of the congressional committees on energy, issued late and perfunctorily, were declined by both Democratic and Republican members of Congress. The press was not briefed in advance of the event and no network media were present at the ceremony.[180]

The president arrived late, in shirt-sleeves and tieless. He bounded upon the plank platform that had been erected by the owners of the drilling rig, looked over the small local crowd of Republican faithful, pulled from his shirt pocket three-by-five cards containing his notes, and said, "The Energy Policy Act will increase domestic energy production, reduce our reliance on foreign energy sources, promote conservation and efficiency, and create American jobs. We will accomplish these goals not by resorting to the failed methods of government control, but by unleashing the genius of private enterprise."[181] The president concluded his speech by promising to "produce more of our energy here at home and import less from abroad."

Then, with Watkins at his side, he affixed his seal and made into law the Energy Policy Act of 1992.[182]

NOTES AND COMMENTS

Congressional committees and subcommittees of oversight of the statutory and programmatic responsibilities of DOE:[183]

Senate Committees

Agriculture, Nutrition and Forestry

Appropriations: Subcommittee on Energy & Water Development; Subcommittee on Interior & Related Agencies

Armed Services: Subcommittee on Strategic Forces & Nuclear Deterrence; Subcommittee on Readiness, Sustainability and Support Banking, Housing and Urban Affairs: Subcommittee on Consumer & Regulatory Affairs

Budget: Commerce, Science & Transportation: Subcommittee on Consumer; Subcommittee on Merchant Marine; Subcommittee on Science, Technology & Space; Subcommittee on National Ocean Policy

*E*nergy and Natural Resources: Subcommittee on Energy Regulation & Conservation; Subcommittee on Energy Research & Development; Subcommittee on Mineral Resources Development & Production; Subcommittee on Water & Power

Environment and Public Works: Subcommittee on Environmental Protection; Subcommittee On Nuclear Regulation; Subcommittee on Superfund, Ocean & Water Protection; Subcommittee on Toxic Substances, Environmental Oversight, Research & Development

Finance: Subcommittee on Energy & Agricultural Taxation; Subcommittee on International Debt

Foreign Affairs: Subcommittee on International Economic Policy, Trade, Oceans & Environment

Government Affairs: Subcommittee on Government Information & Regulation; Subcommittee on

Oversight of Government Management

Labor and Human Resources

Judiciary: Subcommittee on Technology & Law; Subcommittee on
Antitrust, Monopolies & Business Rights
Rules and Administration
Small Business

House Committees

Agriculture: Subcommittee on Conservation, Credit & Rural
Development; Subcommittee on Forests, Family Farms & Energy

Appropriations: Subcommittee on Energy & Water Development;
Subcommittee on Interior & Related Agencies

Armed Services: Subcommittee on Investigations; Subcommittee on
Procurement & Military Nuclear Systems; Panel on Arms Control
& Disarmament; Panel on Defense Policy; Panel on Environmental
Restoration; Panel on DOE Defense Nuclear Facilities

Banking, Finance & Urban Affairs: Subcommittee on Economic
Stabilization; Subcommittee on International Development,
Finance, Trade & Monetary Policy

Budget

District of Columbia

Energy and Commerce: Subcommittee on Commerce, Consumer
Protection & Competitiveness; Subcommittee on Energy &
Power; Subcommittee on Health & Environment; Subcommittee
on Oversight & Investigations; Subcommittee on Telecom-
munications & Finance; Subcommittee on Transportation &
Hazardous Materials; Subcommittee on U.S.-Pacific Rim Trade

Education and Labor

Foreign Affairs: Subcommittee on Arms Control, International Security
& Science; Subcommittee on International Economic Policy & Trade

Government Operations: Subcommittee on Environment, Energy &
Natural Resources; Subcommittee on Government Information,
Justice & Agriculture

Administration

Interior and Insular Affairs: Subcommittee on Energy & the
Environment; Subcommittee on General Oversight & Investiga-

tions; Subcommittee on Mining & Natural Resources; Subcommittee on Water, Power & Offshore Energy Resources

Judiciary

Merchant Marine and Fisheries: Subcommittee on Merchant Marine; Subcommittee on Fisheries and Wildlife Conservation & the environment; Subcommittee on Coast Guard & Navigation; subcommittee on Oceanography; Subcommittee on Oversight & Investigations; Subcommittee on Panama and Outer Continental Shelf

Post Office and Civil Service

Public Works and Transportation: Subcommittee on Aviation; Subcommittee on Economic Development; Subcommittee on Oversight & Investigations; Subcommittee on Surface Transportation; Subcommittee on Water Resources

Rules

Science, Space and Technology: Subcommittee on Energy Research & Development; Subcommittee on Oversight & Investigations; Subcommittee on International Scientific Cooperation; Subcommittee on Natural Resources, Agriculture Research & Environment; Subcommittee on Science, Research & Technology; Subcommittee on Space Science & Applications; Subcommittee on Transportation, Aviation & Materials

Small Business

Veterans Affairs

Ways and Means: Subcommittee on Trade; Subcommittee on Select Revenue Measures

REFERENCES

[1] See note one at end of chapter six for a complete list of committees and subcommittees having jurisdiction over DOE affairs.

[2] DOE, Compendium of Energy-Related Legislation, introduced as of February 18, 1991.

[3] Senator Gore's commitment to higher CAFE standards ended with his election to the vice presidency. During the first two years of the Clinton administration, CAFE standards, which can be raised under existing law, remained at the 27.5 miles per gallon level inherited from the Reagan and Bush administration.

[4] DOE, *Major Energy Issues Before the 101st Congress, Second Session*. Washington DC, December 1990.

[5] Ibid.

[6] Leon Panetta, a former member of Congress from California, served as director of OMB in the first Clinton term and as White House chief of staff in the second Clinton term.

[7] Ibid.

[8] Ibid.

[9] Senator Gore, one of the early proponents of legislatively fixed targets for reduction of greenhouse gases, changed his position when elected to the vice presidency, in support of achievement of stabilization of greenhouse gases by voluntary means. This position represented, in effect, the policy of the Bush administration.

[10] DOE, *Major Energy Issues*, op. cit.

[11] Ibid.

[12] The federal government had subsidized state programs for energy conservation since the Carter administration. Federal funds were also used to finance most of the states' energy offices evidence that governors have historically viewed energy policy as a federal responsibility.

[13] DOE, *Major Energy Issues*, op. cit.

[14] U.S. Senate, Committee on Energy and Natural Resources, *National Energy Security Act of 1991: Hearings on S. 341*, 102nd Congress, lst session, February 21, 1991, part 1, p. 1.

[15] U.S. Senate, Committee on Energy and Natural Resources, *History of the Committee on Energy and Natural Resources, United States Senate as of the 100th Congress, 1816-1988*. Washington DC, 1989, p. xxiii.

[16] U.S. Senate, Committee on Energy and Natural Resources, *National Energy Security Act of 1991*, op. cit., pp. 5-289.

[17] Ibid., p. 2.

[18] Ibid., p. 3.

[19] Ibid., pp. 3-4.

[20] Ibid., pp. 458-459.

[21] Ibid., p. 460.

[22] Ibid., pp. 460-461.

[23] Ibid., p. 462.

[24] Ibid., p. 465.

[25] Ibid., pp. 466-467.

[26] Ibid., p. 470.

[27] Ibid., pp. 471-472.

[28] Ibid., p. 472.

[29] Ibid., p. 477.

[30] Ibid., p. 478.

[31] Ibid., p. 483.

[32] Ibid., p. 484.

[33] Ibid., p. 485.

[34] Ibid., p. 485.

[35] Post-hearing communications from OMB and EPC staff to Stuntz and Stagliano

[36] Ibid., pp. 485-486.

[37] Ibid., p. 486.

[38] Ibid., pp. 489-490.

[39] Ibid., p. 492.

[40] Ibid., p. 538.

[41] Ibid., p. 539.

[42] U.S. Senate, Committee on Energy and Natural Resources, *National Energy Security Act of 1991: Hearings on S. 341* (Title III and Subtitles A and B of Title IV), 102nd Congress, 1st session, February 26, 1991, part 2.

[43] U.S. Senate, Committee on Energy and Natural Resources, *National Energy Security Act of 1991: Hearings on S. 341* (Subtitle C of Title IV and Section 10003 of Title X), 102nd Congress, lst session, February 26, 1991.

[44] U.S. Senate, Committee on Energy and Natural Resources, *National Energy Security Act of 1991: Hearings on S. 341* (Subtitle A of Title XI), 102nd Congress, 1st session, February 28 and March 20, 1991, part 4, p. 1.

[45] Ibid., p. 27.

[46] Ibid., pp. 28-38.

[47] U.S. Senate, Committee on Energy and Natural Resources, *National Energy Security Act of 1991: Hearings on S. 341* (Titles XII and XIII), 102nd Congress, 1st session, March 5, 1991, part 5.

[48] U.S. Senate, Committee on Energy and Natural Resources, *National Energy Security Act of 1991: Hearings on S. 341* (Sections 6003 and 6004 of Title VI and Title X), 102nd Congress, lst session, March 7, 1991,6, pp. 28-31.

[49] Ibid., pp. 28-63.

[50] Ibid., p. 109.

[51] U.S. Senate, Committee on Energy and Natural Resources, *National Energy Security Act of 1991: Hearings on S. 341* (Titles VII and VIII), 102nd Congress, lst session, March 11, 1991, part 7.

[52] U.S. Senate, Committee on Energy and Natural Resources, *National Energy Security Act of 1991: Hearings on S. 341* (Title IX), 102nd Congress, lst session, March 12, 1991, part 8, p. 1.

[53] Ibid., p. 148.

[54] Ibid., pp. 150-151.

[55] Ibid., p. 151.

[56] Ibid., p. 160.

[57] Ibid., p. 169.

[58] U.S. Senate, Committee on Energy and Natural Resources, *National Energy Security Act of 1991: Hearings on S. 341* (Title XV, March 14, 1991, part 9), (Section 5101 of Title V, March 18, 1991, part 10), (Subtitle A of Title V, March 19, 1991, part 11), (Subtitle A of Title III, March 19, 1991, part 12), (Subtitle A of Title IV, March 21, 1991, part 13) 102nd Congress, 1st session.

[59] U.S. Senate, Committee on Energy and Natural Resources, *National Security Act of 1991: Hearings on S. 341* (Appendixes to Parts 1, 2, 3 and 4, part 14), (Appendixes to Parts 5, 6 and 7, part 15), (Appendixes to Parts 8, 9, 10, 11, 12 and 13, part 16) 102nd Congress, 1st session.

[60] *Congressional Staff Directory*, 102nd Congress, Washington DC, 1991.

[61] U.S. House of Representatives, Hearings before Subcommittee on Energy and Power of the Committee on Energy and Commerce, *National Energy Strategy (Part 1)*, Serial No. 102-29, 102nd Congress, 1st session, p. 1.

[62] Ibid., p. 7.

[63] Ibid., p. 15.

[64] Ibid., p. 17.

[65] Ibid., p. 43.

[66] Ibid., pp. 99-101.

[67] Ibid., pp. 102-103.

[68] Ibid., pp. 106-107.

[69] Ibid., pp. 142-144.

[70] Ibid., pp. 157-160.

[71] Sperling served as chairman of the White House National Economic Council in the Clinton administration.

[72] Ibid., pp. 185-223.

[73] Ibid., pp. 243-250.

[74] Ibid., pp. 255-265.

[75] Ibid., p. 255.

[76] Ibid., p. 256.

[77] Ibid., p. 259.

[78] Ibid.

[79] Ibid., p. 300.

[80] Ibid., p. 304.

[81] Ibid., pp. 316-317.

[82] Ibid., p. 323.

[83] Ibid., pp. 332-425.

[84] Ibid., pp. 427-579.

[85] U.S. House of Representatives, Hearings before Subcommittee on Energy and Power of the Committee on Energy and Commerce, *National Energy Strategy (Part 3)*, Serial No. 102-59, 102nd Congress, 1st session.

[86] Internal discussions between Stuntz and Policy staff, which, during the hearings in questions, were held on a daily basis and involved, on a more or less recurrent basis, Stuntz, Stagliano, Peter Saba and Kevin Kelly.

[87] GAO, *Energy Policy: Evolution of DOE's Process for Developing a National Energy Strategy* (GAO Report to the chairman, Subcommittee on Regulation, Business Opportunities, and Energy, Committee on Small Business, House of Representatives), GAO/RCED-91-76, February 1991, p.1.

[88] Victor S. Rezendes, director, Energy Issues, Resources, Community, and Economic Development Division, GAO, Letter to Ms. Linda Stuntz, deputy undersecretary and director, Office of Policy, Planning, and Analysis, DOE, December 3, 1990.

[89] Stephen A. Wakefield, general counsel, DOE, Letter to the Honorable James F. Hinchman, general counsel, GAO, December 14, 1990.

[90] Ron Wyden, chairman, Subcommittee on Regulation, Business Opportunities, and Energy, Committee on Small Business, U.S. House of Representatives, Letter to the Honorable George Bush, president, December 7, 1990.

[91] Frederick D. McClure, assistant to the president for Legislative Affairs, the White House, Letter to the Honorable Ron Wyden, U.S. House of Representatives, December 11, 1990.

[92] W. Henson Moore, deputy secretary of energy, Letter to the Honorable Ron Wyden, chairman, Subcommittee on Regulation, Business Opportunities, and Energy, Committee on Small Business, U.S. House of Representatives, January 25, 1991.

[93] GAO, op. cit., pp. 1-2.

[94] Ron Wyden, chairman, Subcommittee on Regulation, Business Opportunities, and Energy, Committee on Small Business, U.S. House of Representatives, Letter to Admiral James D. Watkins, secretary, DOE, June 26, 1991.

[95] Ron Wyden, congressman, News from Congressman Ron Wyden, Opening Statement before the Subcommittee on Regulation, Business Opportunities & Energy, "The Debate on NES was Short-Circuited", July 8, 1991.

[96] GAO, Testimony, Full Disclosure of NES Analyses Needed to Enhance Strategy's Credibility, Statement of Judy A. England-Joseph, associate director, Energy Issues, Resources, Community and Economic Development Division, July 8, 1991.

[97] The author was the DOE witness. Use of third person in account of this testimony, and in other appearances before congressional committees, is solely for the purpose of maintaining narrative consistency.

[98] Vito A. Stagliano, associate deputy undersecretary, DOE, Testimony before the Subcommittee on Regulation, Business Opportunities, and Energy, Committee on Small Business, U.S. House of Representatives on NES development process, July 8, 1991.

[99] Howard Wolpe, chairman, Subcommittee on Investigations and Oversight, Committee on Science, Space, and Technology, U.S. House of Representatives, Letter to Linda G. Stuntz, deputy undersecretary, Office of Policy, Planning and Analysis, DOE, March 26, 1991.

[100] Howard Wolpe, chairman, Subcommittee on Investigations and Oversight, Committee on Science, Committee on Science, Space, and Technology, U.S. House of Representatives, Letters to J. Michael Davis, assistant secretary, Conservation and Renewable Energy, DOE, and Calvin A. Kent, administrator, EIA, DOE, May 6, 1991.

[101] Howard Wolpe, chairman, Subcommittee on Investigations and Oversight, Committee on Science, Space, and Technology, U.S. House of Representatives, Letter to the Honorable W. Henson Moore, deputy secretary of energy, DOE, May 6, 1991.

[102] Draft of Motion and Statement of Rep. Howard Wolpe, chairman, Subcommittee on Investigations and Oversight, Science, Space and Technology Committee, faxed from Office of the General Counsel, DOE to Paul Colborn, Office of Legal Counsel, DOJ, August 1, 1991.

[103] DOE witnesses were: EIA Administrator Calvin Kent, Deputy Undersecretary Linda Stuntz, Senior Policy Analyst Eric Petersen, Director of Economic Analysis Abraham Haspel, EIA Director of Energy Supply/Conversion Mary Hutzler, Director of Program Review Robert Marlay, and Policy Analysis Director Vito Stagliano, from U.S. House of

Representatives, Committee on Science, Space, and Technology, Hearing before the Subcommittee on Investigations and Oversight, *The National Energy Strategy* 102nd Congress, 1st session [No. 87], October 16, 1991.

[104] Howard Wolpe, chairman, Subcommittee on Investigations and Oversight, Committee on Science, Space, and Technology, U.S. House of Representatives, Letter to the Honorable James D. Watkins, secretary, DOE, October 2, 1991.

[105] DOE records of meetings between DOE staff and Keith Laughlin, special assistant to Howard Wolpe, October 7-11, 1991.

[106] U.S. House of Representatives, *The National Energy Strategy* [No. 87], op. cit., p. 2.

[107] Ibid., p. 8.

[108] Ibid., p. 91.

[109] Ibid., p. 82.

[110] Ibid., p. 224.

[111] Ibid., p. 259.

[112] Ibid., p. 242.

[113] Ibid., p. 261.

[114] U.S. Senate, Calendar No. 106, *National Energy Security Act of 1991*: Report of the Committee on Energy and Natural Resources to accompany S. 1220 together with additional and minority views, Calendar No. 106, Report 102-72, 102nd Congress, 1st Session, June 5, 1991, p. 213.

[115] The Senate bill did not reflect all of the proposals in NES enabling legislation which had been submitted by the White House, (e.g., the elimination of FERC and repeal of some moratoria on OCS leasing).

[116] U.S. Senate, Calendar No. 106, op. cit., pp. 7-8.

[117] Ibid., p. 8.

[118] Ibid., pp. 11-14.

[119] Ibid., pp. 17-39.

[120] Ibid., pp. 238-246.

[121] Ibid., pp. 246-263.

[122] Ibid., pp. 291-323.

[123] Ibid., pp. 323-337.

[124] Ibid., pp. 337-339.

[125] Ibid., pp. 354-362.

[126] Ibid., pp. 345-349.

[127] U.S. House of Representatives, *Comprehensive National Energy Policy Act*: Report of the Committee on Energy and Commerce together with additional and supplemental views

[to accompany H.R. 776], Report 102-474, Part 1, 102nd Congress, 2nd Session, March 30, 1992, pp. 153-155.

128 Ibid

129 Ibid., pp. 133-142, quote on p. 142.

130 Ibid., pp. 145-153.

131 James D. Watkins, admiral, U.S. Navy (Retired) personal communication, March 1, 1994; Linda G. Stuntz, personal communication, March 11, 1994; W. Henson Moore personal communication, March 19, 1994.

132 U.S. House of Representatives, *Comprehensive National Energy Policy Act*. Report from Mr. Brooks, from the Committee on the Judiciary [to accompany H.R. 776], Report 102-474, Part 7, 102nd Congress, 2nd Session, May 5, 1992, p. 3.

133 U.S. House of Representatives, *Comprehensive National Energy Policy Act*. Report from Mr. Miller from the Committee on Interior and Insular Affairs [to accompany H.R. 776], Report 102-474, Part 8, 102nd Congress, 2nd Session, May 5, 1992, p. 64.

134 Ibid., pp. 65-91, quote on p. 91.

135 Ibid., pp. 91-102.

136 Ibid., p. 65.

137 Ibid., pp. 244-269, quotes on pp. 252 and 253 respectively.

138 Manuel Lujan, secretary of the interior, Letter to Honorable George Miller, chairman, Committee on Interior and Insular Affairs, House of Representatives, April 7, 1992.

139 U.S. House of Representatives, *Comprehensive National Policy Act*. Report from Mr. Brown, from the Committee on Science, Space, and Technology together with dissenting views [to accompany H.R. 776], Report 102-474, Part 2, 102d Congress, 2d Session, May 1, 1992.

140 Ibid.

141 Ibid.

142 Ibid., indented paragraph and quote on pp. 201-202, respectively.

143 James D. Watkins, admiral, U.S. Navy (Retired), secretary of energy, Letter to the Honorable George E. Brown, Jr., chairman, Committee on Science, Space and Technology, U.S. House of Representatives, March 30, 1992.

144 U.S. House of Representatives, *Comprehensive National Energy Policy Act*. Report from Mr. Jones from the Committee on Merchant Marine and Fisheries, together with dissenting views [to accompany H.R. 776], Report 102-474, Part 9, 102nd Congress, 2nd Session, May 5, 1992.

145 The Committee had only one vessel in mind, built by the Japanese to transport reprocessed plutonium from France to Japan as fuel for a new generation of reactors, which the Japanese thought would decrease their reliance on insecure sources of uranium.

[146] U.S. House of Representatives, Report H.R. 102-474, Part 9, op. cit.

[147] Ibid., p. 69.

[148] James D. Watkins, admiral, U.S. Navy (Retired), secretary of energy, Letter to the Honorable Dan Rostenkowski, chairman, Committee on Ways and Means, U.S. House of Representatives, April 27, 1992; and to the Honorable Bill Archer, ranking minority member, U.S. House of Representatives, April 27, 1992.

[149] Nicholas F. Brady, secretary of treasury, Letter to the Honorable Dan Rostenkowski, chairman, Committee on Ways and Means, U.S. House of Representatives, April 28, 1992.

[150] Gregg Ward, DOE, Memorandum to: Henson Moore and Roger Porter, Subject: NES, April 29, 1992.

[151] Gregg Ward, DOE, Memorandum to: Henson Moore and Roger Porter, Subject: NES, April 30, 1992.

[152] OMB, Executive Office of the President, "Statement of Administration Policy," S. 1220 - National Energy Security Act of 1991, October 31, 1991.

[153] DOE, assistant secretary for Congressional Affairs, Intergovernmental and Public Affairs, Congressional Record Summary, No. 13, February 5, 1992.

[154] James D. Watkins, admiral, U.S. Navy (Retired), secretary of energy, Letter to the Honorable J. Bennett Johnston, chairman, Committee on Energy and Natural Resources, United States Senate, February 4, 1992; and to the Honorable Malcolm Wallop, ranking minority member, Committee on Energy and Natural Resources, United States Senate, February 4, 1992.

[155] Ibid.

[156] DOE, Congressional Record Summary, op. cit.

[157] Linda Stuntz, DOE, Memorandum to: Henson Moore and Roger Porter, Subject: Update on Today's Action on Energy Bill, February 6, 1992.

[158] Gregg Ward, DOE, Memorandum to: Henson Moore and Roger Porter, Subject: Update on Today's Action on Energy Bill, February 7, 1992.

[159] Notes of Senator George Mitchell, starting with "Mr. President, I ask unanimous consent that the only amendments remaining in order to S. 2166, with the exception of the Murkowski amendment regarding ANWR which is covered under the provisions of a separate agreement, be the following first degree amendments, that the listed first degree amendments be subject to relevant second degree amendments,"

[160] History of NES, 1 page mimeo, July 20, 1992.

[161] OMB, Executive Office of the President, "Statement of Administration Policy," H.R. 776, CONEPA, May 20, 1993.

[162] James D. Watkins, admiral, U.S. Navy (Retired), secretary of energy, Memorandum for the President, Subject: Alternative Minimum Tax (AMT), February 27, 1992.

[163] Handwritten note from the president to Jim from aboard Air Force One, signed "GB", February 28 1992.

[164] James D. Watkins, admiral, U.S. Navy (Retired), secretary of energy, Letter to the Honorable Thomas S. Foley, Speaker of the House of Representatives, May 20, 1992; and Ivan Selin, U.S. Nuclear Regulatory Commission, Letter to the Honorable John D. Dingell, chairman, Committee on Energy and Commerce, United States House of Representatives, May 20, 1992.

[165] Gregg Ward, DOE, Memorandum for: Henson Moore and Roger Porter, Subject: House Floor Action on H.R. 776, CONEPA, May 20, 1992.

[166] James D. Watkins, admiral, U.S. Navy (Retired), secretary of energy, Letter to the Honorable Thomas S. Foley, Speaker, U.S. House of Representatives, May 21, 1992.

[167] Gregg Ward, DOE, Memorandum for: Henson Moore and Roger Porter, Subject: Further House Floor Action on H.R. 776, CONEPA, May 21, 1992.

[168] James D. Watkins, admiral, U.S. Navy (Retired), secretary of energy, Memorandum for the president, Subject: House Passage of Energy Legislation, May 27, 1992.

[169] Ibid.

[170] The White Office, Office of the Press Secretary (Atlanta, Georgia), Statement by the press secretary, May 27, 1992.

[171] James D. Watkins, admiral, U.S. Navy (Retired), secretary of energy, Memorandum for the president, May 27, 1992, with a handwritten note from the president in the upper right-hand margin, dated May 28, 1992.

[172] *DOE* NEW,S For Immediate Release, N-92-029, May 27, 1992.

[173] OMB, Executive Office of the President, "Statement of Administration Policy," H.R. 776, CONEPA, July 23, 1992.

[174] United States Senate, "Dear Colleague," letter, signed by thirteen senators, June 19, 1992.

[175] Title XIX of the Energy Policy Act of 1992 contained revenue provisions designed to offset Treasury losses due to subsidies enacted in the bill. These provisions included: an increase in the per pound tax rate for ozone depleting chemicals, an increase from 20% to 30% in the rate of tax withholding for gambling winnings, an increase from 20% to 31% in the rate of tax withholding when an employee fails to furnish a taxpayer identification number, a disallowance of deductions for travel expenses when travel from home exceeds one year, authorization for use as accidental health benefits of excess assets in black lung trust funds.

[176] James D. Watkins, secretary of energy, Memorandum for Robert B. Zoellick, assistant to the president and deputy chief of staff, Subject: National Energy Legislation Signing Ceremony, with attachment, October 8, 1992.

[177] Ibid., Attachment: Proposal for Publicizing the National Energy Bill Signing Ceremony.

[178] James D. Watkins, secretary of energy, Memorandum for the Honorable Robert Zoellick, deputy chief of staff to the president, Subject: Signing Ceremony for the Energy Bill, 21 October 1992.

[179] "Signing Ceremony for the Energy Bill," White House Agenda, October 23, 1992.

[180] The author attended the ceremony and was privy to all attendant communications between the DOE and the White House.

[181] "Signing Ceremony for the Energy Bill," Op cit., "President's Remarks".

[182] Ibid.

[183] DOE, *Major Energy Issues*, op. cit., Appendix A.

EPILOGUE

The Clinton administration assumed power on January 20, 1993, swept to victory on a campaign slogan that was as clever an indictment of the Bush administration as it was misleading: "It's the economy, stupid!" The new administration was from the outset expected to be exceptionally pro-environment, not only because of the political passion that newly elected Vice President Gore would bring to energy and environmental policy, but also because the Democratic party itself had during the EPAct debate shown itself closely aligned with the environmental community. The Democrats' achievement was not lost on those willing to remember that virtually all U.S. environmental legislation of the latter half of the twentieth century had been proposed and signed into law by Republican presidents.[1]

Hazel O'Leary[2] took office as the seventh secretary of energy in late January 1993. She most recently had been an executive of a Minnesota utility, Northern States Power (now Xcel Energy). O'Leary had a long history of association with DOE and predecessor agencies. In her last post, then known as Hazel Rollins, she had led the Economic Regulatory Administration (ERA) during the Carter presidency. The ERA, functionally a part of DOE, had been responsible for enforcement of oil and gas price controls. Contrary to Watkin's vain hope, O'Leary, a lifelong Democrat, had no interest in seeing the NES as a foundation for further policy refinements. She knew from experience that in Washington's political climate, building on the other party's achievements never pays dividends.

Indeed, the Clinton administration lost no time in seeking to burnish its credentials as energy policymaker of a different breed than its immediate predecessor. In February 1993, the administration made public its intent to support an unprecedented tax on the heat content of fuels, a so-called Btu (British thermal unit) tax. The tax was intended not only to discourage consumption of fossil fuels, but, more importantly, to directly address in a way that the Bush administration had refused to do, U.S. emissions of greenhouse gases. The tax, as expected, proved unpopular.

Profoundly underestimating congressional aversion to energy taxes of any sort, the administration found itself in an early, unwanted battle with Congress, on the Democratic as well as the Republican side of the aisle. The energy industry, already in a heightened state of alert because of the recent legislative battle for EPAct, had no trouble mobilizing its members in opposition to a tax that few understood and that O'Leary herself could not satisfactorily explain. Consequently, it became obvious within a few weeks that the ambitious but inexperienced new administration was engaged in a protracted political battle it was unlikely to win. With the political costs mounting on an issue that in any case did not represent a priority on its agenda, the administration wisely decided to cut its losses and, in mid-March permanently abandoned the ill-conceived, stunningly mistimed tax proposal.

The Btu tax battle would seal the Clinton administration's brief, ill-fated activism on energy policy. His attention taken up by the social issues of his core constituency, his political capital aimed at the defeat of House Speaker Newt Gingrinch's vision of government, Clinton would for the duration of his presidency relegate energy policy to a state of benign neglect not seen since the Reagan administration. Energy policy was by default assumed by EPA, whose rulemakings on the CAAA would prove more central to the energy industry than any provision in EPAct. As for Vice President Gore, his passion for automobile fuel economy (CAFE) and for energy conservation apparently spent while in the Senate, pursued no noteworthy energy policy initiatives during the eight years of his incumbency.

There were, of course, energy issues that the administration could have addressed in a manner consistent with its ideological leanings. Coincident with the timeframe of the Clinton presidency, the United States experienced a virtual explosion of demand for trucks disguised as sport utility vehicles (SUVs), which were and remain exempt from fuel efficiency (CAFE) standards. SUVs, the most fuel inefficient consumer vehicles on the road, in the 1990s entered the national fleet in such numbers as to literally drive higher transportation oil demand.[3] To further aggravate matters, SUVs would counter-intuitively prove to be in many respects less safe than ordinary automobiles. The undesirable characteristics of SUVs should have aroused the National Highway Traffic Safety Administration (NHTSA) from its usual bureaucratic torpor, given the agency's statutory mandate to oversee automotive fuel economy and vehicle safety. The leadership of NHTSA, however, in tune with the Clinton administration's view of energy matters as peripheral to its interests, undertook no automotive safety or fuel economy rulemakings at all from 1993 to 2000.

As expected, Vice President Gore retained control of climate change policy throughout the Clinton administration. Notably, he was instrumental in making it possible for the United Nations to conclude what came to be known as the 1998 Kyoto Protocol. The protocol, drafted literally in the dead of night after lengthy and arduous negotiations, aimed to punish U.S. behavior on climate change, as well as excuse the majority of the world's countries from any obligation to comply with its terms. The protocol might not have been signed at all by the United States or other countries, except for a dramatic eleventh hour appearance by Gore at Kyoto in response to pointed criticism of the administration by the otherwise friendly environmental community. Because of its irrational compliance deadlines, the Kyoto Protocol would have been exceptionally costly to implement and, perhaps because Gore could not defend it, it was never submitted to Congress for ratification.

Alternative transportation fuels, regarded by EPAct's architects as an important instrument of oil displacement policy, were also neglected by the administration. Initially responsive to EPAct provisions requiring large-scale purchases of alternative fuel vehicles for the federal fleet[4], the administration could not subsequently find the will to issue rules requiring owners of largest fleets—the private ones—to comply with the statute. Finally, in January 2000, eight years after EPAct's enactment, the administration published a notice in the Federal Register indefinitely postponing the issuance of regulations by which Congress had intended to literally transform the U.S. transportation sector.[5]

The EPAct-inspired reforms of the electric power sector were carried out by FERC in 1996 with issuance of Order 888, which set the stage for non-discriminatory open access to the transmission grid by all market participants. The order was followed in December 1999 by Order 2000, which called for voluntary creation of regional transmission organizations (RTOs) to assume control of the interstate transmission grid and operate it independently of the wires' owners. The consequences of both Order 888 and Order 2000 remained inconclusive to the end of 2000, engendering highly divergent though generally uneconomic results in different regions of the nation.

California would experience the worst results of electric sector reform. The state, which was the first in the nation to restructure its electric industry, in 1997, committed with FERC assent to a profoundly flawed market model that failed utterly in its aim to promote competition and lower consumer costs of power. The California experiment drove the state's investor-owned utilities to the verge of bankruptcy and saddled the state's taxpayers with restructuring costs in excess of $20 billion. Other RTOs—in New England, New York, the Midwest, and Mid-Atlantic states—would prove more or less workable and somewhat less costly than California's. In all cases, however, the economic benefits that in the NES were forecast to accrue from reform of the industry remained largely unrealized at the turn of the millennium.

Meeting the future

Neglect of policy has consequences. During the Clinton administration, in the absence of policy intervention the petroleum market evolved in the direction that NES and EPAct had intended to prevent. As predicted by NES forecasters, U.S. oil consumption rose from 17 MMB/D in 1990 to nearly 20 MMB/D in 2000. During the same period, domestic oil production fell from 7.3 MMB/D to 5.8 MMB/D. U.S. oil imports rose from about 8 MMB/D in 1990 to nearly 9 MMB/D in 2000. Most critically, imports from members of OPEC, the only producers with excess capacity, rose from 4 MMB/D to 5 MMB/D in the same period.[6]

With oil demand increasing in the United States and throughout the industrialized world and production essentially flat in all producing regions except the Persian Gulf, the members of OPEC in 1999 once again took control of the international oil market. They succeeded in doing so by finding the will that had eluded them for two decades: they disciplined their output and, at greater risk to consumers, actually matched supply to demand. OPEC oil supply, which in 1990 represented about thirty-five percent of world oil production, rose to forty-two percent of world production in 2000. This rise in market share essentially guaranteed, and continues to ensure, the ability of OPEC members to extract from consuming nations rents well above the market price of oil.[7] The consequence of OPEC market control became most evident in the spring and summer of 2000 when, at over $35 per barrel, crude oil prices reached and sustained levels not seen since the Iraqi war.

The Clinton administration reacted to OPEC's newly achieved control of the oil market by doing the only thing it could—send its latest secretary of energy, Bill Richardson, to the Persian Gulf, hat in hand, to beg for relief from the king of Saudi Arabia. While awaiting Saudi largess, which came, as usual, in the form of promises to raise production by inconsequential volumes, the administration was also managing the political calculus of the 2000 electoral campaign. True to historical form, pressure arose from the Northeast political establishment, which by now included New York senatorial candidate (and First Lady) Hillary Rodham Clinton, to mitigate sharply higher price of winter fuels. In response, the president ordered a release of oil from the SPR for the first time in history not in order to redress a supply disruption in the international petroleum market, but in order to moderate the domestic price of heating oil.

For governments in Europe and the United States, a resurgent OPEC came as something of a surprise, given the prevailing wisdom of the 1990s that cartels could not sustain market control over the long term. The analysts, however, had said nothing about a cartel's ability to retain control of a market in the short term and, in that short term, inflict economic damage of significant proportions. Indeed, the OPEC-induced sharply higher oil prices of 2000, combined with exceptional prices for natural gas, slowed the U.S. economy to a crawl for the first time in eight years, with the risk of nudging it into a recession. The predictable part of the oil market's evolution to the year 2000, fully documented in NES, was U.S. failure to increase domestic production or to decrease demand, especially in the transportation sector or, for optimal results, to do both. The Clinton administration had done neither.

Sic Transit Gloria

The cycle of crises in the oil sector seems immune to change. U.S. oil policy, however prudent or radical, seems either ineffectual or unsustainable. The downward slide in U.S. oil production seems irreversible. The rise in demand for oil in U.S. transportation seems unstoppable. The oil policy of industrialized nations in Europe and Asia, based almost entirely on high taxation of fuels, seems no more effective than does U.S. policy in shaping long-term production and consumption trends. OPEC's dominant role in the international oil market and frequent control of it seems immutable, as does the role of Saudi Arabia.

Yet, as a new Bush administration took power in Washington, in January 2001, word once again went forth from the White House that the nation will have—must have—a new energy policy. History, a wise French philosopher once said, never repeats itself, people always do.

REFERENCES

[1] The environmental legislative record of Republican presidents includes: the Clean Air Act, the Clean Water Act, Resource Conservation and Recovery Act (RCRA), Comprehensive Environmental and Resource Conservation Liability Act (CERCLA) and others.

[2] O'Leary served as DOE secretary during the entire Clinton first term. She was succeeded by Federico Peña, who served from 1997 to 1998. Peña was succeeded by Bill Richardson, who served to the end of the Clinton second term.

[1] The environmental legislative record of Republican presidents includes: the Clean Air Act, the Clean Water Act, Resource Conservation and Recovery Act (RCRA), Comprehensive Environmental and Resource Conservation Liability Act (CERCLA) and others.

[2] O'Leary served as DOE secretary during the entire Clinton first term. She was succeeded by Federico Peña, who served from 1997 to 1998. Peña was succeeded by Bill Richardson, who served to the end of the Clinton second term.

[3] EIA: Annual Energy Review 2000.

[4] President Clinton issued an executive order requiring that federal vehicle fleets comply with the alternative fuels requirements of EPAct on December 13, 1996: Executive Order 12844. As a consequence, the federal vehicle fleet comprised 35,000 alternative fuel vehicles in 2000, according to statistics provided by David Rodgers of DOE's Office of Energy Efficiency and Renewable energy.

[5] DOE, Office of Energy Efficiency and Renewable Energy, 10 CFR Part 490, Docket No. EE-RM-99-507, "Alternative Fuel Transportation Program; Requirements for Private and Local Government Fleets," Action: Advance Notice of Proposed Rulemaking; extension of deadline. January 12, 2000.

[6] EIA: Petroleum Supply Monthly, January 2001, and Annual Energy Review 2000.

[7] EIA: Annual Energy Review 2000

INDEX

C

D

Darman, Richard, 85-86
Deal, Timothy, 284
Decision-making framework, 290-291
Demilitarization (nuclear power), 5-6
Department of Energy Organization Act, 48-49, 88
Deregulation, 23, 30, 45, 118, 161, 318, 323, 326
Desert Storm, 282
Deutch, John, 42
Developing countries, 41, 140, 187-189
Disagreements narrowed, 322-325
DOE's role (oil embargo 1990), 210-213
Domestic policy, 46-48, 86, 142
Domestic Policy Council, 86
Domestic production, 293
Drawdowns (SPR), 211, 221-235, 239-241, 244-258, 430
Dundan, Charles, 42

E

Easton, John, 258-264
Economic costs/benefits, 155-156
Economic Policy Council (EPC), 59-60, 96-98, 103-106, 137-204, 215, 219-220, 233-234, 243, 282, 299-304, 309-311, 314-317: Working Group on NES, 96-98, 103-106, 173-174; disagreement (NES interim report), 105-106; public hearing record, 138-143; policy options, 138-143; Troika agencies, 138-143; Troika agencies' control, 144-157; unified policy sought, 157-174; inter-laboratory white papers, 174-189; central intelligence advice, 189-192; notes/comments, 193-198; deliber-ations, 299-304; meetings, 299-304, 309-311, 314-317

Economic Policy Council deliberations, 299-304: January meeting, 300-303; November meeting, 303-304. SEE ALSO Energy security options.
Economic Policy Council Working Group on NES, 96-98, 103-106, 173-174, 282
Economic Regulatory Administration, 46-47, 426
Economic Stabilization Act, 28
Education, 129, 157-158, 298-299
Edwards, James, 46
Efficiency standards, 28-29, 157, 325
Eisenhower, Dwight D., 10-14: oil imports control, 10-14; other policies, 13-14
Electric Power Research Institute, 128, 327
Electric utility industry, 294
Electricity, x, 16, 20, 119-122, 146, 150-151, 153, 159, 164-169, 194, 287, 294-296, 313, 353, 370: policy, 164-169, 194, 313, 353, 370; market, 294-296
Electricity market, 294-296
Electricity policy, 164-169, 194, 313, 353, 370
Electricity Working Group, 150-151
Embargo (1973), xi, xiii, 19-30
Embargo (1977-1978), 34, 39
Embargo (1990), 206-226: DOE's role, 210-213
Emergency authority (Nixon), 25
Emerging technology, 141
Emissions control, 152-153, 176-179, 296-298, 300-301
Energy as enemy within, 397-398
Energy bureaucracy, 2-4
Energy Conservation and Production Act of 1976 (ECPA), 30-31
Energy conservation. SEE Conservation.

K

Kennedy, John F., 15-19: nuclear power vs. fossil fuels, 15-19
Korean War, 6, 8
Krug synfuel program, 8-9
Kuwait, 15, 206-280, 282, 308, 312
Kyoto Protocol (1998), 428

L

Laissez faire approach (Reagan), 43-46
Lake Erie, xi
Land reclamation, 23
Lantzke, Ulf, 226-227
Lawrence Berkeley Laboratory, 47
Lawrence Livermore Laboratory, 47, 177
Leadership in Congress, 402-408: U.S. Senate, 403-404; U.S. House of Representatives, 404-406; fruits of tenacity, 406-407; compromise within sight, 407-408
Leadership role, 140
Less developed countries, 306
Lifting costs, 45
Light water reactors, 18
Liquid petroleum gas, 91
Los Alamos Laboratory, 47, 185
Louisiana (EPAct enactment), 408-410
Lovins, Amory, 32

M

Magnetic levitation (maglev), 311
Magnetohydrodynamic technology, 21
Major producing companies, 256
Mandatory quotas (oil imports), 10-14, 21
Manhattan Project, 24, 47

Market efficiency, 293-296
Market strategy, 146
Martin, William, 57
Means to ends (energy security), 305-308
Melby, Eric, 87-88, 319-320
Methanol, 90, 125, 307
Mexico, 163, 305-306
Mid-Atlantic coast offshore, 160
Miller, George, 397-398
Monopsony price effects, 308
Moore, W. Henson, 76-80, 127, 191-192, 194, 210-211, 213-214, 246-247, 290
Moral equivalent of war (Carter), 31-43
Morgantown Energy Technology Center, 47
Motor Vehicle Fuel Efficiency Act, 241

N

National Academy of Science, 31, 163
National Aeronautics and Space Administration, 21, 48, 185
National Energy Act of 1978, 37-38
National Energy Conservation Policy Act of 1978 (NECPA), 37
National Energy Modeling System, 94
National Energy Policy Plan, 9, 33-37, 40-43, 48-54, 88, 315: first, 33-37, 48-50, 315; second, 40-43, 51-52; third, 52-54
National Energy Security Act of 1991, 236, 357, 379, 389-394, 402-404
National Energy Strategy (NES), xiv-xv, 9, 83, 85-88, 93-99, 102-107, 111, 115, 149-153, 218-219, 247, 269, 281-350: Development Committee, 93; interim report, 102-106; public hearing record, 111; options of discord, 282-289; framework for decisions, 290-291; framework for consideration of options, 292-299; Working Group, 297; EPC deliberations,

O

P

R

Sulfur dioxide, 296

Sulfur oxide control technology, 20

Sum of parts (National Energy Strategy), 333-337

Sununu, John, 79, 85, 145-149, 282, 302, 314-315, 326-329, 331

Supply measures, 216-217

Surface Mining and Reclamation Act, 29

Survey (technology transfer at DOE labs), 185-187

Synthetic fuel (synfuel), 5, 8, 29, 42, 46, 49-50, 52, 174

Synthetic Fuels Corporation, 42, 46, 49-50, 52, 245, 315

Synthetic Liquid Fuels Act of 1944, 8

T

Tariff (imports), 28-29

Tax credits, 302

Tax incentives, 38, 41, 157, 162, 169, 220, 268-269, 286, 293, 302, 319, 324, 330-331, 354-355, 366, 395

Technology diversity, 295-296

Technology transfer, 95, 128-129, 146, 173, 183-189, 194-195, 198, 298-299: white paper, 183-189; process, 185; DOE laboratories, 185-187; developing countries, 187-189, 198

Technology transfer for developing countries, 187-189, 198

Technology transfer white paper, 183-189

Tennessee Valley Authority, 2-3, 166, 295

Terms-of-trade effects, 308

Test drawdown (SPR), 250-252

Texas Railroad Commission, 24-25

Trade Agreement Extension Act of 1955, 11

Transportation energy use, 109-110

Transportation fuels, 109-110, 146, 157, 162-163, 307, 311, 428

Transportation technology, 311

Trends (U.S. energy economy), 107-108

Troika agencies, 59, 82, 100-101, 138-157, 173-174, 219-220, 222, 226, 243, 282-283, 289, 302, 310-311, 314-315, 363, 386: policy control, 144-157, 219-220, 222, 226, 243, 282-283, 289, 302, 310-311, 314-315, 363, 386; options, 173-174

Troika agencies policy control, 144-157, 219-220, 222, 226, 243, 282-283, 289, 302, 310-311, 314-315, 363, 386

Truman, Harry S., 2-4

Twentieth Century Fund, 32

U

U.S. Bureau of Mines, 9

U.S. Bureau of Reclamation, 15

U.S. Congress, 236-248, 351-424: U.S. House of Representatives, 239-242, 246-248; joint session of Congress, 242-243; U.S. Senate, 243-246; Congressional committees, 352-356; bipartisanship in U.S. Senate, 356-371; Sharp hearings, 371-379; political dimensions of policymaking, 379-388; competing bills, 389-396; other views, 396-402; by persuasive margin, 402-408; Louisiana enactment (EPAct), 408-410; notes/comments, 411-413

U.S. Department of Commerce, 22, 286

U.S. Department of Energy (DOE), 30, 38-39, 46-49, 58, 70-136, 174-189, 210-213, 282-283, 292-294, 299-319, 325-326: oil embargo (1990), 210-213

U.S. Department of Health and Human Services, 98

Dedication

This book is dedicated to Jesus, the first Wounded Warrior who broke the glittering-image barrier by choosing to relinquish His crown for thorns. And to all you wounded warriors who want all that Jesus has for you—it's time to find your shine. *Rock on!*

I also give a special appreciation to all those who contributed to this with your words of encouragement, wisdom and validation. You know who you are!

Table of Contents

Preface

This book is not a Christian self-help book. Goodness, I think we have enough of *Five Ways to Break Through*, *Three Keys to Prosperous Living*, or *Seven Ways to Open Heaven*. This book is about the joy of discovering who we are created to be, our true identity for which each individual has a personal process. There are no specific steps. But there is a path, a unique one designed for each of us. Mine took me through experiences I would only eventually look back on and realize they were all a part of the piece of the puzzle to define me. My entire journey was orchestrated by a loving God to bring me into the full realization of who I was.

Seriously, beloved, self-help and following Jesus are, well, two polar opposites. Didn't Jesus say, "Come to me, all you who are weary and burdened, and I will give you rest"? "For my yoke is easy and my burden is light"? "It is more blessed to give than to receive"? "Forgive and you will be forgiven"?

That's pretty straightforward stuff, right? Why do we complicate following Jesus? It is really simple. Accept Him as Lord and Savior, and He will give you the desires of your heart!

OK, sounds simple, but it's not easy. I hear you.

What does this "Lord and Savior" thing actually mean? Lord of what? Savior from what? Or whom?

I have done a pretty amazing job making a mess of my life, with all my failed good deeds and bad choices. You want to be Lord of *this* life? It is all yours—on a silver platter. (Where is that silver platter by the way, and the silver spoon in my mouth? Probably gave them up in some effort to be sacrificial or something.)

So I gave it to Him, good, bad, and ugly, forty years ago. I was twenty-eight, a mother of two, and thinking I wasn't doing so well at life. I asked Him to save me. He did. But I still had a mess to clean up. It would be many years before I would actually get the desires of my heart. God is like that. *Patient*. And *good*. And *kind*. And *loving*. And He finishes what He starts.

He saved me from hell, and as best I could, I gave Him control of my out-of-control life. What did I have to lose? He assured me I was free. If I decided to turn away from Him, that was my choice. There was no stronghold on me, no threats, just a call to trust Him. It was all up to me how much I received and acted upon. Sounds fair enough, right?

Well, fair may not be the operative word, because much of my journey did not feel fair. But unwrapping Jesus caused me to unwrap myself, and I discovered the shine that was already there, covered in all that stuff called life.

I invite you into my life, where it has been messy and painful and always purposeful. My hope is that you will see a piece of your journey here and no longer feel alone. Or maybe you will discover a path to your identity that you haven't explored. In either case, there is always hope.

You are important. You have a purpose. Your identity matters.

Introduction

Glittering images.

The words constantly interrupted my thoughts. What was it that God was trying to tell me?

I knew it was at the core of my pursuit to find words for the deep, visceral understanding of true identity that was struggling to surface.

Glittering images.

A glittering image is the direct antithesis to true identity. I realized my life had too often been a pursuit of glittering images rather than my true identity. Self-help and pulling myself up by my bootstraps hadn't done it, because I still didn't know who I was.

I love glitz and glitter. I love to sparkle. I like dangly earrings and shiny necklaces. God loves to show me off. He likes my style. But nothing is more attractive to Him than that inner glow of Himself reflected through me.

The glittering images had to go.

As believers in Christ, we are meant to look in the mirror each day and see Christ. Each of us carries the identity of Jesus—we are a chip off the old block. And we each have a unique inheritance, or birthright, that defines us individually. Unfortunately, we often prefer someone else's birthright to our own, their glittering images to our own true destinies, and we may fall prey to being an appearance of the real thing.

When I attempted to be something I was not, by putting on a glittering image of what I thought was attractive and desirable, I lost myself. What I was looking for was intimacy, the kind where I am known and loved anyway, which wasn't possible until I was ready to shed the glittering image and let the true me shine through.

No more, I cried out to God one morning. *I am finished. No matter what, I will allow the true identity of who you saw at that moment of creation when you said, "Let there be Angela," and you looked at me and said, "This is good."*

So I decided to shed the glittering image I was wearing and set out to embrace who I really was. I have not looked back, except in gratitude.

I will daily seek to receive your lens, God, not only for seeing myself truly as I am but seeing others as you see them. It is a solemn journey that I anticipate with great joy.

He Knows My Name

Chapter 1

The Vision

Before I formed you in the womb, I knew you.
—Jeremiah 1:5

It was 4:00 a.m. I drowsily came out of a semicomatose sleep. Immediately I had a vivid picture in the window of my mind. I became aware of a young baby girl, about nine months old, sitting on a cold cement floor in a gray cell-like room. She was staring up at a small unreachable opening that reflected a beam of light onto her beautiful blond hair.

God was up to something.

I had dropped into bed several hours earlier in a desperate state of pain, feeling frozen in hopeless despair. It was a new year, I was sixty-seven, and it felt like my life was fading into the shadow of death. I spent the winter fighting with, and struggling to find, peace in the midst of a personal perfect storm—loss, rejection, and fear of death. My blood pressure had soared due to anxiety about my health. I could barely walk from a debilitating case of plantar fasciitis. A ten-year struggle with one of my daughters had elevated into complete rejection.

Yes, a perfect storm.

In desperation, I had prayed a nighttime prayer I had written for a spiritual daughter earlier that month.

I thank you, Father, for you are a good, good Father. Thank you for this time of rest for my soul. I submit myself—body, soul, and spirit—to you, Holy Spirit. Have your way with me. Infiltrate and fill the unhealed parts with your healing balm, and manifest your healing ways in me while I rest in your love. Cause my soul to rest while you restore the cracked parts of my spirit, the parts that feel splintered and lost. I trust you to put me back together into complete wholeness, and I thank you that you will do this even when I don't have a clue what you are doing. You are a good, good Father. Thank you for covering me in your protective wings and guarding my heart from any further wounding. I rejoice in what you are doing, and I thank you for your loving kindness.

Was this my answer, this vision?

I lay still, puzzling over this rather familiar-looking child. I whispered, "God, what is it I am seeing?" My answer came in the form of a shadowy image that I intuitively knew was Jesus. I looked toward him, expecting He might have the answer to my question. Again, with great curiosity mixed with a bit of anxiety, I queried, "Who is this?"

The unloved one, He responded.

What do you mean? How is she the unloved one? My gut tightened, anticipating a response I wasn't sure I was ready for.

She does not know love. She has been forgotten and left here. She is in great need of love.

He paused, and I continued to view this little one, not understanding how this precious child could be unloved.

Would you love her?

I couldn't say no. In fact, I was quickly overwhelmed with the desire to hold this baby and pour into her everything I had in me that even resembled love. It was a deep and emotional love for this little one that was rising up in me, like she was one of my own, only…more.

Of course, I exclaimed in the quiet of my mind, barely hesitating. *I will.*

Jesus picked up the little one and walked toward me to hand me the cherub. I wrapped my arms around her and pulled her into me, crushing her to my chest. As I stared into her angelic, chubby-cheeked face, tears poured down my cheeks. I remembered my daughter's face when her first child was born, how she looked at him like she had just fallen in love for the first time. I fell in love with this beautiful child.

Through my tears, words overwhelmed me. Out loud, in the darkness of my bedroom, I broke the silence with sobs of joy and exclaimed, "You are so, *so* beautiful. Oh my goodness, you are so beautiful, so precious. Oh how I love you." Over and over again I poured into this little one all the love I had in me. I could feel her soft skin against my cheek, her smell of sweetness, as I looked into her pale-blue eyes. Quite clearly, I soon realized, my love capacity depleted, and I moved into an out-of-body love that began to flow from within. I was overwhelmed with joyful tears and held her so tight I might have crushed the life out of her.

After a while, I found my breath and looked at Jesus with another question. *How is it she is so without love?*

Jesus explained that she had been born into a home where love did not come easily. Her parents were incapable of loving her the way she needed, so broken were they from their own painful lives.

Instantly, I thought of my two parents, and shock and awe had no comparison to what my heart was feeling. I was aghast with a dismay that contradicted what I felt for this baby.

"Is this me, Jesus?" I stuttered.

Yes, my child.

"That was *my* birth. Those are *my* parents." The picture was becoming clearer now.

Yes was His simple reply.

I paused to take it all in. I felt anger rise up, and without being able to stop it, I demanded, "Why, Lord? Why would you place me into a loveless home? It doesn't make sense! I have spent my whole life trying to find the love I didn't get, and here I find out you intentionally placed me where that would be impossible!"

I was indignant, somewhat in shock. I knew God to be one who is kind and loving and who meets our needs. How could this possibly be true? I wanted to be loved, and I wanted to love, and it had been so difficult because I'd had no idea what that really looked like. Even after I found Jesus, I had failed over and over again.

With the kindest and most loving voice, I heard Jesus say, **How else could I have shown you to love like me? I created you to be my vessel of love, a full expression of my love on the earth. There was nowhere for you to learn that with these parents I gave you. And yet here you are, living proof that my love is bigger than any lack you could come up against. Even though your love was often unrequited and more often abused and rejected over and over again, yet here you are, still full of enough love for this little unloved one. That is the power of *my* love. When I give good gifts, I don't ever take them away.**

By now the waterworks were beyond control. I was glad my husband was out of sight and hearing.

My whole life played out before me— all the men I'd loved, the children I loved, the friends I'd loved and lost, the people I'd poured into, the churches where I had searched for a spiritual home, often unrequited. I was an endless stream of love poured out and often rejected. I was always getting up again and again, to try once more.

Here, after following Jesus for almost forty years, He showed me my true self, the one He originally designed and had Himself fallen in love with before I was conceived. Only a God of love could take control of my life and then give it back to me in such a glorious way.

Earlier that week my friend had said to me, "You need to love yourself." Those are words you hear a lot in Christian circles. It is the second commandment after all: "Love your neighbor as yourself." So that means you need to love yourself first. I had no idea what that looked like. When you grow up in a narcissistic, alcoholic home, how can you possibly know what that looks like or how to do that? What does love feel like, look like, act like?

14

Jesus. Yes. And He is God, so good luck with that. I had my work cut out for me.

That early morning, I experienced a firsthand revelation of the kind of love Jesus is, and I got to love *me*, with that love. Jesus's love poured through me. I did. I fell in love with me, all of me, the good, the bad, and the ugly. And the honeymoon isn't ending anytime soon.

Who I discovered made all the difference.

Declaration and blessing: I call forth over each of you the fullness of knowing the love that is in you from your Father in heaven, and the infinite joy of knowing that love for yourself. You are a treasure right out of heaven, and I declare that no matter your family circumstances or the conditions of your birth, you are meant to be here, and God is saying, **"You are good!"**

Chapter 2

A New Name

Don't be afraid, I've redeemed you. I've called your name. You're mine.
　　　　—Isaiah 43:1 (The Message)

Just as the vision was fading and I felt ready to go back to sleep, exhausted from the tears, Jesus said, **By the way, your name is not the one I gave you in heaven.**

My response was mixed. I knew that I was named for an aunt, my father's sister, who had died of a childhood disease when she was about twelve. I often wondered what kind of a legacy I had been given, as the decision seemed to be one of pleasing my grandfather. That, and my doctor intimating that I was at risk for a heart attack that year based on family history, all could have contributed to the death grip I was feeling over my life. Needless to say, I did not have an emotional attachment to my birth name. I often contemplated changing my name, more so lately since my father's passing.

Jesus's words intrigued me. It made sense that we have a name in heaven before we are born. Jeremiah 1:5 says, "Before I formed you in the womb I knew you; before you were born I sanctified you." Of course we would have a name. I just never expected to know it this side of heaven.

I looked at Jesus, acknowledging that I wanted to know His name for me.

I called you Angela, He said.

He knew my heart's yearning! I could feel His joyful smile.

My spirit leaped. I was overwhelmed with joy. A new name to go with my newfound love for myself...that was just such a bonus! I *loved* the name Angela and immediately tacked on *Joy* because that is exactly how I felt. I am Angela Joy. I am a new creation. He knew me before I was ever conceived, and He said, "This is *good*!"

The impact of hearing Jesus tell me my true name was beyond words. Eventually, I started using the new name when I introduced myself, and the response was so encouraging. Some people's eyes would light up with agreement. "That is *so you*!"

Names are an important part of our identities. Parents-to-be often pore over books looking for just the perfect name for their future son or daughter. The name has to feel just right, and the final pronouncement may not happen until the child is born. It has to be perfect. That heart comes straight from God.

God is intentional about names. Adam's first assignment in the garden was to name all the animals, and God invited him to join Him in the process.

Many of the names in the Old Testament were chosen because they defined the character of the person, beginning with Adam and Eve. *Adam* means *earth*, as he was created from the earth. *Eve* means *life*, as she was the one through whom life would flow.

Then they gave birth to the brothers, Cain and Abel. *Cain* means *spear*. *Abel* means *breath*. Which one killed the other? Cain speared the breath out of Abel.

The story of Nabal in 1 Samuel 25 is an interesting play on name meaning. Nabal was a rebellious rich man. When asked, he refused David the favor for his men. He didn't want to part with his possessions. David was ready to go to war against him, but Nabal's wife, Abigail, stepped in and begged for mercy for her husband. She brought an offering beyond what David had asked for. David relented and sent her home, releasing Nabal from certain death. She referred to Nabal as a fool, which was what Nabal means. When Abigail returned to her husband, she found him drunk, and ten days later, God struck him dead. Fool indeed!

Sometimes God changed people's names to go along with their new identities.

Abraham's name at birth was Abram. Abram means "high father." Later, when God made a covenant with Abram, He said, "No longer shall your name be called Abram, but your name shall be Abraham; for I have made you the father of a multitude of nations" (Genesis 17:5). To this day he is known to the world as Father Abraham. He became the father of a multitude of nations, definitely an upgrade in identity.

Jacob was a liar and a deceiver in his youth. He manipulated to steal his older brother's (Esau's) birthright so he could get the blessings that belonged to the firstborn. *Jacob* means *supplanter*, which is defined as to *trip up or to overthrow.* After he wrestled with God and reconciled with Esau, his name was changed to Israel: "For you have striven with God and with men and have prevailed" (Genesis 32:28).

In the New Testament, we have Peter, one of the first disciples Jesus called. His given name was Simon, which means *he has heard.* Then, in a conversation about Jesus's identity, Jesus asked, "Who do you say that I am?" Simon declared, "You are the Christ, the son of the living God" (John 11:27). With that Jesus said, "You shall be called Cephas" (*Peter* in Greek), which means *stone* or *pebble.* Peter became part of the foundation of the Christianity we now experience.

Needless to say, when God so beautifully blessed me that night with my name in heaven, and I took that name on as my true name, it definitely felt like a Damascus experience. However, it is important to understand that I do not have something unique. Everyone has a name in heaven. Some of you have been so blessed to have parents who actually prayed and asked God what your name should be. Others, like me, have an opportunity to find out sixty-seven years later.

You may remember Zacharias and Elizabeth, the parents of John the Baptist. The custom was to name the firstborn with the father's name. However, the angel Gabriel had already told Zacharias that this child was to be called John. So at John's circumcision, the pressure was on to name this child Zacharias, which means *priest*, and therefore his son would follow in his father's footsteps. We know that John had a different call on his life, and God make that clear when he gave him a different name than tradition prescribed. Zacharias obeyed God and named him John, which means, *Yahweh is gracious*.

In all of these name changes, there is an identity change or declaration of identity. Abraham got an upgrade to Father of Nations; Jacob became Israel, the Land of the Fathers; John would not just be a priest but would usher in the High Priest, Jesus; Peter became a stone that would be part of the cornerstone of the kingdom of God on earth.

But the name above all names, the name that carries power over all tradition, is the name of Jesus. Jesus tells us in John 14:13–14, "For I will do whatever you ask me to do when you ask me *in my name*; ask me anything *in my name* and I will do it for you." Jesus knew the power of a name. A name carries a legacy, an identity, a birthright. It declares how God sees you.

Jesus's name too was declared in the heavens before He entered Mary's womb. "And at the end of eight days, when he was circumcised, he was called Jesus, the name given by the angel before he was conceived in the womb" (Luke 2:21).

Angela means *messenger of God*. Jesus let me know that morning that He entrusted me to be His messenger. It was a weighty call, and I knew that it needed to be done with joy. From the time I took that name into the world, declaring "I am Angela," my spirit rose with a resounding affirmation. I knew that when I spoke, God wanted to speak through me. I made a point to pay attention to what I spoke and the tone I used. My heart demanded my words to be spoken in love and kindness; anything less would besmirch the name and the message of God Himself. It was an upgrade that I knew I was to step up into.

Declaration and blessing: He knows your name. Listen for Him to speak it to you. Whether in the quiet chamber of intimacy with Him or in the public arena of declaration, we are all His messengers, carrying His name. We are His, and as the church is Christ's bride, we will one day be fully sons and daughters of God.

Chapter 3

The Journey Begins

I am, I said.
—Neil Diamond

Let's go back for a moment to 1975. Imagine a hot August night. I stand in my living room, looking out the picture window, pretend microphone in hand, singing along with Neil Diamond's epic song, "I am, I said." With each word, I feel the cry of my heart. Someone please hear me! Someone please see me! I do feel lost, and I do not know why.

My spirit rose up with determination. I was a survivor. I believe that love can change anything. Maybe it will change this man, this marriage, and I can have the dream I always wanted.

It was in that longing I would find Jesus. Well, at least I finally answered the door He had been knocking on. Again, He saw my need and negotiated me into a place where I could no longer ignore his call. He can be sneaky, and I love that about Him.

At the time I was in the clutches of a seventies cult that was my church of sorts—the one where they locked you in their rented spaces for a weekend and told you that you were god and everything in you was good. They programmed you to think you could have anything your mind thinks, which actually was a Bible verse—"For as he thinks in his heart, so is he" (Proverbs 23:7). It made sense. The leader was a preacher's kid (PK). He told me I had the power!

Right!

This group took us to the top of a mountain and asked us to sign our lives over to them, one mind at a time. Mind control.

When your life is out of control, don't you look for some sort of control? The mantra was that if you just knew that you were god, everything would be amazing. The world would be your oyster, and you could create anything your mind could conceive of. "You are a child of the universe, no less than the trees and the stars; you have a right to be here" is taken from their psalm of truth ("Desiderata," by Max Ehrmann, 1927).

I experienced a sense of belonging I had not known. It felt like home. I was ecstatic at being among seemingly like-minded people who were shining the light of some obscure truth into me and my pathetic world. It was a different kind of an addiction. We learned meditation, but only by opening our minds to whatever in the universe was looking for a home. We turned our money over to the leader, and our women turned their lives over to their husbands—that was happiness. We learned from Marabel Morgan's book, *The Total Woman*, that it was actually possible to bring home the bacon, fry it up in a pan, and let him know he was a man. That is how you became the eight-cow wife.

What is the true definition of a cult? Remove my will so I can succumb to yours. Control. It was an issue I would address over and over again. It was not an easy jump. My life was out of control. So jump I did.

Why? The world I grew up in was not beautiful and peaceful. My mother buried her poor self-esteem in alcohol, while Dad went about proving his manhood by feeding his narcissism with his charmed success in the world of sales. I was left to fend for myself, and I buried my head in the sand when I would come home and find Mom passed out on the bathroom floor. I wanted to run. I felt lost and unlovable, sure I did not belong anywhere.

At the time I discovered the cult, I was newly married to my first husband, and he was pushing the sexual limits in our marriage. I had no idea who I was, so I was easily convinced to try anything in the name of marital harmony. I didn't value myself enough to say no, even though I didn't feel he cared the least bit about my "hang-ups." I just wanted to be loved. I was searching for truth and did not know yet I desperately needed a Savior, someone to show me where the truth really was. For a while I trusted that to be my husband. And then I found the cult.

As it turned out, the gaping hole in my heart never got filled. I kept running into…*me*! Broken, wounded, hurting, and unlovable *me*! Nothing in this cult could have filled the void, could have prevented what was happening at home. I didn't like what I saw when I looked in the mirror. I didn't like that I allowed myself to be manipulated into someone else's idea of good enough, and I wanted to find out whether I was good enough—for God and ultimately for me. I mattered, obscure as that thought was.

In this group, we were taught a meditation technique that involved going into a workshop in your subconscious mind, much like that window of the mind in my vision. Here we created our own personal worlds, rooms we called our "workshops." Into this workshop we invited "assistants" (spirits, I now know) whom we looked to for counsel and help, much like a mentor. I loved my workshop and often enjoyed sharing my experience there with the other members. My husband wanted no part of it.

Imagine my surprise when Jesus showed up as my first "assistant." He was clearly trying to get my attention, even in this place of vain imaginings and spirit beings. At that moment I didn't take advantage of what He was offering, but eventually He won. He always does.

There was somewhat of a spiritual conflict in this organization in the beginning years. I went to an advanced seminar a year later, and they were showing the movie *King of Kings*, a Hollywood version of the story of Jesus. They were promoting the importance of love and sacrifice, but what they wanted was for us to sacrifice our money to get their version of love. Eventually they quit showing that movie, as it was causing too many to turn their allegiance to God and not their cause. Cults don't like that.

Clearly I was on a spiritual journey. Having Jesus show up as an "assistant" felt so good, even for the short time He stayed. And seeing this movie made the temptation toward this group even more inviting for me, at least momentarily. One night at a campfire we all stood around in a circle and sang "He's Got the Whole World in His hands." It lighted a spark in me that eventually led me to the true Jesus.

There are no coincidences with God. He will pursue us relentlessly. God was truly knocking on my door. And I was ready to answer, as tears poured down my cheeks while watching the story of Jesus.

It was at this advanced seminar that the truth was revealed about the true intent of this organization. They gave all of us an exit interview when the week was over and asked us what we thought the purpose of the group was. I gave some hyperspiritual answer such as, "Uniting the world in peace," or something equally mystical. Their response shocked and disappointed me. "We want to take over the world, one mind at a time, and thereby rule and control our society." They then asked for money in the form of homes, life insurance policies, and tithes.

Though deeply disappointed, I saw more clearly after that. I recognized the draw to God was greater than the draw to the group, and I set out to rediscover my roots in God.

Back to the Future

As a young Catholic girl, I had always been drawn to the things of God. I actually liked catechism class. I was the kid who came home with an advent wreath to pray around during advent season (the four weeks before Christmas). I would pick up the family Bible that sat on the coffee table, primarily used to store birth and baptism certificates. (We generally saved Bible reading for Sunday mass). I actually loved to read the red letters, which represented Jesus's words. I could feel my mom's pity when she saw me doing this.

Being raised in a Catholic home and attending a Catholic high school and college did nothing to prevent me from finding rebellious boys attractive. Perhaps my own rebellious heart made me hungry for something exciting. My first husband was one of those. He was persistent and charming, and before I knew it, I was pregnant. Abortion was not an option for this girl, and fortunately it wasn't legal at the time. We had a quick Catholic wedding for the sake of my parents. He didn't take the vows seriously. I had been turned off to Catholicism for a while, but I knew I wanted to be married when the baby was born; I wanted to start out right. He on the other hand was rightfully concerned the church building would fall in on him when he entered. I found out why quite soon.

Michele was born six months later, and I baptized her Catholic, promising the priest I would raise her in the church. But I didn't enter a church again until six years later when our son Michael was born and I baptized him in a local church. It was between these two births that I discovered the cult, which became my substitute religion for a few years. Michael was six months old when I attended the advanced seminar in California where I came home feeling the need to find God again.

When my eyes were opened to the true motive behind the cult, I felt the draw back to God and away from the cult more strongly. Michele was about to turn seven, and I decided to return to church for her to receive her first communion. Catholicism was part of my history, the only spiritual background I knew, so I wanted to have her experience the same. That's what moms do. We want the best for our babies.

My journey took me back to the Catholic church I had attended in high school, a familiar place where I felt at home. It was 1977, right after the Jesus movement and the beginning of the Catholic charismatic movement. The Catholic Church was experiencing a revolution of sorts and looked more Protestant than the Catholicism I grew up with. Jesus was off the cross. The confessionals were no longer little claustrophobic boxes. Women were actually allowed to be secular ministers and didn't have to cover their heads with lace doilies. Everyone was invited to touch the communion wafers and drink the wine. They were attempting to personalize Jesus.

At this church, one brave woman, herself a Catholic charismatic, boldly asked the church leadership if she could announce a charismatic Bible study being held in the home of a college professor in the area. I had heard about the charismatic movement from other friends who had left the cult. So I put my name in the collection basket as an interested party.

This teacher was a retired college professor who had discovered Jesus and was called to teach the Bible. He was not a Catholic, so the idea of a Catholic parish approving a nondenominational, charismatic Bible study for their parishioners was highly unusual. This Bible study was another sign that God was looking out for me and had pressed into my identity to bring me to a place where I would find my true home.

This professor opened my eyes as he taught me about Jesus through the gospel of John. I was ecstatic. I was flying high. Here was the love and hope I had wanted, right in front of me all the time. Jesus was more than just a name on the page of a book called the Bible. He was real. And I was so hungry. At the end of the twelve-week class on the gospel of John, I was the only new student remaining. The professor commented that perhaps the class had been created just for me. He was very aware of my hunger. So I fell in love with the One who had fallen in love with me before I was born twenty-eight years earlier.

Present in that group that met on Sunday night was a woman who would become my spiritual mother. She led the worship on her guitar before the study each night. She showed me love and kindness, taking me under her motherly wing and mentoring me in the truth. She helped me realize I had value, and she gave me the nurture I never received from my own mother. Her relationship with Jesus modeled one I cherished and was jealous for. Her simple faith and passion for Jesus inspired me and gave me hope for myself.

I wanted everything Jesus offered. So in the fall of 1977, I received Him as Lord and was baptized in the Holy Spirit. Then I asked Him what my purpose was. He whispered to me, **Just love—that is all I want you to do**. From the beginning, he had placed love into my identity. Forty years later, I am still discovering the fullness of that whisper.

What an outpouring of love God is! He knew my heart and that my love for my children would bring me back to my roots and to the church of my youth. He knew I would find my true call. This happened over and over in my life. When I was weak and needing someone to anticipate my needs, God stepped in. I was just beginning to discover who I really was.

My motherhood was an identity that carried me on many adventures. There were numerous God-sent opportunities to make choices for the good of my children. Inevitably, the choices would be good for me as well. But the motivation came from my identity, my spiritual and physical DNA, as a mom. In spite of my failure, in spite of my ignorance, in spite of my fears, He was still honoring my mother heart and knew me well enough to know what would get me in a position to find the truth. He was pursuing me, like true love does, helping me to uncover the fullness of what He saw in me before time began.

Declaration and blessing: My beloved, never doubt that your heavenly Father knows exactly what you need and when. He is hovering over you daily, watching where you are going, directing and sometimes correcting your path along the way. I declare to you that you cannot get lost when you have a loving Father who is guarding your every step. You matter.

Chapter 4

I Am Redeemed

Out of that terrible travail of soul,
He'll see that it's worth it and be glad He did it.
Through what He experienced, my righteous one, my
servant, will make many "righteous ones,"
as He himself carries the burden of their sins.
Therefore I'll reward him extravagantly—
the best of everything, the highest honors—
because He looked death in the face and didn't flinch,
because He embraced the company of the lowest.
—Isaiah 53:11

One of the things the Lord showed me so clearly that January morning Jesus told me my name was that my whole life was redeemed, not just the good parts. There was *nothing* He saw that He would throw out, *nothing* He wanted to make me feel guilty about.

Really, I thought? Not the three divorces, the adultery, the lust, the deception, the manipulation, the partying, the negligence of my kids? Even the abortion I eventually succumbed to after Michele was born, when it was legal? Seriously? *None of that stops you from loving me?*

None, not a bit. All is redeemed. All has purpose. All was proof that no matter how I behaved, the core of who I am, what God placed there in my spirit, could not be taken from me. It can get covered in some ugly onion skins, requiring some stinky peeling, but it *all* had purpose. "All things work together for good for those who love Him and are called according to HIS purpose" (Romans 8:28). That is a promise.

Tribulation

One of my favorite Bible verses is, "In the world you will have tribulation, but be of good cheer, I have overcome the world" (John 16:33).

Tribulation? Yes, I knew what that was, and it was more than suffering abuse for my beliefs or experiencing a rough patch in life. Tribulation, according to *Thesaurus.com*, means suffering, distress, trouble, misery, wretchedness, unhappiness, sadness, heartache, woe, grief, sorrow, pain, anguish, agony. Literally, it means travail. Travail is defined as hard work, especially when arduous or involving painful effort, as in the labor of childbirth. We are talking a lifetime of childbirth, folks.

Have you considered that Jesus went through travail to bring you into life? Being born again means you entered into *His* travail—the cross. Every single time someone asks Jesus to enter into them, Jesus again enters the travail of the cross and allows us to see what He did in order to redeem us—in order to fulfill the promise that He had truly overcome the world. "Even when we were dead and doomed in our many sins, he united us into the very life of Christ and saved us by his wonderful grace" (Ephesians 2:5). *Every* time He presents Himself to you on the cross, He dies again, just for you. He never lets you go through anything that He Himself did not experience fully. Because of His travail on the cross, we have victory over the tribulation in the world. Really, really cool!

So now we get to do the same thing. We get to travail with one another over the things we have experienced and been redeemed from. It is called intercessory prayer.

Can I really intercede for someone who is suffering from sexual abuse, for example, really travail with them, if I have not walked that world? There is a level of intercession that allows you to enter into someone's travail and pray for that individual's healing, but most of us don't have that experience. So when a brother or sister is experiencing pain we have experienced and been healed of, we have authority to pray for the person. That certainly brings some sense of redemption to the experience, doesn't it? And it's real payback to the enemy!

But that doesn't even touch the ultimate gift we get from our tribulations. We get to experience the cross. We get to be laid-down, poured-out vessels. That's a fancy way of saying we participate in His suffering. "But rejoice to the extent that you partake of Christ's sufferings, that when His glory is revealed, you may also be glad with exceeding joy" (1Peter 4:13).Why? Because we are one in Him, and He is one in us. It is called intimacy. When we are one with someone, we experience all their joys and sorrows, as in the intimacy of marriage. In John 17:21–22, Jesus prays, "I pray for them to become one with us So that the world will recognize that you sent me. For the very glory you have given to me I have given them, so that they will be joined together as one and experience the same unity that we enjoy." It is similar to the way identical twins feel each other's pains and sorrow and joys. They have a divine connection that begins when they share the same womb.

Any tribulation we experience is an expression of our relationship with Christ. By being willing to be a small part of what He suffered, we get to count it all joy, just as He did. "My brethren, count it all joy when you fall into various trials, knowing that the testing of your faith produces patience" (James 1:2–3).

Earthly Reality

As with every God-centered truth, there is a counterfeit, the twisting of truth that destroys rather than brings life. The joy of intimacy was vacant from my home with my first husband. After

I became a Christian in 1977, God opened my eyes to much of what I was contending with spiritually. Now with two children, Michele and Michael, and one on the way, I felt I had to do all I could to keep this marriage strong, which isn't easy with an unbeliever. But the extent of his sin was yet to be revealed. The things he did and asked me to do for the first several years of our marriage were no less than fornication. Now, as a Christian, I knew this was not acceptable behavior. He was a sex addict.

The symptoms of his addiction started early in our marriage. While I was pregnant with Michele and we were in our first apartment together, he would bring me pornographic magazines to look at as a means to "loosen me up" from my "frigid Catholic upbringing." I felt sick the first time I looked at the lewd pictures. Slowly and insidiously, the darkness began to overtake me, and I allowed him to influence my "prudish" personality.

His idea of intimacy was to share me with other men so I could be more experienced and bring that experience into the bedroom, just for the increased excitement he would feel. It was the seventies, and right along with the Jesus movement and the charismatic renewal, the darkness was raising its ugly head with sexual freedom in something called open marriage. Couples were encouraged to experience other couples sexually to expand the joy of sex. Movies like *Bob and Carol and Ted and Alice* were on the screen, normalizing perverted sex. We devoured the book *The Harrad Experiment*, by Robert Rimmer, about a new-age college campus where endless experiments with sex are explored. Masters and Johnson were normalizing the need for good sex in a relationship. The seduction was real, and I succumbed to the dark side for a season, at times enjoying the adventure that the world had never shown me before. Slowly the darkness became clear to me, and after seven years of compromise, I refused to participate further. But the seed had been planted in our home, and the worst was yet to come.

It would be twenty-three years later, when Michele was thirty and engaged to be married, that I would find out that his addiction had been inflicted on our child. He discovered an early attraction in his own tortured soul toward Michelle, and from the time she was a baby had molested and eventually raped her. She would be lost for years, hiding inside from the horror of what was inflicted on her by force. She would spend many years diligently searching for the original person God had designed her to be.

At the time the truth came out, there were two other daughters, Joanie and Sarah. He had made Michele a slave to his promises that if she just cooperated, he wouldn't touch her sisters. That became a betrayal that borders on unforgiveable. He did eventually molest Joanie and Sarah. While nothing physical happened to Michael, our only son, there is no way to grow up in that environment and not be affected. The whole family had been abused. (It is common in family abuse situations for the predator to leave one untouched).

This truth was shocking. As a mom, there is no greater travail than realizing your husband had been raping your daughter right in the house you lived in, right in the room downstairs from where you slept. Our sex life had pretty much come to a halt after all the kids were born. Clearly, his attention was elsewhere, but never did I suspect toward our daughter. To this day, it is hard for me to comprehend how I didn't know. I was blind.

His affairs with other women through the years should have been enough for me to leave him, but clearly I was as guilty, even though it was with his permission and encouragement. I was determined to make the marriage work—yes, ironically, for the sake of the children. I took the children to church by myself every Sunday while praying God would bring my husband to his knees.

I never questioned his fathering. I never dreamed he would touch his own children. Neither did anyone else in our circle. He seemed to be a "fun" dad. Nobody talked about sexual abuse in those days, except maybe in private therapy. Everything seemed so normal. But the devil has some great cloaking devices called intimidation and fear, and Michele was victim of that manipulation.

Intimidation and fear can make you blind. So how did my identity save me through that? I did mothering really well. I love, love, love being a mom. One thing Michele's therapist had told her sustained me through many days of self-evaluation after the truth surfaced. She told Michele that it was my mother love that had been her safe harbor and that otherwise she would have been much more damaged, an alcoholic or even a prostitute, considering what had happened. Again God banked on my mother love to protect his precious daughter, whether or not I was aware.

Admittedly, I had often found it difficult to connect to Michele. I never knew why and just saw it as one of those style differences. She had a lot of fear in her, fear I didn't understand and often criticized. She cried easily. When most teenagers wanted distance from Mom, she hovered close by. I had translated it to poor self-esteem, and I thought I knew how to fix that.

Trophy Child

When she was seventeen, we encouraged Michele to enter a teen beauty contest, hoping to break through some of that self-esteem issue. She would have an opportunity to shine like the star I knew she was. She was so beautiful and talented. I had no doubt she could win.

The night before the contest, as she headed with her dad to the hotel where the contest was being held, she broke down in tears. I had coached her all that I could and thought she was well prepared. We had shopped for all the right clothes and memorized her speech. She was ready.

Now she was petrified. I had no idea what was waiting for her at the hotel. I only knew I couldn't leave yet because of the other kids. What a price to pay.

How do you stand up in front of hundreds of people and show confidence and poise when your dad just had his way with you in the hotel room? Her identity was buried in her perception of her own shame and guilt, none of which was her doing. Throw in some unintentional abandonment by a mother who is oblivious to what is going on, and you do not have a good formula for confidence. While she did come in third, to this day she buries the trophy in storage.

Taking Off the Blinders

Life began to be unbearable with this predator after eighteen years. The evidence of his addiction was becoming apparent in all of the children. He was angry, and there were no signs of remorse. Revelation started with recognizing the behavior of our daughter. When Michele started to bring home the dark, bad boys, I knew something was really wrong. Even without being consciously aware of the abuse, I could see that my husband's abusive mouth and sexually provocative language had penetrated the innocence of my children. While I didn't know all that Daddy was doing, I knew he was affecting something in Michele for her to bring home the exact opposite we would ever approve of.

The crowning blow came a year later when my mom alarms went off big time. Michele had gone off to a Christian college. The first Christmas break she came home financially and emotionally broken. She shared with her father—but not with me—that she had gotten into some compromising situations with boys at the school. When he later told me, I realized it was best she not go back, as I was concerned about her virginity. The betrayal I felt grew into a realization that my husband was behaving more like a confidant than a protective father. I didn't fully understand the grooming that happens between the predator and the victim, nor that her virginity had already been compromised, but my instinct said she needed to get away. So I sent her out of state to live with a friend of mine and attend college, while I attempted to untangle my marriage. Thank God for mother instinct.

I went into therapy to clarify my options, with separation looming. The idea of therapy frightened him, and he wouldn't go. When I invited him, his response was, "It will just end in divorce."

It was there I began to discover a strength in myself that was crying for the freedom I had declared many times in my mind. This psychologist helped me see my own strength, and I finally was able to ask my husband to leave after nineteen years of marriage. Two years later I moved myself and the three remaining children to the Pacific Northwest, and I filed for divorce. Soon after, he moved to Florida, where his mother now lived. I hoped the separation would be good for us all. Though the girls did visit their dad in Florida a couple of times, Michele tells me she never let him touch her again. The sexual abuse stopped. But the emotional trauma would take many more years to unwrap.

Light in the Darkness

For Michele the journey to wholeness took her to several counselors. Finally, at age thirty, Michele was able to uncover the truth about her experience. The memories that had been blocked and buried, from the time she'd been a baby, began to flow into conscious memory. Now she was engaged and planning her wedding, and the prospect of her father walking her down the aisle so terrified her that the blinders came off and she could face the truth. She needed to let him know, but first she had to tell me.

The day Michelle came to grips with the truth and was able to reveal what I had begun to fear, I ran to her in dismay. Mama bear wanted to protect her cub, but it seemed so, so late. I was devastated, and she was numb. I was thrown into a roller-coaster ride of self-evaluation and fear for my other daughters. How did that happen before my eyes? But the truth set us on the journey to finding our freedom.

Michelle finally sent her dad a letter telling him that since he never really behaved like her father, she was not comfortable having him walk her down the aisle. She finally faced the reality of what her psyche had buried, the thing I would have done anything to prevent. Hell, literally, broke loose.

At the time, Joanie was living with her father in Florida, and I was fearful he may have abused her. She assured me he had not touched her, but his knee-jerk response to the letter was to run away and threaten suicide. I quickly sent her a plane ticket home.

Sarah was a senior in high school, and we had a serious talk that night. She was able to finally tell me the truth that she and Joanie had talked about only in the privacy of their bedroom. Fortunately, she agreed to go into therapy. Our son, Michael, was the only one who remained in contact with his dad from that time on. Neither my ex-husband nor his mother ever again contacted the three girls, and eventually they both passed away. Shame and guilt won.

Blessedly, Michael agreed to walk Michele down the aisle for her wedding. The crisis was temporarily contained, but the ripple effect would continue.

Now it was my turn.

Joy Is Not a Feeling

Once the marriage of my daughter was over and Sarah was safely headed to college, I broke down under all I was carrying. It felt like a tsunami of emotion had hit me from all sides. I got some needed help from a good Christian counselor.

I learned much about my blindness. The betrayal to me as a wife and mother hit my core identity. As I discovered through my journey that my identity as a mom was a huge part of who I was, it became clearer how sinister and evil sexual perversion is.

My father never touched me sexually, but his eyes said everything. The abuse was covert. His father had been an elder in their church and a womanizer, which was an embarrassment to my dad, so he'd been determined to be true to his wife, at least by appearances. He was the personification of glittering images. But everything else about him wandered and cheated. I watched him flirt and leer at women he worked with, and often felt his leers personally. He told some pretty nasty jokes, often denigrating women with his humor. You think you are Daddy's favorite, but only when he doesn't have to share you with anyone. Dating was a nightmare. That was not a concerned father waiting up for me. No, it was a jealous man. If I was one minute late on a date, he would be sitting up, face demonically set in a frown of disapproval, growling at me under his breath, screaming into my face how much trouble I was in. Jealousy.

So how do you count all this as joy? There was no joy in realizing my daughters were abused. There was no joy in *being* abused. But joy is not a feeling; it is an act of faith. Love is not a feeling; it is an act of will. Tribulation is allowed by God so that we can exercise our faith in the fact that He has overcome the world. Done deal. It is finished!

My tribulation was a process of disentangling that would take lots of time, love, and patience. And God was the originator of all of that. "In the world you will have tribulation; but be of good cheer, I have overcome the world" (John 16:33) was my life scripture during this time. Facing reality was a necessary part of it. I was often reminded of Jesus on the cross as this family walked through what we all faced in those days. He knew. He understood. And most of all, His loving Father was right there through it all. I was finally able to crawl up on my heavenly Father's lap for comfort and love. I found peace there.

Only God knew what my Michele needed. One blind guide in her corner did not seem fair. I don't even try to understand fairness. But I do understand a God who is bigger than all of it and who stands beside us in the dark and in the light, always shining the light of truth in the darkest places. He never leaves us or forsakes us. His truth sets us free. He only sees the beautiful treasure he originally created. And He continues to make that creation a reality every time. Michele has found Jesus and freedom from the tortured life she grew up in. She is safe.

God has placed in each of us exactly what we need to become what He created us to be. "His divine power has given to us all things that pertain to life and godliness, through the knowledge of Him who called us by glory and virtue" (1 Peter 2:3). The life we are given is for the purpose of shaping us into that perfection He saw in heaven.

Declaration and blessing: I bless each of you with the revelation of the strength, the courage, the endurance in you to rise up against the enemy and stand as a warrior over the injustices that life brings. God is good all the time. And I declare that He is with you, He is fighting for you, and He is aware of everything you struggle with. He cares so much.

He Knows My Name

Chapter 5

New Eyes

God has predestined every single one of us for fruitfulness (John 15). We need to be familiar with a place of divine intimacy in which we are so consumed by the Holy Spirit that we will nurture and protect the seed He places in us. We need to fearlessly step out and activate His promises. It is intimacy that gives us the grace and strength we need to push through suffering, pain and inconvenience.
—Heidi Baker, *Birthing the Miraculous*

I am a survivor. My dream as a young girl was to experience love. I wanted to have children and love them well, and I wanted to be loved. Not because I was evil, or perverted, or sex starved. No. Because God made me his love bubble and I couldn't help but pour it out on whoever wanted it. I wanted intimacy. And love.

Unfortunately, my experience with men taught me that they wanted love and intimacy in the form of sex, and that added a dimension I was not prepared for. Somehow sex and love got enmeshed together in my mind, and so to get love, it seemed that sex was part of the deal. My dad had me so scared of what bad boys do (and they were all bad), it took me a while to let go of my virginity. It was love that made the difference—or so I'd thought.

It is a paradox that God says to love others as you love yourself. It certainly was for me. So I tried to love and decided that would define me. I would love, and it would change those people. He (hubby number one) would stop wanting other women. He (hubby number two) would stop drinking. He (hubby number three) would stop abusing me physically and spiritually. And Daddy would finally love me.

The problem is that the real me got buried under all those expectations, even the ones that I thought God had of me. He doesn't though. Have expectations. He has love. Our earthly parents can mess up our sense of love, filling our minds with what we must do to earn love. Or lose love. Or never get love. I spent a lifetime searching in other men for the love I didn't get from my dad.

Each of my journeys with men brought me a piece of the puzzle that God was putting together. Each represented a place of brokenness that needed healing. And my identity as a love bubble got me into relationships that desperately needed love. I just didn't know how unable I was to fulfill that need.

After separating from and divorcing husband number one, I flourished in my new freedom. With Michele safely away from home, I raised the three remaining children on my own. Jesus was my husband, my all and all. Unfortunately, until we moved to the Pacific Northwest, Joanie and Sarah were subject to occasional overnights with their dad, which were not always reported to me as pleasant. Eventually the visits stopped.

I decided to move to the Pacific Northwest for a new beginning. Joanie felt the loss of Dad's presence the hardest. She had begun to rebel by running away and hanging out with teenage gangs and was nearly uncontrollable. Being a runaway was against the law, and she actually had a record. I thought a new environment would be healthy. Unfortunately, she took her rebellion with her, and she found teenage gangs in our new community in the Pacific Northwest. The teenage versions of the Bloods and the Crips became her family.

Husband number two was the father of another rebellious teenager, and we were drawn to each other as mutual crutches to deal with our runaways. We met while searching for our daughters one early Saturday morning. Pain makes strange bedfellows. But he was an alcoholic—an angry and abusive one. And I foolishly thought my love could "fix" him, much as I had wanted to fix my mom. This one didn't last long. Fortunately, I had found some inner strength and healing from my walk with the Lord, and before two years had passed, he was out of my life.

Free again, I continued my journey to wholeness. By now Michael had moved to Florida to be near his dad. Michele was living on her own and going to college. Joanie was still on the run, living with her gang boyfriend, and only Sarah remained at home. I discovered an opportunity to return to college at night to complete the degree I had left behind when I'd gotten pregnant with Michele. I found a Christian Bible college (I had left the Catholic Church many years earlier) that would accommodate my earned credits through their degree completion program. There in Bible college sat husband number three, searching for his perfect Christian wife. After two years of night school, we graduated together and got married.

This was supposed to be my dream marriage, two Christians who knew Jesus and attended church regularly. Again my hopes and dreams were dashed. A new reality set in. It was in the midst of this marriage that the truth about the abuse to my daughters came to light. Since they were struggling with their abuse, I needed to be available to them in their healing. However, at home I was being asked to abandon them and put my husband above all that, to choose him and reject my family, to prove I loved him. His psychological instability had already manifested in physical violence, causing me to walk around on egg shells. To be cut off from my children was unbearable. He was a deeply troubled and angry man who demanded more than I had to give. And my failures caused some truly violent and ugly responses. I was even too afraid to call 911.

Nine years into the marriage, on my knees, I ran to Jesus. I was done, at least in my flesh. I pulled myself up from the agony of despair for the last time. Love and care had completely drained from my heart. I was empty. And out of that emptiness, I gave over the marriage. I gave up on the fear of rejection because of "another divorce." I gave up on "not being good enough to make him love me." I gave up on my love being enough. I gave up the part of my identity dictating to me that being married somehow legitimized me and that divorce was the ultimate failure. I was forgetting the truth about me. God loved me and hated violence against His women. "Take heed then to your spirit, and let no one deal treacherously against the wife of your youth. 'For I hate divorce,' says the LORD, the God of Israel, 'and him who covers his garment with wrong and violence,' says the LORD of hosts. 'Therefore keep watch on your spirit, so that you do not deal treacherously [with your wife]'" (Malachi 2:16 AMP).

When I turned over the marriage and released it to God, I held on to the promises I knew were mine. On my hands and knees in my living room, I confessed my failure to trust God with my marriage, and I gave it back to Him, all of it, willing to let it go completely if that was what was necessary to be free. God was going to have to save this marriage, in His way. In my spirit I knew that He was far more concerned about how the marriage was treating me. I had come to understand how God saw me and what He desired for me. It just might not have been possible there.

I so wanted Jesus to fix the marriage. It never occurred to me that God also wanted me to stop being complicit in the abuse by being silent. Speaking up carried a huge risk, but I was finally strong enough to verbalize my intent: I said no. I would not reject my children for the sake of his fragile ego. Enough. And that was all it took. We were in marriage counseling, and I walked in to what would be our last meeting and said I was done. Sadly, there was no protest. I truly had been holding it together by myself.

God rescued me. Again.

Single again, my pursuit of my identity continued. My life flourished, financially and spiritually. I had begun to understand that Jesus wanted intimacy with me just as I did with Him. With my history, that was no less than a frightening prospect. I had to learn what true intimacy was.

Intimacy

Intimacy means vulnerability, and to this point that did not feel like a safe place. How do you make the transition from abuse to intimacy with Jesus?

I simply had to let Him do the heavy lifting of pouring into me all the validation and love and kindness I could contain. I buried myself in the Bible and in counseling in an effort to fill this empty vessel. Men were not easy to trust, but Jesus proved Himself to be trustworthy. I slowly allowed him into the dark and dirty places that needed healing so I could be whole again.

In time, I realized I understood what He wanted. I wanted it too. Intimacy was the most elusive side of the love I sought. Oh, to be known and to know, to pour out your dreams and passions and be validated and encouraged. Now *that* had to be love.

It turns out you can have sex without intimacy and love, but it is not fulfilling. The intimacy Jesus talks about, when we are his beloved and He is our bridegroom—that's a whole different experience. Wowsie! I was in for that. I wanted it all. I couldn't get enough of knowing who He was and what He was about. Morning and night, I searched for the fullness of who He was. He was calling me. And I was responding.

Arise, my love, my beautiful companion,
And run with me to the higher place.
For now is the time to arise
And come away with me.

—Song of Solomon 2:1

In the beginning of my walk with Jesus, there was no way I could imagine Jesus wanting to be intimate with me the way I was. Come away with *this*? That is the limitation of seeing yourself through the eyes of people. The journey ahead of me would be to see myself the way God saw me, the way He saw me in heaven when He conceived of me. There was much to learn about that person and much to shed about the old me. I thought I was so undeserving of such favor.

So while I had fallen in love with Jesus those many years ago, I had a ways to go to accept that He was crazy in love with me. I had to come to love myself before I could believe I was loveable and able to receive His love. And now forty years later, I finally fell in love with me.

Declaration and blessing: I bless any of you reading this who are suffering at the hand of an abusive person, to rise up and declare the majesty of God over yourself. You are created in His image, and when that violence strikes you, it is striking Jesus. Your greatest act of faith and securing your identity could be in finally saying enough is enough. I bless you with the same courage of Jesus as He walked to the cross, the same confidence, as Father whispers in your ear, "I am here. Walk with me."

Beloved, the banner over you is *love*. Your name is written in heaven. Our good Father is smiling over you, and He knows your name. I declare over you a refreshing of your identity as a child of the King, crowned in His glory and blessed by His inheritance. Your story matters.

Chapter 6

Wholeness

*To give to them beauty for ashes, the oil of joy for
mourning, the garment of praise for the spirit of
heaviness, that they might be called trees of righteousness,
the planting of the Lord, that He might be glorified.*
 —Isaiah 61:3

NOTE: This may not be an easy chapter for those of you who have experienced sexual abuse or are not comfortable with the subject. Tread gently and be kind to yourself. You are free to skip it and return when you are ready, if at all.

The devastation of sexual abuse rocked my world. You have "heard" me use words such as "memories blocked" and "what her psyche had buried" and "the blinders came off" in describing what Michele experienced. This is common with all sexual abuse survivors.

Sexual abuse is the greatest destroyer of identity and destiny, period. Whether it is sex trafficking, prostitution, rape, molestation, verbal denigration, gender mutilation, infanticide, sterilization...it hits a woman at her core identity. Some abuse is so devastating that it divides one literally into many pieces, leaving an often-lifetime journey of putting humpty back together again. That is the reality of dissociative identity disorder (DID).

This would be part of the journey to wholeness my daughters and I were to walk through. Sometimes it is easier to let a part of you disappear in order to cope with life. But God clearly wants us each to know the beautiful creation He saw in heaven. The journey to the original self, fully integrated as we were seen in heaven, is necessary and worthwhile.

Gift of Dissociation

DID is a gift from God to assist the innocent in living through a terrifying and destructive experience and still stay functional. Think of it as a wall that goes up to hide behind while watching ourselves experience something we can't emotionally handle. We can detach from the reality for as long as it takes to again feel safe to return to our "original self."

Violent sexual experiences can trigger this response easily, especially when we are too young to have cognitive understanding (usually under three years old), though our spirits always remember. The conscious memory often gets tucked away for a later time when it is ready to be addressed, as was the case with Michele at the age of thirty. Meanwhile, it may express itself in denial, confusion, and pain and cause us to act out in ways contrary to our natures, often being unable to explain our unhealthy reactions.

The parts of us that are hiding are our cores, our original identities. The ones God saw before we entered our mothers' wombs. The journey to finding that core generally requires digging back through all the pain, denial, confusion, and shame. It is an arduous task.

Dissociation has broad ranges. Some will discover there are more parts that have broken away. Sometimes it is like a replay of the movie *Seven Faces of Eve*. For others it is as simple as denial.

We all dissociate at times. It is sometimes called *zoning*. Have you ever driven a familiar path to or from work and suddenly realized you had arrived with no conscious memory of the journey? That is a form of dissociation.

For many it looks like post-traumatic stress disorder (PTSD), which occurs when the shock of a current unrelated event (trigger) causes you to relive the shock and pain over and over again months and years later. The term originated with military soldiers returning from war zones, like Vietnam. They can be resting comfortably in their homes and hear a car backfire, and they'll run under the table for cover or grab their rifles for defense. It is as if they are back in Vietnam and hearing gunfire. PTSD for someone who has been abused can be as simple as a man coming up behind you to give you a hug, and you recoil because that is a trigger of a more violent experience.

While I don't want to minimize the seriousness of this process, I also want to normalize it. With the level of abuse that is being discovered since we started measuring and talking about it in the last thirty years, DID is more common than we realize.

For me it could be a word said by a man in my life. The words would trigger something from a memory I wasn't immediately conscious of, and my emotions would go to such an extreme that I would be screaming at this man, when he was not the perpetrator. It is very difficult if no one understands the symptoms. It was with a knowledgeable counselor that I was able to see and discover my original self. Today, I sometimes don't recognize the woman I was. But God was invested in my wholeness, as was I. The battle was worth the fight. We have an amazing advocate in the Holy Spirit, who knows exactly what we need.

Satanic Ritual Abuse

The most complex and destructive level of dissociation is SRA, satanic ritual abuse. This goes beyond the abuse we read about in the news today—priests molesting boys, fathers molesting daughters, families selling their children for money... All of this we read about and are much more aware of than when I was a young mom. I am very grateful for that exposure, giving abused men and women a voice that neither I nor my daughters ever had.

The complexity of SRA is beyond the scope of this book to address. Briefly, SRA is mind (will), body, and spirit control to such a level that when offered an opportunity to be free, the fear of punishment is so deeply engrained or programmed, trusting God, much less anyone else, seems impossible. Satan and his accompanying darkness are presented as more powerful than God. The victim is taught to fear God, follow Satan (as represented by the programmers' insistence on being the only source of truth), and trust no one except those who had literally programmed them by using dark sexual rituals for control. It distorts the joy of sex God intends and becomes a religious cult experience. In fact, it is often what is happening in the religious cults we have become aware of where everyone is a concubine of the "king of the house," like David Jones and Michael Karesh.

I have been through much inner healing, for which there are many styles and names. It is grueling and often painful to face the lies I grew up believing about myself and to recover the suppressed memories. Imagine if there were more than one part to deal with, each with a broken identity. What if there are three, ten, fifty, or one hundred broken parts to deal with? Seems overwhelming and impossible, doesn't it?

SRA attacks at your core identity and often before you have any cognition. If you are fortunate enough to find someone who can help you, the unraveling can still take years. The purpose, like with DID, is to find your original self, part by divided part; to find that one that God created before you were even placed in your mother's womb, that one who is filled with all the goodness that God intended. In the meantime, you are walking out your life through the veil that the parts have provided in an effort to appear normal.

SRA reduces you to a thing, an object, living only to meet the needs of others who exploit you and lie to you in the name of love. Because the perpetrators are often people who know you and are in a position of authority or power over you, and are people who are supposed to love you, the mind gets confused about love and identity. If you had to give yourself away to any available man just to feel wanted, you did. If you drank or did drugs to bury the hurt, you did. Whatever survival mechanism you could find, just to bury the awful self-hate, you gravitated toward it.

Women everywhere are fighting desperately to stop the pain of their wounding and to truly discover who they are. They often fight to have the world around them change ("if he would stop saying that, I would be OK"), when it is in fact a journey they must indulge in for personal inner transformation. The correct question to ask is, "What needs to be healed in me so I don't react so strongly?" We each have to fight for who we are and find that original self, no matter to what degree it has been stolen. That is why I think SRA belongs in the discussion of identity.

My Hero

I met Jackie at a conference where she boldly stood up and declared before everyone, "I have DID because of sexual abuse." And then she sat down. My heart broke for her. Few were able to feel her pain or were so stunned they couldn't respond. I wanted to let her know I heard her heart. I went to her, gave her a hug, and told her I loved her and understood how hard that was. That one gesture created a mother-daughter bond that is strong to this day. No one had ever truly embraced Jackie as a daughter.

Jackie had an inner strength that kept her safe from the worst scenarios. She'd come to know Jesus in her life as a young woman long before she knew the fullness of what had happened to her. Her pursuit of healing revolved around dispelling the lies about who she was and to whom she belonged.

In Jackie's case it was her father and a whole cult of Satan worshippers who had started programming her from the moment of her birth. These perpetrators, including her mother, convinced her that they knew what was best for her, and as long as she did what she was told, including the lowest level of sexual acts, she would live. When that is all you know, that is who you are, a slave to lies and fear. And you do unspeakable things.

Jackie has fought to be whole like no one I have yet to encounter. And yet today she has heard the voice of Jesus call her *daughter* and *bride*, and she has responded to the call. It is never too late. And it is always God's heart to respond in kind.

What a difference it would have made to Jackie to have been lovingly called *daughter* by those that instead chose to use her and thereby almost destroy her identity. All those parts of her also disguised the true wonderful woman she is. Her self-destructive behaviors were used to cope with life, because survival was all that mattered.

I am so grateful for all the wonderful friends and counselors who guided me and participated in my healing. Jackie was one of them. Her pain has made her an authority on the self-degradation of sexual abuse SRA can bring. She gave me and many others courage.

Jackie has tremendous revelation about who she is becoming, and now as she lives as a more integrated self, her healing becomes about her and not only about her divided parts. She now has to deal with the emotions and situations that caused her to divide and make parts in the first place. Finding the initial impact of pain is the hardest, because Jackie is a warrior for others and just isn't used to fighting on her own behalf. She continues to seek every lie that could have ever been believed about herself and is discovering the true amazing woman of God that she is. She is one of my heroes. I am blessed to be a part of her journey, if for no other reason than to validate and believe in her.

In My Own Backyard

Michele was a daughter and a wife all in one. Love didn't look the same from two different parents. I didn't know at the time what had stolen her self-esteem, but I did what I could to give it back to her. Jesus knew who she was, and because of Him she is finding her way home. I am grateful she calls God her Father and that she is also called *daughter* by Him. She has transformed into a beautiful wife and mother and is learning each day what normal is. She has raised her children with the love of a mama bear. I am so very proud of her.

For me, I knew I had to be a daughter before I could truly be a mother. My understanding of mothering was skewed, so I needed to touch the hem of Jesus's robe many times before I truly heard the word "Daughter" and believed it. To know myself as daughter has enriched me as a mother and grandmother.

For those who have been wounded by the horrific experience of sexual abuse, you are my personal heroes. For if you are reading this, perhaps you are recovering and maybe even have found your wholeness.

Declaration and blessing: I declare victory over each of you. I declare God's love and healing power to be exploded in your soul, bringing you to the fullness of your identity. You are precious children of God, created for a divine purpose that may not yet be evident but is unfailing and unrelenting in its pursuit of you. Yes, your identity pursues you. Jesus pursues you into a place where you have only him, and I bless each of you with finding that hiding place and letting Him complete the work He so loves to do.

Chapter 7

I Am Woman

The Anointed One has set us free— not partially, but completely and wonderfully free!
—Galatians 5:1

Women take a lot of heat for being the one who "ate the apple of temptation" and brought mankind into sin. It really wasn't quite that simple.

In the beginning, the fullness of creation was resident in one body called *man*: "Then God said, 'Let Us make man in Our image, according to Our likeness'" (Genesis 1:26). Adam was the fullness of God's desire to create a being in His image. When the man got lonely looking for companionship, there was none found suitable among the rest of creation. There was no other creature in paradise who could quite meet his companionship needs. So, genius that God is, He took a part of Adam's side and created (wo)man (the womb of man). Now from one we have two. How inspiring is it that the institution of marriage has set about to return two to one, through a true act of spiritual and physical intimacy.

Now the man rejoices (Gen2:23): "This at last is bone of my bones and flesh of my flesh; she shall be called Woman, because she was taken out of man." Brilliant!

We were created spirit, soul, and body. That didn't change when God separated woman from man. Now the two had a choice to make, each with a complete, though separate, spirit, soul, and body. Together they were to increase and multiply and expand the world of the garden. They had one commandment only. Do not eat of the tree of the knowledge of good and evil. It is notable that this commandment was given to the man before God separated woman from his flesh. After they became two separate beings, the serpent showed up.

The serpent was a created being. He was one of the animals they named: "For the serpent was more crafty than any other wild animal that the Lord God had made" (Genesis 3:1). So does that mean that evil already existed before God created this earth? Apparently so, because there was this tree of the knowledge of good *and* evil that they were not to eat from.

So the serpent, in his craftiness, chose to tempt the woman, and not the man, who was apparently a silent observer. Why? Have you ever wondered? I think it had to do with her identity.

God said that man needed a companion, a helper. Who did God say the Holy Spirit would be for us after Jesus was ready to return to heaven? The Helper. "And I will ask the Father, and He will give you another Helper (Comforter, Advocate, Intercessor—Counselor, Strengthener, Standby), to be with you forever" (John 14:16 AMP). Women represent the Holy Spirit in the relationship.

What else do we know about woman? She is a procreator. "And Adam called his wife's name Eve, because she was the mother of all living" (Genesis 3:20). All future generations would come into being through the woman, including Jesus. Did the serpent know that? More than likely, as these were not animals like we have today. Obviously there was a form of communication between man and the other creatures that we don't experience today. After all, God looked among them to find a proper companion for Adam. So they were definitely a higher level of creation than we see today.

Could the serpent know God's plan? Or did he just know that if there were too many of these humans, he would lose power? I don't know. But it was her he went after. And Eve was a nurturer. She was responding out of her identity. Having not encountered "evil" yet, she listened to this creature, the serpent. She could only think the best of him. That's what nurturers do. That is an obvious response out of her identity as procreator. Nurture, care, and feeding all come through the woman.

All of this made her an easy target for temptation. The serpent knew that if he could appeal to the woman's nature to help and nurture, by giving her wisdom equal to God, he could convince her that she misunderstood God's commandment. Why would a loving God deprive them of knowledge of good and evil? And of course we know Adam was silent on the matter. He deferred to her. Perhaps her beauty blinded him to the truth. We only know that he partook of the fruit as well when she handed it to him.

So the serpent tempted her with having the wisdom of God, and she forgot God's command. She believed the lie.

Adam also forgot who he was—the leader, the guide, the protector, the provider. In Ephesians we are reminded that men are called to be sacrificial to the woman, to give their lives for her. "Husbands, love your wives [seek the highest good for her and surround her with a caring, unselfish love], just as Christ also loved the church and gave Himself up for her." He was the one who needed to protect and strengthen Eve and to seek the highest good for her as God had created him to do. He stood silent as his wife became a pawn to the schemes of the enemy.

Consequences

No excuses here. They all blew it. And now the serpent was condemned to writhe on his belly and eat dust all the days of his life. (Could one conclude he was a two-footed upright creature until then?) Then comes this prophetic pronouncement and curse, foretelling the coming of Jesus: "I will put enmity between you and the woman, and between your seed and her seed; he shall crush your head, and you shall nick his heel" (Gen 3:15 AMP).

Women would now have an increase of pain during childbirth yet would be drawn to men, and they would rule over them. This, apparently, was not the case in the garden before they sinned. They were one flesh. They had shared responsibility and equal submission. But now she must submit.

Men were cursed to toil over the land that until that moment was meant to be a land-maintenance project. The ground was now cursed to produce thistles and thorns: "And you shall eat the plants of the field." Basically, you are dirt, and to dirt you shall return.

The proof of the break from God was when their eyes were opened and they knew that they were naked. Until then the glow of their countenance had blinded them, and they felt no shame. But sin opened the doors to the flesh. Suddenly they needed to "cover" themselves. Shame entered the heart of mankind. Sex became an obligation, an urge, a means of procreation, but not a celebration of oneness. And worst of all, they were thrown out of the garden, for they were in no condition to eat of the tree of life.

Jesus Restores Intimacy

And so it was for thousands of years. God showed up on occasion, but that daily intimate relationship had changed. The hope of it returning arrived in the form of the God/Man, Jesus. And with him came a new identity of women that we have yet to fully grasp.

When Jesus came to earth, the people of the world had failed on all fronts to fulfill their godly call. For the most part, the biblical age was one of male dominance, though there were some amazing stories of women who became heroines and even judges. But now it was time to reinstate the promises in the garden. Man would again have daily access to God and be able to walk in the fullness of his identity. Jesus came to save them from themselves. And He reinstated the woman to her rightful place next to the man, not under his feet. It has been a long two thousand years seeing the fruition of that mandate. Satan is still prowling around seeking to destroy, determined to nick Jesus's heel by subduing women. He doesn't like that he was told woman would crush His head.

Jesus, fully God, was birthed through the seed of the Holy Spirit, born of a woman, born to destroy the works of the enemy. That is our mandate. That is our collective identity. We are the bringers of light into the darkness. Jesus completely turns upside down the culture of the day to show us how He sees women.

Jesus had His Father's heart for women and never meant for the crushing of women to continue. The curse was reversed at the cross.

Declaration and blessing: Step into your truthful place of dignity. I declare all your shame has been redeemed. Hiding has ended. Come out into the light and declare the fullness of who you are, woman of God.

Chapter 8

Daughters Restored

For this reason I say to you, her sins, which are many,
have been forgiven, for she loved much; but he who is
forgiven little, loves little.
—Luke 7:47

This restoration of dignity and redemption from shame is exemplified throughout the New Testament. Whenever Jesus encounters a woman, we see honor and dignity portrayed, the antidote to shame.

Mary and Martha, with their brother, Lazarus, were clearly close friends of Jesus's. He treated them like his family, often staying at their home. Jesus so loved this family that He wept when Lazarus died, for He knew the pain of loss the sisters were feeling, and it was a personal loss for Him as well.

Mary and Martha were two very different sisters. Martha was a do-er, and Mary was a be-er. Jesus honored them both. Mary just wanted to sit at Jesus feet getting filled up with His words. Martha wanted to serve Him and spent her time in busy meal preparation. Martha complained that she was having to do all the hard work and wanted Jesus to correct Mary. He didn't correct Martha or Mary. Instead, He called her higher. "Mary has chosen the better part, which shall not be taken from her." He understood Martha and her need to serve and was kind in reminding her of the "better" way as Mary, her sister, sat at His feet, absorbing every word He taught. No shame, but a simple lens adjustment.

Mary Magdalene is often referred to as a prostitute. There is no clear evidence of that being true, though she is the woman from whom Jesus cast out seven demons. "The twelve were with

Him, and also some women who had been healed of evil spirits and diseases: Mary, called Magdalene [from the city of Magdala in Galilee], from whom seven demons had come out, and Joanna, the wife of Chuza, Herod's household steward, and Susanna, and many others who were contributing to their support out of their private means [as was the custom for a rabbi's disciples]" (Luke 8:2–3 AMP).

While she may have been tormented, she seems to have held some place of honor in the community as she was apparently contributing to his support. Of all the ladies mentioned, however, she is the only one we know of, besides His mother, who followed Him to the cross.

It was this Mary to whom the resurrected Jesus first spoke. She is anxiously searching for his body, believing someone got there before her. He comforts her. "Jesus said to her, 'Mary.' She turned and said to Him, 'Rabboni!' [Teacher]" (John 20:16). Such intimacy! The object of her greatest affection says her name in such a familiar way that she immediately recognizes Him. I can feel the joy that must have bubbled up inside of her!

The woman whom Jesus met at Jacob's well (John 4) was a Samaritan, a woman, and unmarried yet living with a man. Just one of these would make her an outcast to a Jewish man. When Jesus spoke to her at the well where she was drawing water, no one could be more surprised than she. Their interchange was reverent and honoring on both sides. She was a learned woman, no matter what her lifestyle betrayed, and let him know it. "I know that Messiah is coming (who is called Christ). When He comes, He will tell us all things" (John 4:25). Jesus doesn't care about her lifestyle. He cares about her heart to such an extent he shares with her the keys to the kingdom of God. "Jesus said to her, 'I who speak to you am He'" (v. 26). I don't see anywhere before where that exact information had been shared in public. He actually identified Himself to her, a female Samaritan. He honored her, knowing her history, and consequently she was honored in the community that had rejected her. People came to see Jesus because of what she said. In current circles, that would make her an apostle. So He stayed in that town two more days, to the dismay of the disciples, who "marveled that He was talking with a woman."

In John 8 we find the story of the woman caught in adultery. While the law stated that both the man and the woman who are caught should be stoned, the male-dominant culture had deteriorated to only stoning the woman, a huge injustice. So the righteous men of the town dragged her to Jesus, carrying stones of death, determined to catch Jesus off guard.

In His wisdom, without any words of condemnation, Jesus squatted down to write in the sandy ground. There is no mention of what He wrote, though I believe He was taking a moment to talk with His Father. His tender heart toward women must have made it difficult not to stone these accusers Himself! But again He waited, while the crowd grew in anticipation of what Jesus would say. Rocks and boulders were being tossed up and down as the accusers impatiently glared at the sinful woman. They were sure Jesus would agree. Instead, Jesus said, "Let him who is without sin among you be the first to throw a stone at her." No one could. Stones as big as boulders were dropped in place as one by one they walked away, under total conviction. And as she stood there in dismay, her face still wet with the tracks of fearful tears, He removes condemnation from her. "Where are your accusers? Did no one condemn you?" With chattering teeth, she replied, "No one, Lord." And with that, Jesus says, "Neither do I condemn you. Go and sin no more." He simply directs her to change her lifestyle, to correct her view of herself and her identity. She would never have to hide in this culture again. No one would call her adulteress. She could now proudly walk in the town as a woman forgiven.

In Luke 7:36–50, we learn of an unnamed woman, a known sinner, who came into the house of a Pharisee to anoint Jesus's feet. Overcome with weeping, she washed His feet with her tears, for she realized He had not received the foot washing when He entered the room, which was the custom. Using her hair as a towel, she finished the cleansing and began to anoint His feet with the expensive oil from the alabaster jar she'd brought. This is highly significant, since a woman's hair was her crown, her covering. Jesus spoke about her to the Pharisees who were indignant at His allowing her to touch Him, much less kiss His feet. "Her sins which are many are forgiven, for she loved much." And to her, "Your sins are forgiven. Your faith has saved you. Go in peace." She received a new name. Not prostitute, not sinner, but rather a woman of faith, a woman who loved much.

Mary the mother of Jesus carried a burden that no other woman could have understood. The woman who had by faith become an outcast of her community by agreeing to be impregnated by the Holy Spirit; the woman who said to God, "Be it done to me according to Thy will"; the woman who watched her son grow up knowing the call of God was on Him; the woman who watched her son be crucified on the cross to the end. There is no greater honor than that of a child to His mother, and Jesus sets the standard. Hanging on the cross, He speaks to His dearest friend, John, points to His mother, and says, "Behold your mother." He watched her suffer while He was scourged and beaten. Now, hanging before her on the cross, He looks into her face wrenched with sorrow and remembers who she is. He takes care of her with the love of a true Son.

Daughter Revealed

My favorite story of God's women in the New Testament by far is about a woman I will call Veronica. She was the woman with the twelve-year bleeding disorder that caused her to be banished from society. Allow me to set the stage.

Veronica lay prostate on the dirt floor of her humble abode, worshipping YHWH, her God. She was praying once again, desperately crying out to Father in heaven. "Lord God, you know the years I have endured this affliction and the money I have spent on cures that have failed. I have nowhere else to go but to you. I am without a husband, for no man will come near me or touch me. Only my one daughter remains. I ache to be normal again, to be looked at by a man as something more than filth and impure. I do not know what to do anymore. Any attempt at healing only exposes others to my contamination. I beg your forgiveness and ask for undeserved favor. I cry out for your healing."

About this time, Veronica heard about the man Jesus, who was coming right through her town. The story was that a certain government official had asked Jesus to come to his home to heal his child. *This man is said to be the Messiah, but who can be sure?* she thought. Jesus was well known for his healing power, for rumors abounded about those He had already made whole.

She wanted to be one of them, so she plotted how to get near him without contaminating him or drawing attention to herself. *If I could just go to him, just for a moment, no one would notice. There will be so many surrounding him. I know I can remain hidden. I will make myself appear to be a man. I'll wrap layers around myself and crawl on the ground, through the crowd. I just want to touch the hem of his cloak—just a slight, unnoticeable touch—and get healed. No one would know. No one would care. Oh, to live a normal life again. I must...I must try!* He was her last hope.

In the morning dawn, she heard He had arrived. As she peeked through her window, she spotted Him on the horizon and was overcome by His kind face. Quickly, she gathered the material she had put aside for her camouflage, making sure there was no evidence of the persistent bleeding.

The crowd was bigger than she anticipated. She struggled, getting on her knees, desperately holding on to the cloths surrounding her, and keeping her head well covered. She endured getting kicked and stepped on by the demanding followers. All she saw were the bottoms of the crowd's cloaks and their sandals. Which one was Jesus?

Suddenly, there He was. She just knew it was Him, and as quickly and intentionally as she could, she reached for and touched the bottom of his cloak. Breathlessly, she withdrew, suddenly aware that something happened.

"There, there, I did it. Yes, I did it," she whispered to herself. "Oh, I can feel the difference already! I must hurry home and prove myself healed."

She stopped suddenly when she heard Jesus say, "Who touched me?"

So many thoughts ran through her mind. *Wait, what? He is talking to the crowd and asking who touched Him. How could He know? I was so careful! No! I cannot let anyone know it was me.*

Oh! He so persists in knowing. I cannot run and hide. I must declare myself, no matter the consequences. God have mercy.

"It is I," she stutters as she rises to her feet, hesitating to meet His eyes.

He looks at her, He sees her, and He speaks one word into her eyes.

"Daughter" was all He said.

Tears coming from years of pain covered her cheeks as she tried to brush them away, leaving streaks of dirt behind. *This was not the plan! I am seen. He knows me. I can't escape.* The thoughts ran through her mind in anguish over her dilemma.

Slowly, she began to take in the word He spoke. *Daughter? How could this young man call me daughter?* she thought. *I could be his mother! Is He truly the Messiah, speaking for our Father God? He called me Daughter!*

Finally, she was able to look at Him, tell her story, and receive the gift she was seeking.

"Your faith has made you well. Go in peace, and be healed of your disease."

Suddenly out of nowhere, townspeople were gathering around her, holding her up as she slumped to the ground, fainting under the power of the encounter. "He called me Daughter!" was all she could say as they led her back to her home.

I absolutely love this story. Veronica pushed against all oppression possible in her culture to just touch the hem of Jesus's robe. She had completely gone through all of her known resources and was at a place of desperation. She was tired of being identified as "unclean." The identity society labeled her was not who she was and there was something visceral inside her that knew that.

Where does one get the gumption and courage to venture into a mobbed city of people trampling over each other to see Jesus? What was inside her that convinced her that her only hope was in this man? She knew she was not simply "unclean," that she was more. She went after the truth. She went after healing because under that healing was her true identity. She did not see herself as a woman who was supposed to be shut up in a room for the rest of her life and labeled unclean, untouchable as a filthy rag.

Jesus was the one who knew who she was and how to open that door. He spoke that truth to her. And He was intentional in his declaration to her. How was it that among all of the people, mostly men, surrounding Jesus, it was her He focused on? If Jesus only did what His Father said, then could it not be true that Father God whispered into Jesus at that moment? "Son, you will feel your power go out to heal this one woman here who is afraid to be seen because she fears she will make you unclean. She is reaching for the hem of your garment. Heal her." And Jesus immediately felt the pull of His Spirit, and the woman was healed.

But He wasn't finished. He spoke up, asked who it was, even though He knew. But He had more to give her than she had come for. Beauty for ashes was waiting for her. Finally with great hesitation, she rose up to expose herself and admitted it was she. His response is "Daughter." He calls her *Daughter*. He gives her a new identity that very moment, and it redeemed all the years of pain and rejection she had lived through. The words *had* to be spoken. He *had* to call her out so that she could hear what He wanted her to understand.

When He called her "Daughter," she was transformed from unclean to whole, from dirty to beautiful, from outcast to a full member of the family of God. One word declared her identity. Not just from anyone, but from the one who gave her life. Only a Father could call her a daughter.

The opposite of shame is dignity. Every one of these stories of the women Jesus encountered is a story of dignity restored and shame rebuked.

He does the same for all of us.

Declaration and blessing: Beloved child of God, rise up to the stature He placed in your heart to be the fullness of what he saw when He conceived you in heaven. Come to the garden and spend time with the one true God. He wants to restore you to the original way He created you to be, with dignity and honor and love. No more shame, no more guilt, no more condemnation. In Jesus, you are completely free.

Chapter 9

I Am

The truth will set you free.
—John 8.32

Jesus has a lot to say about His own identity. It is fascinating. For being the most humble of people who ever lived, He spoke boldly of who He is, and no one who followed Him thought He was arrogant. Remember when He stood up in the temple and opened the scroll to teach from it for the day?

And He was handed the book of the prophet Isaiah. And when He had opened the book, He found the place where it was written:

"The Spirit of the LORD is upon Me,
Because He has anointed Me
To preach the gospel to the poor;
He has sent Me to heal the brokenhearted,
To proclaim liberty to the captives
And recovery of sight to the blind,
To set at liberty those who are oppressed;
To proclaim the acceptable year of the LORD."
Then He closed the book and gave it back to the
attendant and sat down. And the eyes of all who
were in the synagogue were fixed on Him. And He
began to say to them, "Today this Scripture is
fulfilled in your hearing" (Luke 4:17–21).

Truth shines like nothing else. Of course His enemies made tremendous accusations toward Him, but He also modeled how to deal with that. It was easy for Him to ignore them. He knew better. He knew who He was.

The gospel of John was written by Jesus's close friend and disciple. John and Jesus had an intimacy that was recognized by all the disciples. He saw Jesus in ways the other gospel writers didn't. He walked with Jesus. He shared details in a way that only one who walked with Him would have known. The book of Revelation is the masterpiece fulfillment that came out of that intimacy.

That makes John a pretty credible witness of the Jesus he writes about. Because of this gospel, Jesus became real and tangible to me. It became apparent that knowing Jesus intimately was necessary in understanding my identity.

I Am

There are 7 "I am" statements in the gospel of John. When you read these in context, you will find a profound expression of Jesus and His identity and purpose.

1. John 6:35: "I am the Bread of Life. Come every day to me and you will never be hungry. I am the true Bread of Life. Your ancestors ate manna in the desert and died. But standing here before you is the True Bread that comes out of heaven, and when you eat this Bread you will never die."

Here is Jesus giving himself as food for our spiritual hunger. While we seek daily nourishment, He is saying there is a food that will give you eternal life.

2. John 8:12: "I am the light of the world and those who embrace me will experience life-giving light, and they will never walk in darkness."

Darkness surrounds us daily, and here we have the Son of God offering His light to shine in a dark world. He would not only shine in the darkness, but He would be a change agent of darkness, causing those who walk in hopelessness and despair to be free to walk in the light of life.

3. John 8:58: "I give you this eternal truth: I have existed long before Abraham was born, for I AM."

Jesus makes no mystery of His equality with God. These words draw us back to Moses's query of God in Exodus—"And God said to Moses, 'I AM WHO I AM.' And He said, 'Thus you shall say to the children of Israel, I AM has sent me to you.'"

4. John 10:11, 14: "I am the Good Shepherd who has come to give my life as a sacrifice for the sheep. I alone am the Good Shepherd, and I know those whose hearts are mine, for they recognize me and know me."

He knows us by name! This is blessed assurance from a loving Shepherd, the only Good Shepherd.

5. John 11:25: "I am the Resurrection and I am Life Eternal. Anyone who clings to me in faith, even though he dies, will live forever."

Jesus gives Martha words of reassurance as she questions Jesus about Lazarus's death. This is the same assurance we have of eternal life.

6. John 14:6: "I am the Way, I am the Truth, and I am the Life. No one comes next to the Father except through union with Me."

There is no more potent statement than this one. Jesus is the only way to God.

7. John 15:5: "I am the sprouting vine, and you are my branches. As you live in union with me as your source, fruitfulness will stream from within you."

And lest you think you are on your own, He offers Holy Spirit to help you remain connected to Him as well.

Jesus walked in the fullness of his identity. He knew who He was and what his purpose was. He walked the earth in order to show us how to do the same. He is the fullest expression of who we are called to be.

My Friend

There are many words to describe Jesus—Savior, Redeemer, Christ, Son of God, the second Adam, Son of Man, Messiah, Servant, Rabbi. I like to call Him Friend, which is what he told his disciples He was to them, on the eve of his death. "Now you will call me friend, because I have made myself known to you through the words of my Father" (John 15:15).

True friendship comes out of true intimacy. He revealed Himself intimately to them; He let them know Him in His weakness and His strength. Consequently, they now had permission to call Him friend.

There was that cry of my heart again—to know and be known by God. We get to have that because He left us Holy Spirit.

Jesus did not come to condemn the world but to save it (from the evil one). John 3:17, the verse right after the infamous 3:16, says, "For God did not send the Son into the world to judge the world, but that the world might be saved through him." It was not a condemnation. He was here to save us from an eternal life in hell. He let the serpent crawl around seeking whom he could destroy from the day of creation. And it was time to take away his rule and replace it with a Savior. It was time to crush his head.

He didn't remove the serpent from the earth. He simply said that He, Jesus, would be the one who would save us from Satan's attacks. He told us to pray these words in the Lord's Prayer, "deliver us from evil." That was why Jesus came to the earth—for deliverance from the works of Satan.

So often we want Jesus to remove our struggles, when what He wants is to let Him save us through them. Like He did for Moses when He split the sea for the Israelites to walk through and escape Pharaoh. God could have lifted them above the water. He certainly had authority over all things. He could have slain Pharaoh or at least made him hear the truth. Instead, as they stepped into the water, He caused them to walk through the Red Sea as He held the sides of water up to make a way to freedom.

Our freedom is hugely important to Jesus. And He allows us to be a part of the victory. Remember that in the midst of all those miracles, He (God) blinded Pharaoh's eyes. So who were the miracles for, I wonder?

Not Condemned

Jesus knew what His Father said about Him. He knew His purpose in walking on the earth, and He made choices that were in alignment with that destiny. The last time we hear the word "repent" is from the mouth of John the Baptist, who came to prepare the Jews for the coming Savior. When Jesus was baptized and the Father said, "Behold my Son, in whom I am well pleased," the focus changed. Now we enter into a time of beholding. To repent means to change your view. But God said, "Behold." Look—there He is! God the Father was pointing at Jesus. Here was a living being who was God, who would save the people from their enemies. Only they didn't really know who the true enemy was. They thought it was Caesar. God knew it was Satan, the one who seeks to destroy. So He sent Jesus to show them the way.

Jesus calls people to repentance by His very essence. Awareness of freedom and healing drew people to Him. Suddenly they didn't have to wait for feast days to be clean; they could just step into His presence and know they were forgiven.

Yes, he confronts their sin, by his presence and often indirectly by simply saying "go and sin no more." You see, He knew who He was. He was the Savior, so His purpose was to save people from their incorrect lenses of sin and condemnation that was prompted by a vicious enemy. He raised people up to a higher view of love and forgiveness. Every time they got close to Him, their sin betrayed them. He didn't have to say anything really.

So how does the Savior act differently than a condemner? Throughout His time on earth, He met people where they were and showed them a higher way of life. He told them they would be in the world but not of it. He expanded the commandments to include the heart, not just the behavior. "This is My commandment, that you love one another as I have loved you" (John 15:12). He sent us the Holy Spirit to make it possible to live out what He was calling us to do. He let us know that "greater works than these will you do, for I go to the Father" (John 14:12).

There was never a word of condemnation out of his mouth. The woman caught in adultery, sitting at the feet of her accusers, was simply told to go and sin no more. And His word to her accusers, who were obviously accomplices in her sin, was to challenge them to throw the first stone if they were without sin. In a culture that centered on sinfulness, this was an equalizing way of bringing truth. So many times we condemn ourselves by our actions. Jesus gave them the freedom to own their sins. No one threw a stone. He gave them dignity in spite of their condemning behavior. Jesus doesn't shame us. So if you ever feel ashamed of your behavior, look somewhere else for the accuser.

He was the same with Zacchaeus, the tax collector. Everyone in the town hated this little man. He was a relentless, unmerciful tax collector who charged more than required and skimmed off the profits. He was worthy of condemnation, but instead Jesus called him out as he hid in the tree, and said He wanted to come spend time with him at his house. His kindness brought Zacchaeus to repentance. "Or do you think lightly of the riches of His kindness and tolerance and patience, not knowing that the kindness of God leads you to repentance?" (Romans 2:4).

It is His kindness that calls us also out of hiding in order to give us a chance to truly partake of His goodness.

While Jesus did have a few things to say to the Pharisees, he didn't tell them to repent. They already considered themselves above sin. And it was for that reason Jesus called them blind guides. He holds spiritual leaders to a much higher standard. He exhorted them to stop looking at the Scriptures to find the Messiah and instead look at Him. But they were too proud.

How often do we flippantly excuse ourselves with, "Well, of course He lived the perfect life. He was God." It is important to understand that He was also fully man, so He struggled just as we do. He knew the only way He could be perfect was to stay connected to the Father. So we read in the gospel of John, "I do only what my Father tells me" (John 12:49). How many times did He enter places where people were in need but healed only those the Father pointed out? How does one do that? We know it was His heart to heal them all. God's desire is that *all* be saved.

He knew His destiny. He knew He was the Savior. He had something so much more valuable than any earthly healing could have been. He was going to give them eternal life, and therein, perfect healing. While they wanted an earthly king, He knew what He would leave behind for them could more than satisfy their need for an earthly king. So while they grabbed at him and questioned him, He could let go of His own will and only do the Father's. He was secure in who He was.

There is a scene in the movie *The Passion of Christ* depicting Jesus's scourging, where Jesus is getting whipped almost to the point of death. We see Him passed out on the ground, soaking in His own blood. Anyone would have understood if He'd chosen to stay there and die. But we watch this agonizing resurrection from the ground, as He wills Himself to get up and not give up, desperately grabbing hold of the whipping post, grasping relentlessly as His bloody hands slip and he drops to the ground again and again. Finally, He is standing up again, just in time to receive more blows.

After loading the cross on his back, the weight causes Him to fall over and over again, and he relentlessly crawls along, often on one knee, determined to complete the course. Each time it is the cross that He holds on to that gives him the leverage to stand once more. He knew His destiny. He was determined to finish what He started. I believe Father God was whispering to His Spirit over and over again: "You will make it. You are my beloved Son. I am pleased with you." Until finally on the cross Jesus could say, "It is finished."

That is what knowing your core identity, knowing your truth, knowing your purpose, does. It keeps you on your feet, no matter how many times you fall. And we aren't finished until God says, "Well done. It is finished." Without an identity, hopelessness and despair set in. And that brings all kinds of problems with it.

I am a child of the King just because Jesus lives in me. That identity helped me through a lot of struggles. When you have been slapped across the face, or cussed at, or ridiculed, how do you rise up again unless you know who you really are? Father God stands there and says, "Not to my child, you don't." And if we aren't in agreement with Him, we step right back into the mess because some part of us believes it is the best we deserve. God's hand is right there to rescue us, and we can't even see it if we are so blind to who we are.

When Jesus sees me, He sees Himself in me. That is all He sees. He doesn't see my failures, my weaknesses, or any of the sins the world sees. He laid all that at the cross. He sees Himself reflected in me. He sees me as He created me to be. He died for all that junk that I see in the mirror. But until I was willing to see myself as He did, the sinner, the old man, won.

Angela Is

At one time I went through the process of creating my own personal identity statements. Here they are, ever evolving though they may be. These reflect a piece of how God created me and who He is calling me to become.

- I walk in the fear of the Lord, taking back territory with the vengeance of the Lion of Judah.
- I am a ferocious lover, prowling around, taking back what the locusts have eaten.
- I wake each day with strategy for empowering the beloved in their destiny.
- I am a dreamer, receiving divine strategies for overcoming the fiercest of battles.
- I worship with the intensity of a lion, while joyfully declaring the majesty of God.
- I am a glorious kingdom warrior, exploding in light and truth that shines through to the nations.
- I see a Rahab, and know it is the great-great-great-great-grandmother of Jesus.
- I am a Sarah, full of promises for an inheritance of thousands of daughters.

Declaration and blessing: Daughter, you are a child of the King. I declare it is payback time, time to take back what the enemy has stolen. I bless you with the courage and the determination to go after your birthright, your inheritance, with the intensity of a child whose whole identity was stolen. God gave it to you, unique one, and only you. Receive it back now, precious daughter.

He Knows My Name

Chapter 10

Finding Your Tribe

Now Jabez called on the God of Israel, saying, "Oh that You would bless me indeed and enlarge my border, and that Your hand might be with me, and that You would keep me from harm that it may not pain me!" And God granted him what he requested.
—1 Chronicles 4:10

Many stories in the Bible are about identity, calling, destiny, birthright. Use whatever name you want—there is much in the Bible that says it is important to know who we are in Christ and in our spiritual and physical DNA. God placed each of us on this earth for a purpose, but how do you discover that if you don't know foundationally how God sees you? That is why we often end up doing what everyone else expects.

Moses Finds Himself

Moses faced some huge identity issues. He was born in a tumultuous time. The pharaoh of Egypt was an evil man. He made a decree to kill all the babies of the Israelites. Moses's mother was an Israelite, and she loved her son. So she decided that the only way to save him was to send him across the Nile River in a basket and hope that the Egyptians would find him and keep him safe. He was discovered by the Pharaoh's daughter, to his mother's great relief. The daughter immediately knew he was Hebrew, so they invited his mother to be his nursemaid. Later, Moses's mother returned him to the princess, and the pharaoh adopted Moses. He grew up in the king's household and lived like a king, like an Egyptian.

But Moses couldn't escape his identity as a Hebrew. When he was grown and saw an Egyptian beating a Hebrew slave, his heart was wrenched and he went after the Egyptian. He was ostracized and ended up hiding in a foreign land, though still presenting himself as an Egyptian. He named his son "Gershom," for he said, "I have been a sojourner in a foreign land."

Only when Pharaoh died was Moses able to come out of hiding and become who God created him to be, and fulfill his birthright. And it took a face-to-face encounter with the true God, who proclaimed "I am that I am" to convince Moses to obey, fighting all the way. Though his name was given him by a princess of Egypt, his true birthright was to be savior of the Israelites, his people. His mother saved him from destruction, and now he was to save his tribe from the very people who saved him from death. Only God can tell that kind of a story.

It is in our nature to seek out our tribe, those that we can connect to, relate to, and feel that we belong with. That is what I sought in the cult. That is what I sought in many varied churches. Everyone is looking for belonging. Moses was grateful to his Egyptian family, but was never one of them. He found his destiny among his own people. When he found out who he was, he was available for God's call on his life. Pretty astounding, isn't it? Right place, right time made all the difference.

Where Your Treasure Is

Sometimes your destiny, your identity, is right in your backyard. There was a story I read years ago called *Acres of Diamonds* (Russell H. Conwell, 1915). Here's the gist of it:

There was once a wealthy man named Ali Hafed who lived not far from the River Indus. He was contented because he was wealthy, and wealthy because he was contented. One day a priest visited Ali Hafed and told him about diamonds.

Ali Hafed heard all about diamonds, how much they were worth, and went to his bed that night a poor man. He had not lost anything, but he was poor because he was discontented, and discontented because he feared he was poor.

Ali Hafed sold his farm, left his family, and traveled to Palestine and then to Europe, searching for diamonds. He did not find them. His health and his wealth failed him. Dejected, he cast himself into the sea. One day, the man who had purchased Ali Hafed's farm found a curious sparkling stone in a stream that cut through his land. It was a diamond. Digging produced more diamonds—acres of diamonds, in fact. This, according to the parable, was the discovery of the famed diamonds of Golconda.

There are many ways to look at this story, but my point is that much of what we are missing in our identities can be found already within our grasps. Perhaps we just haven't looked in the right place. Our tribe may be living right next door, or in our family.

In my case, one key to my identity showed up when I became a grandmother. After raising four kids, often alone, I was pretty sure I wanted to "get a life" after they were grown, and find myself and my purpose. I told my kids so. I think Michelle might have been cheated by this declaration because I didn't give her kids that much time and attention in their early years. I was pretty busy trying to get whole and deal with the abusive relationship I was in. But Joanie found herself in a predicament, and since I was single at the time, I was in a position to help her.

She was pregnant with her first child and needing to continue to work. I agreed to watch her son a couple times a week. It wasn't long and she was pregnant again, so we decided it would be advantageous to get a house together.

I had no idea how much I would enjoy being "Gramma." It seemed to redeem all the failure I felt I had been to my own children. I had nothing to prove with grandchildren. I just loved them the way they were, and they did the same. I renewed my belief that indeed I was a good mom, and now a wonderful grandma.

Living arrangements have changed over these ten years, but I still get great joy being a part of their lives. It astounds me still whenever I go to their house, because they are always excited to see me. That does much for my sense of self, and it also contributes immensely to define my destiny. I can feel my inner shine whenever I see their glowing faces!

Through them I was reminded of who I was as a mother, something I feared was lost in my failure to protect my own children. You can never make up for your failings. There are not enough good things that can cover letting your daughters suffer abuse from their father. However, it did redeem my identity as a woman of love and nurture, and I love the relationship I have with all of them. Being a part of their lives has enhanced mine beyond anything I could have hoped for.

Thankfully, I didn't stick to my declaration of never being one of "those doting" grandmothers, a declaration made from pain and exhaustion, or I would have missed out on one of the treasures of my life. God knew. I am glad I listened to my heart, not my head.

Sisters

Other opportunities to discover my inner joy were found beyond my immediate family. As an independent introvert, I tended to be a loner. Relationships did not come easy. I was the one who reached out to the needy of the world, but when I was in need, there was no one there. Choosing needy people did not expand my horizons; it just drained me.

I am thankful to the counselor who reminded me that I needed other healthy women in my life. She challenged me to look in my immediate arena to find the very people I needed to make a part of my inner circle. So I took the challenge. She was so right.

When I opened myself up to the possibility of healthy, mutually satisfying friendships with women, which by itself was a bit scary, I found more people like myself. My relationships expanded quickly, and women searching for fellowship showed up in my community. It required me stepping out of myself, joining groups, and reaching out. I am always one to reach out to the underdog, the lost puppy, or the hurting child. Reaching out in friendship was a new adventure.

I discovered that I was a pursuer. Where I saw pain and hurt and weakness, I pursued and offered myself sacrificially as a life giver. I thought I wanted to be a counselor, and did so for several years. My spirit was tweaked whenever I came across an unloved and unappreciated daughter. I offered myself sacrificially to bring them love and acceptance. And a few of those became friends with whom I too could share my life. It was a whole new place of God meeting me where I was.

Today I am surrounded by wonderful women who validate and appreciate me regularly. Yes, some were found on Facebook, and many were from groups and organizations that I joined or started in order to expand my horizons. None were very far away, and with my eyes open, I could begin to trust and enjoy other people.

My dearest and best friend became so in a much unexpected way. Our church was offering training on prophetic gifting, something that my heart just leaped at. She was someone I knew to be advanced in that gifting, and to my delight I was put in her group for extended training after the formal classes ended. We would meet with a few others at my apartment, and she would teach and encourage. I really loved how she caused me to believe in my gifting.

The next year, an opportunity arose at the church to go to Israel. This was a dream opportunity! My recent divorce had left me with a little cash settlement, so I invited her to go to Israel with me. She said yes, and our friendship was bound into eternity after that trip. When two women can travel together and still stay friends, you know there is something special going on!

Friends are a great way of finding who we are. True friends will tell us when we are being hard on ourselves and will reflect how God sees us. They will correct our negative self-talk with words of affirmation. They will bless our spirits and give us hope. Friends are fiercely important. Wouldn't we be lost without them?

Declaration and blessing: I bless you to take a look around your immediate community. What pieces of your identity are you missing? Where do you feel empty and unfulfilled? Could the answer be right where you are and you are missing a blessing? I declare an expansion of territory for you and a drawing of caring and loving friends to walk with you through a life that is meant to be full of exuberant joy.

Chapter 11

Hearing God

I love what God's voice does inside of us. It is so forming, so connecting, so relating. There is the original version of us that God the Father intended, and his voice helps to reestablish the feeling of true self or original self.
—Shawn Bolz, *Translating God*

Prophecy has been a part of my relationship with Jesus from the beginning of my Christian journey. Jesus now lived within me. He loved me from the inside out. He started speaking to me in the spirit of my mind, whispering prophetic truths about my life and about Himself. Before computers and word processing, I would write endlessly what I believed God was speaking to me. It was like I held a magic pen. I would lift it up, dedicate it to God, and then start writing or typing what I would hear. I learned much about my identity through those whispers. I saved many of my earlier words. This tidbit was written around 1980 (unedited):

> You cannot prove to anybody that I love them—only I can do that job. You can only love them, and that I do too, by the power of the Holy Spirit in you. Do not, never, be afraid to love, especially the unlovable. I do my greatest miracles in the hearts of the unlovable. How you worship me is of no concern to me. The highest form of worship to me is to aim to love one another as I loved you and do love you. Everything else in your life will then fall into place. This was and still is my greatest commandment. Without it, everything else is meaningless—great teachings, good

works, tithing, prophecy, discipleship. Seek the highest way. As I spoke through Paul, this is no different today. You want to be in my favor—this is how. Let my love abide in you. Open your heart to receive my love and to let it flow through, and even if you feel like the least child in my kingdom, you will be the greatest. This is not easy. Only my Spirit can do it in you. Ask and you shall receive. Do you want to walk in my way? Ask for the Holy Spirit to fill you with himself, and your walk will be easier and the results will be better. You cannot love this way on your own power. I did not create you that way. Do not believe that by doing good works you are fulfilling this commandment. Abiding in me fulfills this commandment. Let my Spirit free in you to love one another. Watch and see what I will do when you obey. Do not be concerned about the other things. Seek first the kingdom of God; these words are for today. The kingdom is never so present as when my love is flowing in it.

My identity was already being shown to me as a young Christian, and it has taken a lifetime to really understand the journey of letting go and doing it His way. It has never been easy but has always been rewarding.

Abba Father

I value the voice of prophesy that is encouraged in the New Testament. Jesus told us we were to follow Him, and then He said, "I do only what the Father tells me." That is pretty profound considering Jesus was fully God and probably had a pretty good spiritual head on His shoulders. I see this as Him modeling for us the importance of always checking in with Abba Father before doing or speaking anything. Always.

A friend of mine beautifully expressed her perspective on the value of prophesy in discovering your identity. Victoria captures the essence of prophecy and identity: "Prophecy can reveal how heaven sees us for who we are now and in the future. Identity is about who we are and who we are becoming, and prophecy is about where/how that identity will be revealed. Prophecy is an invitation into a journey of discovering how we are known in heaven, and then how to partner with the Holy Spirit to become that on earth" (used by permission).

I like the simplicity of that description. A pastor I know said, "Prophecy is simply hearing God and then speaking what you hear." That sounds simple, but it's not easy. We have complicated it in our churches because we have elevated the prophetic gift to a place where it is seen as "for the specially gifted."

All Can Hear God

Paul the apostle said, "Now I want you all to speak in tongues, but even more to prophesy" (1 Corinthians 14:5). He simply means that everyone can hear the voice of God. No one is more gifted. It's about learning to listen. "So then faith comes by hearing, and hearing by the word of God" (Romans 10:17).

Hearing God well grows out of intimacy, and intimacy grows out of hearing. The more we become intimate with Him, the better we will hear Him. A mother's ear is always tuned to her baby's cry. New lovers lock on to every word the object of their affection speaks. And God is daily revealing Himself to us in the hope that the more we understand who He is, the more we will listen to Him. Good communication is always the hallmark of a strong relationship. We must remember—He loved us first, and He is patiently waiting for us, His Beloved, to return His affection by experiencing His intimate love that He speaks over us each day.

When I discovered the joy of personal prophesy, my search for identity and wholeness accelerated. There is nothing more life giving than hearing God speak through another person whom we have never met. When it touches a place in me, when it resonates as truth in my spirit, my confidence takes a leap and my faith grows. Wow, is that how God sees me? How do I live up to that?

One misunderstanding about personal prophecy is this: if God said it, it is a done deal. The tendency is to just sit back waiting for all that to happen. Then it doesn't, and we cry foul. False prophet! God lied! Unfortunately, that is just an indication that we don't really understand.

You see, God can only see us through Jesus, because when Jesus died, everything that was us died also. God sees us as He created us, and all He sees is your fullness, your destiny, your birthright and purpose. All God sees is that shining star inside of you that reflects Him.

In reality we are still living in this body and dealing with the history we came in with, the good, bad, and ugly. We don't easily let go of the junk that the old man in us remembers so well and reminds us of so often. He is just so darn familiar. So when we hear God's heart concerning us, it helps to remember the process is about becoming in the future the one Jesus sees in heaven.

Graham Cooke, in his CD "Living Your Truest Identity" (April, 2012), calls this living present future, not present past. "Present-past is when you allow everything from your history, your background, your upbringing and your past to come into your present and affect you, and it stops you from actually realizing your true future in God. When you embrace what God says you are, you are set free of being present-past and you become present-future!" That prophetic word is a future word, and God is in the business of cooperating with you to bring it to fulfillment. There is no time limit on prophecy because God is eternal.

Let's say someone gives you a prophetic word like this: "God wants you to know that He has seen you pray and that He is increasing your ability to see things in the Spirit." This is speaking to potential, as it turns out, because this person has not yet experienced "seeing in the Spirit." If the next time he prays he expects that prophecy to come true, he will be disappointed. But as he practices listening and watching, God will bring the prophecy to reality. As his capacity grows, God trusts him with more to "see," and a new adventure begins. It is like a baby walking for the first time. All those efforts pay off. And the Father's joy is no less than Daddy and Mommy cheering the toddler to get up and try again. It is a joy-filled, exuberant experience that binds us to God more deeply than before. *Now* you can actually start to hear God about yourself, and true revelation unfolds. God just loves being part of the journey. That is intimacy.

Many years ago I was told I would write a book. I made a few attempts, even joined a writers' club for a season. Life events took me places that forced me to set it aside. However, the idea never left my mind. I was just waiting for the right time and place. Then last year, my very prophetic friend said, "I see you sitting at a desk, and there is a swarm of angels around you, encouraging you as you write your book. I think it's time!" Not being one to waste angelic power, I received that and sat down and started this book. I hope there will be more. Again, I am finding that as I write, the words flow from within my spirit. That is God fulfilling His promises!

Prophecy Reveals Our Identity

In August of 2016, I went to the School of the Prophets at Bethel Church and was given a prophecy that really turned me sideways. This young man said that I would be praying for small businesses that were struggling and that, when I prayed for them, they would get back on track and begin to prosper. He called it the Ezekiel anointing, based on the biblical story of Ezekiel speaking to the dry bones and calling them to life (Ezekiel 37:1–14).

This prophecy caused me to frown. There was nothing in my radar that felt this was a fit. This was the first time a prophetic word didn't resonate, so I was tempted to toss it out.

Significantly, I was a woman of business, as I owned a bookkeeping service for thirty years. I often waved it off as "just the way I make money to pay bills." I spent years doing that, along with my counseling service.

Wisely, I did not discard the prophecy, though I sadly did not give that prophet a high score on the evaluation sheet. One day I hope to let him know that he was spot on!

In our community groups at that same school, we were talking about the seven spheres of influence, or metrons, we were to minister in. The choices were church, government, education, media, entertainment, business, and family. I was so sure I would end up in the church sphere, but because of that word, and other clues that inspired me, I went into the business sphere. I was as surprised as anyone could be!

Later that day I was having dinner with a spiritual son who lived in the area, and I shared the prophecy with him. He is an entrepreneur, and I found myself being tugged at in my spirit to invest in this man, as I knew he was struggling financially. So I pulled out my checkbook and wrote him a check and prayed for him. He says that is the first time the "Christian" world ever felt Christlike in his life. He began to prosper at his business. God was sealing the deal.

Back home was another young entrepreneur that I intentionally began to bless and pray for, and she is finding success. The prophecy was being fulfilled before my eyes! It is fascinating what happens when we step out of our comfort zones. I like how Graham Cooke expresses it—stepping off your map.

I am watching what God is doing with this prophetic word, including putting myself back in the business world. It is more comfortable for me to support other businesses, and I am open to His direction in my own enterprise. There was a reason He has kept me in the bookkeeping business. It gives me a sense of relevance to the business world of these entrepreneurs. Without that prophecy, I would have never turned my head and looked in this direction. Now I am involved in a church that has started a ministry for that exact purpose of supporting entrepreneurs, just within months of my getting that prophecy. I am surrounded by people carrying that same message. God knew.

Inheritance Words

God also speaks to us about our identities through Scripture. This can occur when we are reading the Bible and a verse just seems to pop off the page. Sometimes it is an indicator that God is showing us something about Himself. And often it is Him showing us something about ourselves. He is sending us a love letter through His word to communicate His heart toward us.

This I call an inheritance word, sometimes referred to as a rhema (an utterance from God) word.

My first inheritance word from the Bible is Isaiah 50:4. One night early in my walk with Christ, this Scripture literally jumped off the page and seared into my heart. My ears perked up, and I wanted to claim it. I was attending the professor's home Bible study at the time, so I took it to him to test. (This is always a good idea when you believe you are hearing God.) He prayed over me, acknowledging what I heard was from God, while reminding me that every call came with a price. And I knew it was a God promise that I have carried into today.

> The Lord God has given me the tongue of those who are taught
> That I may know how to sustain the weary with a word
> Morning by morning He wakens—wakens my ear
> To listen as those who are taught. (Isaiah 50:4)

I would remember this word years later when I found myself always drawn to the believer in crisis. Opportunities to sustain the weary with a word have abounded in my life, starting with my own children and now my spiritual family as well. Each time those moments of despair would show up, I would be reminded of His promise.

A couple years ago, I received this blessing, which went with that inheritance Scripture.

> Beloved, I bless you with knowing that you are teachable. As you wake up each morning, the words of the Lord are singing in your heart, mind, and spirit. Those words are life to you, and as they bear fruit, they are life to those the Lord places in your life.
>
> Be bold in sharing the wisdom God has placed in you in the night season. You are a life giver. Your words are life to those around you. As you sleep and dream, Holy Spirit is placing words of wisdom into your spirit so that you will know exactly what to say when the time comes. That moment of encouragement could be the thing that

lightens the load of someone who is tired in the journey, feeling hopeless and forgotten.

I bless you with being always ready with a word of life to those who are downtrodden and wounded and in need of strength. I bless you with knowing where those needs are and with listening with God's ears for the right words and the right timing. I bless your going out and coming in. I bless you with releasing those words once given and resting in Holy Spirit to complete the process. I bless you with freedom to explore the bounteous expression of how God talks to you in the night season, and as your dreams and visions increase, so will your message.

You never get done with the heart of God's love for you spoken through His words in the Scripture. We are the beloved of God. His love is so constant and pure, and His vision of us is His primary purpose in why He pursues us. And the bonus is, I have not used an alarm clock for years, apart from emergencies. He truly does wake me each morning to speak to me!

Your Turn

Perhaps you have a prophecy that someone spoke over your life. If so, pull it out and dust it off. If it hasn't been fulfilled, it is not too late. Time is eternal to God. What are the gifts and motivations inside of you that you can tap into that will be a catalyst to this prophecy? If it was that you were to be a healer, how many people have you prayed for to be healed? How could you start agreeing with that prophecy in the here and now?

If you have never had a personal prophecy, there is an easy way to begin to interact with God about who you are. The Bible is an amazing book full of prophetic identity statements. Psalm 139:13–18 is a good place to start, only I have flipped it to be God talking to you.

I formed your innermost being,
Shaping your delicate inside
And your intricate outside,
And wove them all together in your mother's womb.
Be thankful for I made you so mysteriously complex!
Everything I do is marvelously breathtaking!
It is simply amazing to think about it!
How thoroughly I know you!
I even shaped every bone in your body,
When I created you in the secret place,
Carefully, skillfully shaping you
From nothing to something!
I saw who I created you to be,
Before you became you!
Before you had ever seen the light of day,
The number of your days I planned for you
Were all recorded in My book.
Every single moment I am thinking of you!
Isn't it precious and wonderful to consider,
That I cherish you constantly in my every thought!
My desires toward you are more
Than the grains of sand on every shore!
When you awake each morning I am still thinking of you.

As you ponder each verse, pay attention to what words jump out at you and feel personal. Make note of those and talk to Holy Spirit about it. Ask, "Is this how you see me? How do I become more like this?" The Holy Spirit loves conversations like this. He can't wait to tell you how amazing you are and what He loves about you. It is quite an adventure.

Song of Songs in the Passion Translation gives us the bride, a beautiful picture of how God sees us. Take this personally, and let it be released into your identity.

Look at you, my dearest darling,
You are so lovely!
You are beauty itself to me.
Your passionate eyes
Are like loyal, gentle doves. (Song of Songs 1:15)

That's *you,* beloved!

Declaration and blessing: Daughter, be relentless in your pursuit. You see, He has been pursuing you far longer and waits tirelessly for you to receive the treasures He has been holding for you. And guess what? He knew the distractions and interruptions that would come your way. Nothing surprises Him about your life. I break off shame and guilt over your failures of the past and release a spirit of joy over your heart to receive everything waiting for you.

Chapter 12

I Am Spirit

Christ in me, the hope of my glory.
—Misty Edwards, singer/songwriter in "Garden"

The first picture of our identities comes from our heavenly Father, through Jesus, and was planted in us in heaven. Jeremiah 1:5 (TLB) says, "I knew you before you were formed within your mother's womb; before you were born I sanctified you and appointed you as my spokesman to the world." In one swoop, God sanctified and placed in Jeremiah's spirit an identity.

My personal declaration is this: "He knew me before I was formed in my mother's womb; before I was born He sanctified me and appointed me as His prophetic love bomb to the world." That is in my spiritual DNA.

I recently found this in an article in *Charisma Magazine*, "What happens to Your DNA When Holy Spirit and Your Human Spirit Merge," written by Matt Sorger, September 27, 2016. I am so excited to see that the importance of understanding our core DNA is spreading in the Christian community. It is so, *so* important. This excerpt presents a great visual:

> 1 Corinthians 6:17 declares, "But he who is joined to the Lord becomes one spirit with Him" (MEV). This revelation was in Scripture the whole time! I became one spirit with the Holy Spirit and I now have a new holy, divine nature.
>
> This is Christ in me, the hope of glory (Col 1:27; 2 Pet 1:4). Divine DNA from God was fused into my human spirit causing me to become a

partaker of God's divine nature! I was truly a brand new creation. As Holy Spirit became one with my human spirit, I was "born again" and Christ was formed inside of me. I was much more than a better version of myself. I was something brand new!

When you receive Christ as your Savior and the Holy Spirit takes up residence inside of you, He actually fuses Himself together with your spirit. You become one with God! You have His divine nature inside of you. You are a brand new creation, with new desires and a new life. Your core identity is completely transformed. Christ's very nature and identity is now completely formed in your spirit. It's a glorious transformation! This is why you are holy, righteous and clean!

I can't emphasize more the importance of what he is saying. "I was much more than a better version of myself. I was something brand new!" How much I want to be a better version of myself. But God doesn't want to fix the old (wo)man. He wants to increase and embrace the new (wo)man. In order to do that, He doesn't see me as I was before Christ. That, in and of itself, is a miracle. He sees me just as He did on the day He said in heaven, "Let there be Angela." That is not the way the world works, however.

Once we are in the womb, and our physical DNA (body and soul) joins with our spirit, we become a new physical creation, carrying the DNA of our parents. That can be awesome and wonderful, and sometimes it can be not so beautiful. But it all makes us who we are. We also will pick up what's going on in Mom's world—all her fears, her joys, her nurture for us will come through way before we are actually born.

In the womb, this new creation is aware of the physical environment in and out of the womb. It is our first opportunity to know we are wanted, loved, and anticipated.

Wise parents do all they can to bless this unborn child so that they have the best possible start as a human being. The birth process is the final release, and it is not an easy journey for everyone. I believe that an unborn child has a will because they are spirit, soul, and body. There are some incredible testimonies of babies in the womb responding to outside stimulus and literally changing the course of their births. One that I will share is of a family whose baby was breach. The parents understood that the child could hear and had a spirit connection to Daddy and Mommy because they had been blessing and speaking over her for nine months. Now her life was in danger. So the father spoke to the baby and blessed her, and with what he said, she responded and turned in the womb, experiencing a safe birth.

Spirit First

In 1 Thessalonians 5:23–24 we read, "May God himself, the God of peace, sanctify you through and through. May your whole spirit, soul and body be kept blameless at the coming of our Lord Jesus Christ." Notice the order; spirit first, then soul, then body.

Our human spirit is the part of us that connects to the Holy Spirit, and when we grow our spirit, we also grow our ability to hear God. This is critically important if you want to know how He sees you and why He made you.

If we only listen to our souls (our mind, emotions, and will), we may miss the best part of who we are. Our soul will also often veto what the spirit is receiving because it is so well fed. We have to learn to subdue our soul into submission to our spirit.

Most soul information comes from our experiences and our physical DNA, making up the "old man" (see Colossians 3:9–10) that died on the cross when we were reborn. That old man has a lot of bad habits and unhealthy responses ingrained in its mind. We need new habits; we need to renew our minds. But that doesn't mean we simply say things differently all the time hoping for a different result. You know what you get when you do that, right? Insanity!

True permanent change comes through our spirits. Rarely are our religious cultures blessing and growing our spirits, unless you count Sunday church and school. The rest of the time we are put through a lot of behavior modification and disciplines that can be very helpful in our ability to live our lives, but not really affecting our spirits in any redemptive way.

So present in the new man is the human spirit. In the Matt Sorger article excerpt mentioned earlier, he refers to DNA being fused into the human spirit, causing us to become a partaker of God's divine nature. He understands that our connections to God are most accessible through our human spirits.

Most of us grow up relating to God through our souls. "Bless the Lord, oh my soul." But since we are created spirit, soul, and body, we need to allow our spirits to have dominion over our souls. That means we have to enlarge our spirits so that they will have a chance at dominion over our souls.

The Human Spirit

Arthur Burk of the Sapphire Leadership Group in Anaheim, California, did a seminar on Nurturing the Human Spirit in 2006. It was a powerful part of my transition into accepting the fullness of who I was created to be.

Arthur began his study on the human spirit as a result of his practice of blessing the spirits of babies in the womb. He stumbled on this purely in an effort to help a mother who was struggling over her current pregnancy. It was his search for truth that brought him to the place of discovering the value of recognizing the power of the human spirit.

What Arthur discovered was not new but was a new emphasis he hadn't grasped before. There is an eternal connection to heaven in our spirits, the connection that started in heaven before we were born, as I mentioned earlier. Since we become inundated with our physical and emotional DNA upon being conceived by two imperfect beings, who we were created to be can get buried in a lot of generational data. Mama and Daddy may be either really happy or really sad they are pregnant, and those messages will be sent to the soul. But when some negative commentary hits the spirit at a very early time, we can be already wounded with no capacity to cope with or veto the negativity. So we come screaming into the world already with a load of baggage. Sadly, the ones that don't make it to birth or get aborted have a much different tale.

So Arthur started to speak to this woman's baby in the womb. Once a week he would call the mom. He would search for Scriptures about joy that he could use to bless the baby. Mom would put her hand on her stomach and put the phone next to the baby, and Arthur would bless her with whatever the Lord would show him to do. He made this a weekly practice whenever possible. Eventually, the mother reported that the baby anticipated the time for the phone call by leaping in the womb with excitement when she heard the phone ring at a particular time. Consequently, the birth went profoundly well, and Arthur reported that he has never held a more joy-filled baby in his life. Out of that came an incredible ministry to babies in the womb.

It's All about Inheritance

As children of the King, we have an inheritance that exceeds anything we receive from and through our earthly parents. What

Jesus declared over you before you entered your mother's womb is still the absolute unadulterated truth, and each of us deserves to know the fullness of that truth so that we can walk in the inheritance we have been promised from the beginning. This is why God selected and ordained us to be his own inheritance through our union with Christ! Before we were even born, he gave us our destiny—that we would fulfill the plan of God who always accomplishes every purpose and plan in his heart (see Ephesians 1:11).

If you were the child of a wealthy king and suddenly all of it was stolen from you before you received your inheritance, would you not do anything to get it back? The devil is creeping around every day seeking to destroy your God-given identity. It is a battle worth pursuing to get it back, because knowing who you are is the single most precious gift you have, and no one has a right to steal it. Have you ever had your wallet stolen, with all your identifying information inside? Who doesn't go to great lengths to redeem what has been stolen?

A few months after my mom passed away, my youngest daughter, Sarah, came home from a visit to my brother's house, with some of my mom's jewelry. Her aunt had given them to her under the auspice of suddenly and mysteriously being "found" and wanted me to have them out of the generosity of her heart. This was curious to me because a few months earlier, on the eve of my mother's funeral service, we all had gathered in my parents' living room planning her service the next day. My sister-in-law invited me to go upstairs and go through my mom's jewelry while I was there so I could choose what I wanted to take home with me. Awkwardly, I followed her and discovered nothing but costume jewelry. Somewhat surprised, I asked my sister-in-law where the valuable jewelry was. She let me know this was all there was and that the pieces I was thinking of must have been stolen.

As it turned out, my mom and dad had given her my mom's valuable jewelry, and she unabashedly received it like a true interloper. I was the only daughter, and while I wasn't as free to go visit my parents in their later years as this sister-in-law was, I realized this woman stepped into my role as daughter and "stole" my inheritance, such as it was.

The warrior in me rose up. I knew enough about who I was at this time to see an opportunity to stand up and battle for my inheritance. This was not about greed. It was about receiving my rightful inheritance as the only daughter. The enemy does truly seek to kill and destroy.

I realized the true betrayal was my dad's. He had to have known. So I chose to expose the truth and get everything back in proper order. I wrote my dad a letter and told him that I wanted him to go to my sister-in-law and ask her for the jewelry back and then to send it to me. It wasn't long after that I received a package with much of the treasured jewelry enclosed. I was satisfied. The rubies from one necklace now sit in mine and my husband's wedding rings. And my daughters were able to receive some nice pieces of jewelry as a remembrance of their grandmother.

It was one of the most difficult things I have done. I'd felt beaten down by men most of my life, so when I put aside fear of rejection to declare what needed to be made right, I felt like a stronger, more vibrant person. I took my case to God's court, and he gave me a verdict of favor. It was one more step toward my freedom.

Your freedom to be who you were created to be is your birthright. It is your inheritance. No one can take it from you. Sometimes you have to fight to get it back. But you have help. Jesus sees you as you were created to be, and He is faithful to guide you to the path of freedom if you let him. There really is abundant life waiting for each of us.

Declaration and blessing: I bless you with the courage to go after your true God-given identity. You are not to be a buried treasure. Your light is needed in this world. Go after it. Ask the hard questions: Who am I? What do you see, Father God, when you look at me? I bless your spirit to reach into the heavenly treasure box and pull out what God has there for you. As my friend Arthur says, go be dangerous!

Chapter 13

I Am Blessed

Whoever has no rule over his own spirit is like a city
broken down, without walls.
—Proverbs 25:28 NKJV

Imagine two figures. One is a thin waif of a human, looking like the undernourished refugees you see on TV. The other is a three-hundred-pound man, overstuffed and solid to the core. Imagine walking up to that undernourished refugee with a partial McDonald's hamburger you had just pulled out of the garbage and dropping it on the ground in front of him. Can you see him scramble to salvage whatever bits of the sandwich he could, so starved was he for nourishment? It is doubtful the overstuffed man would even notice the food.

That is a picture of what becomes of us when we fail to feed our spirits and concentrate only on nourishing our souls. My understanding of God has been fed with rituals, rules, and religion. My failures were wrapped in my inability to do all the "right" things to find happiness and please God. Spirit food was rare and showed up often in the rituals, but it was not lasting and always left me wanting more.

After watching the DVD from the seminar "Nurturing Your Spirit," presented by Arthur Burk, I was pretty sure I was touching a heavenly concept of truth. I came alive! As I got started blessing my spirit with the help of a little book called *Blessing Your Spirit*, by Arthur Burk and Sylvia Gunther, I enjoyed giving my soul a rest from all the soul food that was keeping me bound in performance. I wanted my spirit to be blessed and to grow.

In the introduction to the book, Arthur says, "The spirit had no chance to implement the will of God in this person's life because the soul had been so overfed for so long. The Scripture says, 'Whoever has no rule over his own spirit is like a city broken down, without walls' (Proverbs 25:28). A city that is broken down and without walls lacks clear identity, clear boundaries, and the means to protect itself. Similarly, someone who is controlled by his soul will not have the proper identity, nor will he have solid boundaries that will protect him. God designed our spirit to be dominant and the soul to be subordinate to the spirit, but when a culture feeds the soul and ignores the spirit, it develops a misrepresentation."

Blessing for Your Identity

Here is the first blessing from the book, reprinted with permission. When you speak this out loud, preferably in front of a mirror with your eyes open, you will begin to engage your spirit and experience the fullness of this place where the Holy Spirit wants to enter. Of course, doing this with another person is always the best, as both of you will be blessed.

[Fill in the name], I call your spirit to attention in the name of Jesus of Nazareth. Listen with your spirit to God's Word for you. "For you created my inmost being; you knit me together in my mother's womb. I praise you because I am fearfully and wonderfully made; your works are wonderful, I know that full well. My frame was not hidden from you when I was made in the secret place. When I was woven together in the depths of the earth, your eyes saw my unformed body. All the days ordained for me were written in your book before one of them came to be (Psalm 139:13–16).

_____, your Father made you special. You are a very special person, created and crafted and designed by God *your Father. Before the foundation of the world, your Father planned for you. You are no accident. You did not have to exist, but your Father willed you into existence. He chose the day and the time you would start your life. He chose your parents and wove you together in your mother's womb. He planned your birth order and put you in your family. He chose every one of your 23 pairs of chromosomes. He chose every one of your 10,000 plus genes. He chose every part of your spiritual heritage. He reached back into your father's bloodline and your mother's bloodline, and from generations past, your heavenly Father chose different parts of your heritage. Some parts are not so beautiful and some parts are absolutely gorgeous. Yet your Father wove it all together and gave you everything you need in the package of your life to be an overcomer, a victor, to take the negative parts of your heritage and triumph over them, to walk in the beauty of all that God has placed within you. Your father made you beautiful and beloved.*

I bless you, _____, because you are fearfully and wonderfully made. God invested an incredible amount of effort and concentration in designing you. You are unique, one of a kind. There is nobody else like you. God has thought extensively about you. Every detail of your body, every organ, and every cell is the result of God's thoughts. Every facet of your personality is the result of His kind intention. You are beautiful, and you are beloved. God has blessed you with His love. God smiled on the day He created you. He had been waiting for millennia for the particular point in time when you were conceived. He had great joy in His heart when His plans actually came together. He nurtures your spirit; He watches over you. Your world needs you. You bring something to your family that no other person has. They need the gifts you bring. Your family would not be complete without you. Others in your circle need the deposit that God has placed in your life.

_____, *your Father wrote your days in His book. He has already read the final chapters, although we have not had that privilege. Your life is not a random thing. He is looking forward to the chapters of the story He has already written. He designed your spiritual heritage. Your generational blessings go back a thousand generations. There is a spiritual treasure chest of generational blessings with your name on it. Those are being released to you incrementally over the course of your life at the appointed, appropriate time. All this is God's master plan. God has foreseen your pain. He promises that because of His love, His power, and His blessing upon you, He causes pain and negative things to be transformed into good things before the end of the story of your life. We don't know everything about who you are going to be or what you are going to do, but you are loved, you are a blessing to your family and you are a life giver in the world. You are special, and we celebrate God's miraculous design of who you are. I bless you in the name of Jesus of Nazareth.*

I have found this blessing technique to be very effective and you will see that I use it in the blessings at the end of my chapters. The more you practice blessing yours or someone else's spirit, the more effective it will be. As your spirit grows, you will begin to notice how much easier it is to hear God more clearly.

Dividing Soul and Spirit

What is the struggle that keeps our souls in control? Being so overfed on our thoughts and feelings, the person we truly are is blocked. The mental talk, our will, out-of-control feelings, all contribute to keeping our true human spirits small. The other piece is that our souls are directly connected to our "old man," our preredeemed man. Our spirits are more easily connected to the "new man," postredemption (biblical reference is in Romans 6). The war is between two kingdoms, the spirit and the soul, the old man and the new man. Hebrews 4:12 says, "For the word of God is alive and powerful. It is sharper than the sharpest two-edged sword, cutting between soul and spirit, between joint and marrow. It exposes our innermost thoughts and desires."

Janelle Brown, in her forthcoming book *Living Your Original Design*, shared,

> My basic premise is that since our human spirit is the place where we connect with God (John 4:23–24), we must consider it of prime importance to discover the true condition of our spirit not only before we invite Him to live in our heart, but after this life-changing experience as well. For the first 32 years of my Christian walk, I believed my spirit was made new through Christ—which it indeed was. However, my assumption was that there is nothing more to be done with my human spirit than to be the passive recipient of God's life. Oh, how incomplete that understanding was! I no longer assume that our spirit is made completely healed and perfect at our first heart surrender to Jesus. In reality, I believe that there is an enormous amount of healing and deliverance that needs to take place within our spirit, as well as our soul. This comes as we increase our capacity to open our spirit to the Living Lord. Because God never pushes His will upon us, He waits patiently until we invite Him in the deepest places of our spirit. However, if we are unaware that we have this deep need in our personal spirit, His knocking at the door

our heart (spirit) is misinterpreted and largely goes unanswered.

As we increase our willingness to open our spirits to the Living Lord, we increase our capacity to receive all that God has for us. We can actually start living as we were originally created to live, as our original selves that God first envisioned. And if we continue to only seek our food from things that feed our souls, life can still be good, but I do not believe it will be the best it can be.

I prayed that the Lord would free my spirit by separating my soul and all its fleshly attachments from my spirit so that my spirit could reign supreme and not fall prey to the voice of my old man. It was a process, and afterward I wrote in my journal, "I am relearning who I am. I have discovered that I have lived only a facade of who I really am. I wore a mask to make me pleasing and acceptable, but it was not my real self. I am starting to live from the heart that Jesus gave me." Those glittering images could finally take a backseat.

A dear friend described her revelation of her spirit/soul dilemma as follows. By permission, I include below a few excerpts.

The inner and the outer world have always collided. I've tried for so long to be what I thought everyone wanted me to be. I am what psychologists call a high self-monitor, meaning that I look at society and my circumstances and formulate the expectations of those around me and then do my best to meet those expectations.

Inside where no one else sees, I am vibrant passionate, and alive. Outside I am a perfectionist, analytical. I am administrative and neat and orderly. Inside I color outside the lines, throw paint on the canvas and see where it lands, and then throw on a handful of glitter for good measure—because everything should sparkle and shine.

Outside I dress like I think a good businessperson or woman of God should. Inside I am clothed in color—paint splattered, lively.

It is in recognizing the importance of our spirits that true freedom to be fully ourselves is made more immediately possible. A strong, large, and ever-present spirit is the greatest antidote to the old man that shouts all that negativity at us, triggered by wounded places we have yet to heal. Those negative words we keep hearing repeated in our heads were all buried at the cross when we entered the kingdom of heaven and declared Jesus on the cross. That is all dead, and the new man needs to have a chance to experience the newness of life that is being offered. Your spirit needs to be fed so that the old man stays dead and the voices become less intrusive.

Soul Food

Words I used to hear that beat me down were, "You're not loveable"; "You made your bed, so lie on it"; "What's wrong with you? No one will love you if you are fat"; and "Don't try too hard—you will just be disappointed." On and on the voices would come. When I first started to read the above blessing, it helped my soul somewhat, but I still didn't believe the words were about *me*. But as my spirit has been nurtured and comes forward to listen, something in me rises up with a resounding *"Yes!* That's me! I know her!" And suddenly the dark voices go away and hope returns.

You may not get that resounding yes right away, but don't quit. Don't give up. Find someone you trust to say these words to you. A daily dose of this will overcome so much that your soul has been struggling to solve. My soul wants to fix me, but my spirit wants to bless me. When we know how God sees us and it penetrates our spirit, the lies are so much easier to dissipate.

Declaration and blessing: I bless you to receive the fullness of how God sees you. You are a unique and beautifully made daughter (son) of the King. He rejoices to see you rising up into your *yes*, your identity, and your birthright. He is ready to resource you in every way to take that journey into how He sees you. Take His hand, and enjoy the ride.

Chapter 14

Why Am I Here?

I am what I am, and that's all that I am.
—Popeye the Sailor

God created us to know him in a specific way and to communicate with him according to our spiritual DNA. Some people hear God in the shower and others when they are walking or driving. I always get a download for a particular spiritual daughter whenever I am driving south on I-5. Others need a quiet place, with no noise and no motion. How we hear God best is important, because knowing who you are, who you were created to be, must first come from God who created you, not from people who didn't. Everyone will have an opinion of you, but no one knows your purpose here on this earth more than He that created you. Knowing your particular gift you carry is part of your spiritual DNA.

Years ago I rediscovered chapter 12 in the book in the Bible called Romans. In verses 6–8, there is a list of gifts, and it reads something like this (I have added the gift title I use in brackets): "We have different gifts according to the grace given us. If a man's gift is prophesying, let him use it in proportion to his faith [prophet]; if it is serving, let him serve [servant]; if it is teaching, let him teach [teacher]; if it is encouraging, let him encourage [exhorter]; if it is contributing to the needs of others, let him give generously [giver]; if it is leadership, let him govern diligently [ruler]; if it is showing mercy, let him do it cheerfully [mercy]."

Charles R. Wale, Jr. describes these gifts in his book *Designed for Fulfillment* (Free to Be Ministries Inc., 2007): "These seven gifts in Romans 12 shape our views on life circumstances, others, ourselves and God. It is the mindset that God gives us through which we interpret life and respond, make decisions, choose ministry, enjoy friends, choose a mate, et cetera. Our dominant gift causes us to see life through a particular point of view with certain spiritual assumptions."

Unlike the manifestation gifts of the spirit listed in 1 Corinthians, these gifts are part of our DNA. I call them the redemptive gifts. The manifestation gifts are ministry gifts. They come as a result of the Holy Spirit coming into us when we have received Jesus. They come and go, and sometimes a person will express a particular manifestation during a particular season of their life. These occur at the will of the Holy Spirit for the benefit of the recipient of the gift.

The redemptive gifts are also different than the five gifts or callings mentioned in the book of Ephesians: "And he has appointed some with grace to be apostles, and some with grace to be prophets, and some with grace to be evangelists, and some with grace to be pastors, and some with grace to be teachers. And their calling is to nurture and prepare all the holy believers to do their own works of ministry, and as they do this they will enlarge and build up the body of Christ" (Ephesians 4:11–12). These are often referred to as the fivefold governmental gifts. I think of them more as callings. These are designated for the maturing of the body of believers. Certain men and women are raised up to walk in the authority of serving as apostle, prophet, evangelist, pastor, or teacher. These are not part of their DNA but rather come out of their maturity and character development.

The redemptive gifts in Romans 6 are gifts of grace, showing us our particular bent, or drive. These are sometimes called motivational gifts. Inherent in discovering our redemptive gifts (RG) is discovering our birthrights, our purposes, why we were placed in the world, in these bodies, in this time period, with these parents and these people, for such a time as this. I was designed for a purpose, and my journey in life is to discover that and walk in it. Life is so much more than what we currently walk out each day. I deeply desired to know my manifest destiny, what would make me go "Yes, this is who I am. This is what I was made to do. I was born for this."

This is as important as knowing your family tree. From whom did you get that understanding of math? Why are your eyes blue? What is your family health history? Adopted children have a difficult time when they don't know their histories should a medical or behavioral problem come up.

Knowing our spiritual DNA is just as important. Why do I want to rearrange every shelf in the store? Why do I criticize that speaker when he says "uh" too often? What makes me so intolerant of wishy-washy people? Why do I always have to win? Why do I always say "yes" and feel so unappreciated? Why do I like to study the Bible randomly, while others like nice orderly question-and-answer studies? Why do I get my best revelations in the shower?

More Than a Test

There are other tests available that have been used for centuries that will give you a clue about how you are bent—for example, Enneagram, Myers Briggs, DISC, et cetera. I find all of them helpful, but I do think they fluctuate depending on where I am in my life journey. When I first tested with the Myers Briggs Temperament Indicator, I tested INFJ (introverted intuitive feeling judgment). (There are tests online that you can take for this indicator, and I do recommend it, as it is very helpful in understanding your personality.) I now lean more toward extrovert in many areas of my life, and it has changed because of my discovery of how God sees me. Life and wounding can cause us to think we are one way when that is merely us responding the way we think we have to in order to survive. So the score on that test can change.

These redemptive gifts stay the same and are not about personality. They instead reflect how we are bent in our spirits to participate in the world we live in. Change occurs in me when I learn to live beyond the negative aspects and behave more Christlike, rather than excuse my ungodly behavior as being "just the way I was born."

At that time I listened to a CD teaching set called "Redemptive Gifts" (Plumbline Ministries, 2003) by Arthur Burk. He compiled years of study and testing into some very basic indicators that help you know what your redemptive gift is and what that means in walking out your life.

Lens Change

When I recognized myself as a redemptive gift (RG) of prophet, I too decided to pay attention to the indicators and confirm it was indeed true. I was not too keen on one of the statements I read about the prophet RG in Mr. Wale's book, which stated that "God often calls the prophet to a higher level of sacrifice in his personal disciplines, faith and commitment." That did not sound like much fun! Nor did I like the list of weaknesses stated there, especially "Tends to value principles and truth as more important than relationships." Ouch!

What I did like is that the prophet RG is hugely committed to design. Anything that is out of order, unjust, unfair, or just simply wrong must be corrected. And sooner is far better. That quality kicked in big when I went to sunny California for a seminar on the redemptive gifts, led by one of Arthur Burk's protégés.

First of all, we don't wear a huge amount of light summery clothing in June where I live. I brought the lightest clothing I could find in my closet. When I arrived and was looking at what I had planned to wear to the conference on the beach the next day, alas, nothing looked inviting in my suitcase. That designer in me was not going to show up at this California seminar in *that*!

I had spotted a mall within walking distance upon arrival at my hotel, so I quickly headed over to see what I could find. Well, the sales were phenomenal, and the service was delightful. I ended up with a whole new outfit, very Cali, reasonably priced, and I was now comfortably delighted to be dressed appropriately and in alignment with my gift for the next day. It was so fun to see that blossom.

It was on the airplane ride home from that trip that I read that statement about prophets and sacrifice, discipline, and commitment, and difficulty with relationships. I felt I was stepping up into a higher calling and that revelation addressed many of the struggles life had brought, putting them in perspective in a way that brought me peace. Several *aha!* moments occurred. "Oh, that is why this happens all the time! It's about my design, not my faults!"

The intensity for right and wrong was part of my DNA, not just some judgmental side of me. Wanting to rearrange furniture and redecorate rooms came out of my DNA for design. My love for the underdog that everyone else abandoned was legitimized. My "cheerleader" personality was me saying, "You have no idea how awesome you are." This book, I believe, is a part of my destiny and a healing balm to my struggle with relationships throughout my life.

Identity means so much. How God sees you, the gifts and opportunities placed in you, are life changing. I had the confidence to move forward in loving myself a bit more, even liking myself, because it was apparent God created me this way and He liked me...a lot!

The best thing about discovering my redemptive gift was that it gave me purpose. It showed me my birthright. It confirmed that there was a particular assignment on my life, the reason I was here at this time in history. None of my life was accidental, and the more I healed, the more I could believe I would complete my journey. Oh, how I wanted to hear "Well done!"

Declaration and blessing: I bless you with the revelation of the truth about yourself and who God created you to be. I declare over you the freedom to explore who you are with joy and courage. It makes all the difference. And it is a fun journey.

Chapter 15

Identity Is a Weapon

Whoever welcomes a prophet as a prophet receives a prophet's reward.
—Matthew 10:41 (NIV)

Bam! The words stung. "You know, Angela, I really don't know you. I think we need to restart our relationship. In order to feel comfortable with you ever again being in leadership, we want you to step back and submit to our pastoral team for the next five to six months. I don't want you to do any leadership, and I want you to meet with my women's pastor regularly until she feels you are ready again to be a safe person for leadership and ministry." This pastor then proceeded to share with me negative comments he had received about me and some corrections of his own.

I sat in his office in shock. I couldn't believe what I was hearing. After five months of being validated, receiving favor, sharing my heart, and even leading a small group at this pastor's encouragement, I was being told in one swoop that I wasn't trusted, I was not to lead, and on top of that, I had some mending of fences to do with some of my accusers.

I made this appointment with the pastor because of what I thought was a shared vision for developing a prophetic community in our church. This was not a foreign idea to the pastor. Having pursued my prophetic gifting for several years, while attending schools and training to support my understanding of this gift, I felt I had brought back with me a blueprint for success and wanted to bring that to this church so that all could know and experience this awesome spiritual gift. I came with a love offering to help lead this church into becoming a prophetic community. He and others clearly welcomed my prophetic gift on a weekly basis, and the pastor was well aware of what I was proposing before I made the appointment. So it was with excitement I entered the room that day.

After pouring out my vision, this response was the last thing I'd expected. Apparently, there were people who had crossed paths with me that didn't like my style. Perhaps they didn't understand prophecy or didn't like my confidence; I actually don't know. But they started running to the pastor with accusations, which caused him to wonder if I had some "issues." As it turned out, he was harboring his own issue with a prophetic word I had spoken to his daughter, and it appeared to make him vulnerable to these other negative comments. Rather than giving me an opportunity to respond to the individual complaints, all was received as confirmation of his own criticism. Suddenly I was deemed unfit, in need of correction and discipline.

Finding a church home has been a journey of disappointment most of my life. Belonging is a big part of everyone's identity, so belonging to a body of believers who actually "got" me and let me "be" me was unusual. Within three years of becoming a follower of Jesus, I no longer felt comfortable in the Catholic Church. I have since been to Presbyterian, Baptist, Assembly of God, Vineyard, and nondenominational churches. I have always stayed in fellowship with believers but often became disillusioned with what I called churchianity. Still, I valued the need for the fellowship of believers and never quit seeking a place of worship that would be a true home. I thought this church was it. So to hear the pastor say those words, a man I had prayed for and received prayer from, that he suddenly didn't know who I was and wanted me to submit to such harsh discipline, left me stunned, hurt, and angry for a while.

I now had a choice. A part of me wanted to walk away, shake the sand off my feet, and consider the whole thing a big mess, big mistake. "I am out of here!" I sought the counsel of people who knew my heart, and no one responded with anything but shock. These were people who would have called me on any error, who knew my heart and my journey. Some suggested I walk away, others that I confront my accusers, which is what I chose to do.

I am all for righteous correction. If I was in that leadership, I certainly would have set about validating the truth before giving such a stern correction. So for me this was an affront from the enemy. Now, what to do?

When it ceased to be personal and instead was a spirit of gossip, I took the posture of war. I got out my sword of truth and proceeded to right the wrongs. If I wasn't going to get my day in court, I would go find the answers and clear my reputation, if for no one else than myself.

Now I grant you, not all would agree this was necessarily the most Christlike posture. Jesus did preach to turn the other cheek. I get that. This however was an attack against my identity. Persecution and tribulation are part of what we should expect as believers. I also understand that. Here was a church, followers of Christ, attacking my identity as a prophetic voice. They wanted me to be quiet while they controlled my behavior. I wasn't to pray for people or prophesy during prayer time until they decided the Holy Spirit gave them the thumbs-up. This is not the character of the Holy Spirit I know. Holy Spirit is a gentleman, and I know when He is convicting. No, this was an attack, and I wasn't going to lie down. So I went to each of my accusers one by one. There was no substance anywhere, and where there was willingness to reconcile, we did.

Fear of Rejection

Fear of rejection is a huge inroad to pain and wounding. I have known it well. I have had my share of rejection in my life. Starting with my mom and dad, and even siblings, I knew how it felt to be deemed "not good enough." I think that is why I often helped the underdog or the younger people in school, because they needed a friend and I was a friend to the downtrodden. That is how I roll. That is the RG prophet in me.

There is darkness in the form of a lie underlying the spirit of rejection that needs to be exposed. We need to find the truth about why we think we are being rejected. If someone didn't like you, were you ugly, too fat, too skinny? Did it occur to you that maybe they just had bad taste? Generally, a fear of rejection digs at all the lies you feel about yourself and makes them bigger.

The core rejection often occurs when you are born into a family that can't nurture or make you feel welcome. You are a burden, wrong hair color, too much trouble, unwanted, a mistake, et cetera. That goes deep and needs revelation to clear it out, a revelation of identity. Only Jesus can show you the root of that one and pull it out.

This pastoral rebuke occurred after that January morning when Angela was revealed, and I now knew how God saw me. So I was either to walk away or allow them to continue to desecrate my identity that I had fought so hard to discover. To walk away would be to let the enemy win.

Fight from Your Identity

When we fight with our identity, we are not doing it from ego. We are doing it from the Spirit of Truth in us. When we know who we are, when we finally believe what God says about us and it is now burned into our spirits and our hearts, nothing can knock us over. I was like that blow-up, round-bottomed punching doll we played with as kids—it went down and then came right back up because the bottom was weighted. I was weighted in truth.

We apparently weren't on equal ground. Professing Christians decided they were my judge and jury. But I understood the importance of identity. There was a sense from this leadership that if my gifting was upsetting the people, it is false. If my enthusiastic words of prophecy rub people the wrong way, I must be a false prophet. If I offer words of encouragement, I am out of bounds. No consideration was given to examine the motivation of the accusers or to the need for a conversation to clarify the heart issues.

Despite an attempt to reconcile and be at peace, the truth was that every bad statement about me was believed by the leadership. Loyalty was elevated above truth. Eventually, I felt I had no choice but to leave. Shut down your gift so that we are more comfortable? No, I don't think so.

Without knowing clearly and with confidence who I am, this would have been a life-sucking and depressing experience. I know I would have doubted my gift, believed the lies of man, and be set back in my walk in a devastating way. While I had some forgiving to do, I also knew I was free to step away.

The enemy of our souls doesn't like it when we know how to hear God and pray accordingly. He likes milquetoast prayers like "Oh God, if it be your will, would you please _____?" God, on the other hand, has given us permission to pray from our identities. "Lord, You made me to be a child of the King, freely endowed with all the rights of kingship. As your child I stand on the reality of who I am and declare that no weapon formed against me shall prosper. I am a new woman. The old woman has been crucified. Lies and deception have no place in my spirit, soul, or body. Leave now in Jesus name and taunt me no more."

Consequently I am no longer in shock and awe that such an attack came. I now accept this as normal, have a good laugh, and move on. If this is how God made me, then He has prepared a place for my gifting to be accepted and valued, and for success to be built under me, not for control to keep me quiet.

God's light shines the brightest in the darkness. Always. So I look for the light in the darkness, and sometimes I have to *be* the light in the darkness. I go there willingly if I am sent, but for now I wait while He dispels the darkness around me. I will step forward when my light blends with His so that together that piece of territory is redeemed.

I was blessed recently to read a prophetic word that clarified what I had experienced. The essence was that the reason you are not flourishing where you thought you were supposed to is because the right place was yet to be found. The old program in my brain of "grin and bear it" did not fit with my new paradigm of truth about myself. I had a choice. Isn't it awesome that God is always after the best for us, a place where we can shine and grow rich in maturity?

I now find myself in a new church home that has welcomed my gift and my heart. What a truly loving God. He wants me in relationship with like-minded people and shining with the gifts he has placed in me. I am elated to know such a loving God.

Declaration and blessing: For all those who have sought to have their identity validated by the local church and have been wounded and betrayed, I bless you with the resilience that only the Holy Spirit can bring. Rise up! Take your place in the kingdom. You matter. You are chosen. You have yet to see the glory of God in the land of the living. That setback is rather a catalyst to the next forward move of God, taking you to a new place of inheritance, a closer look at your purpose. Be of good cheer. Jesus has overcome the world.

Chapter 16

God Bless the USA

Nations will come to your light, and kings to the brightness of your rising.
—Isaiah 60:3 NASB

We have a new president, and it is a true identity adjustment for America.

I think America has lost her true identity over the last many years, and I don't blame it on any particular president or political party. We the people are in control of where America is. America is a country that was created to stand up against bondage but has swung the pendulum so far that we forgot that we are a nation under God. We have passed laws that approve things that are completely against our Judeo-Christian foundation. Whether you are a Christian or a Muslim or an atheist, there are basic inalienable rights based on being a country that truly believed all men were created equal.

We got confused along the way. Equality doesn't mean do anything you want. It doesn't mean that you can kill or vandalize because you don't like the way something turned out. Our country right now is experiencing an outrage from people who don't really know the foundation of America at its roots, and they have come to the conclusion that she is a country that gives relentlessly while expecting nothing in return. Tolerance has been the cry of our young, and yet those same people declare their own intolerance in their protest against those who don't agree with them. Perhaps they do not know or haven't learned about the foundational identity of this country, and don't like that Mommy took away their piggy bank. Using social media as the primary source of truth may contribute to and exacerbate the problem.

Perhaps the season of grace truly is moving toward truth, as I have been noticing lately. We don't know what to say to these young Americans who have lived only one ideology and who are uncomfortable with the likes of Donald Trump, who is clearly a radical change from the previous administration. And they are passionate about what they believe. But do they believe what is real, or do they believe a virtual reality? Do they want to know the truth? I wonder but have no real answers. Clearly, we are in the middle of a paradigm shift in perception of truth.

"We the People of the United States, in order to form a more perfect union, establish justice, insure domestic tranquility, provide for the common defense, promote the general welfare, and secure the blessings of liberty to ourselves and our posterity do ordain and establish this constitution for the United States of America."

The United States is a country of pioneers, innovators, creative thinkers. It is a prophet redemptive gift nation. She understands design and lobbies for the underdog. The preamble stated above speaks to our identity as a nation. Whatever we may think greatness is, we have to want it to be true.

Freedom Isn't Always Pretty

In the sixties I was one of the baby boomers that rebelled against the establishment. We hippies wanted our freedom, the blacks wanted their freedom, and women wanted their freedom. We were sure it was all in alignment with the original plan. Our parents didn't like our responses either. Their response of "love it or leave it" wasn't well received.

World War II was the season of great heroes who were now looking at their children, the baby boomers, and wondering where the dream went. While Vietnam was a big mistake and a waste of time and money, there was good reason to be angry at the death and destruction of so many Americans. However, those who fought were not seen as heroes but fools. They were hurt and angry and traumatized, bringing drugs and rebellion into America. Divorce and abuse became more prominent. Broken people do broken things.

So yes, we need a new, revitalized identity. We need a reminder that we are still the country our forefathers sought to create as a place of destiny and inheritance for the generations to come. And if God is not the center of that identity, anarchy happens.

It will all balance out. Identity keeps everything in balance. The boat can rock, but eventually it settles down and resumes its journey. Pendulums swing, only to finally return to the middle to start the process again.

I have confidence in the identity that is in the blood that has been shed in America. But more than that, I believe God heard our forefather's cry for a country where freedom reigned and all men truly were created equal. Our country fought for women to vote and for African Americans to be equal citizens. They now are. We had a black president. And a woman ran for president. Some day we will have a woman president. But first we must swing the pendulum to bring balance back. And that is rocking the ship a bit. It is all good.

At the inauguration of our forty-fifth president, Donald J. Trump, I was enjoying the patriotic music. It was wonderful to hear these stirring words from "The Battle Hymn of the Republic" reminding me that we are a republic first.

Glory! Glory! Hallelujah!
Glory! Glory! Hallelujah!
Glory! Glory! Hallelujah!
His truth is marching on.

In the beauty of the lilies Christ was born across the sea,
With a glory in His bosom that transfigures you and me:
As He died to make men holy, let us live to make men free, While God is marching on.

A republic is a type of government that has no king, queen, or other monarch and where the people are sovereign, protecting the minorities by rule of law. "I pledge allegiance to the flag of the United States of America, and to the *republic* for which it stands." In America we are submitted under rule of law, not public opinion, as outlined in the Constitution. And our right to vote gives us the opportunity to choose a government that meets our desires for justice.

Declaration and blessing: I truly bless this country with the wholeness of living out its true identity. It is a work in progress, as we are quite young, like our millennial friends, and may not really know who we are as a nation. I pray God will show us how He sees America so that she can stand for liberty and freedom, under God, as never before.

Chapter 17

Yes I Can

For all the promises of God find their Yes in Him.
—2 Corinthians 1:20

Yes is a wonderful word. Did you know that we each have a *yes* encrypted into our spiritual DNA? It is God's *yes* about you.

Do you know that one of the first words we learn as babies is *no*? Why? Because it is the word a toddler hears most. Think about it. They mimic us. So if *no* is what we have heard most, how hard it becomes for us to hear or say *yes*.

I said the following to a friend in a phone conversation. I asked her to write it down and send it to me because I thought there was something profound about it: "We have spent so much of our life fighting to be heard instead of fighting to find out what our *yes* is."

It came out of a conversation about her struggles to do the right thing for an aging parent who seemed to neither care nor appreciate the help. My friend was determined to keep pressing on to be the good daughter because it seemed right, even if her mom didn't ask for or care if she did so. The need for order in her mom's life was more important to my friend than to the mother, and some of it was important enough for her to intrude for health reasons.

What we discovered in the conversation was that my friend has a strong negative reaction to being told no. That word screamed rejection, stupidity, and degradation. It hurt. The need to be heard would turn into a battle of words with strong feelings of anger and rejection. At the end of it all, division occurred. Neither heard the other side; neither liked to hear no.

The Fight for Equality

Fighting to be heard goes back in my generation to the women's movement. Women were vehemently declaring their right to break the glass ceiling, to get paid the same as men, to not be confined to home and babies (just because I gave birth to them doesn't mean I want to raise them), to have abortions, to have divorces if they didn't like the way he smelled or she looked. Seriously, it took on all kinds of views, some of them good and some of them cringe worthy. I realize we unwittingly ended up turning some beautiful, meaningful women into bombastic, narcissistic penis-envying creatures. Gender confusion? Perhaps. But the pendulum had to swing. When you need to change a mindset, that is often what it takes. And swing it did.

Now a woman has run for president. That is a really good thing, and a lot of men were cheering her on. Gay rights also grew out of that rebellion, as did the passing of Roe v. Wade to allow abortion on demand. Today we are dealing with transgender rights. What happened?

I think when we tried to make women like men, we forgot how God originally created them. Any time we step out of our true identities, something gets corrupted. That really wasn't the point. Men weren't free either. If they were, this would not have been an issue to begin with. So why try to be equal to someone who himself was missing his identity and purpose? A secure man has no issue with a woman in leadership, and many companies and churches recognized that.

So were we screaming to be heard rather than releasing the *Yes* of God in us? It is worth consideration.

I know that I found myself often in the shadow of my husband. My belief was that my need to strike out and find myself needed to wait for my husband to first find his destiny. I lost many years waiting and endured much abuse in the process.

That was my errant response to the Christian view of submission to your husband. Don't make more money and don't be more successful, because it castrates a man's masculinity, and who wants to be married to a eunuch? So repress I did, until I couldn't. The *Yes* in me was of a woman of substance who had purpose and value, and it had nothing to do with how much money I made but everything to do with my sense of self, my purpose, and my birthright. That is what identity does for you.

So what if, instead of spending all that energy protesting and demanding equality, we had instead fought for our personal *Yes*, our identities, our purposes, our birthrights. I was right back to "I am, I said." What is it about us that wants to change the outside circumstance and then expects that to change the inward person? I am all for behavior modification when the behavior is socially and personally unacceptable, if not dangerous. My alcoholic husband number two knew that he would not make any inward changes until he stopped drinking. But the alcohol was more important than self-improvement.

I wish I could go back to the women who headed the feminist movement and say, "You are already magnificent and more than equal. You are a unique and one-of-a-kind magnificent creature that God created and chose from before time for a purpose. He sees your potential as a woman like no other because He created you for greatness. Would you be so dissatisfied with the way you are treated if you truly knew how God saw you?"

That is what I was saying to my friend that day. If you knew the immensity of who you are in God's sight, would it be so hard to hear someone say no to what you want and to recognize they too are responding from their identity? Perhaps your need for acknowledgment encroached on their value system.

I found that I had a lot of people saying *no* to me and not enough saying *yes*. So I set out to change that. I believed I had so much to give and just needed a place or a person who would receive what I had. So I gave and gave and loved and counseled and befriended. Then I needed a friend, and they all disappeared. People don't like weakness in those they count on to be strong. Kids hate their parents getting old because it says that someday they will be gone, and it is scary. But I needed *yes* people, at least a few, that would speak life and truth into me and stick around when I wasn't feeling so strong.

They started showing up in my fifties. Thanks to my wonderful counselor, I found female friends for the first time, and I released those who only wanted to take but who gave nothing in return. While Jesus was so full of love that He was all I really needed, He also knew I needed people in order to be fulfilled. He created us for relationship. That is love. He knew what I needed when I had no clue.

No Is Sometimes *Yes*

The process of transformation to a culture of *Yes* starts in the first three years of life. The toddler begins to explore his environment and explore food and discover what he or she likes and doesn't like, what she enjoys playing with and what she doesn't. Yes, this makes me happy. No, that makes me sad. No, that hurts. Yes, I like it when you do that.

When curiosity gets dangerous, *no* shows up more.

I used to babysit my grandson a couple of times a week. He was a pretty unhappy baby for the first six months. Eventually, with much persistent love and words of affirmation, he began to appreciate Gramma. Then he turned three, and separation anxiety again set in. He now understood that Mommy was leaving and acted squeamish, disliking anyone who tried to replace her—that is, Gramma. As soon as I arrived, he would immediately switch from contented to fearful, crying, and demanding: "No Gramma!" He actually started saying that the minute he heard Mommy turn on the shower to get ready for that dreaded word "work."

Once Mom was out the door, he would calm down, and we would have a wonderful time, until the next time I arrived.

At first I was hurt by his rejection. I had poured a lot into this child, as I was no slouchy grandma. But all my good could not replace Mommy and Daddy going away and leaving him. I wanted to be angry, to reason with him. But instead I figured out it was best to comfort him. "Oh, poor fella. So sorry Mommy and Daddy have to go to work. We are going to have a great time playing and singing and watching your favorite shows. It will be OK." Eventually, as he was breaking into tears, he was simultaneously walking toward me as he shook his head saying "No Gramma" with his arms outstretched, wanting to be held in his pain. Now, when he teases me with "No Gramma," I tease back with "No Edgar," and we both break into giggles. One day he crawled up on my lap and said, "I love Gramma." There was no doubt. He just needed reassurance that I would love him even when he said no.

It explains to me why we don't like to hear no. It strikes at the core of our being to be going for something and then told no. And with God it is even more formidable when all those prayers are still sitting in no and not yes. But are they really?

The greatest misstatement of our identities is in believing we deserve everything we ask for. It is a true idol. And it is tricky ground because I am telling you that your identity is the most precious gift you have and in the same paragraph telling you that you will sometimes hear no from God. If you think of the scenario of a father and child, when love is in the center of it, that no could save that child's life. On the other hand, saying yes to every desire of a two-year-old can be very dangerous to their health and well-being. That is not to say that we are all two-year-olds in need of a daddy to guide every step of our days. There comes a time when our heavenly Father trusts us to make the right choices. His apparent no may be an opportunity to trust the yes He already has in mind. Let me explain.

What if the cold shoulder we think God is giving us is really yes, but because we are not getting a clear answer, we think it is no. What if it is, "I have taught you well. You have experience here. Why don't you just assume yes until you actually hear no? Or perhaps search the Scriptures to see if I have already answered you there?" How would that change your decision? What would you pray differently if you knew you had the agreement of God?

God is not a dictator. He is a loving Father. He makes us a part of the conversation. Just as we were once little children climbing up on Daddy's lap so he could hold us or tell us a story, our heavenly Father wants us to climb up on his lap and talk with Him. When we truly understand that we are rightfully daughters and sons of the Most High God and that He has given us access to him personally, how confident should that make us to ask? In God, even a *no* may be a hidden *yes*.

He Said *Yes*

There is one sure way to always get a yes from God. Ask Him what He wants in the current situation. And be willing to agree with Him. Graham Cooke has a wonderful little book called *Crafted Prayer*, where he goes into this idea in great detail and helps us learn how to write a prayer that is always answered with God's yes. It may not be now, but it will be yes if He is in it. So maybe what we are asking for isn't God's best for right now. And who knows that better than our Creator?

My experience at that church burst some bubbles for a while in defining where I thought God was taking me. I saw myself as a prophetic voice to the leadership by training others in the gift of prophecy so that all could hear God. It is a cry of my heart. When it all fell apart and I heard no instead of the yes I had hoped for, I wondered if I had missed God. Since then He has been redirecting my path, a path I would have totally missed had I persisted in what I thought He was doing. That would have been good, but I had asked God for the best He had for me, for what would reflect my true identity. I am still discovering that, and it is a great adventure.

I encourage you to redirect your attention from the *no* places of your life. If you are surrounded by people who give you more no than yes responses, who deplete your shine rather than build it up, find the freedom to let go, and in letting go, you will find those who are your *yes* in God. And if you have some prayers that seem to be always no, ask again. What are you doing here, God, and how can I pray in a way that would agree with your yes?

Declaration and blessing: I bless you to seek God for *yes* and trust God with the *no*. Listen to His heart for you and find the yes that has been waiting there all the time. Those *yes* responses contribute greatly to coming into alignment with who you truly are. Yes validates what God has seen in you all along. I declare a resounding *yes* over your life, in agreement with our heavenly Father, who is cheering you on into the *yes* of His heart.

Chapter 18

I Am Complete

But the fact is, it was our pains He carried—
our disfigurements, all the things wrong with us.
—Isaiah 53:4

Living with pain can become way too comfortable. Having adjusted to life in a wheelchair, how sure are you that walking again is what you want? My husband is legally blind with macular degeneration. He has adapted well and does not cry out for God's healing. I know that seems wrong, but just look at how we respond to getting rid of the pain when given the opportunity. When we hear, "God can heal that, my friend," a common response is, "That's OK. I am fine—God will take care of me." We adapt to pain quite easily. God has built into us a strong sense of survival.

What if you needed bypass surgery because the veins to your heart were blocked? You know it will be painful, but you do it because the alternative is possibly dying if you have another heart attack. God has given you a doctor to help you fix your heart issue. When you know that the clogged arteries can be replaced with healthy arteries, you are quick to want surgery so that you can live a fuller life.

Yet some of us are having emotional and spiritual "heart" attacks daily when we have been abused or deeply hurt. And instead we often choose to shove it away. That's called denial. We think we are so strong that we can deal with the feelings. "If only everyone else would just behave in a way that doesn't set off those horrible feelings of defensiveness and shame," we tearfully scream into our pillows at night.

Get Real

I had to get real to heal. Denial wanted to just move my issues to a later date, not realizing that it would just get more painful to recover and heal. I believed that all those sucker punches that caused me to become defensive were the fault of that person in front of me who just said the thing that hurt. He would take the brunt of my hurt and anger, whether he meant it or not.

It could be something as benign as him saying, "You left the stove on again." And the thought in my head would be, "Why doesn't he just turn it off? Why does he have to say anything? Everyone makes mistakes." And begrudgingly I would go turn off the stove and say a sarcastic "*Sorry!*" which would hit a nerve in him, and off we'd go.

Having been a victim of never doing anything right at home, from spilling stuff at the table to laziness in my chores, I was pretty sure I was worthless. So when I would forget to do the most mundane things, I would get defensive and go into fight mode.

Did you know that defensiveness is a signal for self-hate? Yes, that one got to me too. Defensiveness waves a big *I am not OK, so bug off* flag that causes people to want to walk on eggshells around you. How in the midst of that are you able to hear, "You are my beloved. I love you with an everlasting love"? Hmmm? Not so much. My self-value was so low, I couldn't even hear those words, even when I read them in the Bible. Oh, I was in love with Jesus, but I was pretty sure He was not so crazy about me.

Here is how my mind worked. "If I can love someone else who is unlovable enough, maybe they will love me the way I need to be loved and I will be OK again." So I threw myself into relationships that emptied me, and eventually I had nothing left to give. The cycle to being unlovable started again.

We don't know how to fill up our love vessel in ourselves, and we can't get them filled when we surround ourselves with people who sap us dry. Eventually, relationships fall apart.

Pain Is a Pain

Productive pain has been invaluable to my finding out who I was. It was so much easier for me to blame the person across the room, expecting him to just love me the way I needed so I would feel fixed. It always backfired. No man completes anyone. You are already complete in Jesus. He wasn't asking for me to do anything or to be anyone; I am complete. He is, however, asking me to clean up the mess that is getting me into trouble. It is time to own the responsibility for that defensive, reactive behavior and set things right. It may not change the other person. Sometimes it may even cause the individual to be angry. But for myself, I had to step into the place of healing.

I spent three years in counseling after the abuse of my daughters came to light. I had a lot to work through. I'd married a predator, and then I'd married an alcoholic, and now I was married to a psychotic control freak. Something in me was drawn to these wounded vessels, or they to me, and it more than likely was my own wounding. So I started to unwrap the onion, and it got real stinky at times. It still does.

I faced the fact that my father crossed boundaries with me. And it started with his father, who physically beat and verbally abused him. I discovered in my healing journey this grandparent had touched me inappropriately when I was a little girl. My father never overtly touched me inappropriately, but he did groom me to be more of a wife than a daughter. He would make me his marriage counselor and presented me as his public luncheon date while Mom drank herself into oblivion at home. I came to understand this was called grooming and was a huge part of the fabric of abuse. It was very flattering at the time, and I didn't see what was wrong. When you are surrounded by a broken mirror, you tend to see things in a broken way.

God became reality. When I got real with Him, I could allow Him to get real with me. And He always did so in such a kind and loving way. Conviction is not meant to be destructive; when the Holy Spirit convicts, we have already been waking up to what we know is broken. He just confirms what we have been denying. And then the healing comes. The lie is exposed. The truth is laid gently in our hearts. Hope is restored. I belong to Him and Him to me. I can rest in that truth.

When we make the decision to commit to being the amazing person God saw when He created us, He brings into our arenas all the resources we need to make the changes and to move toward wholeness. I grabbed on to any tool I could find and then started healing others. Each day became a new adventure, and I got to share it with the most wonderful God and friend, Jesus. There wasn't anything He wouldn't do for me. He died for me, and so each day I return the favor. I give back what He gave me. This book is my giving back. Everything He has given me for life and holiness I want to give back to those who don't know how awesome they are.

Beloved, He sees you the way He originally created you. He is relentless in seeing you find that fullness of truth about yourself. Step into that painful place, and let him be your Healer. Ask Father God to shed light on the place that hurts, that yucky place where you feel like you have been sucker punched. Ask him to show you where that feeling (stupid, abandoned, worthless, invisible, etc.) originated, and ask Jesus to change the lie into the truth (you are brilliant, loveable, valued, and important).

Embracing Pain

One of my spiritual sons recently wrote this from a place of pain.

> In being present with any pain or sickness, we must come to know that Jesus did not only weep FOR us, as in the story of Lazarus, but He weeps WITH us. God's character then cannot be separated from now. I think Lazarus's healing began with Jesus's tears. How does God feel for us now? I don't want to try and faith my way through pain rather than know His tears now. That would be separation, and He neither leaves us nor forsakes us.

And this from a spiritual daughter:

> When I don't know where I belong, I remember God has prepared a place for me. The transition from old to new can be lonely if all we see is emptiness. But in that space where nothing exists, the fullness of God resides. I can't allow myself to be drawn to the memories of past days or expectations of future moments. Instead to dwell in the present awareness of something more powerful and fulfilling...the realization that Jesus is the only friend I need to satisfy the desires of my heart, and that as I walk with Him, I'll let go of those things from the past that weren't healthy anyway. And the hope that is in my heart for connection will never be satisfied in the future by a man but by being my truest self in this moment with God alone. Only then can the future be laid out. Because it is when I am fully me the future

can make a way for what I carry. I draw to myself what I carry, and transition is meant to build the right space so I can recognize and fulfill my destiny.

A Servant Heart

I can't close a chapter about pain without remembering who Jesus was in the midst of His pain. Isaiah 53 is an often ignored passage by the Jews. But it is our answer as believers. We must never forget who He is if we want to truly know who we are. Journeying through pain has a reward. Embrace it and see that the Lord is *good*!

> The servant grew up before God—a scrawny seedling,
>   a scrubby plant in a parched field.
> There was nothing attractive about him,
>   nothing to cause us to take a second look.
> He was looked down on and passed over,
>   a man who suffered, who knew pain firsthand.
> One look at him and people turned away.
>   We looked down on him, thought He was scum.
> But the fact is, it was our pains He carried—
>   our disfigurements, all the things wrong with us.
> We thought He brought it on himself,
>   that God was punishing him for his own failures.
> But it was our sins that did that to him,
>   that ripped and tore and crushed him—our sins!
> He took the punishment, and that made us whole.
>   Through his bruises we get healed...
> Through what He experienced, my righteous one, my servant,
>   will make many "righteous ones,"
>   as He himself carries the burden of their sins.

Therefore I'll reward him extravagantly—
the best of everything, the highest honors—
Because He looked death in the face and didn't flinch,
because He embraced the company of the lowest.
He took on his own shoulders the sin of the many,
He took up the cause of all the black sheep. (Isaiah
53, MSG)

Declaration and Prayer: The pain you have suffered does not compare to the glorious freedom and wholeness you have waiting for you. I declare over you a renewed strength in the battle, your journey into wholeness. I bless you to receive all the strength of heaven to get up and out of that painful past and into the glorious future waiting for you. Arise!

Chapter 19

I Am Perfect

All our righteous acts are like filthy rags.
—Isaiah 64:6

Performance is a human condition, not just a spiritual one. We turn to performing because that is the way to get approval and validation. The apostles only knew performance because all they had were zillions of commandments, and none of those gave them the peace they needed. They asked Jesus, "What must we do to *perform* the works of God?" Jesus said to them, "This is the work of God; that you *believe* in him whom He has sent" (italics mine) (John 6:28–29). No performance. *Believe.*

The word "believe" in this case is not just a head-knowledge belief—it is a word in the Greek that means *acknowledge* and *obey*. Earlier in John 3:36, Jesus said, "Whoever believes in the Son has eternal life; whoever disobeys the Son will not see life, but must endure God's wrath." Clearly, the opposite of *believe* is *disobey*. Jesus was making it clear that he was asking for submission to His Lordship. We are to be in a state of submission to the one and only true Jesus, whom God sent and placed all things in His hands. In Him we have everything that entitles us to heaven on earth and after death.

The journey to our true identity starts with Jesus. Do you understand that God only sees you through Jesus? He can't see the person you were before Jesus because that person was crucified on the cross with Him. He only sees you as the person you are *in* Jesus. And when we answer the door that He has been knocking on and we allow Him to take our messy lives into his hands, He not only changes us—He takes charge of the rest of the changing that will eventually look like how He already sees you. I love that!

There is no magic here. Relationship that leads to intimacy starts messy sometimes. But God knew that when He created us. He knew we were flesh, that we would have a problem being obedient from the beginning. And He already had a plan for all that…Jesus. So He endowed us with some basic DNA that would define who we are and how we needed to see the world.

God took me on an adventure down many varied and treasure-filled paths to show me who I was. I was excited to follow because I believed this life was worth living and that there was some reason I was here. God chose me because He wanted relationship with me. He thought I was pretty cool. Do you think God wants to be in relationship with someone who isn't cool? Of course not. He only created really cool people, like us. "And He chose us to be his very own, joining us to himself even before He laid the foundation of the universe. Because of his great love, He ordained (predestined, set apart) us as one with Christ from the beginning, so that we would be seen as holy in his eyes with an unstained innocence" (Ephesians 1:4). See? We are super cool, because we are one with Him.

Now here's the *really* cool part: "For it was always in his perfect plan to adopt us as his delightful (cool) children, so that his tremendous grace that cascades over us would bring Him glory—for the same love He has for his Beloved One, Jesus, He has for us!" (Ephesians 1:5–6, *insertion mine*).

In His Eyes

If all of that is true, then why are we sometimes so far from living like it is? The bumpy part comes from living life through what others think. Trying to live up to that standard is impossible. With every failure, we fall deeper into a pit of self-abuse, leaving us open to be abused by others in one way or another.

So it is helpful to find out who we are before we start giving ourselves over to the greatest idol of the world, OPOs (other people's opinions). That is a form of control, and all forms of control are idols.

Perhaps you have found yourself at a crossroads of conscience. You did it wrong. You are devastated. You performed and gave it your best, and approval was denied. "If only" runs through your mind, trying to grab hold of the one thing you could have done better to get the desired result.

I know the feeling. When I allow approval of my performance to be the measurement of my identity and sense of worth, I feel like a failure and a loser. "When am I going to get it right?" I cry.

The truth is we don't have to perform to be a follower of Jesus. He did all the performing needed. He lived, He died, He resurrected, and then He knocked on the door of our hearts until we answered. Yes, He does say "follow me." That does require some action on our part. Pray like this, be generous, sacrifice, and most of all, love and forgive. Yes, He asks all of that of us. But He never said to do it under your own strength and ability. Goodness, if we could have done that with the Ten Commandments, He wouldn't have had to come and die.

God does seem to have expectations. The Beatitudes from the Sermon on the Mount (Matthew 5:2–10) is a huge one. You are blessed, happy, if you do the things Jesus reminds us to do.

Blessed are the poor in spirit,
 For theirs is the kingdom of heaven.
Blessed are those who mourn,
 For they shall be comforted.
Blessed are the meek,
 For they shall inherit the earth.
Blessed are those who hunger and thirst for
righteousness,

For they shall be filled.
Blessed are the merciful,
For they shall obtain mercy.
Blessed are the pure in heart,
For they shall see God.
Blessed are the peacemakers,
For they shall be called sons of God.
Blessed are those who are persecuted for
righteousness' sake,
For theirs is the kingdom of heaven.

We all want to be blessed. In Matthew 6:33, Jesus tells us to seek first the kingdom and all these things will be added to you. There is a lot that Jesus talked about when He was walking with his disciples that in many ways seem contradictory.

The thing is, He knew we couldn't do it. His chosen tried to for thousands of years and came up short. God knew that the only way we could succeed is to have the Holy Spirit fully indwelling us. Holy Spirit is the *how* to make it. He is no longer visiting His people on occasion but is now residing within us, the very power of creation. With all the commands He has given us to love our enemies, to love ourselves, to forgive others (490 times, for starters), turn the other cheek…it is all impossible in our own strength. We just don't have any of that in us naturally. The Holy Spirit was given so that we could at least begin to resemble Jesus, but only if we let him do the heavy lifting.

Burden Bearers

We carry a lot on our shoulders that we aren't supposed to, a whole lot. We carry our children, our spouses, our parents, our country, our job, our finances. There are so many expectations that overwhelm us and cause us great anxiety if we don't do them well. We must run the race to win. We are surrounded by the results of striving. We are fully aware every day of what success looks like based on what we do, where we live, how awesome our kids are, how many people love us, or even like us on Facebook. It is endless.

Being ruled by how well we perform is the same as being ruled by our souls. Our minds, wills, and emotions set us on a track for success, and when things fall apart, we pedal harder to get back on track. Even Paul writes to Timothy, "I have fought the good fight, I have finished the race, I have kept the faith."

But what if it was the wrong track? What if we are becoming someone else's idea of "good enough," but we never take the time to find out for ourselves if that really is what He wants for us?

Rebellion

I have shared that I was a baby boomer. The sixties were all about finding ourselves. Sensitivity training was big as we gathered around in our "sensitivity" circles and challenged each other to be honest and real. It was a good thing, a great way to figure out what drove us and made us happy. At the same time it can be upsetting to those around us who think they know what is best for us, like our well-meaning parents and friends.

I was a well-meaning parent to my youngest daughter, Sarah. I wanted her to find herself. She rode on my coattails for a long time without me realizing I was shaping her the way I wanted her to be or assumed she wanted to be. When she figured it out, she was angry and stayed angry for a long time.

I often favored her since she was the youngest. I could see early on she didn't feel like she belonged in the family she was born into. She had good reason.

You may recall that my first husband believed in open marriage. That is when you allow each other to experience sex with other couples just for fun. After I turned my marriage over to

Jesus along with my life, the open-marriage thing was not for me. He continued to experiment. Knowing something is wrong does not always translate to making good choices. My spirit was weak.

A newly born-again man started attending a Wednesday night Bible study with my professor. The attraction was strong. I was hungry for a like-minded man in my life. And He was one of those wounded puppies I loved to help. It didn't feel like adultery; I had clearly been anesthetized.

As a result I soon became pregnant. After a few months, seeing the destruction to my family, he disappeared quietly, never to be seen or heard from again. Though legal at the time, I refused to get an abortion.

Sarah never knew until she was seventeen. The very night Michelle came out of hiding about her father's abuse is the night I told Sarah the circumstances of her birth. That was not a stellar night for her. And for years she toughed it out, until she couldn't anymore.

I had overcompensated throughout those seventeen years. At one point in my single motherhood, it was just she and I. It was such a relief to have only her, and I probably treated her a bit more like a friend than a mother. She and I generally got along great, and I was grateful for her companionship. She started acting out, as all middle school kids do. I am sure to this day I don't know everything she did, and perhaps didn't want to know. I liked being the *cool* mom.

Through high school I let her do things that I shouldn't have; I so wanted her to *like* me. She could disrespect me like none of the others could. That's what happens when you don't respect yourself. I was lost in my own insecurities, and she was part of the mirror that made me feel OK. She wasn't OK, but I gave her the freedom she wanted and didn't need. She needed more of me, and I was busy fixing my own problems. Single moms, we have a unique struggle, don't we?

She went off to college and still needed me. I wasn't very available, as my life at home was a mess with third husband. I was sorting through all my stuff, which eventually left me single again. I invited Sarah to live with me, thinking it would be good for both of us. She was not the least interested. In fact, she was annoyed at the pattern I was not aware of—all those times I had put her aside when she inconvenienced me. It had happened before with husband number two. She didn't like the idea that she was my yo-yo, and it was the last straw. So one Christmas everything blew up. The anger she had put off for too long exploded, and I lost her. I tried and tried and pushed for reconciliation. Letting go was my only hope, and so I finally did. Though we moms, really, we never completely let go, at least not of hope.

She found her solace in a world that was the complete opposite of mine and seemingly far from God. I felt so responsible, even though I didn't know why. Not really. Not then. She had a right to be angry, and she expressed it in my being an awful mother who didn't protect her daughters from the abuse. The pain had come full circle.

Her need to find out who she was became part of my painful journey. My input was no longer welcome. I had messed her up, and she was going to trust anyone but me and my God. So I needed to find out who exactly I was and put myself together again. Only this time, it was going to be God who did the redemption, not me.

Living in regret and self-condemnation is not part of God's plan. It is what we do to ourselves because we take failure really hard. I made her pain my failure. Letting go meant that her pain was her pain and mine was mine.

Redemption

The morning I became Angela, Jesus took me through my whole life, the good, the bad, and the ugly. I was given absolution as He washed his blood of forgiveness over my life one more time. He understood all the perceived failures and difficulties in my life were choices I made while I was searching for who I was. And through it all, that identity as His love bomb remained intact, whether or not others saw it that way. He did. He saw who I was created to be, and He took charge of the messes and cleaned them up behind me. The places where I loved too much, loved too little, and didn't love enough. I was not in charge of the outcome of this story. He was. And He was knitting it all together into this beautiful tapestry that would be a reflection of my life. Now I get to put the finishing touches on it, and with a more astute awareness of who that was all those years and what a better (though incomplete) version of myself I am now.

Each of us has an individual journey to completeness. No matter what others did to mess us up, it is our responsibility to do the forgiving and the letting go that comes with the cleaning up. There are always consequences to our bad choices. But God uses clay pots. God loves broken vessels. When He heals, the cracks are unseen. When He looks at me, He sees only what God saw when He first thought of me. I was a thought and then a word. "Let there be Angela," and it was good.

Declaration and blessing: I declare wholeness to you who have messed up in this life and failed in your performance mandate. Take a ride on the shoulders of our God, and take a look at your life from His perspective. Look at how He turned all the ashes into beauty, all the sadness into joy. You are unique, and so is your journey. All of it, you and the journey, have all been orchestrated by God, and He isn't finished yet. I bless you with the joy of the journey and the peace of knowing that all God is looking for is you to turn to him daily and say, "OK, Daddy, what are we going to do today?" and then skip off to the next adventure. Entrust the rest to Him.

Chapter 20

I Am Forgiven

Lead us not into temptation but deliver us from evil.
—Matthew 6:13 (the Lord's Prayer)

Les Miserables. The title of the movie caught my eye as I was closing down my office for the night. That is not so unusual, except this time I saw no other title on my eight-foot shelf of CDs and DVDs, and there were many stacked horizontally and vertically. That and the ping in my spirit soon caused me to know that God was up to something. "Don't forget about forgiveness," He whispered. "You can't close a book on identity without it."

Les Miserables is the story of Jean Valjean and his nemesis, Javert. It takes place during the French Revolution.

The next morning I sat down and watched the movie again. My emotions were immediately and intensely captured by this amazing story of forgiveness and letting go that I have not seen so beautifully portrayed except by Jesus. It is a fascinating story of redemption.

The words in Jean Valjean's soliloquy in the opening are stunning and powerful. He has been released from prison and taken in by a kind priest. He has no life outside of prison, as his incarceration follows him wherever he goes. Instead of gracefully receiving from this kind man, he fearfully steals all the silver utensils from him and goes on the run again. Caught in his crime, he is returned to the priest by the police. Jean Valjean is sure he is destined for prison again, where he will die.

Instead he is met with love. The priest refuses to file a complaint. Rather, he apologizes to Valjean for failing to also include the two silver candlesticks on the dining table in his bag before he left so suddenly. The police have no choice but to leave, extremely confused.

Valjean is overcome. He laments in despair over the last twenty years of absolute torture and pain he had endured over stealing a mouthful of bread. He realizes that nothing remained but his hate. He wonders, *Is it too late to change? Is God truly giving him another chance?*

A new identity begins. Valjean takes the candlesticks, breaks his parole, leaves again, and starts a new life with a new name. He begins giving back to society as a man of honor and becomes a successful businessman.

The power of redemption through identity is amazing. Later in the movie, there is a scene where you realize he never did sell the two silver candlesticks. He made a new beginning without them. It gave me goose bumps.

That is just part of the story. His despicable legalistic jailer, Javert, believes he is living up to God's expectation by making sure this criminal is returned to justice. He is relentlessly hunting him down. Every time he finds Valjean and tries to destroy him or take his freedom away, Valjean forgives him. When the moment arrives for Valjean to finally get his revenge and he has an opportunity to kill Javert, he releases him. It so reminds me of David and Saul in the Bible.

In the end, this forgiveness is too painful for Javert, for he is so locked into right or wrong that he has shut off his own nature's capacity to forgive. Having finally captured Valjean, he lets him go in a moment of forgiveness but immediately rebukes himself for his weakness. He can no longer live with himself and the lie he has become. The identity he had chosen was to be a man of justice, which did not fit with being a man of forgiveness. So he takes his own life, throwing himself off a cliff, a broken man. The failure to fulfill what he thought was his destiny causes him to believe he is not forgivable. A tragic ending.

Forgiveness Transforms

Changing his name and his lifestyle isn't what changed Jean Valjean. It was the forgiveness of that priest that Valjean kept paying forward.

Forgiveness is, for me, the most complicated of God's dictates. Jesus Himself says in the Lord's Prayer, "Forgive us our trespasses as we forgive those who trespass against us." Or substitute the word *debts* for *trespasses*. Forgive us for what goes unpaid to others in the same way we forgive those who are indebted to us. Forgive us in the same way we forgive. The implication is that there is no forgiveness for us until we first forgive. Or is it? It would be easy to see how a religious, legalistic lens would lay a pretty heavy load on each of us when we find ourselves unable to forgive. Have we therefore lost our salvation, *our* forgiveness? We accepted God's forgiveness of everything when we asked Jesus into our hearts. Why now are we being tested in that place that is guaranteed also by Scripture? Jesus forgave constantly. "Go and sin no more." He didn't ask the woman caught in adultery to first forgive the accusers. Forgiveness was a direct gift from God. So why would Jesus tell them to pray in that way?

Nothing can replace the fact of your forgiveness because of the cross of Christ. However, our experience of forgiveness is an ongoing process that depends on our willingness to be the forgiving people we are called to be. God forgave, He forgives, and He will forgive. We can't take this out of context. He expects us to forgive because He did. We are to forgive in the same way He did, an intentional choice born out of love. He died. We are forgiven. And so are those that "trespass" against us. They are already forgiven. We are just to come into agreement with the truth. And because we have Holy Spirit abiding in us, it is possible.

Honor Your Father

I had a rocky relationship with my father. He was very inappropriate to me and my children. He thought it was fun to push my buttons by offering them beer. He would taunt them by calling his dog their brother. He teased them if they were overweight, and he flirted with the pretty ones. I bless the psychologist I saw years ago who told me I was under no obligation to encourage my children to have a relationship with their grandfather if he was being inappropriate.

For me, "Honor your father and your mother" was a commandment that translated, "Suck it up. He's your father. You love and respect him, period." I was now being given permission to say, "No, being around you is not healthy for me or my kids."

Eventually I did the ultimate distancing and moved thousands of miles away from him. However, I still had a journey to forgiveness. I wasn't so sure about reconciliation. I only knew that when he touched me or tried to hug me, I felt dirty. That is not a way a daughter wants to feel around her father. So we communicated from a distance. When my mother got sick and eventually passed, I thought in some strange way that it would bring my dad and I closer. It didn't. However, I did go through the process of forgiving him as best as I was able. And I came to realize that my unconscious choice of marrying a predator directly related to the way my father treated me.

Dad remarried rather quickly, and all my feelings of obligation to take care of him were redeemed. However, in the process, he bitterly and intentionally took all the inheritance set aside for me and my two brothers and willed it to his new wife. That was painful, and a wise boss of mine said, "It's his money. He can do with it what he wants." There's that reality of choice again, and I had to release the freedom to let him choose that route. Money was my dad's love currency—he withheld it as punishment and gave freely when it served his narcissistic need.

To say his removing us from his inheritance didn't hurt would be a lie. However, the truth is that there is a gracious and generous God who is my true Father and has an inheritance for me that no earthly father could compare to. That is where I rest.

Closure

Finally, when my dad was past ninety, it was clear he was close to death. We had celebrated his ninetieth birthday just months before, but his quality of life was failing. I decided to visit him on Father's Day in the rehab hospital. I was determined to make my last meeting with my dad a positive one.

I only had one day, so I asked his wife if I could have some time alone with him. She left, and I sat next to the bed and took my dad's hand. This was not a man I had much sentiment toward. I could never find any cards for birthday or Father's Day that I could honestly give him if they carried any of the classic "Where would I be without you? I am so grateful to have such an awesome Dad in my life." I had long reconciled with the fact that my forgiveness and love for him came strictly from the fact that this was the father God had given me, and if the best I could do was say thank you for being my father, then that was enough.

That is what I said. It is all I had. "Dad, I just wanted to thank you for being my dad." Of course, I still held this little-girl hope that the response would be, "I am so glad you are my daughter," or something along those lines. His response was cold and cut deeply, a wound I would later process in privacy. "You're welcome." That was it. The rest of the time there, he kept asking for my sister-in-law and barely knew I was there. When he did, he just kept saying he wanted to die. And he did, two weeks later.

I was blessed to have a dear pastor friend help me take the first step to healing from that rather shocking moment at my dad's bedside. He saw my pain, and he stood in the place of my dad and said the words in his place that I so wanted to hear. "I am so blessed to have had you for a daughter." My tears flowed in gratitude.

Yes, I forgave dad. I never received what I had hoped to from my earthly father. But the process was not over.

Declaration and blessing: Jesus is all about forgiveness. He wants us to walk free of bitterness and unforgiveness, and He did His part to show us the importance by dying on the cross. I bless you to find a place inside to be willing to forgive where forgiveness has been difficult. And I declare that your forgiveness is a done deal, from the day you said yes to Jesus. Be free, and choose forgiveness, allowing Holy Spirit to complete the process.

Chapter 21

Freedom

For as he thinks in his heart, so is he.
—Proverbs 23:7

The movie had me spellbound. Knowing my husband loved war stories, I thought *Hacksaw Ridge* was a good compromise, as it was new and I didn't have to watch it for the tenth time, as I have done with so many of Joe's favorite war movies. I had no idea this one was going to open a door into a darkness of my soul I didn't even know was there.

The main character, Desmond Doss, has a compelling story. Driven by his own realization of how violent he could be, thanks to his violent, alcoholic father, Desmond finds himself at a crossroads. He had almost killed his brother when they were kids when he violently, in a brotherly fist fight, hit him in the head with a brick. His pain and remorse brought him to his knees when he was drawn to a poster on the wall of the house. It was a depiction of the sixth commandment: "Thou shalt not kill." Desmond vows that he will never in his life kill anyone or pick up a rifle.

The movie is a true story of the battle he goes through to keep that promise as a medic in World War II, fighting at Hacksaw Ridge in Okinawa. He battles the army as well as his peers and is almost dishonorably discharged for disobeying orders when he even refused to shoot a rifle. Eventually he ends up a medic on the front lines, carrying the wounded to safety and struggling to fulfill his promise to God.

There is a scene in the movie when Doss and one of his fellow soldiers are resting in a trench together at the end of an exhausting and hard-fought battle. Desmond begins to share about his decision to never pick up a gun or kill again.

He relays the story (via flashback video) of the night his father, in one of his drunken rages, was attacking and threatening his mother with a gun pointed at her. Desmond, wanting to protect his mother, stormed out of his bedroom, confronts his dad, and grabs the gun away from him, instantly turning it on his father. His father's face contorts into one of sarcasm and taunting as he challenges Desmond to shoot, calling him cowardly names to egg him on while his mother is in the background, horrified at what is being played out. It is all Desmond can do to stop himself from pulling the trigger and keeping the vow he had made years earlier: "Thou shall not kill."

His buddy asks Desmond, "But you did not kill him?"

Desmond replied, "In my heart I did."

I was struck by the thrust of those words. That all-too-familiar sucker punch resurfaced, and I knew I had an appointment with Papa.

Heart Issues

In his heart he'd killed his father, just as Cain killed Abel.

Something inside me broke. The tears flowed from a deep, deep sorrow of a broken heart. What was it that was in my heart that God was breaking open right now? What had I done in my heart that I had not yet been able to see, much less repent of?

Tearfully, hiding my emotions from my husband, not wanting to distract from the rest of the movie, I got through it to the end. I was so struck by this young man's raw belief in the absolutes of the Bible. He knew in his heart of hearts that he had killed his father in spirit. And I knew in that moment that I was harboring a deep, uncontrollable hate for my earthly father, one that was covered with my glittering image of holiness and forgiveness. I hated what I saw. But I could no longer escape the truth.

I was taken back to the Scriptures called the Sermon on the Mount, Matthew 5:21 (MSG): "You're familiar with the command to the ancients, 'Do not murder.' I'm telling you that anyone who is so much as angry with a brother or sister is guilty of murder." And this in 1John 3:15: "Whoever hates his brother is a murderer, and you know that no murderer has eternal life abiding in him."

Another part of that Sermon on the Mount, verses 27–28, says, "You know the next commandment pretty well, too: 'Don't go to bed with another's spouse.' But don't think you've preserved your virtue simply by staying out of bed. Your *heart* can be corrupted by lust even quicker than your *body*. Those leering looks you think nobody notices—they also corrupt."

And that is where the hate came from. Those jealous, leering eyes had corrupted this innocent teenager fifty years ago. I had found all the excuses, the explanations, the need to forgive. I had healed every way I knew how. And here I was confronting such a deep hatred for the man, not just for what he did. I wish it were that I was that holy. No, I hated *him*, and I spent a couple hours wrestling with God and this hate. Fifty years of hate that had held me back from loving as I could have loved. Fifty years of darkness, blindness, denial. I simply didn't know, but here it was in my face—a true reviling hate that I couldn't ignore. I wish I hated the devil the way I hated my father at that moment.

I gave myself permission to own the hatred. My journey into wholeness and identity so far had taught me that lying to me only prolonged the inevitable. Enough. The hate had to go, but first I had to own it. It all came out. What his sin against me had created, affecting my choice of marrying the predator who would steal the innocence of my children. Sin has a way of accelerating as it transfers forward in the generations.

I begged God to forgive me for hating so deeply. I found it inconceivable that I could hate that deeply when I had loved equally as deeply. Who was this woman, this person, who could feel such raging hate? She was me. No more denial. That hate was coming from me. The rage felt righteous and true and indignant. I embraced it for a time.

Jesus Shares My Sorrows

I went into the pit of hell. Jesus came with me, and we wrestled that demon out of me. I remembered my dad's leering looks and touches, his inappropriate crude jokes, his flattery, his jealous rages when I dated, his anger when I got married, his stealing of any financial inheritance, and worst of all that last time I saw him when he could not find a thing inside of him to say the words of healing I so needed to hear. I seriously and truly did not think I was capable of that level of hate. ISIS comes to mind. *That* is what I was feeling. And I didn't try to make it pretty.

It seemed to take forever to be willing to let go of what had made me so strong for all these years. I believed I could handle anything. "I am woman—hear me roar" was my mantra. Hate is a powerful control mechanism. I was an amazing survivor, always throwing my love out there as an antidote to any hate that came my way. It was exhausting, and I mostly failed.

Out of that pit a snaky, ugly black thing was extricated, and I handed all my hate to Jesus. It wasn't easy letting go of such a huge part of my defense mechanism. But it had to go. And I was left with this vessel so empty and so needing to be filled, and I had nowhere to go to fill it except to Jesus.

Suddenly I felt like Mary Magdalene, with seven demons removed. I became immediately mindful of the fact that I better fill that void with lots of Jesus before it came back with double force. That was easier said than done. Forgiveness was still on the table. And having made a case for forgiveness in these pages, I owed it to myself and God to face that sooner than later.

I knew the forgiveness was for me, for my benefit. Dad had passed away eighteen months earlier, and quite honestly, in my encounter with hatred, I didn't care if he was in heaven or hell. I just did not ever want to see him again. But God cared. He cared about me. I was His love bomb. Love forgives.

Jesus stood in the room in my mind, between me and my dad. I sent my dad out of the picture, as a pathetic stick figure of a man, weak and pitiful. I looked at him, and not only in my heart but also out loud, I said, "You foolish, foolish, feeble man. You had no idea what a treasure you held in your hands when I was born. You could have had a real relationship with a devoted daughter, but you forgot who I was. I know who I am now. God forgive you for what you did to me...you weak, pathetic shadow of a man."

All ties of expectation, of hope, of a false love covenant, had to be broken, and Jesus took the sword of truth and cut through the marrow of deception that had kept me tied to my father by hate.

I owed Dad nothing. I understood why all I had for him on his death bed was to thank him for being my father—basically, for giving birth to me. It was finished.

Strangely, memories began to surface, memories that were out of the norm of his usual narcissistic behavior. Pleasant memories, rare but occasional times when there was something fatherly and redeemable. I could not fit them into the paradigm of reality I now saw before me, but I embraced the few positive memories that Jesus brought to mind.

I ran to my music once again for solace and for grounding. I found and played songs that encouraged and strengthened me at the moment. To stand for what I believed and knew I was. God reminded me that He was good all the time, that I could trust Him in this journey to forgiveness.

Now it was time. I had been there before, and I could feel the nudge. Jesus needed an answer, to know I was willing to do the next thing. The best I had was to be willing to forgive. It wasn't in me, but it was enough. Jesus drew my father toward us, and this shadow of a man joined the circle, making three of us. "Dance with Me, Oh Lover of My soul" was now playing, and Jesus was dancing with me, holding me gently and looking into my eyes with kindness, unlike what I had experienced fifty years earlier when my father was dancing with me at a dinner party where I had felt so unsafe and uncomfortable. With Jesus I was comfortable and safe. I allowed my father to be there, at a distance, thankful that Jesus stood between me and him. In the safety of Jesus's arms, I looked at Dad and said, "I forgive you." He quickly faded from view. It was finished.

Bed was a welcome friend, and yet I still woke up drained. Prayer at church helped a bit, but I was still pretty raw. I was still struggling with the level of hate that I had carried, being hard on myself, the good Christian woman and all her glittering images. *You seriously loved me all this time, knowing this was here, waiting for release?* It was beyond my ability to comprehend that kind of love. Yet I knew it was true. I needed to forgive myself.

It was never my behavior God cared about. It was my willing heart, willing to be free, to be able to receive the fullness of love being offered. I needed way more of His love inside me in order to carry out the mandate of love for the remainder of my life. That hate had blocked the grid.

I was aware of the purity of God's love and understood for the first time the words "Amazing grace...that saved a wretch like me."

But Misty Edward captured what I could not express in her song, "Killing Me with Mercy." It is a song of forgiveness and renewed love.

What are You doing, Lord, kneeling in front of me?
I feel indignant, Lord, that You'd ever wash my feet
I'll never let You see the dark and dirty
It's just too much for me
I know who You are, and I know where I have been
It offends me, Lord, that Your knees are bent
I'd rather You be strong and make me pay
But this is too much for me
(Chorus)
You're killing me with mercy, I can't breathe
You're wrecking me with Your kindness, I can't receive
What am I supposed to do with a God so humble?
It's breaking me
It's crushing me

Verse 2
I'd draw a sword for You, I said I'd fight unto the death
I'd lose it all for You, I swore I'm not like the rest
But then the cock crows and I've let You down
I can't face You now…I can't face You now
(Chorus)
You're killing me with mercy, I can't breathe
You're wrecking me with Your kindness, I can't receive
What am I supposed to do with a God so humble?
It's breaking me
It's crushing me
(Bridge)
I'm a fragile stone,
I'm a vow that's broken,
I'm a rock that's crumbled at Your feet
But You still want me

You say my love is real, though my love is weak
You still believe, the vows I make, I break, I make
You still want me
(Chorus 2)
You're killing me with mercy, I can't breathe
You're wrecking me with Your kindness, I'll just receive
What am I supposed to do with a God so humble?

I'll just believe
And let You love me

Oh, how I related to these words. I felt Peter's pain! One minute ready to die for Jesus, and the next in full denial that he even knew Him. And then that fateful day at the end of the gospel of John, as Jesus took Peter aside and asked him three times, "Do you love me?" Three times, "Yes, of course!" And as simple as that, Jesus entrusted Peter to feed His sheep. Many would be fed by Peter.

Peter and I had much in common. My cock had crowed. The sword was rendered useless. And there I was, like Peter, embarrassed by my failure, in awe that Jesus could love me all these years knowing this ugliness dwelled in me. And He whispers, "Do you love me? Feed my sheep."

God has now opened up a huge vacuum inside, one that is available to be filled with His unfailing, unconditional love. I can scarcely handle it even now. How deeply entrenched is the idea that we have to deserve this love. He knew on the cross that I would face this ugliness at this time. He had waited until I finally knew I was created good.

That hate is a passion that still overwhelms me, only now it is toward the enemy of my soul. I had been convinced that I was evil, that my dad was evil, and that I was undeserving of this kind of love. Hate cannot control me.

That void left in my soul, formerly filled with hate, made room for a new and profound experience of love. That love that I had for that baby, me, is again needing to be poured into me, to a greater and more powerful capacity. The reality is, even that love is nothing compared to the love Jesus expressed to me on the cross. Now I have more room for that love I was called to walk in.

So I let myself off the cross.

My Elegant Journey Continues

My search for identity as a beloved daughter of my earthly father was never fulfilled in this life. We don't always get what we want. However, Jesus promised us fathers and mothers and sisters and brothers and sons and daughters—a spiritual family that he knew we would need this side of heaven.

Being the beloved daughter of our heavenly Father fills a void that no man can.

My kids also didn't get the fathering they needed, and I pray they will find the Father heart of God in their lives.

Declaration and blessing: I cry out for the unfathered and unmothered children of this land, they who find it so difficult to reach out to God because of the lack of a good image of a Father. I bless you to be kind to yourself regarding the need to forgive. Baby steps are fine. Sometimes we just have to trust in God's timing. Sometimes it takes fifty years. You will understand it all in heaven, but God has a particular purpose for you on this earth, and it is to your benefit to free yourself from feeling bitterness and resentment that can only come between you and your destiny.

God is the judge.

And He is the Healer.

We need both.

Chapter 22

What Does Love Look Like?

Choose this day whom you will serve.
—Joshua 24:15 (ESV)

How can I believe in a good, loving God when all this awful stuff happened to me and my children? That's a good question, a really good question.

Simply speaking, He, this good, loving God, didn't do those horrible things. Men and women operating from their own free will did. So did God allow it all? In a sense He did, by not intervening. It really wasn't an issue of allowing though. He hated it. In the same way I hated finding out what happened to my daughters. But when the Triune of God got together and created man, they made one decision that was a bottom line. Man was to have a free will. They wanted their creation to choose to love them. Father, Son, and Holy Spirit could have endowed us with all wisdom, love, and ability to forgive. But they were seeking a companion, a relationship with us, and it was important to their plan that this creation would choose to love. We were created in His image. And God chooses each day to love us with an unconditional love.

The Gift of Free Will

Choice is an amazing gift. Without it, we would all be robots, like Stepford wives. Each and every day I get to choose to love God, love my husband, love my enemies, and love my children. It is a commandment because it is important to God that we recognize the importance of choosing to love, rather than to hate, or worse, to be indifferent. If we are lukewarm, He actually vomits us from his mouth. Yes, it is in the Bible! (See Revelation 3:16.)

Choice without God delivers some ugly results. Broken people do broken things. Abused people abuse others. Angry people get angry. Hurt people hurt.

Love received is love given; forgiveness received is forgiveness given; you reap what you sow. These are the principles of God, and when they are followed, good things happens. When they are not, unnecessary pain is created.

A Father asking his Son to die a violent death doesn't sound like love. We are all appalled at the Bible story of Abraham prepared to sacrifice his son on the altar. Choosing to let your son die as an act of love is unparalleled except by Jesus, who obediently chose to be that Son. Listen to how this is expressed in Philippians 2:6 (TPT):

> He existed in the form of God, yet He gave no thought to seizing that alone as his supreme prize. Instead He emptied himself of his outward glory by reducing himself to the form of a lowly Servant. He became human! He humbled himself and became vulnerable, choosing to be revealed as a Man. He listened to the Father and was obedient to everything He heard. He was a perfect example, even in his death—a criminal's death by crucifixion! Because of that obedience, God exalted him and multiplied his greatness! He has now been given the greatest of all names!

It is because of this love that we too are given the privilege of making our own choices. Watching someone make bad choices is heartbreaking, especially as parents. The most beneficial changes in life occur by making choices for good, not for evil. Every day we make a thousand choices, and those decisions shape today and the days to come.

Sometimes those choices feel like a punishment rather than freedom. I remember when my middle daughter, Joanie, was in her rebellion years. She returned to my nest after the tragedy of the abuse had been revealed. But she kept pushing the boundaries, and when she started bringing alcohol home and exposing my teenage daughter Sarah to the alcohol, I had to make a difficult choice. I told her to move out. She hated me at that moment. She was really hurt. I stood there in tears as she removed her things from the bedroom. She found a place to stay, and eventually she asked me to come and see where she was. Years later, she was finally able to tell me I did her a favor. It sure didn't feel like it at the time. That was the second time I had done that with her.

Now, Joanie is the mother of three of my beautiful grandchildren, and I am proud of what she has done with her life.

The best choice we can ever celebrate is the choice that God made for us to be born. I keep trying to imagine that moment in heaven when God said, "Let there be Angela, who will eventually settle into her true identity and will love because she chooses to be like me." We are never prepared for what life brings, but we always have a choice.

Even we abused have a choice. Oh, not when the abuse is being perpetrated on us. But we have a choice of what to do with what happened. We have a choice to blame and be a victim or to heal and be a victor.

Heart-Wrenching Choices

My dearest friend is in the middle of one of those crises of choice. She has an unmarried daughter, whom I'll call Rachel, who had undergone surgery years ago that ended up disabling her and taking away her ability to work. Rachel had adopted a special-needs child who was the apple of Grammy's eye. Rachel's parents were supplementing Rachel's income and realized they could not keep two households any longer as they approached retirement age. So they bought a home that could accommodate all of the family and moved everyone together. It was a brilliant plan, meant to save them a lot of money.

The reality has been much harder than anticipated. The emotional instability of Rachel, exacerbated by pain medication, often put the grandchild in jeopardy, and what seemed so simple became more difficult. The drugs to ease the discomfort caused by her disability triggered angry outbursts, and life at home has become challenging, to say the least. The brilliant idea just didn't feel so brilliant.

What does a mother do? Her daughter needs her and yet bites the hand that feeds her. How often do you turn the other cheek? Is there a threshold where enough is enough? Is this what God had in mind when my friend's husband presented the plan to her?

There are consequences for letting abuse continue. And there are consequences for saying enough is enough. Is there enough grace in heaven to live in this turmoil? Absolutely. My friend knows who she is. She understands that her strength is only in her identity as a daughter of the King. He knows her limits, and He will continue to hold on to her as she walks out this season of her life. It doesn't seem fair. She has already lived through so much pain. These were the years to reap some of the benefits of all that blood, sweat, and tears.

I haven't walked in her shoes exactly. I certainly have experienced abuse, but I was able to walk away. That is not an option here. So every day my friend has to make choices to draw lines and boundaries around her grown daughter, who is seemingly incapable of self-control.

How do you trust God with the lives of those we love and not feel guilty for not doing enough? What does love look like in this situation? Only God knows. And I know He loves my friend and her family and at the same time hates seeing what this is doing to her.

There comes a time in the search for purpose and identity that we realize God is bigger than all of what we see and experience. We see through a glass darkly, and He sees all things clearly. Knowing who we are allows us to trust. Without knowing her true identity, she would not be able to trust Him with this situation. She would be making emotional choices that may or may not be fruitful. So I pray for God to show her what to do and to give her the strength to maintain inner peace when making those one thousand choices each day.

Whose Will?

God will not impose His will on us. As mentioned before, He gave us free will so that we would know what it was to choose Him and to choose love. My friend chooses each day to serve the one true God who is good and wants only good for her. Is there a higher place in heaven for those who suffer more than others? Suffering isn't a popular Christian concept these days. As I write these words, I can see prayer warriors reading this and pulling out their swords. I am one of them. But I don't really know what God has in mind here. I only know He loves my friend with outrageous love and He will not abandon her. We may not know the fullness of this story this side of heaven. But no matter what, God's love remains and will never leave my friend and her family. Love endures all things.

I find myself in a similar new season. With the aging of my spouse, choices that were easy become harder. I am not as free. I don't like it. Sometimes God confines us in order to get our attention. Freedom happens on the inside, not the outside. I was reminded by this same friend that Paul wrote most of his letters from prison. I am the same person more confined to home as I was on all those fun jaunts around the country. I can love from here as well as from an airplane or a conference. That is freedom.

I end this book with 1 Corinthians 13, from The Message Translation. Love is what began this journey, and love is what has kept me moving. I Corinthians 13 tells us what love is to look like.

Love never gives up.
Love cares more for others than for self.
Love doesn't want what it doesn't have.
Love doesn't strut,
Doesn't have a swelled head,
Doesn't force itself on others,
Isn't always "me first,"
Doesn't fly off the handle,
Doesn't keep score of the sins of others,
Doesn't revel when others grovel,
Takes pleasure in the flowering of truth,
Puts up with anything,
Trusts God always,
Always looks for the best,
Never looks back,
But keeps going to the end.

It is a revelation to see that God's view of love has nothing to do with feeling. It has to do with choosing.

When I put my name in the place of the word *love*, I can see that God has His work cut out for Him. This *is* who I am. I can only hope and pray to catch up in reality to what Jesus sees in eternity.

Angela never gives up.
Angela cares more for others than for self.
Angela doesn't want what she doesn't have.

Angela doesn't strut,
Angela doesn't have a swelled head,
Angela doesn't force herself on others,
Angela isn't always "me first,"
Angela doesn't fly off the handle,
Angela doesn't keep score of the sins of others,
Angela doesn't revel when others grovel,
Angela takes pleasure in the flowering of truth,
Angela puts up with anything,
Angela trusts God always,
Angela always looks for the best,
Angela never looks back,
Angela keeps going to the end.
SELAH, and AMEN

Epilogue

I am a voice, a messenger, among many.
—Angela Joy Chapman

There is no purpose to knowing your identity if it doesn't lead to knowing your birthright and finding what you are called to do. Discovering that is necessary to feel fulfilled, to be able to say "my life meant something."

There is a reason I was born in this season and at this time. I have an assignment on my life given to me before I was conceived in my mother's womb. I am not done here until I complete that.

And on any given day, I am not always sure what that is exactly.

Some people have a public call to ministry, mission work, or evangelism. Their names are big in the stars. But recognition in the world does not define a call.

My call as a mom reaches further than my own four children. Truth be told, they are the hardest for me to reach. Their journey is incomplete, and I may still be part of their healing and they mine.

There are many women who do not have moms for various reasons. Or they have moms who are (or were) incapable or unable to give them the nurture they needed. So God places some of us in their paths to be moms in the spirit and to give them chances to experience being daughters.

I don't have a fancy platform. I have a heart that loves God and wants to see the women in my life walking out their destinies in fullness and wholeness. I have a choice each day to act in that call, depending on where I am and who I am in relationship with. I let God bring the people, and I pray that I am ready to be His heart to them. It's nothing fancy. But recently I was reminded it was an elegant journey.

This is my inheritance Scripture for this next season:

Arise, shine, for your light has come,
and the glory of the Lord has risen upon you.
For the darkness shall cover the earth
and deep darkness the peoples;
but the Lord shall rise upon you,
and His glory shall be seen upon you.
The nations shall come to your light
and kings to the brightness of your rising. (Isaiah 60:1–3)

True shine comes from within and allows God's glory to shine through. The world is attracted to glittering images. God is attracted to our light because He put it there.

We can shine because He first shined into us His glorious light of truth. As in the garden of Eden, we don't need to cover up with any glittering image or leaves of shame, because when we are truly reflecting the glory of God, no one can see anything past that glow of his presence. That is the ultimate law of attraction.

I like to contemplate, go back to the future so to speak, that moment in heaven when Jesus and Father and the Holy Spirit conceived me and blew into me all that they saw in me to become. I want to see what it was they saw when they created me before I was placed in that love-starved home.

I want the eyes to see what *you* saw, God. Thank you for the peeks into that picture as I walk out this elegant journey. I package that glittering image daily and return it to you in a divine exchange and ask for you to continue to create in me the beauty from the ashes of my life that you promised.

Thank you, God, for calling my name.

A Note about Spiritual Warfare

I come from a spiritual warfare community that looks for tools to overcome the darkness we inevitably find on our journeys. Jesus gave us tools of warfare, as did Paul in his letters. Jesus instructs us to bind and loose. Our light is to shine in the darkness. Darkness is real. I have read and studied many books and have used many of the tools most of you have to bring freedom into my life and the life of those I love.

None of those have had such a profound impact on my healing than the discovery of my identity.

Standing on the truth of who we are gives the enemy no place to attack. He looks for openings where we believe lies. He prowls around seeking whom he can destroy. What does he want to destroy? Our identities—the firstfruits of our creation that God gave us when He first saw us in heaven. The truth of who we are replaces those lies in an instant. Even physical healing is directly connected to identity, the identity of our sovereign King, Jesus. He is the Healer.

Pursue with a vengeance who you are, whose you are, how God sees you, and what His birthright is to you. It is an adventure of immense proportions. And remember He has given you everything you need!

Please contact me at angelajoy48@gmail.com. I would love to hear from you! Or visit my blog on angelajoychapman.com.

Be blessed!

Made in the USA
Middletown, DE
04 November 2017